Street by Street

WEST SUSSEX
PLUS BRIGHTON, HASLEMERE, HAVANT, HOVE, PETERSFIELD
Enlarged Areas Bognor Regis, Chichester, Crawley, Horsham, Worthing

Ist edition May 2001

© Automobile Association Developments Limited 2001

This product includes map data licensed from Ordnance Survey® with the permission of the Controller of Her Majesty's Stationery Office. © Crown copyright 2000. All rights reserved. Licence No: 399221.

Published by AA Publishing (a trading name of Automobile Association Developments Limited, whose registered office is Norfolk House, Priestley Road, Basingstoke, Hampshire, RG24 9NY. Registered number 1878835).

Mapping produced by the Cartographic Department of The Automobile Association.

A CIP Catalogue record for this book is available from the British Library.

Printed by G. Canale & C. S.P.A., Torino, Italy

The contents of this atlas are believed to be correct at the time of the latest revision. However, the publishers cannot be held responsible for loss occasioned to any person acting or refraining from action as a result of any material in this atlas, nor for any errors, omissions or changes in such material. The publishers would welcome information to correct any errors or omissions and to keep this atlas up to date. Please write to Publishing, The Automobile Association, Fanum House, Basing View, Basingstoke, Hampshire, RG21 4EA.

Ref: MX020

Key to map pages	ii-iii
Key to map symbols	iv-1
Enlarged scale pages	2-13
Street by Street	14-223
Index – towns & villages	224
Index – streets	225-246
Index – featured places	246-250

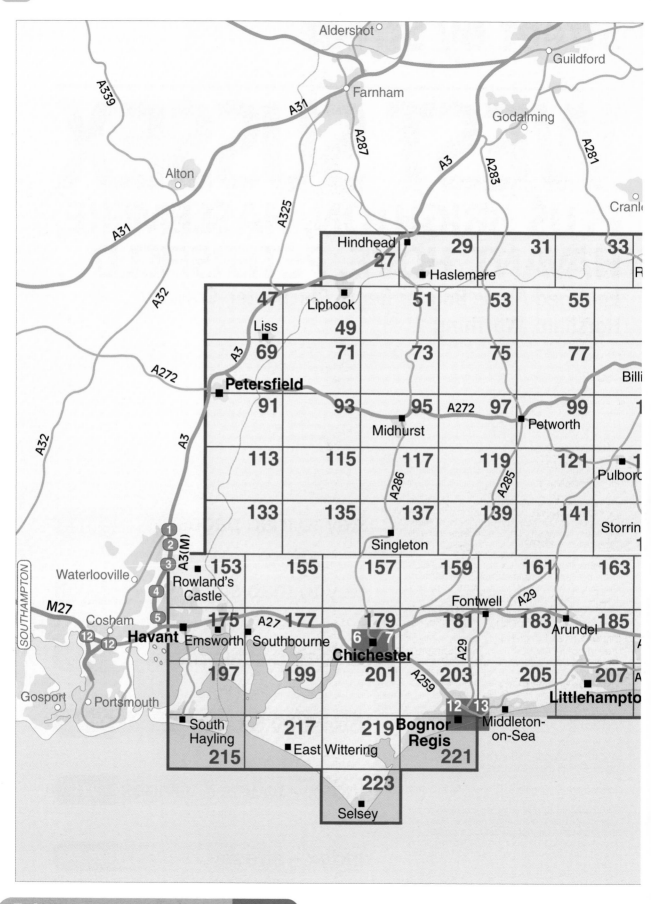

Aldershot
Guildford
A339
A31
Farnham
A287
A31
A3
A283
A281
Godalming
Alton
A325
Cranl
A32
Hindhead **29** **31** **33**
27
Haslemere R
A31
A32
Liphook **47** **51** **53** **55**
Liss
49
A3
A272
69 **71** **73** **75** **77**
Petersfield Billi
A3
91 **93** **95** A272 **97** **99**
Midhurst Petworth
A286
A285
113 **115** **117** **119** **121**
Pulbor
A32
133 **135** **137** **139** **141**
Singleton Storrin
1 A3(M)
2
153 **155** **157** **159** **161** **163**
SOUTHAMPTON
3
Waterlooville Rowland's
Castle
Fontwell A29
4
M27
5
175 A27 **177** **179** **181** **183** **185**
Cosham
12 Emsworth Southbourne A29 Arundel
12 Havant 6 7
Chichester
Gosport **197** **199** **201** **203** **205** **207**
A259
Portsmouth
12 13 Littlehampto
Middleton-
on-Sea
South **217** **219** Bognor
Hayling East Wittering Regis **221**
215
223
Selsey

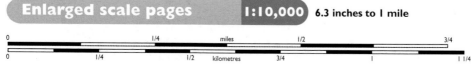

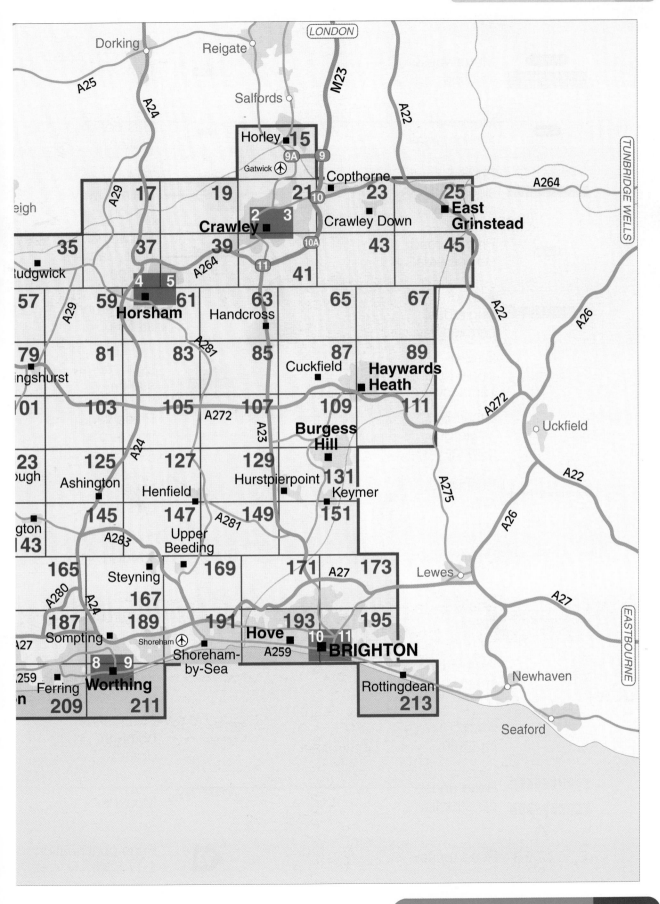

3.6 inches to 1 mile **Scale of main map pages 1:17,500**

| 0 | 1/2 | miles | 1 |
| 0 | 1/2 | kilometres | 1 1/2 | 2

Junction 9	Motorway & junction
Services	Motorway service area
	Primary road single/dual carriageway
Services	Primary road service area
	A road single/dual carriageway
	B road single/dual carriageway
	Other road single/dual carriageway
	Restricted road
	Private road
← ←	One way street
	Pedestrian street
	Track/ footpath
	Road under construction
	Road tunnel
P	Parking

P+	Park & Ride
	Bus/coach station
	Railway & main railway station
	Railway & minor railway station
	Underground station
	Light railway & station
++++++++++	Preserved private railway
LC	Level crossing
•—•—•—•—•	Tramway
------------	Ferry route
....	Airport runway
— · — · — · —	Boundaries- borough/ district
vvvvvvvvvvv	Mounds
93	Page continuation 1:17,500
7	Page continuation to enlarged scale 1:10,000

	River/canal lake, pier			Toilet with disabled facilities
	Aqueduct lock, weir			Petrol station
465 ▲ Winter Hill	Peak (with height in metres)		PH	Public house
	Beach		PO	Post Office
	Coniferous woodland			Public library
	Broadleaved woodland		_i_	Tourist Information Centre
	Mixed woodland			Castle
	Park			Historic house/ building
	Cemetery		Wakehurst Place NT	National Trust property
	Built-up area		M	Museum/ art gallery
	Featured building		†	Church/chapel
⊓⊔⊓⊔⊓⊔⊓	City wall			Country park
A&E	Accident & Emergency hospital			Theatre/ performing arts
	Toilet			Cinema

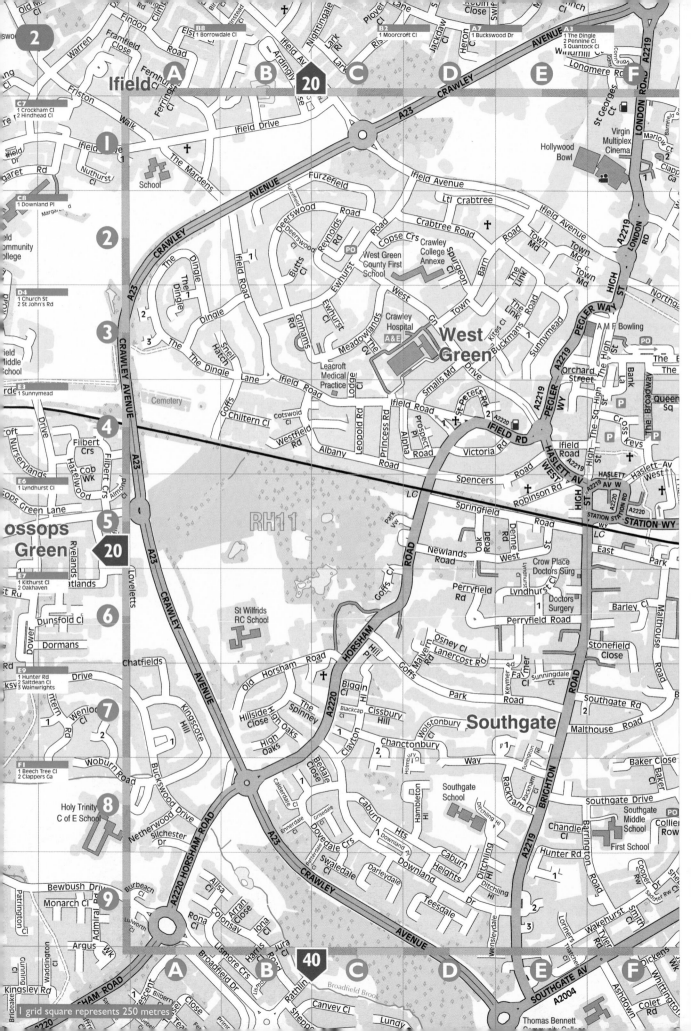

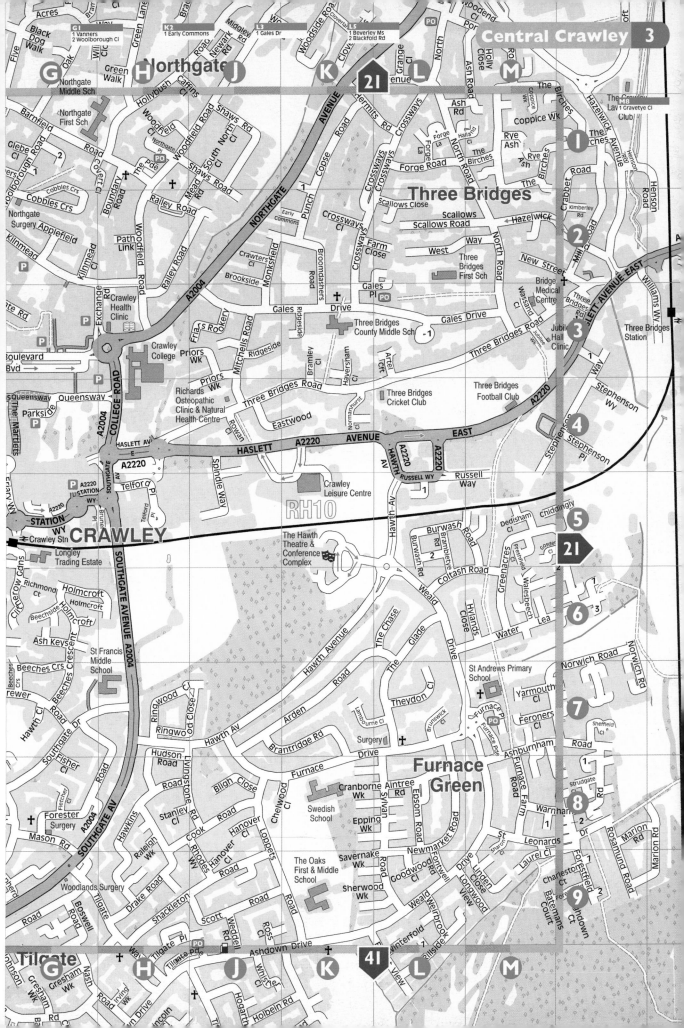

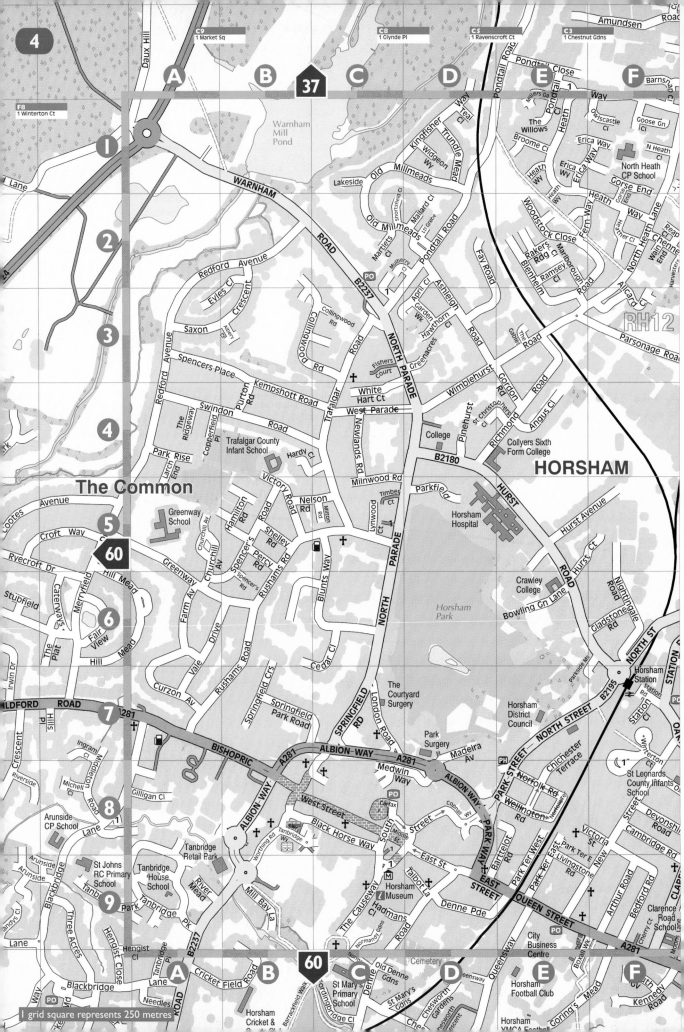

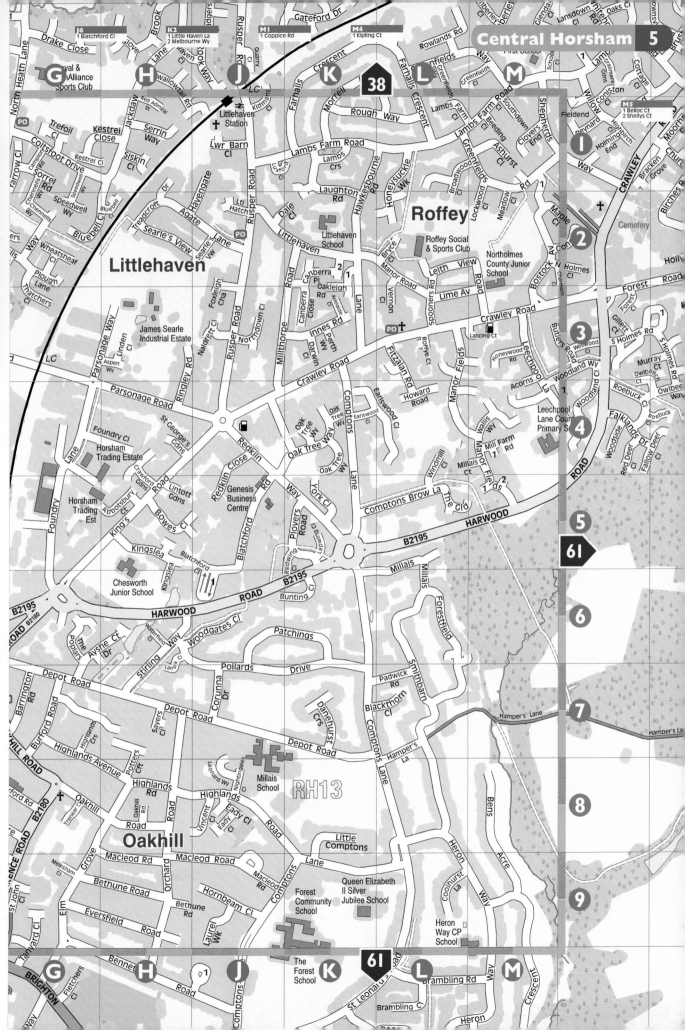

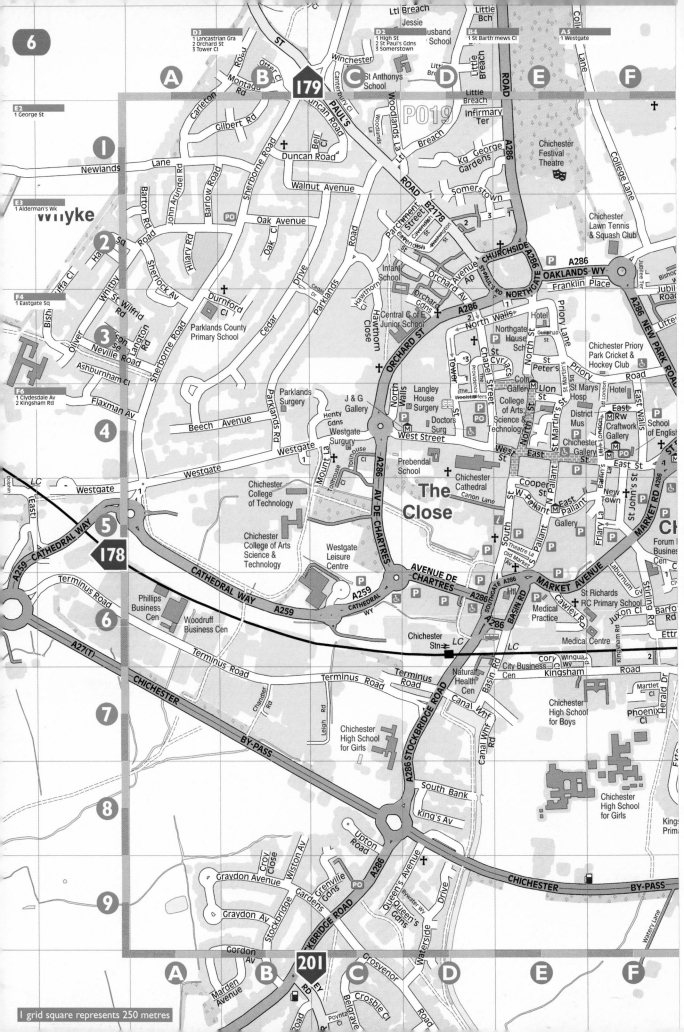

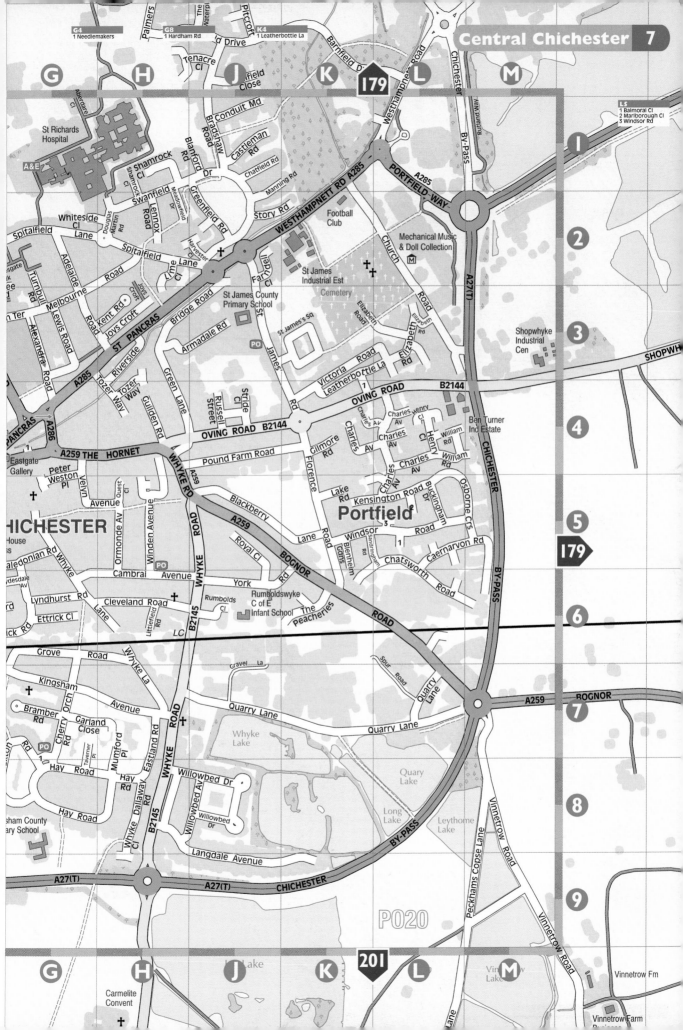

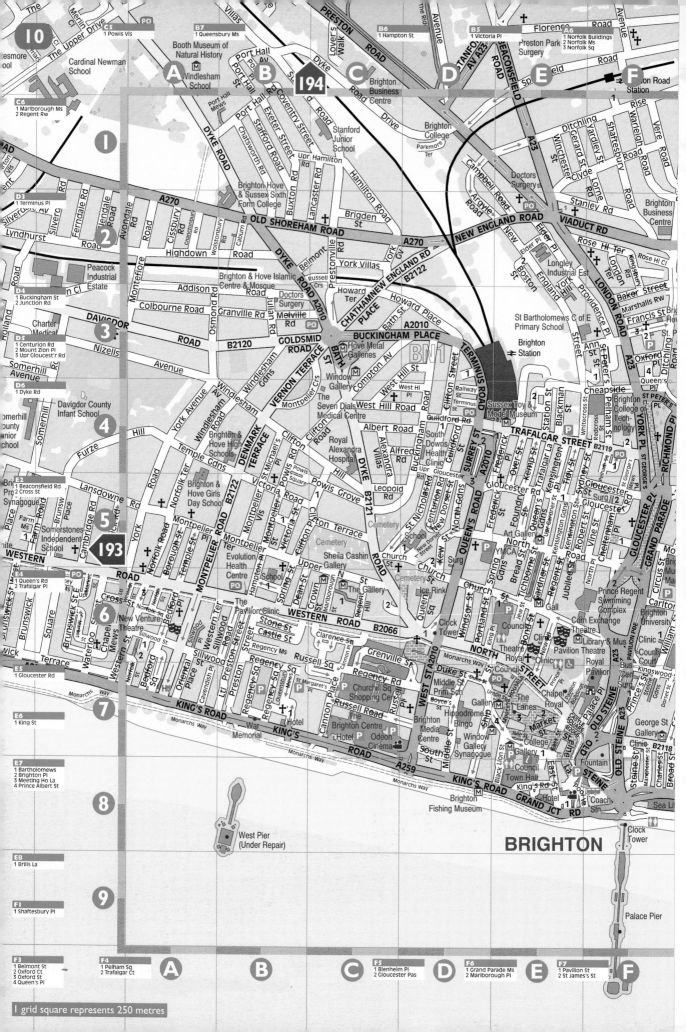

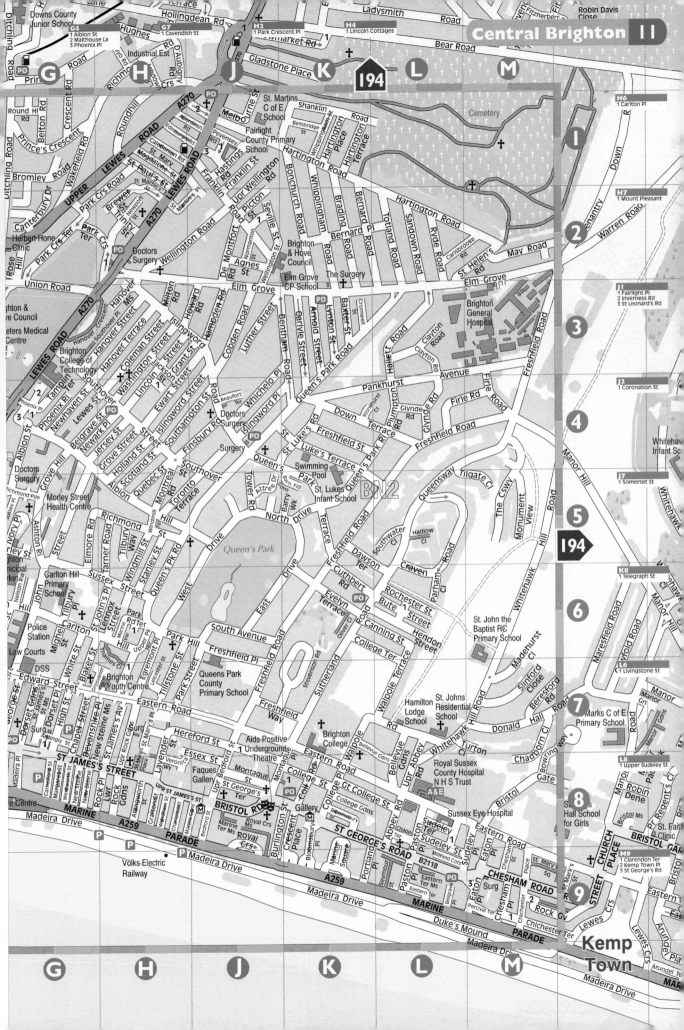

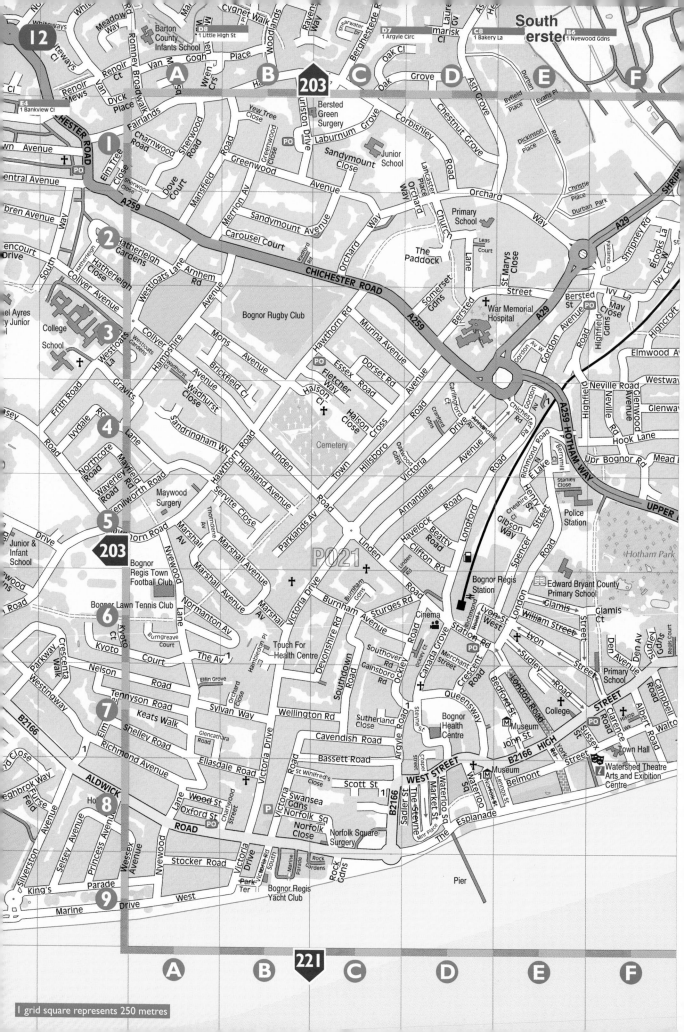

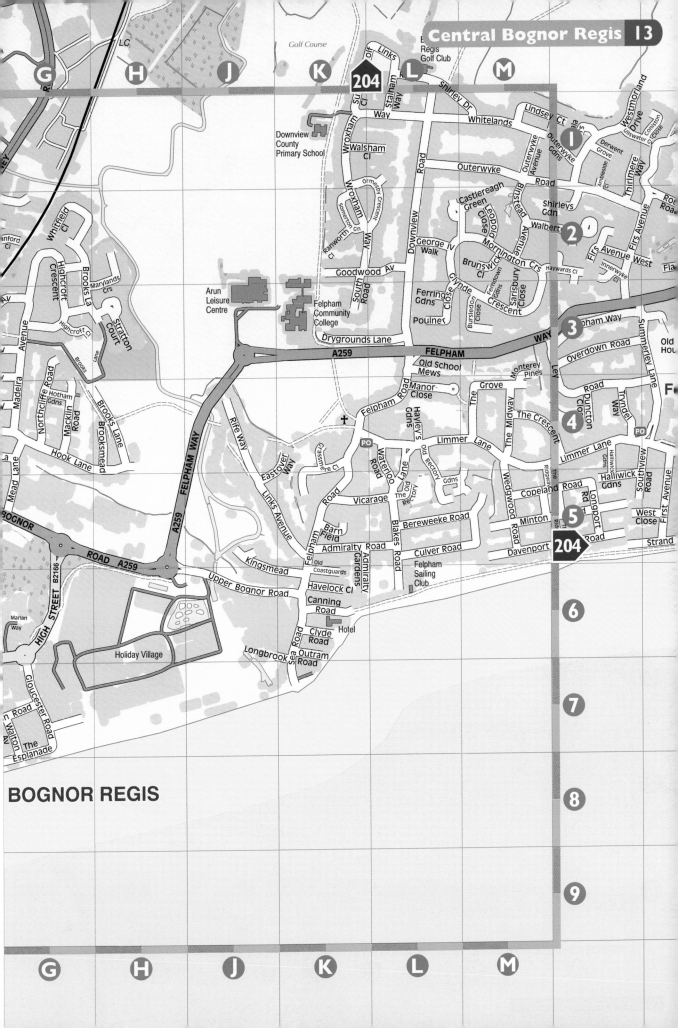

BOGNOR REGIS

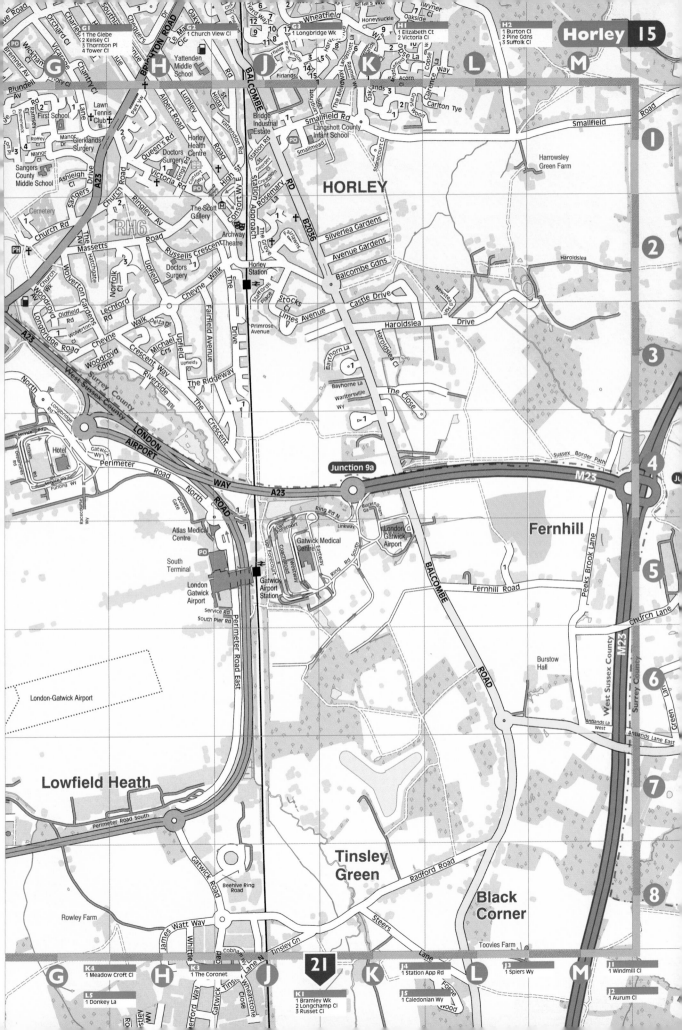

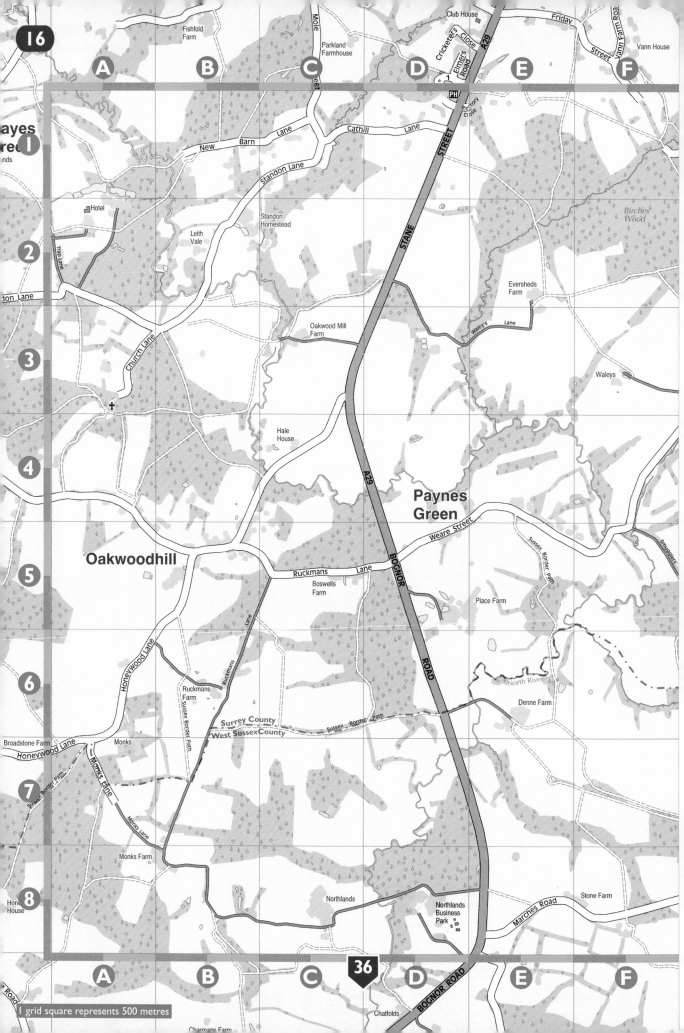

Clark's Green

Vann Lake

Vann Lake

G

Grenehurst Park

H

J

K

L

M

Pleystowe Farm

Rusper Road

1

Tiphams

Weare Street

Taylors

2

Knoll Farm

HORSHAM ROAD

Clock House

Holbrook Farm

Osbrooks

A24

Gages Farms

3

Ridge Farm

Sussex Border Path

Sussex Border Path

Muggeridge's

4

Sussex Border Path

Surrey County

West Sussex County

18

Oakdale Farm

Sussex Border Path

Lane

Wattlehurst Farm

Stammerham Business Centre

Friday Street

5

Old Barn

Hewells Farm

6

Tickfold Farm

Kingsfold

DORKING ROAD

Friday Street

Great Benhams

7

Marches Road

The Marches

Green Lane

A24

Langhurst Close

Langhurst

8

Joanland Farm

Boldings Brook

Langhurst Road

Mayes Lane

G

Durfold

H

J

37

K

Langhurstwood Road

L

M

Old Holbrook

L7
1 Abbotsfield Rd
2 Fulmar Cl
3 Hunstanton Cl
4 Moor Park Crs
5 The Orchards
6 Prestwick Cl
7 Puffin Rd
8 Troon Cl

L8
1 Coniston Cl
2 Kittiwake Cl
3 Langdale Rd
4 Sandpiper Cl
5 Woodcroft Rd

M6
1 Galahad Rd
U 2 Guinevere Rd
P 3 Lancelot Rd
4 Merlin Cl
F 5 Stanbridge Cl

G H J K L M

Ivyhouse Farm

Oaklands Park

Orltons

Orltons Lane

Sussex Border Path

Naldretts Farm

Prestwood Lane

Lower Prestwood Farm

Ifieldwood

The Mount

The Mount

Langhurst

Langhurst Lane

Langhurst Lane

Hilvbarn Road

Ifield Wood

River Mole

Bonwycks Place

Old Barn

20

Aldingbourne Close

Chowles

Burnt House Lane

Rusper Road

Lambs Green

Cobnor

Axmas Farm

Lambs Green Road

River Mole

Stumbleholm Farm

Rusper Road

Ifield Golf & Country Club

St Andrews Road

Birkdale Drive

Fairway

Fairway

Kilnwood End

Carylls

Hoylake Close

Bonnings Rd

Peverel Rd

Whitehall Drive

Hyde Drive

Middleton Way

Hanbry Rd

Collins Road

Rother Crs

Waterfield Gdns

Waterfield School

Kilnwood

39

Kilnwood Lane

Faygate

The Millbank

The Hollow

Rother

Gemini Cl

Casson

Callisto

Booth Rd

M8
2 Comper Cl
3 Harmony Cl
3 Hyperion Ct
4 Lutyens Cl
5 Neptune Cl
6 Peacemaker Cl
7 Samaritan Cl
8 Saturn Cl
9 Soane Cl

Street Names for these grid squares are listed at the back of the index

Bewbush Community Middle School

First School

G H J K L M

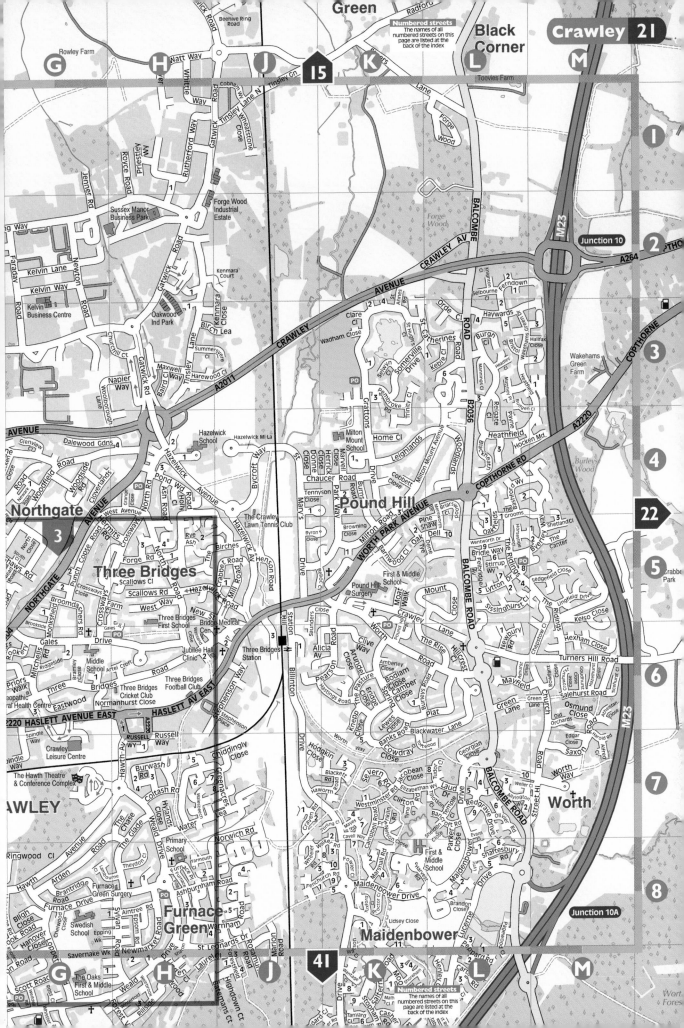

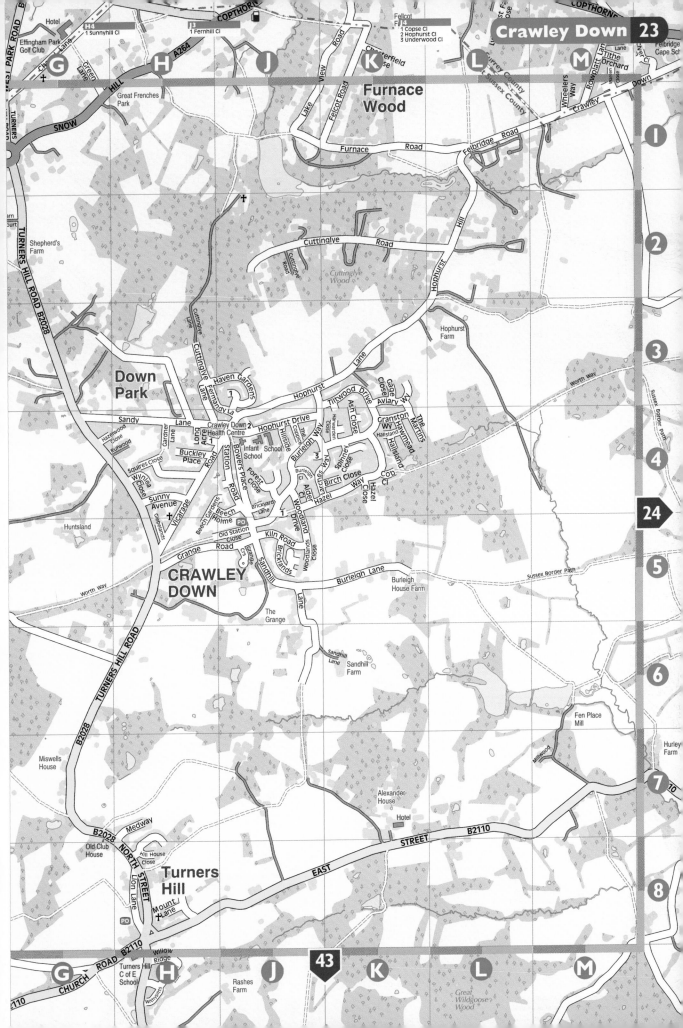

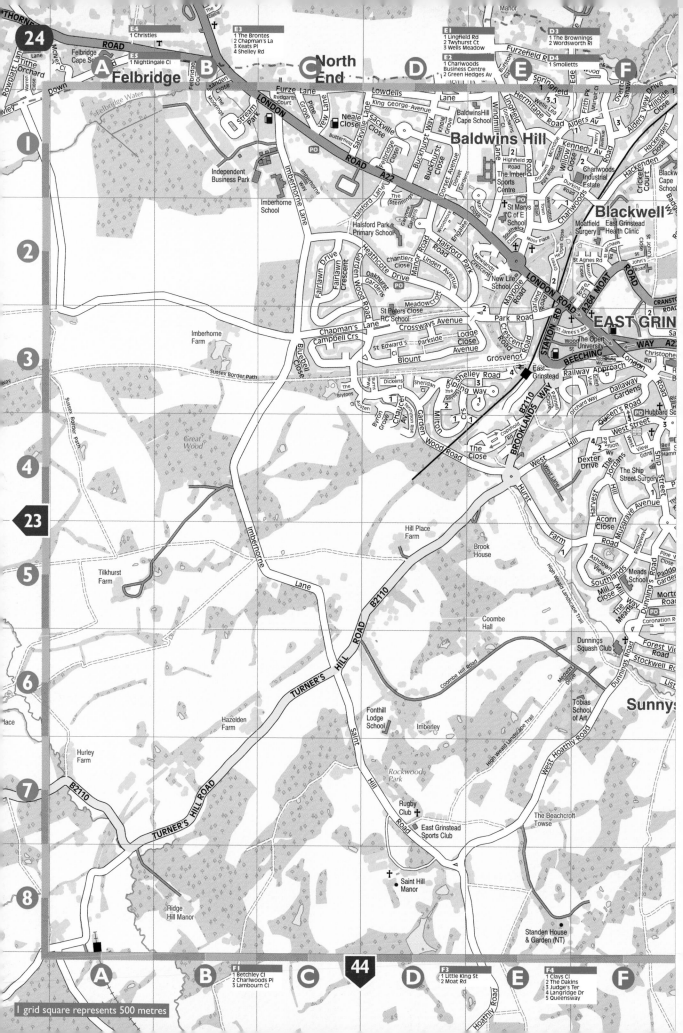

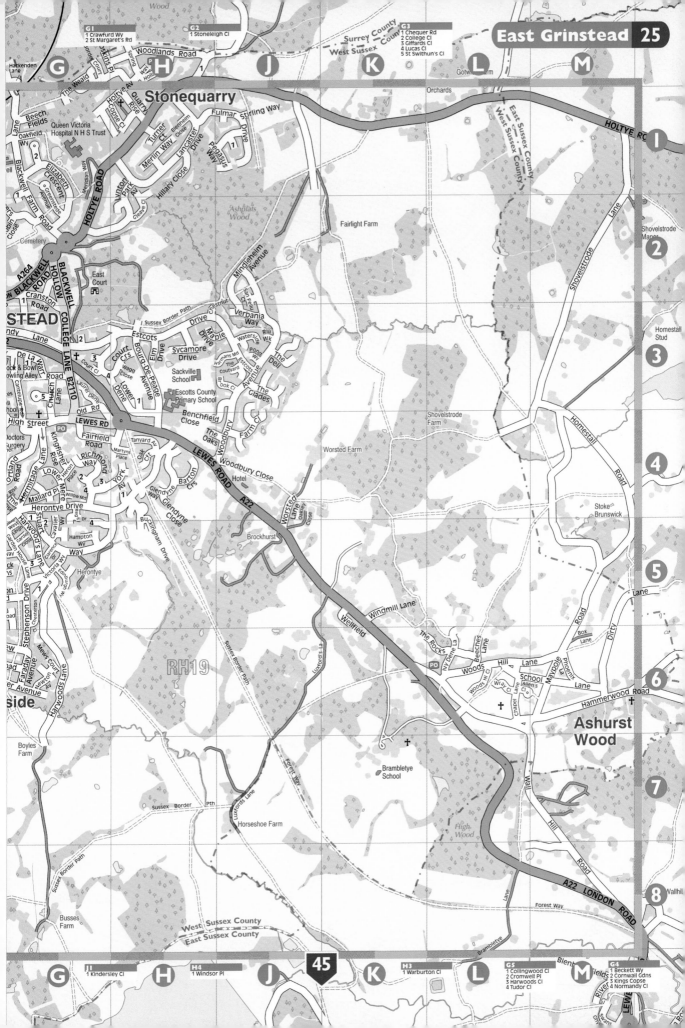

B3002

GU26

G **H** **J** **K** **L** **M**

I

2

3

4

28

5

6

7

8

HEADLEY ROAD

K1
1 Jubilee La

L1
1 Rockdale Dr

Whitmore Vale Road

L2
1 The Rowans

The Spinney
Waggoners Wy
Saddlers Scarp
Waggoners
Wheelwrights La
Beech La
Bridle Cl
Halters End
Horseshoe Bend
Beech Hanger End
Grayshott Clinic
School Rd
Grayshott Primary School
Vale Wood Lane
Vicarage Gdns
Chestnut Cl
Church La
Glen Rd
Glen Rd
Hurstmere Cl
Tarn Rd
B3002
Grayshott Council Office
Grayshott Surg
Forestdale
St Edmunds School

Grayshott Hall

Grayshott

HEADLEY ROAD

Hill Road
PO
Stoney
Bottom
Kingswood Firs
Kingswood Firs
Tudor Cl
Cypress Wy
Hazel Gv

Lacygate Drive
Waggoners Wells Road

Hunters Moon

Kingswood Lane

Nutcombe

Mount Alvernia

High Pitfold

High
Pitfold

Hazel Grove

Amesbury School

Nutcombe Lane

Glenlea

HINDHEAD ROAD A287

Summerden

Waggoners Wells

High Pitfold Farm

A3(T)

Lion Lane

Bramshott Chase

PORTSMOUTH ROAD

Knockhundred Lane

Sandy Lane

Woolmer Hill Road

Woolmer Hill School

Hollow

Glenlea

Critchmere

Holy Cross Hosp

Terry Tree Avenue

Bramshott Common

Hatchetts Drive

Rockfield

Woolmer Hill

Critchmere Hill

Shottermill County Middle Sc

Shottermill

Sandy Lane

Lower Hanger

Woolmer Hill Rd

Pitfold Av

Dolphin Cl

Critchmere Vale

Deep Well Dr

Redwood Copse

Butterbeds La

Fox Rd

Foxcote

Old Rd

Fir Tree Avenue
Sunvale Av
Oak Tree Lane
Border Rd

Cemetery

Mnr Cl
Mnr Cl
Critchmere Lane

Thur Cl
2
1
4
3

Hercott
Elliot Dr
Fox Rd

HINDHEAD

LIPHOOK RD

Meadows

The Millstream

Hammer Lane

Moor Rd

Copse Road
Pegasus Cl

Hammer Bottom

Hammer Lane

Heath Rd

B2131

LINCHMERE ROAD

Hammer

Cemetery

B2131

Penwith Drive

Marley Lane

B2131

Springfarm Rd

Row Rd

School

Hillside

7

C

Hewshott Lane

Hampshire County
West Sussex County

Gillham's Lane

Gillham's Lane

Hammer Hill

Hewshott House

LIPHOOK ROAD

Danley Lane

Linchmere Common

Sussex Border Path

M6
1 Lucas Fld
2 Mallard Cl
3 Mill Cl
4 Pitfold Cl

L7
1 Hammerwd Cps
2 Puttock Cl

L6
1 Sunvale Cl

G **H** **J** **K** **L** **M**

Sussex Border Path

Sussex Border Path

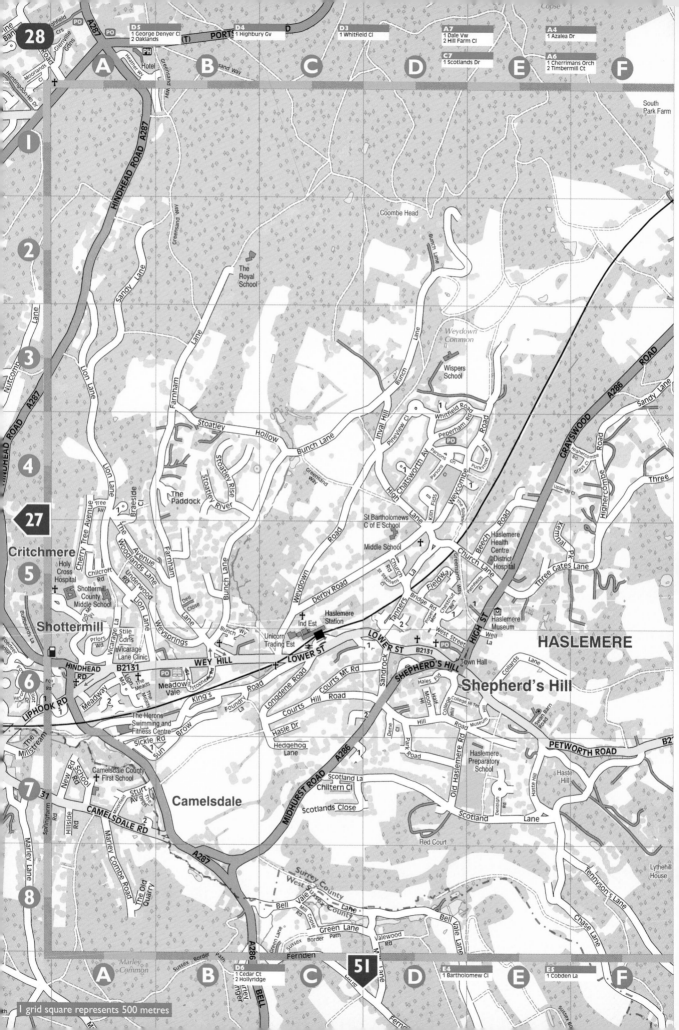

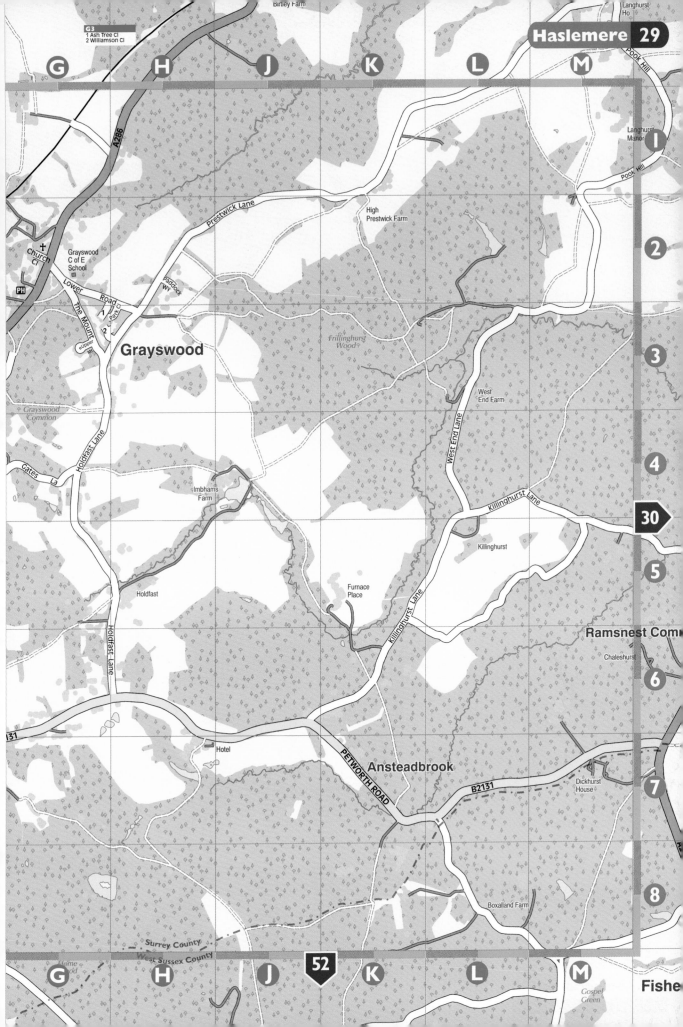

G H J K L M

Langhurst
Ho

Pook Hill

1 Ash Tree Cl
2 Williamson Cl

A286

Langhurst
Manor

I

Pook Hill

Prestwick Lane

High
Prestwick Farm

2

Church
Cl

Grayswood
C of E
School

PH

Lower Road

Paddock
Wy

Park Cl

1
2

Upper M

Grayswood

Frillinghurst
Wood

3

The Mount

West
End Farm

West End Lane

4

Grayswood
Common

Holdfast Lane

Gates La

Imbhams
Farm

Killinghurst Lane

30

Killinghurst

5

Holdfast

Furnace
Place

Killinghurst Lane

Ramsnest Comm

Chaleshurst

6

Holdfast Lane

131

Hotel

Ansteadbrook

PETWORTH ROAD

B2131

Dickhurst
House

7

Boxalland Farm

8

Surrey County
West Sussex County

Home
ood

G H J **52** K L M

Gospel
Green

Fishe

Langhurst
Ho

30

Ridgley Road

Ballsdown

The As... Combe

Rose... Road

The Surgery
Pathfield

school Lane

Coxcombe Lane

A283

Pockford Road

A

B

C

D

E

F

PO

St Marys
C of E First
School

The Green

PH

I

Langhurst
Manor

Pook Hill

Mill Lane

Turners Ma

Pickhurst Road

Hazel
Bridge

Sydenhurst

Bethwins Farm

A283

Pickhurst Road

High Street Gr

2

PETWORTH ROAD

Cherfold

Pickhurst

Folli

3

Chiddingford
Golf Club

4

29

5

Gostrode
Farm

Robins Farm

Shillinglee
Park Golf
Club

Ramsnest Common

Gostrode Lane

Chaleshurst

CRIPPLECRUTCH HILL

6

Surrey County

West Sussex County

Plaistow Rd

Sussex Border Path

khurst
se

7

Shillinglee Road

Broadlands

Stilland
Farm

Shillinglee
Home Farm

A283

Shillinglee Road

Gaston's Farm

8

Deer
Tower

A

B

C

53

D

E

F

Fisherstreet

Gospel
Street

Eastland Farm

I grid square represents 500 metres

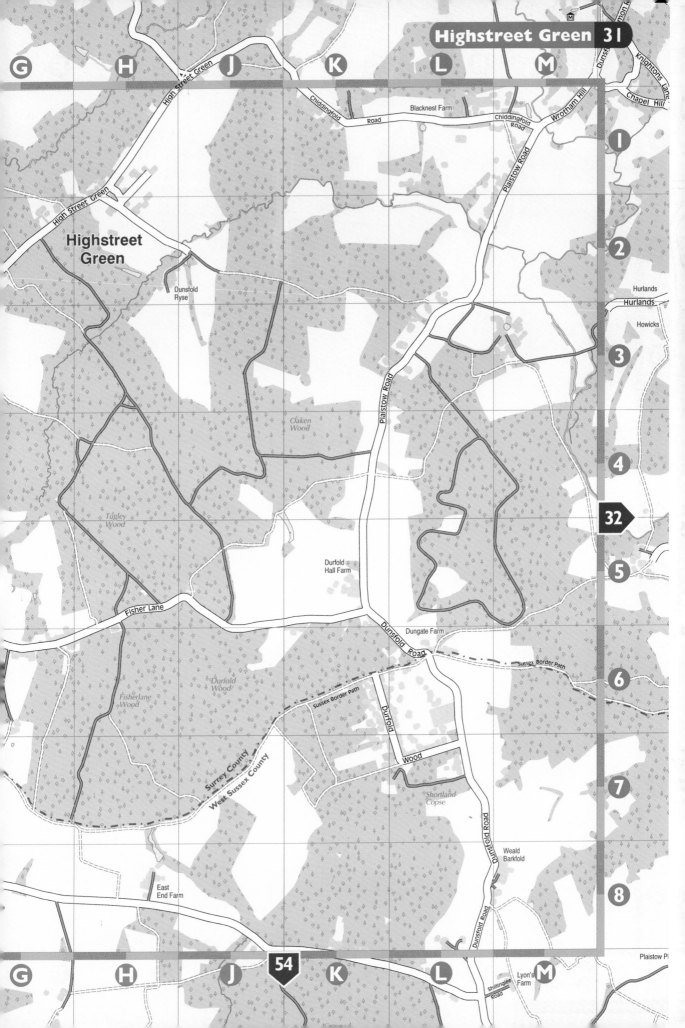

Dunsfold Common R
Afold Road
Common House
A K ans Lane
Dunsfold Common
B
C Barnfield
Benbow Lane
D
E
F
Wrotham Hill
Chapel Hill
Alfold Road
Dunsfold Road

1

Sachel Court Road

Rams Lane
Wey South Path
Sachel
Court

2

Hurlands
Hurlands Lane
Howicks
Knightons
Sidney Wood
Springbok Farm

3

Wey south Path

Wey South Path
Rosemary Lane

4

Oakhurst

31

Upper Ifold

5

er Path

6

Oakhurst Farm

Surrey County
West Sussex County
Sydney Farm
Wey South Path

7

Hog Wood
Sussex Border Path

The Ifold Bridge Lane

8

Plaistow Place
A
B
C
55
D Hogwood Road
E
F
Pound field
Thistledown Vale
Lo

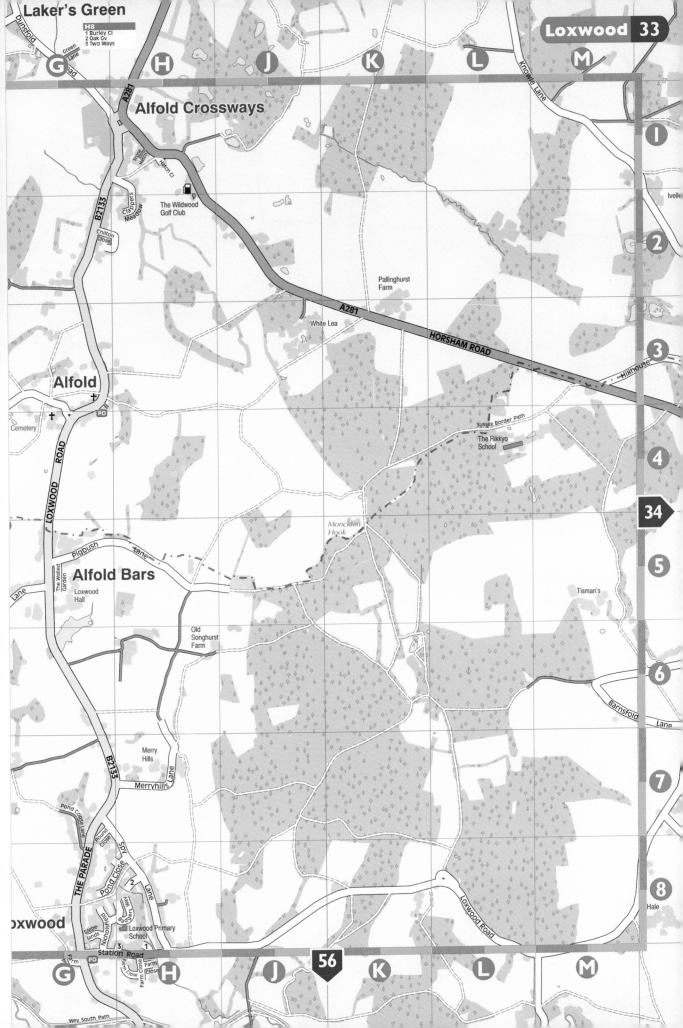

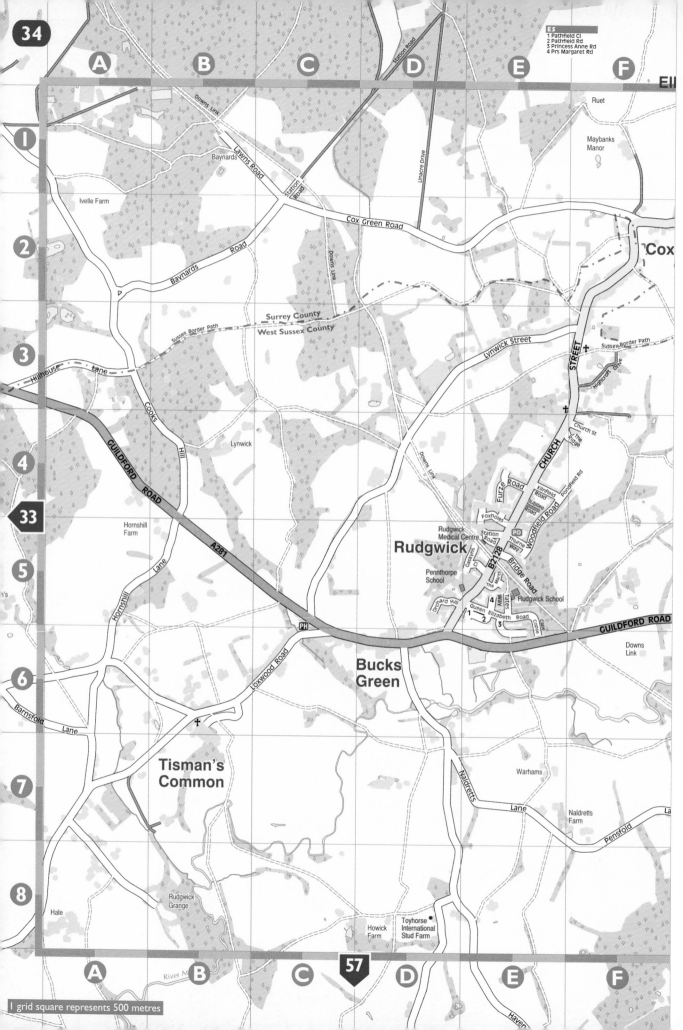

A B C D E F

A B C D E F

E5
1 Pathfield Cl
2 Pathfield Rd
3 Princess Anne Rd
4 Prs Margaret Rd

Ell

Ruet

Maybanks
Manor

Cox

Cox Green Road

Ivelle Farm

Baynards

Lawns Road

Station Road

Linacre Drive

Downs Link

Baynards Road

Downs Link

Surrey County
West Sussex County

Sussex Border Path

Lynwick Street

STREET

Sussex Border Path

Highcroft Drive

Hillhouse Lane

Cooks Hill

Lynwick

Downs Link

Church St
The Ridge

CHURCH

Furze Road

Kilnfield Road

Pondfield Rd

Jubilee Road

Woodfield Road

Pondfield Rd

33

Hornshill Farm

GUILDFORD ROAD

A281

Foxnoles

Rudgwick
Medical Centre

Station Road

PO

Thurne Way

Rudgwick

Gaskyns Cl

B2128

Pennthorpe
School

Bridge Road

Hornshill Lane

Orchard Hill

The Marts

New Way

Tates

Rudgwick School

Queen Elizabeth Road

Copse

Cope

4

1

2

3

GUILDFORD ROAD

Downs Link

PH

Loxwood Road

Bucks
Green

Warhams

Barnsfold Lane

Naldretts Lane

Naldretts Farm

Pensfold

Tisman's
Common

Rudgwick
Grange

Hale

Howick
Farm

Toyhorse
International
Stud Farm

River Ar

Haven

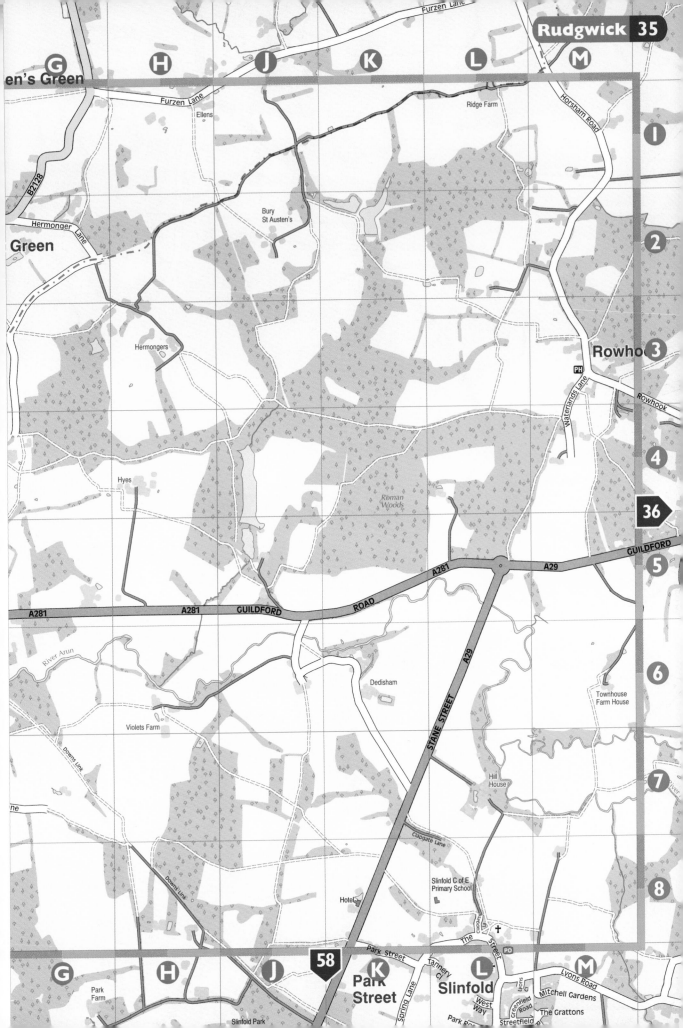

G   H   J   K   L   M

en's Green

I

2

3

4

36

5

6

7

8

Furzen Lane

Ellens

Bury
St Austen's

Ridge Farm

Horsham Road

B2128

Hermonger Lane

Green

Hermongers

Rowhoo

PH

Rowhook

Waterlands Lane

Hyes

Roman
Woods

A281   GUILDFORD

A281

A29   GUILDFORD

River Arun

Dedisham

Stane Street

A29

Townhouse
Farm House

Violets Farm

Downs Link

Hill
House

Clapgate Lane

Downs Link

Slinfold C of E
Primary School

Hotel

58

Park street

The Clapham

G   H   J   K   L   M

Park
Farm

Park
Street

Spring Lane

Tannery
Cl

Slinfold

Lyons Road

West
Way

Greenfield
Road

Lyons
Road

Mitchell Gardens

The Grattons

PO

Street

Streetfield

Park Ro

Slinfold Park

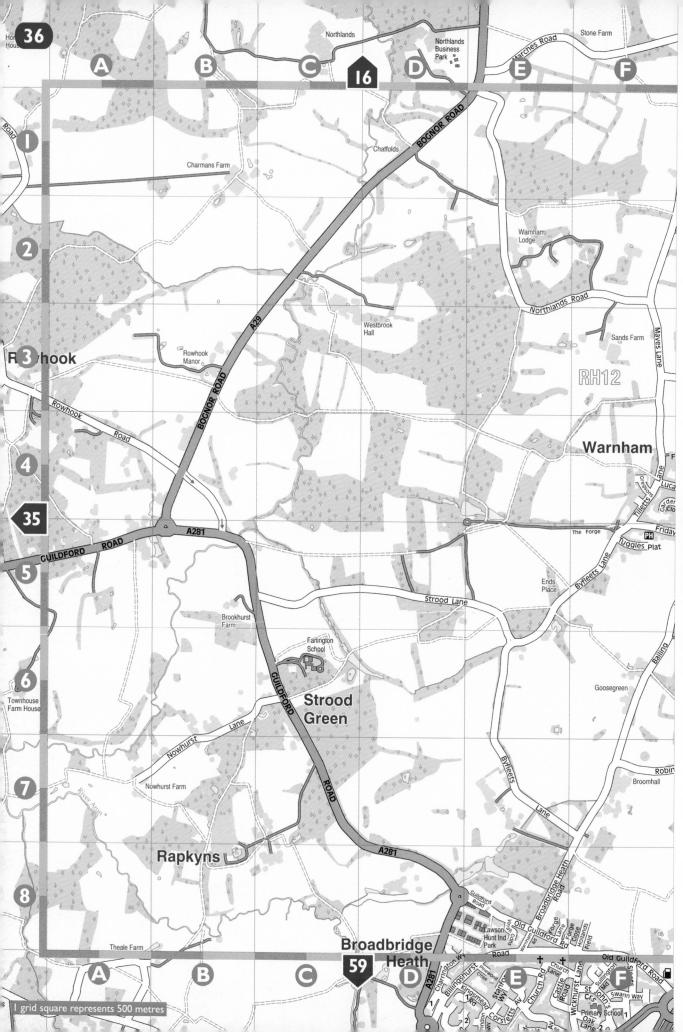

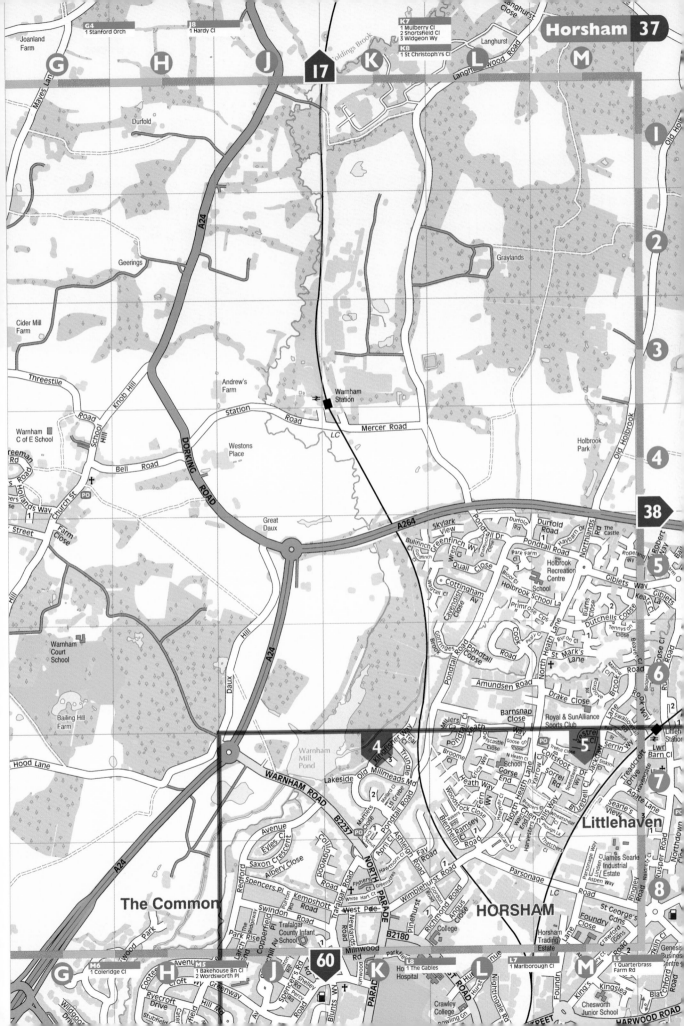

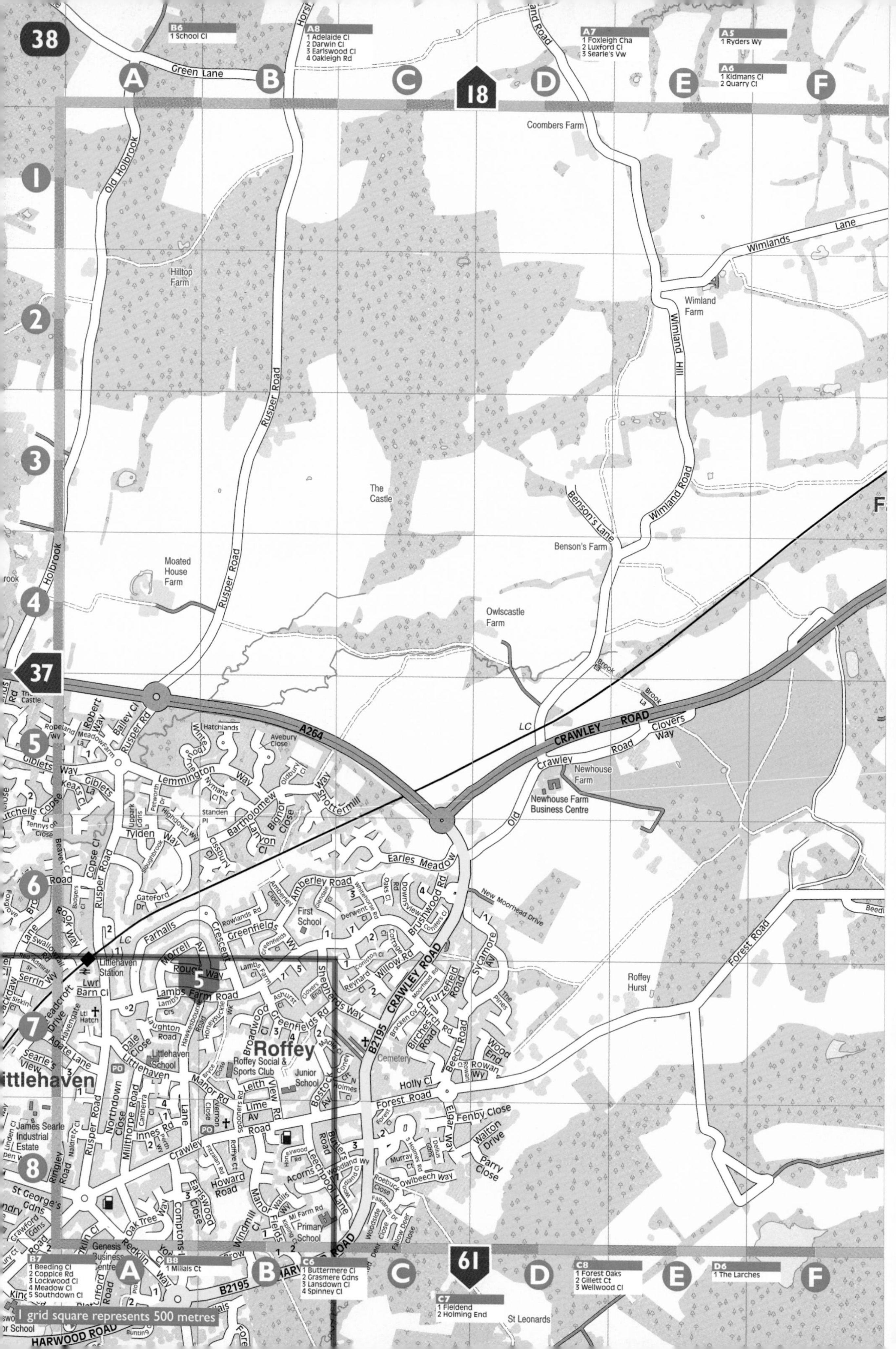
B6
1 School Cl
A8
1 Adelaide Cl
2 Darwin Cl
3 Earlswood Cl
4 Oakleigh Rd
A7
1 Foxleigh Cha
2 Luxford Cl
3 Searle's Vw
A5
1 Ryders Wy
A6
1 Kidmans Cl
2 Quarry Cl
Green Lane
18
Coombers Farm
Old Holbrook
Hilltop Farm
Rusper Road
Wimlands Lane
Wimland Farm
Wimland Hill
Wimland Road
The Castle
Benson's Lane
Benson's Farm
Moated House Farm
Owlscastle Farm
Holbrook
37
A264
Brook La
CRAWLEY ROAD
Clovers Way
Crawley Road
Newhouse Farm
Newhouse Farm Business Centre
Old
LC
Robert Way
Bailey Cl
Rusper Rd
Hatchlands
Avebury Close
Giblets Way
Lemmington Way
Bartholomew
Bignor Close
Shottermill
Tennyson Close
Tylden Way
Earles Meadow
New Moorhead Drive
Amberley Road
First School
Greenfields
Brushwood Rd
Gateford Dr
Farnhalls
Crescent
Littlehaven Station
Lambs Farm Road
Shepherds Way
B2195 CRAWLEY ROAD
Sycamore Av
Roffey Hurst
Forest Road
Roffey
Roffey Social & Sports Club
Junior School
Littlehaven School
Cemetery
Wood End
Rowan Wy
Holly Cl
Forest Road
Fenby Close
Walton Drive
Parry Close
Owlbeech Way
Crawley Road
Howard Road
Littlehaven
James Searle Industrial Estate
Ringley Road
St George's Gdns
Primary School
Genesis Business Centre
B2195 HARWOOD ROAD
61
B7
1 Beeding Cl
2 Coppice Rd
3 Lockwood Cl
4 Meadow Cl
5 Southdown Cl
B8
1 Millais Ct
C6
1 Buttermere Cl
2 Grasmere Gdns
3 Lansdown Cl
4 Spinney Cl
C8
1 Forest Oaks
2 Gillett Ct
3 Wellwood Cl
D6
1 The Larches
C7
1 Fieldend
2 Holming End
St Leonards
1 grid square represents 500 metres

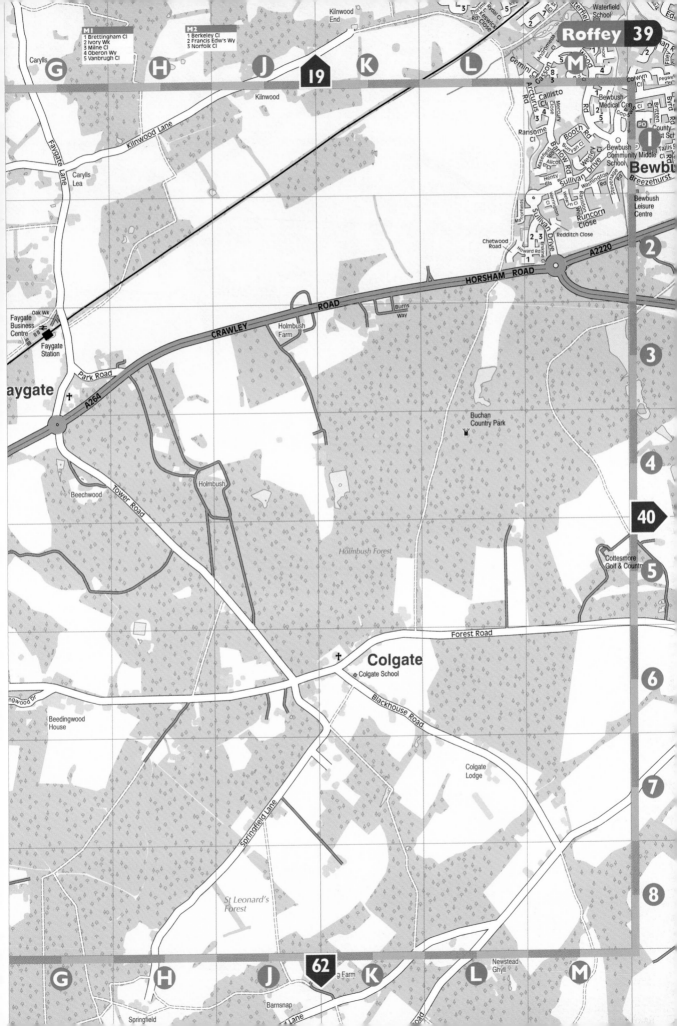

G H J **19** K L M

M1
1 Brettingham Cl
2 Ivory Wk
3 Milne Cl
4 Oberon Wy
5 Vanbrugh Cl

M2
1 Berkeley Cl
2 Francis Edw's Wy
3 Norfolk Cl

Carylls

Kilwood
End

Waterfield
School

Kilwood

Kilnwood Lane

Faygate Lane

Carylls
Lea

Gemini Cl

Callisto

Colwyn Rd

Bewbush
Medical Cen

I

Bewbu

Ransome
Cl

Booth Rd

Barlow Rd

Arcturus Rd

Casson Rd

Mercury

Bewbush
Community Middle
School

County
st Sch

Bewbu

Masefield

Alicott

Henty
Cls

Wesley

Van Cl

Sullivan Drive

Washington

Tallis

Breezehurst

Sullivan Drive

Runcorn
Close

Redditch Close

Bewbush
Leisure
Centre

Chetwood
Road

2

Burns
Way

HORSHAM ROAD

A2220

Faygate
Business
Centre

Oak Wk

Faygate
Station

CRAWLEY ROAD

Holmbush
Farm

3

Park Road

aygate

A264

Buchan
Country Park

4

Beechwood

Tower Road

Holmbush

40

Cottesmore
Golf & Countr

5

Holmbush Forest

Forest Road

6

ngwood Dr

Beedingwood
House

Colgate

Colgate School

Blackhouse Road

Colgate
Lodge

7

Springfield Lane

St Leonard's
Forest

8

Newstead
Ghyll

G H J **62** K L M

g Farm

Barnsnap

Springfield

Lane

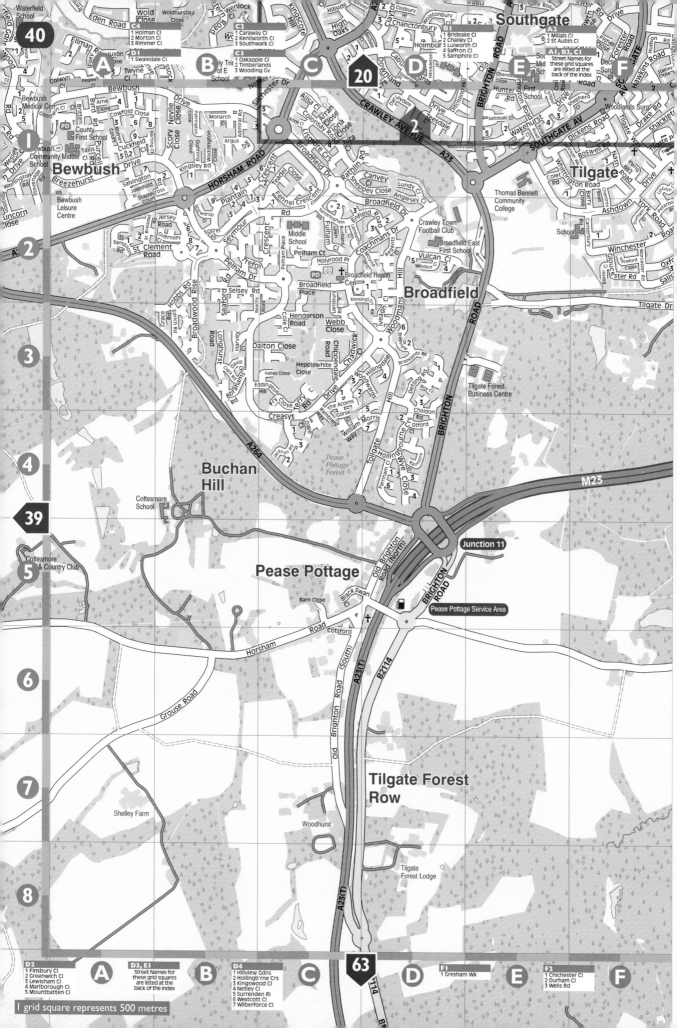

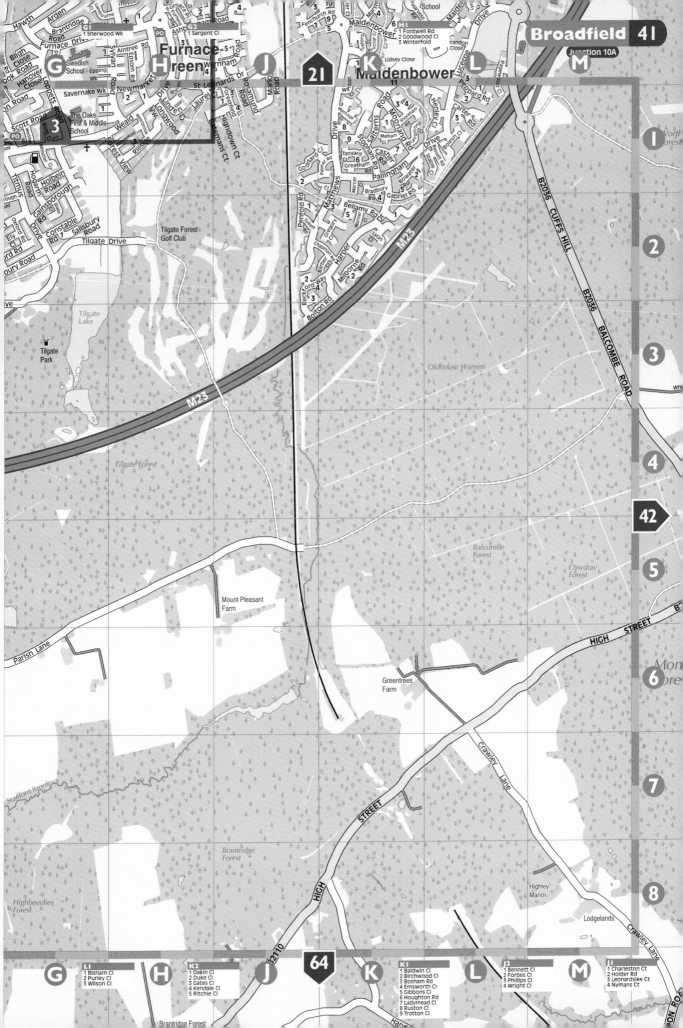

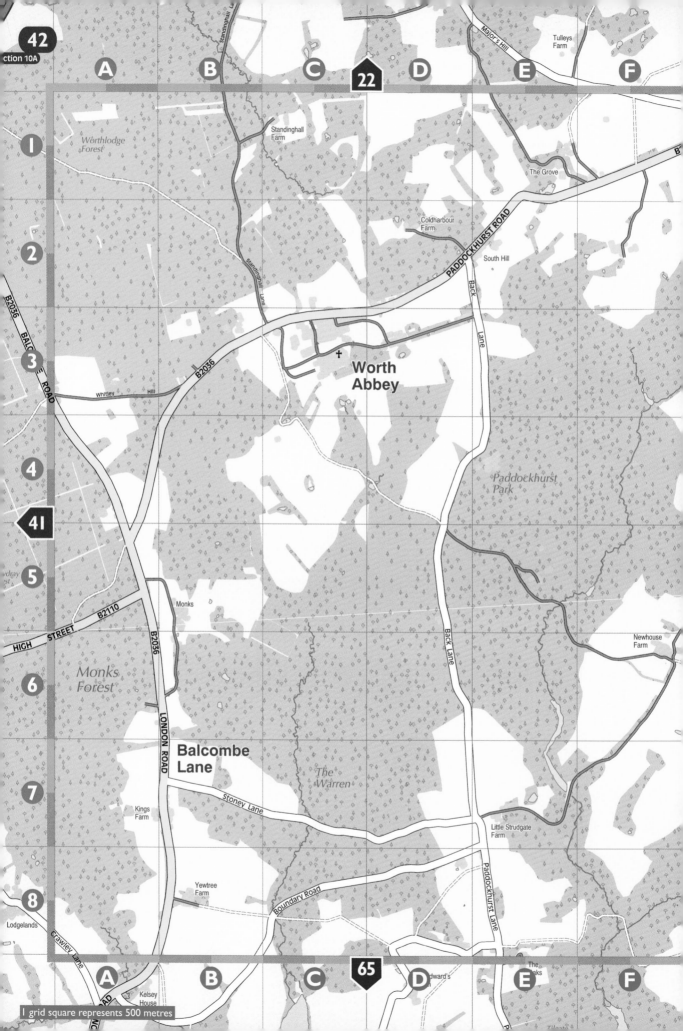

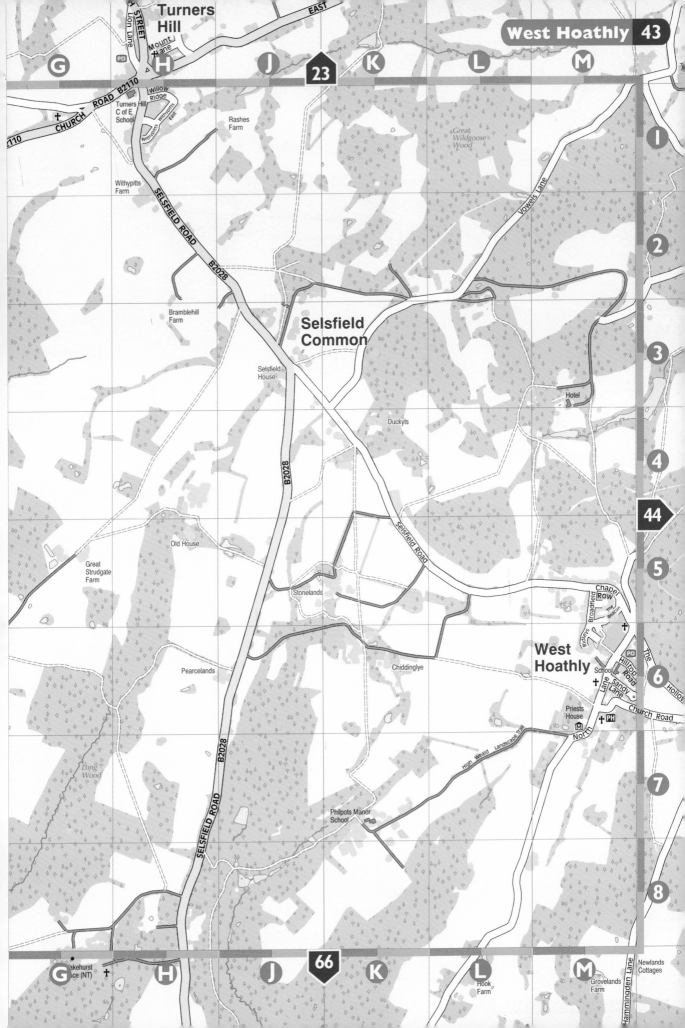

Turners
Hill

G   H   J   **23**   K   L   M

Lion Lane

Mount Lane

EAST

CHURCH ROAD B2110

B2110

PO

Turners Hill
C of E
School

Willow
Ridge

Witmorts East

Witmorts

Rashes
Farm

Great
Wildgoose
Wood

I

Withypitts
Farm

SELSFIELD ROAD

B2028

Vowels Lane

2

Bramblehill
Farm

**Selsfield
Common**

3

Selsfield
House

B2028

Hotel

Duckyls

4

44

Great
Strudgate
Farm

Old House

Selsfield Road

5

Chapel
Row

Broadfield

The
Beacon

Stonelands

Ridleys

6

School

Pearcelands

Chiddinglye

**West
Hoathly**

Hill Top Road

PO

Sandy
Lane

The Hollow

Lane

Church Road

Priests
House

M

PH

North

High Weald Landscape Trail

7

Long
Wood

B2028

SELSFIELD ROAD

Philpots Manor
School

8

akehurst
ce (NT)

G   H   J   **66**   K   L   M

Hook
Farm

Grovelands
Farm

Hammingden Lane

Newlands
Cottages

Ⓐ Ⓑ Ⓒ **24** Ⓓ Ⓔ Ⓕ

Saint Hill Manor

✝

tanden House & Garden (NT)

Ridge Hill Manor

1

2

Mill Place

Bluebell Railway

High Weald Landscape Trail

Admiral's Bridge Lane

West Hoathly Road

Weir Wood Resevoir

3

Birch Farm

Neylands Farm

Charlwood

4

43 ◄

Giffard's Wood

Blackland Farm

Mayes

Grinstead Lane

East Sussex County

West Sussex County

Plaw Wood

5

New Coombe Farm

Chapel Row

Broadfield

The Beacon

6

PO

School

Hilltop Road

ndy Lane

The Hollow

Church Road

✝ PH

✝

✝

Bavhams Field

Maripit Road

Harmsey Road

Station Road

Sharpthorne

Home Platt

Highcroft Road

Tyes Cross

Plawhatch Hall

Bulldogs Bank

Top Road

PO

Top Road

Plaw Hatch Lane

7

Courtlands

Horsted Lane

Bluebell Railway

Chilling street

Horncastle Wood

8

Han gden Lane

Newlands Cottages

Grovelands Farm

Ⓐ Ⓑ Ⓒ **67** Ⓓ Wickenden Farm Ⓔ Ⓕ

Deanlands Farm

Northwood

1 grid square represents 500 metres

G H J K L M

25

West Sussex County
East Sussex County

Lane

Sharpthorne

A22

Blenheim Fields

Riverside

LEWES ROAD

I

Swans Ghyll

Ashdown Forest
Health Centre

PO

Gilham Lane

Highfields

Cemetery

Priory Road

Colchester Vale

Freshfield

Michael Flds

Gage Ridge

Bank

Hatch

Upper Clo

2

Woodcote Road

LEWES ROAD

Chequer Grange

Spring Mead

Highgate Road

3

Tomtits Lane

Michael Hall
School

Kidbrooke
Park

Balfour Gdns

Tompsets

A22

4

Greenfield
School

RH18

5

Kidbrooke
Wood

Legsheath
Farm

6

Hindleap
Warren

Legsheath Lane

Priory Road

Coldharbour
Manor

Hindleap Farm

7

Wych
Cross

A22

Cripps Manor

Wych Cross
Place

8

Ashdown Forest
Farm

G H J K L M

Hillsd...m

A275

Press

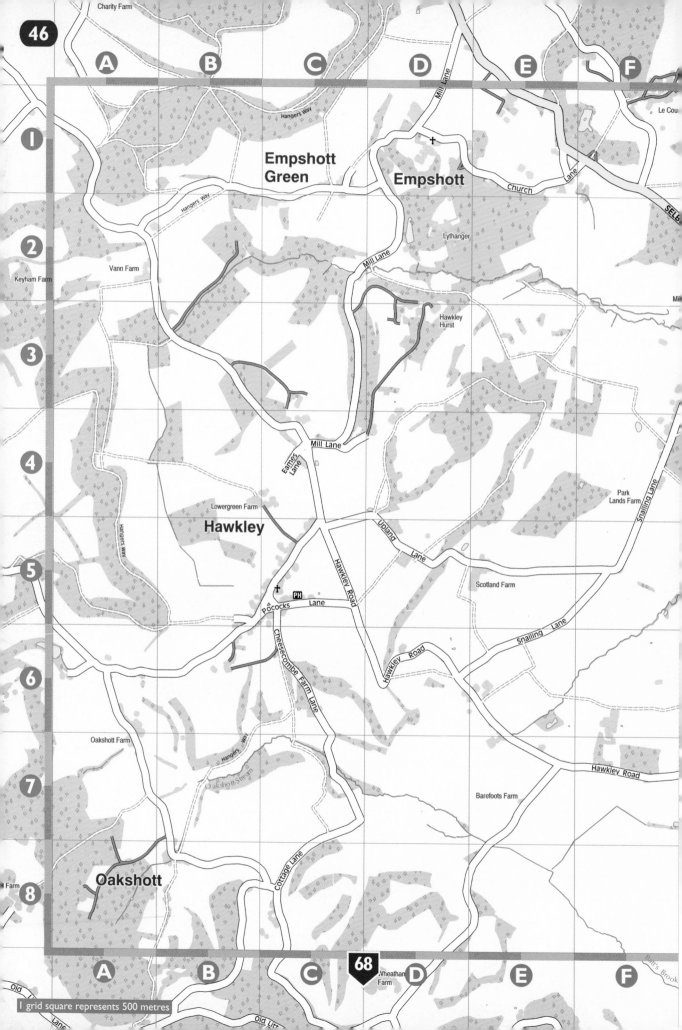

A   B   C   D   E   F

1

Charity Farm

Hangers Way

**Empshott
Green**

Empshott

Church Lane

Mill Lane

SELB

Le Cou

2

Keyham Farm

Vann Farm

Hangers Way

Mill Lane

Lythanger

3

Hawkley
Hurst

Mill

4

Mill Lane

Eames Lane

Park
Lands Farm

Shalling Lane

Lowergreen Farm

Hawkley

Upland Lane

5

PH

Pococks Lane

Scotland Farm

Hawkley Road

Snailing Lane

6

Oakshott Farm

Cheesecombe Farm Lane

Hawkley Road

7

Hangers Way

Oakshott Stream

Hawkley Road

Barefoots Farm

Cottage Lane

8

Farm

Oakshott

A   B   C   D   E   F

Wheatham
Farm

Bell's Brook

Old

Old Litt

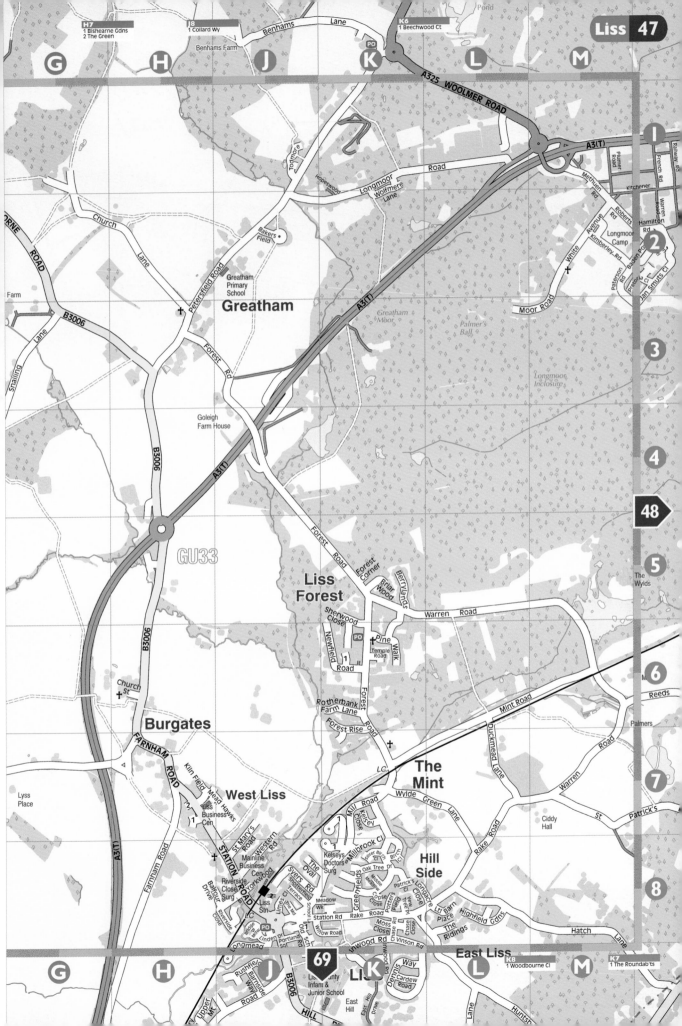

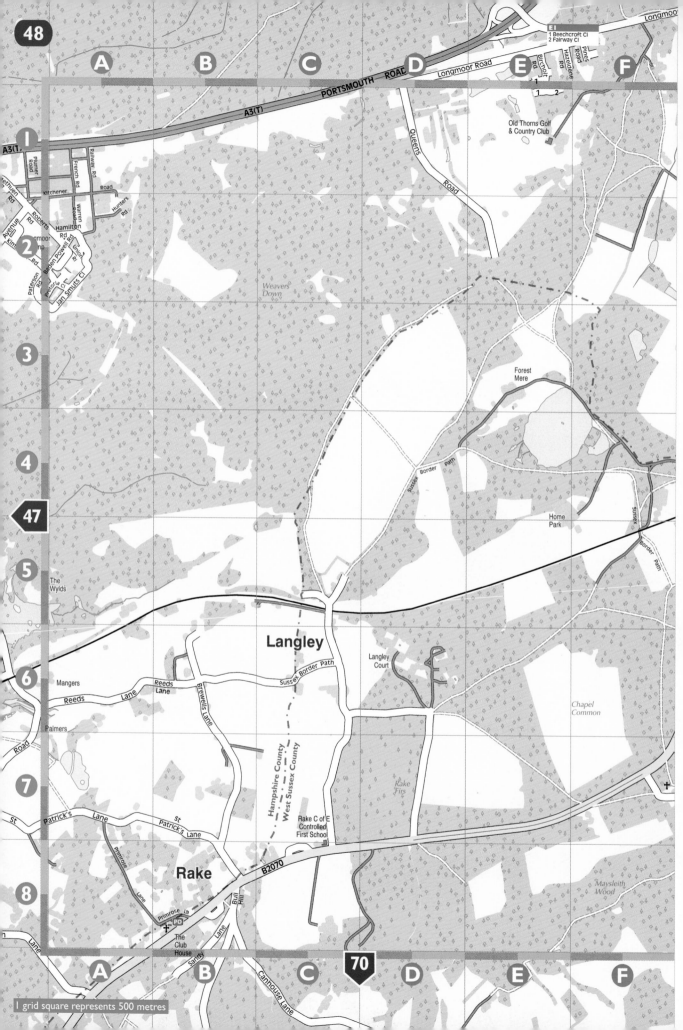

A   B   C   D   E   F

PORTSMOUTH ROAD

A3(T)

Longmoor Road

1 Beechcroft Cl
2 Fairway Cl

Old Thorns Golf
& Country Club

Birchott Rd
Hazeldene
Pines Road

A3(T)

Plumer Road
French Rd
Railway Rd
Road

Kitchener

Methuen Rd
Roberts Rd
Hunters Rd

Avenue
Kimp
Hamilton Rd

2

Baden Powell Rd
Union Rd

Paterson Rd
Pretoria Cl
Jan Smuts Cl

Weavers Down

Queens Road

3

Forest Mere

4

Sussex Border Path

47

Home Park

Sussex Border Path

5

The Wylds

Langley

Langley Court

Chapel Common

6

Mangers

Reeds Lane

Reeds Lane

Brewells Lane

Sussex Border Path

Reeds Lane

Palmers

Road

Hampshire County
West Sussex County

Rake Firs

7

St Patrick's Lane

St Patrick's Lane

Rake C of E
Controlled
First School

Maysleith Wood

8

Rake

Primrose Lane

Primrose Ln

PO

The Club House

Santy Rd

Bull Hill

B2070

Canhouse Lane

Lane

A   B   C   70   D   E   F

1 grid square represents 500 metres

Griggs Green

1 Shipley Ct

Longmoor Road

Liphook Junior School

1 Enfield Cl
2 Willow Cl

Ave

The Gv

Contour Gallery

Bohunt Community School

The Maltings

B2131

Manor Ho

Hazelbank Cl

Chappell

HASLEMERE

G   H   J   K   L   M

The Ship House Surgery

LIPHOOK

Larch Cl

Court Cl

Midhurst

Chiltlee Mnr

Grenville

Chiltlee Cl

Ash Gv

Willow

Chestnut

Golden Flds

Devils

Highfield Lane

I

The Firs

Bohunt Manor

Fletchers Fld

Newtown Road

Shepherds

Way

Chiltley Lane

Brookham School

Highfield School

2

Beaver Industrial Est

Newtown

Station Rd

ROAD

Newtown Surg

PORTSMOUTH

Midhurst Rd

Liphook Stn

Gunns Farm

Hollycombe Cl

Chiltley Way

Littlefield School

Highfield Lane

Sussex Border Path

Foley Manor

B2070

Aamers Crescent

Gunns Farm

Midhurst Road

South Road

3

Wheatsheaf Common

Sussex Border Path

GU30

Shufflesheeps

4

PORTSMOUTH RD

Sussex Border Path

50

Liphook Golf Club

Hollycombe

5

Ripsley House

B2070

Hatch Farm

Milland Lane

6

Milland House

Home Farm

Upper Wardley

7

Maysleith

Milland Lane

Wardley

Elmers Copse

8

Hollycombe School

Northend Farm

G   H   J   K   L   M

71

Mill Vale Meadows

Midhurst Road

Lambourne

A   B   **HOOK** C   D   E   F

GILLHAM'S   **ROAD**

PENWITH DR

27

LANE

Linchm   Road

I

Highfield Lane

Sussex Border Path

Danley   Lane

Sussex Border Path

Marley House

Sussex   Border   Path

Linchmere

Linchmere on

Sussex Border Path

2

Highfield School

Cognor Wood

Sussex Border Path

3

Stanley Common

4

Stanley Farm

Greenhill Wood

49

Parkgate Rough

5

Oakreeds Wood

6

Lower Lodge Farm

7

Elmers Marsh

Minepit Copse

Elmers Copse

8

Upper North Park Farm

Amon's Copse

A   B   **72**   C   D   E   F

Woodmansgreen

WHITES

LINCH RO

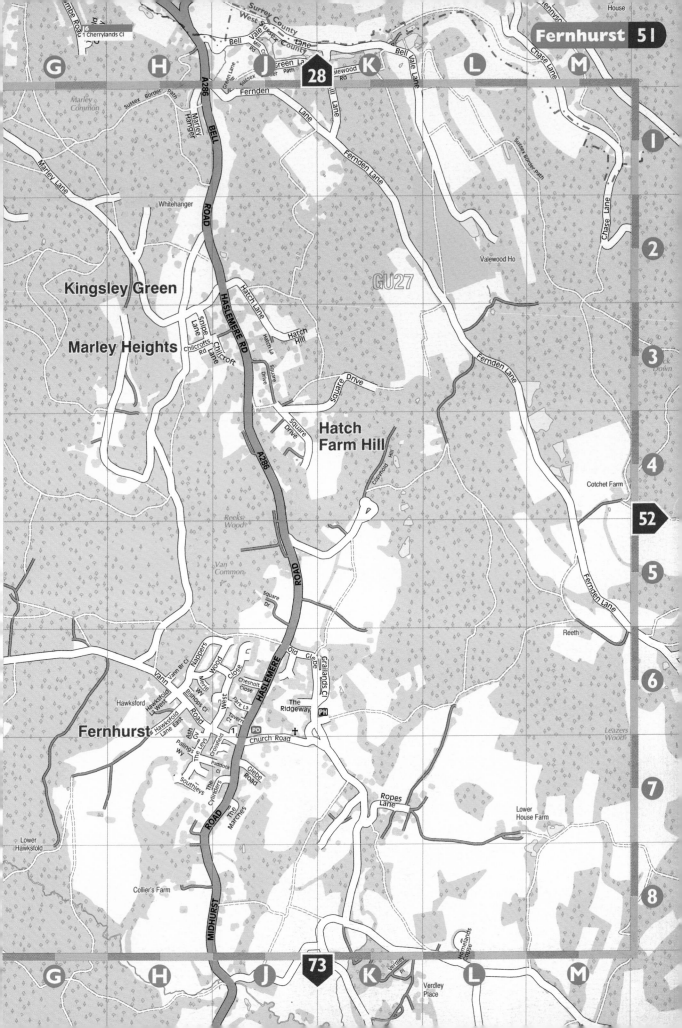

G   H   J   K   L   M
28

Surrey County
West Sussex County
Lane
Bell Vale Lane
Chase Lane
House

Marley Common
Sussex Border Path
Marley Hanger
BELL ROAD
A286
Green Lane
Fernden
Mill Rd
Valewood Rd
Bell Vale Lane

1 Cherrylands Cl

Marley Lane

Whitehanger

Kingsley Green

Hatch Lane
Snipe Lane
Chilcrofts Rd
Chilcroft
HASLEMERE RD
Square Drive
Hatch La
Hatch Hill

Marley Heights

A286
ROAD
Square Drive

Hatch Farm Hill
Copthold Hill
Square Drive
Drive

GU27

Valewood Ho

Fernden Lane

Ferndon Lane

Cotchet Farm

52

Reeks Wood

Van Common

Square Dr

Reeth

Vann
Vann Br Cl
Nappers Cl
Merle Wy
Bishops Cl
West
Park La
Wood Close
Cheshott Close
Old Glebe
Grailands Cl
The Ridgeway
PH

Hawksfold
Hawksfold La West
Hawksfold Lane East
Tavern Cl
Crossfield
PO
1
Church Road
+

Fernhurst
Ash Gv
The Leys
Palings
Wy
Paddock Cl
Southley's
The Cwilnders
Glebe Road
The Marshes
ROAD
HASLEMERE

Ropes Lane
Lower House Farm
Leazers Wood

Lower Hawkstold

Collier's Farm

MIDHURST

Verdley Pl
Verdley Place
Homelands Copse

G   H   J   K   L   M
73

I
2
3
4
5
6
7
8

Chase Lane
Down

A   B   C **29** D   E   F

Lythehill
House

Boxalland Farm

Surrey County
West Sussex County

Home
Wood

Gospel
Green

1

Chase Lane

Tennyson's Lane

Barfold

Jay's Lane

Jay's
Copse

Jobson's Lane

2

Tennyson's Lane

Aldworth Ho

Sussex Border Path

Roundhurst
Farms

Roundhurst
Common

3

Black
Down

Greenland Farm

Jobson's Lane

Black
Down

Upper
Diddlesfold
Farm

4

Cotchet Farm

280
▲
Blackdown Hill

Abesters

Ferndon Lane

5

Ferndon Lane

Shopp
Hill

Hookhams Farm

6

Blackdown
Farm

Hillgro

Leazers
Wood

7

Navant Hill

8

Windfallwood
Common

Park Farm

A   B   C **74** D   E † F

Great
Brockhurst
Farm

**Dial
Green**

PH

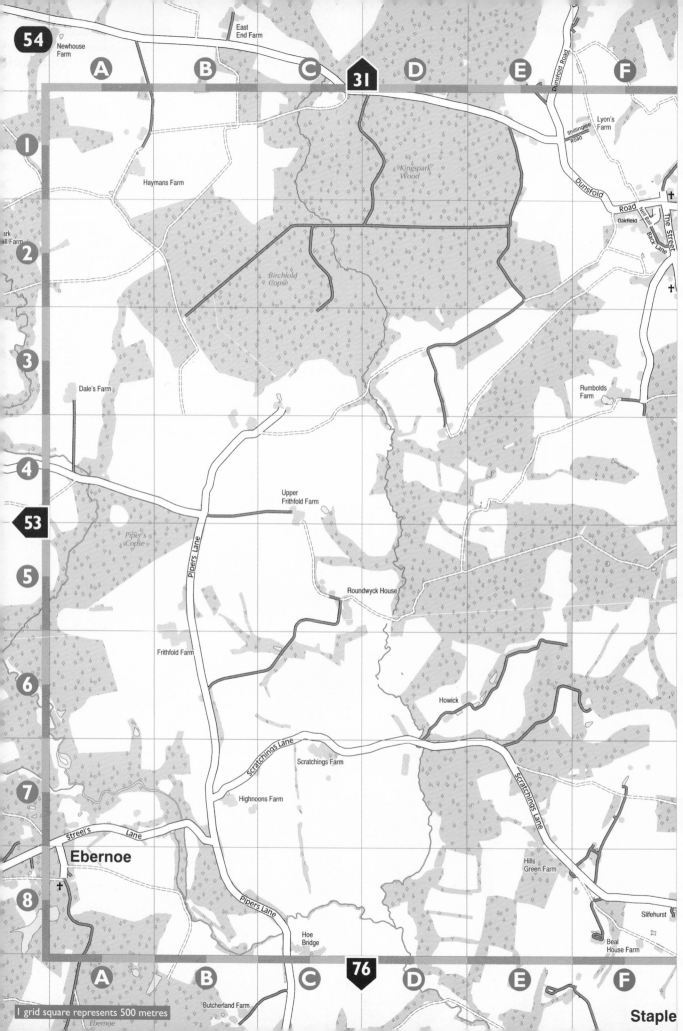

Newhouse
Farm

East
End Farm

A   **B**   **C**   **31**   **D**   **E**   **F**

Dunsfold Road

I

Haymans Farm

*Kingspark
Wood*

Shillinglee
Road

Lyon's
Farm

Dunsfold

Road

2

Oakfield

Neil Ball

Back Lane

The Street

*Birchfold
Copse*

ark
ill Farm

3

Dale's Farm

Rumbolds
Farm

4

Upper
Frithfold Farm

53

*Piper's
Copse*

Pipers Lane

5

Roundwyck House

Frithfold Farm

6

Howick

Scratchings Lane

Scratchings Farm

7

Highnoons Farm

Scratchings Lane

Streel's   Lane

Ebernoe

Hills
Green Farm

8

Slifehurst

Pipers Lane

Hoe
Bridge

Beal
House Farm

A   **B**   **C**   **76**   **D**   **E**   **F**

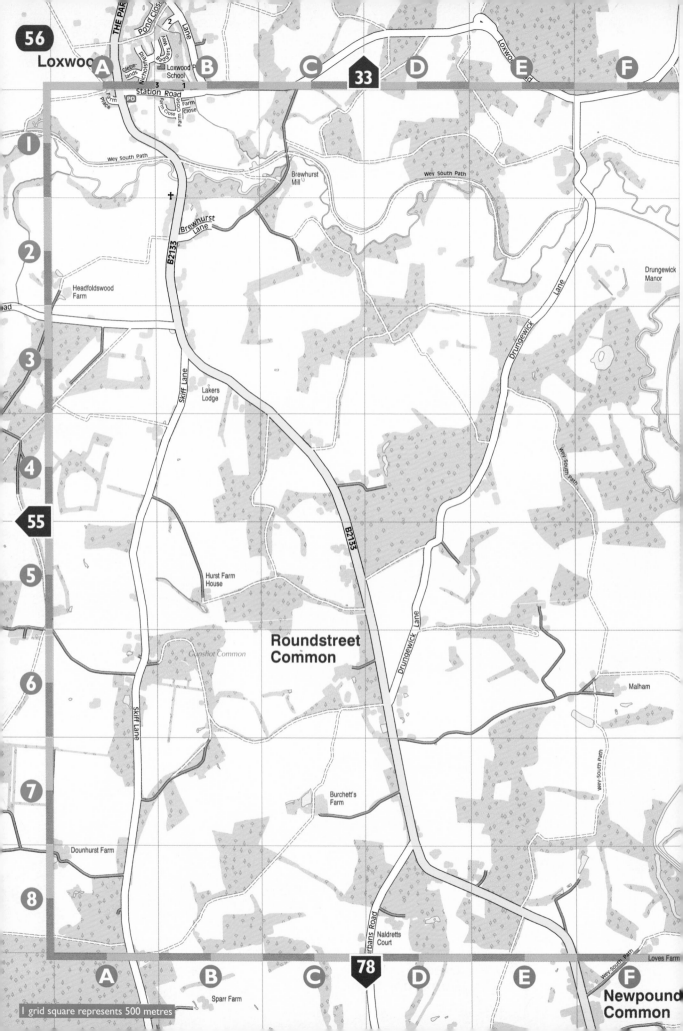

THE PARK

Pond Close

Lane

Glebe-lands

Nicholsfield

Loxwood School

Station Road

Farm Piece

PO

Farm Close

Farm Close

Loxwood Road

I

Wey South Path

Brewhurst Mill

Wey South Path

2

Headfoldswood Farm

Brewhurst Lane

B2133

Drungewick Manor

3

Skiff Lane

Lakers Lodge

Drungewick Lane

55

4

Wey South Path

5

Hurst Farm House

B2133

Roundstreet Common

6

Skiff Lane

Gunshot Common

Drungewick Lane

Malham

7

Burchett's Farm

Wey South Path

Dounhurst Farm

8

Naldretts Court

Urbans Road

Loves Farm

Sparr Farm

Newpound Common

1 grid square represents 500 metres

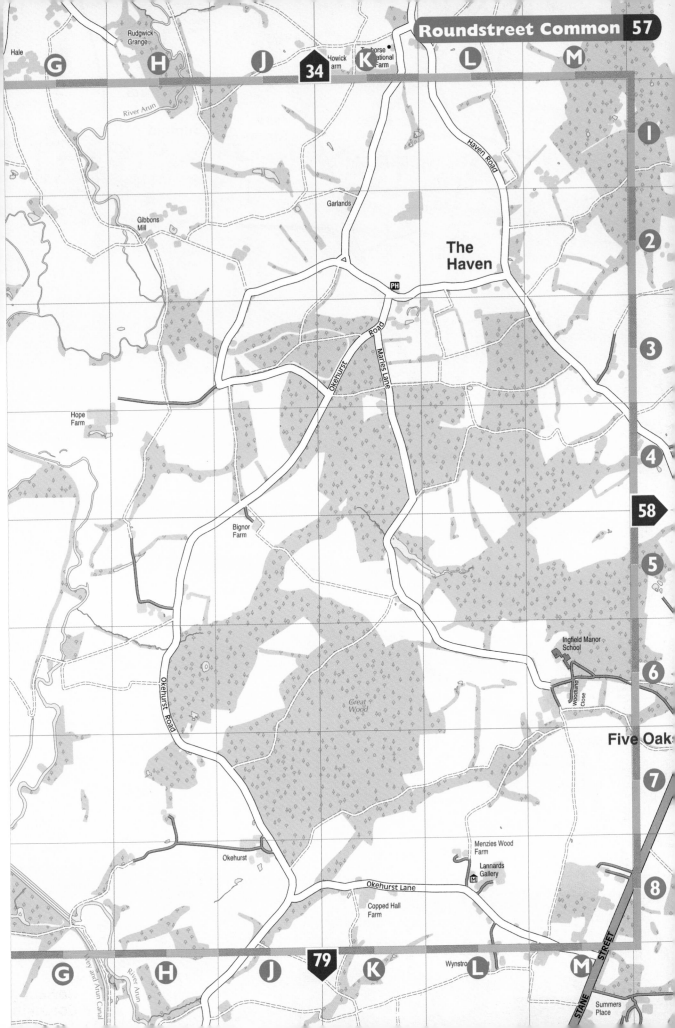

I

The
Haven

2

3

4

58

5

6

Five Oak

7

8

Hale

Rudgwick
Grange

River Arun

Gibbons
Mill

Garlands

Howick
Farm

Horse
National
Farm

Haven Road

PH

Hope
Farm

Okehurst Road

Marles Lane

Bignor
Farm

Great
Wood

Okehurst Road

Ingfield Manor
School

Woodland
Close

Menzies Wood
Farm

Lannards
Gallery

Okehurst

Okehurst Lane

Copped Hall
Farm

Wynstro

Summers
Place

STANE STREET

Wey and Arun Canal

River Arun

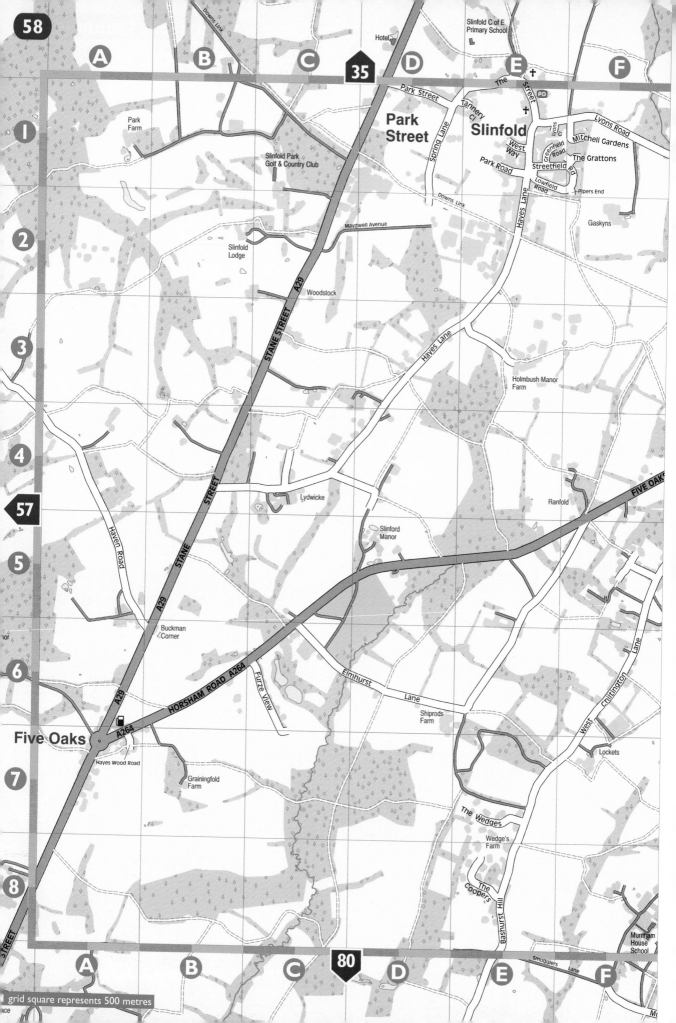

A   B   C   **35**   D   E   F

Downs Link

Hotel

Slinfold C of E
Primary School

I

Park Farm

Park Street

Park
Street

Tannery Cl

Spring Lane

Slinfold

West
Way

PO

Lyons

Mitchell Gardens

Greenfield Road

The Grattons

Streetfield

Slinfold Park
Golf & Country Club

Park Road

Lowfield
Road

Pipers End

Downs Link

Gaskyns

Lyons Road

Hayes Lane

2

Slinfold
Lodge

Maydwell Avenue

STANE STREET   A29

Woodstock

3

Holmbush Manor
Farm

Hayes Lane

4

57

Haven Road

Lydwicke

Slinford
Manor

Ranfold

FIVE OAKS

5

STANE   STREET

A29

6

Buckman
Corner

HORSHAM ROAD A264

A29

Furze View

Elmhurst
Lane

Shiprods
Farm

West Chiltington Lane

Lockets

Five Oaks

A264

Hayes Wood Road

7

Graningfold
Farm

The Wedges

Wedge's
Farm

8

STREET

The
Coopers

Bashurst Hill

Muntham
House
School

Smugglers Lane

A   B   C   **80**   D   E   F

grid square represents 500 metres

G   H   J   `36` dbridge Heath   K   L   M   I

H4 1 Itchingfield Rd   **K1** 1 Newbridge Cl

Guildford Road

Broadbridge H Road

Lawson Hunt Ind Park

Charrington Wy

Billingshurst Road

A281

Stanford Wy

Pinewood Close

Kingsmead Rd

Findon NW

Corsletts Av

Snelley Dr

Thelton

St. John's Av

Wickhurst Lane

Castle Road

Church Lane

Bearsden Way

Oak Lane

Primary School

Swann Way

Forge Cl

Forge Close

Hollands Field

Old Guildford Road

A264

Old-Guildford Road

Tanbridge House School

2

Lyons Road

Pinkhurst La

Lyons Farm Estate

Wellcross Grange

Pinkhurst

A264

Wickhurst Lane

Broadbridge Heath Leisure Centre

A24

3

Hills

Fen

Stoneybr

Farm

Downs Link

A264

Old Broadbridge Farm

River Arun

4

Bashurst Copse

A264

ROAD

Downs Link

Fulfords Farm

Christ's Hospital Station

T

60

A24

5

Grigg's Farm

Bashurst

Weston's Farm

Christ's Hospital Road

Station Road

Kg Edward Cl

King Edward Rd

Bluecoat Pond

The Christs Hospital Sports Centre

Infirmary

6

Christs Hospital Infirmary

Itchingfield

Itchingfield County Primary School

Westons Hill

The Av

The Avenue

Christ's Hospital (Sch)

West Gln Copse Rd

East Gun

Copse Rd

Downs Link

Two Mile Ash Road

7

Plumtree Cross Lane

Sandhills Road

Marlands

Sharpenhurst Farm

Lanaways Farm

8

G   H   J   `81`   K **Southwater Street**   L   M **Two Mile Ash**

M1 1 Heath Cl 2 St John's Crs

L1 1 Kingsmead Pl 2 Singleton Rd

ntham Dr

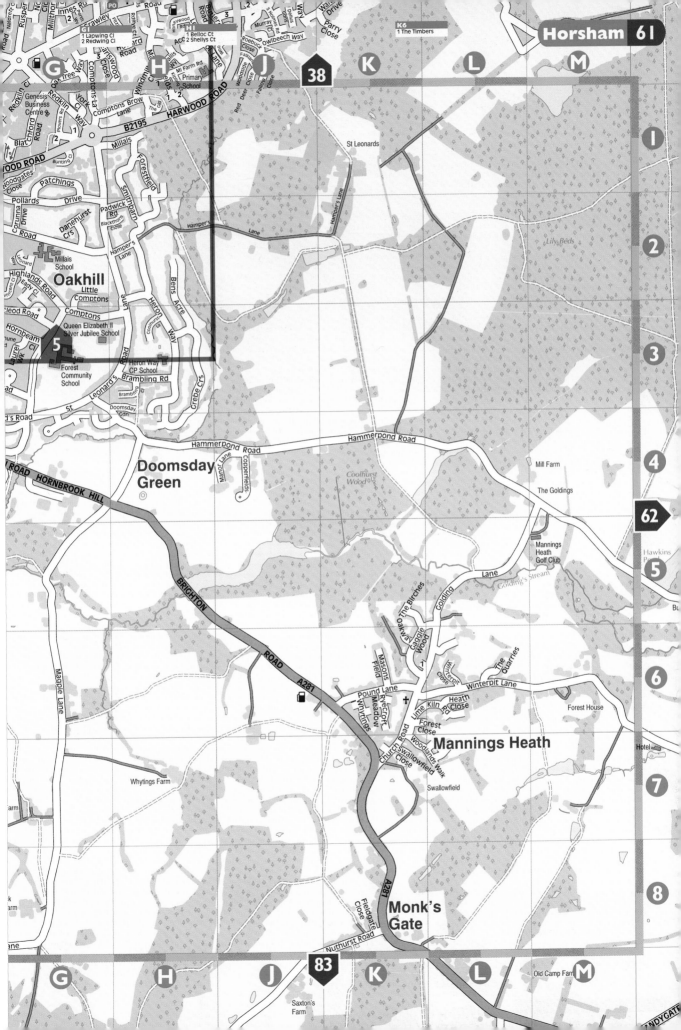

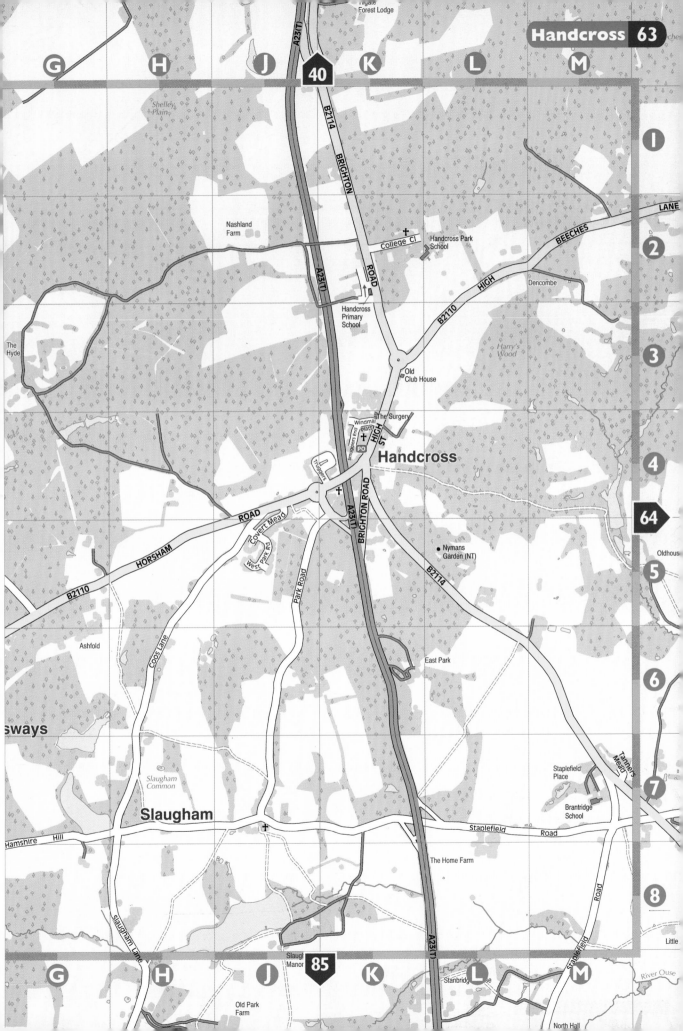

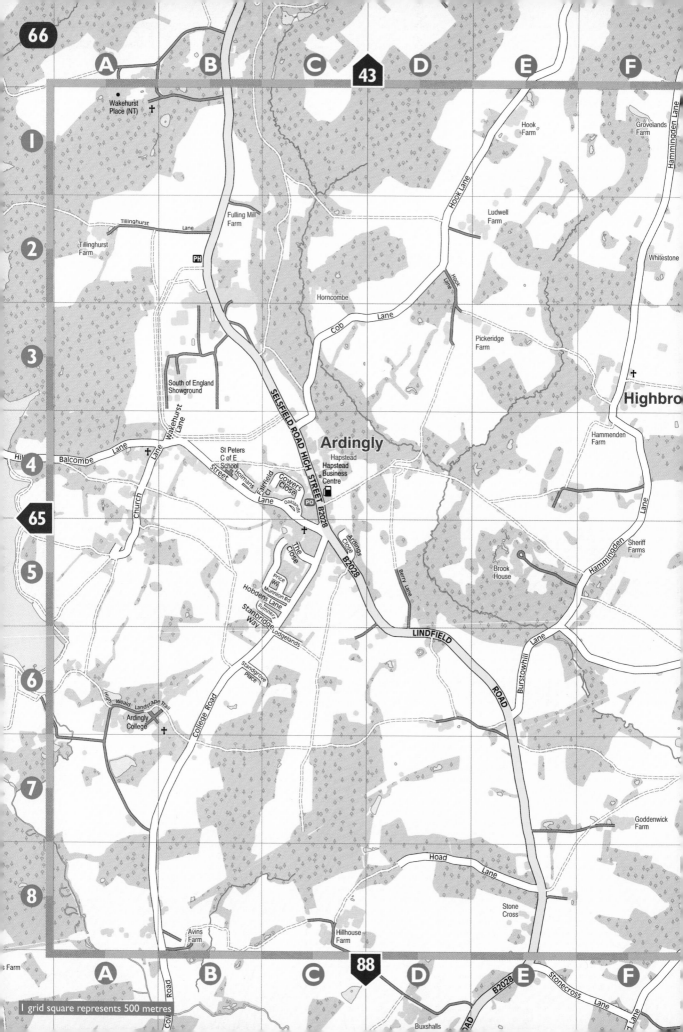

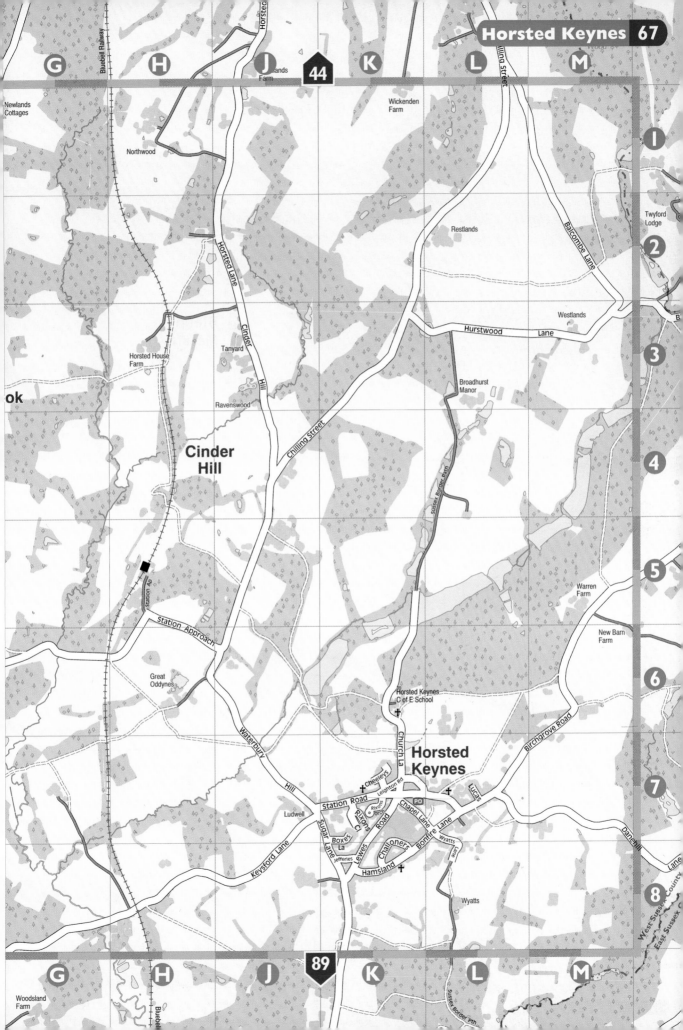

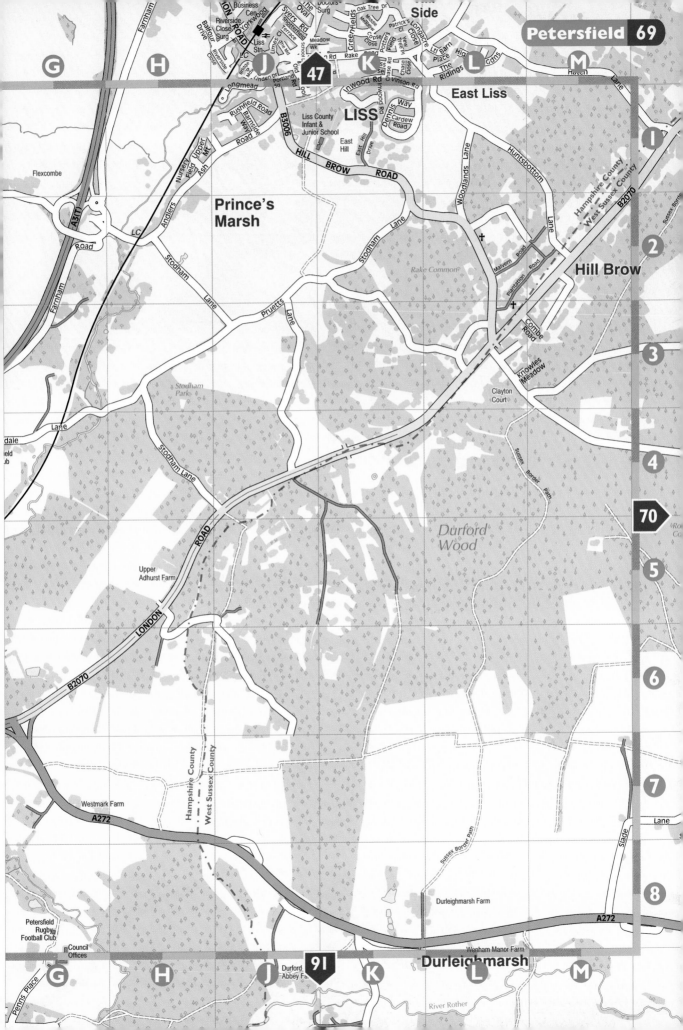

Rake

70

A B 48 C D E F

Hampshire County
West Sussex County

B2070

Sussex Border path

Primrose Lane
The Club House
PO
Sandy
Bull Hill
Lane
B2...

Canhouse Lane

Goldring

Canhouse Lane

1

Hill Brow 2

3

Harting Combe

4

Tullecombe

69

Rogate Common

Trotten Ma...

5

Rondle Wood

6

Rogate Lodge

Halecommon

Terwick Common

Dangstein

7

Fyning

Lane

Slade Farm

Slade

8

A272

PO
A272
Red House Ct
Rogate C of E
Controlled School
Parsonage Est
Habin
Carditts Lane

Rogate

A B C 92 D E F

1 grid square represents 500 metres

G H J **49** K L M

1

2

3

Titty Hill
4

72

Queen's
Corner
5

6

7

8

Mill Farm

Mill Vale
Meadows
Fernhurst Road

Greensand
Copse

Stretton's
Copse

Milland Rd

Drawdry's
Pennels

Meade

Milland

Rake Road

Iping Road

Lyford Farm

Waldergrove Farm ✝

Lambourne Lane

Lambourne Lane

Great
Trippetts Farm

Chorley
Common

Rake Road

Hurst
Farm

New
Barn Farm

Cook's Pond Road

Bobbolds
Farm

Kingsham
Wood

Iping Road

Hammer Stream

Borden
Wood

Robins
Lane

Robins

Bowley
Farm

Moorhouse Lane

arsh

Borden   Lane

Borden

Gatehouse Lane

Chithurst Lane

Tentworth

Iping Lane

Ash House

Gatehouse Farm

Cumber's Farm

Hammer
Wood

G H J **93** K Hammer   Lane Stanwater   Lane L M Hammerwood House Crouchhous

Northend

Hollycombe
School

Chithurst

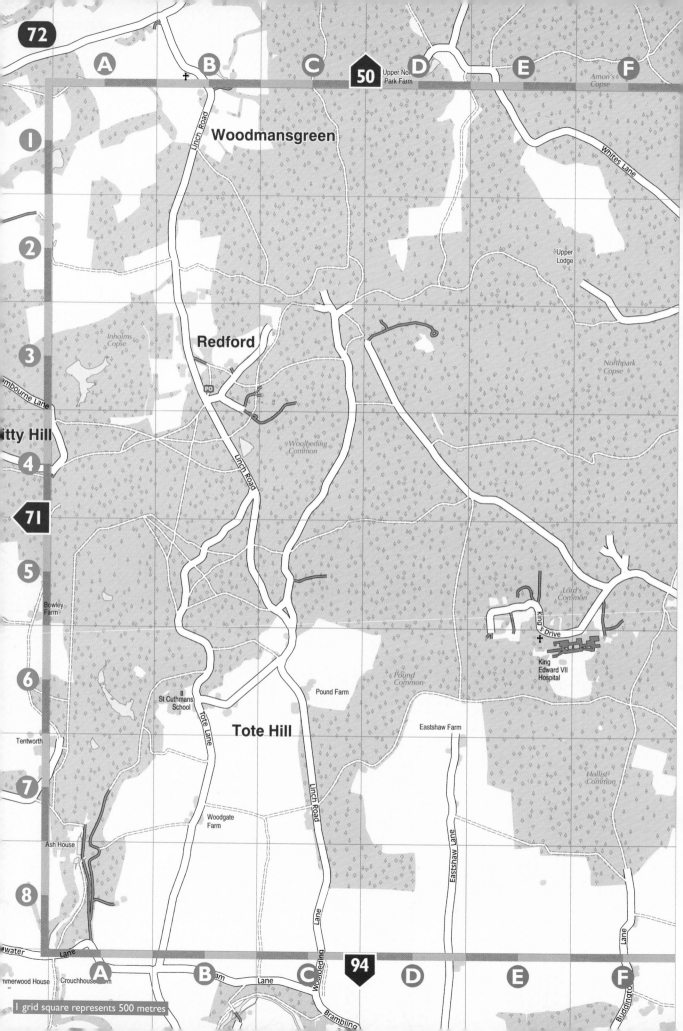

A   B   C   **50** D   E   F

Upper No...
Park Farm

Woodmansgreen

Linch Road

†

I

2

Inholms
Copse

Redford

...mbourne Lane

PO

...itty Hill

4

Amon's
Copse

Whites Lane

Upper
Lodge

Northpark
Copse

Woolbeding
Common

71

5

Bowley
Farm

Lord's
Common

King's Drive

†

King
Edward VII
Hospital

6

St Cuthmans
School

Pound Farm

Pound
Common

Tentworth

Eastshaw Farm

Tote Hill

Tote Lane

Linch Road

Hollist
Common

7

Ash House

Woodgate
Farm

Eastshaw Lane

8

...water   Lane

A   B   **94** C   D   E   F

...mmerwood House Crouchhouse...

...am   Lane

Woolbeding
Lane

Brambling

Buddingto...
...Lane

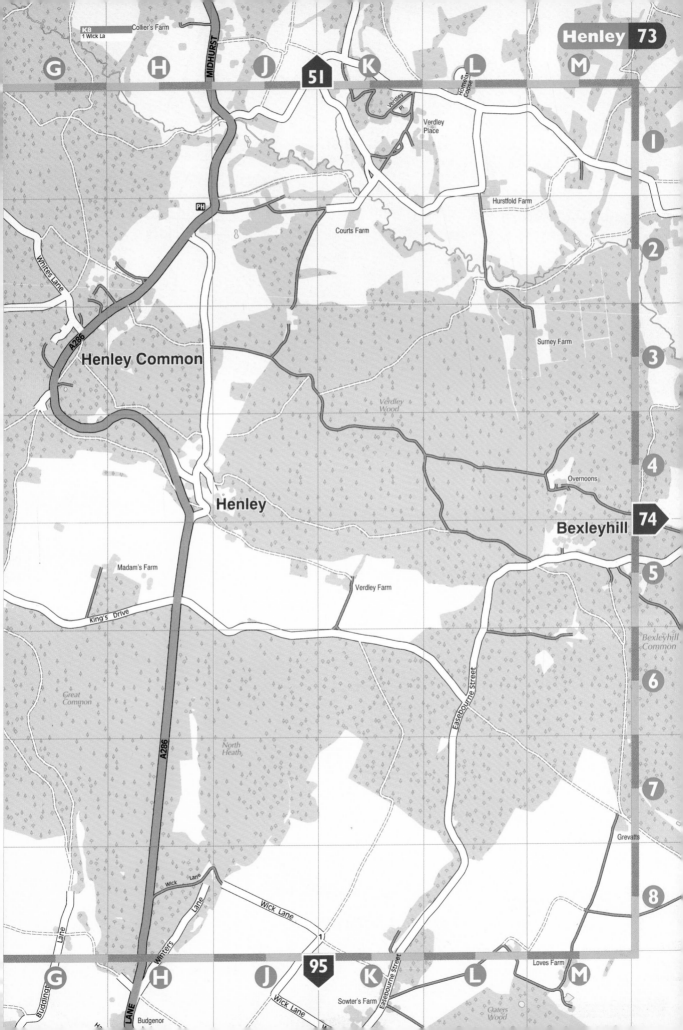

K8
1 Wick La

Collier's Farm

G H **MIDHURST** J **51** K L M

Verdley Pl

Verdley Place

Homefield Copse

I

Hurstfold Farm

2

PH

Courts Farm

Surney Farm

3

Henley Common

A286

Verdley Wood

4

Overnoons

Bexleyhill **74**

Henley

5

Madam's Farm

Verdley Farm

Bexleyhill Common

King's Drive

6

Great Common

A286

North Heath

Easebourne Street

7

Grevatts

8

Wick Lane

Budding

Winters

Wick Lane

95

Lane

G H J K L M

Lane

Budgenor

Wick Lane

Sowter's Farm

Easebourne Street

Loves Farm

Oaters Wood

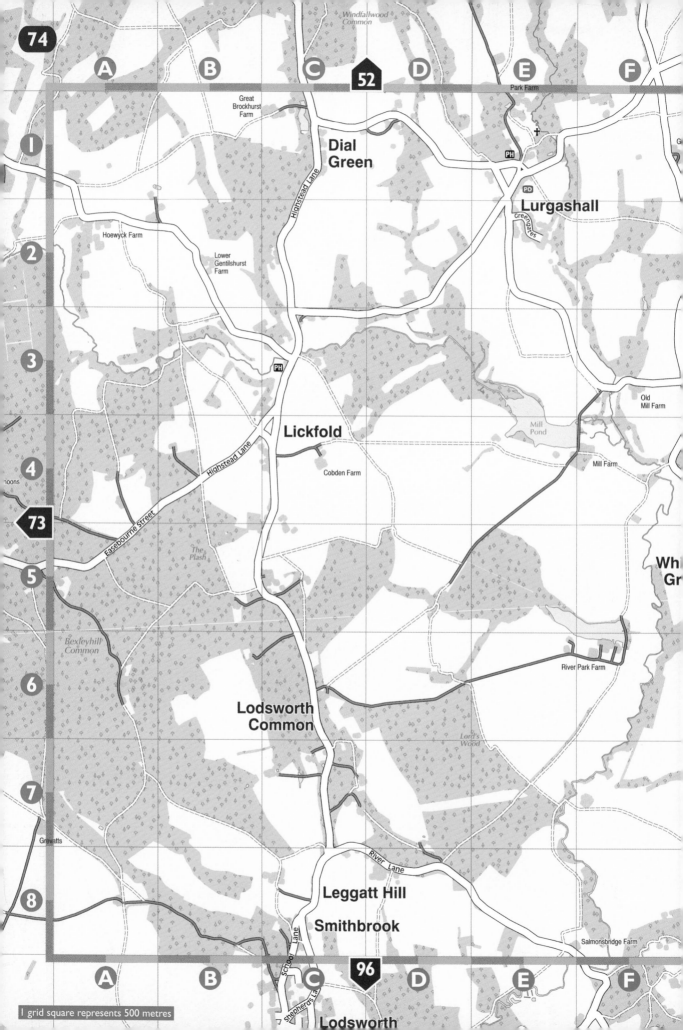

A B C 52 D E F

1

Windfallwood
Common

Park Farm

Great
Brockhurst
Farm

Dial
Green

PH

Lurgashall

PO

Greenores

2

Hoewyck Farm

Lower
Gentilshurst
Farm

3

PH

Old
Mill Farm

Mill
Pond

Lickfold

Mill Farm

Cobden Farm

4

Highstead Lane

73

Easebourne Street

The
Plash

Wh
Gr

5

Bexleyhill
Common

River Park Farm

6

Lodsworth
Common

Lord's
Wood

7

Grevatts

River Lane

8

Leggatt Hill

School Lane

Smithbrook

Salmonsbridge Farm

A B C 96 D E F

Shepherds La.

Lodsworth

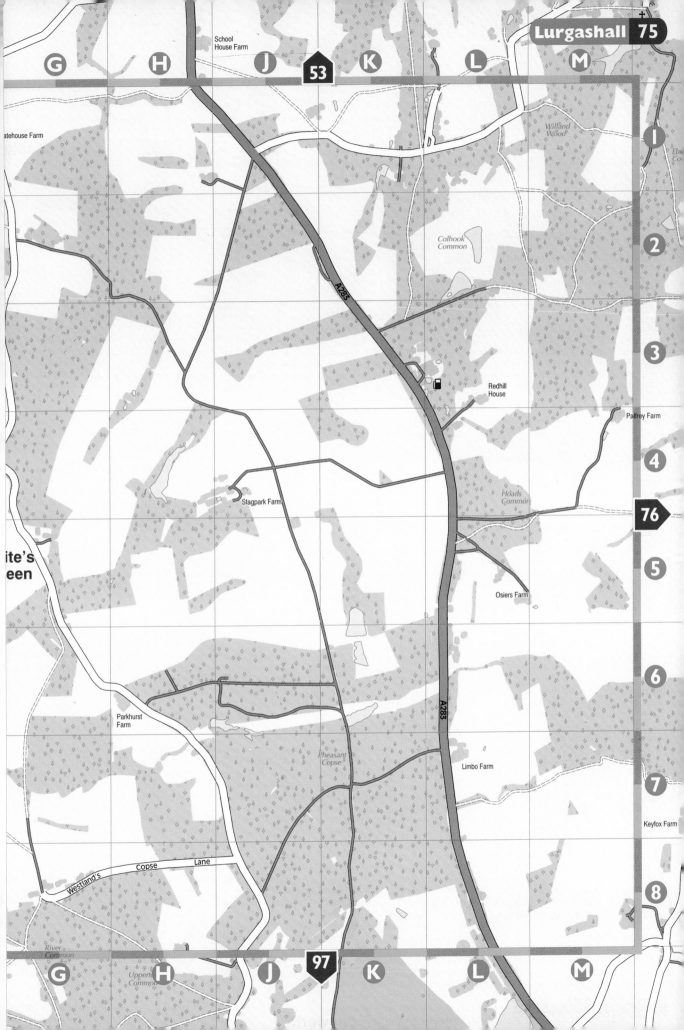

G H J **53** K L M

I
2
3
4
76
5
6
7
8

School
House Farm

atehouse Farm

Willand
Wood

Ebe
Co

Colhook
Common

Redhill
House

Palfrey Farm

Stagpark Farm

Hoads
Common

ite's
een

Osiers Farm

Keyfox Farm

Parkhurst
Farm

Pheasant
Copse

Limbo Farm

Westland's   Copse   Lane

River
Common

Upperto
Common

A283

A283

A

B

C

D

E

F

Pipers Lane

Slifehurst

Bea
House Farm

1

Butcherland Farm

*Ebernoe
Common*

Staple

2

High
Buildings Farm

Pipers Lane

Allfields Farm

**Balls
Cross**

3

Crawfold
Farm

Palfrey Farm

Langhurst Farm

4

5

Medhone
Farm

Blackhouse Lane

*Holland
Wood*

6

7

Keyfox Farm

Blackbrook Farm

Bennyfold Farm

8

Gunter's Bridge

Moor Farm

*Pondtail
Copse*

Blackhouse Lane

A

B

C

D

E

F

I grid square represents 500 metres

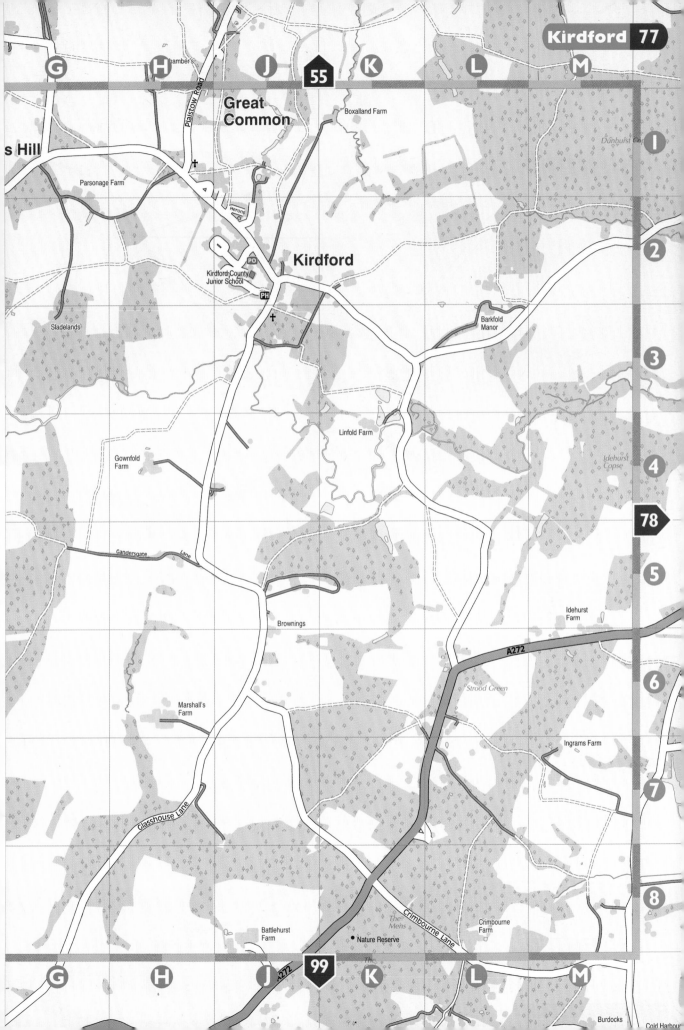

G   H   J   55   K   L   M

I

Plaistow Road

Great
Common

Boxalland Farm

Dunhurst Cop

Parsonage Farm

s Hill

Herons

2

Kirdford

PO

Kirdford County
Junior School

PH

Barkfold
Manor

3

Sladelands

Linfold Farm

Idehurst
Copse

4

Gownfold
Farm

78

Gandersgate   Lane

5

Idehurst
Farm

Brownings

A272

6

Strood Green

Marshall's
Farm

Ingrams Farm

7

Glasshouse Lane

A272

Crimbourne Lane

8

Battlehurst
Farm

The
Mens

Nature Reserve

Crimbourne
Farm

G   H   J   A272   99   K   L   M

Burdocks   Cold Harbour

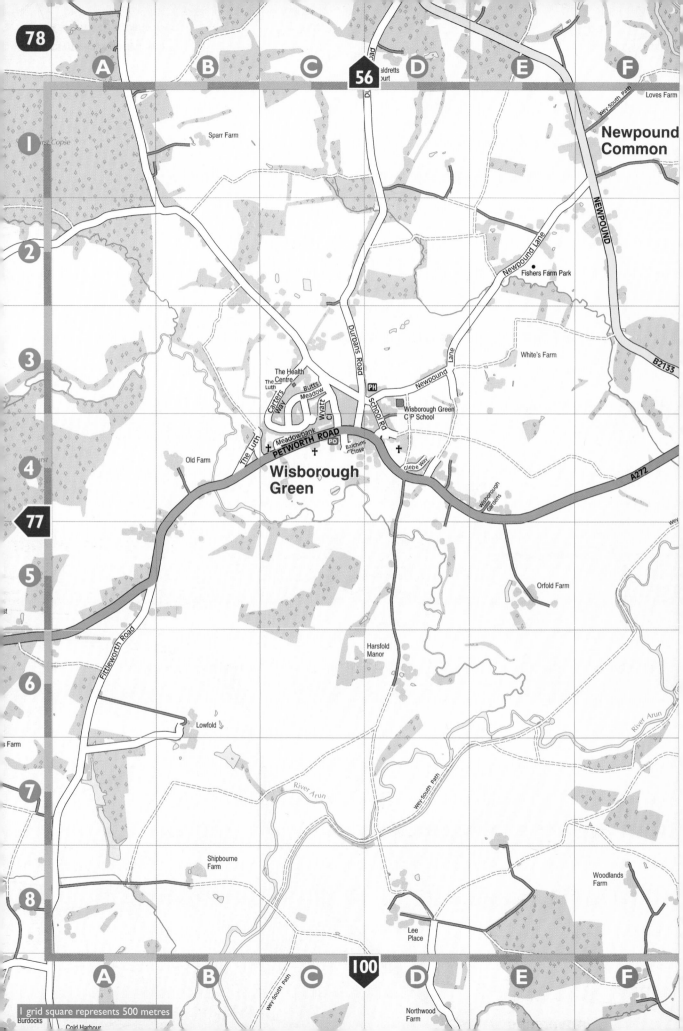

A B C D E F

56

I

2

3

4

77

5

6

7

8

A B C **100** D E F

Hurst Copse

Sparr Farm

Baldretts Court

Loves Farm

Newpound Common

Newpound Lane

NEWPOUND

Fishers Farm Park

B2133

White's Farm

Durbans Road

The Health Centre
The Luth
Carters Way
Butts Meadow
Wyatt Cl
Meadowbank
PETWORTH ROAD
PO
PH
School Rd
Wisborough Green C P School
Newpound Lane

Balchins Close

Glebe Way

Wisborough Gardens

A272

Old Farm

The Luth

Wisborough Green

Orfold Farm

Fittleworth Road

Harsfold Manor

River Arun

Lowfold

West Farm

Burdocks

River Arun

Wey South Path

Shipbourne Farm

Woodlands Farm

Lee Place

Northwood Farm

Wey South Path

Cold Harbour

Burdocks

1 grid square represents 500 metres

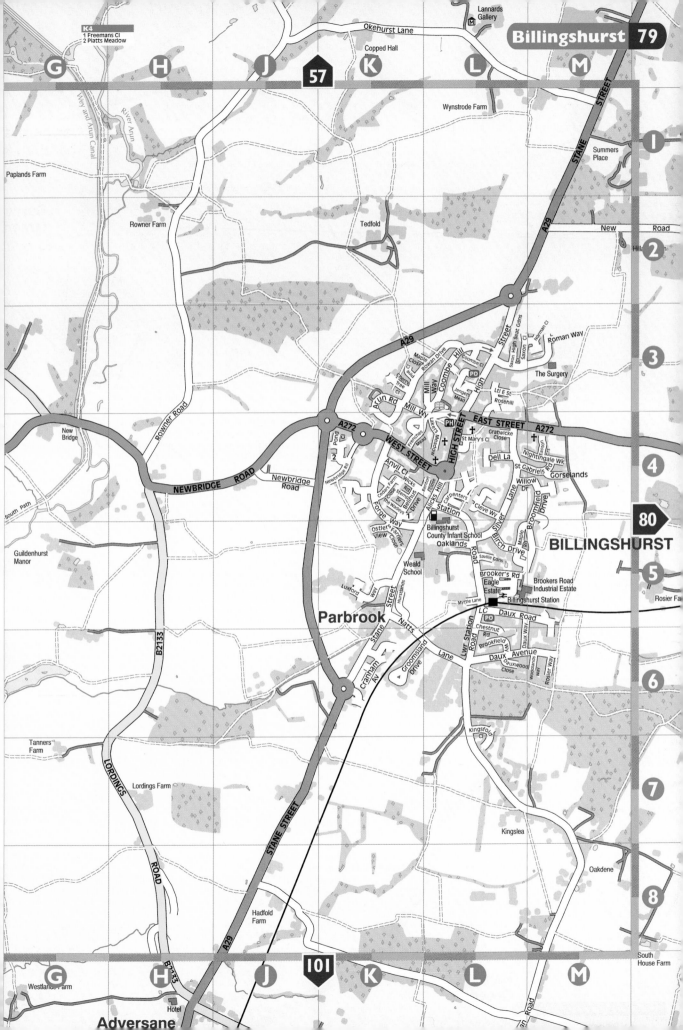

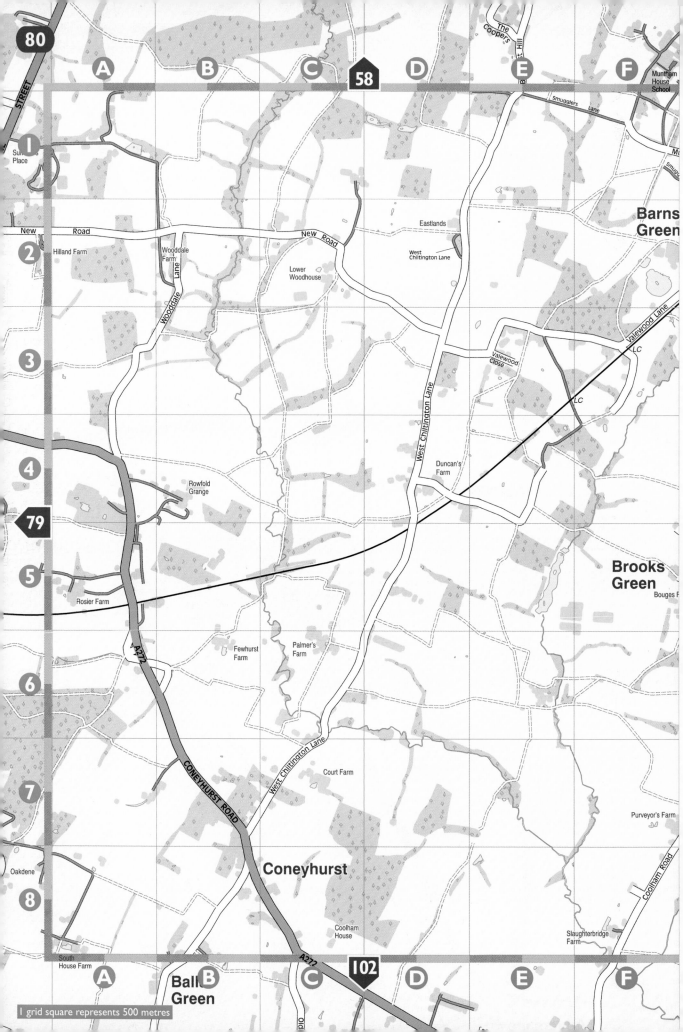

A B C 58 D E F

The Coopers

Muntham House School

STREET

1 Sunte Place

Barns Green

New Road

New Road

Eastlands

2 Hilland Farm

Wooddale Farm

Lower Woodhouse

West Chiltington Lane

smugglers Lane

Wooddale Lane

3

Valewood Close

Valewood Lane

LC

LC

West Chiltington Lane

4 Rowfold Grange

Duncan's Farm

79

5

Rosier Farm

Brooks Green

Bouges F

A272

Fewhurst Farm

Palmer's Farm

6

7

West Chiltington Lane

Court Farm

Purveyor's Farm

CONEYHURST ROAD

Coolham Road

Oakdene

8

Coneyhurst

Coolham House

Slaughterbridge Farm

South House Farm

A Ball Green B C A272 102 D E F

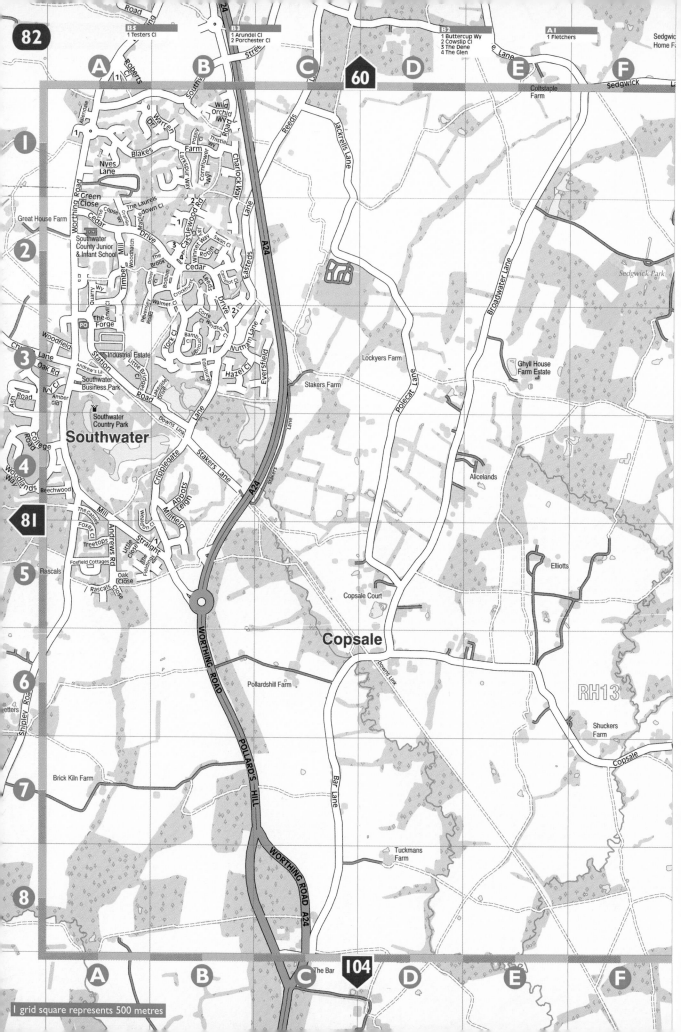

B5
1 Testers Cl

B3
1 Arundel Cl
2 Porchester Cl

B2
1 Buttercup Wy
2 Cowslip Cl
3 The Dene
4 The Glen

A1
1 Fletchers

A   B   60   C   D   E   F

Sedgwick
Home Fa

Coltstaple
Farm

Sedgwick

I

Great House Farm

Sedgwick Park

2

3

4

81

5

6

7

8

A   B   104   C   D   E   F

Allendale

Roberts Cl

Warren Drive

Nyes Lane

Blakes Farm

Green Close

Worthing Road

Cedar

Southwater County Junior & Infant School

PO

The Forge

Industrial Estate

Station

Southwater Business Park

Woodfield

Oak Rd

Ash Road

IVY Cl

College Road

Woodlands Way

Beechwood

The Gables

Foxes Cl

Treetops

Foxfield Cottages

Rascals

Andrews Rd

Mill

Oak Close

Rascals Close

Southwater Country Park

Cripplegate

Abbots Leigh

Millfield

Little Close

Wealdon

The Straight

The Fieldings

Downs Link

Stakers Lane

Downs Link

Wild Orchid Road

Southern

Street

A24

Charlock Way

Reeds

Jackrells Lane

Lane

Coltsfoot

Poppy

Thistle

Cornflower

Larkspur

The Laurels

Maple

The Copse

Grove

Castlewood Rd

Winnet Way

Swan Cl

Dover

The Brook

Bodiam

Crockmyrt

Leggs

Corfe

Windsor

Camelot Cl

York Cl

Bamboo

Pevensey Road

Walmer

Anvil

Quarry Wy

Timber Mill

Cedar Drive

Easteds Lane

Nutham Lane

Eversfield

Hazel Cl

Edinburgh

Lakeside Drive

Little Bridges

Andrew's La

Amber Gdn

Downs Link

A24

Stakers Lane

Worthing Road

Pollard's Hill

WORTHING ROAD A24

Lockyers Farm

Stakers Farm

Broadwater Lane

Polecat Lane

Ghyll House Farm Estate

Alicelands

Elliotts

Copsale Court

Copsale

Pollardshill Farm

Bar Lane

RH13

Shuckers Farm

Copsale

Tuckmans Farm

The Bar

Brick Kiln Farm

Shipley Road

etters

Rascals

Chu   Lane

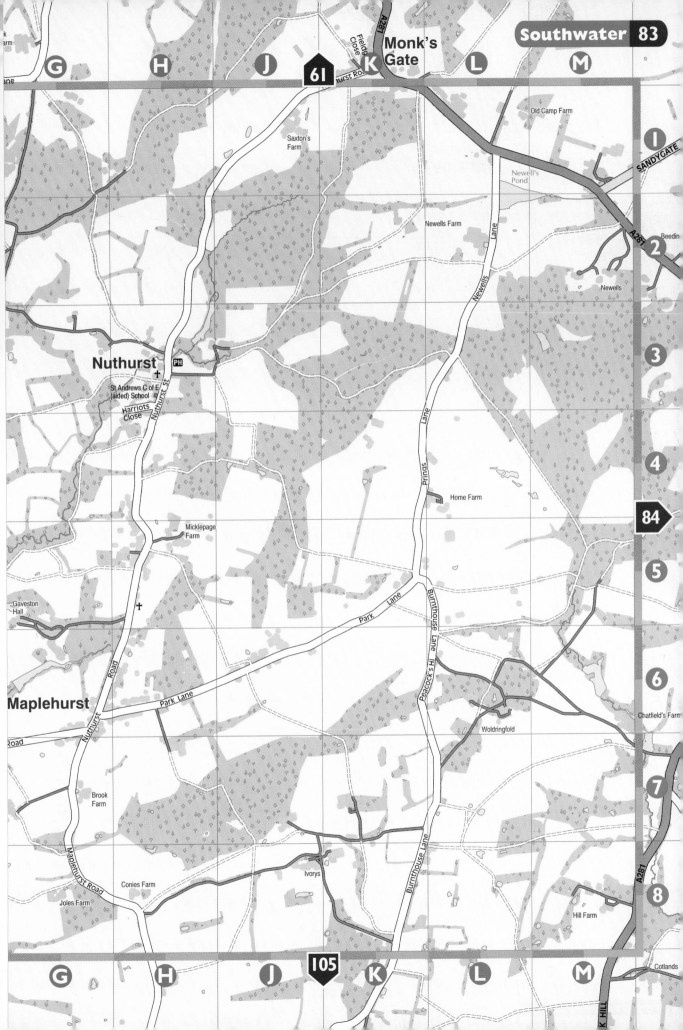

G
H
J
61
K
Monk's Gate
L
M

Field
Close

Old Camp Farm

1
SANDYGATE

Saxton's
Farm

Newell's
Pond

Beedin

2
A281

Newells Farm

Newells
Lane

Newells

3

Nuthurst
PH

Prings Lane

4

St Andrews C of E
(aided) School

Harriots
Close

Nuthurst St

Home Farm

84

5

Micklepage
Farm

Gaveston
Hall

Park Lane

Burnthouse Lane

Peacock's Hi

6

Chatfield's Farm

Maplehurst

Park Lane

Woldringfold

Road

Nuthurst Road

7

Brook
Farm

Maplehurst Road

A281

Conies Farm

Ivorys

8

Joles Farm

Hill Farm

Cotlands

G
H
J
105
K
L
M
K HILL

A   B   B2110   C   **62**   D   E   Bell's Farm   F

HANDCROSS ROAD   WARNINGLID LANE

I
SANDYGATE LANE B2115
Brick Kiln
Close
Church
Close
Lower Beeding Church of England Primary School
Lower Beeding
LEECHPOND HILL
B2115

Eastland Farm

2
A281
Beedinglee
Leech Pond
B2110
Newells

Copyhold

3
Selehurst
LONG HILL

Leonardslee

4

83
New Pond

Crabtree
Hotel
Mill Close
PH
5
Mill Lane
Free Chase

Peppersgate
Furnace Pond

Peppersgate
Drewitts

Earwig Lane

6
Chatfield's Farm
A281
Perryfield Lane

7
Picts Lane
Long House
Earwig La.

Frithknowle
Colwood Manor

8
A281
Picts Lane
Spronkett's
Spronkett's Lane
Cotlands
Wallhurst Manor
Bull's Lane

A   B   C   **106**   D   E   F

Barnfield

1 grid square represents 500 metres

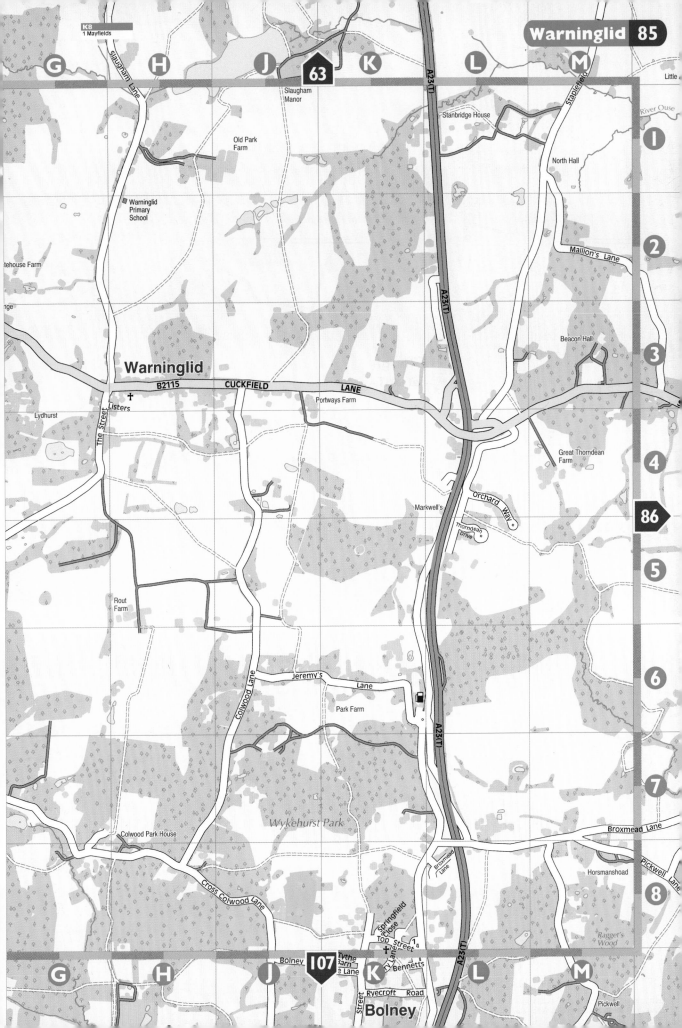

G   H   J   63   K   L   M

K8
1 Mayfields

Slaugham Lane

Slaugham Manor

Stanbridge House

A23(T)

Stanglefield

Little

River Ouse

I

Old Park Farm

North Hall

Warninglid Primary School

Mallion's Lane

2

tehouse Farm

Beacon Hall

3

nge

Warninglid

B2115   CUCKFIELD   LANE

Portways Farm

Lydhurst

The Street

Listers

Great Thorndean Farm

4

Markwell's

Orchard Way

Thorndean Drive

86

Rout Farm

5

Colwood Lane

Jeremy's   Lane

Park Farm

A23(T)

6

Colwood Park House

Wykehurst Park

Broxmead Lane

7

Cross Colwood Lane

Broxmead Lane

Horsmanshoad

Pickwell Lane

8

Springfield Close

Top Street

Tythe Barn Lane

Bennetts

Ragget's Wood

Pickwell

G   H   J   107   K   L   M

Street   Ryecroft Road

A23(T)

Bolney

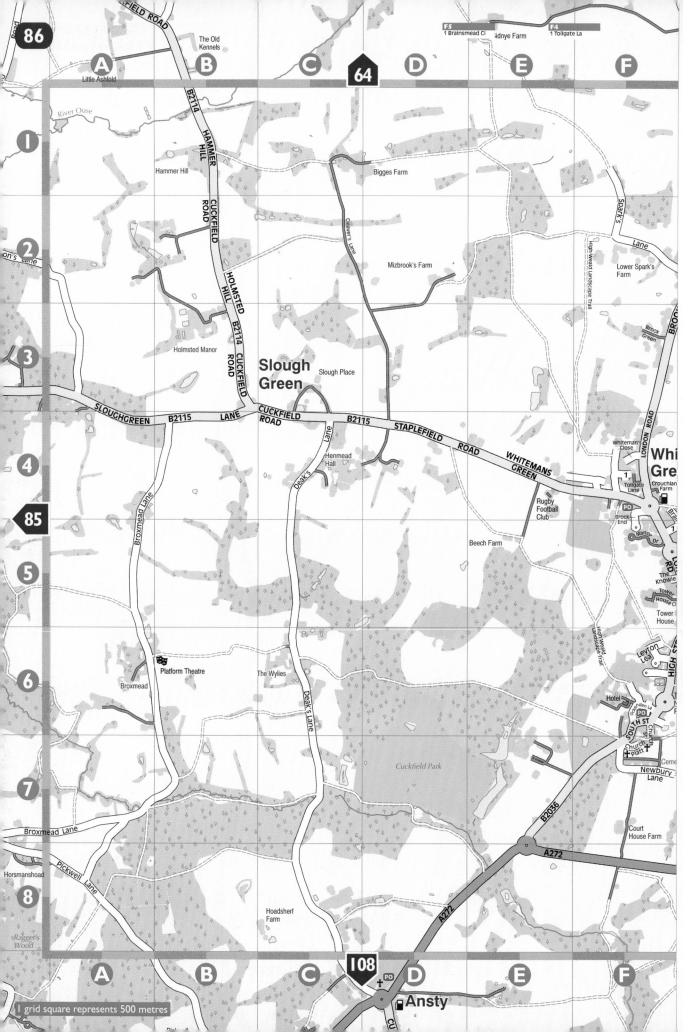

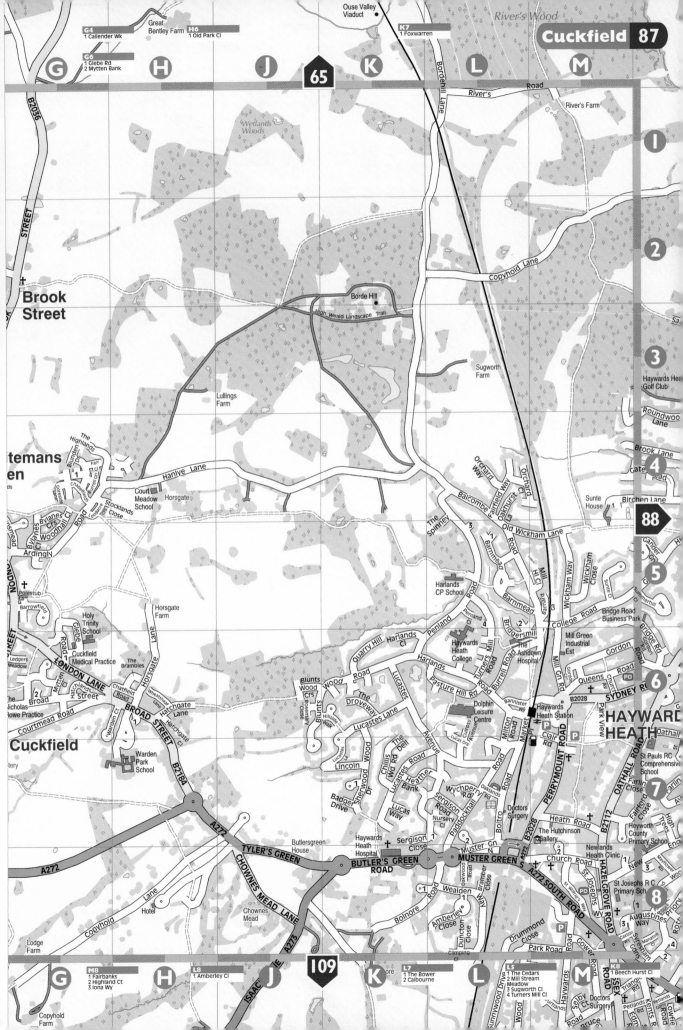

G
H
J
65
K
L
M

Ouse Valley Viaduct

River's Wood

River's Road

River's Farm

G6
1 Glebe Rd
2 Mytten Bank

Wetlands Woods

Copyhold Lane

Sa

I

2

3

Borde Hill

Brook Street

High Weald Landscape Trail

Sugworth Farm

Haywards Hea Golf Club

Roundwoo Lane

Lullings Farm

Brook Lane

4

Gate

The Highlands

Haniye Lane

Orchard Way

Orchard Way

Fairfield Way

Balcombe Road

Orchard

Oakhurst

Sunte House

Birchen Lane

88

temans en

Court Meadow School

Horsgate

Old Wickham Lane

The Spinney

3

College Road

Wickham Way

Summerhill

5

ArdingN

Stocklands Close

Barnmead

Mill Clo

Wickham Close

Sunte Cl

Bridge Road Business Park

Polestub

Horsgate Farm

Harlands CP School

Barnmead

Bridgersmill

College Road

Gordon

Mill Green Industrial Est

Summerhill

6

Barrowfield

Holy Trinity School

Quarry Hill

Harlands Cl

Penland

Haywards Heath College

Turners Mill Rd

Gordon

Queens Rd

PO

SYDNEY R

Cuckfield Medical Practice

Glebe

Penland Cl

The Ashdown Hospital

Burrell Road

B2028

HAYWARD HEATH

Ledgers Meadow

The Brambles

Chatfield Road

Harlands Road

Park View

Oathall

LONDON LANE

Horsgate Lane

Harlands

Pasture Hill Rd

Milton Road

Haywards Heath Station

Clair Rd

St Pauls RC Comprehensive School

Nicholas owe Practice

Wheatsheaf Lane

Blunts Wood Crs

Rosemary

The Droveway

Lucastes Lane

Avenue

Dolphin Leisure Centre

Market

P

Farli Close

7

Broad Street

Hatchgate

Warden Ct

Blunts Wood

Hillside

Lucastes Lane

Lucas Clo

Bannister Wy

P

Heath Road

Fairford Close

Cuckfield

B2184

Warden Park School

Lincoln

Chilli Wd Rd

The Dell

Heather Bank

Sherwood Dr

Lucas Way

Sergison Road

Nursery Cl

Paddockhall

Oaklands Rd

Doctors Surgery

Boltro Road

B2028

The Hutchinson Gallery

Heyworth County Primary School

Heath Road

Heyworth

7

Badge Drive

Sergison Close

Muster Gn

Church Road

Newlands Health Clinic

New

High Trees

8

A272

Butlersgreen House

TYLER'S GREEN

Haywards Heath Hospital

BUTLER'S GREEN ROAD

MUSTER GREEN S

Muster Grn

A272 SOUTH ROAD

Church Road

St Josephs RC Primary Sch

Mansf

Augustines Way

A272

CHOWNES MEAD LANE

Chownes Mead

Bolnore

Wealden Way

Amberley Close

Duncton Close

Bramber Close

HAZELGROVE ROAD

P

St Josephs RC Primary Sch

3

St Josephs RC Primary Sch

Caxton

8

Copyhold Lane

A273

Lodge Farm

Copyhold

Drummond close

Park Road

Gower Road

Caxton

Climping

Sryesian

Edn

owe

Copyhold Farm

109

G
H
J
K
L
M

M8
1 Fairbanks
2 Highland Ct
3 Iona Wy
L8
1 Amberley Cl
L7
1 The Bower
2 Calbourne
L5
1 The Cedars
2 Mill Stream Meadow
3 Sugworth Cl
4 Turners Mill Cl
K8
1 Beech Hurst Cl

Doctors Surgery

G   H   J   67   K   L   M

I
2
3
4
5
6
7
8

Woodsland Farm

Bluebell Railway

Keys

Hamsla

Wya

Sussex Border Pth

Latchetts

Treemans Road

Great Plummerden Farm

Lane

Hill

Montes

Cockhaise Mill Farm

Monteswood Lane

Freshfield Crossways

Freshfield Lane

Stoaches Farm

Northla

Town Place

Ketche's Lane

Sussex Border Path

Bluebell Railway

Great Walstead School

PH

Henfield Wood

Pegden

Nash Farm

Nash Lane

Butterbox Lane

Sussex Border Path

Massetts

Sennotts Farm

Scayn Hill

Vicarage Lane

Church Road

G   H   J   III   K   L   M

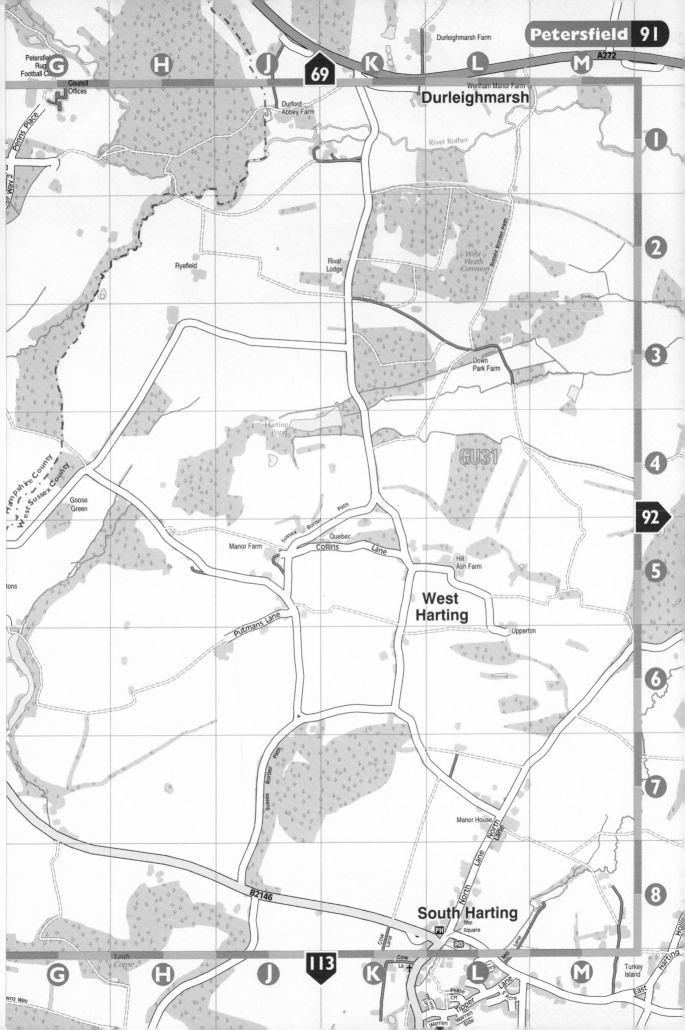

G H J **69** K L M A272

Petersfield
Rugby
Football Club

Council
Offices

Penns Place

Durleighmarsh

Wenham Manor Farm

Durford
Abbey Farm

Durleighmarsh Farm

River Rother

I

Ryefield

Rival
Lodge

West
Heath
Common

Sussex Border Path

2

3

Down
Park Farm

Harting
Pond

GU31

4

Hampshire County
West Sussex County

Goose
Green

Sussex Border Path

Quebec

92

Manor Farm

Collins Lane

Hill
Ash Farm

5

West
Harting

tons

Upperton

Putmans Lane

6

Sussex Border Path

7

Manor House

North Lane

8

B2146

South Harting

PH
The
Square

PO

G H J **113** K L M

Cow Lane

Cow
La

Turkey
Island

East Harting

Leith
Copse

Downs Way

The
Cro

Pease
Cft

Tipper Lane

Mill Lane

Warren
Side

Warren

S Acre

Holl

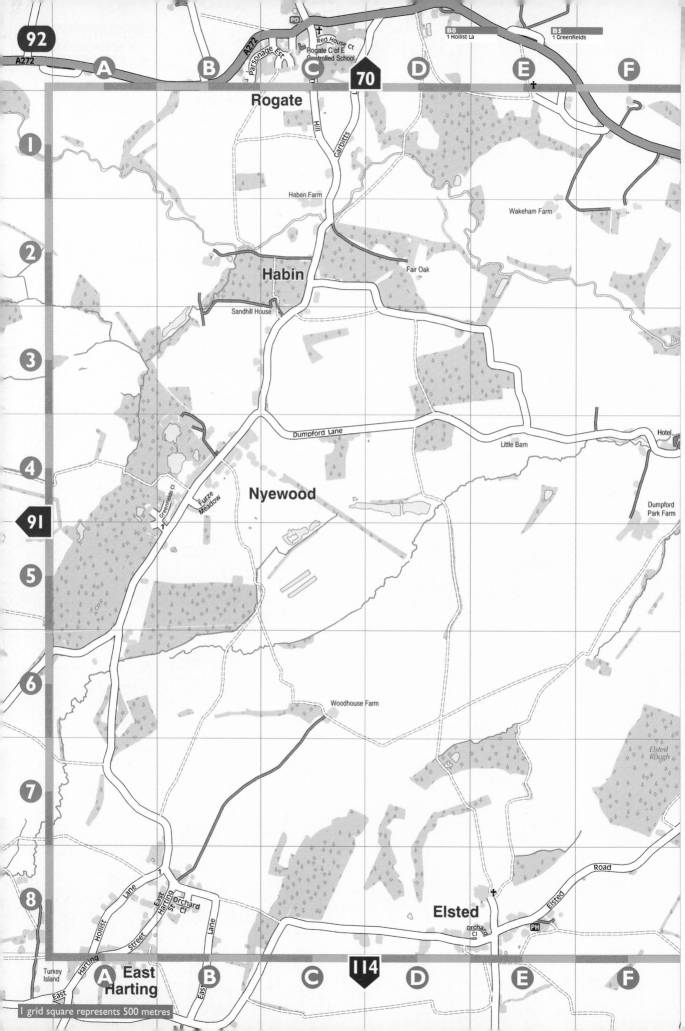

92
A272

70

91

114

1 grid square represents 500 metres

A272
Parsonage
PO
Red House Ct
Rogate C of E
Controlled School

B8
1 Hollist La
B5
1 Greenfields

Rogate

Hill
Garbitts

Haben Farm

Wakeham Farm

Habin
Fair Oak

Sandhill House

Dumpford Lane
Little Barn
Hotel

Greenfields Cl
Furze
Meadow
Nyewood
Dumpford
Park Farm

Woodhouse Farm

Elsted
Rough

East
Harting St
Orchard
Cl
Lane
Hollist
Street
Lane
Road
Elsted

Elsted
Orchard
Cl
PH

Turkey
Island
**East
Harting**
East

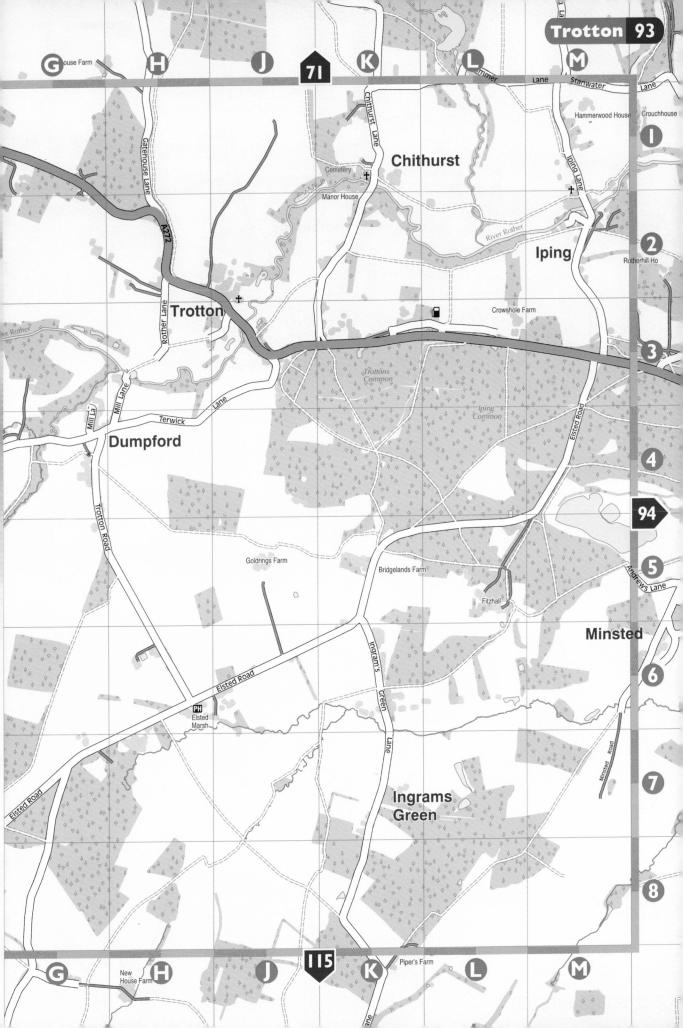

G
H
J
71
K
L
M

ouse Farm

Hammerwood House

Crouchhouse

1

Chithurst Lane

Iping Lane

Chithurst

Cemetery

Manor House

River Rother

Iping

Rotherhill Ho

2

Gatehouse Lane

A272

Crowshole Farm

Trotton

Rother Lane

3

Trotton Common

Iping Common

Elsted Road

Dumpford

Mill La

Mill Lane

Terwick

Lane

4

94

Andrews Lane

5

Minsted

Goldrings Farm

Bridgelands Farm

Trotton Road

Fitzhall

6

Elsted Road

Ingram's Green Lane

PH
Elsted Marsh

Minsted Road

7

Elsted Road

Ingrams Green

8

G
H
115
J
K
Piper's Farm
L
M

New House Farm

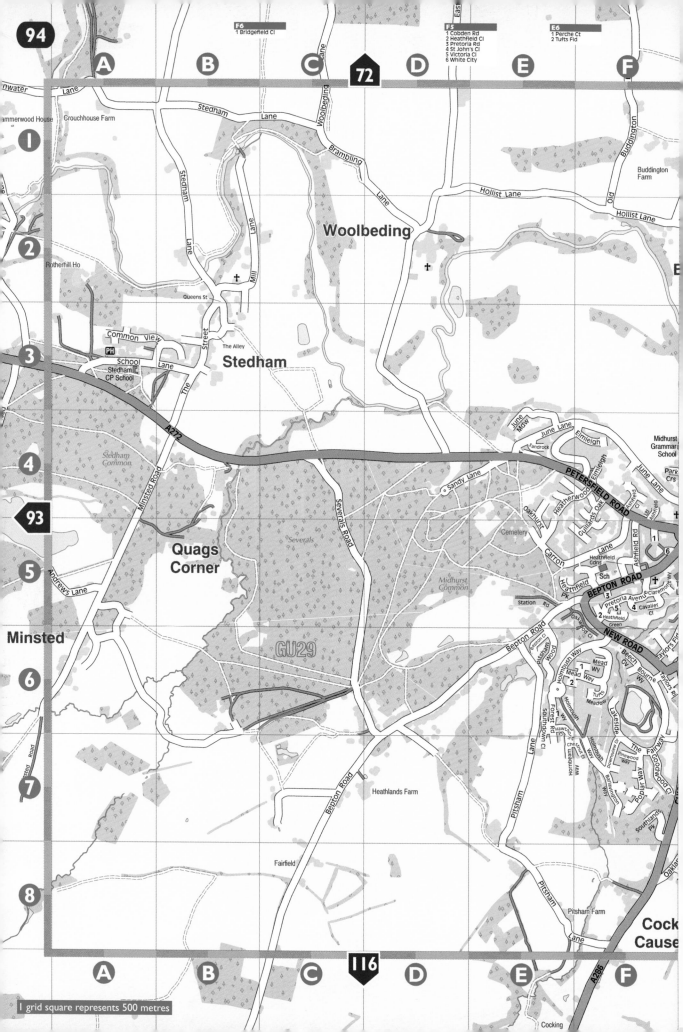

F6
1 Bridgefield Cl

F5
1 Cobden Rd
2 Heathfield Cl
3 Pretoria Rd
4 St John's Cl
5 Victoria Cl
6 White City

E6
1 Perche Ct
2 Tufts Fld

I

Hammerwood House
Crouchhouse Farm

Stedham Lane

Woolbeding Lane

Brambling Lane

Hollist Lane

Buddington Farm

Old Hollist Lane

2

Rotherhill Ho

Stedham Lane

Mill Lane

Woolbeding

Queens St

3

Common View
PH
School Lane
Stedham CP School
The Street
The Alley

Stedham

A272

4

Stedham Common

Minsted Road

June Mdw
Sandrock
June Lane
Emleigh
Emleigh
Midhurst Grammar School
Park Crs

93

5

Andrews Lane

Quags Corner

Severals

Severals Road

Sandy Lane

Oakhurst
Heatherwood
Carron
Cemetery
Midhurst Common
Guillards Oak
Heathfield Gdns
Heathfield Pk
Ashfield Rd
Ashfield
PETERSFIELD ROAD
1
6

Minsted

GU29

Station Rd

Heathfield
Sch
Hethfield Pk
BEPTON ROAD
Pretoria Avenu
5
2 Heathfield Green
Claremont Wy
Cavalier Cl

6

Minsted Road

Bepton Road

Bepton Road
Bepton Cl
Pitsham Wood

NEW ROAD
Holmbush Way
Mead Wy
1 Mead Way
2 Tufts Meadow
Beech Cv
Bourne Wy
Lakeside
The Fairway
Woodown
Poplar Way

7

Minsted Road

Bepton Road

Heathlands Farm

Southdown Cl
Forest Rd
Holmbush
Hawkcroft
Holmbush Way
Barlavington Way
Downsview Dr
Pinewood Way
Southlands Pk

8

Fairfield

Pitsham Lane

Pitsham Lane

Pitsham Farm

Oaklands

**Cock
Cause**

Cocking

1 grid square represents 500 metres

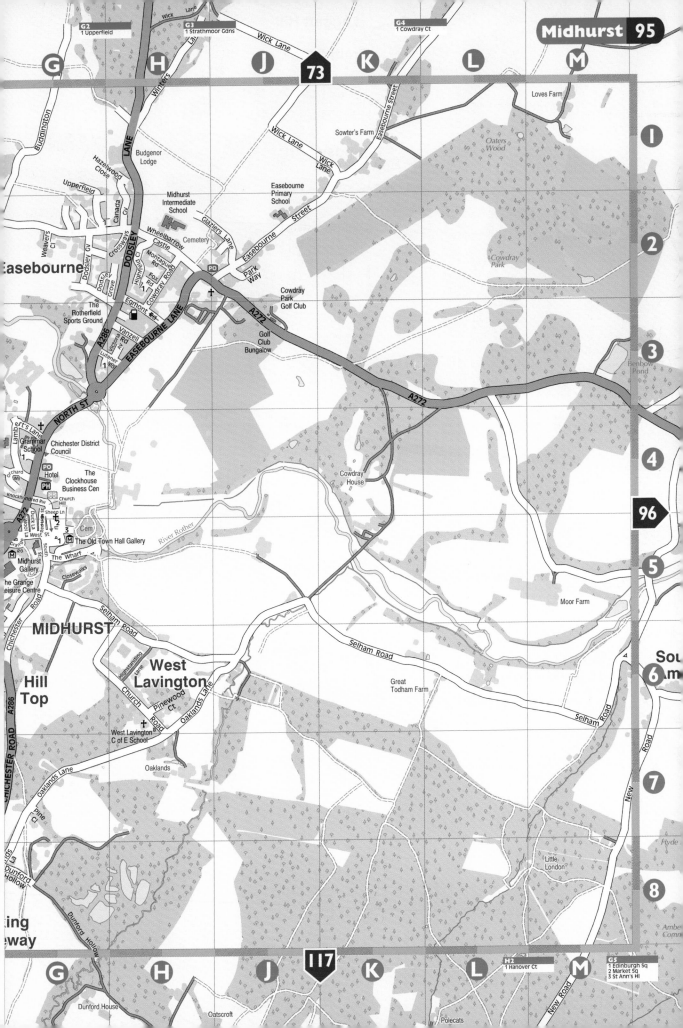

G   H   J   **73**   K   L   M

I

Wick Lane

Loves Farm

Oaters Wood

Sowter's Farm

Easebourne Street

Budgenor Lodge

Hazelwood Close

2

Upperfield

Midhurst Intermediate School

Easebourne Primary School

Cowdray Park

Weavers Ct

Cemetery

Glaziers Lane

Easebourne

Wheelbarrow Castle

Dodsley Gv

Crossways

Montague Rd

Fox Rd

Highfield Cl

PO

Park Way

Cowdray Park Golf Club

3

Benbow Pond

The Rotherfield Sports Ground

Egmont Rd

Vanzell Rd

Victoria Rd

A272

Golf Club Bungalow

A286

Lutener Rd

EASEBOURNE LANE

Cowdray Road

NORTH ST

Lambert's Lane

Grammar School

Chichester District Council

Cowdray House

4

PO

Hotel

The Clockhouse Business Cen

PH

Knockhundred Rw

Church Hill

Sheep Ln

96

River Rother

Cem

The Old Town Hall Gallery

West St

5

Duck La

Union La

M

Midhurst Gallery

The Wharf

Closewalks

Moor Farm

The Grange Leisure Centre

A272

Selham Road

MIDHURST

Selham Road

6

**Sou...
...m...**

Hill Top

Selham Road

Highstanding Lane

West Lavington

Great Todham Farm

A286

Church Road

Pinewood Ct

Oaklands Lane

New Road

7

Selham Road

West Lavington C of E School

Oaklands

Oaklands Lane

Pine Rd

Hyde...

Little London

8

Dunford Hollow

...ing
...eway

Dunford Hollow

Amber
Comm...

G   H   J   **117**   K   L   M

Dunford House

Oatscroft

Polecats

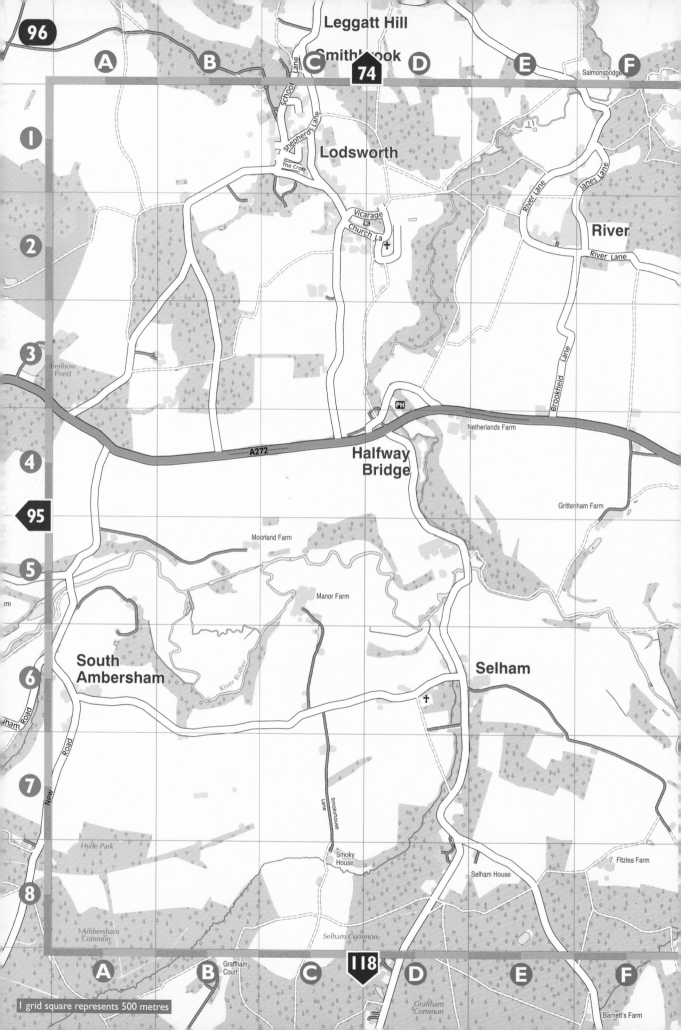

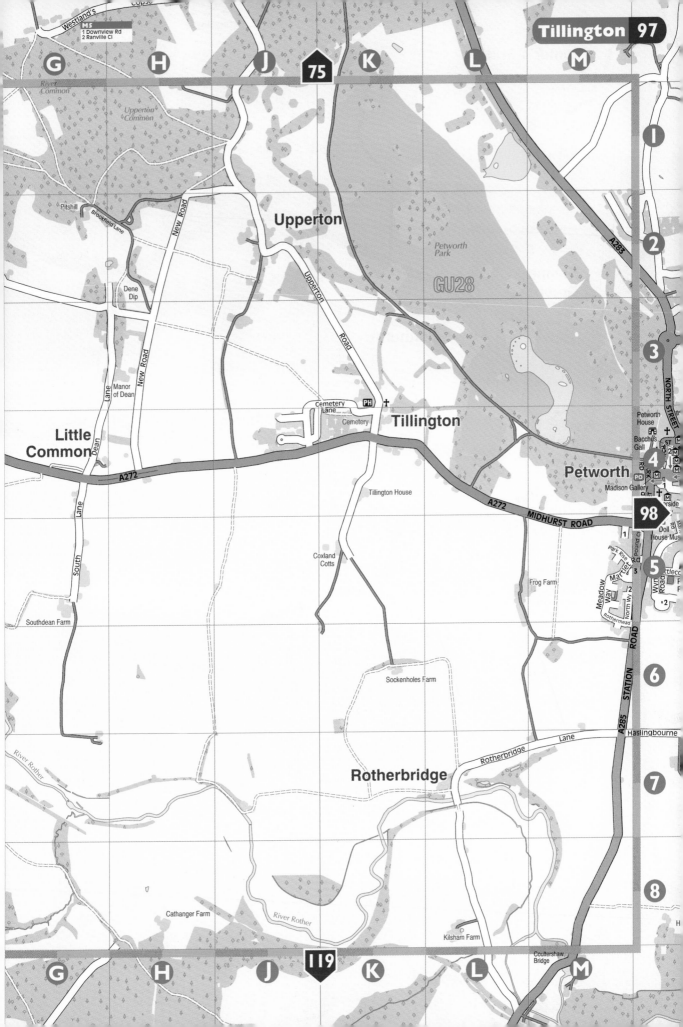

M5
1 Downview Rd
2 Ranville Cl

G   H   J   75   K   L   M

Westland's Copse
River Common

Upperton Common

Pitshill

Brookfield Lane

New Road

Dene Dip

Upperton

Petworth Park

GU28

Manor of Dean

Dean Lane

New Road

South Lane

Little Common

Cemetery Lane

PH

Cemetery

Tillington

Petworth

Petworth House
Bacchus Gall

NORTH STREET

Madison Gallery

A272

A272 MIDHURST ROAD

Tillington House

98

Coxland Cotts

Frog Farm

Park Rise
Pound Cl
Meadow Way
Martlet
North Wy
Rothermead

STATION ROAD

Southdean Farm

Sockenholes Farm

A283

Haslingbourne

River Rother

Rotherbridge Lane

Rotherbridge

6

7

8

Cathanger Farm

River Rother

Kilsham Farm

Coultershaw Bridge

G   H   J   119   K   L   M

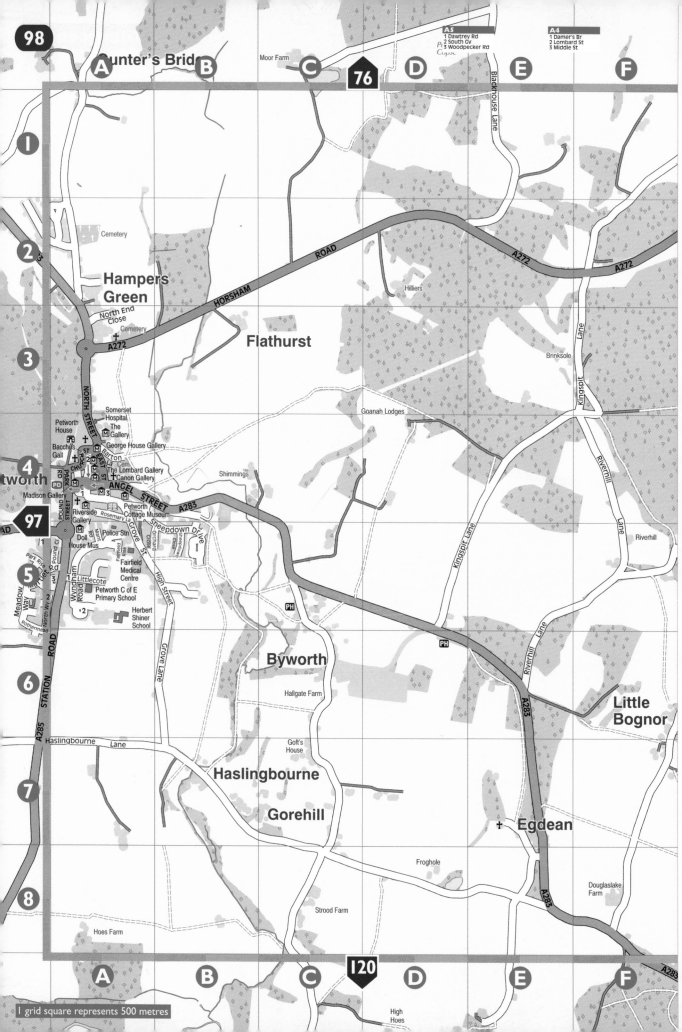

A   B   C   **78**   D   E   F

Woodlands Farm

I   Burdocks

Cold Harbour Farm

Wey south Path

Northwood Farm

Horsebridge Hill

Pallingham Lane

2

Snape Farm

3

River Arun

Pallingham Manor Farm

Black Gate Lane

Stablebarn Farm

Toat House

4

Pallingham

99

Lane

Toat Monument

Toat

River Arun

5

A29

Pickhurst Lane

6

Pickhurst

Pythingdean

STANE STREET

Broomers

LC

7

Hill Farm Lane

Codmore Hill

Cray Lane

Hill Lane

Codmore Hill Farm

Mason's Way

8

Coombelands

Coombelands Lane

Stane St Close

STANE STREET

A29

Broomers Hill Lane

A   B   C   **122**   D   E   F

1 grid square represents 500 metres

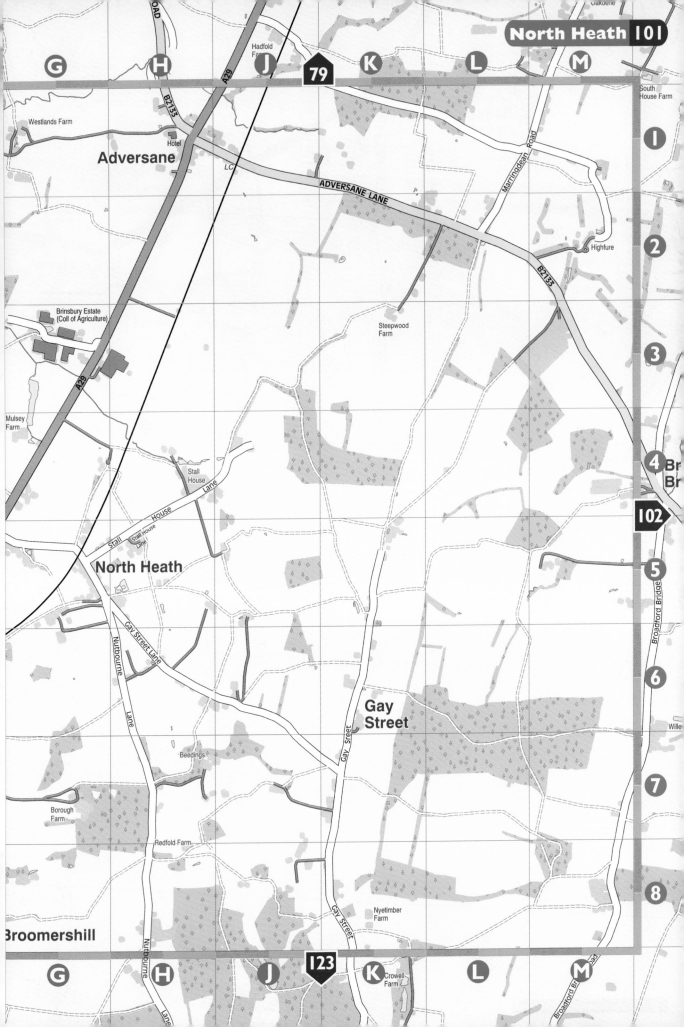

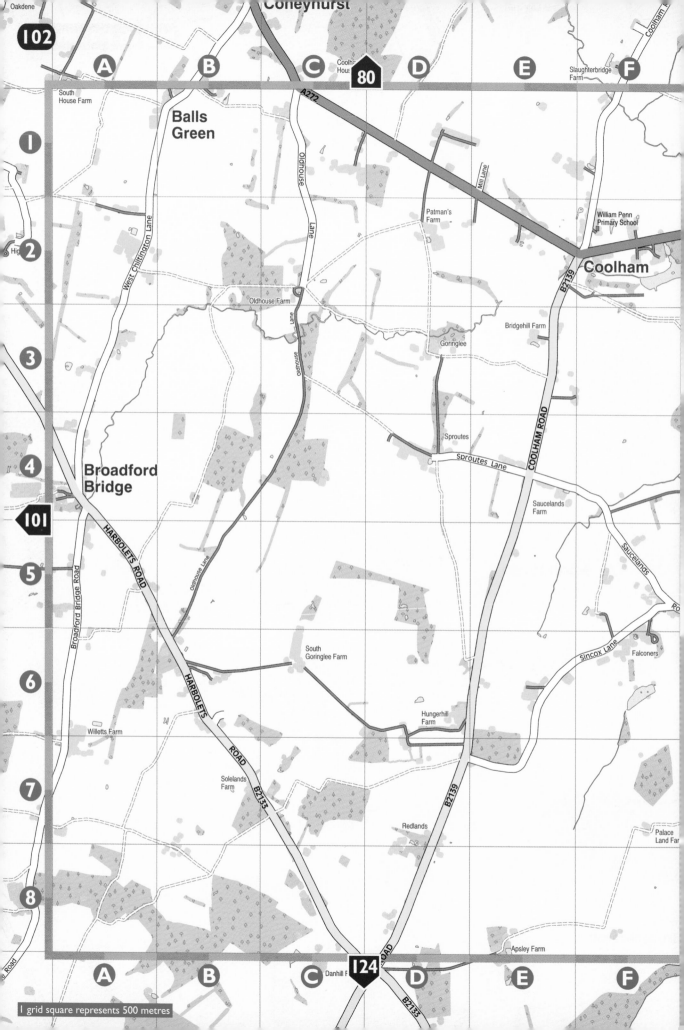

Coneyhurst

Oakdene

A **B** **C** **D** **E** **F**

80

South House Farm

Balls Green

I

Coolham House

Slaughterbridge Farm

Hig

2

Patman's Farm

Mill Lane

A272

Oldhouse Lane

William Penn Primary School

Coolham

B2139

3

Oldhouse Farm

Oldhouse Lane

West Chiltington Lane

Goringlee

Bridgehill Farm

4

Broadford Bridge

Sproutes

Sproutes Lane

Saucelands Farm

101

Coolham Road

5

Broadford Bridge Road

Oldhouse Lane

Harbolets Road

Saucelands Road

Sincox Lane

Falconers

6

South Goringlee Farm

Willetts Farm

Hungerhill Farm

Harbolets Road

7

Solelands Farm

B2133

Redlands

B2139

Palace Land Far

8

Apsley Farm

A **B** **C** **D** **E** **F**

124

Danhill F

B2133 ROAD

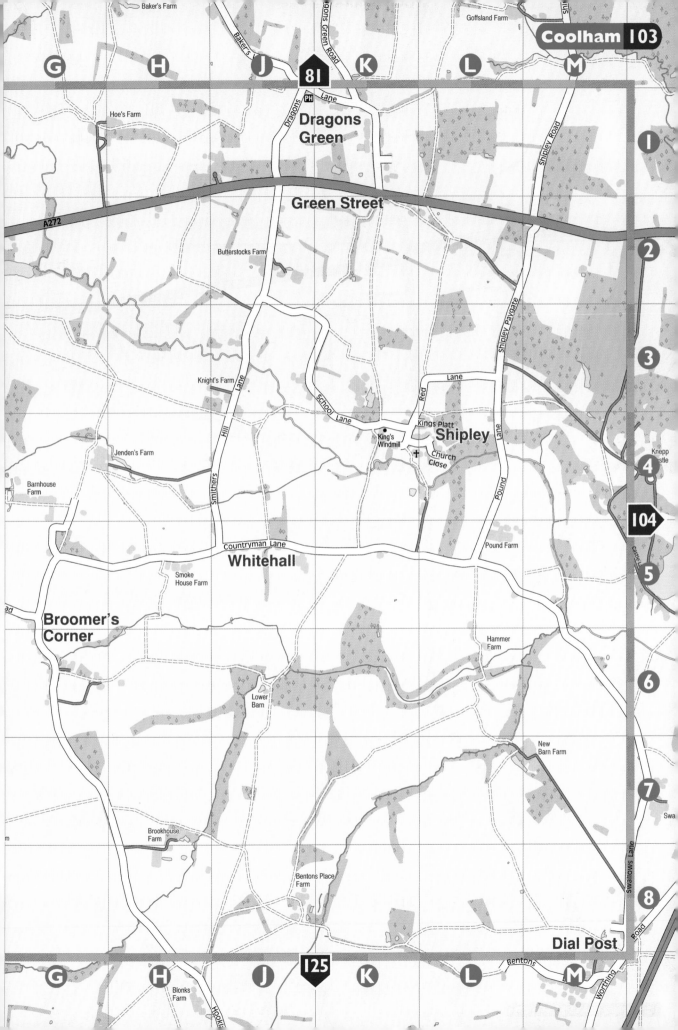

G   H   J   **81**   K   L   M

1

Goffsland Farm

Baker's Farm

Hoe's Farm

PH

Dragons Green

Shipley Road

2

Green Street

A272

Butterstocks Farm

3

Knight's Farm

Lane

School Lane

Red

Lane

Kings Platt

Shipley

King's Windmill

Church Close

Jenden's Farm

Hill

Smithers

Lane

Shipley Paygate

Pound Lane

Knepp Castle

4

104

Barnhouse Farm

Countryman Lane

Whitehall

Pound Farm

Castle La

5

Smoke House Farm

Broomer's Corner

Hammer Farm

ad

6

Lower Barn

New Barn Farm

7

Brookhouse Farm

Swa

8

Bentons Place Farm

Swallows Lane

Worthing Road

Dial Post

Bentons

G   H   J   **125**   K   L   M

Blonks Farm

Hook

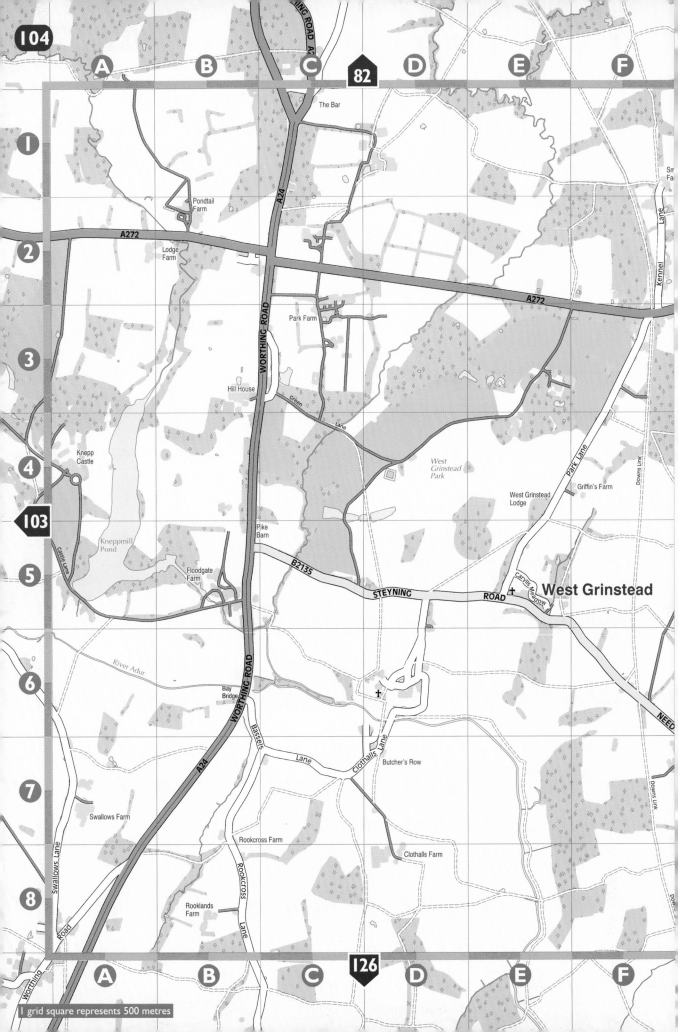

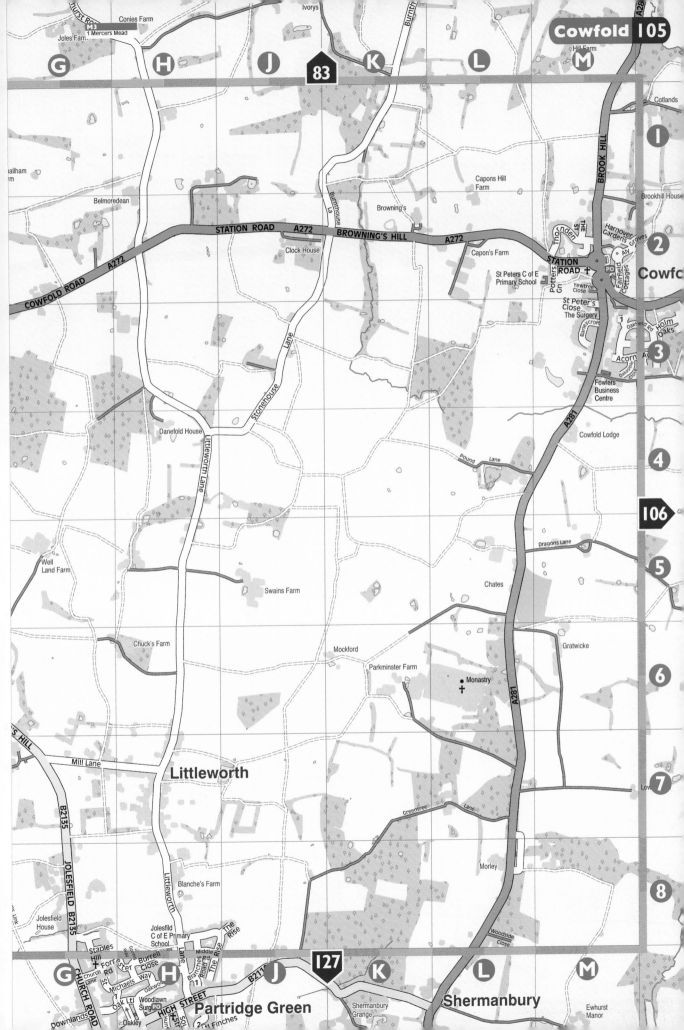

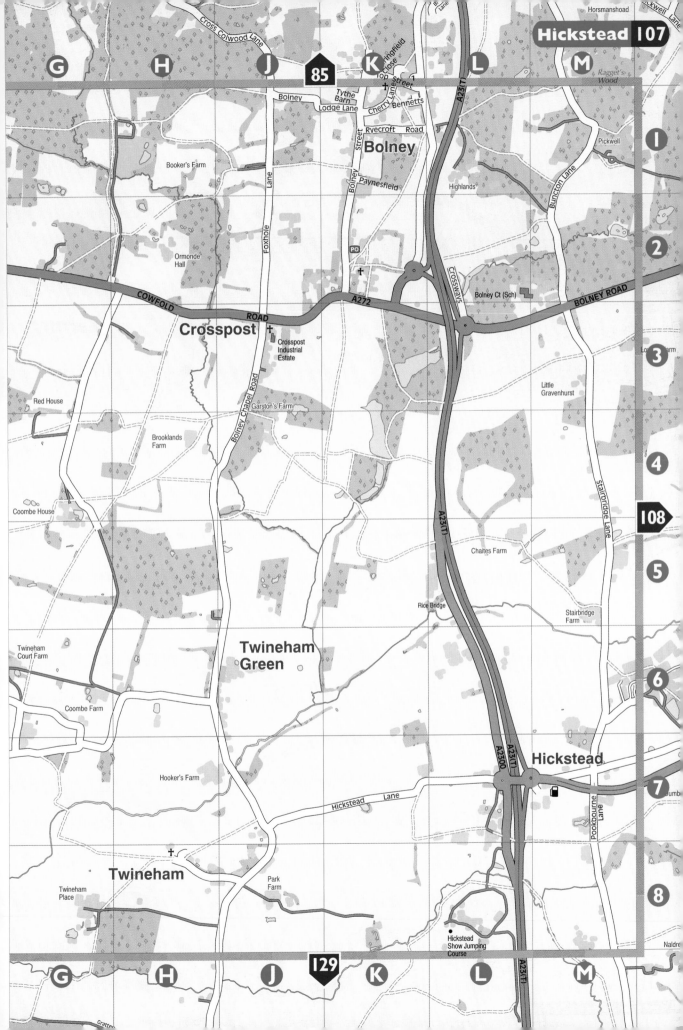

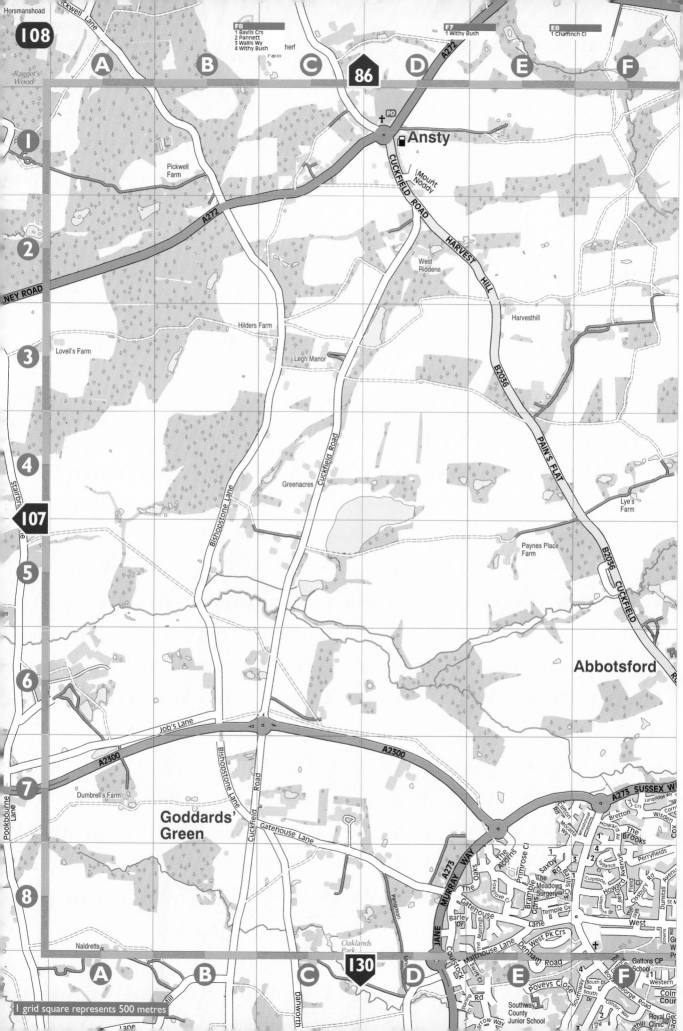

Horsmanshoad

Ragget's Wood

ickwell Lane

F8
1 Baylis Crs
2 Pannett
3 Wallis Wy
4 Withy Bush

F7
1 Withy Bush

E8
1 Chaffinch Cl

PO

Ansty

Pickwell Farm

NEY ROAD

A272

CUCKFIELD ROAD

Mount Noddy

West Riddens

HARVEST HILL

Harvesthill

Hilders Farm

Lovell's Farm

Legh Manor

Stairbl

Greenacres

Cuckfield Road

B2036

PAIN'S FLAT

Lye's Farm

107

Bishopstone Lane

Paynes Place Farm

B2036 CUCKFIELD

Abbotsford

Job's Lane

A2300

A2300

A273 SUSSEX W

Bretton

The Brooks

Dumbrell's Farm

Bishopstone Lane

Cuckfield Road

Gatehouse Lane

JANE MURRAY WAY

A273

Clifton Rd

Saxby Rd

Primrose Cl

The Acorns

Langridge Wy

Wisden

Perryfields

Goddards' Green

Pookbourne Lane

The Meadows Surgery

Bramble Gdns

Foxglove Cl

Howard Avenue

Royal Oak Cl

Temple Gv

Field

The Cleshey

Dunstall

Culpeper

Pangdean

Naldretts

The Oaks

Gatehouse Lane

Barley Dr

Matthing Lane

Malthouse Lane

Dennam Road

West Pk Crs

Oaklands Park

130

Poveys Close

Southway County Junior School

Gattons CP School

1 grid square represents 500 metres

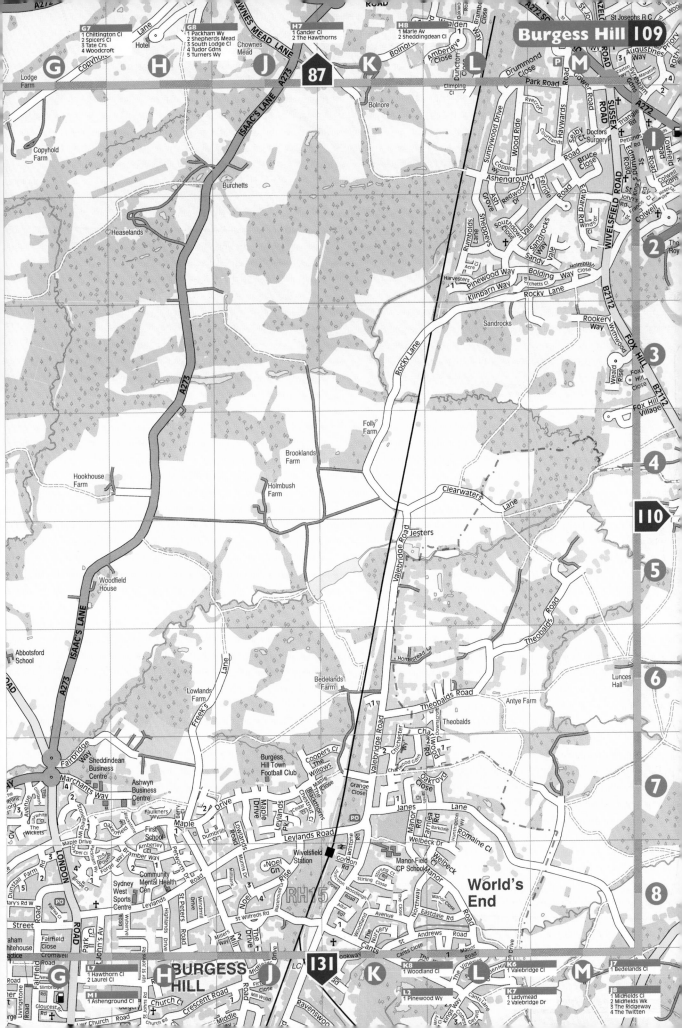

G7
1 Chittington Cl
2 Spicers Cl
3 Tate Crs
4 Woodcroft

G8
1 Packham Wy
2 Shepherds Mead
3 South Lodge Cl
4 Tudor Gdns
5 Turners Wy

H7
1 Gander Cl
2 The Hawthorns

H8
1 Marie Av
2 Sheddingdean Cl

87

Park Road

WIVELSFIELD ROAD

FOX HILL

B2112

110

World's End

RH15

BURGESS HILL

131

G
1 Hawthorn Cl
2 Laurel Cl

H1
1 Ashenground Cl

J
1 Slimbridge

K8
1 Woodland Cl

L2
1 Ladymead
2 Valebridge Dr

K6
1 Valebridge Cl

K7
1 Pinewood Wy

J8
1 Midfields Cl
2 Midfields Wk
3 The Ridgeway
4 The Twitten

M8
1 Bedelands Cl

G1
1 Awbrook Cl
2 The Coppice
3 Orchard Cl
4 St Augustine Cl

Scaynes
Hill

Nash
Farm

Butterbox Lane

89

Vicarage Lane

Church Road

Clearwater Lane

Hammond's
Farm

Sennotts
Farm

Lindfield
Farm

Warr's
Farm

Inces

Pellingbridge
Farm

Banks Road

New
Heritage

Vale
Farm

Great Noven
Farm

West Sussex County
East Sussex County

Teague's
Farm

A275

Warren
Lane

Leylands
Farm

Holford
Manor

North
Common

STATION ROAD

Chailey Heritage
Clinical Services

Old
Heritage

Chailey
Heritage
School

North
Chailey

A272

Downs Vw
Close

Lewes Road A272

B2183

North Common Road

BEGGAR'S WOOD ROAD

A275

Broadstone
Farm

Newhouse
Farm

Townings
Farm

Longridge

Breens
Cottages

Hole Farm

**Godleys
Green**

St Peters
Primary
School

Chailey

A B C **90** D E F

1
2
3
4
5
6
7
8

A B C **132** D E F

Hangers Way

Road

South Downs

Coulters
Dean Fm

South Downs Way

Forty Acre
Lane

Sunwood Fm

South Do

Head
Down Plantation

Hampshire County
West Sussex County

Oakham
Bottom

Downley

West
Harting
Down

Newbarn Road

Ditcham
Park Sch

Glass
Brow

Sussex Border Path

Staunton Way

Ladyholt

Eckensfield

Sussex Border Path

Harris La

Sussex Border Path

Woodcroft
Fm

Sussex Border Path

Cowdown Fm

Cow

1 grid square represents 500 metres

B2146

South Harting

91

G H J K L M

I

Leith Copse

Cow
La

Col...
Lane

PH

PO

Turkey
Island

East

Harting

2

Sussex Border Path

South Downs Way

Foxcombe Fm

Warren
Side

Warren
Side

Tipper

Pease
Cft

S Acre

Culvers

Mill Lane

New
Lane

Hill Lane

Down
Place

South

B2146

South Downs Way

B2141

South Downs Way

3

4

114

5

B2141

Round
Down

NT Uppark

0

Up Park

Hale Wood

6

7

8

Fernbeds
Down

Hucksholt Fm

B2146

Pads
Wood

Little Green
School

...down
Lane

Fernbeds Fm

Bevis's
...omb

133

G H J K L M

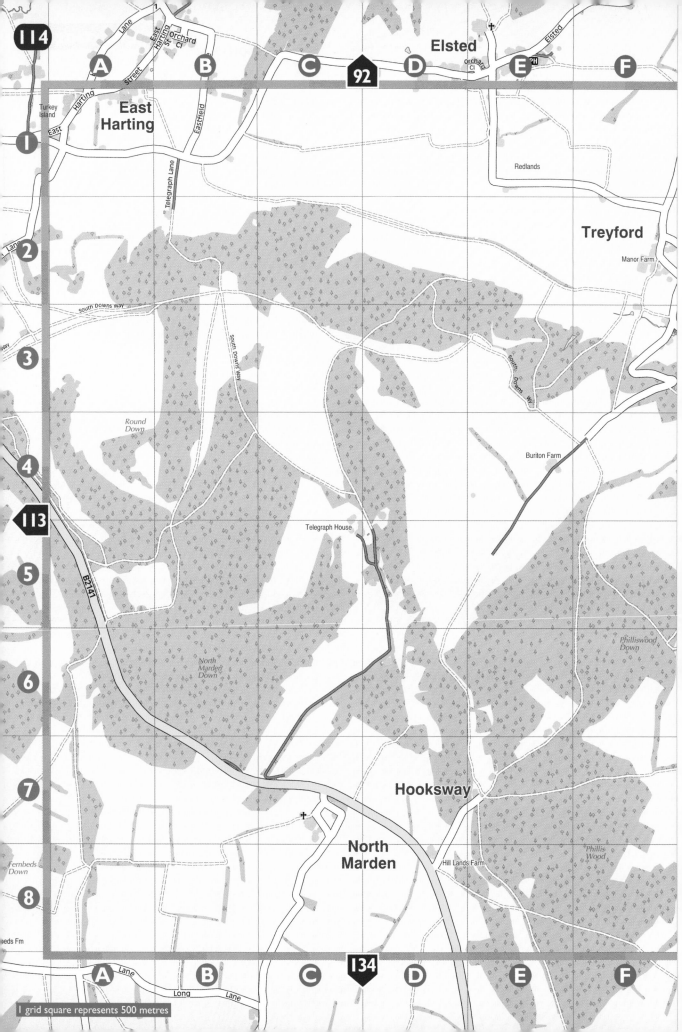

A   B   C   92   D   E   F

Elsted

Turkey Island

East Harting

Redlands

Treyford

Manor Farm

1

Telegraph Lane

South Downs way

2

South Downs Way

3

Round Down

South Downs Wy

Buriton Farm

4

Telegraph House

B2141

5

Philliswood Down

North Marden Down

6

Hooksway

7

North Marden

Hill Lands Farm

Phillis Wood

Fernbeds Down

8

eds Fm

A   Lane   B   C   134   D   E   F

Long Lane

1 grid square represents 500 metres

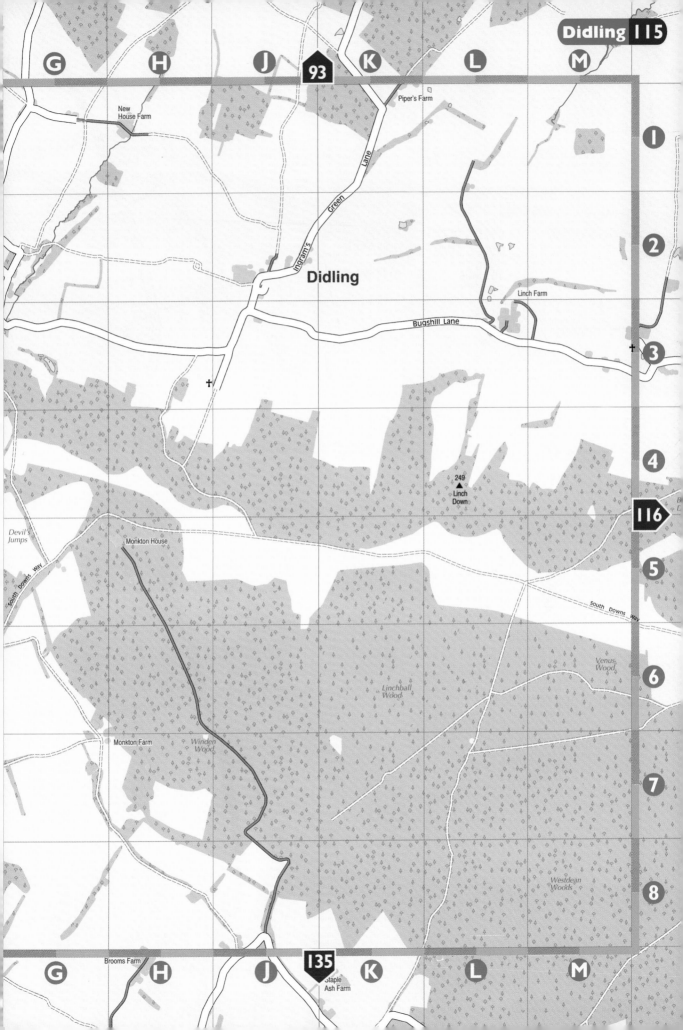

G H J 93 K L M

1

2

Piper's Farm

Green Lane

Ingram's

Didling

Linch Farm

Bugshill Lane

3

†

†

4

249
▲
Linch
Down

116

Devil's
Jumps

Monkton House

South Downs Way

South Downs Way

5

Venus
Wood

6

Linchball
Wood

Monkton Farm

Winden
Wood

7

Westdean
Woods

8

G Brooms Farm H J 135 K L M

Staple
Ash Farm

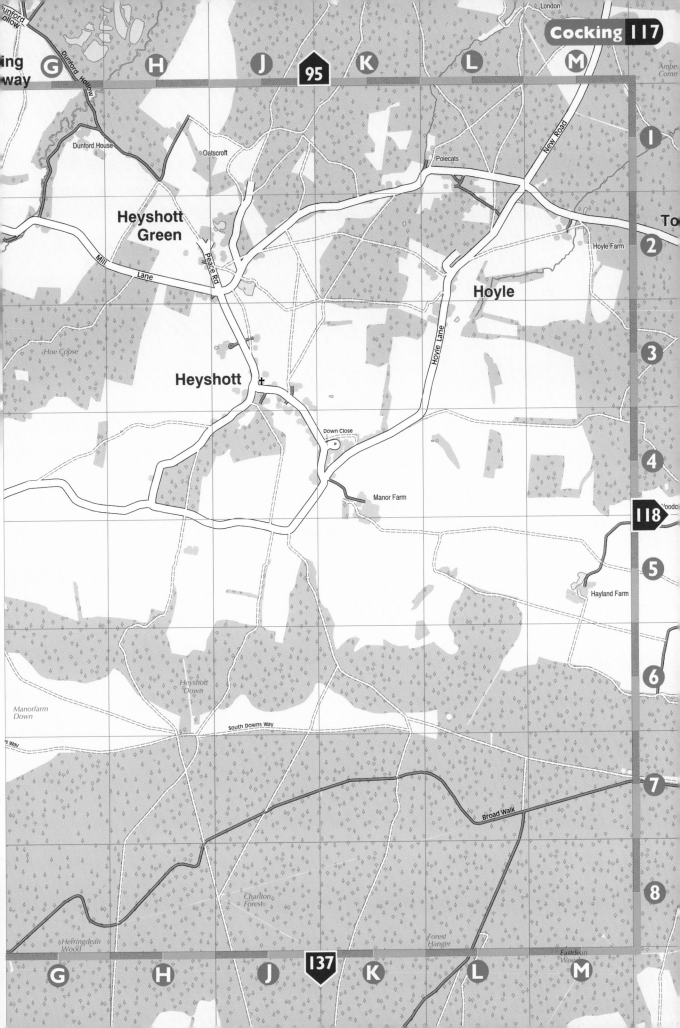

G H J 95 K L M

Dunford Hollow

Dunford House

Oatscroft

London

Polecats

To

Hoyle Farm

New Road

Heyshott
Green

Mill

Lane

Peace Rd

Hoyle

Hoe Copse

Heyshott

Hoyle Lane

Down Close

Manor Farm

Hayland Farm

Woodc

118

Heyshott
Down

Manorfarm
Down

South Downs Way

s Way

Broad Walk

Charlton
Forest

Forest
Hanger

Herringdean
Wood

Eastdean
Wood

G H J 137 K L M

I
2
3
4
5
6
7
8

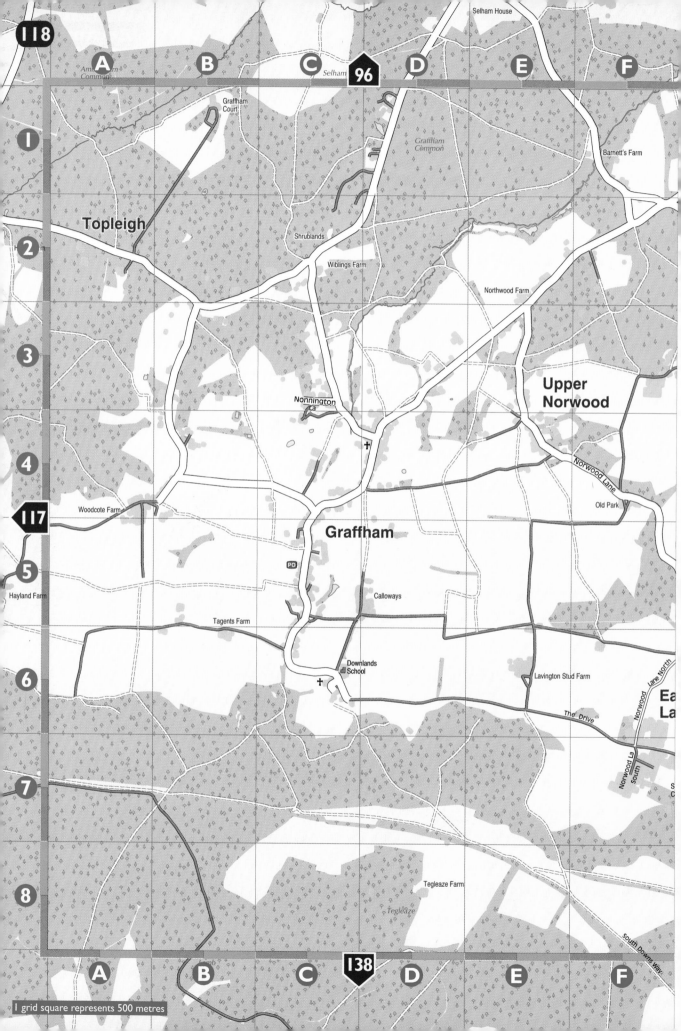

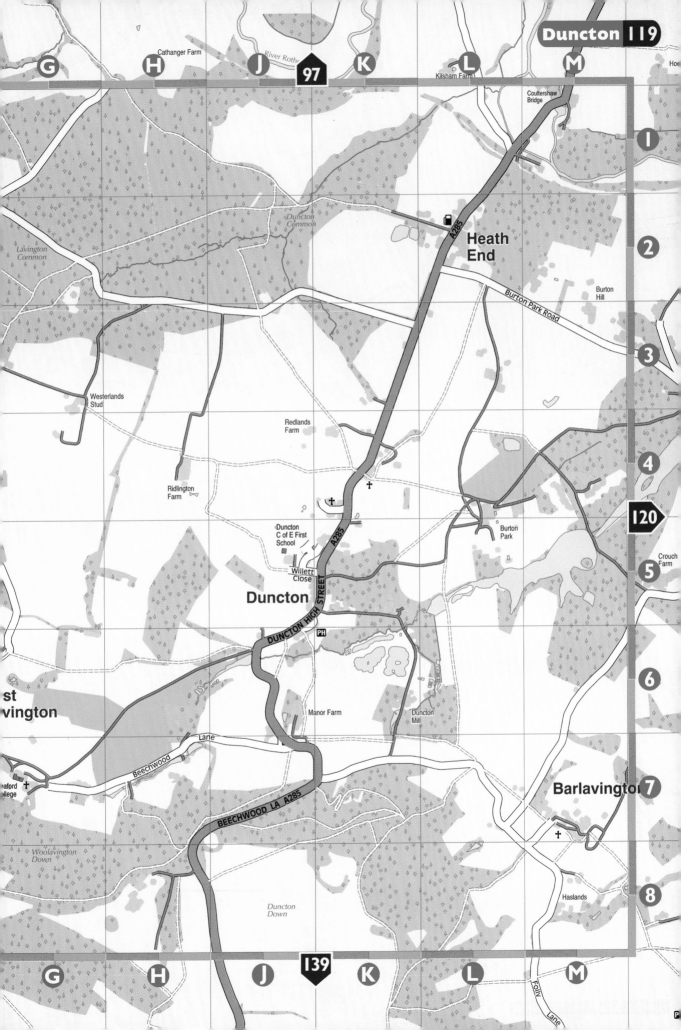

G   H   J   **97**   K   L   M

Cathanger Farm

River Roth

Kilsham Farm

Coultershaw Bridge

1

2

Duncton Common

Heath End

A285

Burton Park Road

Burton Hill

Lavington Common

3

Westerlands Stud

Redlands Farm

4

120

Ridlington Farm

Duncton C of E First School

Burton Park

Crouch Farm

5

Willett Close

Duncton

A285

PH

DUNCTON HIGH STREET

6

st vington

Manor Farm

Duncton Mill

Lane

Beechwood

Seaford College

BEECHWOOD LA A285

Barlavington

7

Woolavington Down

Haslands

8

Duncton Down

Folly Lane

120

A   B   C   **98**   D   E   F

Strood Farm

Douglaslake
Farm

A283

A28

1

High
Hoes

Hesworth Common

River Rother

2

Burton
Hill

Shopham Bridge

Bigenor Farm

3

Burton Park Road

Coates

4

Burton
Mill
Pond

Coates
Castle

Coates Lane

119

Crouch
Farm

Coates
Common

5

Broad
Halfpenny

6

Bignor
Park Cott

**Sutton
End**

7

Bignor
Park
Road

Bignor Park Road

8

School Lane

Sutto   **140**

A   B   C   **140**   D   E   F

Bignorpark

1 grid square represents 500 metres

PH

Churchwood

L7
1 Piers Secombe Cl

G **H** **J** 99 **K** **L** **M**

Fittleworth

UPPER STREET

† Churchfield
Fairmead Cl
Greppin Cft
School Cl
School Cl
A283
Wyncombe Cl
The Gdns
Fittleworth C of E First School
Limbourne Lane
Church Wood
THE FLEET

† Stopham

B2138

Fittleworth Common

PO
Sandy Lane
Lea Farm Lane

A283

I

Lee Farm

Stopham House

2

Wey South Path

STOPHAM ROAD

3

Lower Fittleworth

LOWER STREET

B2138

Wey South Path

Lower Horncroft

Tripphill Farm

HILL

Horncroft Farm

TRIPP

LC

122 Ha

4

5

Kings Lane

Old London Rd

Coldwaltham

Wey South Path

6

Ashurst

Coldwaltham Farm

Waltham Park Road

St James C of E School

† Church Lane

Malthouse Leaf

Silverdale

A29

Arun

PO

Greatham Bridge

7

Sandy Lane

Colebrook Lane

LONDON ROAD

Brookview

Brookland Way

Arun Vale

Brook Lane

Quell Farm Industrial Estate

Watersfield

B2138

River Lane

†

BEACON HILL

A29

River Arun

8

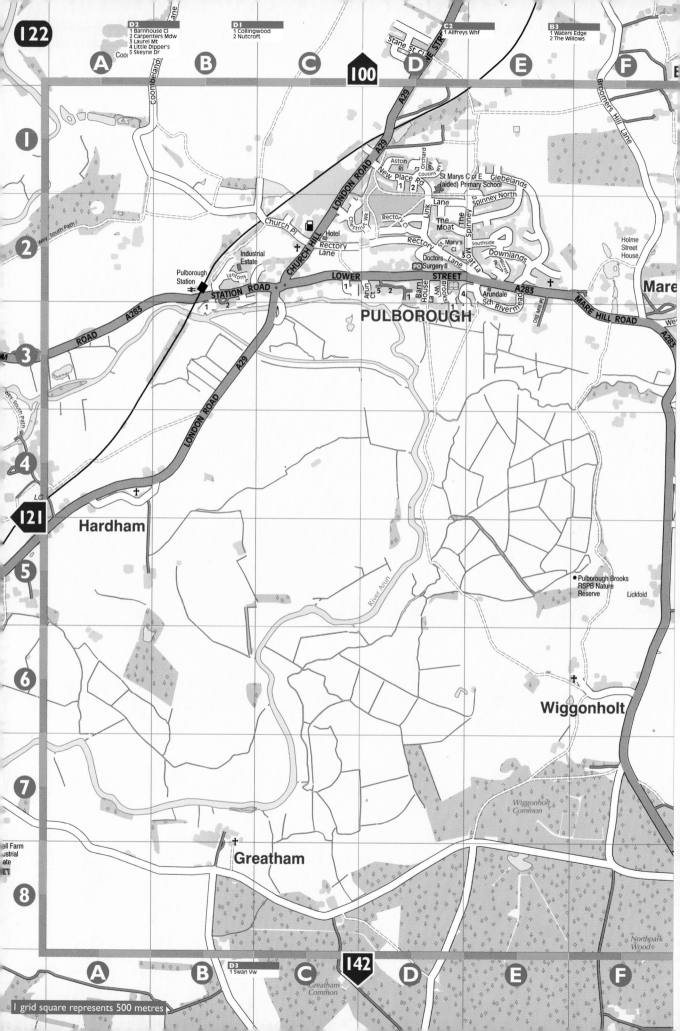

100

A B C D E F

Coombelands Lane
Cool

Wey South Path

London Road

A29

Church Pl

Church Hill

Pulborough Station

Industrial Estate

Lyntons

STATION ROAD

A283 ROAD

London Road

A29

Wey South Path

LG

121

Hardham

Stane St

Aston Ri

New Place Rd

Orchard Wy

Cousins

St Marys C of E (aided) Primary School

Glebelands

Spinney North

Chestnut Wlk

Rectory

Link Lane

The Spinney

The Moat

Southside

Downlands

Hotel

Rectory Lane

Rectory

Mary's Cl

Moat La

Pewtrees

Doctors Lane

Southside

LOWER STREET

PO Surgery

Arun Ct

Barn House La

Brooks

Arundale Sch

Rivermead

A283

Mare Hill Road

A283

Wey

PULBOROUGH

Mare

Holme Street House

River Arun

Pulborough Brooks RSPB Nature Reserve

Lickfold

Wiggonholt

Wiggonholt Common

Greatham

ll Farm ustrial ate

Greatham Common

Northpark Wood

142

A B C D E F

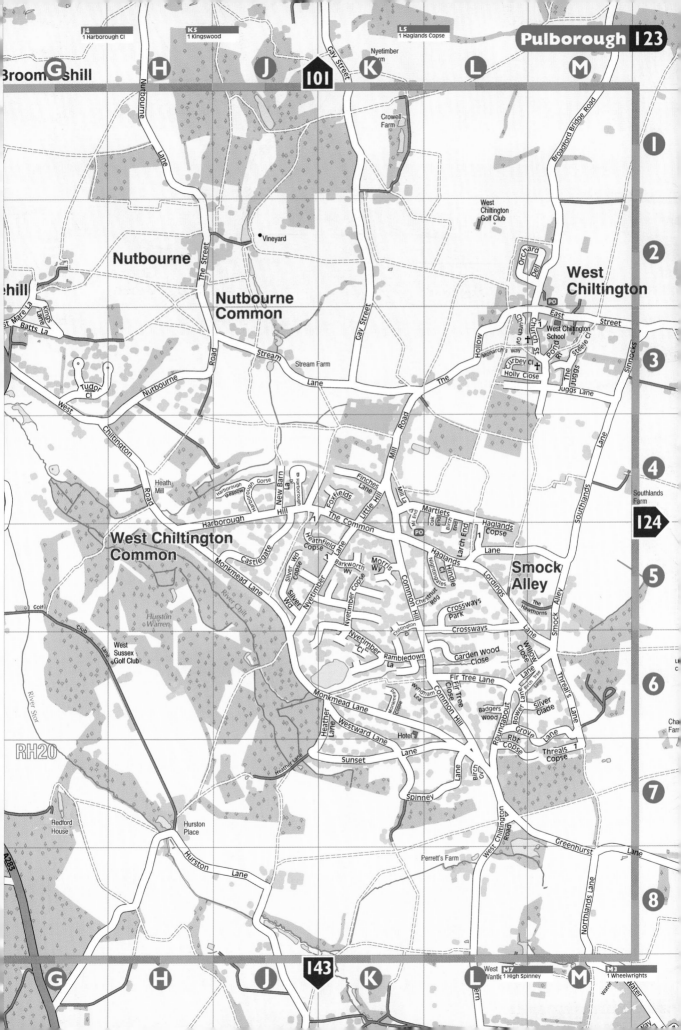

J4
1 Harborough Cl

K5
1 Kingswood

L5
1 Haglands Copse

G Broomershill

H

J

101

Gay Street

K Nyetimber Farm

L

M

Crowell Farm

West Chiltington Golf Club

Broadford Bridge Road

1

Nutbourne

The Street

Vineyard

Orchard Dell

West Chiltington

2

ehill

West Mare La

Kings La

Batts La

Nutbourne Common

Nutbourne Road

Stream

Stream Lane

Stream Farm

Gay Street

Mill Road

Hollow

Monarch's Way

PO

Church Ov

Church St

East Street

West Chiltington School

Curbey Cl

Holly Close

Pond Rd

Steele Cl

The Juggs

Sinnocks

Juggs Lane

3

Tudor Cl

West Chiltington Road

Heath Mill

Harborough Meadow

Harborough Gorse

Harborough Hill

New Barn La

Harborough

Foxfields

Finches Lane

Little Hill

The Common

Mill La

Mill La

Martlets

Oak End

Birch End

Elm End

Haglands Copse

Southlands Farm

124

4

West Chiltington Common

Harborough

Castlegate

Monkmead Lane

Silver Wd Copse

Heathfield Copse

Barkworth Wy

Morris Wy

Nyetimber Copse

Common Hill

PO

Nightingales

Haglands Cl

Hindle

Larch End

Lordings

Chestnut Rdg

Lane

Smock Alley

5

Golf Club Lane

Hurston Warren

River Chilt

Silver Wld

Nyetimber

Nyetimber Cl

Chillington

Rambledown La

Crossways Park

Crossways

Garden Wood Close

The Hawthorns

Willow Close

Smock Alley Lane

West Sussex Golf Club

Monkmead Lane

Wingham Lea

Morkmead Copse

Common Hill

Fir Tree Close Lane

Birch Tree Lane

Badgers Wood

Bower Lane

Grove Lane

Silver Glade

Threal's Lane

6

River Stor

RH20

Heather Lane

Westward Lane

Sunset Lane

Hotel

Spinney

Birch Gv

Roundabout

Rbt Copse

Threals Copse

7

A283

Redford House

Hurston Place

Hurston Lane

Perrett's Farm

West Chiltington Road

Greenhurst Lane

Northlands Lane

8

G

H

J

143

K

L West Wantley 1 High Spinney

M7

M 1 Wheelwrights

M3

Water Way

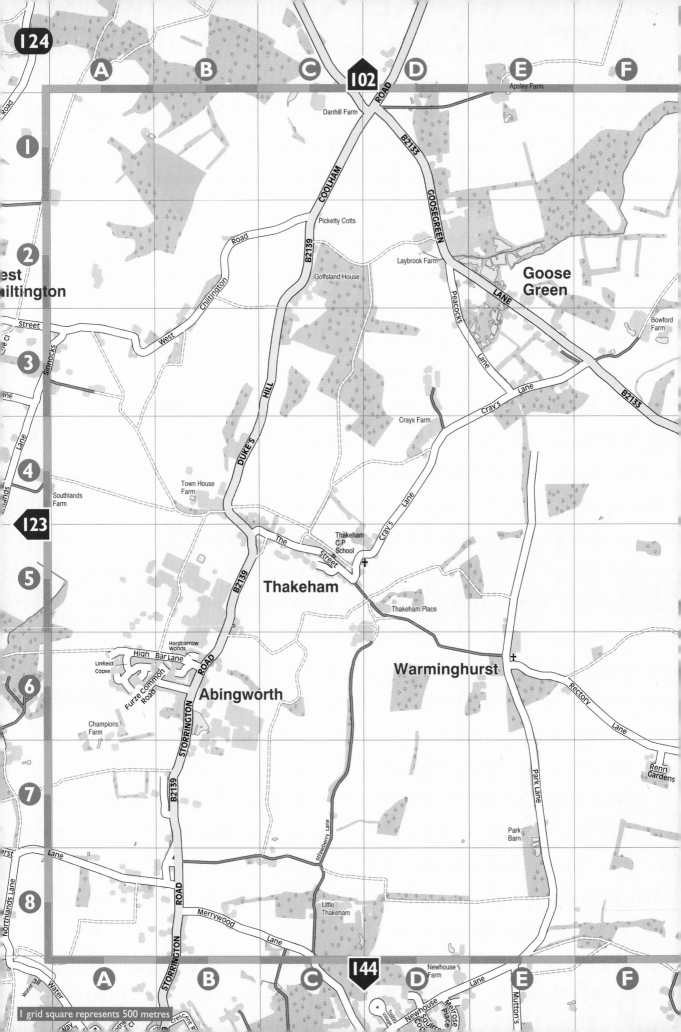

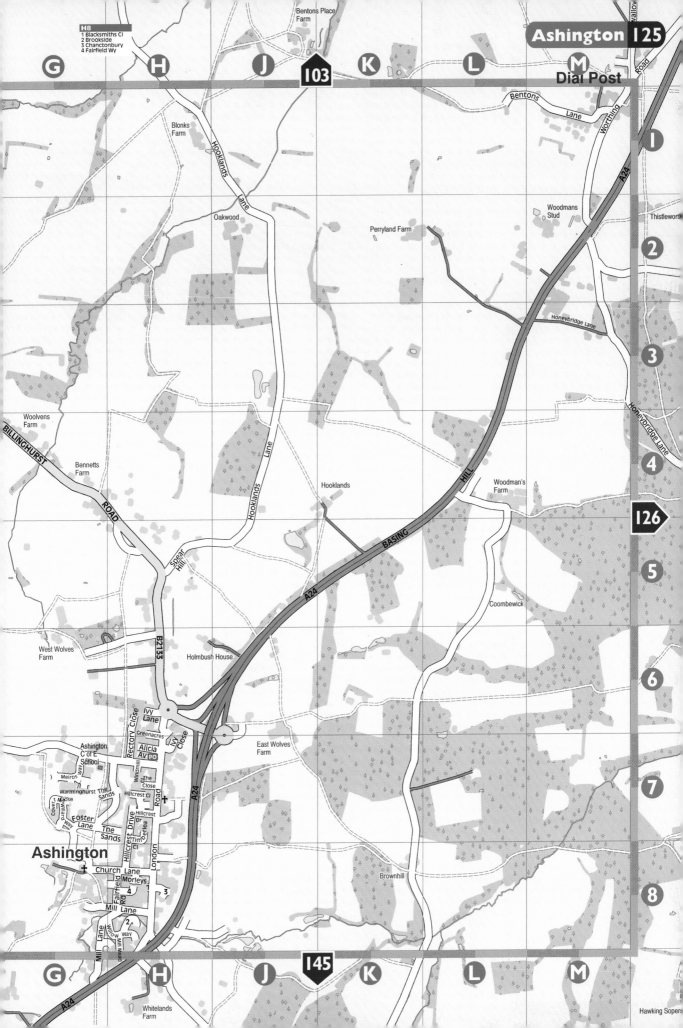

104

A B C D E F

1

2

3

125

4

5

6

7

8

A B C D E F

146

Swallow

Worthing Road

A24

e Lane

Honeybridge Lane

ROOKCROSS Lane

Rooklands Farm

Hobshort's Farm

Thistleworth Farm

Sands Farm

Eder Farm

The Capite

Daylands Farm

Honeybridge Farm

Honeybridge Lane

Brookwood Farm

Sopers Farm

King's Barn Farm

Pepper's Lane

Ashurst

Lock Farm

Pinlands Farm

Ford

Claylands Farm

Godsmarks Farm

Ford Lane

Golden Lane

Church Lane

School Lane

Ashurst Primary School

Sweethill Farm

PH

B2135

Blakes Farm

Spithandle Lane

Beggars Bush

G1
1 St Georges Rd

H1
1 Blanches Wk
2 Finches Cl

G H J 105 K L M

Jolesfield BR
Littleworth
Blanche's Farm

Jolesfield House

The Rise

B2116

Partridge Green

Shermanbury

Shermanbury Grange

Ewhurst Manor

Staples Hill
Forrester
Church Lane
Burrell Close
Michaels Way
Oak Ltd
Oakwood
Woodlawn Surg PO
Oakley Surgery
HIGH STREET
South Street
Hunter's Mw
Hazelwood Rd
Ltd Finches

CHURCH ROAD
Downlands
Mevins

Star Road Trading Est

Star Road

Tristar Business Centre

B2135

Downs Link

Homelands Farm

Downs Link

Shermanbury Place

Wychwood Farm

A281

Nymans Farm

Bottings Farm

Kidders

Lane

Lloyts Farm

Pinland

Road

Brigtham's Farm

Lidde Hill Farm

128

CROUCH HILL
LONDON RD A281

B2135

River Adur

Bines Green

Great Betley Farm

Downs Link

Parsonage Farm

Henfield C of E Primary School

Cresham Place

Fawn Rise

Mallard Cl
Stag Cl
Maidment Cl

Chess Gre

Park

Deer Park

Chantry Close

Manor Way
Manor Close

Wantley Hill Est

A281

Eatons Farm

Chates

Lashmars Hall

End Lane

Stonepit Lane

West End

West End Lane

Lawyer's Lane

Catsfold Farm

Hollands Lane
Buckwish Lane

Leeches

Staples Barn

Flower Farm Close

Fablans Way

Staples Barn Lane

Northcroft

Upper Station Road

Lower Fablans

Station Lane
Lower Faircox
Faircox

Beeching

Hollands Road

Batt Drive

Lwr Station Road

Broomfield Road

Chanctonbury
Holms

Sandy Lane

Nep End

Chopping

Hooks

Nep Town Road

Henfield & District Leisure Centre

Parsonage Road

Martyn Close

Church St

The Laurels

Bishops Cl PO

Park Rd
Cagefoot Lane

Hewitts

South View Terrace

Windmill Lane

Furners Mead

Cedar Wy
Mill Rd

BARROW HILL
HIGH ST

Nep Town

Rye Farm

A B C 106 D E F

Fryland Lane
Ervl Lane

Wineham Lane
Gratten Lane

Furzefield House

Wyndham Farm

1
...hurst ...anor

Sakeham Farm

Abbeylands Farm

Great Wapses Farm

2
Shermanbury ...se

Shiprods

3
...ns

Fieldlands Farm

Lane

Firsland Farm

Chestham Park

Heatenthorn Farm

4

Ride
Cake

ALBOURNE ROAD B2116

Morley Farm

127
...Hill Farm

CROUCH HL LONDON RD A281

5

Park Farm

Blackstone Gate Farm

B2116

Chess Brook Green

Maidment Cl

Mallard Wy

...sta...

6
Park

Wantley Hill Est

Manor Way

Manor Close

Barn End

Woodhouse

Bylsborough Farm

Blackstone Lane

Chantry Close
...nurst
Road

A281

NYEs

The Tofts

Parsonage

Benson Rd

7
Church St

HENFIELD

Furners Lane

Furners Farm

Blackstone St

Blacksto...

...esto...k Wy
Craofts

Bisnops Cl
PO

Park Rd
Cagefoot Lane

Furners Mead

The Daisycroft
...pps Way

8
...Blackgate...
Hewh...

Town Road

HIGH ST

Cedar Wy

Mill Drive

BRIGHTON ROAD A281

BARROW HILL A2...

A B C 148 D E F

A281

Holedean

Woodmancote Place

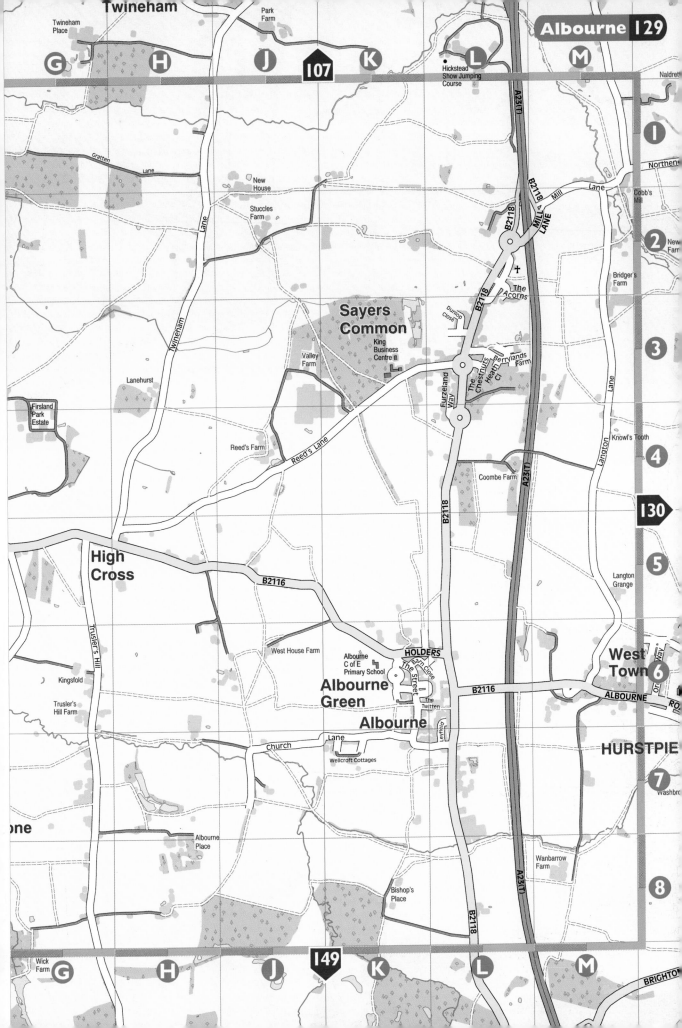

Twineham

Park Farm

Twineham Place

Hickstead Show Jumping Course

Naldret

Northen

I

Gratten Lane

New House

Cobb's Mill

Mill Lane

Stuccles Farm

B2118

The Acorns

Bridger's Farm

New Farm

2

Sayers Common

King Business Centre

Dunlop Close

Berrylands Farm

3

Valley Farm

Furzeland Way

The Chestnuts

Heath Cl

Langton Lane

Knowl's Tooth

Firsland Park Estate

Lanehurst

Twineham Lane

Reed's Farm

Reed's Lane

Coombe Farm

A23(T)

4

B2118

130

High Cross

B2116

Langton Grange

5

Trusler's Hill

Kingsfold

West House Farm

Albourne C of E Primary School

HOLDERS

Barn Close

West Town

6

Trusler's Hill Farm

Albourne Green

The Street

The Twitten

B2116

ALBOURNE RD

Albourne

Church Lane

Wellcroft Cottages

Leylands

HURSTPIE

7

Washbro

Albourne Place

Bishop's Place

Wanbarrow Farm

8

Wick Farm

B2118

BRIGHTON

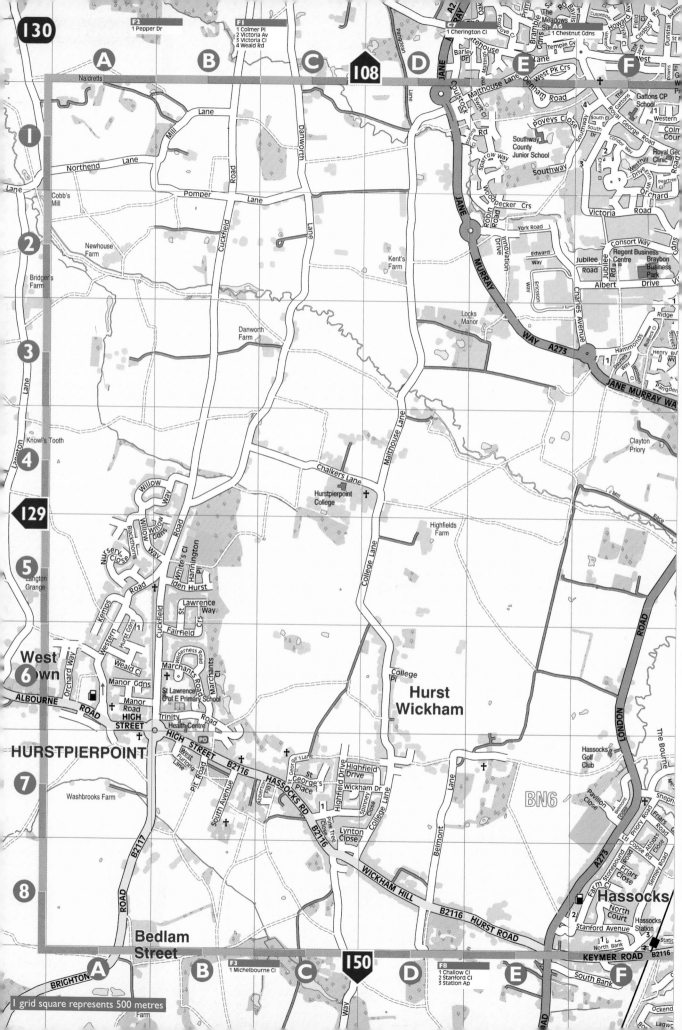

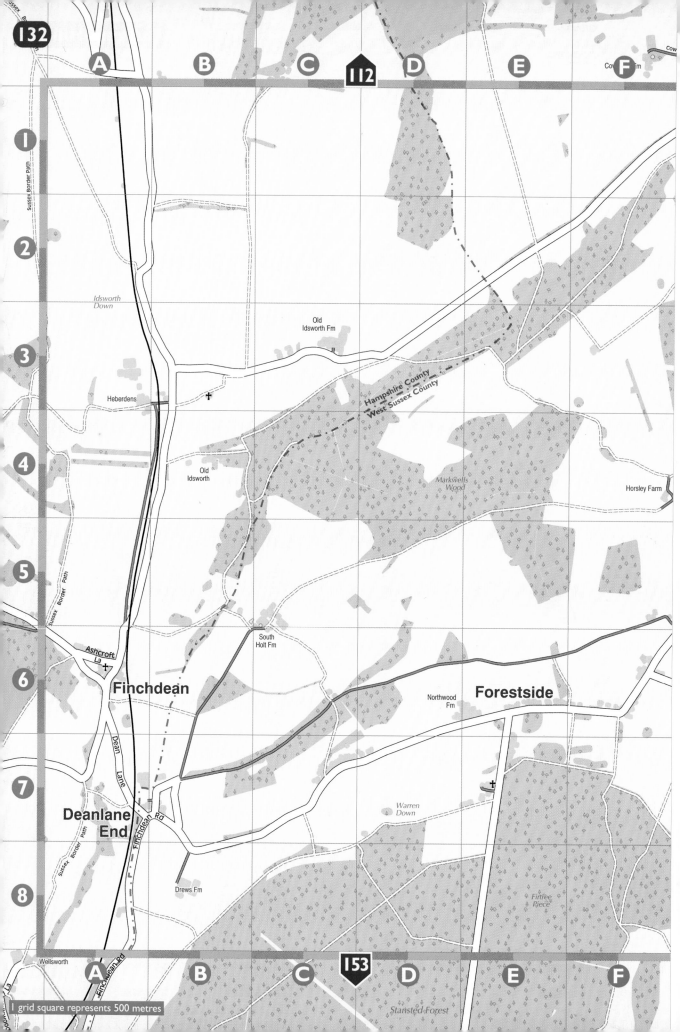

A B C **112** D E F Cow

I

2

3

4

5

6

7

8

A B C **153** D E F

Sussex Border Path

Idsworth Down

Old Idsworth Fm

Heberdens

Old Idsworth

Hampshire County
West Sussex County

Markwells Wood

Horsley Farm

Sussex Border Path

Ashcroft La

Finchdean

South Holt Fm

Northwood Fm

Forestside

Dean Lane

Warren Down

Deanlane End

Sussex Border Path

Finchdean Rd

Drews Fm

Firtree Piece

Wellsworth

Finchdean Rd

1 grid square represents 500 metres

Stansted Forest

Cow Fm

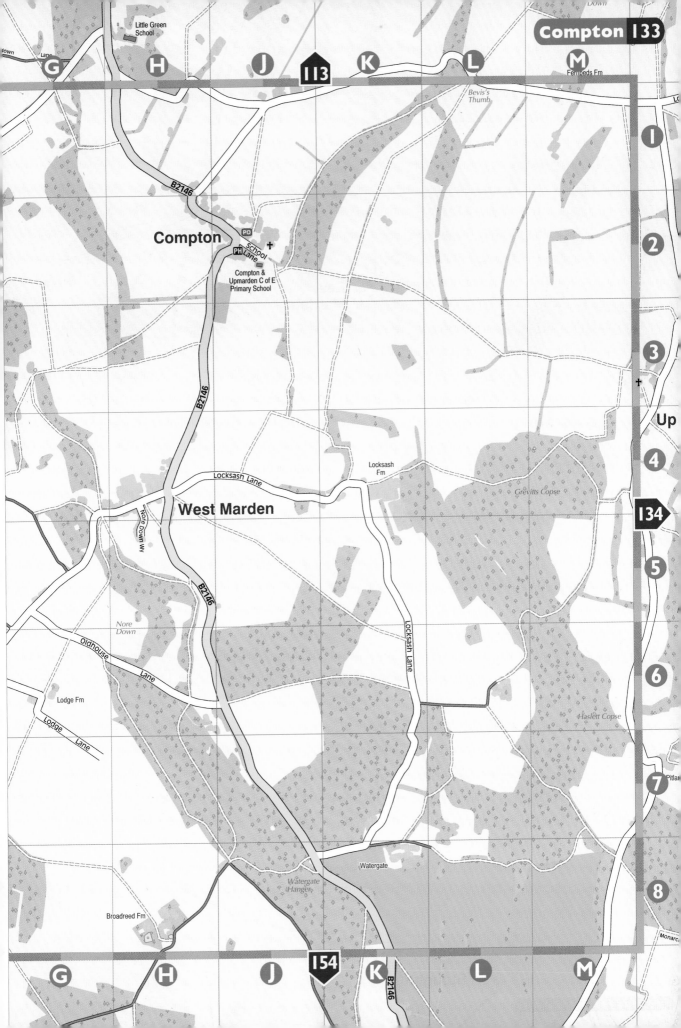

G H J 113 K L M
Ferrbeds Fm

Down

I

Bevis's Thumb

2

B2146

Compton

PO

School Lane
PH

Compton & Upmarden C of E Primary School

3

Up

4

Locksash Fm

Locksash Lane

Grevitts Copse

West Marden

134

Nore Down Wy

5

B2146

Nore Down

6

Locksash Lane

Haslett Copse

Oldhouse Lane

Lodge Fm

Lodge Lane

7

Pitla

Watergate Hanger

Watergate

8

Broadreed Fm

Monarc

G H J 154 K L M
B2146

Ⓐ   Ⓑ   Ⓒ   **114**   Ⓓ   Ⓔ   Ⓕ

Down

beds Fm

Long Lane

Long Lane

East Marden

East Marden Down

Philliswood La

B2141

Hillbarn

Up Marden

133

Wildhams Wood

Lowerfarm Copse

lett Copse

Inholmes Wood

Pitlands Fm

Stoughton Down

Mo

Monarch's Way

Monarch's Way

Church Path

Ⓐ   Ⓑ **Stoughton**   Ⓒ   **155**   Ⓓ   Ⓔ   Ⓕ

1 grid square represents 500 metres

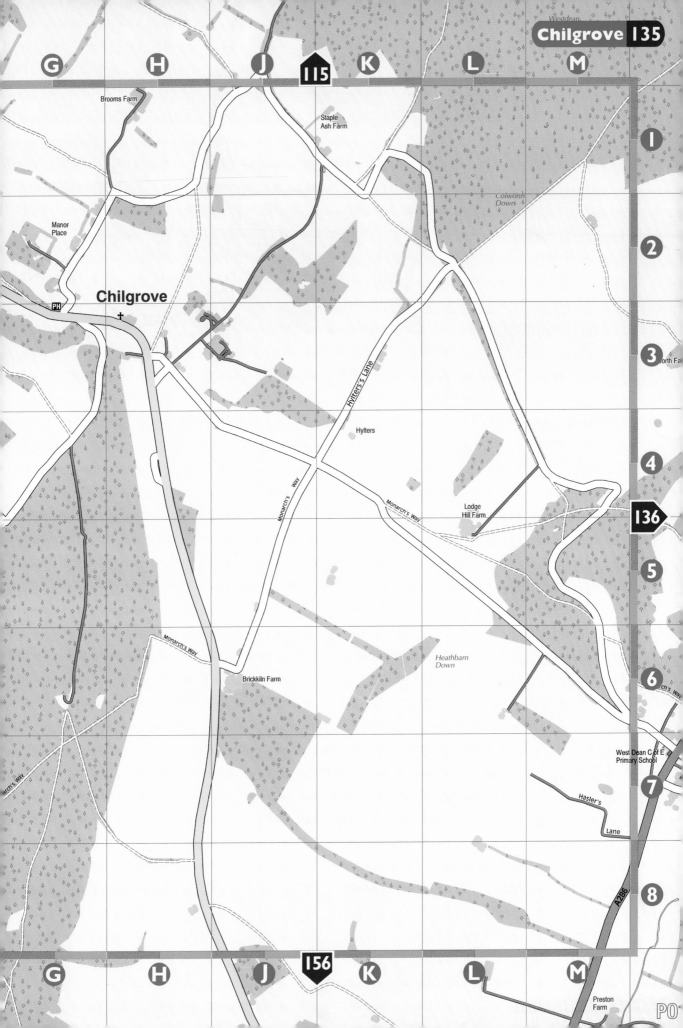

Westdean

G   H   J   115   K   L   M

I

Brooms Farm

Staple
Ash Farm

Colworth
Down

2

Manor
Place

PH Chilgrove
†

3   orth Fa

Hylters's Lane

Hylters

4

Monarch's Way

Monarch's Way

Lodge
Hill Farm

136

5

Monarch's Way

Heathbarn
Down

Monarch's Way

6

ch's Way

Brickkiln Farm

West Dean C of E
Primary School

7

arch's Way

Hasler's

Lane

A286

8

G   H   J   156   K   L   M

Preston
Farm

PO

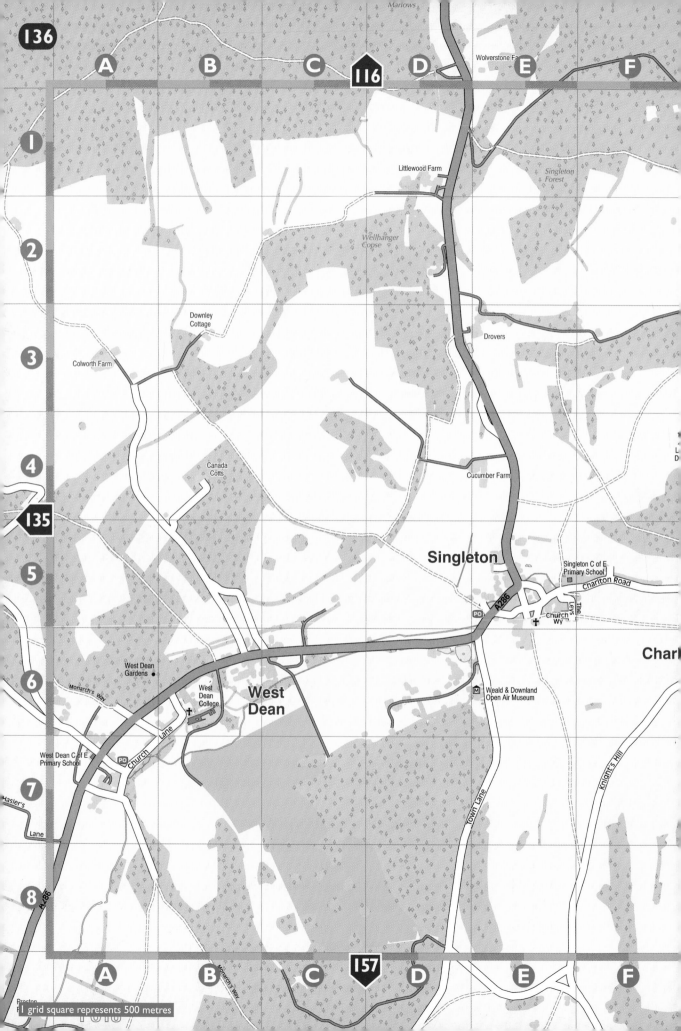

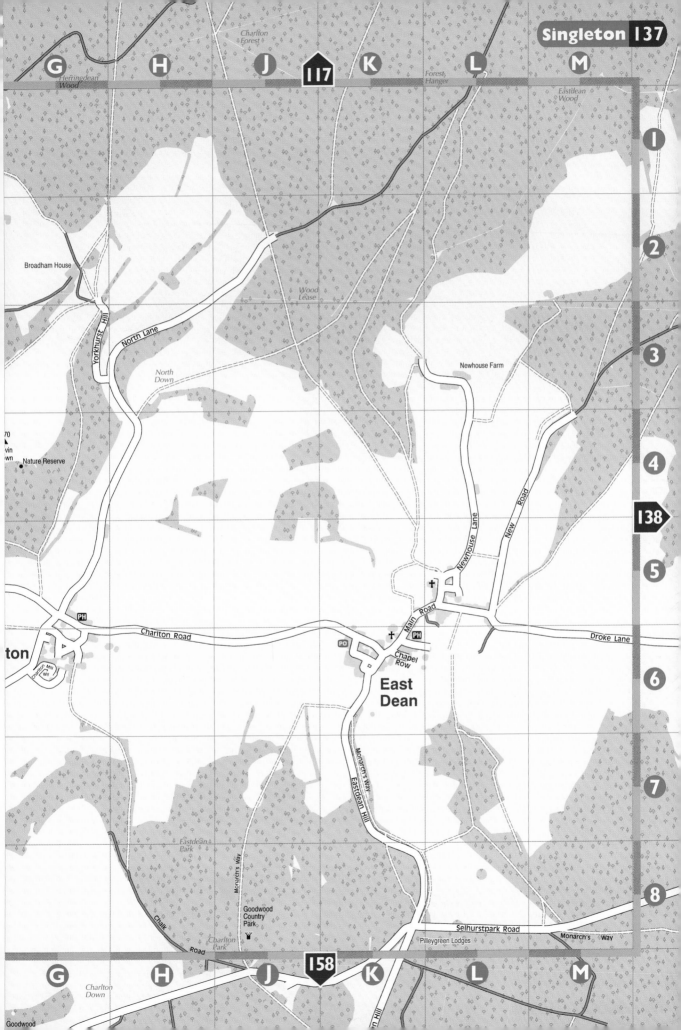

G   H   J   **117**   K   L   M

1

2

3

4

138

5

6

7

8

Herringdean Wood

Charlton Forest

Forest Hanger

Eastdean Wood

Broadham House

Wood Lease

Newhouse Farm

Yorkhurst Hill

North Lane

North Down

Nature Reserve

Newhouse Lane

New Road

PH

Charlton Road

PO

Chapel Row

PH

Droke Lane

ton

Charlton Hill

East Dean

Monarch's Way

Eastdean Hill

Eastdean Park

Monarch's Way

Chalk Road

Charlton Park

Goodwood Country Park

Selhurstpark Road

Monarch's Way

Pilleygreen Lodges

G   H   J   **158**   K   L   M

Charlton Down

Goodwood

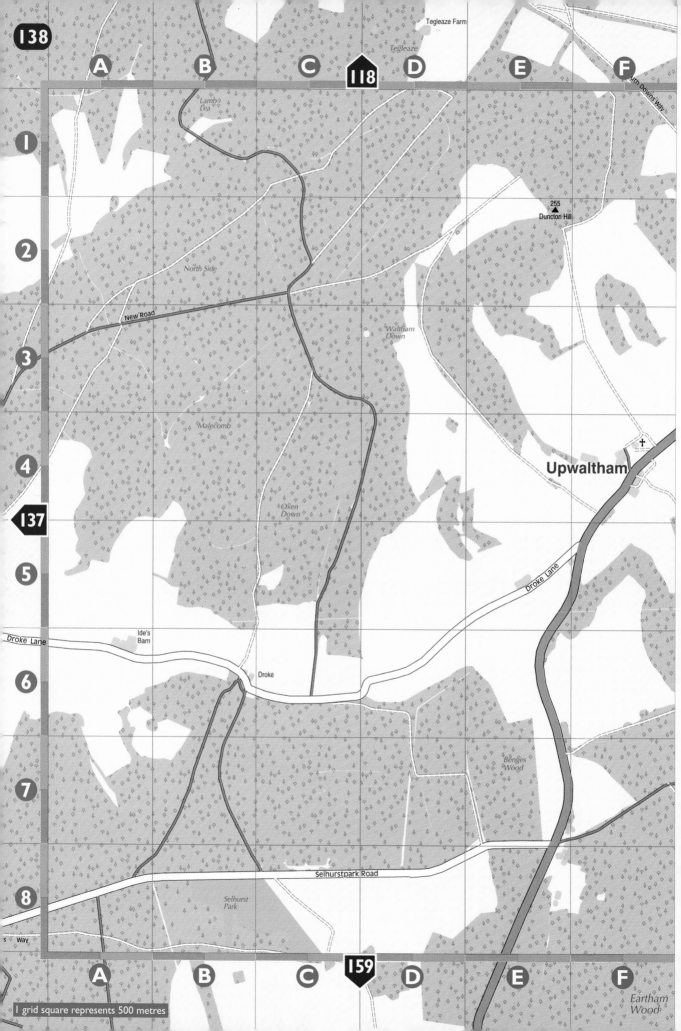

A   **B**   **C**   118   **D**   **E**   **F**

Tegleaze Farm

Tegleaze

uth Downs Way

1

255
Dunton Hill

2

North Side

New Road

Waltham
Down

3

Malecomb

Upwaltham

4

137

Oxen
Down

Droke Lane

5

Droke Lane

Ide's Barn

Droke

6

Benges
Wood

7

Selhurstpark Road

8

Selhurst
Park

s Way

A   **B**   **C**   159   **D**   **E**   **F**

Eartham
Wood

1 grid square represents 500 metres

119

G H J K L M

I

Green

2

3

4

140

5

6

7

8

Folly Lane

Glatting Lane

Glatting Farm

Coldharbour Farm

Glatting Lane

South Downs

South Downs Way

Monarch's Way

Great Bottom

Monarch's Way

Gumber Farm

Stammers

Dogkennel Cottages

Duncton Down

Littleton Farm

A285

South Downs Way

West Wood

Burton Down

North Wood

120

139

161

Sutton

Bignor

West Burton

School Lane

PH

Greenfield

Bignor Mill

Hadworth Farm

West Burton Lane

W Burton Lane

West Burton

Coldharbour Farm

225
▲ Bignor Hill

South Downs Way

South Downs Way

Lane

South Downs Way

Monarch's Way

South Downs Way

The Denture

Houghton Forest

Stammers

Monarch's Way

A29

Park Road

A B C D E F

I
2
3
4
5
6
7
8

A B C D E F

1 grid square represents 500 metres

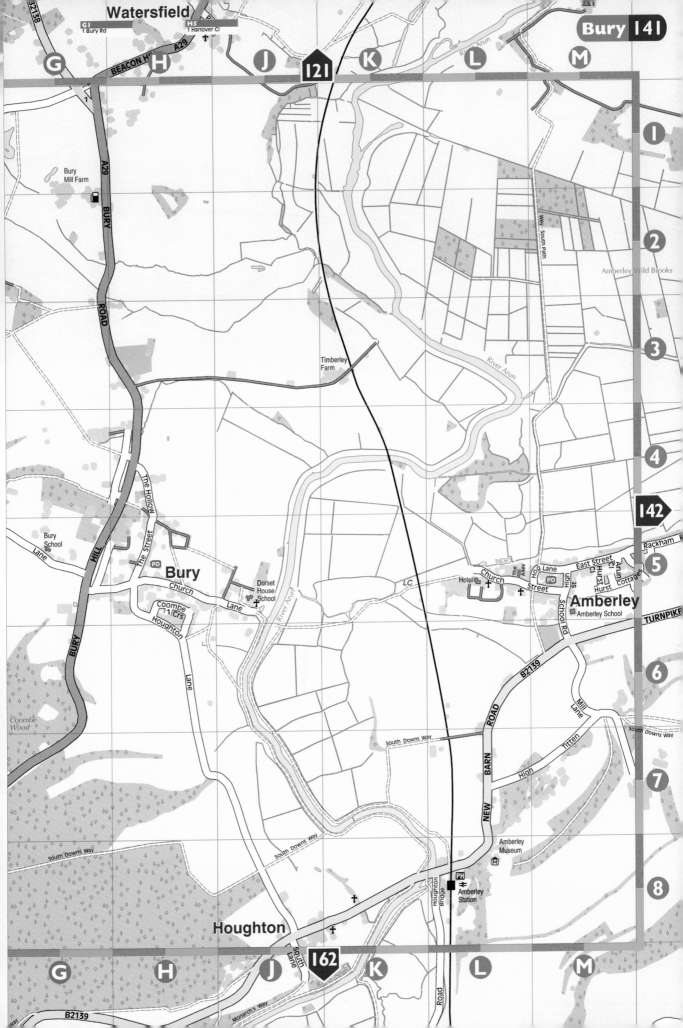

Watersfield

G1 1 Bury Rd   H5 1 Hanover Cl

G   BEACON HILL   A29   **H**   **J**   **121**   **K**   **L**   **M**

River Arun

I

2

Amberley Wild Brooks

Bury Mill Farm

A29 BURY ROAD

3

River Arun

Wey - South Path

Timberley Farm

4

142

Rackham

The Hollow

Bury School

Lane

The Street

PO

Bury

Church Lane

Coombe Crs

Houghton Lane

BURY HILL

Dorset House School

River Arun

LC

Hotel   Church   The Alley   Hog Lane   East Street   Hurst   Arun Cl   Cottages

PO   Hurst Street

High St

Amberley School

School Rd

Amberley

5

TURNPIKE

B2139

NEW BARN ROAD

Mill Lane

Titten

High

6

South Downs Way

south Downs Way

7

Coombe Wood

South Downs Way

South Downs Way

Amberley Museum

Houghton Bridge

PH

Amberley Station

8

Houghton

G   **H**   **J**   **162**   **K**   **L**   **M**

South Lane

River Arun

Road

B2139   Monarch's Way

A B C D E F

Northpark
Wood

1

Greatham
Common

2

Amberley Wild Brooks

3

Parham
Historic
House

✝

4

Rackham Street

Rackham

Springhead
Farm

Rackham Road

Cross
Gate

5

st Str
HURST
Hurst
Cottages

mberley

berley School

B2139

TURNPIKE ROAD

6

South Downs Way

South Downs Way

7

Downs
Farm

8

A B C D E F

The Burgh

1 grid square represents 500 metres

123

144

164

J2
1 Hormare Crs

J3
1 Greenacre Cl

K2
1 Holly Ct
2 Shermanbury Dr

M3
1 Chantry Cl
2 Wisborough La

L2
1 Frenches
2 Riverside

K3
1 Holly Cl

1 Brewers Yd
2 Chanctonb'ry Wk
3 Manor Cl
4 Mant Cl
5 Rectory Rd
6 Rectory Wk
7 Rosemary Cl

Cootham

STORRINGTON

Fryern Hall

West Wantley Farm

Chanctonbury Leisure Centre

Spierbridge School

The Glebe Surgery

Storrington Lawn Tennis Club

Cemetery

Kithurst Park

Kithurst Farm

Gerston Business Park

Greyfriars

The Chantry

212
Kithurst Hill

South Downs Way

PULBOROUGH ROAD

A283

B2139

AMBERLEY ROAD

WEST STREET

HIGH ST

MANLEY'S HILL

SCHOOL HILL

Chantry Lane

Greyfriars

Clay Lane

Hurston Lane

THAKEHA

Sulk
War

Sullir

Sullin

G H J K L M I 2 3 4 5 6 7 8

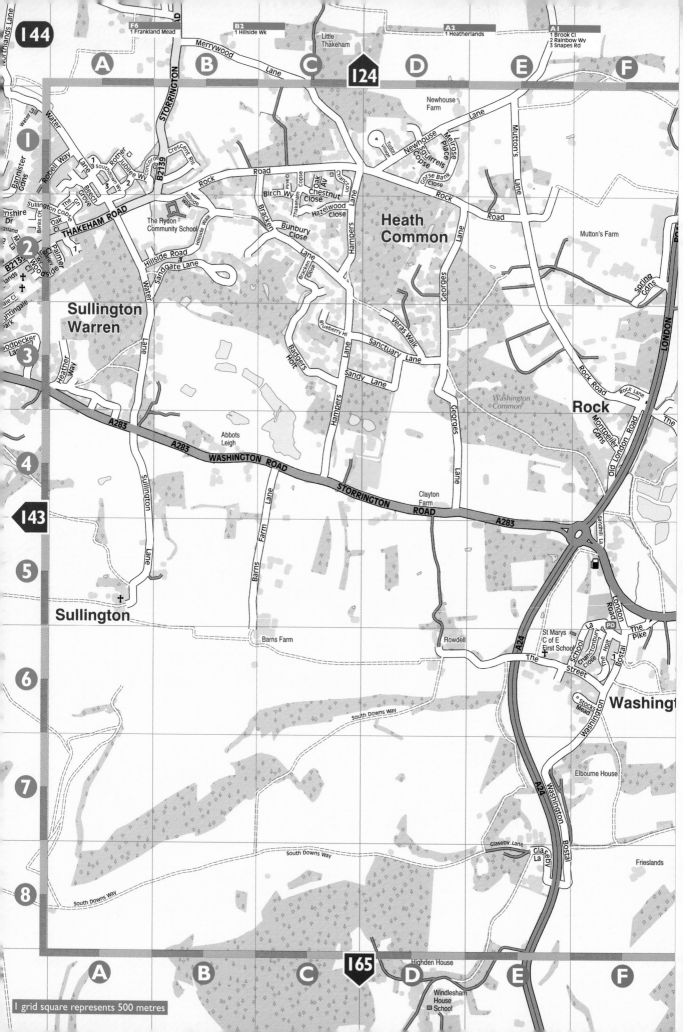

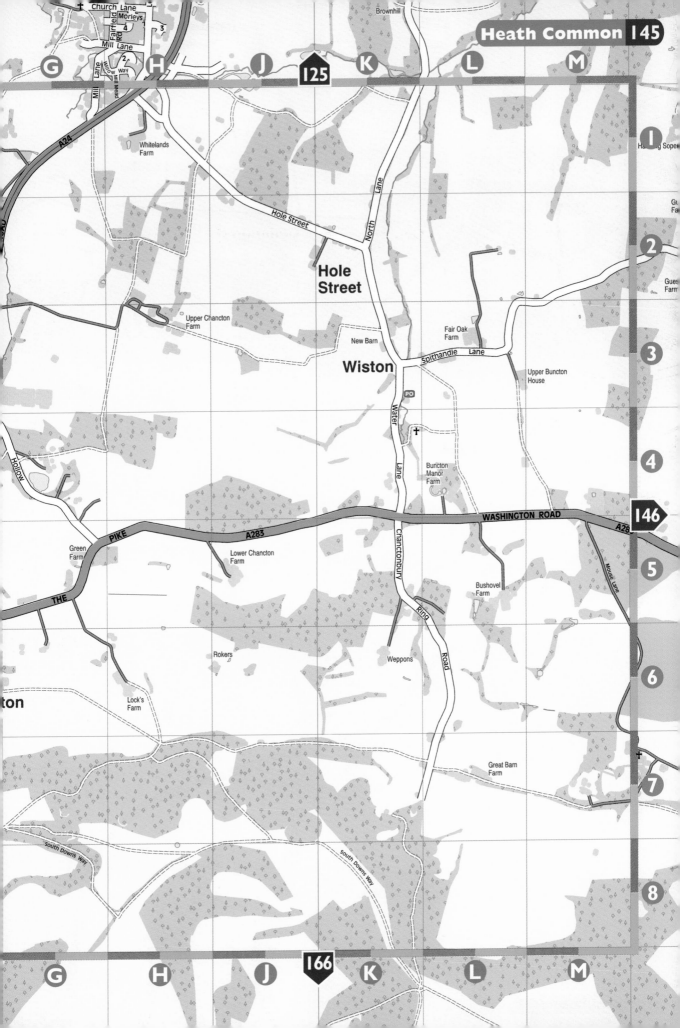

G H J **125** K L M

I

2

3

4

146

5

6

7

8

G H **166** J K L M

Church Lane
Morleys
Fairfield Rd
Mill Lane
Willow Mill Mead
Way

Brownhill

Whitelands
Farm

Hole street

North Lane

Hole
Street

Upper Chancton
Farm

New Barn

Fair Oak
Farm

Spithandle Lane

Wiston

Upper Buncton
House

PO

Water Lane

Buncton
Manor
Farm

Hollow

WASHINGTON ROAD

A28

A283

THE PIKE

Green
Farm

Lower Chancton
Farm

Chanctonbury

Mouse Lane

Ring

Bushovel
Farm

Rokers

Weppons

Road

Lock's
Farm

ton

Great Barn
Farm

South Downs Way

South Downs Way

126

145

167

A B C D E F

1

2

3

4

5

6

7

8

A B C D E F

King's Barn Farm

Sweethill Farm

F8
1 Henderson Wk

E8
1 Mimmack Cl
2 Thornscroft

Blakes Farm

Hawking Sopers

Spithandle Lane

Beggars Bush

Horsebridge Common

Guesses Farm

Doves Farm

Calcot Wood

Northover Farm

Spithandle Lane

Guessgate Farm

College Wood Farm

Calcot Farm

Wappingthorn Wood

B2135

Huddlestone Farm

Wappingthorn

HORSHAM ROAD

Ham Farm

Wiston Park

Staplefields

Greenfields

Mouse Lane

BN44

A283

Horsham Road

STEYNING

Toomey Rd

Charlton Court

Mouse Lane

Steyning St Andrews C of E Primary School

Steyning Sports Centre

Steyning Grammar School

Middle Rd

Canons Way

BY-PASS

Wiston Barn

Charlton Court

Coxham Lane

Steyning Town Football Club

Penns Ct

Steyning Health Centre

St George's

Tanyard Lane

Vicarage La

Market Fd

Station Rd

Steyning Athletic Club

Charlton St

High St

Church St

Church Lane

Grammar School

King's Barn Lane

Rosemary Close

1 grid square represents 500 metres

127

168

148

Nep Town

Catsfold Farm

Leeches

Harwoods

West End Lane

Hollands Lane

Buckwish Lane

Sandy Lane

Windmill Lane

ChancConbury View

Mill

Hook

Barrow Hill

A2037

Cedar Wy

Mill Rd

Town Road

South View Terrace

Dagbrook Lane

Brookside Farm

Downs Link

Rye Farm

Newbarn Lane

New Barn Fa

Newbarn Lane

Wyckham Wood

River Adur

Downs Link

Stretham Manor

West Mill Farm

SHOREHAM ROAD

Hoe Wood

Bee Wo

Shelleys

Downs Link

Newhall Farm

New Hall Lane

Downsview

Wood La

Tottington

Wyckham Farm

PO

Sands Lane

Small D

Mae Esta

A2037

Hillside Lane

Henfield Road

Tottington Manor Farm

ring's

Barn Lane

Kings Barn Farm

River Adur

Saxon Road

Avenue

The Priory

Farm Walk

Horton Hall

G H J K L M

I

2

3

4

5

6

7

8

148

High St
Cedar Wy
Mill Drive
Town Road
View
BARROW HILL A2037
IGHTON
A ROAD
B
C
128
D
E
F

Hackgate Fm
Town

A281

1
agbrook Lane

Holedean
Farm

Woodmancote
Place

†

Blackstone Lane

2
Newbarn Lane
Newbarn
Lane
New
Barn Farm
BN5
A2037

Terry's
Cross

Woodmancote

A281

3
Newbarn
Lane

The Henfield
Business
Park

Oreham
Common

Horn Lane

Bramlands Lane

Bramlands

Holmbu

4
A2037
Woods
Mill

Catsland
Farm

147

silver
Birches

Oreham
Manor

Catsland Lane

Catslands Lane

5
SHOREHAM
Hoe wood
Beech
Wood
Downsview
Wood La
Lane

Edburton Drove

6
Tottington Drive
Orchard
Close
Sands Lane
PO

Small Dole

South
Tottington Sands

Truleigh
Sands

Lower Edburton Barn

Perching
Sands Farm

Mackley Industrial
Estate

Edburton Drove

7
e Lane

Perching Drove

Paythorne
Drove

8
ngton
or
Farm

Truleigh
Manor Farm

Edburton
†

169

Perching
Manor Farm

A
B
C
D
E
F

1 grid square represents 500 metres

G H J **129** K L M

BRIGHTON

1

Wick
Farm

Bishop's
Place

Wanbarrow
Farm

Muddleswood

Brighton Rd

B2117

2

Shaves Farm

Shaves
Wood

Shaves Wood Lane

B2117

Locks Green
Farm

London Road

Random
Copse

3

Holmbush
Farm

ush Lane

Park
Wood

LONDON ROAD

4

150

Badger
Wood Farm

Clappers Lane

Poynings
Grange Farm

A281

Church Lane

5

WEST ROAD

A28

6

Brook
House

Mill
Cl

Mill La

The Good
Start School

Beggar's Lane

Manor
Farm Business
Centre

7

Poynings

PH

PO

8

Wickhurst
Barns

Fulking

Stammer's Hill

Saddlescomb

G H J **170** K L M

Devil's

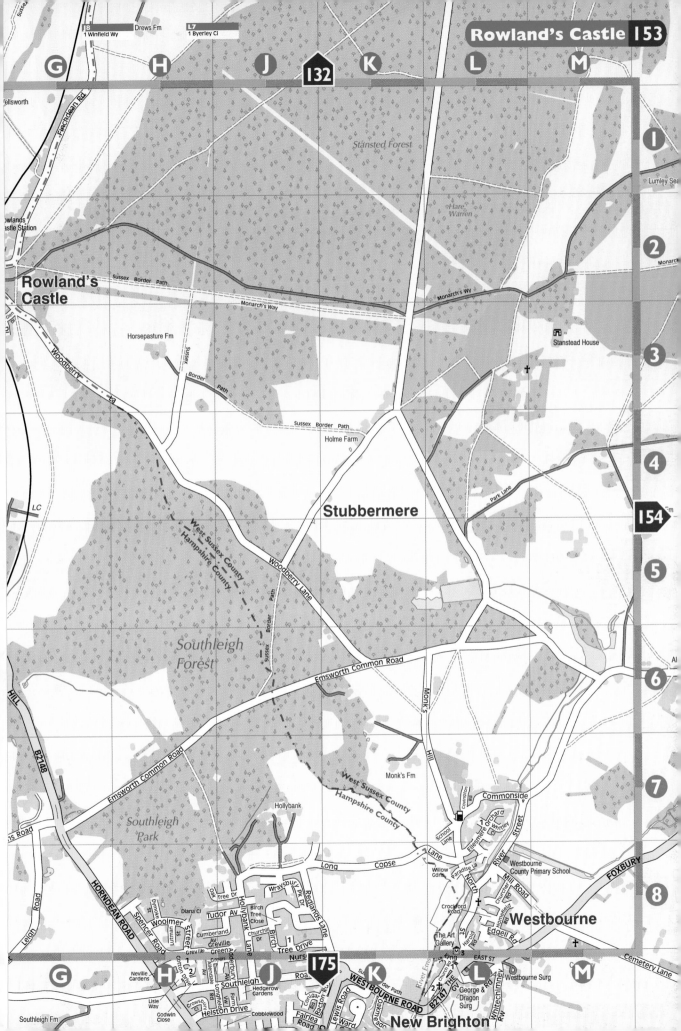

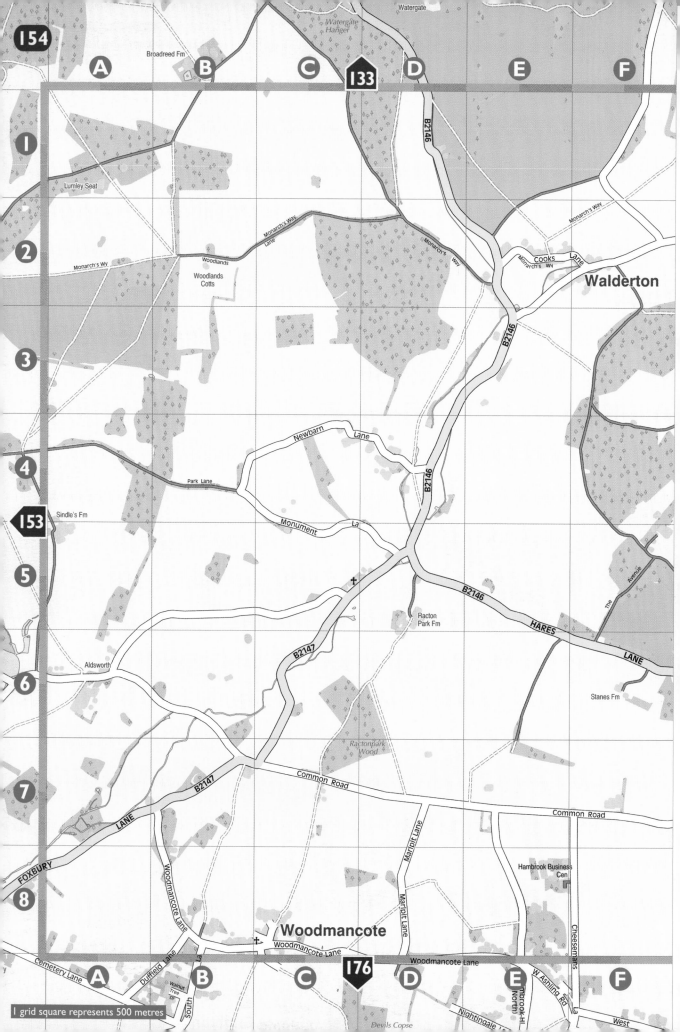

G   H   J   **134**   K   L   M

Monarch's Way

Monarch's Way

Church Path

Stoughton

I

2

Kingley
Vale (Nature
Reserve)

3

*Walderton
Down*

Stoke
Down

4

156

Adsdean Ho

5

Downs Farm

Bowhill Lane

Bowhill

West
Stoke
House

*Funtington
Down House*

Downs Road

Woodend

6

Funtington

The Broad Walk

Downs Road

Lynch
Down

Lynch
Down

Five Acres

Haresfoot Cl

Weston La

B2146

7

PO
Dukes
Meadow

Church La

Admirals
Walk

Watery

Northbrook
Farm

Lane

B2146

B2178

Lye Lane

8

Balsam's Fm

Sandy Lane

**East
Ashling**

G   H   J   **177**   K   L   M

School Dell

Down

Thickdders Lane

Merrow's Lane

Funtington
County
Primary
School

Heather
Cl

**West
Ashling**

A   B   C   **135**   D   E   F

F6
1 Downview Cl

1

Crows Hall Farm

B2141

Binderton Lane

2

3

Langford Farm

4

Stoke
Clump

5

Lavant Down

Gaston Wy

Heron Cl

Hayes Cl

Eastmead
Industrial Est

Northside

West
Stoke
House

Trumley
Copse

**West
Stoke**

St Nich

Tyndale Cl

**Mid
Lavant**

6

Downs Road

Two Barns Lane

Lavant C of E
Primary School

A286

7

Lye Lane

Lavant
House
School

8

Lye Lane

st
hling

Lye Lane

A   B   C   **178**   D   E   F

Densworth

Chapel Lane

West Road

Oldwick Farm

Hunters Race

Huntersrace

G H J **136** K L M

P018

I
Goodwood
Race Course

2

Monarch's Way

Monarch's Way

Monarch's Way

206
▲
The
Trundle

Park Rd.

Haye's
Down

Lavant
Down

Kennel Hill

Prince's Dr

Monarch's Way

3

4

158

Middlefield Lane

Middlefield Lane

Kennel Hill

5

Forage
Yard

Goodwood
Golf Club

The
Valdoe

6

St Mary's Cl
East Vw Cl
St Roche's Cl

Staple Lane

Marsh Lane

Springfield Cl

Churchmead Cl

Douglas Rd

River Lavant

PO

Sheepwash
Lane

Pook Lane

Shop
La

Lower Rd

East Lavant

Fordwater Road

7

The
Close

Oldwick
Mdw

Raughmere
Drive

Raughmere
Farm

Fordwater Road

Stocks Lane

New Road

Woodcote

8

A286

LAVANT

Rew
Lane

Keepers
Wood

Halberton Crs

The
Marchwood

Compton Cl

Selsey

Maple

Road

River

G H **179** J K

Chichester
Airfield

L

Claypit Lane

M

Richmond Rd

W

157

180

Charlton Down

Goodwood Race Course

Goodwood Country Park

Charlton Park

Road

Pilleygreen Lodges

Sel Park Road

Monarch's Way

Eastdean Hill

Open Winkins

Molecomb Broadwalk

Prince's Dr

Park Rd

Park

Road

Molecomb

New Barn Hill

New Barn Hill

Halnaker Park

Goodwood Park

Park

Road

Goodwood House

Home Farm

Marriott Goodwood Park Hotel & Country Club

Waterbeach

New Barn Hill

Park Lane

A285

PH

Halnaker

Tinwood Lane

The Street

A285

Strettington

New Road

St Mary's Road

St Blaises Road

Boxgrove C of E Primary School

Crouch Cross Lane

Kirkby Cl

The Close

PO

Priory Close

Priors

Richmond Rd

Westerton

Strettington Lane

Temple Bar

STANE STREET

Boxgrove

1 grid square represents 500 metres

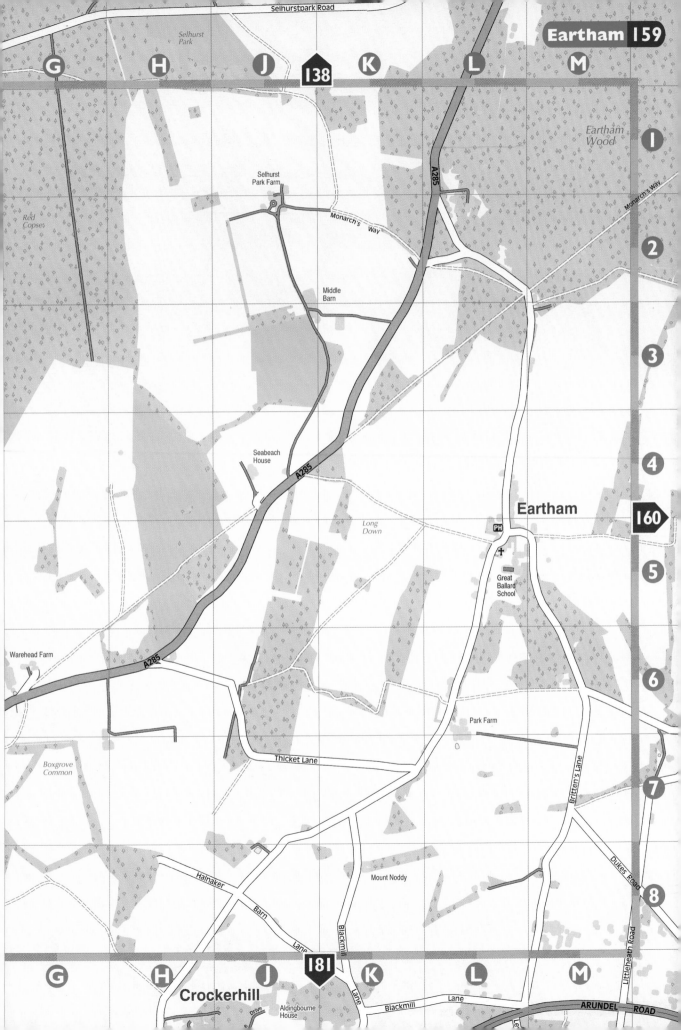

Selhurstpark Road

Selhurst
Park

I

Eartham
Wood

Selhurst
Park Farm

Red
Copse

Monarch's Way

2

A285

Middle
Barn

Monarch's Way

3

Seabeach
House

A285

4

Eartham

160

PH

Long
Down

5

Great
Ballard
School

Warehead Farm

A285

6

Park Farm

Britten's Lane

Thicket Lane

7

Boxgrove
Common

Dukes Road

Mount Noddy

Halnaker

8

Barn Lane

Blackmill Lane

Littleheath Road

Crockerhill

Aldingbourne
House

Drive

Blackmill Lane

ARUNDEL ROAD

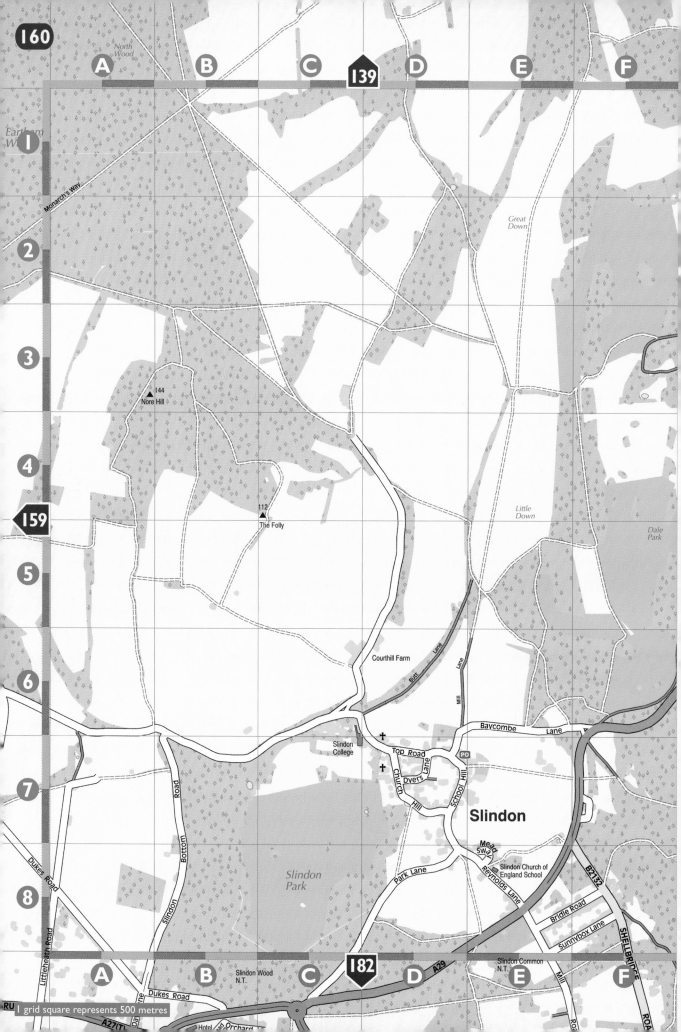

A   B   C   **139**   D   E   F

Eartham W.

I

Monarch's Way

2

North Wood

Great Down

3

▲ 144
Nore Hill

4

159

▲ 112
The Folly

Little Down

5

Dale Park

6

Courthill Farm

Baycombe   Lane

Butt   Lane

Mill   Lane

Slindon
College

Top Road

Dyers   Lane

Church   Hill

School   Hill

PO

7

Slindon

Bottom   Road

Dukes Road

Park Lane

Mead
SW

Reynolds   Lane

Slindon Church of
England School

B2132

*Slindon
Park*

8

Littleheath Road

Bridle Road

Sunnybox Lane

SHELLBRIDGE ROA

A   B   *Slindon Wood
N.T.*   C   **182**   D   A29   E   *Slindon Common
N.T.*   Mill   F

Dukes Road

RU   I grid square represents 500 metres

A27(T)

Hotel   *Orchard*

G   H   J   140   K   *Houghton Forest*   L   M

Stammers

Monarch's Way

A29

A284

LONDON ROAD

Monarch's Way

Whiteways Lodge

I

2

3

Parletts Farm

A29

A29

FAIRMILE BOTTOM

Madehurst

New Barn Farm

Cemetery

A29

BOTTOM

Fairmile Bottom

FAIRMILE

Punchbowl

Sherwood Rough

LONDON ROAD

A284

162

BN18

4

5

6

Rewell Wood

Rewell House

Long Lane

Long Lane

LONDON ROAD

7

8

G   H   J   183   27(T)   K   CHICHESTER RD   L   M   Farm

Paine's Wood

CHICH

A   B   Hough **C**   141   D   E   F

A29

1

Monarch's Way

B2139

South Lane

River Arun

Monarch's Way

Houghton Bridge

PH

Amberley Station

2

A284

LONDON R

Stoke Road

North Stoke

3

Monarch's Way

Monarch's Way

4

A284

South Stoke

161

ON R

5

Arundel Park

River Arun

LC

J18

LONDON

6

Offham

ROAD

7

Monarch's Way

Swanbourne Lake

Monarch's Way

8

Friends of Arundel Castle Cricket Club

Wildfowl Reserve

ark Farm

A   B   **ARUNCEL**   **184**   D   E   F

A284 ARUNDEL BY-PA

ndon

Primary Sch

Arundel Castle

Cemetery

Arun District Council

Arundel Football Club

King

Road

Arundel & District

Town

High Stre

Arundel Hotel

LC

1 grid square represents 500 metres

The Burgh

Wepham Down

Peppering High Barn

Burpham High Barn

Coombe Lane

Peppering Lane

Peppering Farm

Hotel

Burpham

Wepham

New Down

Wepham Wood

Monarch's Way

Warningcamp

A B C 143 D E F

1

2

Lee
Farm

3

167
▲
Harrow
Hill

4

163

5
Lower
Barpham

Upper
Barpham

6

Monarch's Way

Myrtle Grove
Farm

Michelgrove

7
Monarch's Way

Monarch's Way

BN

8

Longfurlong
Lane

Angmering
Park

LONG FUR

A ...ering
...rk Farm
B C 186 D E F

1 grid square represents 500 metres

G   H   J   146   K

K1
1 Sir George's Pl

L1
1 Tunsgate

L2
1 Coombe Dro

M

Mouse Lane

Wiston Barn

Charlton Court

Coxham Lane

Steyning Grammar School

Steyning Football

Penns Ct

Sir George's Pl

Charlton St

Mill Road

Tanyard Lane

Steyning Health Centre

Steyning Athletic Club

High Street

Charlton Street

Elm Gv

Church Street

Museum

Grammar School

Sheep Pen La

Dog Lane

Dukes Meadow

Vicarage La

Station Rd

Holland Rd

Rosemary Close

King's Barn Vs

Canons Way

Bowmans Cl

Abbey Rd

BY-PASS

Castle Way

Saxon Road

Roman Road

De Braose Way

King's Stone Ave

I

Bra

STEYNING

Newham

Hills Road

Laines Road

Chandlers Way

Godstalls La

Perrots La

Penfold Way

Ingram

The Furlongs

Portway

Penlands Rise

Penlands

Coombe Rd

Penlands Way

Andrew

Little Grove

Goring Road

Bramber Rd

The Crescent

College

Castle La

Clays

Hill

Castle Lane

Pepperscoombe

Penlands

Combe Drive

The Ridings

Maudlyn Park

Maudlyn Close

Monarchs Way

Annington Road

Maudlin Lane

Kingsmead Close

2

A283

The Hotel

3

Bostal Road

Bostal Road

Maudlyn Parkway

Sopers Lane

Upper Maudlin Farm

Annington

Monarch's Way

4

168

New Hill Barn

South Downs Way

Steyning Bowl

Sopers Lane

South Downs Way

5

South Downs Way

Annington Hill Barn

6

7

8

Titch Hill

Steep Down

Valley Barn

Farm

G   Beggars Bush   H   J   189   K   L   M

M2
1 Castle Cl

M1
1 Southdown Ter

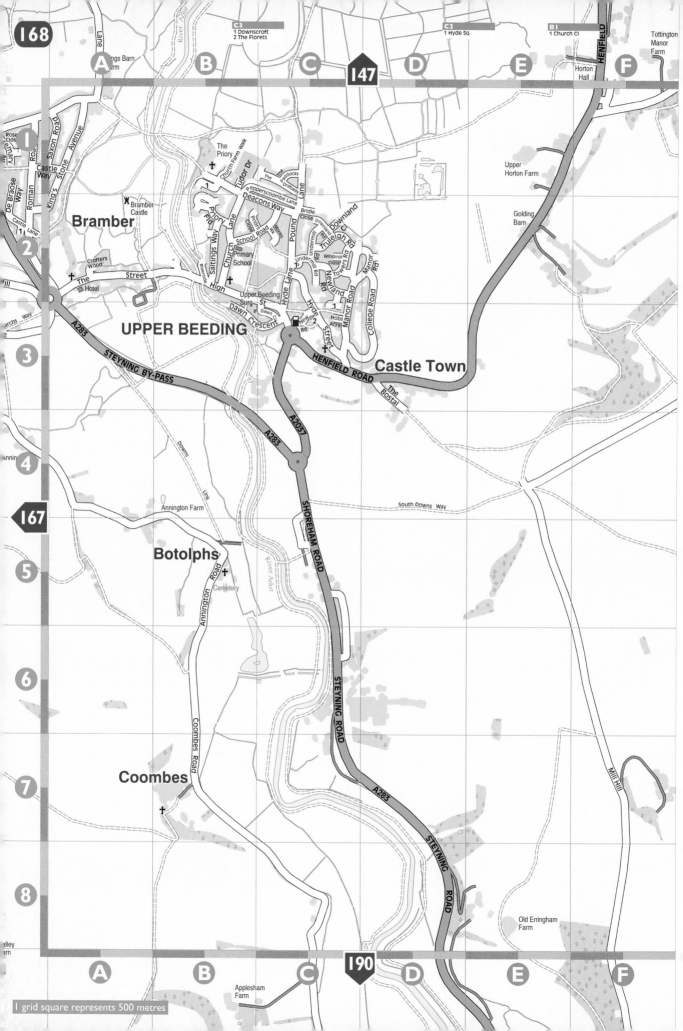

M8
1 Nursery Cl
2 Westway Cl

G H J K L M

148 Edburton

Manor Farm

Perching
Manor Farm

1

2

213
Truleigh
Hill

Tottington
Barn

South Downs Way

Freshcombe
Farm

West Sussex
Brighton a

3

4

170

The
Warren

Bushy
Bottom

5

Monarchs Way

West Sussex County
East Sussex County

6

Sussex Border Path

New Erringham
Farm

7

Mile Oak
Farm

8

BN43

Oakdene
Ri

Oakdene
Cl

Oakdene
Wy

Oakdene
Crs

christdory Rd

Oakdene
Av

Oakdene
Gdns

PO

Monarchs Way

Mile Oak
South

scombe

L7
1 Deneside
2 Downside

M6
1 Highview Rd

M7
1 Grangeways

West Sussex County
Brighton and Hove

Pangdean
Farm

West Sussex County
Brighton and Hove

I

South
Hill Farm

2

Sussex Border Path

3

Sussex Border Path

A23(T) LONDON ROAD

Braypool Lane

4

172

A27(T)

5

LONDON ROAD

A23(T)

Court Close

Church Hill

The Village Barn

Ashley Cl

Vale

Craignair Avenue

Barrhill Av

Sussex Border Path

Waterhall
Golf Course

Waterhall

Brighton
Rugby Club

Mill Road

Watername Road

PATCHAM BY-PASS

Old Patcham Mews

PO

Ladies' Mile

Highview Av North

Highview Way

Mile

6

Patcham CP Scho

First School

Patcham
High Sch

Doctor
Surge

A27(T)

Windmill Drive

Fernwood Rise

Bramble Rise

Highbank

Copse Hill

Brangwyn Crescent

Brangwyn Av

Brangwyn Drive

A23

AEM

Brompton Cl

Old London Rd

Audrey Cl

Overhill Way

Highview Av S

Patcham Grange

Patcham Drive

Dale

7

Green Ridge

Glen Rise

Millcroft

Westdene Drive

Hillcrest

Mill Rise

Bankside

Westdene
Primary
School

Barn Rise

Dene Vale

Eldred

The Cl

Old London Rd

Old Mi Cl

Ridgeside Av

Overhill Gdns

Graham
Road

Old Farm
Road

Hill Top

Glen Rd

Cl

Redhill Cl

Redhill Drive

Fairview Rise

Dene Vale

Avenue

PO

LONDON ROAD

Avenue

Old Ct Cl

Whitethorn Dr

Valley Drive

Hillside Lane

Hillbrow Road

Colebrook Road

Doctors
Surgery

The Deneway

Withdean

8

The Hs

Crott Rd

The Cl

Surrey

Westdene

DYKE ROAD AVENUE

Tongdean Lane

Tongdean

Shepherds Crt

Wayland Av

P+

Tongdean
Lane

Peacock Lane

A2038

KING GEORGE VI

George VI

Sandringham

Queen

Mary Av

Alexandra

Victoria

Woodland Drive

Deanway

Downside

The Spinney

DYKE ROAD

Wayland Avenue

Dyke Rd Pl

Station

LONDON ROAD

Surrenden Crescent

Withdean Court Gdns

Cedars Gardens

Varndean Gardens

Walnut Close

Braxmont Rd

G H J K L M

1
Buckland
Bank

2
St Mary's
Farm

Stanmer
Down

3
East Sussex County
Brighton and Hove

Ridge Rd
Ridge Road

Balmer
Farm

4

5
A27(T)

University
of Sussex

Falmer House Road
Park Street

Mill Street

Middle
Street

Falmer

Ridge
Road

A27(T)

LEWES ROAD
Station
Falmer
Station

South
Park St

East St

6

B2123

Village Way

University
of Brighton

THE DROVE

Loose
Bottom

7

A270

University
of Brighton

Egginton
Close

Lucraft Road
Egginton Road
Ashurst Road

Woburn Pl

Ovingdean Lane

Barcombe Rd

Ringmer Rd
Road
Halland Road
Bolney Rd
Stonecross Rd

Sullington Way
Sportsgate Cl
Appledore
Axminster

Lidwood W
Wharfield

**East
Moulsecoomb**

B2123

East Sussex County
Brighton & Hove

8

G H J K L M

H1
1 Barwell Gv
2 Panton Cl

J2
1 Emsbrook Dr

J4
1 Frobisher Gdns
2 King's Ter
3 Orange Rw

Westbourne
County Primary School

FOXBU

Westbourne

The Art Gallery

Cemetery

Cemetery Lane

New Brighton

George & Dragon Surg

Westbourne Surg

I

P010

A27(T)

2

Bourne Vw Cl

Haslemere Road

The Bourne Community College

3 rea

St John's Rd

Lumley

Manor Gdns

Hermitage

LC

4

Alfrey Cl

A259

Emsworth Primary School

Glenwood School

Emsworth Station

Victoria Cottage Hosp.

Victoria Road

Havant Road

EMSWORTH

I 76

Prinsted

5

The Promenade

Western Parade

Roundhouse Meadow

Heron Quay

Osprey Quay

Thorney Road

Thornham Lane

6

Fowley Island

Sweare Deep

Great Deep

7

Wickor Point

Emsworth Road

8

G H J K L M

K4
1 The Fishermans
2 Frankland Ter
3 Harbour Wy
4 Marina Cl
5 Pelham Ter

K
1 Church Vw
2 Old Rectory Cl
3 The Square

K2
1 Westbourne Cl

Thorney Island

176

A   B   W **C**dma**e**te   D   E   F

Woodmancote Lane   154

Woodmancote Lane

Cheesemans

Marlpit

Cemetery Lane

Duffield Lane

Walnut
Tree
Df

Woodmancote Lane

W Ashling Rd

Lane

South La

Hambrook Hl
(North)

West As

I

Devils Copse

Nightingale Lane

Hambrook Ho

Lane

A27(T)

A27(T)

A27(T)

Scant

Stein Rd

South

Hither
On

Hambrook

Hambrook Hl (South)

Broad Road

Scant Road (West)

2

Cheshire W

Lauder
Cl

Fraser
Gdns

PO

Conifer
Dr

The Avenu

Bourne
Vw Cl

Haslemere
Road

Breach Avenue

East
Fld
Cl

Oak Tree
Farm

Priors Leaze Lane

Yeomans Fld

Road

Clovelly Road

Park Road

Barnfield

Kelsey
Cl

Priors Leaze

Broad Rd

The Bourne Community
College

Mountwood
Road

smallcutts Av

Glenwood
Rd

Plumston Road

Priors Leaze Lane

Drift

3

St. John's Rd

Manor Road

Hartland
Ct

PO

Priors
Cl

Priors Leaze Lane

Breach

Manor
Gdns

Manor
Way

Cooks
Lane

Hurstwood Av

Inlands Road

LC

LC

Acre

LC

Guildford
Cl

LC

Nutbourne
Station

LC

First Av

Lazy
Acre

Second

Southbourne Station

LC

LC

4

Carsons Road

Longlands
Road

The Drive

Lodgebury
Close

Southbourne County
Junior & Infant School

Flatt
Rd

Flatt Rd

AD

A259

The Crescent

New
Rd

Mosdell
Rd

Goodwood
Court

Flatt Rd

Pottery La

175

Ham La

Prinsted Lane

Frarydene

Church Rd

Surgery

Southbourne

A259

Ivydene
Crescent

MAIN

A259

Prinsted

Farm La

School La

Main Rd

PO

A259

Maybush

5

Nutbourne

Maybush Drive

Cot Lane

Chidham Pa
Primary Sc

Chidham Lane

6

Chidham Point

7

Prinsted
Point

Steels Lane

Chidham

PH

Marsh
La

Eastfi

8

Marsh
Lane

A   B   C   198   D   E   F

198

1 grid square represents 500 metres

G   H   J   155   K   L   M

1 Stream Cl

J7

Gam's Fm

Down Street

Funtington
County
Primary
School

Heather
Cl

**West
Ashling**

Mt
Ashling

School Dell

School Dell

West
Ashling
Rd

West Ashling
Road

Scant
Road

Southbrook

Newells Lane

Maltmo's
The Gardens

Sandy Lane

1

2

Waterloo Farm

Road

ad (East)

RATHAM
LANE

CLAY LANE

Ratham
Mill

Ratham
Lane

Clay Lane

Mourney's Lane

Road

27(T)

A27(T)

A27

3

Newells Lane

Mudberry Lane

Green
La

LC

LC

RATHAM LANE

B2146

Brooks
Lane

4

Newells Lane

Green
Lane

LC

LC

LC ≷ Bosham
Station

178

ROAD

A259   MAIN ROAD

Old Br
Hamilton
Gdns
Rd

STATION RD

Arnold Wy
Williams Road

North Rd

Gifford Rd

Brooks Lane

Barnside

Broadbridge

5

Broadbridge Ct

Grenwarden
Wy

arochial
ool

Broadbridge Farm

PO

Southfields
Industrial
Estate

Lane

Chequer

MAIN

6

d Fm

Delling

Delling
Close

Green
La

Elm
Pk

Crede La

Lane

7

Marcuse
Flds

Westbrook Fld

Critchfield
Brook Av
Rd
Merryfd

Lane

Fairfield Rd

Bosham
Football Club

School La

Walton

Bosham County
Primary School

Stonewall Farm

Old Park

Windmill
Fld

Critchfield

Hotel

Bosham

Sunny
Wy

Fairfield
Cl

Westward

Leandel

Astra

Stumps Lane

Bosham

Manor
Vis

arbour
Way

Church
Meadow

Canute
Rd

Cambria
Ct

Manor

Harbour

8

Bosham Abbey

High St

Shore
Road

Harbour
Way

Harbour
Way

The Drive

Taylor's Lane

Old Park

Bosham
Sailing Club

Shore
Road

Stumps
Lane

G   H   J   199   K   L   M

Shore Road

Southwood Farm

Old
Park Farm

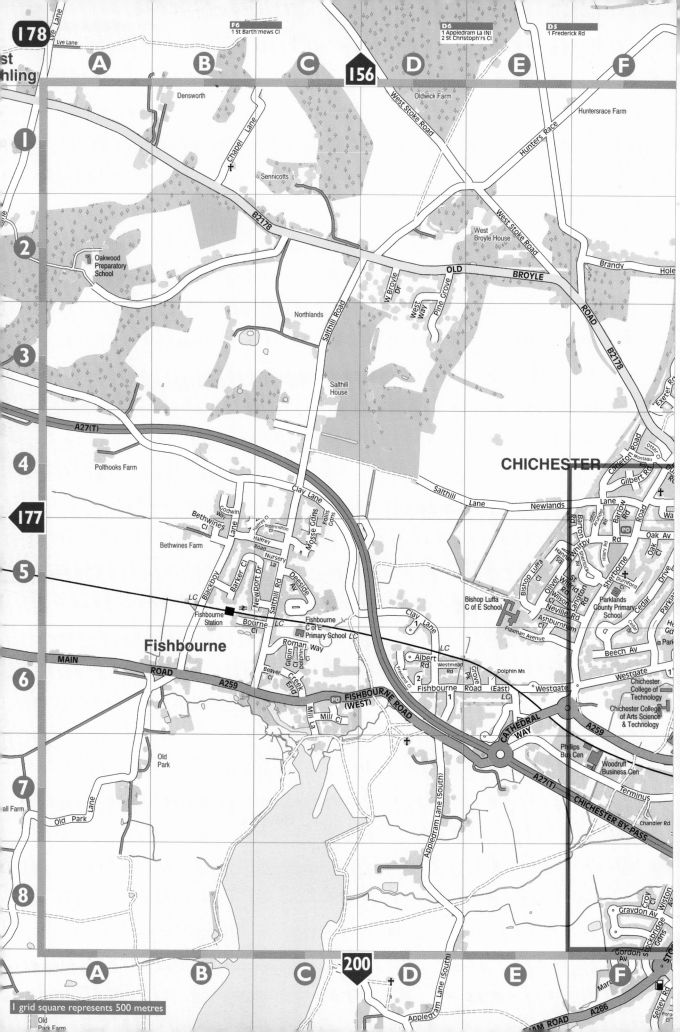

G1
1 Stavely Gdns

G3
1 Hereford Cl
2 Salisbury Wy

G5
1 Cavendish St
2 Lancastrian Gra
3 Orchard Gdns
4 The Providence
5 Tower Cl
6 Washington St

G6
1 The Woolstaplers

G8
1 Bywater Wy

157

I   We

2   Maudlin

3   Westhampn

Chichester Airfield

March C of E Primary School

Oldplace Farm

180

4

5

6   Portfield

Shopwhyke Industrial Cen

SHOPWHYKE ROAD

Ben Turner Industrial Est

Mechanical Music & Doll Collection

Cemetery

Portfield Football Club

St James Industrial Est

WESTHAMPNETT RD

PORTFIELD WAY

River Lavant

Keepers Wood

Summersdale

Fordwater School

Marchwell Industrial Estate

Chichester Health Authority

Graylingwell Hospital

Chichester Rugby Club

The Broadway

Lavant Road Surgery

Highland Road

The Avenue

Chichester Festival Theatre

P019

St Richards Hospital

A&E

Chichester Lawn Tennis & Squash Club

St Paul's Road

OAKLANDS WAY

Franklin Pl

Chichester Priory Park Cricket & Hockey Club

St James County Primary Sch

St Paul's Road

NEW PARK RD

Melbourne Rd

ST PANCRAS

OVING ROAD

Victoria Road

B2144

Chichester Cathedral

Eastgate Gallery

Forum House Business Cen

THE HORNET

Pound Farm Road

A259

BOGNOR ROAD

Westgate Leisure Centre

Chichester Station

Natural·City Health Cen Business Cen

Chichester High School for Boys

Chichester High School for Girls

Kingsham County Primary School

Whyke

Rumboldswyke C of E Infant School

WHYKE ROAD

A27(T) CHICHESTER BY-PASS

Quarry Lake

Long Lake

Leythome Lake

A259 BOGNOR

7

8

Stockbridge

201

G
1 Blenheim Gdns

H
1 The Waterplat

J7
1 Clydesdale Av
2 Littlefield Rd

K

K4
1 Farndell Cl
2 Harvester Cl
3 St James's Sq

K6
1 Balmoral Cl
2 Marlborough Cl
3 Sandringham Rd
4 William Rd

L6

H7
1 Martlet Cl
2 Winguard Wy

J5
1 Doug's Martin Rd
2 Meadowfield Dr

L
1 Cooper St
2 East Rw
3 East Walls
4 Little London
5 New Town
6 North St
7 St Martin's St

M
1 Dunstan Cl

H5
1 Alderman's Wk
2 Guildhall St
3 St Cyriacs

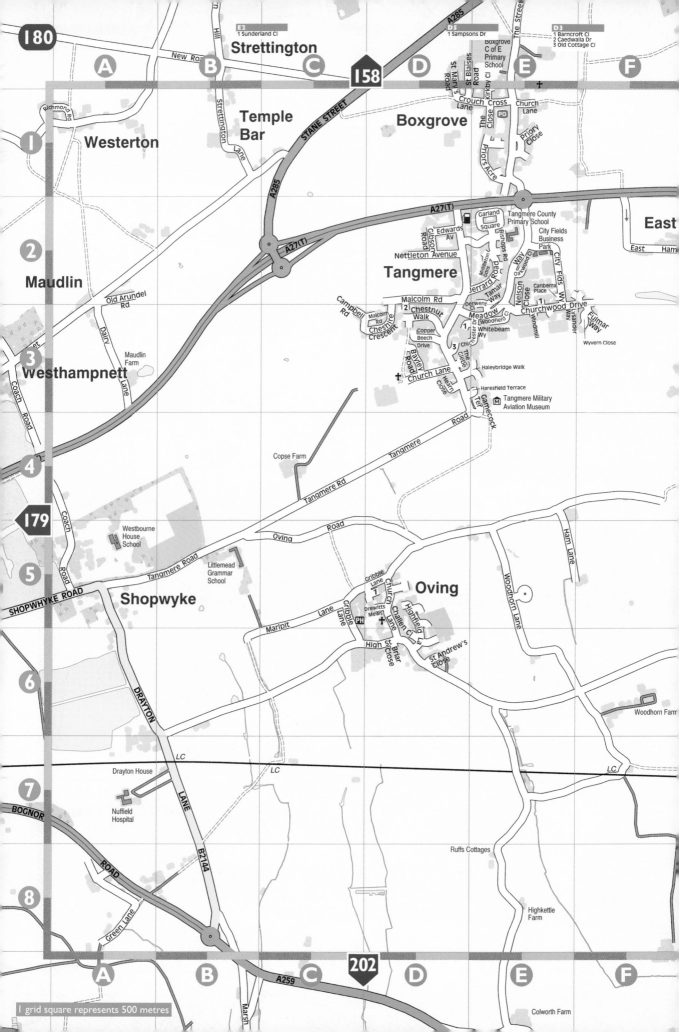

G · H · J · K · L · M

159

1 Beech Cl
L5

1 Lamorna Gdns
L6

Halnaker

Mount Noddy

Littleheath Road

Barn Lane

Blackmill Lane

Crockerhill

Aldingbourne House

Aldingbourne Drive

Aldingbourne Dr

ARUNDEL ROAD

1

2

Hampnett

...nett Lane

Marsh Lane

Oldbury Farm

A27(T)

NYTON ROAD

B2233

Level Mare Lane

Denmans Lane

Level Mare Lane

Northfields Farm

3

Norton

Lane

Norton Lane

Glebe Cl

Murrayfield House

4

Church Road

Nyton

B2233

NYTON ROAD

Northfields Lane

Tudor Dr

Barnett's Field

Westergate Mews

Barnett Close

NYTON ROAD

PO

Cherry Tree Drive

182

Highview

Old Rectory Drive

School Lane

5

Aldingbourne

Park Lane

Hook Lane

Westergate

A29

Victoria Gdns

Watson Way

Ivy Lane

Olivers Meadow

Westergate Community College

Eastergate C of E Primary School

Close

Elm Road

Baron Cl
Old Farm Dr
Oaks Close

St Richards Rd

Elmcroft Place

6

Park Farm

Meadow

WESTERGATE STREET

Aldingbourne County Primary School

St Johns Cl

Elmcroft Park

1

Orchard Gdns

Belle Meade Cl

PO

Cohen Cl

LC

LC

Oak Tree Lane

Woodgate Rd

Woodgate Close

7

Woodgate

A29

8

Reed's Farm

Aldingbourne Rife

Headhone Farm

A29

G   H   J   161   K   L   M

CHICHESTER ROAD
A27(T)

Park Farm

CHICHESTER

I

Paine's Wood

Binsted Lane

Jarvis Road
Hill Terrace
Dukes Close
Ellis
Pear

Arundel C of E Primary School

2

Binsted Wood

Hazel Grove
Oak End

Birch Close

Dalloway Road
Stewards

High Ridge Close

3

Church Farm

Tortington Common

Priory Farm

Binsted

✝

4

Binsted Lane

Walberton Farm

Meadow Lodge

184

Tortington

5

Goose Green

Hoe Lane

Binsted Lane

✝

Manser Road
Hedgers Hill

Ford PK Rd
Yapton Lane B2132
Henty Close
eet

Lower Farm

Marsh Farm

Ford Road

6

Yapton Lane B2132

Lake Lane
LC

Maypole Lane
North End Road

LC

North End

Gaugemaster Way

Ford Station
LC

7

Wicks Farm

Ford Lane

Ford Road

Ford La

8

Yapton C of E School
The Croft

Church Lane
The Lychgates
The Friars
Close

✝

St Marys
Meadow
James Close
church

Yapton

Ford Road

Ford Road
Rodney Crs
Penney Crs

Ford

✝

Nelson

G   H   J   205   K   L   M

MAIN ROAD
✝
The Pines
B273
Tack Lee

Briar Close
Downview Close
Downview

Burndell

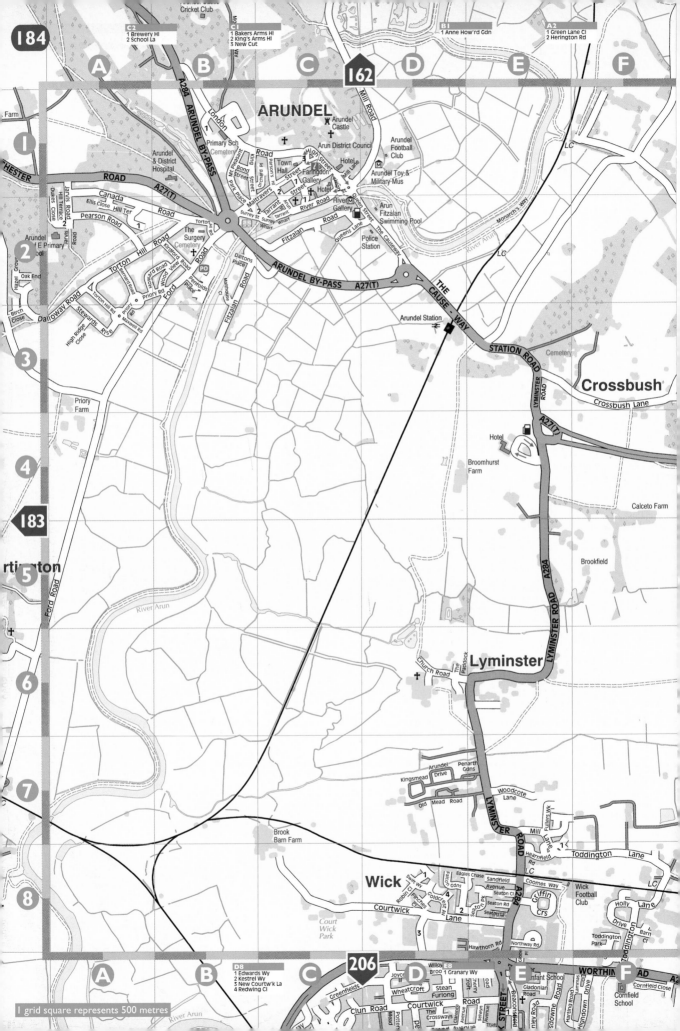

Warningcamp

G   H   J   **163**   K   L   M

I
2
3
4
5
6
7
8

Monarch's Way

Blakehurst Lane

Blakehurst

Clay Lane

Blakehurst Lane

The Dover

Priorsleas Farm

A27(T)

A27(T)

ARUNDEL ROAD

Poling Corner

Newplace Farm

186

B2225

Poling Street

Decoy Drive

Palmer Road

Peckhams

Poling Street

Poling

ANGMERING

Primary School

Cemetery

Rectory Lane

Old Place Farm

Thatchway

The

BN16

Black Ditch

Ham Manor Golf Course

Manor Way

Ham Manor Ci

Blue Cedars Cl

Toddington

A259

LC

Norway Lane

Camella

Bluebell Drive

Bluebell Drive

Windsor Drive

Montfort Dr

Blenheim

Cowdray Dri

Penfold Lane

Club House

Ham Manor Farm

West Drive

East Drive

North Drive

South Drive

STATION ROAD

Greenwood

A280

G   H   J   **207**   K   L   M

Oakcroft Gardens

Cemetery

Timbers

WORTHING

Lupin Cl

Summerlea County Primary

X Avenue

Brookside Avenue

Dominion Way

NEW ROAD

Rustington Retail Park

A259

G   H   J   165   K   L   M

Clapham Wood

High Salvington

Clapham

Cote

Holt Farm

A27(T)   ARUNDEL   ROAD   A27(T)   ARUNDEL   ROAD

Swandean Hospital

Broadview Gardens

188

Durrington

Forest Barn

Northbrook College

Highdown Tower

Durrington High School

Highdown School

Rodmell Road

English Martyrs RC School

Harwood Avenue

Orchards Middle School

The Hawthorns School

TITNORE LANE   A2700

LITTLEHAMPTON-ROAD   A2032

LITTLEHAMPTON-ROAD   A259   A2032

BN12

209

167

190

211

Beggars Bush

Titch Hill Farm

Lambleys Barn

Sompting Abbotts

SOMPTING

LANCING

SOUTH LANCING

East Worthing

BN15

North Lancin

B4
1 Old Shoreham Rd

A7
1 Cowley Dr
2 The Saltings

A6
1 Brierley Gdns

A5
1 Mckerchar Cl

1

Valley
Barn

Applesham
Farm

2

River Adur

Lancing
College
Chapel

The Drive

Coombes Road

A283

Old Erringham

Mill Hill
Cl

Mill Hill Drive

3

College Farm

The Drive

Hoe

A27(T)

Old Shoreham Road

Old Shoreham

The Street

Lesser Foxholes

The Paddock

Adur Avenue

Street Lodge Ct

Erringham Rd

Ountway
Ring Road

Boxgrove
Close

Swanbourne
Close

Heyshott
Close

Norbury
Close

Court

SHOREHAM

ROAD

A27(T)

St Nicolas La

Upper Shoreham Ro

Mill Road

Drive

Norbury
Close

The
Moorings

St Nicolas

PO

Colvil
Av

Greenacres

Connaught Av

Adur Ave

Cemetery

4

**North
Lancing**

The Street

Old Shoreham Rd

189

Manor
Close

Mash Barn Lane

OLD SHOREHAM ROAD

A283

Shoreham
County
First School

Overmead

Avenue

Orchard Av

First

A2025

Lisher Road

Woodard
Rd

Road

Road

Cecil Pashley Way

Museum

Chelsea
College

Riverbank
Business
Centre

Swiss
Gdns

Victoria Rd

West St

Hebe Rd

HIGH ST

5

Curvins
Wy

Shadwells

Daniel
Close

Gravely Cres

Cecil Pashley Way

New Salts Farm Road

Nature
Reserve

Marlipins
Museum

Lane

Grinstead Av

Monks Avenue

Haglow
Way

Barfield Park

Links
Road

North Farm

Farm Rd

LC

Old Salts Farm Road

Windsor Rd

Millennium Cl

Downs Cl

Drakes

Manor
Rd

Sussex Rd

Adur Cl

Swallows Cl

Kings Crs

BRIGHTON ROAD

PO

Ormonde Wy

Beach Green

River
Cl

6

GRINSTEAD LANE

Freshbrook
First School

Monks Close

Freshbrook

The Paddocks

Larkfield Close

George V Avenue

Bristol Avenue

The Broadway

Orient Rd

West Beach Road

Kings
Gap

Woodards
View

Marchke

Havenside

Beach

Kings Walk

7

The
Framing
Studio &
Gallery Bri

New
Pond Row
Surgery

Ingleside

Russells

Mirch
Cl

Caron
Close

Kings Close

Brook
Way

Seaside
Road

Larkfield
Close

Seaside
Avenue

Alexandra
Rd

Queens
Rd

Thornberry Middle
School

West
Avenue

Prince
Avenue

Boundary Road

PO

A259

The Fairway

**South
Lancing**

Penleigh
Crs

Beachcroft
Place

PENHILL RD

The Close

Road

Queens

Shoreham

Salts Farm Road

ROAD

West

8

A259   BRIGHTON

D7
1 Wenceling
Cottages
2 Widewater Cl
3 Willow Cl

E7
1 Fishermans Wk
2 Mariners Cl
3 Seahaven Gdns

F5
1 Buckingham St
2 Little High St

1 grid square represents 500 metres

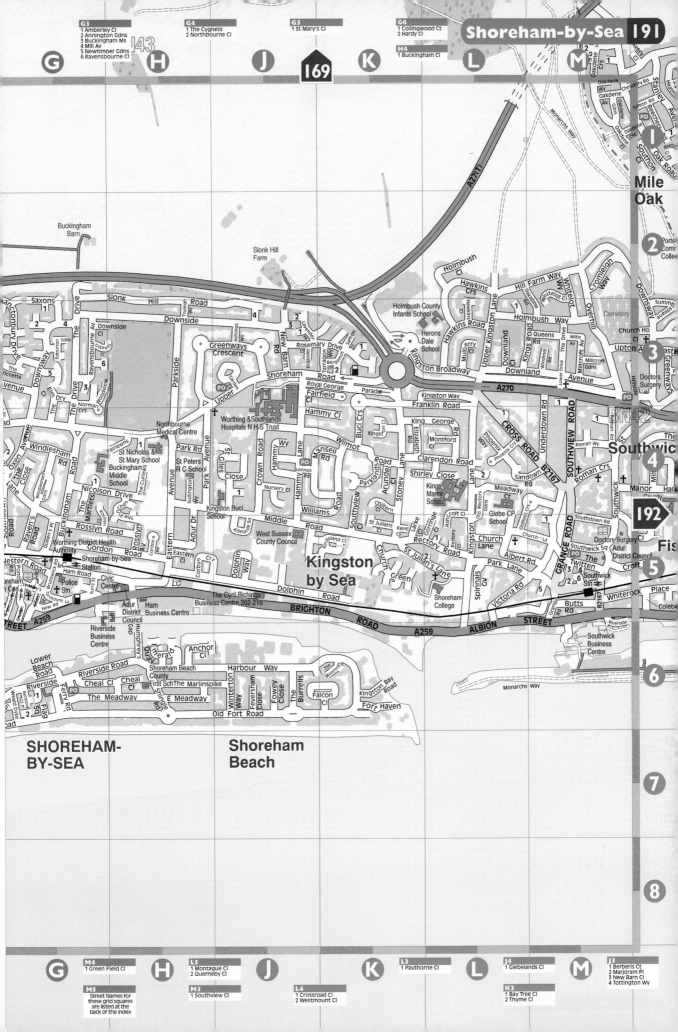

143

169

G H J K L M

I
Mile
Oak

2

3

4

192

5

6

7

8

Buckingham
Barn

Slonk Hill
Farm

Holmbush County
Infants School

Herons
Dale
School

Cemetery

Church Ho

Upton Av

Doctors
Surgery

Southwic

Manor
Hal

Fis

Saxons

Downside

Greenways
Crescent

Rosemary Drive

Shoreham   Road

Royal George
Fairfield
Cl

Parade

Kingston Broadway

A270

Franklin Road

Kingston Way

Downland   Avenue

Northbourne
Medical Centre

Worthing &Southlands
Hospitals N H S Trust

Hammy Cl

King George

Clarendon Road

CROSS ROAD B2161

SOUTHVIEW ROAD

BN42

Doctors Surgery

Windlesham
Rd

St Nicholas &
St Mary School

St Peters
R C School

Crown Road

Kings Manor
School

Meadway
Ct

Glebe CP
School

Nicolson Drive

Buckingham
Middle
School

Kingston Buci
School

Middle   Road

West Sussex
County Council

Kingston by Sea

Rectory   Road

Church
Lane

Albert Rd

Worthing District Health
Authority

Shoreham-by-Sea
Station

Police
Stn

Civic
Centre

Dolphin   Road

St Julian's Lane

Shoreham
College

Southwick
Stn

Butts

Whiterock   Place

The Cyril Richings
Business Centre 202-210

BRIGHTON   ROAD

A259   ALBION   STREET

B2161

Southwick
Business
Centre

STREET A259

Adur
District
Council

Ham
Business Centre

Riverside
Business
Centre

Lower
Beach
Road

Emerald
Quay

Anchor
Cl

Harbour Way

Monarchs Way

Riverside Road

Shoreham Beach
County
First Sch The Marlinspike

Riverside

Cheal Cl   Cheal
Cl

The Meadway   E Meadway

Old Fort Road

Winterton
Way

Feversham
Close

Fowey
Close

The
Burrells

Falcon

Kingston Bay
Road

Fort Haven

SHOREHAM-
BY-SEA

Shoreham
Beach

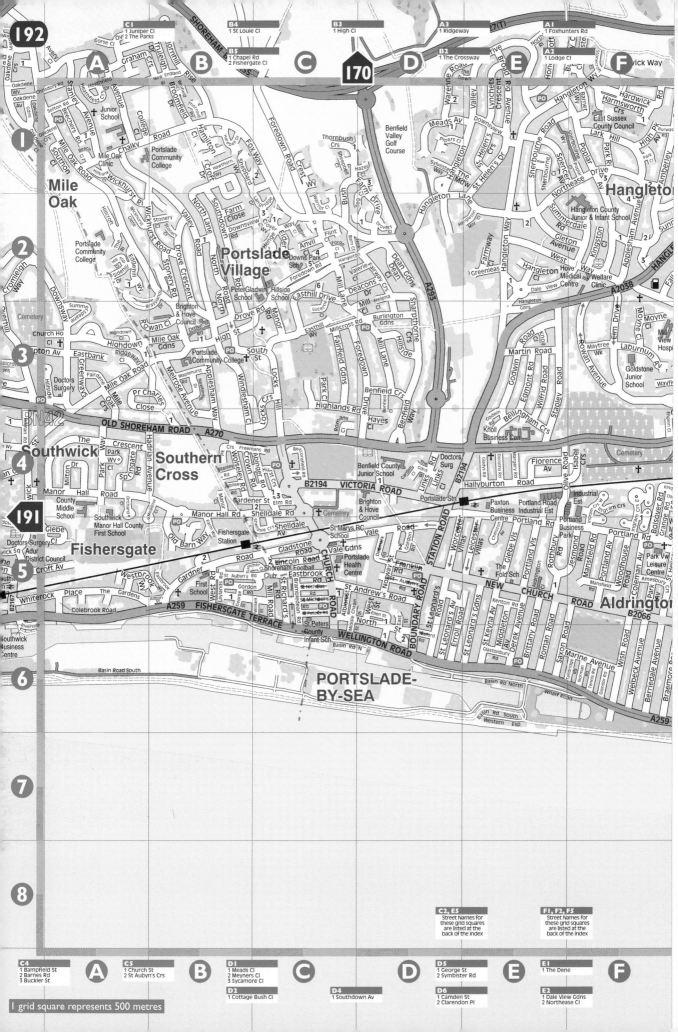

G5
1 Pulborough Cl
2 Sevelands Cl
3 Sompting Cl
4 Swanborough Pl

G6
1 Horsham Cl
2 Pett Cl
3 Selmeston Pl

G7
1 Selmestone Rd

G East Moulsecoomb

H

J

173

K

L

M

I

Moulsecoomb

Bevendean

Kenilworth Close
Knepp Cl
Norwich Close
Norwich
Norwich Drive
Bamford Close
Bodiam Close
Bodiam Close

Bevendean County Primary School
PO
Leybourne Road
Durham Close
Heath Hill Avenue
Bodiam Avenue
Walmer Crs

The Willow Surgery
Heath Hi Av
Taunton
Hornby Rd
Auckland
Road
Drive
Drive

Plymouth Av
Dartmouth Close
Dartmouth Drive
The Hyde

East Sussex County
Brighton & Hove
B2123
FALMER ROAD
Drive
Avenue

197 ▲ Newmarket Hill

Norton Drive
Bexhill Road
Suttton Cl
Treyford Cl
Langley Crescent
Sandhurst Av
Norton Drive

Upper Bevendean

Drove
Road
Farm Hill
Ivor Rd
McWilliam Road
Downsway
B2123
Warren Way
Ridgway Close
Baisdean Road
Newells Cl
Bexhill Road
Drive

Warren Av
Downsview Avenue
Vernon Avenue
Bush Cl
Rudyard Cl
Catherine Vale
Crescent
Downs
Heronsdale Rd
Willow Sycamore
Drove
Downland
Rosebery Gdns
Baywood Gdns
Seaview Avenue
Midway Road
Warren Rd
PO
Falmer Gdns
The
Rudyard Rd
Deans Cl
North

Drove
Road
Channel View Rd
Warren Rd
Holtview Rd
Warren Road
Hazel Cottage Clinic
Downs View School
Falmer Gdns
Brow
Villiers Cl
Kevin Gdns
Nolan Rd
Cowley Drive
Truleig Cl
Rise

Warren Road
1
3
Warren Road
Sussex Nuffield Hospital
Woodingdean School
FALMER ROAD
Pitt Gdns
Briar Rd
Ridgway
Lockwood Cres
Dudwell Rd
Rudyard Kipling Primary School
Foxdown

Warren Road
Brighton Racecourse
Lodsworth Cl

Woodingdean

Briarcroft Road
Millyard Crs
Kipling Avenue
Batemans Road
Valley Road
Shipley Rd
Maple Close
Fir Cl
Littleworth Close

Swanborough Drive
Wilson Avenue
Whitehawk
Wiston WY
Wiston Road
Pilastow
Vines Cross Rd
Seabourne WY

Holton Hill
Connell Drive
Dudwell Rd
Drive
Drive
Broadway
Littleworth Close

Aldrich
Pittdown Rd
Colgate Cl
Sadlers WY
Desmond WY
Nuthurst Rd

Whitehawk

Crescent
Rosedene Close
Shipley Rd
PO
Green
Ravens
Road Drive
La
Stanmstead Cres

Brownleaf Road
Abinger Road
Pinfold Close
Donnington Road
Merston Rd
B2123
FALMER ROAD
Cowley Drive

Whitehawk Clinic
Danehill Rd
Alan Way
Findon Road
Wilson Avenue
Whitehawk Avenue

Sheepcote Valley

Wick Bottom
BN2

Golf Course

Mount Pleasant

Ovingdean Close

Stanley Deason Leisure Centre

Wadhurst Rd
Broadway Surgery
Peel Rd
Marlow Rd
Henley Rd

Woodland Walk
Ovingdean Hall School
Longhill Road
Wanderdown Road
PO
The Vale
Longhill School
Rowan Way
Elvin Crescent
B2123

Bristol Gdns
Tower
Eley
Eley Crs

Roedean Road
The Cliff
Roedean
Roedean
Roedean Crescent
Roedean Vale
Greenways
Ainslie
Longhill Rise
Wanderdown WY
Wanderdown Close
Wanderdown Drive
Dean Court Rd
New Barn
H3

Cliff Way
Marina Way
A259
Marina Way

G
Black H Hock
212
J
K
L
M

M5
1 Ridgeway Gdns

K
1 Helena Rd

L4
1 Downland Cl
2 Hylden Cl
3 Warren Cl

M
1 Leybourne Cl
2 Taunton Wy

Trafalgar Gate
Victoria
Roedean School

A   B   C   D   E   F

174

B8
1 Aubrey Cl
2 Grayland Cl
3 Lexden Gdns
4 Newtown La
5 Spinnaker Cl

Spinnaker
Grange

North

Northney La

St Peter's Rd

Clovelly
Rd

Pycroft
Close

Church
Lane

North

St Peter's Av

New Cut

HAVANT ROAD

Island Cl

Kingsway

Queensway

Avenue Road

Meadow
Cl

Rogers Md

Victoria Road

Mill
Close

HAYLING ISLAND

Stoke

Northwood
Lane

Croft
Lane

Castlemans Lane

Chiches

Tye

Gutner

Wooddason Lane

West Lane

PO

Copse Lane

Fleet

Yew Tree Rd

HAVANT ROAD

Daw   Lane

A3023

Mill   Rythe
La

PO11

Manor Ho

A3023

A3023

Rest-A-Wyle Av

Pound
Lea

Road

Kings Road

Woodlands
La

Brights La

PO

Higworth La

Lulworth Cl

Church

Road

Tournerbury

Dundonald

Eastwood Cl

Lane

Poplar Grove

Beech Grove

Hawthorne
Gv

Laburnum Grove

Saltmarsh La

Denhill
Cl

West

Lane

Dover
Court

Glebe Cl

Atherley
Road

Wardens Cl

Katrina
Gdns

ithica Cl

Burwood Cl

Burwood
Rd

ROAD

Hayling Billy
Business
Cen
Station Theatre

North Shore Road

Charleston Cl

Dances Way

Gilbert Mead

Sycamore Cl

West

Lane

Avenue

MANOR

A3023

Hamfield Drive

Fathoms Reach

PO11

Southleigh Gv

St Mary's

Road

Legion
Rd

Mengham Infant
School

Palmerston
Rd

St Leonards

Mengham
Junior
School

Warren Cl

Warren

Park Road

Catherine's

Ferry Road

St Aubin

St Thomas
Av

St Thomas

Close
Fernhurst

Richmond Dr

PO

Station
Road

Hamfield Drive

Hollow

Garden

St Mary's
Road

South Rd

Cherrywood Gdns

Oakwood

Hayling
Health Centre

Elm

Margarets Rd

PO

Mengham Rd

St Leonards
Avenue

Mengham La

Simmons Gn

Salterns Cl

St Helen's

Avenue

BEACH ROAD

West Town

Wes Bown

B

214

C

D

E

F

Mongham

8

7

6

5

4

3

2

1

A   B   C   D   E   F

G
H
J
175
K
L
M

Hayling

Hampshire County
West Sussex County

Sussex Border Path

Hunter
Swift Road
Meteor
S Bay N Bay
Sabre Rd
Sparlan Cl
Javelin Road
Canberra Rd
Hornet Road
Emsworth Rd

Thorney County
Primary School

Thorney Island

Emsworth Rd

Thorney Island
Airfield

Smith Lane

Church

Pleasant Lane

Marker Point

Emsworth Channel

Mill Rithe

198

Sussex Border Path

Longm
Po

Pilsey
Sand

Stocker's Lake

G
H
J
215
K
L
M

East Hea

Mengham
Salterns

1
2
West
3
4
5
6
7
8

A   B   C   **176**   D   E   F

1

Stanbury
Point

2

West Thorney

Thorney Island
field

Cobnor Fm

New
Barn

Gerald Da
Sailing
Club

Smith
Lane

Church

Victor Rd

Road

Vulcan
Road

Varsity Road

Pleasant Lane

Vallant
Road

Valetta Road

Thorney
Channel

Cobnor Ho

3

Cobnor
Point

Chichester Channel

4

197

5

Path

We

Longmere
Point

6

Pilsey
Island

Itchen

7

Chichester Harbour

8

East He   A   B   C   **216**   D   E   F

Rookwood
Lane

Rookwood Lane

Sheepwash Lane

2179

I grid square represents 500 metres

H5
1 Chandlers Reach
2 Waterstone Cl

L8
1 Old School Cl

M7
1 Claytons Cnr
2 Kewell's Cnr

G H J K L M

177

I

Old
Park Farm

Shore Road

Southwood Farm

Old Park Lane

Hook   Lane

Church Farm

2

Bosham
Channel

iel

Hone   Lane

Lowerhone Farm

Taylor's Lane

Park   Lane

Oldpark
Wood

3

Lower

Smuggler's Lane

Hart's Farm

Hoe Farm

Hoe   Lane

Fletcher's Lane

4

Bosham Hoe

200

st Itchenor

Itchenor
Sailing
Club

1

The   Street

Orchard Orchard
Lane
2

Longmore
Point

Birdham
Pool

5

Chic
Yach

Ho

Itchenor   Road

Spinney   Lane

Oldhouse Farm

Westlands Farm

The   Causeway

LOC

6

Birdham

Court Barn Lane

The Sp

Chalkdock
Lane

Glebe
Field
Road

Westlands   Lane

Oak
Meadow

tins La

7

St James's La

Church   Lane

Crooked La

Cherry   La

Springf

M

Shipton
Green

Pescott's
Cl

Birdham C of E
Primary School

Longmeadow
Gdns

A286

Lippering Farm

The Saltings

Chaffer La

Florence Close

Crooked   Lane

Farne Lane

MAIN   ROAD

Whitestone
Farm

8

Redlands Fm

h
Lane

Itchenor   Road

Shipton

Green   Lane

Burlow
Cl

Farne Cl
PO

217

Holt Place

B2179

G H J K L M

B2198

Pinks Lane

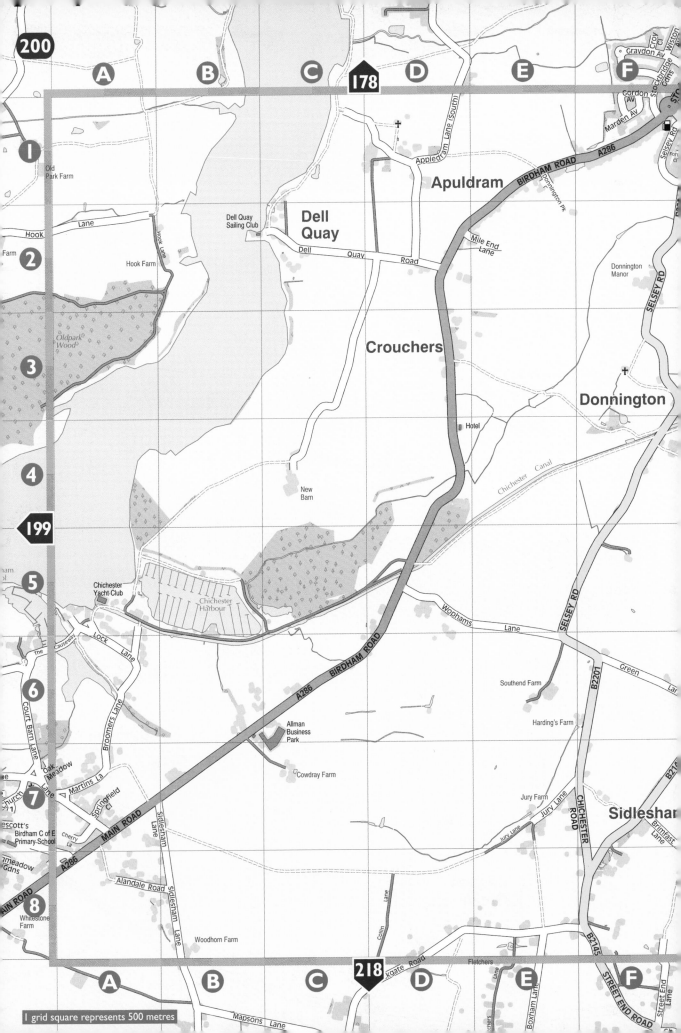

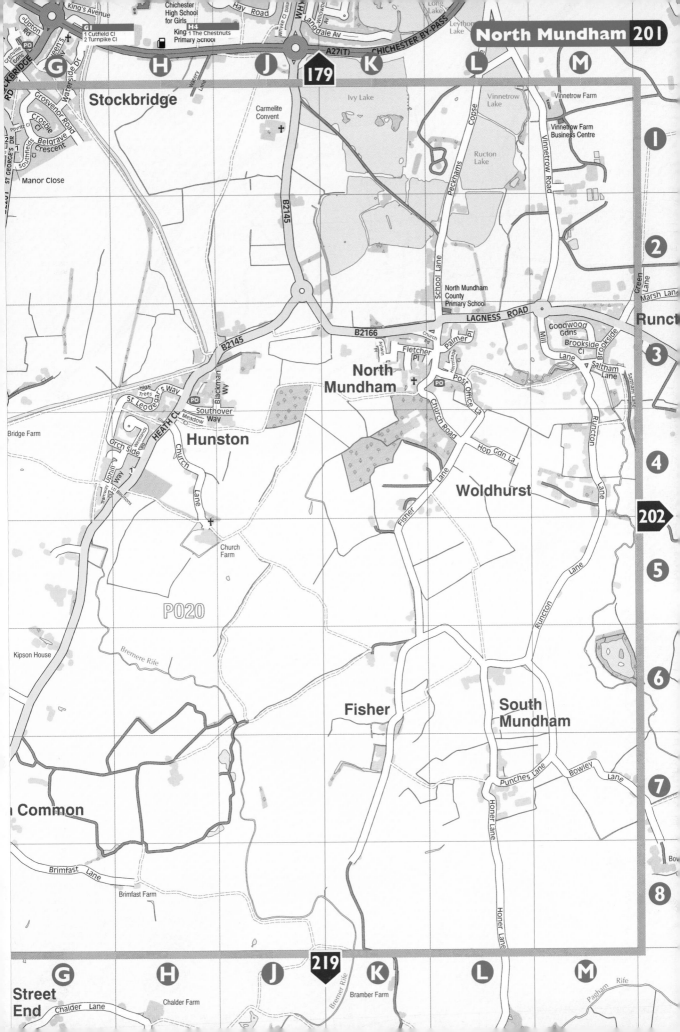

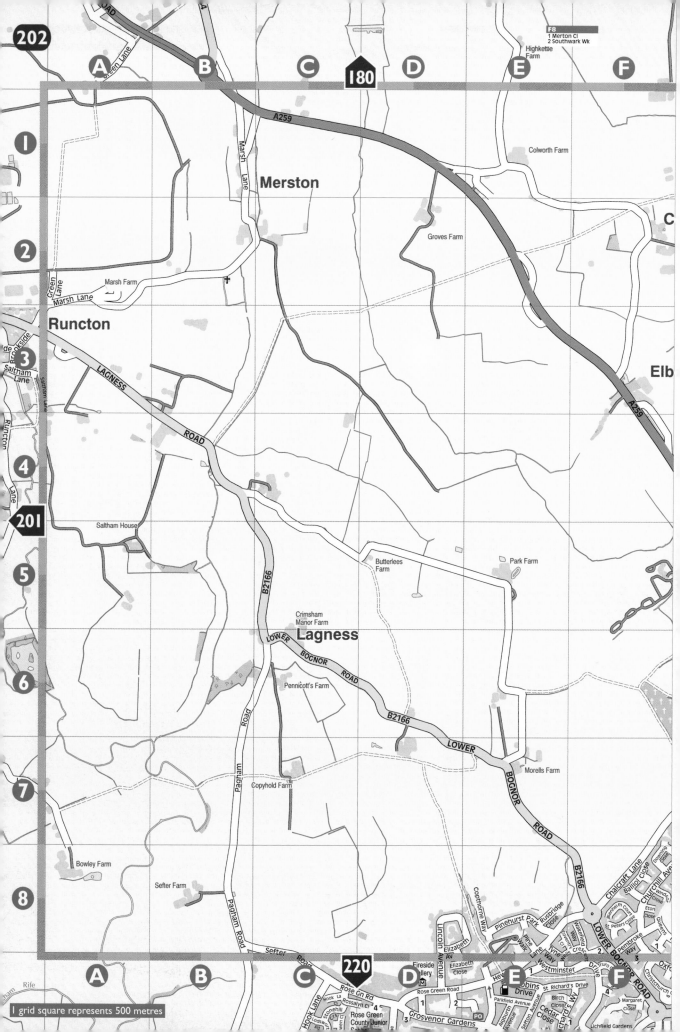

G H J **183** K L d M

I

Yapton C of E
School

Yapton

Burndell

Climbing

Rudford
Industrial
Estate

Rudford
Industrial
Estate

Horsemere
Green

Apple
Tree
Walk

Bilsham

CROOKTHORN LANE

St Marys C of E
Primary School

206

Ryebank Rife

Middleton Business
Park

Ancton

Elmer

Poole
Place

Hotel

Middleton
Medical Centre

ETON
SEA

The Jetty

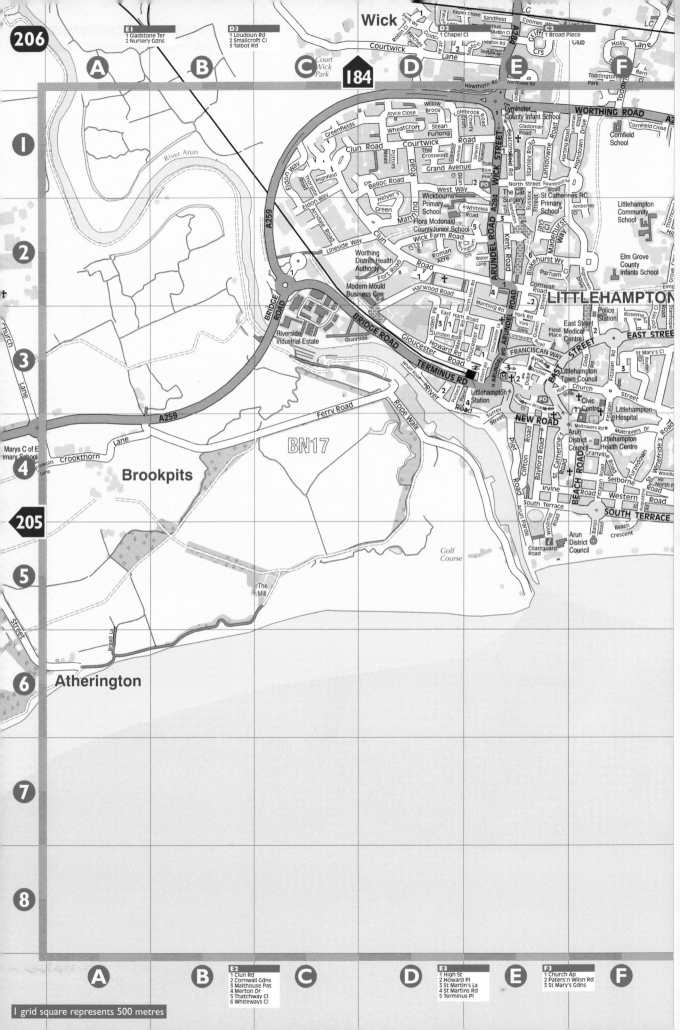

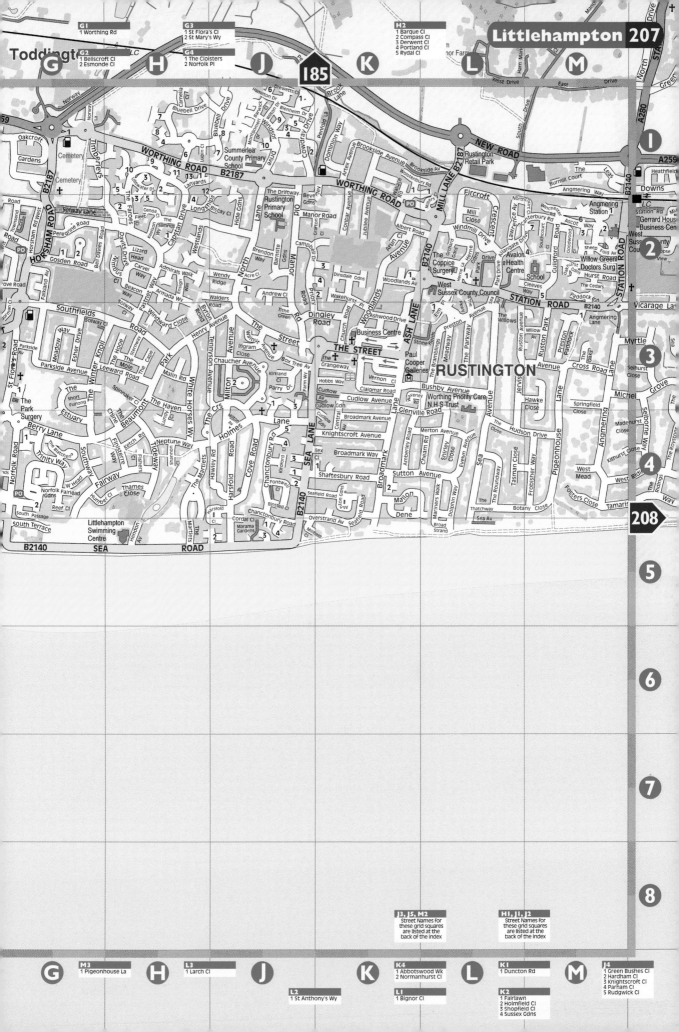

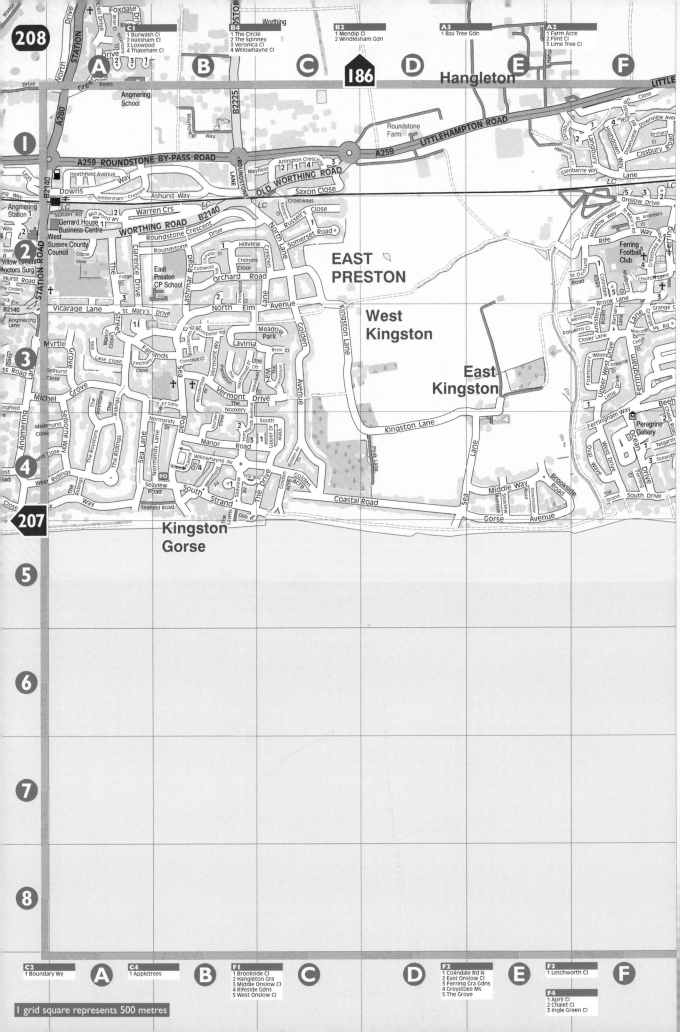

G3
1 Beehive Cl
2 Laburnum Cl

G4
1 Chalet Gdns
2 Doone End
3 Florida Gdns
4 Guernsey Rd
5 Lamorna Gdns
6 Milbury Cl

H2
1 Thakeham Cl

J1
1 Denton Cl
2 Galsworthy Cl
3 Southwater Cl
4 Steyning Cl

L3
1 Warnham Cl

L2
1 Marlborough Wy

L1
1 Avondale Cl
2 Grenville Av

K2
1 Barrington Cl
2 Goring Rd
3 Mersham Gdns
4 Mulberry Gdns
5 Ryecroft Gdns

K1
1 Alexandra Ct

J2
1 Aldsworth Ct

West Tarring

188

WORTHING

1 grid square represents 500 metres

A ROEDEAN ROAD

B

C 195

D

E

F

MARINE DRIVE

Henley Rd

Princes's

Marlow Rd

BRISTOL GDNS

Bell
Tower
Ind Est

Cliff Rd

Marina Way

The Cliff

A259

Marina Way

Virgin Cinemas

Marina Way

Black Rock

Trafalgar
Gate

Victory
Mews

The
Strand

Brighton
Marina

B2118

Roedean Hts

Roedean

Crescent

Roedean
Path

Roedean
Road

Roedean
Vale

Roedean
School

Roedean

MARINE

DRIVE

A259

Woodland
Walk

Ovingdean
Hall
School

Greenways

Down Road

Longhill

Ainsworth Close

Dower Road

Ainsworth Avenue

Greenways

Longhill

Wanderdown Way

Wanderdown Close

Rowan Way

Rowan Way

Eley Crs

Eley
Crescent

Eley
Court

Beacon Hill

Ovingdean

Longhill
School

PO

Down Road

1 grid square represents 500 metres

G3
1 Vicarage La
2 Vicarage Ter
3 Whipping Post La

J3
1 Abbotsbury Cl

G H J K L M

I

2

3

4

5

6

7

8

Pickers Hill Farm

Coombe Farm

Brighton & Hove
East Sussex Cou...

Upper Bannings Road

Coombe Vale

Westfield Av
Westfield Av
Westfield
Vale Rd
Stanmer Av
Stanmer Av
Westfield Rise
Coombe Av
North
Coombe Rise

Pedlersburg

FALMER ROAD

Meadow...
...ingdean
Surgery

Rottingdean
Football Club

Bazehill Road
Welesmere Rd
Court
Road
Whiteway Lane

Gorham Avenue
Dean
Royles Cl

The Rotyngs
Challoners Ms

ROTTINGDEAN

Rottingdean
Primary School

Our Lady of
Lourdes School

Whiteway Lane

The Green

Olde Pl
MS

Steyning Road

Nevill
Road

Nevill Road

Sheep Wlk

St Aubyns
School

St Aubyn's
Md

Newlands Road

Chailey Av

Knole Rd

Grand Crescent

Cranleigh Avenue

MARINE DRIVE

Marine
Clinic

Lenham Rd W

Romney Rd

Little Crs

Eileen Av

Marine Cl

Saltdean Park Rd

Westmeston Avenue

Chorley Av

Ashdown Avenue

Lenham

Lenham Rd E

Saltdean

Chichester Dr West

Founthill
Road

Founthill Dr

Arundel Dr West

Chichester Dr East

Arundel Drive East

Withyham Av

Crowborough Rd

Longridge

Lynwood Rd

Wanderdown Rd

Falmer Av

Bishopstone Dr

Falmer Av

Lustrells

Lustrells Cl

Tumulus

Wivelsfield Road

Perry Hill

Winton Av

Crescent

Chiltington Way

School Lane

Saltdean County
School

Hawthorn Close

Tremola Avenue

Vale West

Linchmere

Oaklands

Ridgewood Avenue

Hempstead Road

Arlington Gdns

Heathfield Av

Mount Dr

Glynde Av

Vale

Greenbank

Shepham Av

Bevendean Avenue

Wicklands Avenue

Brambletyne Avenue

Nutley

Ardingly

Cowden Rd

Bannings Vale

Hamsey Rd

Tye Close

Doctors
Surgery

A259 SOUTH COAST ROAD

A259

SOUTH COAST

Rye Cl

Field Close

Crescent

Findon Avenue

Northwood Avenue

Bannings Rd

Chailey Crs

Lewes

Rodmell Avenue

Homebush Avenue

Cissbury Avenue

Ashurst Avenue

Springfield

Gorham Way

Highview Rd

Tyedean Road

Amhurst Rd

Broomfield Av

Saltdean

PO11

A **B** **C** **D** **E** **F**

Station Theatre

Business
Cen

Tournerbury

Legion
Rd

Park Road

St Thomas

Station

A3023

St Mary's Road

Mengham Infant
School

Mengham
Junior
School

1

St Catherine's

St Aubin's Park

St Helen's Road

Richmond Dr

West Town

St Mary's

Garden

Elwell Rd

Oakwood Rd

Hayling Island
Health Centre

St Leonard's Avenue

Mengham Road

Mengham

St George's
Road

Staunton Avenue

Bacon Lane

Stamford Av

Magdala Rd

Green Lane

Beach Road

Hollow
Lane

Garden Cl

Hollow Lane

Selsmore
Avenue

Mengham La

Salterns Lane

Ilex Walk

Selsmore Avenue

Westmead

Westfield Avenue

Victoria Av

Alexandra Avenue

Chichester Avenue

Sea Grove Av

Webb Lane

Mengham Avenue

Bound Lane

Orchard
Rd

North Crs

Norman Rd

Blackthorn Dr

Kingfisher

Fishery Lane

Foreland
Ct

Sea Front

Westfield

Ramsey Rd

Lyndhurst Cl

Manor Wy

Tudor Cl

Webb Cl

1

Wyborn Cl

Grand Pde

St Andrew's Road

Harold Road

St Hermans Rd

Silversands Gdns

Old School Dr

Sea
Front

Easto

2

SOUTH HAYLING

Sea Front

Old School Dr

Southwood

Bembridge Drive

The Clade

Meath Cl

Sea
Front

The Strand

Road

3

Hayling Bay

4

5

6

7

8

A **B** **C** **D** **E** **F**

1 grid square represents 500 metres

H3
1 Wheatlands Crs

East Hea

I

East Head

2

Mengham
Salterns

Marine

aview   Road

Selsmore

Black Point

Bracklesham
Rd

3

Rowin Close

Avenue

Eastoke

Fishermans
Wk

Wittering Road

Earnley

Selsey Cl

Sidlesham Cl

Pagham
Gdns

Itchenor Rd

Bracklesham
Road

West Sussex County

Hampshire County

Avenue

Eastoke

Creek

Burgess Cl

Birdham
Rd

Haven Road

Nutbourne Road

Bosmere Rd

Haven   Road

Haslemere Gdns

Point

Road

West
Haye   Road

Sandy

Coronation
Rd

Treloar   Rd

Road

Winsor Cl

Wheatlands   Avenue

1

Treloar
Rd

Eastoke Point

Southwood Road

4

216

5

6

7

8

Shipton Green

G   H   J   K   L   M

199

Redlands Fm
Redlands Lane
Ichenor Road
Shipton Green Lane
Holt Place
Burlow Cl
Farm
Chapel Lane
Acre Street
Piggery Hall Lane
B2179
Pinks Lane
First Avenue

I

Holmes Fm
Hale Farm
Somerley
Bell Lane
Hundredsteddle La
Carthagena Farm
Batchmere's

2

Piggery Hall Lane
Somerley Lane
Second Avenue

3

Furzefield
Briar Av
Tile Barn Lane
Mill House
Stubcroft Lane
B2198
Bookers Lane
Third

Church Farm Lane
Hilton Park
Church Farm Lane
Stubcroft Farm
Ioddington Lane

4

Church Farm Lane
Church Road
Clayton Lane
Earnley Road
Earnley Grange

218

NORTHERN ...RS
...am Road
Ascot Cl
Eton Dr
Oxford Cl
Bennetts
Mill Gdns
Harrow Dv
East Wittering County Primary School
Barn Rd
Fld Rd
Meadow Rd
Wessex Av
Downview Close
Stubcroft Lane
Holden's Farm
Earnley Mnr Close

5

Windmill Court
STOCKS LA
Oakfield Av
B2179
Coney Six
East Wittering
BRACKLESHAM LANE
Barton Wy
Clappers Lane
Earnley Mnr Close

Solent Rd
Oakfield Av
Coney Cl
Seafield Way
Middleton Close
Grayswood Av
Earnley

Longlands Road
Charlmead
Nab Wk
Shingle Wk
Coney Six
Kimbridge Rd
Peerley Rd
Peerley Close
Hale Cl
B2198
Elm Close
6

Barn Wk
Tamarisk Wk
Charlmead
Coney Six
Kimbridge Rd
Legion Way
Kestrel Cl
Plover Close
Beech Av
Garden Av
Woodborough Cl
Drove Lane

West Bracklesham Drive
Cormorant Way
Pond Rd
Sandringham
Bracklesham Close
PO
Elcombe Cl
Shalbourne Cl
Wilton Cl
Manton Cl
Bracklesham

First Av
Secon
Harmony Dr
Avebury Cl

7

East Bracklesham Drive
Seafi...
Third Av
Sussex Gv
Marin Fields
Silver Wy
Walmsleys Wy
Marsh Farm

Seafi...
Lane
Stoney
8

Sussex Beach Holiday Village

G   H   J   K   L   M

A **B** **C** **200** **D** **E** **B2145** **F**

ROAD

Alandale Road

Sidlesham Lane

Wo___ Farm

Lane

1

Mapsons Lane

Lockgate Road

Fletchers

Street End Lane

STREET END ROAD

Hillands Farm

Mapsons Farm

Fletchers Lane

Boxham Lane

Rotten Row

Church Lane

Highleigh Road

First Avenue

2

Batchmere Road

Batchmere's Farm

PO

SELSEY ROAD

Church

Highleigh

Second Avenue

3

Critchel's Lane

Green Lane

Third Avenue

Almodington Lane

4

Almodington

Keynor House

Keynor Lane

Sidlesham County Primary School

Cow Lane

Chalk Lane

5

Earnley Grange

Oldhouse Lane

Easton Farm

Easton Lane

Ham Road

Bakers Farm

6

The Elms

7

Oakhurst Farm

8

Greenwood Farm

Porthole Farm

A **B** **C** **222** **D** **E** **F**

Ham Farm

Brimfast Lane

Brimfast Farm

G H J **201** K L M

Street End

Chalder Lane

Chalder Farm

Bremer Rife

Bramber Farm

Honer Lane

Pagham Rife

1

Horns

2

Sidlesham

3

B2145

Marsh Farm

Honer Farm

May Cl

Rookery Lane

Rookery Farm

Halsey's Farm

Church Lane **Pagham**

Sidlesham Football Club

Manhood Lane

PH

Mill Lane

SELSEY ROAD

Venus Lane

220

Saxon

Heron Md

Mallard

Wythering Cl

5

Lagoon

Harbour

Pagham Lagoon

6

Visitor Centre

Pagham Harbour (Nature Reserve)

Pagham Harbour

Ferry House

B2145

7

Home Farm

Church Norton

8

Norton

G H J **223** K L M

202

Rose
Green

Nyetimber

Aldv

gham

219

P O 21

F3
Street Names for
these grid squares
are listed at the
back of the index

1 grid square represents 500 metres

Home Farm

hurch
Norton

Norton

219

Coles Farm

Greenlease Farm

Grange Lane

Rectory Lane

Grange Farm

B2145

ROAD

Park Farm

Park Lane

East Beach

Inner Owers

Park Copse

Golf Links Lane

Upways Cl

CHICHESTER

St George's Close

Manor Farm Cl

Delfshare Rd

The Willows

Manor Farm Cl

St Peter's Crs

Park Lane

Wheatfield Rd

Roundstone Wy

Drift Road

Park Road

Park Crs

Newfield Rd

Harcourt Wy

Fontwell Road

Chichester Way

Gillway

Beach Road

Manor Road

Marisfield Pl

Mountwood Road

Church Road

Wellington Gdns

Allandale Rd

Elm Tree Cl

Broomfield Rd

The Cl

East

PO

Beach

Robin's

Denny's Close

Glen Crs

Malthouse Cl

Coach House Cl

Seal County Primary School

North Road

Gainsborough Drive

Orpen Pl

Landseer Dr

Constable Dr

E Bank Wy

Marine Drive

Broad View

Lingfield Way

Littlefield Cl

Manor Road

Lewis Rd

East Street

Hanover Cl

Merryfield Drive

Ruskin Av

Kingsway

Fisherman's Wk

Pretawn Gdns

St Itha Rd

Western Rd

Cotland Rd

Sunnymead Drive

Albion Road

Grove Road

Windsor Rd

Orchard Av

James Street

Lawrence Cl

SELSEY

Jones Sq

Tythe Barn Rd

Grafton Road

York Rd

Lifeboat Wy

Sparshott Rd

Wight Wy

pennycord

Selsey Bill

J4
1 St Wilfreds Cl

H5
1 Beverley Cl
2 Holford Gn
3 Kilnwood Cl
4 Romney Garth
5 Turner Wy

Abbotsford 108 F6
Abingworth 124 B6
Adversane 101 C1
Albourne 129 K6
Albourne Green 129 J6
Aldingbourne 181 C5
Aldrington 192 F5
Aldwick 220 F2
Alfold 33 G3
Alfold Bars 33 G5
Alfold Crossways 33 H1
Almodington 218 A4
Amberley 141 M5
Ancton 205 G6
Angmering 185 M6
Ansteadbrook 29 K7
Ansty 108 D1
Apuldram 200 D1
Ardingly 66 C4
Arundel 184 C1
Ashfold Crossways 62 F6
Ashington 125 C8
Ashurst 126 D7
Ashurst Wood 25 M6
Atherington 206 A6
Balcombe 65 H2
Balcombe Lane 42 B7
Baldwins Hill 24 D1
Balls Cross 76 C3
Balls Green 102 B1
Barlavington 119 M7
Barnham 182 D7
Barns Green 80 F2
Bedham 99 J4
Bedlam Street 130 A8
Beggars Bush 189 G1
Bell Hill 68 B7
Bepton 116 B3
Bevendean 195 H2
Bewbush 40 A1
Bexleyhill 73 M5
Bignor 140 C2
Billingshurst 79 M5
Bilsham 205 G3
Bines Green 127 G5
Binsted 183 H3
Birdham 199 M6
Black Corner 15 L8
Black Rock 212 B1
Blackstone 128 F7
Blackwell 24 F2
Bognor Regis 13 G8
Bolney 107 K1
Borden 71 G6
Bosham 177 K7
Bosham Hoe 199 J4
Botolphs 168 A5
Boxgrove 180 D1
Bracklesham 217 K6
Bramber 168 A2
Bramshott 26 D6
Breach 176 A3
Brighton 10 E8
Broadbridge 177 L5
Broadbridge Heath 36 C6
Broadfield 40 D2
Broadford Bridge 102 A4
Broadwater 188 E6
Brockhampton 174 A4
Brookpits 206 A4
Brooks Green 80 F5
Brook Street 87 G2
Broomer's Corner 103 C5
Broomershill 100 F8
Buchan Hill 40 B4
Bucks Green 34 C6
Burgates 47 H6
Burgess Hill 131 H1
Buriton 90 B7
Burndell 205 J1
Burpham 163 H6
Bury 141 H5
Byworth 98 C6
Camelsdale 28 B7
Castle Town 168 D3
Causeway 90 B2
Charlton 136 F6
Charlwood 14 A5
Charlwood 44 F3
Chichester 6 F5
Chidham 176 B4
Chilgrove 135 G2
Chithurst 93 K1
Church Norton 219 J8
Churchwood 99 H8
Cinder Hill 67 H4
Clapham 187 G3
Clayton 150 F4
Climping 205 L2
The Close 6 D5
Coates 120 D4
Cocking 116 F4
Cocking Causeway 94 F8
Codmore Hill 100 D7
Cold Ash Hill 26 F7
Coldean 172 E7
Coldwaltham 121 K6
Colgate 39 K6
Colworth 202 F2
The Common 37 H8
Compton 133 H2
Coneyhurst 80 C8
Conford 26 A5
Coolham 102 F2
Coombes 168 A7
Cootham 143 H3
Copsale 82 C6
Copthorne 22 C1
Cote 187 K4
Cowfold 106 A2

Cox Green 34 F2
Crabtree 84 B5
Crawley 3 G5
Crawley Down 23 H5
Critchmere 27 M5
Crockerhill 181 H1
Crossbush 184 F3
Cross Gate 142 B5
Crosspost 107 H3
Crouchers 200 C3
Cuckfield 87 G7
Deanlane End 132 A7
Dell Quay 200 C2
Denne Park 60 D5
Denvilles 174 F2
Dial Green 74 C1
Dial Post 103 M8
Didling 115 J2
Ditchling 151 L1
Donnington 200 F3
Doomsday Green 61 H4
Down Park 23 H3
Dragons Green 103 J1
Dumpford 93 H4
Duncton 119 J5
Durleighmarsh 91 K1
Durrants 152 E4
Durrington 187 L5
Earnley 217 K6
Eartham 159 L4
Easebourne 94 F2
East Ashling 155 M8
East Beach 223 J3
East Dean 137 K6
Eastergate 182 A5
East Grinstead 24 F3
East Hampnett 180 F2
East Harting 114 A1
East Kingston 208 D3
East Lavant 157 H7
East Lavington 118 F6
East Liss 69 L1
East Marden 134 C2
East Moulsecoomb 173 G8
Eastoke 214 F2
East Preston 208 C2
East Wittering 217 H6
East Worthing 211 J1
Ebernoe 54 A8
Edburton 148 D8
Egdean 98 E7
Elbridge 202 F3
Elmer 205 J7
Elmers Marsh 50 B7
Elsted 92 D8
Empshott 46 D1
Empshott Green 46 C1
Emsworth 175 H5
Falmer 173 L6
Faygate 38 F3
Felpham 204 C7
Fernhill 15 M5
Fernhurst 51 G6
Ferring 209 G2
Finchdean 132 K4
Findon 165 M5
Findon Valley 188 C2
Fishbourne 178 A6
Fisher 201 K6
Fishersgate 192 A5
Fisherstreet 53 C1
Fittleworth 121 H1
Five Oaks 57 M7
Flansham 204 D5
Flathurst 98 B3
Fleet 196 C4
Fontwell 182 B2
Ford 183 L8
Forestside 132 E6
Fulking 149 G8
Funtington 155 H6
Furnace Green 3 L8
Furnace Wood 23 K1
Fyning 70 D7
Gay Street 101 K6
Goddards' Green 108 B7
Godleys Green 111 C8
Goose Green 124 E2
Gorehill 98 C7
Goring-by-Sea 209 K1
Graffham 118 C5
Grayshott 27 J1
Grayswood 29 H3
Great Common 77 J1
Greatham 47 J3
Greatham 122 B8
Green Street 103 J2
Griggs Green 26 A8
Gunter's Bridge 76 A8
Habin 92 C2
Halecommon 70 B7
Halfway Bridge 96 C4
Halnaker 158 F2
Hambrook 176 D2
Hammer 27 K7
Hammer Bottom 27 J7
Hammerpot 186 A4
Hampers Green 98 A2
Handcross 63 K4
Hangleton 186 D8
Hangleton 192 F2
Hardham 122 A5
Haslemere 28 E6
Haslingbourne 98 B7
Hassocks 130 F8
Hatch Farm Hill 51 K4
Havant 174 B1
The Haven 57 L2
Hawkley 46 B5
Hayling Island 196 E6

Haywards Heath 87 M6
Heath Common 144 D2
Heath End 119 L2
Henfield 128 A7
Henley 73 J4
Henley Common 73 G3
Hermitage 175 K3
Heyshott 117 H3
Heyshott Green 117 H2
Hickstead 107 L7
Highbrook 66 F3
High Cross 129 G5
Highleigh 218 D3
High Salvington 187 K3
Highstreet Green 31 G2
Hill Brow 69 M2
Hillgrove 52 F6
Hill Side 47 K8
Hill Top 95 G6
Hole Street 145 K2
Hollingbury 172 C7
Hollingdean 194 C1
Hooksway 114 D7
Hookwood 14 D2
Horsemere Green 205 K3
Horsham 4 E3
Horsted Keynes 67 K7
Houghton 141 H8
Hove 193 J7
Hoyle 117 L2
Hunston 201 H4
Hurstpierpoint 129 M7
Hurst Wickham 130 D6
Ifield 20 B4
Ifield Green 20 B3
Ifieldwood 19 L3
Ifold 55 K2
Ingrams Green 93 K7
Iping 93 M2
Itchingfield 59 G6
Kent Street 106 D5
Keymer 131 J8
Kingsfold 17 J6
Kingsley Green 51 G2
Kingston by Sea 191 J5
Kingston Gorse 208 B5
Kirdford 77 J2
Lagness 202 C6
Lambs Green 19 G6
Lancing 189 L6
Langley 48 C6
Langley Green 20 C2
Langstone 174 B6
Leggatt Hill 74 C8
Leigh Park 152 A8
Lickfold 74 C4
Lidsey 203 L1
Linchmere 50 B1
Lindfield 88 C4
Liphook 49 H1
Liss 69 K1
Liss Forest 47 J5
Little Bognor 98 F6
Little Common 97 G4
Littlehampton 206 E2
Littlehaven 5 H2
Littleworth 105 H7
Lodsworth 96 C1
Lodsworth Common 74 B6
Lower Beeding 84 B1
Lower Fittleworth 121 G3
Lower Horncroft 121 G4
Lowfield Heath 15 G7
Loxwood 32 F8
Lumley 175 K3
Lurgashall 74 E2
Lyminster 184 E6
Mackerel's Common 55 H7
Madehurst 161 J3
Maidenbower 21 K8
Mannings Heath 61 L7
Manor Royal 20 F2
Maplehurst 82 F6
Marehill 122 F2
Marley Heights 51 G3
Maudlin 179 M2
Mengham 214 E1
Merston 202 C1
Middleton-on-Sea 204 F7
Midhurst 95 G6
Mid Lavant 156 F6
Mile Oak 192 A1
Milland 71 H2
Minsted 93 M6
The Mint 47 K7
Monk's Gate 61 K8
Moulsecoomb 195 G1
Navant Hill 52 E7
Nepcote 166 A7
Nep Town 147 M1
New Brighton 175 K1
Newpound Common 78 F1
Newtown 49 J2
New Town 60 E4
North Bersted 203 H5
North Chailey 111 L6
Northchapel 53 H5
North Common 111 M5
North End 165 L4
North End 183 H7
Northgate 21 G4
North Hayling 196 F1
North Heath 101 G5
North Lancing 190 A4
North Marden 114 C3
North Moulsecoomb 172 E8
North Mundham 201 K3
Northney 174 F8
North Stoke 162 D2
Norton 181 J2

Norton 223 H1
Nursted 90 F5
Nutbourne 123 H2
Nutbourne 176 C5
Nutbourne Common 123 J2
Nutcombe 27 L2
Nuthurst 83 G3
Nyetimber 220 B2
Nyewood 92 B4
Nyton 181 K4
Oakhill 5 H8
Oakshott 46 A8
Oakwoodhill 16 A5
Offham 162 E6
Old Shoreham 190 F3
Oving 180 D5
Ovingdean 212 F1
Pagham 219 M4
Parbrook 79 J5
Park Street 58 D1
Partridge Green 127 H1
Passfield 26 A3
Patcham 172 A6
Patching 186 E2
Paynes Green 16 D4
Pease Pottage 40 B5
Petersfield 90 A1
Petworth 97 M4
Plaistow 55 G2
Poling 185 J6
Poling Corner 185 H4
Portfield 7 K5
Portslade-by-Sea 192 C6
Portslade Village 192 B2
Pound Hill 21 K4
Povey Cross 14 D3
Poynings 149 J7
Preston 193 M3
Prince's Marsh 69 J2
Prinsted 175 M5
Pulborough 122 C3
Pyecombe 150 C6
Quags Corner 94 B5
Queen's Corner 71 M4
Rackham 142 D4
Rake 48 B8
Ramsnest Common 29 M6
Rapkyns 36 B8
Redford 72 B3
Red Hill 152 E3
River 96 F2
Robins 71 K5
Rock 144 E3
Roedean 212 D1
Roffey 5 L2
Rogate 92 B1
Rose Green 220 D1
Rotherbridge 97 K7
Rottingdean 213 H2
Roundstreet Common 56 C6
Rowhook 35 M3
Rowland's Castle 153 G2
Rudgwick 34 D5
Runcton 202 A3
Rusper 18 D5
Rustington 207 L3
Saddlescombe 170 F1
Saltdean 213 L2
Salvington 188 B5
Saxby 182 F7
Sayers Common 129 K3
Scayne's Hill 110 F1
Selham 96 E6
Selsey 223 H6
Selsfield Common 43 J3
Selsmore 215 G2
Sharpthorne 44 B6
Sheet 68 E7
Shepherd's Hill 28 D6
Shermanbury 127 L1
Shipley 103 L4
Shipton Green 199 H8
Shopp Hill 52 D6
Shopwyke 180 A5
Shoreham Beach 191 J7
Shoreham-by-Sea 191 G7
Shottermill 27 M6
Shripney 203 L3
Sidlesham 219 G3
Sidlesham Common 200 F7
Singleton 136 D5
Slaugham 63 H7
Slindon 160 E7
Slinfold 58 E1
Slough Green 86 C3
Small Dole 147 M6
Smithbrook 74 C8
Smock Alley 123 L5
Somerley 217 K2
Sompting 189 J6
Sompting Abbotts 189 H4
South Ambersham 96 A6
Southbourne 176 B4
Southern Cross 192 B4
Southgate 2 D7
South Harting 91 K8
South Hayling 214 B2
South Lancing 189 M7
South Mundham 201 L6
South Stoke 162 E4
Southwater 82 A4
Southwater Street 81 K1
Southwick 191 M4
Stanmer 172 C3
Staplefield 64 A7
Staples Hill 76 F1
Stedham 94 B3
Steep 68 B5
Steep Marsh 68 D3
Steyning 167 L2

Stockbridge 201 G3
Stockheath 174 B1
Stoke 196 D2
Stonequarry 25 H1
Stopham 121 L2
Storrington 143 K4
Stoughton 155 H1
Street End 219 G1
Strettington 158 B6
Strood Green 36 C6
Stubbermere 153 K4
Sullington 144 A5
Sullington Warren 144 A3
Summersdale 179 H2
Sunnyside 24 F6
Sutton 140 B1
Sutton End 120 A6
Tangmere 180 C2
Temple Bar 180 B1
Terwick Common 70 F2
Thakeham 124 C5
Thorney Island 197 M4
Three Bridges 3 L2
Tilgate 40 E1
Tilgate Forest Row 40 D7
Tillington 97 K4
Tinsley Green 15 K8
Tisman's Common 34 B7
Titty Hill 71 M4
Toddington 185 G8
Topleigh 118 A2
Tortington 183 M5
Tote Hill 72 B7
Tower Hill 60 A4
Treyford 114 C7
Trotten Marsh 70 F5
Trotton 93 H3
Tullecombe 70 B4
Turners Hill 23 H8
Twineham 107 C8
Twineham Green 107 A6
Two Mile Ash 81 L1
Tye 196 F3
Up Marden 134 C4
Upper Beeding 168 A3
Upper Ifold 32 B5
Upper Norwood 118 E3
Upperton 97 J2
Upper Wardley 49 K7
Upwaltham 138 E4
Walberton 182 E4
Walderton 154 F2
Warblington 174 E4
Wardley 49 K8
Warminghurst 124 F4
Warnham 36 F4
Warningcamp 185 J3
Warninglid 85 H3
Washington 144 F6
Waterbeach 158 B7
Watersfield 121 H4
Wepham 163 H6
West Ashling 177 K1
West Blatchington 193 C3
Westbourne 153 L2
West Burton 140 E3
West Chiltington 123 M2
West Chiltington Common .. 123 H5
West Dean 136 B6
Westdene 171 J7
West End 127 K7
Westergate 181 K5
Westerton 180 A1
Westfield 214 B2
West Green 2 D3
West Grinstead 104 C5
Westhampnett 179 M3
West Harting 91 K5
West Hill 65 K3
West Hoathly 43 M6
West Itchenor 198 F5
West Kingston 208 D3
West Lavington 95 H6
West Leigh 152 D7
West Liss 47 J7
West Marden 133 H4
Westmeston 151 M4
West Stoke 156 B6
West Tarring 8 B1
West Thorney 198 A2
West Town 129 M6
West Town 214 B1
West Wittering 216 D3
West Wittering 216 E4
West Worthing 210 A4
Whitehall 103 J5
Whitehawk 195 G6
Whitemans Green 86 F4
White's Green 74 F5
Wick 184 D8
Wiggonholt 122 E6
Wineham 106 E7
Wisborough Green 78 C4
Wiston 145 K3
Withdean 171 M8
Wivelsfield 110 B7
Woldhurst 201 L4
Woodgate 181 L7
Woodingdean 195 K5
Woodmancote 148 E2
Woodmancote 154 C8
Woodmansgreen 72 B3
Woolbeding 94 C2
Woolmer Hill 27 K5
World's End 109 L8
Worth 21 M7
Worth Abbey 42 C5
Worthing 8 F1
Wych Cross 45 M8
Yapton 205 H1

USING THE STREET INDEX

Street names are listed alphabetically. Each street name is followed by its postal town or area locality, the Postcode District, the page number, and the reference to the square in which the name is found.

Example: Abbotsbury CI *ROTT* BN2..................213 J3 **◨**

Some entries are followed by a number in a blue box. This number indicates the location of the street within the referenced grid square. The full street name is listed at the side of the map page.

GENERAL ABBREVIATIONS

ACC ...... ACCESS	CTYD ...... COURTYARD	HLS ...... HILLS	MWY ...... MOTORWAY
ALY ...... ALLEY	CUTT ...... CUTTINGS	HO ...... HOUSE	N ...... NORTH
AP ...... APPROACH	CV ...... COVE	HOL ...... HOLLOW	NE ...... NORTH EAST
AR ...... ARCADE	CYN ...... CANYON	HOSP ...... HOSPITAL	NW ...... NORTH WEST
ASS ...... ASSOCIATION	DEPT ...... DEPARTMENT	HRB ...... HARBOUR	O/P ...... OVERPASS
AV ...... AVENUE	DL ...... DALE	HTH ...... HEATH	OFF ...... OFFICE
BCH ...... BEACH	DM ...... DAM	HTS ...... HEIGHTS	ORCH ...... ORCHARD
BLDS ...... BUILDINGS	DR ...... DRIVE	HVN ...... HAVEN	OV ...... OVAL
BND ...... BEND	DRO ...... DROVE	HWY ...... HIGHWAY	PAL ...... PALACE
BNK ...... BANK	DRY ...... DRIVEWAY	IMP ...... IMPERIAL	PAS ...... PASSAGE
BR ...... BRIDGE	DWGS ...... DWELLINGS	IN ...... INLET	PAV ...... PAVILION
BRK ...... BROOK	E ...... EAST	IND EST ...... INDUSTRIAL ESTATE	PDE ...... PARADE
BTM ...... BOTTOM	EMB ...... EMBANKMENT	INFM ...... INFIRMARY	PH ...... PUBLIC HOUSE
BUS ...... BUSINESS	EMBY ...... EMBASSY	INFO ...... INFORMATION	PK ...... PARK
BVD ...... BOULEVARD	ESP ...... ESPLANADE	INT ...... INTERCHANGE	PKWY ...... PARKWAY
BY ...... BYPASS	EST ...... ESTATE	IS ...... ISLAND	PL ...... PLACE
CATH ...... CATHEDRAL	EX ...... EXCHANGE	JCT ...... JUNCTION	PLN ...... PLAIN
CEM ...... CEMETERY	EXPY ...... EXPRESSWAY	JTY ...... JETTY	PLNS ...... PLAINS
CEN ...... CENTRE	EXT ...... EXTENSION	KG ...... KING	PLZ ...... PLAZA
CFT ...... CROFT	F/O ...... FLYOVER	KNL ...... KNOLL	POL ...... POLICE STATION
CH ...... CHURCH	FC ...... FOOTBALL CLUB	L ...... LAKE	PR ...... PRINCE
CHA ...... CHASE	FK ...... FORK	LA ...... LANE	PREC ...... PRECINCT
CHYD ...... CHURCHYARD	FLD ...... FIELD	LDG ...... LODGE	PREP ...... PREPARATORY
CIR ...... CIRCLE	FLDS ...... FIELDS	LGT ...... LIGHT	PRIM ...... PRIMARY
CIRC ...... CIRCUS	FLS ...... FALLS	LK ...... LOCK	PROM ...... PROMENADE
CL ...... CLOSE	FLS ...... FLATS	LKS ...... LAKES	PRS ...... PRINCESS
CLFS ...... CLIFFS	FM ...... FARM	LNDG ...... LANDING	PRT ...... PORT
CMP ...... CAMP	FT ...... FORT	LTL ...... LITTLE	PT ...... POINT
CNR ...... CORNER	FWY ...... FREEWAY	LWR ...... LOWER	PTH ...... PATH
CO ...... COUNTY	FY ...... FERRY	MAG ...... MAGISTRATE	PZ ...... PIAZZA
COLL ...... COLLEGE	GA ...... GATE	MAN ...... MANSIONS	QD ...... QUADRANT
COM ...... COMMON	GAL ...... GALLERY	MD ...... MEAD	QU ...... QUEEN
COMM ...... COMMISSION	GDN ...... GARDEN	MDW ...... MEADOWS	QY ...... QUAY
CON ...... CONVENT	GDNS ...... GARDENS	MEM ...... MEMORIAL	R ...... RIVER
COT ...... COTTAGE	GLD ...... GLADE	MKT ...... MARKET	RBT ...... ROUNDABOUT
COTS ...... COTTAGES	GLN ...... GLEN	MKTS ...... MARKETS	RD ...... ROAD
CP ...... CAPE	GN ...... GREEN	ML ...... MALL	RDG ...... RIDGE
CPS ...... COPSE	GND ...... GROUND	ML ...... MILL	REP ...... REPUBLIC
CR ...... CREEK	GRA ...... GRANGE	MNR ...... MANOR	RES ...... RESERVOIR
CREM ...... CREMATORIUM	GRG ...... GARAGE	MS ...... MEWS	RFC ...... RUGBY FOOTBALL CLUB
CRS ...... CRESCENT	GT ...... GREAT	MSN ...... MISSION	RI ...... RISE
CSWY ...... CAUSEWAY	GTWY ...... GATEWAY	MT ...... MOUNT	RP ...... RAMP
CT ...... COURT	GV ...... GROVE	MTN ...... MOUNTAIN	RW ...... ROW
CTRL ...... CENTRAL	HGR ...... HIGHER	MTS ...... MOUNTAINS	S ...... SOUTH
CTS ...... COURTS	HL ...... HILL	MUS ...... MUSEUM	SCH ...... SCHOOL

SE ...... SOUTH EAST
SER ...... SERVICE AREA
SH ...... SHORE
SHOP ...... SHOPPING
SKWY ...... SKYWAY
SMT ...... SUMMIT
SOC ...... SOCIETY
SP ...... SPUR
SPR ...... SPRING
SQ ...... SQUARE
ST ...... STREET
STN ...... STATION
STR ...... STREAM
STRD ...... STRAND
SW ...... SOUTH WEST
TDG ...... TRADING
TER ...... TERRACE
THWY ...... THROUGHWAY
TNL ...... TUNNEL
TOLL ...... TOLLWAY
TPK ...... TURNPIKE
TR ...... TRACK
TRL ...... TRAIL
TWR ...... TOWER
U/P ...... UNDERPASS
UNI ...... UNIVERSITY
UPR ...... UPPER
V ...... VALE
VA ...... VALLEY
VIAD ...... VIADUCT
VIL ...... VILLA
VIS ...... VISTA
VLG ...... VILLAGE
VLS ...... VILLAS
VW ...... VIEW
W ...... WEST
WD ...... WOOD
WHF ...... WHARF
WK ...... WALK
WKS ...... WALKS
WLS ...... WELLS
WY ...... WAY
YD ...... YARD
YHA ...... YOUTH HOSTEL

POSTCODE TOWNS AND AREA ABBREVIATIONS

ANG/EP ...... Angmering/East Preston	EDN/EASTW ...... East Dean/Eastbourne west	HOVE ...... Hove	PETW ...... Petworth
ARUN ...... Arundel	EGRIN ...... East Grinstead	HPPT/KEY ...... Hurstpierpoint/Keymer	PEV ...... Pevensey
BAT ...... Battle	EMRTH ...... Emsworth	HRTF ...... Hartfield	POLE ...... Polegate
BEX ...... Bexhill	EPSF ...... Petersfield east	HTHF ...... Heathfield	POY/PYE ...... Poynings/Pyecombe
BEXW ...... Bexhill west	FERR ...... Ferring	HWH ...... Haywards Heath	PSF ...... Petersfield
BIL ...... Billingshurst	FIN/BW ...... Findon/Broadwater	LAN/SOMP ...... Lancing/Sompting	PTSD ...... Portslade
BOGR ...... Bognor Regis	FROW ...... Forest Row	LEW ...... Lewes	PUL/STOR ...... Pulborough/Storrington
BRI ...... Brighton	GSHT ...... Grayshott	LGNY ...... Langney	RBTBR ...... Robertsbridge
BUR/ETCH ...... Burwash/Etchingham	HAIL ...... Hailsham	LHPTN ...... Littlehampton	RCCH ...... Rural Chichester
BURH ...... Burgess Hill	HAS ...... Hastings	LIPH ...... Liphook	RGODL ...... Rural Godalming
CCH ...... Chichester	HASM ...... Haslemere	LISS ...... Liss	RHAS ...... Rural Hastings
CRAN ...... Cranleigh	HAV ...... Havant	LW/ROSE ...... Lower Willingdon/Roselands	RHWH ...... Rural Haywards Heath
CRAWE ...... Crawley east	HAWK ...... Hawkhurst	LYDD ...... Lydd	RING/NEW ...... Ringmer/Newick
CRAWW ...... Crawley west	HFD ...... Henfield	MAYF ...... Mayfield	ROTT ...... Rottingdean
CRBK ...... Cranbrook	HISD ...... Hayling Island	MIDH ...... Midhurst	RRTW ...... Rural Royal Tunbridge Wells
CROW ...... Crowborough	HORL ...... Horley	MIDOS ...... Middleton-on-Sea	RTON ...... Rural Tonbridge
EAST ...... Eastbourne	HORN ...... Horndean	NEWHV ...... Newhaven	RTW ...... Royal Tunbridge Wells
EDEN ...... Edenbridge	HORS ...... Horsham	NROM ...... New Romney	RTWE/PEM ...... Royal Tunbridge Wells east/Pembury
		PEAHV ...... Peacehaven	

RYE ...... Rye
SALV ...... Salvington
SBGH/RUST ...... Southborough/Rusthall
SEAF ...... Seaford
SELS ...... Selsey
SHOR ...... Shoreham
SLVH ...... Silverhill
STEY/UB ...... Steyning/Upper Beeding
STHW ...... Southwick
STLEO ...... St Leonards
STPH/PW ...... Staplehurst/Paddock Wood
SWTR ...... Southwater
TENT ...... Tenterden
UCK ...... Uckfield
WADH ...... Wadhurst
WSEA ...... Winchelsea
WTHG ...... Worthing

Index - streets

A

Abberton Fld HPPT/KEY BN6 ... 130 C7
Abbey Cl LAN/SOMP BN15 ... 190 B6
Abbey Rd LAN/SOMP BN15 ... 189 K5
ROTT BN2 ... 11 L8
STEY/UB BN44 ... 146 F8
WTHG BN11 ... 8 D8
Abbotsbury Cl ROTT BN2 ... 213 J5
Abbotsbury Ct SWTR RH13 ... 5 H5
Abbots Cl HPPT/KEY BN6 ... 130 F8
Abbotsfield Rd CRAWW RH11 ... 19 L7
Abbots Leigh SWTR RH13 ... 82 B4
Abbotstone Av HAV PO9 ... 152 D8
Abbotswood Wk
ANG/EP BN16 ... 207 K4
Abbotts Cl WTHG BN11 ... 8 F5
Abbotts Vw LAN/SOMP BN15 ... 189 K4
Abbotts Wy LAN/SOMP BN15 ... 190 A6
A'becket's Av BOGR PO21 ... 220 C2
Aberdare Cl CCH PO19 ... 179 J4
Aberdeen Rd BN2 ... 11 H1
ROTT BN2 ... 195 M6
Abinger Rd PTSD BN41 ... 192 C4
ROTT BN2 ... 195 M6
Abrahams Rd CRAWW RH11 ... 40 B1
Acacia Av HOVE BN3 ... 193 L8
SALV BN13 ... 188 A5
Acer Wy HAV PO9 ... 152 E8
Acorn Av SWTR RH13 ... 105 M3
Acorn Cl ANG/EP BN16 ... 186 A8
EGRIN RH19 ... 24 C4
SELS PO20 ... 222 E2
Acorn End BOGR PO21 ... 220 C2
The Acorns CRAWW RH11 ... 40 C3
HPPT/KEY BN6 ... 108 B8
HPPT/KEY BN6 ... 129 L2
The Acre Cl WTHG BN11 ... 8 C6
Acre St SELS PO20 ... 217 G2
Adams Cl BRI BN1 ... 194 C2
Adastra Av HPPT/KEY BN6 ... 131 M8
Addison Cl LAN/SOMP BN15 ... 189 M6
Addison Rd HOVE BN3 ... 10 A3
Addison Wy MIDOS PO22 ... 203 J3
Adelaide Cl CRAWW RH11 ... 20 E3
HORS RH12 ... 5 K3
SALV BN13 ... 187 K6
Adelaide Crs HOVE BN3 ... 193 K7
Adelaide Rd CCH PO19 ... 7 G2
Adelaide Sq SHOR BN43 ... 191 J5
Adelphi Cl CRAWE RH10 ... 21 L8
Adhurst Rd HAV PO9 ... 152 D8
Admers Crs LIPH GU30 ... 49 K2
Admiral Rd CRAWW RH11 ... 40 B1
Admiral's Bridge La
EGRIN RH19 ... 44 D2
Admirals Wk ANG/EP BN16 ... 207 H2
RCCH PO18 ... 155 H7
Admiralty Gdns MIDOS PO22 ... 13 K5
Admiralty Rd MIDOS PO22 ... 13 K5
Adsdean Cl HAV PO9 ... 152 B8
Adur Av SALV BN13 ... 187 K4
SHOR BN43 ... 190 D7
Adur Cl LAN/SOMP BN15 ... 190 D7
Adur Dr SHOR BN43 ... 191 H5
Adur Rd BURH RH15 ... 109 K8
SHOR BN43 ... 190 F4
Adversane La BIL RH14 ... 101 J1
Adversane Rd FIN/BW BN14 ... 188 C7
Agate La HORS RH12 ... 5 H2
Aglaia Rd WTHG BN11 ... 210 A3
Agnes St ROTT BN2 ... 11 J2
Aigburth Av BOGR PO21 ... 220 E1
Ailsa Cl CRAWW RH11 ... 2 A9
Ainsdale Cl SALV BN13 ... 187 L6
Ainsdale Rd SALV BN13 ... 187 L6
Ainsworth Av ROTT BN2 ... 212 E1
Ainsworth Cl ROTT BN2 ... 195 L8
Aintree Rd CRAWE RH10 ... 3 L8
Airport Wy HORL RH6 ... 15 H4
Ajax Pl MIDOS PO22 ... 204 D7
Akehurst Cl CRAWE RH10 ... 22 B1
Alandale Rd LAN/SOMP BN15 ... 189 K4
SELS PO20 ... 200 A8
Alan Wy ROTT BN2 ... 195 G6
Albany Cl WTHG BN11 ... 8 B7
Albany Ms HOVE BN3 ... 193 J6
Albany Rd CRAWW RH11 ... 2 C4
Albany Vls HOVE BN3 ... 193 J7
Alberta Rd SALV BN13 ... 187 L6
Albert Cl HWH RH16 ... 88 B8
Albert Dr BURH RH15 ... 130 F2
Albert Ms HOVE BN3 ... 193 J6
Albert Rd ANG/EP BN16 ... 207 K2
BOGR PO21 ... 12 F7
BRI BN1 ... 10 C4
CCH PO19 ... 178 D6
HORL RH6 ... 15 H1
LHPTN BN17 ... 206 E3
STHW BN42 ... 191 L5
Albery Cl HORS RH12 ... 4 B3
Albion Cl CRAWE RH10 ... 21 L7
Albion Ct BURH RH15 ... 131 G2
Albion Hl ROTT BN2 ... 11 H5
Albion Rd SELS PO20 ... 223 H6
Albion St PTSD BN41 ... 191 L6
ROTT BN2 ... 11 G4
STHW BN42 ... 192 B5
Albion Wy HORS RH12 ... 4 B8
SWTR RH13 ... 60 E3
Alborough Wy BOGR PO21 ... 220 E2
Albourne Cl ROTT BN2 ... 194 F5
Albourne Rd HFD BN5 ... 128 A5
HPPT/KEY BN6 ... 129 M6
Aldbourne Dr BOGR PO21 ... 220 E2
Alder Cl CRAWE RH10 ... 23 J4
SALV BN13 ... 187 K7
Alderfield PSF GU32 ... 90 B1
Alderman's Wk CCH PO19 ... 6 E3
Aldermoor Av PUL/STOR RH20 ... 143 M2
Alderney Rd FERR BN12 ... 209 G4
Alders Av EGRIN RH19 ... 24 C4
Alders View Dr EGRIN RH19 ... 24 F1
Alder Wy MIDOS PO22 ... 204 F6
Aldingbourne Cl CRAWW RH11 ... 20 A5
Aldingbourne Dr RCCH PO18 ... 181 H1
SELS PO20 ... 181 J1
Aldrich Cl HAV PO9 ... 195 L8
Aldrington Av HOVE BN3 ... 193 H4
Aldrington Cl HOVE BN3 ... 192 E5
Aldsworth Av FERR BN12 ... 209 J2
Aldsworth Ct FERR BN12 ... 209 J2
Aldwick Av BOGR PO21 ... 221 G3
Aldwick Cl ANG/EP BN16 ... 207 J5
Aldwick Felds BOGR PO21 ... 221 G1
Aldwick Gdns BOGR PO21 ... 221 G1
Aldwick Hundred
BOGR PO21 ... 220 F3
Aldwick Pl BOGR PO21 ... 221 G1
Aldwick Rd BOGR PO21 ... 220 F2
Aldwick St BOGR PO21 ... 220 F2
Alexander Cl BOGR PO21 ... 220 F2
Alexandra Av HISD PO11 ... 214 C2
Alexandra Ct FERR BN12 ... 209 K1
Alexandra Rd BURH RH15 ... 131 K2
CCH PO19 ... 7 G3
LAN/SOMP BN15 ... 190 A7
WTHG BN11 ... 9 M5
Alexandra Vls BRI BN1 ... 10 C4
Alford Cl FIN/BW BN14 ... 188 B5
Alfred Cl CRAWE RH10 ... 21 M7
MIDOS PO22 ... 205 G7
Alfred Pl WTHG BN11 ... 9 K6
Alfred Rd BRI BN1 ... 10 C4
Alfrey Cl EMRTH PO10 ... 175 M4
Alfriston Cl FIN/BW BN14 ... 188 C7
MIDOS PO22 ... 204 D6
ROTT BN2 ... 195 G6
Alfriston Rd FIN/BW BN14 ... 188 C7
Alice Av HOVE BN3 ... 193 L7
Alicia Av CRAWE RH10 ... 21 J6
PUL/STOR RH20 ... 125 H7
Alicks Hl BIL RH14 ... 79 L4
Alinora Av FERR BN12 ... 209 L2
Alinora Cl FERR BN12 ... 209 L2
Alinora Crs FERR BN12 ... 209 K4
Alinora Dr FERR BN12 ... 209 K3
Allandale Cl SELS PO20 ... 223 G4
Allandale Ct HAV PO9 ... 152 A6
Allangate Dr ANG/EP BN16 ... 207 L2
Allbrook Ct HAV PO9 ... 152 A6
Allcard Cl HORS RH12 ... 4 F2
Allcot Cl CRAWW RH11 ... 39 M1
Allee Dr LIPH GU30 ... 26 C7
Allendale SWTR RH13 ... 82 A1
Allendale Av EMRTH PO10 ... 175 H1
FIN/BW BN14 ... 188 B3
Allen Rd HWH RH16 ... 88 B7
Allen's Cl EGRIN RH19 ... 25 L6
Alley Groves SWTR RH13 ... 105 M2
Alleyne Wy MIDOS PO22 ... 205 J7
The Alley ARUN BN18 ... 141 L5
MIDH GU29 ... 94 B3
Allfreys Whf PUL/STOR RH20 ... 122 C2
Allington Rd FIN/BW BN14 ... 188 F5
Allwood Crs RHWH RH17 ... 110 D8
Allyington Wy CRAWE RH10 ... 21 L7
Alma Rd HWH RH16 ... 88 C4
Alma St LAN/SOMP BN15 ... 189 M8
Almodington La SELS PO20 ... 218 A4
Almond Cl CRAWW RH11 ... 20 B7
Alpha Rd CRAWW RH11 ... 2 C4
Alpine Rd HOVE BN3 ... 193 G6
Alresford Rd HAV PO9 ... 152 B8
Alverstone Rd WTHG BN11 ... 9 L3
Amber Gld SWTR RH13 ... 82 A3
Amberley Cl BURH RH15 ... 109 H8
CRAWE RH10 ... 21 K6
HWH RH16 ... 88 B7
HORS RH16 ... 87 L8
Amberley Dr BOGR PO21 ... 203 G8
FERR BN12 ... 209 J3
HOVE BN3 ... 192 F1
Amberley Ga PUL/STOR RH20 ... 143 J3
Amberley Rd ANG/EP BN16 ... 207 K4
HORS RH12 ... 38 B6
PUL/STOR RH20 ... 143 H4
Ambersham Crs ANG/EP BN16 ... 208 A2
Ambleside Cl CRAWW RH11 ... 19 L7
MIDOS PO22 ... 204 C6
Ambleside Rd
LAN/SOMP BN15 ... 189 K7
Ambrose Pl WTHG BN11 ... 9 G5
Amelia Rd WTHG BN11 ... 8 F5
America La HWH RH16 ... 88 B7
Amesbury Crs HOVE BN3 ... 192 F5
Amherst Crs HOVE BN3 ... 193 G4
Amport Ct HAV PO9 ... 152 A6
Amundsen Rd HORS RH12 ... 37 L6
Anchor Cl SHOR BN43 ... 191 H6
Anchor Springs LHPTN BN17 ... 206 E3
Ancren Cl FERR BN12 ... 187 G8
Ancton Cl MIDOS PO22 ... 205 G7
Ancton Dr MIDOS PO22 ... 205 H6
Ancton La MIDOS PO22 ... 205 G6
Ancton Lodge La MIDOS PO22 ... 205 H7
Ancton Wy MIDOS PO22 ... 205 H7
Anderson Cl HAV PO9 ... 174 D1
Andlers Ash Rd LISS GU33 ... 69 H2
Andrew Av MIDOS PO22 ... 204 D7
Andrew Cl ANG/EP BN16 ... 207 J2
STEY/UB BN44 ... 167 L2
Andrews La MIDH GU29 ... 93 M5
SWTR RH13 ... 82 A3
Andrews Rd SWTR RH13 ... 82 A5
Andromeda Cl CRAWW RH11 ... 19 M8
Angel St PETW GU28 ... 98 A4
Anglesea St WTHG BN11 ... 8 E4
Anglesey Cl CRAWW RH11 ... 40 D1
Angmering Ms ANG/EP BN16 ... 207 M3
Angmering Wy ANG/EP BN16 ... 207 M1
Angola Rd FIN/BW BN14 ... 9 L1
Angus Cl HORS RH12 ... 4 E4
Angus Rd FERR BN12 ... 209 M2
Annandale Av BOGR PO21 ... 12 C5
Ann Cl HPPT/KEY BN6 ... 131 H7
Anne Howard Gdns
ARUN BN18 ... 184 B1
Annington Gdns SHOR BN43 ... 191 G3
Annington Rd
LAN/SOMP BN15 ... 168 B6
STEY/UB BN44 ... 167 M3
Ann St BRI BN1 ... 10 E3
WTHG BN11 ... 9 H6
Annweir Av LAN/SOMP BN15 ... 189 H6

Anscombe Cl WTHG BN11 ...... 210 A3 🔟
Anscombe Rd WTHG BN11 ...... 210 A3
Ansisters Rd FERR BN12 ...... 208 F3
Anson Rd BOGR PO21 ...... 220 C2
  FERR BN12 ...... 187 K8
Ansty Cl ROTT BN2 ...... 194 F7
Antlands La East HORL RH6.... 15 M7
Antlands La West HORL RH6 .... 15 M6
Anvil Cl BIL RH14 ...... 79 K4
  PTSD BN41 ...... 192 C1
  SWTR RH13 ...... 82 A3
Appledore Gdns HWH RH16 .... 88 A6
Appledore Rd ROTT BN2 ...... 173 C8
Appledram La (North)
  CCH PO19 ...... 178 D6 🔟
Appledram La (South)
  SELS PO20 ...... 178 D8
Applefield CRAWE RH10 ...... 3 G2
Apple Gv BOGR PO21 ...... 220 C3
  EMRTH PO10 ...... 175 L4
Applesham Av HOVE BN3 ...... 192 F2
Applesham Wy PTSD BN41 ...... 192 B3
Appletree Dr MIDOS PO22 ...... 182 C6
Appletrees ANG/EP BN16 ...... 208 C4 🔟
Apple Tree Wk LHPTN BN17 .... 205 L3
The Approach BRI BN1 ...... 193 M1
April Cl FERR BN12 ...... 208 F4 🔟
  HORS RH12 ...... 4 D3
Apsley Av SALV BN13 ...... 187 H7
Arcade Rd LHPTN BN17 ...... 206 E5
Archibald Rd WTHG BN11 ...... 211 H1
Arcturus Rd CRAWW RH11 .... 19 M8
Ardale Cl WTHG BN11 ...... 210 A2
Arden Cl CRAWE RH10 ...... 3 K7
Ardingly Cl CRAWW RH11 ...... 20 C4
Ardingly Dr FERR BN12 ...... 209 J3
Ardingly Rd HWH RH16 ...... 87 G5
  RHWH RH17 ...... 87 G5
  ROTT BN2 ...... 213 L3
Ardingly St ROTT BN2 ...... 11 C7
Ardings Cl RHWH RH17 ...... 65 C5
Ardsheal Cl FIN/BW BN14 ...... 188 C1
Ardsheal Rd FIN/BW BN14 ...... 188 D6
Argus Wk CRAWW RH11 ...... 40 B1
Argyle Circ BOGR PO21 ...... 12 D7 🔟
Argyle Rd BOGR PO21 ...... 12 C8
  BRI BN1 ...... 10 C8
Ariadne Rd WTHG BN11 ...... 8 C8
Arlington Av FERR BN12 ...... 209 J4
Arlington Cl EGRIN RH19 ...... 23 J3
Arlington Crs ANG/EP BN16 .... 208 C1
  BRI BN1 ...... 172 F7 🔟
Arlington Gdns ROTT BN2 ...... 213 L2
Armadale Rd BOGR PO21 ...... 7 H3
Armada Wy ANG/EP BN16 ...... 207 H2
Armdale Rd LHPTN BN17 ...... 206 C2
Arne Cl CRAWW RH11 ...... 40 A1
Arneli Av SELS PO20 ...... 223 C6
Arnfield Cl CRAWW RH11 .... 19 M7 🔟
Arnhem Rd BOGR PO21 ...... 12 A2
Arnold St ROTT BN2 ...... 11 K3
Arnold Wy RCCH PO18 ...... 177 K7
Arnside Cl LAN/SOMP BN15 .... 189 K7
Aron Cl PSF GU32 ...... 90 D2
Arran Cl CRAWW RH11 ...... 2 B9
Artel Cft CRAWE RH10 ...... 3 L3
Artex Av ANG/EP BN16 ...... 207 K1
  SWTR RH13 ...... 4 F9
Arthur Rd CRAWW RH11 ...... 19 M6
Arthur St HOVE BN3 ...... 193 H4
Arun Cl ANG/EP BN16 ...... 207 K2
  ARUN BN18 ...... 141 M5
  EPSF GU31 ...... 90 B2
  LAN/SOMP BN15 ...... 189 K5
  SALV BN13 ...... 187 L5
Arun Ct PUL/STOR BN20 ...... 122 D2
Arun Crs ARUN BN18 ...... 157 L3
Arundel By-pass ARUN BN18 .... 184 B1
Arundel Cl BOGR PO21 ...... 203 H8 🔟
  CRAWE RH10 ...... 21 K6
  SHOR BN43 ...... 191 K4
  SWTR RH13 ...... 82 B3 🔟
Arundel Dr East ROTT BN2 ...... 213 K3
Arundel Dr West ROTT BN2 ...... 213 J3
Arundel Pl ROTT BN2 ...... 194 F8
Arundel Rd ANG/EP BN16 ...... 186 A5
  ARUN BN18 ...... 181 M1
  LHPTN BN17 ...... 206 E2
  ROTT BN2 ...... 194 F8
  SALV BN13 ...... 187 L4
Arundel Wy MIDOS PO22 ...... 205 J7
Arun Pde LHPTN BN17 ...... 206 E4
Arun Rd BIL RH14 ...... 79 K3
  BOGR PO21 ...... 203 H8
Arunside HORS RH12 ...... 60 B3
Arun St ARUN BN18 ...... 184 C2
Arun V PUL/STOR BN20 ...... 121 K7
Arun Wy BOGR PO21 ...... 220 C6
  SWTR RH13 ...... 60 F3
Ascot Cl SELS PO20 ...... 217 G4
Ascot Wk ANG/EP BN16 ...... 207 M2
Ashacre La SALV BN13 ...... 188 A5
Ashacre Ms SALV BN13 ...... 188 A5
Ashacre Wy SALV BN13 ...... 188 A5
Ashburnham Cl BRI BN1 ...... 172 F7 🔟
  CCH PO19 ...... 178 E5
  SALV BN13 ...... 187 J7 🔟
Ashburnham Dr BRI BN1 ...... 172 E6
Ashburnham Rd CRAWE RH10 .... 3 M8
Ash Cl CRAWE RH10 ...... 23 K3
  FIN/BW BN14 ...... 165 M6
  HOVE BN3 ...... 193 K1
Ashcroft Av SHOR BN43 ...... 191 L5
Ashcroft La HORN PO8 ...... 132 A6
Ashcroft Wy BOGR PO21 ...... 220 B5
Ashdown Av ROTT BN2 ...... 213 J3
Ashdown Cl ANG/EP BN16...... 186 A8
  HWH RH16 ...... 88 C8
Ashdown Dr CRAWE RH10 ...... 40 F2
Ashdown Rd ROTT BN2 ...... 194 C4
  WTHG BN11 ...... 9 H3
Ashdown Vw EGRIN RH19 ...... 24 E5
Ashenground Cl HWH RH16 .. 109 M1 🔟
Ashenground Rd HWH RH16 .. 109 L1
Ashe Rd HAV PO9 ...... 152 E7 🔟
Ashfield Cl MIDH GU29 ...... 94 F4
Ashfield Rd MIDH GU29 ...... 94 F5
Ashfold Av FIN/BW BN14 ...... 188 B3
Ashford Rd BRI BN1 ...... 194 B2

Ash Gv HASM GU27 ...... 51 H7
  HWH 109 L2
  LIPH GU30 ...... 49 L1
  MIDOS PO22 ...... 203 K5
  WTHG BN11 ...... 9 J5
Ash Keys CRAWE RH10 ...... 3 G6
Ash La ANG/EP BN16 ...... 207 K3
  HORL RH6 ...... 15 G1
Ashleigh Cl ANG/EP BN16 ...... 186 A6
  HORL RH6 ...... 15 G1
Ashleigh Rd HORS RH12 ...... 4 D2
Ashley Cl BRI BN1 ...... 171 M5
  HAV PO9 ...... 152 A8
Ashlings Wy HOVE BN3 ...... 192 F2 🔟
  SHOR BN43 ...... 191 J3
Ashmere Gdns MIDOS PO22 .... 204 E7
Ashmere La MIDOS PO22 ...... 204 E7
Ashmore Cl HORS RH12 ...... 18 D6
Ash Rd CRAWE RH10 ...... 3 L1
  CRAWE 21 H4
  SWTR RH13 ...... 81 M3
Ashton Gdns ANG/EP BN16 .... 207 K4
Ashton Rd ROTT BN2 ...... 11 G5
Ash Tree Cl HASM GU27 ...... 29 G3 🔟
Ashurst Av ROTT BN2 ...... 213 M4
Ashurst Cl BOGR PO21 ...... 203 H6
  FERR BN12 ...... 209 J3
  HORS RH12 ...... 5 M1
Ashurst Dr CRAWE RH10 ...... 21 L6
  FERR BN12 ...... 209 J3
Ashurst Rd ROTT BN2 ...... 173 C2
Ashurst Wy ANG/EP BN16 ...... 208 A2
Ashway BURH RH15 ...... 131 H2 🔟
Ashwood Cl HISD PO11 ...... 214 D1
  WTHG BN11 ...... 9 M2
Ashwood Dr ANG/EP BN16 ...... 207 K3
Aspen Cl HWH RH16 ...... 88 C8
Aspen Wy HORS RH12 ...... 5 M1
  MIDOS PO22 ...... 204 F6 🔟
Aston Ri PUL/STOR BN20 ...... 122 D1
Astra Cl HISD PO11 ...... 214 F1
Astrid Cl HISD PO11 ...... 214 F1
Athelstan Cl CRAWE RH10 .... 21 M6
Athelstan Rd SALV BN13 ...... 8 A2
Atherley Rd HISD PO11 ...... 196 B7
Atkinson Cl CRAWE RH10 .... 21 K8 🔟
Atlingworth St ROTT BN2 ...... 11 H8
Attree Dr ROTT BN2 ...... 11 J5
Aubrey Cl HISD PO11 ...... 196 B8 🔟
Auckland Cl CRAWW RH11 .... 20 E3 🔟
Auckland Dr ROTT BN2 ...... 195 G3
Audrey Cl BRI BN1 ...... 171 M1
Augusta Pl WTHG BN11 ...... 9 G7
Augustines Wy HWH RH16 .... 87 M8
Aurum Cl HWH RH16 ...... 15 J2 🔟
Austen Cl EGRIN RH19 ...... 24 C3
Avalon Wy SALV BN13 ...... 187 L6
Avebury Cl HORS RH12 ...... 38 B5
  SELS PO20 ...... 217 K7
Aveling Cl CRAWE RH10 .... 21 K8 🔟
The Avenals ANG/EP BN16 .... 186 B7
Avenue Ap CCH PO19 ...... 6 D2
Avenue Cl LIPH GU30 ...... 26 C8
Avenue De Chartres CCH PO19.... 6 C5
Avenue Gdns HORL RH6 ...... 15 K2
Avenue Rd GSHT GU26 ...... 27 L1
  HISD PO11 ...... 196 C1
The Avenue BOGR PO21 ...... 12 A6
  CCH PO19 ...... 179 C2
  EPSF GU31 ...... 90 C1
  FERR BN12 ...... 187 K8
  CSHT GU26 ...... 27 L1
  HASM GU27 ...... 28 A5
  HORL RH6 ...... 15 G2
  LIPH GU30 ...... 26 B8
  RCCH PO18 ...... 154 F5
  RCCH PO18 ...... 176 E3
  ROTT BN2 ...... 179 C2
  SHOR BN43 ...... 190 F3
  SWTR RH13 ...... 59 L6
Avery Cl PTSD BN41 ...... 170 A8
Avian Gdns BOGR PO21 ...... 220 C2 🔟
Aviary Cl CRAWE RH10 ...... 23 K3
Avisford Park Rd ARUN BN18 .... 182 F4
Avocet Quay EMRTH PO10 .... 175 K5
Avon Cl LAN/SOMP BN15 ...... 189 J6
  MIDOS PO22 ...... 204 D7
  PSF GU32 ...... 90 B2
Avondale Cl FERR BN12 ...... 209 L1 🔟
Avondale Rd HOVE BN3 ...... 193 L5
Avonhurst BURH RH15 ...... 131 J1
Avon Rd LHPTN BN17 ...... 206 E3
Avon Wk CRAWW RH11 ...... 20 A7
Awbrook Cl RHWH RH17 ...... 111 G1 🔟
Aylwin Pl SELS PO20 ...... 201 K3
Aymer Rd HOVE BN3...... 193 H6
Ayshe Court Dr SWTR RH13 .... 5 G6
Azalea Cl HAV PO9 ...... 152 F8
Azalea Dr HASM GU27 ...... 28 A4 🔟

B

Babsham La BOGR PO21 ...... 203 G4
Back La BIL RH14 ...... 54 F2
  CRAWE RH10 ...... 42 D2
  RHWH RH17 ...... 88 D5
Backwoods Cl HWH RH16 ...... 88 B8
Backwoods La HWH RH16 ...... 88 A8
Bacon La HISD PO11 ...... 214 A1
Baden Powell Rd LISS GU33 .... 47 M2
Baden Rd ROTT BN2 ...... 194 E4
Badger Cl PTSD BN41 ...... 192 C2
Badger Dr RHWH RH17 ...... 87 K7
Badgers Cl HORS RH12 ...... 88 C3
Badgers Holt PUL/STOR RH20.. 144 C3
Badgers Wk BURH RH15 ...... 131 L2 🔟
Badgers Wy BIL RH14 ...... 33 H8
  EGRIN RH19 ...... 24 E3
Badgers Wd PUL/STOR BN20 .... 123 L6
Badger Wy BRI BN1 ...... 172 F6
Baffin's La CCH PO19 ...... 6 F5
Bailey Cl ANG/EP BN16 ...... 207 H1 🔟
  HORS RH12 ...... 38 A5
Bailing Hi HORS RH12 ...... 36 F6
Baird Cl CRAWE RH10 ...... 41 H4
Bakehouse Barn Cl
  HORS RH12 ...... 37 M5 🔟
Baker Cl CRAWE RH10 ...... 2 F8
Bakers Arms Hi ARUN BN18 .... 184 C1 🔟

Bakers Fld LISS GU33 ...... 47 J2
Baker's La SWTR RH13 ...... 81 J8
Baker St BRI BN1 ...... 10 F3
Bakery La BOGR PO21 ...... 12 C8 🔟
Balchins Cl BIL RH14 ...... 78 C4
Balcombe Av FIN/BW BN14 .... 188 D7
Balcombe Gdns HORL RH6 .... 15 K2
Balcombe La RHWH RH17 ...... 66 A4
Balcombe Rd CRAWE RH10 .... 21 L5
  CRAWE 41 M3
  HWH 87 L4
Baldwin Cl CRAWE RH10 .... 41 K1 🔟
  LHPTN BN17 ...... 204 E6
Balfour Dr LISS GU33 ...... 47 H8
Balfour Gdns FROW RH18 .... 45 M4
Balfour Rd BRI BN1 ...... 194 A1
  CRAWE RH10 ...... 21 L3 🔟
Balliol Cl BOGR PO21 ...... 202 F8
  CRAWE RH10 ...... 21 L3
Balmoral Cl BOGR PO21 ...... 220 C2
  CCH PO19 ...... 7 L5 🔟
Balmoral Wy PSF GU32 ...... 68 C8
Balsdean Rd ROTT BN2 ...... 195 L3
Bamborough Cl SWTR RH13 .... 82 B3
Bamford Cl ROTT BN2 ...... 195 H2
Bampfield St PTSD BN41 ...... 192 C4 🔟
Bancroft Rd CRAWE RH10 ...... 21 L7
Banjo Rd LHPTN BN17 ...... 206 F5
Bank La CRAWE RH10 ...... 2 F3
Bank Pas STEY/UB BN44 ...... 167 L1
Banks Cft PUL/STOR BN20 ...... 143 M2
Bankside BRI BN1 ...... 171 K7
  HPPT/KEY BN6 ...... 131 G7
Banks Rd CRAWE RH10 ...... 21 K7
  RING/NEW BN8 ...... 111 M3
Bankview Cl BOGR PO21 .... 12 E4 🔟
Bannerman Rd PSF GU32 ...... 68 C8 🔟
Bannings V ROTT BN2 ...... 213 L4
Bannister Gdns
  PUL/STOR RH20 ...... 143 M1
Bannister Wy HWH RH16 ...... 87 L6
Banstead Cl FERR BN12 ...... 209 K3
Barancraig Av BRI BN1 ...... 172 A5
Barbary La FERR BN12 ...... 208 F3
Barber Cl CRAWE RH10 ...... 41 K2
Barfield Pk LAN/SOMP BN15 .... 190 A6
Barford Rd CCH PO19 ...... 6 A1
Barham Rd PSF GU32 ...... 90 C1
Barkdale BURH RH15 ...... 109 L7
Barker Cl RCCH PO18 ...... 178 D5
Barkworth Wy
  PUL/STOR RH20 ...... 123 K5
Bar La SWTR RH13 ...... 82 C7
Barlavington Wy MIDH GU29 .... 94 F7
Barley Cl BOGR PO21 ...... 220 A2
  CRAWE RH10 ...... 2 F6
Barleycroft SWTR RH13 ...... 105 M3
Barley Dr BURH RH15 ...... 108 F3
Barlow Rd CCH PO19 ...... 6 A2
  CRAWW RH11 ...... 39 M1
Barnard Ga HWH RH16 ...... 87 M5
Barn Cl CRAWW RH11 ...... 40 C5
  EMRTH PO10 ...... 175 G4
  HPPT/KEY BN6 ...... 129 K6
  LHPTN BN17 ...... 184 F4
  SALV BN13 ...... 188 A5
Barn Cottage La HWH RH16 .... 88 B7
Barn Ct CRAWE RH10 ...... 3 G7
Barncroft Cl SELS PO20 .... 180 D3 🔟
Barncroft Wy HAV PO9 ...... 174 A1
Barn End HFD BN5 ...... 128 A7
Barnes Rd PTSD BN41 ...... 192 C4 🔟
Barnett Cl SELS PO20 ...... 181 M4
Barnett Rd BRI BN1 ...... 194 C2
Barnett's Fld SELS PO20 ...... 181 L5
Barnet Wy HOVE BN3 ...... 192 F1
Barn Fld MIDOS PO22 ...... 13 K5
Barnfield Cl EMRTH PO10 ...... 176 B2
Barnfield Dr CCH PO19 ...... 179 K4
Barnfield Gdns
  HPPT/KEY BN6 ...... 151 M1 🔟
Barn Field Gdns ROTT BN2 .... 11 K5
Barnfield Rd CRAWE RH10 .... 2 F1
Barnham La MIDOS PO22 ...... 182 D5
Barnham Rd SELS PO20 ...... 182 A5
Barnhouse Cl
  PUL/STOR BN20 ...... 122 D2 🔟
Barn House La
  PUL/STOR BN20 ...... 122 D2
Barn La MIDOS PO22 ...... 203 L3
Barnmead HWH RH16...... 87 L5
Barn Meadow RHWH RH17 .... 65 H3
Barn Ri BRI BN1 ...... 171 L7
  MIDOS PO22 ...... 182 D6
Barn Rd SELS PO20 ...... 217 G5
Barns Farm La
  PUL/STOR RH20 ...... 144 C5
Barnsfold La HORS RH12 ...... 33 M6
Barnside RCCH PO18 ...... 177 L5
Barnside Av BURH RH15 ...... 131 L5
Barnside Wy LISS GU33 ...... 69 J1
Barnsite Gdns ANG/EP BN16.... 207 J2
Barnsnap Cl HORS RH12 ...... 37 L6
Barn Wk SELS PO20 ...... 217 G6
Barnwood Cl CRAWE RH10 .... 21 K5
Baron Cl SELS PO20 ...... 181 L5
Barons Ct BURH RH15 ...... 131 J2
Barons Md BOGR PO21 ...... 220 B4
Barque Cl ANG/EP BN16 .... 207 H2 🔟
Barrack La BOGR PO21 ...... 220 C2
Barrhill Av BRI BN1 ...... 193 J1
Barrington Cl FERR BN12 .... 209 K2 🔟
  HWH RH16 ...... 88 B4
Barrington Rd CRAWE RH10 .... 2 E1
  FERR BN12 ...... 209 K2
  SWTR RH13 ...... 5 G7
Barrington Wd HWH RH16 .... 88 A4 🔟
Barrow Cl BRI BN1 ...... 194 D2 🔟
Barrowfield RHWH RH17 ...... 87 G5
Barrowfield Cl HOVE BN3 .... 193 K1 🔟
Barrowfield Dr HOVE BN3 .... 193 K2
Barrow Hi BRI BN1 ...... 194 D2
  HFD BN5 ...... 128 A8
Barry Cl CRAWE RH10 ...... 40 F1
Barry Wk ROTT BN2 ...... 11 K5
Bartholomew Cl HASM GU27 .... 28 B4
Bartholomew BRI BN1 ...... 10 E7 🔟
Bartholomew Wy HORS RH12.. 38 B6

Barton Cl BOGR PO21 ...... 220 B3
  SALV BN13 ...... 188 B7 🔟
Barton Crs EGRIN RH19 ...... 25 K4
Barton La PETW GU28 ...... 98 A4
Bartons Rd HAV PO9 ...... 152 D7
Barton Wy SELS PO20 ...... 217 J6
Barttelot Rd HORS RH12 ...... 4 D9
Barwell Gv EMRTH PO10 .... 175 H1 🔟
Barwick Cl ANG/EP BN16 ...... 207 J1
Bashfords La FIN/BW BN14 ...... 9 J2
Bashford Wy CRAWE RH10 .... 21 L4
Bashurst Copse SWTR RH13 .... 59 C4
Bashurst Hi SWTR RH13 ...... 58 E8
Basildon Wy CRAWW RH11 .... 39 M1
Basing Hi PUL/STOR RH20 .... 125 K5
Basin Rd HAV PO9 ...... 152 B7
Basin Rd CCH PO19 ...... 6 A6
Basin Rd South PTSD BN41 .... 192 A6
Bassels Rd SWTR RH13 ...... 104 B6
Bassett Rd BOGR PO21 ...... 12 C8
  CRAWE RH10 ...... 41 L1
Batchmere Rd SELS PO20 ...... 218 A2
Batemans Cl SALV BN13 .... 187 J7 🔟
Batemans Ct CRAWE RH10 .... 3 M9
Batemans Rd ROTT BN2 ...... 195 M5
Bates Rd BRI BN1 ...... 194 A2
Bath Pl WTHG BN11 ...... 9 H7
Bath Rd EMRTH PO10 ...... 175 J4
  WTHG BN11 ...... 8 C8
Bath St BRI BN1 ...... 10 C8
Bathurst Cl HISD PO11 ...... 214 B1
Battens Wy HAV PO9 ...... 152 C8
Batts Dr HFD BN5 ...... 127 L7
Batts La PUL/STOR RH20 ...... 123 G3
Bavant Rd BRI BN1 ...... 193 M2
Baxter Cl CRAWE RH10 .... 21 J8 🔟
Baxter St ROTT BN2 ...... 11 K3
Baybridge Rd HAV PO9 ...... 152 C8
Baycombe La ARUN BN18 .... 160 E6
Bayford Rd LHPTN BN17 ...... 206 E4
Bayhams Rd EGRIN RH19 ...... 44 A6
Bayhorne La HORL RH6 ...... 15 K3
Bayley Rd SELS PO20 ...... 180 D3
Baynards Rd HORS RH12 ...... 34 B2
Baythorn La HORL RH6 ...... 15 K3
Baytree Cl SELS PO20 ...... 179 C2
Bay Tree Cl SHOR BN43 .... 191 K3 🔟
Bay Tree Gdn ANG/EP BN16 .... 208 A3 🔟
Bay Wk BOGR PO21 ...... 220 D4
Baywood Gdns ROTT BN2 .... 195 K3
Bazehill Rd ROTT BN2 ...... 213 H1
Beach Cl BOGR PO21 ...... 220 D3
Beach Crs LHPTN BN17 ...... 206 F5
Beachcroft Pl
  LAN/SOMP BN15 ...... 189 M8
Beach Gdns SELS PO20 ...... 222 F7
Beach Gn SHOR BN43 ...... 190 E6
Beach Pde WTHG BN11 ...... 9 K6
Beach Rd BOGR PO21 ...... 220 B5
  EMRTH PO10 ...... 175 H4
  HISD PO11 ...... 214 B1
  LHPTN BN17 ...... 206 F4
  SELS PO20 ...... 223 H4
  SHOR BN43 ...... 190 F7
Beachside CRAWE RH10 ...... 3 J4
Beachy Rd CRAWW RH11 ...... 40 B3
Beacon Cl BRI BN1 ...... 194 B2
Beacon Gn HOVE BN3 ...... 190 G6
Beacon Hurst HPPT/KEY BN6.... 151 J1
Beaconsfield Cl MIDOS PO22 .... 204 F7 🔟
Beaconsfield Rd BRI BN1 ...... 10 E2 🔟
  LHPTN BN17 ...... 206 E1
  PTSD BN41 ...... 192 C4
Beaconsfield Vis BRI BN1 ...... 194 A3
Beacon Sq EMRTH PO10 ...... 175 H5
The Beacon EGRIN RH19 ...... 43 M5
Beacon Wy LHPTN BN17 ...... 207 H2
Beagle Dr ARUN BN18 ...... 205 J2
Beal Crs BRI BN1 ...... 194 C2
Beale St BURH RH15 ...... 130 F3
Bear Rd ROTT BN2 ...... 194 D4
Bearsden Wy HORS RH12...... 59 L1
Beatty Av BRI BN1 ...... 172 E5
Beatty Rd BOGR PO21 ...... 12 D5
Beaufield Cl SELS PO20 ...... 222 F7 🔟
Beaufort Rd HAV PO9 ...... 174 A2
Beaufort Ter ROTT BN2 ...... 11 J4
Beaulieu Av HAV PO9 ...... 152 A6
Beaumont Cl CRAWW RH11 .... 19 M7 🔟
Beaumont Pk LHPTN BN17 .... 207 H4
Beaumont Rd FIN/BW BN14 .... 188 E7 🔟
Beaver Cl CCH PO19 ...... 178 C6
  HORS RH12 ...... 37 M6
Beccles Rd WTHG BN11 ...... 8 D5
Becket Rd FIN/BW BN14 ...... 8 B3
Beckett La CRAWW RH11 .... 20 E3
Beckford Wy CRAWE RH10 .... 41 J3
Beckham La PSF GU32 ...... 68 A8
Beckley Cl ROTT BN2 ...... 194 F7
Beckworth Cl HWH RH16 ...... 88 B6
  SALV BN13 ...... 187 J7 🔟
Beckworth La HWH RH16 ...... 88 B6
Bedale Cl CRAWW RH11 ...... 2 C8
Bedales Hi HWH RH16 ...... 88 E7
Bedelands Cl BURH RH15 .... 109 J7 🔟
Bedenscroft BOGR PO21 ...... 221 H1
Bedford Av BOGR PO21 ...... 203 H6
Bedford Cl HAV PO9 ...... 174 E4
Bedford Pl BRI BN1 ...... 10 A6
Bedford Rd PSF GU32 ...... 90 A1
  SWTR RH13 ...... 4 F9
Bedford Rw WTHG BN11 ...... 9 J6
Bedford Sq BRI BN1 ...... 10 A7
Bedford St BOGR PO21 ...... 12 D7
  ROTT BN2 ...... 11 J8
Bedham La PUL/STOR BN20 .... 99 H8
Bedhampton Wy HAV PO9 .... 152 C8
Beech Av CCH PO19 ...... 6 A4
  SELS PO20 ...... 222 F7
Beech Cl FIN/BW BN14 .... 165 M5 🔟
  PTSD BN41 ...... 192 A1
  SELS PO20 ...... 181 L5 🔟

Beechers Rd PTSD BN41 ...... 192 A1
Beeches Av WTHG BN11 ...... 188 C5
Beeches Crs CRAWE RH10 ...... 3 C1
The Beeches BRI BN1 ...... 193 L1
Beechey Cl CRAWE RH10 ...... 22 C1
Beechey Wy CRAWE RH10 ...... 22 C1
Beech Flds EGRIN RH19 ...... 25 C1
Beech Gdns CRAWE RH10 ...... 23 H5
Beech Gv HOVE BN3...... 196 E8
  MIDH GU29 ...... 94 F6
  PUL/STOR BN20 ...... 144 A1
  ROTT BN2 ...... 194 F1
Beech Hanger End GSHT GU26.... 27 J3 🔟
Beech Hi HWH RH16 ...... 110 C1
Beech Holme CRAWE RH10 .... 23 H4
Beech Hurst Cl SWTR RH13 .... 87 K8 🔟
Beechings HFD BN5 ...... 127 L7
Beeching Wy EGRIN RH19 .... 24 E3
Beechlands Cl ANG/EP BN16 .... 208 A3
Beech Rd FIN/BW BN14 ...... 165 M6
  HASM GU27 ...... 28 A5
  HORS RH12 ...... 38 C7
Beechside CRAWE RH10 ...... 3 J4
Beech Tree Cl CRAWW RH11 .... 2 F1 🔟
Beech Vw ANG/EP BN16 ...... 186 A5
Beech Wd HFD BN5 ...... 148 A5
Beechwood SWTR RH13...... 81 K4
Beechwood Av BRI BN1 ...... 172 A8
  SALV BN13 ...... 188 A5
Beechwood Cl BRI BN1 ...... 172 A8
Beechwood Ct LISS GU33 .... 47 K6 🔟
Beechwood La LISS GU28 .... 119 H7
Beechwoods BURH RH15 ...... 131 H3
Beechworth Rd HAV PO9 .... 174 D3
Beeding Av HOVE BN3 ...... 193 C1
Beeding Cl HORS RH12 ...... 5 M1
  LAN/SOMP BN15 ...... 189 L4
Beedingwood Dr HORS RH12.. 38 C6
Beehive Cl FERR BN12 .... 209 C3 🔟
Beehive La FERR BN12 ...... 208 F3
Beehive Ring Rd CRAWE RH10.. 15 J8
Beggar's La POY/PYE BN45 .... 149 L1
Beggar's Wood Rd
  RING/NEW BN8 ...... 111 K6
Behenna Cl CRAWW RH11 .... 19 M7 🔟
Belfast Cl HOVE BN3 ...... 193 L6
Belgrave Crs CCH PO19 ...... 201 C1
Belgrave Pl ROTT BN2 ...... 11 L9
Belgrave St ROTT BN2 ...... 11 C4
Belinus Dr BIL RH14 ...... 79 K4
Bellair Rd HAV PO9 ...... 174 D3
Bellamy Rd CRAWE RH10 ...... 41 K2
Bell Cl CCH PO19 ...... 6 C1
Bell Ct BOGR PO21 ...... 220 D2
Bell Davies Rd LHPTN BN17 .... 207 H4
Belle Meade Cl SELS PO20 .... 181 L7
Bellevue Gdns ROTT BN2 ...... 11 K7
Bellevue La EMRTH PO10 ...... 175 J2
Bell Hammer EGRIN RH19 .... 24 E3
Bell Hi PSF GU32 ...... 68 A7
Bell Hill Rdg PSF GU32 ...... 68 B7
Bellingham Crs HOVE BN3 .... 192 E4
Bell La MIDH GU29 ...... 116 C4
  SELS PO20 ...... 217 L2
Belloc Cl CRAWE RH10 ...... 21 J5
Belloc Ct SWTR RH13 ...... 5 M5 🔟
Belloc Rd LHPTN BN17 ...... 206 D1
Bell Rd HASM GU27 ...... 51 H1
  HORS RH12 ...... 37 H4
Bellscroft Cl LHPTN BN17 .... 207 G2 🔟
Bell Vale La HASM GU27 ...... 28 C8
Bellview Rd SALV BN13 ...... 188 B7
Belmont BRI BN1...... 10 E3
Belmont Cl HWH RH16 ...... 130 F7
Belmont La HPPT/KEY BN6 .... 130 D7
Belmont St BOGR PO21 ...... 12 E8
  BRI BN1 ...... 10 E3
Belmont Ter ARUN BN18 ...... 205 H2
Belsize Cl WTHG BN11 ...... 8 C4
Belsize Rd WTHG BN11 ...... 8 C4
Belton Rd ROTT BN2 ...... 11 L5
Belvedere Av
  LAN/SOMP BN15 ...... 189 L6 🔟
Belverdere Cl PSF GU32 .... 68 C8 🔟
Belyngham Crs LHPTN BN17 .... 206 D2
Bembridge Dr HISD PO11 ...... 214 F3
Bembridge St ROTT BN2 ...... 11 K1
Benbow Cl SHOR BN43 ...... 191 H4
Benchfield Cl EGRIN RH19 ...... 25 H4
Benedict Cl WTHG BN11 ...... 211 H1
Benedict Dr WTHG BN11 ...... 211 H1
Benett Av HOVE BN3 ...... 193 J2
Benett Dr HOVE BN3 ...... 193 J2
Benfield Cl PTSD BN41 ...... 192 D4
Benfield Crs PTSD BN41 ...... 192 D3
Benfield Wy PTSD BN41 ...... 192 D4
Bengairn Av BRI BN1 ...... 172 B5
Benjamin Cl CRAWE RH10 .... 21 L8 🔟
Bennett Cl CRAWE RH10 .... 41 J2 🔟
Bennett Rd ROTT BN2 ...... 194 F8
Bennetts Cl SELS PO20 ...... 223 H4
Bennetts La RHWH RH17 ...... 107 K1
Bennetts Rd SWTR RH13 ...... 60 F3
Bens Acre SWTR RH13 ...... 5 M8
Benson Rd HFD BN5 ...... 128 A7
Benson's La HORS RH12 ...... 38 D3
Bentham Rd ROTT BN2 ...... 11 J3
Bentley Ct HAV PO9 ...... 152 E7 🔟
Bentons La SWTR RH13 ...... 125 L1
Bentswood Crs HWH RH16 .... 88 B7
Bentswood Rd HWH RH16 .... 88 A7
Bepton Cl MIDH GU29 ...... 94 E6
Bepton Down EPSF GU31 ...... 90 C1
Bepton Rd MIDH GU29 ...... 94 E6
Berberis Ct SHOR BN43 .... 191 J3 🔟
Beresford Rd ROTT BN2 ...... 11 M7
Bereweeke Cl MIDOS PO22 .... 13 L5
Bergamot Crs SHOR BN43 .... 191 J3
Berghestede Rd MIDOS PO22.. 203 L6
Berkeley Cl CRAWW RH11 .... 39 M2 🔟
Berkeley Rw BRI BN1 ...... 172 D5
Berkeley Sq HAV PO9 ...... 174 B5
  WTHG BN11 ...... 8 B6
Bernard Pl BRI BN1 ...... 10 F1
Bernard Rd ARUN BN18 ...... 184 A2
  ROTT BN2 ...... 11 L4
  WTHG BN11 ...... 210 A3
Berriedale Av HOVE BN3 ...... 192 F6 🔟
Berriedale Cl LAN/SOMP BN15.. 189 K5
Berriedale Dr LAN/SOMP BN15.. 189 K5

errybarn La SELS PO20 216 C4
erry Cl BURH RH15 109 H7
errylands LISS GU33 47 K5
errylands Farm
HPPT/KEY BN6 129 L3
Berry La LHPTN BN17 207 G4
MIDOS PO22 203 H5
RHWH RH17 66 D5
Berrymill Cl BOGR PO21 12 E4
Bersted St MIDOS PO22 12 D3
Berwick Rd ROTT BN2 213 L1
Bessborough Ter
LAN/SOMP BN15 189 L8 1
Betchley Cl EGRIN RH19 24 F1 1
Bethune Cl CRAWE RH10 21 L7 2
Bethune Rd SWTR RH13 5 G9
Bethwines Cl RCCH PO18 178 B4
Betts Wy CRAWW RH11 20 E2
Bevendean Av ROTT BN2 213 L3
Bevendean Crs ROTT BN2 194 F2
Bevendean Rd ROTT BN2 194 E4
Beverley Cl SELS PO20 223 H5 1
Beverley Gdns ANG/EP BN16 207 J2
Beverley Ms CRAWE RH10 3 L5 1
Bewbush Dr CRAWW RH11 40 A1
Bewley Rd ANG/EP BN16 186 A6
Bexhill Rd ROTT BN2 195 L3
Bex La MIDH GU29 116 F2
Biggin Cl CRAWW RH11 2 C7
Bignor Cl ANG/EP BN16 207 L1 1
HORS RH12 38 B6
Bignor Park Rd
PUL/STOR RH20 120 E8
Bigwood Av HOVE BN3 193 L5
Bilberry Cl CRAWW RH11 40 C1 1
Billinghurst Rd
PUL/STOR RH20 124 F4
Billingshurst Rd HORS RH12 59 K1
Billinton Dr CRAWE RH10 21 J6
Billy Lawn Av HAV PO9 152 C8
Bilsham La ARUN BN18 204 F3
Bilsham Rd ARUN BN18 205 G3
Binderton La RCCH PO18 156 E2
Binney Ct CRAWE RH10 21 M3 1
Binstead Av MIDOS PO22 13 M1
Binstead Cl CRAWW RH11 20 C4 1
Binsted Cl ANG/EP BN16 207 J4
Binsted La ARUN BN18 183 H2
Birch Av HWH RH16 110 B1
Birch Cl ANG/EP BN16 186 A8
ARUN BN18 183 M3
BOGR PO21 220 E1
CRAWE RH10 23 K4
HWH RH16 110 C1
LAN/SOMP BN15 189 L8
LISS GU33 47 K8
Birch Dr BIL RH14 79 L5
Birch End PUL/STOR RH20 123 L5
Birchen La HWH RH16 87 M4
Birches Cl SALV BN13 187 K7
SELS PO20 222 E5
Birches Rd HORS RH12 38 C7
The Birches CRAWE RH10 3 M1
SWTR RH13 61 K5
Birch Gv PUL/STOR RH20 123 L7
Birch Grove Crs BRI BN1 172 B7
Birchgrove Rd RHWH RH17 67 L7
Birch Lea CRAWE RH10 21 H3
Birch Tree Cl EMRTH PO10 153 J8
Birch Tree Dr EMRTH PO10 153 J8
Birch Tree La PUL/STOR RH20 123 L6
Birch Wy HWH RH16 110 B2
PUL/STOR RH20 144 C2
Birchwood Cl CRAWE RH10 41 K1 2
Birchwood Grove Rd
BURH RH15 131 J3
Birdham Cl BOGR PO21 203 G7
CRAWW RH11 20 C4 2
Birdham Rd HISD PO11 215 H2
ROTT BN2 194 F1
SELS PO20 200 C6
Birkdale Cl SALV BN13 187 L6
Birkdale Dr CRAWW RH11 19 L7
Birkdale Rd SALV BN13 187 L6
Birling Cl ROTT BN2 194 E3
Biscay Cl ANG/EP BN16 207 J2
Bisham Cl CRAWE RH10 41 L1 1
Bishearne Gdns LISS GU33 47 H7 1
Bishop Luffa Cl CCH PO19 178 E5
Bishopric HORS RH12 4 A7
Bishops Cl BOGR PO21 220 B4
HASM GU27 51 H6
HFD BN5 127 M7
Bishopsgate Wk CCH PO19 6 F2
Bishops Rd HOVE BN3 193 K3
SELS PO20 180 E2
Bishopstoke Rd HAV PO9 152 B7
Bishopstone Dr ROTT BN2 213 J2
Bishopstone La
HPPT/KEY BN6 108 B7
RHWH RH17 108 B5
Bitmead Cl CRAWW RH11 19 M7 4
Bittern Cl CRAWW RH11 19 L7
Bitterne Cl HAV PO9 152 C6
Blackberry La CCH PO19 7 J5
Blackboy La RCCH PO18 178 B5
Blackbridge La HORS RH12 60 B3
Blackcap Cl CRAWW RH11 2 C7
HAV PO9 152 D3
Black Dog Wk CRAWE RH10 20 F4 1
Blackdown Crs HAV PO9 152 B8
Blackdown Rd SALV BN13 188 A5 1
Blackett Rd CRAWE RH10 21 K7
Blackfold Rd CRAWE RH10 3 L5 2
Blackgate La HFD BN5 127 M8
Black Gate La PUL/STOR RH20 100 D3
Blackheath CRAWE RH10 21 L4
Black Hl HWH RH16 88 B5
Black Horse Wy HORS RH12 4 B8
Blackhouse La BURH RH15 109 J8
PETW GU28 76 E6
Blackhouse Rd SWTR RH13 39 K6
Black Lion St BRI BN1 10 E8
Blackman St BRI BN1 10 E4
Blackman Wy SELS PO20 201 J3
Blackmill La RCCH PO18 159 K8
Blacksmiths Cl
PUL/STOR RH20 125 H8 1
Blacksmiths Crs
LAN/SOMP BN15 189 J6
Blackstone La HFD BN5 128 F7
Blackstone St HFD BN5 128 E7
Blackstone Wy BURH RH15 109 H7
Black Swan Cl CRAWW RH11 40 C5
Blackthorn Cl BRI BN1 193 L1 1
CRAWW RH11 20 D4
PTSD BN41 192 C2 1
SWTR RH13 5 K7
Blackthorn Dr HISD PO11 214 F1
Blackthorn Rd HISD PO11 214 F1
Blackthorns HPPT/KEY BN6 130 A5
HWH RH16 88 B5
Blackthorns Cl HWH RH16 88 B5
The Blackthorns BURH RH15 109 J7
Blackwater La CRAWE RH10 21 K7
Blackwell Farm Rd EGRIN RH19 25 G1
Blackwell Hollow EGRIN RH19 25 G2
Blackwell Rd EGRIN RH19 25 G2
Bladon Cl HAV PO9 174 F1 1
Blake Cl CRAWE RH10 41 G2
Blakehurst La ARUN BN18 185 H2
Blakehurst Wy LHPTN BN17 206 E2
Blakemyle BOGR PO21 221 G2
Blaker St ROTT BN2 11 G7
Blakes Farm Rd SWTR RH13 82 A1
Blakes Rd MIDOS PO22 13 L5
Blanches Rd SWTR RH13 127 H1
Blanches Wk SWTR RH13 127 H1 1
Blanford Rd CCH PO19 7 H1
The Blatchen LHPTN BN17 207 G4
Blatchford Cl SWTR RH13 5 J6 1
Blatchford Rd SWTR RH13 5 J5
Blatchington Rd HOVE BN3 193 J5
Blendworth Crs HAV PO9 174 B1
Blenheim Av SALV BN13 187 M6
Blenheim Cl ANG/EP BN16 207 J1 1
CRAWE RH10 21 L3 2
EGRIN RH19 25 H1
Blenheim Ct BOGR PO21 202 F8
Blenheim Dr ANG/EP BN16 207 J1
Blenheim Flds FROW RH18 45 M1
Blenheim Gdns CCH PO19 7 K5
HAV PO9 174 E2
Blenheim Pl BRI BN1 10 F5 1
Blenheim Rd ARUN BN18 205 G2
HORS RH12 4 E2
LAN/SOMP BN15 189 L8
Bligh Cl CRAWE RH10 3 J8
Blindley Rd CRAWE RH10 21 L3 3
Blissford Cl HAV PO9 152 E6 1
Blomfield Dr CCH PO19 179 H3
Blondell Dr BOGR PO21 220 E1
Bloomsbury Pl ROTT BN2 11 K9
Bloomsbury St ROTT BN2 11 K9
Bloor Cl HORS RH12 37 L5
Blount Av EGRIN RH19 24 D3
Bluebell Cl CRAWW RH11 40 C1 2
EGRIN RH19 24 C3
HORS RH12 5 G2
HWH RH16 88 A8 1
Bluebell Dr ANG/EP BN16 207 J1
Blueberry Hl PUL/STOR RH20 144 C3
Blue Cedars Cl ANG/EP BN16 185 M8
Bluecoat Pond SWTR RH13 59 L6
Blundell Av HORL RH6 15 G1
Blunden Dr RHWH RH17 87 G4
Blunts Wy HORS RH12 4 C6
Blunts Wood Crs RHWH RH17 87 J6
Blunts Wood Rd RHWH RH17 87 J6
The Blytons EGRIN RH19 24 C3
Bob La RHWH RH17 106 F6
Boddingtons La
HPPT/KEY BN6 151 L1 1
Bodiam Av FERR BN12 209 H2
ROTT BN2 195 J3
Bodiam Cl CRAWE RH10 21 K6
ROTT BN2 195 J2
SWTR RH13 82 B2
Bodmin Cl SALV BN13 187 L4 1
Bodmin Rd SALV BN13 187 L4
Bognor Rd CCH PO19 7 J5
HORS RH12 36 B4
RDKG RH5 16 D5
Bolding Wy HWH RH16 109 L2
Boleyn Cl CRAWE RH10 41 L1
Boleyn Dr BOGR PO21 220 C3
Bolney Chapel Rd RHWH RH17 107 J4
Bolney Ct CRAWW RH11 40 A1
Bolney Lodge La RHWH RH17 107 J1
Bolney Rd RHWH RH17 107 M3
ROTT BN2 173 G8
Bolney St RHWH RH17 107 K1
Bolnore Rd HWH RH16 87 K8
Bolsover Rd HOVE BN3 192 F5
SALV BN13 209 M1
Bolton Rd CRAWE RH10 41 J3
Boltro Rd HWH RH16 87 L7
Bonchurch Rd ROTT BN2 11 K1
Bondfields Crs HAV PO9 152 C6
Bond St ARUN BN18 184 B1
BRI BN1 10 E6
Bones La EPSF GU31 90 A7
Bonfire La RHWH RH17 67 K8
Bonnar Cl SELS PO20 222 E6
Bonnar Rd SELS PO20 222 F6
Bonnetts La CRAWW RH11 20 B1
Bonny Wood Rd
HPPT/KEY BN6 150 F1
Bookers La SELS PO20 217 K4
Booth Rd CRAWW RH11 39 M1
Borage Cl CRAWW RH11 40 B2 1
Bordehill La HWH RH16 65 L8
Borden La LIPH GU30 71 G6
Border Cha CRAWE RH10 22 B2
Border Rd HASM GU27 27 L6
Bordon Rd HAV PO9 152 C7
Borough Gv PSF GU32 90 B2
Borough Hl PSF GU32 90 B1
Borough Rd PSF GU32 90 A2
Borough St BRI BN1 10 A6
Borrowdale Cl CRAWW RH11 2 B8 1
Borrow King Cl ROTT BN2 194 E3 1
Bosham La RCCH PO18 177 J7
Bosham Rd CRAWE RH10 41 K1 3
Bosmere Gdns EMRTH PO10 175 H3
Bosmere Rd HISD PO11 215 H2
Bostal Rd STEY/UB BN44 167 J3
The Bostal STEY/UB BN44 168 D3
Bost Hl FIN/BW BN14 187 M1
SALV BN13 187 M2
Bostock Av HORS RH12 5 M3
Boston Rd HWH RH16 88 B7
Boston St BRI BN1 10 E2
Boswell Rd CRAWE RH10 3 G9
Botany Cl ANG/EP BN16 207 L4
Botley Dr HAV PO9 152 A7
Bough Beeches BURH RH15 131 K3 1
The Boulevard CRAWE RH10 2 F3
FERR BN12 187 M8
SALV BN13 187 L7
Boundary & Station Roads
PTSD BN41 192 D6
Boundary Cl WTHG BN11 8 C7
Boundary Rd CRAWE RH10 3 H2
GSHT GU26 27 L1
LAN/SOMP BN15 190 C7
RHWH RH17 42 C8
WTHG BN11 8 B7
Boundary Wy ANG/EP BN16 208 C2 1
HAV PO9 174 B3
Bound La HISD PO11 214 D2
Boundstone Cl
LAN/SOMP BN15 189 L5
Boundstone La
LAN/SOMP BN15 189 L6 2
Bourg-de-peage Av
EGRIN RH19 25 H3
Bourne Cl CCH PO19 178 B5
SALV BN13 187 J6 1
The Bourne HPPT/KEY BN6 130 F6
Bourne View Cl EMRTH PO10 176 A2
Bourne Wy MIDH GU29 94 F6
Bowater Rd CRAWE RH10 41 K1
Bower La PUL/STOR RH20 123 L6
Bowers Pl CRAWE RH10 23 J4
The Bower HWH RH16 87 L7 1
Bowes Cl SWTR RH13 5 H5
Bowes Hl HAV PO9 152 F1
Bowhill La RCCH PO18 155 L5
Bowley La SELS PO20 201 M7
Bowling Green La HORS RH12 4 E6
Bowmans Cl STEY/UB BN44 146 E8
Bowness Av LAN/SOMP BN15 189 K7
Bowring Wy ROTT BN2 11 M8
Boxall Wk SWTR RH13 60 E3
Box Cl CRAWW RH11 40 D3
Boxes La RHWH RH17 67 K8
Boxgrove FERR BN12 187 J8 1
Boxgrove Cl LAN/SOMP BN15 190 A6
Boxgrove Gdns BOGR PO21 220 D2
Boxham La SELS PO20 218 E1
Box La EGRIN RH19 25 M6
Box Tree Av ANG/EP BN16 207 J3
Boyce's St BRI BN1 10 D7
Brackenbury Cl PTSD BN41 192 C2 2
Bracken Cl CRAWE RH10 20 F4
CRAWE RH10 22 C2
PUL/STOR RH20 144 C2
Bracken Gv HORS RH12 38 C7
Bracken La PUL/STOR RH20 144 B2
Bracken Rd EPSF GU31 90 F2
Bracklesham Cl SELS PO20 217 J6
Bracklesham La SELS PO20 217 J6
Bracklesham Rd HISD PO11 215 J3
Bradbury Rd CRAWE RH10 41 K1
Brading Rd ROTT BN2 11 K2
Bradley Ct HAV PO9 152 E7
Bradlond Cl BOGR PO21 221 H2
Bradshaw Rd CCH PO19 7 J1
Braemar Wy BOGR PO21 203 G5
Braemore Rd HOVE BN3 192 F6
Braeside Av BRI BN1 172 A5
Braeside Cl HASM GU27 28 A4
Brainsmead RHWH RH17 86 F4
Brainsmead Cl RHWH RH17 86 F5 1
Brairwood Gdns HISD PO11 214 C1
Braishfield Rd HAV PO9 152 D8
Bramber Av HOVE BN3 193 G1
PUL/STOR RH20 143 K2
Bramber Cl BOGR PO21 203 H8 2
CRAWE RH10 20 F4 2
HWH RH16 87 L8
LAN/SOMP BN15 189 L4
Bramber Rd CCH PO19 7 G7
FIN/BW BN14 188 F5
STEY/UB BN44 167 L2
Bramber Wy BURH RH15 109 H8
Bramble Cl CRAWE RH10 22 C1
HAV PO9 174 F1 2
SALV BN13 187 L5
Bramble Crs SALV BN13 187 L4
Brambledean Rd PTSD BN41 192 C5
Bramble Gdns BURH RH15 108 E8
Bramble Hl RHWH RH17 65 G3
Bramble La SALV BN13 187 L5
Bramble Md RHWH RH17 65 G3
Bramble Ri BRI BN1 171 K7
Bramble Rd EPSF GU31 90 F1
Brambles HPPT/KEY BN6 131 G7 1
The Brambles RHWH RH17 87 H6
Brambletye La FROW RH18 45 L1
Brambletye Rd CRAWE RH10 3 L5
Brambletyne Av ROTT BN2 213 L5
Brambletyne Cl
ANG/EP BN16 186 B6 1
Brambling Cl SWTR RH13 61 H3
Brambling La MIDH GU29 94 C1
Brambling Rd HAV PO9 152 E3
SWTR RH13 61 H3
The Bramblings ANG/EP BN16 207 L3
Bramdean Dr HAV PO9 152 A7
Bramfield Rd MIDOS PO22 204 D8
Bramlands La HFD BN5 148 D3
Bramley Cl CRAWE RH10 3 K3
FIN/BW BN14 188 E6 1
Bramley Gdns EMRTH PO10 175 L4
MIDOS PO22 203 J5
Bramley Rd FIN/BW BN14 188 E6
Bramley Wk HORL RH6 15 K1 1
Brampton Cl SELS PO20 222 F5
Bramshaw Ct HAV PO9 152 E7 3
Brandon Cl CRAWE RH10 21 L8
Brandy Hole La CCH PO19 178 F2
Brangwyn Av BRI BN1 171 M6
Brangwyn Crs BRI BN1 171 M6
Brangwyn Dr BRI BN1 171 L6
Brangwyn Wy BRI BN1 171 M7
Brantridge La RHWH RH17 64 A7
Brantridge Rd CRAWE RH10 3 J7
Brasslands Dr PTSD BN41 192 A3
Braybon Av BRI BN1 172 A8
Bray Cl CRAWE RH10 21 L8 3
Braypool La BRI BN1 171 L4
Brazwick Av BOGR PO21 203 G5
Breach Av EMRTH PO10 176 A2
Breach Cl STEY/UB BN44 167 L1
Bread La LHPTN BN17 206 A6
Bread St BRI BN1 10 E6
Bream La SELS PO20 222 D4
Brecon Cl SALV BN13 188 A5
Brede Cl ROTT BN2 194 F7
Breezehurst Dr CRAWW RH11 40 A1
Brendon Rd SALV BN13 187 M4
Brendon Wy ANG/EP BN16 207 J2
Brent Ct EMRTH PO10 175 H4
Brent Rd BOGR PO21 203 H8
Brentwood Cl BRI BN1 194 C1 1
Brentwood Crs BRI BN1 194 C1
Brentwood Rd BRI BN1 194 C1
Brettingham Cl CRAWW RH11 39 M1 1
Bretton BURH RH15 108 F7
Brewells La LISS GU33 48 B6
Brewer Rd CRAWE RH10 2 F7
Brewer St ROTT BN2 11 H2
Brewers Yd PUL/STOR RH20 143 L3 1
Brewery Hl ARUN BN18 184 C2 1
Brewhurst La BIL RH14 56 B2
Briar Av SELS PO20 217 G3
Briar Cl ANG/EP BN16 186 A8
ARUN BN18 205 G1
CRAWW RH11 20 D3
ROTT BN2 195 L4
SELS PO20 180 D6
Briarcroft Rd ROTT BN2 195 L5
Briarswood Cl CRAWE RH10 21 L4
Briar Wd LISS GU33 47 K5
Brickfield Cl BOGR PO21 12 A3
Brick Kiln Cl SWTR RH13 84 B1
Bricklands CRAWE RH10 23 J5
Brickyard La CRAWE RH10 23 J4
Brideake Cl CRAWW RH11 40 B1 1
Bridge Cl BURH RH15 109 G8
FERR BN12 209 K1
LAN/SOMP BN15 189 M7
Bridgefield Cl MIDH GU29 94 F6 1
Bridgefoot Pth EMRTH PO10 175 J4
Bridgelands CRAWE RH10 22 A1
Bridge Mdw LISS GU33 47 J8
Bridge Rd CCH PO19 7 H3
EMRTH PO10 175 J3
FIN/BW BN14 9 G3
HASM GU27 28 D5
HORS RH12 34 E5
HWH RH16 88 A5
LHPTN BN17 206 C3
Bridgersmill HWH RH16 87 L5
The Bridgeway SELS PO20 222 F6
Bridgnorth Cl SALV BN13 187 J7
Bridle Cl GSHT GU26 27 H1
STEY/UB BN44 168 C2
Bridle Rd ARUN BN18 160 E8
Bridle Wy CRAWE RH10 21 L5
The Bridle Wy SELS PO20 222 F5
Bridorley Cl BOGR PO21 220 C2
Brierley Gdns
LAN/SOMP BN15 190 A6 1
Brigden St BRI BN1 10 C2
Brigham Pl MIDOS PO22 204 E8 1
Brighton Pl BRI BN1 10 E7 2
Brighton Rd CRAWE RH10 40 D5
CRAWW RH11 2 E8
CRAWW RH11 40 D4
HFD BN5 128 A8
HORL RH6 15 G1
HPPT/KEY BN6 149 L2
HPPT/KEY BN6 150 E2
LAN/SOMP BN15 190 A8
RHWH RH17 63 K5
SHOR BN43 190 E6
SWTR RH13 60 F4
WTHG BN11 9 J6
WTHG BN11 211 K1
Brighton Road Hornbrook Hl
SWTR RH13 61 G4
Brights La HISD PO11 196 C7
Brills La BRI BN1 10 E8 1
Brimfast La SELS PO20 200 F7
Brisbane Cl CRAWW RH11 20 E3 3
SALV BN13 187 J6
Bristol Av LAN/SOMP BN15 190 C7
Bristol Cl CRAWE RH10 21 L3
Bristol Gdns CCH PO19 179 G2
ROTT BN2 194 F8
Bristol Ga ROTT BN2 11 M8
Bristol Ms ROTT BN2 194 F8
Bristol Pl ROTT BN2 194 F8
Bristol Rd ROTT BN2 11 J8
Bristol St ROTT BN2 194 F8
Brittany Rd FIN/BW BN14 8 F1
HOVE BN3 192 E6
Britten Cl CRAWW RH11 40 A1
Britten's La ARUN BN18 159 M7
Broadbridge Ct RCCH PO18 177 K5
Broadbridge Heath Rd
HORS RH12 36 E8
Broad Cft HAV PO9 152 F2
Broadfield EGRIN RH19 43 M5
Broadfield Dr CRAWW RH11 40 C1
Broadfield Pl CRAWW RH11 40 C2
Broadfields ROTT BN2 194 F1 1
Broadfields Rd ROTT BN2 194 F1 2
Broadford Bridge Rd BIL RH14 102 A6
PUL/STOR RH20 123 M1
Broad Gn ROTT BN2 195 M6
Broad Green Av BURH RH15 131 K2
Broadlands BURH RH15 131 J4
Broadmark Av ANG/EP BN16 207 K4
Broadmark La ANG/EP BN16 207 K4
Broadmark Wy ANG/EP BN16 207 K4
Broadmere Av HAV PO9 152 C7
Broad Piece LHPTN BN17 206 C2 1
Broad Rig Av HOVE BN3 170 E8
Broad Rd RCCH PO18 176 E4
Broad Strd ANG/EP BN16 207 L5
Broad St RHWH RH17 87 G6
ROTT BN2 10 F8
Broad Vw SELS PO20 223 H5
Broadview Gdns SALV BN13 187 M4
Broad Wk RCCH PO18 117 L7
The Broad Wk RCCH PO18 155 K6
Broadwater La SWTR RH13 82 E3
Broadwater Rd FIN/BW BN14 9 G1
Broadwater St East
FIN/BW BN14 188 E7
Broadwater St West
FIN/BW BN14 188 E7
Broadwater Wy FIN/BW BN14 188 E6
Broadway SELS PO20 222 E4 1
The Broadway CCH PO19 179 H2
CRAWE RH10 2 F4
HWH RH16 87 L7
LAN/SOMP BN15 190 C7
Broadwood Cl HORS RH12 5 L2
Broadwood Ri CRAWW RH11 40 B3
Brock End RHWH RH17 86 F4
Brockenhurst Av HAV PO9 152 A6
Brockhampton La HAV PO9 174 B3
Brockhampton Rd HAV PO9 174 A3
Brockhurst Cl HORS RH12 60 A3 1
Brocklands HAV PO9 174 A3
Brockley Cl FIN/BW BN14 8 E2
Brock Rd CRAWW RH11 20 C3
Bromley Cl HPPT/KEY BN6 131 H8
Bromley Rd ROTT BN2 11 G1
Brompton Cl BRI BN1 171 M6
The Brontes EGRIN RH19 24 E3 1
Bronze Cl MIDOS PO22 203 K5
Brook Av HPPT/KEY BN6 151 G1
RCCH PO18 177 J7
Brook Barn Wy FERR BN12 209 M3
Brook Cl BOGR PO21 203 G8
EGRIN RH19 25 J3
PUL/STOR RH20 144 A1 1
WTHG BN11 189 H8
Brookdean Rd WTHG BN11 211 J1
Brookenbee Cl ANG/EP BN16 207 J1 2
Brooker Pl HOVE BN3 193 H5
Brooker's Rd BIL RH14 79 L5
Brooker St HOVE BN3 193 H5
Brookfield Cl HAV PO9 174 B2 1
Brookfield La PETW GU28 96 E3
Brookfield Wy BIL RH14 79 L6
Brook Gdns EMRTH PO10 175 G4
Brook Gn RHWH RH17 86 F3
Brook Hl SWTR RH13 105 M1
Brookhill Cl CRAWE RH10 22 B1
Brookhill Rd CRAWE RH10 22 B2
Brooklands BOGR PO21 220 B3
Brooklands Rd CRAWW RH11 40 D3
Brooklands Wy EGRIN RH19 24 E4
Brookland Wy PUL/STOR RH20 121 K7
Brook La ANG/EP BN16 207 K1
FERR BN12 208 F3
HORS RH12 38 E5
HWH RH16 88 A4
PUL/STOR RH20 121 K7
Brooklyn Av WTHG BN11 210 A2
Brookmead Wy HAV PO9 174 C5
Brookpits La LHPTN BN17 205 M4
Brook Rd HORS RH12 37 M6
Brookside CRAWE RH10 3 J2
CRAWE RH10 22 B1
PUL/STOR RH20 125 H8 2
SELS PO20 201 M3
Brookside Av ANG/EP BN16 207 K1
Brookside Cl FERR BN12 208 F1 1
SELS PO20 201 M3
Brookside Rd ANG/EP BN16 208 E4
HAV PO9 174 A4
Brooks La MIDOS PO22 13 G2
RCCH PO18 177 L4
Brooks La West MIDOS PO22 12 F2
Brooksmead MIDOS PO22 13 H4
The Brooks BURH RH15 108 F7
Brook St RHWH RH17 86 F3
Brooks Wy PUL/STOR RH20 122 D2
The Brook SWTR RH13 82 B2
Brookview CRAWE RH10 22 B1
PUL/STOR RH20 121 K7
Brookway BURH RH15 131 K1
HWH RH16 88 B4
Brook Wy LAN/SOMP BN15 190 A7
Broomcroft Rd MIDOS PO22 204 D8
Broomdashers Rd CRAWE RH10 3 K2
Broome Cl HORS RH12 4 E1
Broomers Hill La
PUL/STOR RH20 100 F8
Broomers La SELS PO20 200 A7
Broomfield Av FIN/BW BN14 188 C7
Broomfield Dr BIL RH14 79 M5
PTSD BN41 170 B8
Broomfield Rd HFD BN5 127 L7
SELS PO20 223 H4
Broom Rd EPSF GU31 90 F2
Brou Cl ANG/EP BN16 208 C3
Brougham Rd WTHG BN11 211 H1
Brow Cl PUL/STOR RH20 143 J3
Browning Cl CRAWE RH10 21 K5
Browning Rd LAN/SOMP BN15 189 M4
WTHG BN11 8 D4
Browning's Hl SWTR RH13 105 K2
The Brownings EGRIN RH19 24 D3 1
Brownleaf Rd ROTT BN2 195 M6
Brown's La PUL/STOR RH20 143 L3
The Brow BURH RH15 131 H2
ROTT BN2 195 L4
Broxhead Rd HAV PO9 152 D6 1
Broxmead La RHWH RH17 85 M7
Broyle Cl CCH PO19 179 G3
Broyle Rd CCH PO19 179 G3
Bruce Av WTHG BN11 210 A2
Bruce Cl HWH RH16 109 M1
Bruce Wy WTHG BN11 210 A1
Brunel Pl CRAWE RH10 3 H5
Brunswick Cl CRAWE RH10 3 L7
MIDOS PO22 13 M2
Brunswick Gdns HAV PO9 174 A2
Brunswick Ms HOVE BN3 193 L7 1
Brunswick Pl HOVE BN3 193 L6
Brunswick Rd HOVE BN3 193 L6
SHOR BN43 191 G5
WTHG BN11 8 E8
Brunswick Sq HOVE BN3 193 L7
Brunswick St East HOVE BN3 193 L7
Brunswick St West
HOVE BN3 193 L7 2
Brunswick Ter HOVE BN3 193 L7
Brushes La HWH RH16 88 C4
Brushwood Rd HORS RH12 38 C6
Bryce Cl HORS RH12 5 L2

Buchans Lawn *CRAWW* RH11 ...... 40 C2
Buci Crs *SHOR* BN43 ...... 191 K4
Buckhurst Cl *ARUN* BN19 ...... 24 C1
Buckhurst Wy *EGRIN* RH19 ...... 24 D1
Buckingham Av *SHOR* BN43 ...... 190 F6
Buckingham Cl *SHOR* BN43 ...... 191 H4 🔢
Buckingham Dr *CCH* PO19 ...... 7 L5
EGRIN RH19 ...... 25 H5
Buckingham Ga *HORL* RH6 ...... 15 K4
Buckingham Ms *SHOR* BN43 ...... 191 G3 🔢
Buckingham Pl *BRI* BN1 ...... 10 C3
Buckingham Rd *BRI* BN1 ...... 10 D4
PSF GU32 ...... 90 A1
SHOR BN43 ...... 191 G5
WTHG BN11 ...... 9 G6
Buckingham St *BRI* BN1 ...... 10 D4 🔢
SHOR BN43 ...... 190 F5 🔢
Buckland Dr *BOGR* PO21 ...... 220 C2
Bucklers Ct *HAV* PO9 ...... 152 A5
Buckler St *PTSD* BN41 ...... 192 C4 🔢
Buckley Cl *HOVE* BN3 ...... 170 F8
Buckley Pl *CRAWW* RH11 ...... 23 H4
Buckmans Rd *CRAWW* RH11 ...... 2 D3
Buckmore Av *PSF* GU32 ...... 68 A8
Bucknor Rd *BOGR* PO21 ...... 220 D2
Bucksham Av *BOGR* PO21 ...... 203 G5
Buckshead Hl *STWR* BN13 ...... 62 A5
Buckswood Dr *CRAWW* RH11 ...... 2 A7 🔢
CRAWW RH11 ...... 20 B8
Buckwish La *HFD* BN5 ...... 127 K8
Buddington La *MIDH* GU29 ...... 95 G1
Budgen Cl *CRAWE* RH10 ...... 21 L3
Buffbeards La *HASM* GU27 ...... 27 M5
Bugshill La *MIDH* GU29 ...... 115 K3
Bulkington Av *FIN/BW* BN14 ...... 8 D2
Bulldogs Bank *EGRIN* RH19 ...... 44 M3
Buller Rd *ROTT* BN2 ...... 194 E3
Bullfinch Cl *HORS* RH12 ...... 37 K5
Bull Hl *LISS* GU33 ...... 48 B8
Bull's La *SWTR* RH13 ...... 84 E8
Bunbury Crs *PUL/STOR* RH20 ...... 144 C2
Bunch La *HASM* GU27 ...... 28 B5
Bunch Wy *HASM* GU27 ...... 28 B6
Buncton La *RHWH* RH17 ...... 107 M2
Bunting Cl *SWTR* RH13 ...... 5 J6
Bunyan Cl *CRAWW* RH11 ...... 39 M1
Burchetts Cl *HWH* RH16 ...... 109 L2
Burchett Wk *BOGR* PO21 ...... 203 G7
Burch Gv *ARUN* BN18 ...... 182 E3
Burdale Dr *HISD* PO11 ...... 215 G1
Burdett Cl *CRAWE* RH10 ...... 21 L7 🔢
Burdock Cl *CRAWW* RH11 ...... 40 B2 🔢
Burford Cl *SALV* BN13 ...... 188 B5
Burford Rd *SWTR* RH13 ...... 5 G7
Burgate Cl *HAV* PO9 ...... 174 A1
Burgess Cl *HISD* PO11 ...... 215 G3
Burghclere Rd *HAV* PO9 ...... 152 E6
Burgh Cl *CRAWE* RH10 ...... 21 L3
Burgh Hill Rd *LIPH* GU30 ...... 26 A5
Burlands *CRAWW* RH11 ...... 20 B3
Burleigh Cl *CRAWE* RH10 ...... 23 J4
Burleigh La *CRAWE* RH10 ...... 23 K5
Burleigh Wy *CRAWE* RH10 ...... 23 J4
Burley Cl *BIL* RH14 ...... 33 H8 🔢
HAV PO9 ...... 152 E6 🔢
LAN/SOMP BN15 ...... 189 M6 🔢
Burley Rd *MIDOS* PO22 ...... 204 A3
Burleys Rd *CRAWE* RH10 ...... 21 L6
Burlington Gdns *PTSD* BN41 ...... 192 D3
SELS PO20 ...... 223 H6
Burlington Rd *FERR* BN12 ...... 209 H4
Burlington St *ROTT* BN2 ...... 11 J9
Burlow Rd *ROTT* BN2 ...... 194 F7
SELS PO20 ...... 199 L8
Burma Cl *HWH* RH16 ...... 88 D6
Burns Gdns *MIDOS* PO22 ...... 204 E7
Burnside Crs *LAN/SOMP* BN15 ...... 189 K7
Burns Rd *CRAWE* RH10 ...... 21 K4
Burns Wy *EGRIN* RH19 ...... 24 D3
HORS RH12 ...... 39 K3
Burnthouse Bostall
HPPT/KEY BN6 ...... 151 K5
Burnt House La *HORS* RH12 ...... 19 G5
Burnthouse La *SWTR* RH13 ...... 83 K8
Burrell Av *LAN/SOMP* BN15 ...... 189 L7
Burrell Cl *SWTR* RH13 ...... 127 H1
Burrell Gn *RHWH* RH17 ...... 87 G4
Burrell Rd *HWH* RH16 ...... 87 L6
The Burrells *SHOR* BN43 ...... 191 J6
Burrows Cl *HAV* PO9 ...... 174 D1
Bursledon Cl *MIDOS* PO22 ...... 13 M3
Burstead Cl *BRI* BN1 ...... 194 C1
Burstowhill La *RHWH* RH17 ...... 66 E6
Burton Cl *HORL* RH6 ...... 15 H7 🔢
Burton Park Rd *PETW* GU28 ...... 119 L2
Burton Vls *HOVE* BN3 ...... 193 L4 🔢
Burwash Cl *ANG/EP* BN16 ...... 208 C1 🔢
Burwash Rd *CRAWE* RH10 ...... 3 L5
HOVE BN3 ...... 192 F1
Bury Dr *FERR* BN12 ...... 209 J2
Bury Hl *PUL/STOR* RH20 ...... 141 G6
Bury Rd *PUL/STOR* RH20 ...... 141 G1 🔢
Bushby Av *ANG/EP* BN16 ...... 207 L3
Bushby La *LAN/SOMP* BN15 ...... 189 K7
Bush Cl *ROTT* BN2 ...... 195 L3
Bush Farm Dr *PTSD* BN41 ...... 192 C2
Bushfield Cl *HAV* PO9 ...... 55 G2
Busticle La *LAN/SOMP* BN15 ...... 189 K5
Bute St *ROTT* BN2 ...... 11 L6
Butler Ct *SALV* BN13 ...... 188 A6 🔢
Butler's Green Rd *HWH* RH16 ...... 87 K8
Butlers Rd *SWTR* RH13 ...... 5 M3
Butterbox La *RHWH* RH17 ...... 89 L8
Buttercup Wk *BRI* BN1 ...... 172 C6
Buttercup Wy *SWTR* RH13 ...... 82 B2 🔢
Butterfield *EGRIN* RH19 ...... 24 D1
Buttermere Cl *HORS* RH12 ...... 38 C6 🔢

Buttermere Wy
ANG/EP BN16 ...... 207 H1 🔢
Butt La *ARUN* BN18 ...... 160 D6
Butts Cl *CRAWE* RH10 ...... 2 B2
Butts Meadow *BIL* RH14 ...... 78 C3
Butts Rd *STHW* BN42 ...... 191 M5
Buxshalls Hl *HWH* RH16 ...... 88 D3
Buxted Ri *BRI* BN1 ...... 172 C7
Buxton Rd *BRI* BN1 ...... 10 D3
Bycroft Wy *CRAWE* RH10 ...... 21 J4
Byerley Cl *EMRTH* PO10 ...... 153 L7 🔢
Byerley Wy *CRAWE* RH10 ...... 21 M5
The Bye Wy *SELS* PO20 ...... 216 D3
The Byeway *SELS* PO20 ...... 216 D3
Byfleets La *HORS* RH12 ...... 36 E7
Bylanes Cl *RHWH* RH17 ...... 87 G5
Bylanes Crs *RHWH* RH17 ...... 87 G5
Byne Cl *PUL/STOR* RH20 ...... 143 M3
Byrd Rd *CRAWW* RH11 ...... 40 A3
Byron Cl *CRAWE* RH10 ...... 21 J5
HORS RH12 ...... 37 M6
MIDOS PO22 ...... 204 E6
Byron Gv *EGRIN* RH19 ...... 24 D4
Byron Rd *ANG/EP* BN16 ...... 207 H3
WTHG BN11 ...... 8 E6
Byron St *HOVE* BN3 ...... 193 H5
By Sunte *HWH* RH16 ...... 88 A4
Bywater Wy *CCH* PO19 ...... 6 C9
Byways *SELS* PO20 ...... 222 F7
The Byway *BRI* BN1 ...... 172 F7
MIDOS PO22 ...... 204 F7
Byworth Cl *ROTT* BN2 ...... 195 G6

C

Caburn Hts *CRAWW* RH11 ...... 2 C8
Caburn Rd *HOVE* BN3 ...... 10 B2
The Cackstones *CRAWE* RH10 ...... 21 L5 🔢
Caedwalla Dr *SELS* PO20 ...... 180 D3 🔢
Caernarvon Rd *CCH* PO19 ...... 7 L5
Caffins Cl *CRAWE* RH10 ...... 20 F4
Cagefoot La *HFD* BN5 ...... 127 M8
Caister's Cl *HOVE* BN3 ...... 193 K4
Cakeham Rd *SELS* PO20 ...... 216 D4
Cakeham Wy *SELS* PO20 ...... 216 F5
Calbourne *HWH* RH16 ...... 87 L7 🔢
Calderdale Cl *CRAWW* RH11 ...... 2 B8
Caledon Av *MIDOS* PO22 ...... 204 E7
Caledonian Rd *CCH* PO19 ...... 6 F5
ROTT BN2 ...... 11 H1
Caledonian Wy *HORL* RH6 ...... 15 J5 🔢
Callender Wk *RHWH* RH17 ...... 87 G4 🔢
Callisto Cl *CRAWW* RH11 ...... 39 M1
Callon Cl *SALV* BN13 ...... 187 J6 🔢
Calluna Dr *CRAWE* RH10 ...... 22 B2
Calvecroft *LIPH* GU30 ...... 26 D8
Camber Cl *CRAWE* RH10 ...... 21 K6
Cambrai Av *CCH* PO19 ...... 7 H6
Cambria *RCCH* PO18 ...... 177 K7
Cambridge Av *SELS* PO20 ...... 216 F4
Cambridge Dr *BOGR* PO21 ...... 203 C8
Cambridge Gv *HOVE* BN3 ...... 193 K5
Cambridge Rd *HOVE* BN3 ...... 193 L6
SWTR RH13 ...... 4 F8
WTHG BN11 ...... 4 E5
Camden St *PTSD* BN41 ...... 192 D6 🔢
Camelford St *ROTT* BN2 ...... 11 G8
Camelia Cl *ANG/EP* BN16 ...... 207 H1
HAV PO9 ...... 174 E1
Camelot Cl *SWTR* RH13 ...... 82 B2
Camelsdale Rd *HASM* GU27 ...... 28 A7
Campbell Crs *EGRIN* RH19 ...... 24 C3
Campbell Dr *ANG/EP* BN16 ...... 207 J2
Campbell Rd *BOGR* PO21 ...... 12 F7
BRI BN1 ...... 10 D1
CRAWE RH10 ...... 21 K8
SELS PO20 ...... 180 C2
Campion Dr *HORS* RH12 ...... 5 G1
Canada Gv *BOGR* PO21 ...... 12 D7
MIDH GU29 ...... 95 H2
Canada Rd *ARUN* BN18 ...... 184 A1
Canal Rd *ARUN* BN18 ...... 205 C2
Canal Whf *CCH* PO19 ...... 6 D7
Canal Wharf Rd *CCH* PO19 ...... 6 D8
Canberra Cl *CRAWW* RH11 ...... 20 E3 🔢
HORS RH12 ...... 5 K3
Canberra Pl *HORS* RH12 ...... 5 K2
SELS PO20 ...... 180 E2
Canberra Rd *EMRTH* PO10 ...... 197 K1
SALV BN13 ...... 187 K6
Canfield Cl *ROTT* BN2 ...... 194 E3
Canfield Rd *ROTT* BN2 ...... 194 E3 🔢
Canhouse La *LISS* GU33 ...... 70 C1
Canning Rd *MIDOS* PO22 ...... 13 K6
Canning St *ROTT* BN2 ...... 11 K6
Cannon Pl *BRI* BN1 ...... 10 C7
Canon La *CCH* PO19 ...... 6 D5
Canon's Cl *BOGR* PO21 ...... 220 E3
Canons Wy *STEY/UB* BN44 ...... 146 E8
Cantelupe Rd *EGRIN* RH19 ...... 24 D4
Canterbury Cl *BOGR* PO21 ...... 220 B3 🔢
CCH PO19 ...... 179 G4
Canterbury Ct *SALV* BN13 ...... 210 A1 🔢
Canterbury Dr *ROTT* BN2 ...... 11 G2
Canterbury Rd *ANG/EP* BN16 ...... 207 L2
CRAWE RH10 ...... 40 F2
SALV BN13 ...... 210 A1
The Canter *CRAWE* RH10 ...... 21 M5
Cants Cl *BURH* RH15 ...... 131 K1
Cants La *BURH* RH15 ...... 109 K8
Canute Rd *ROTT* BN2 ...... 177 J7
Canvey Cl *CRAWW* RH11 ...... 40 D1
Cape Copse *HORS* RH12 ...... 34 E5
Capel La *CRAWW* RH11 ...... 20 A7
Capel Rd *HORS* RH12 ...... 18 C4
Capenors *BURH* RH15 ...... 131 G3
The Cape *LHPTN* BN17 ...... 207 H3
Capricorn Cl *CRAWW* RH11 ...... 19 M8
Capsey Rd *CRAWW* RH11 ...... 19 M7
Capstan Dr *ANG/EP* BN16 ...... 207 H2
Caraway Cl *CRAWW* RH11 ...... 40 C2 🔢
Carden Av *BRI* BN1 ...... 171 M8
Carden Cl *BRI* BN1 ...... 172 B6
Carden Crs *BRI* BN1 ...... 172 B6
Carden Hl *BRI* BN1 ...... 172 C7
Cardew Rd *LISS* GU33 ...... 69 K1
Cardinal's Dr *BOGR* PO21 ...... 220 B3

Carfax *HORS* RH12 ...... 4 C8
Cargo Forecourt Rd *HORL* RH6 ...... 14 E5
Cargo Rd *HORL* RH6 ...... 14 E4
Carisbrooke Cl *HAV* PO9 ...... 174 E2
Carisbrooke Dr *SALV* BN13 ...... 189 M4 🔢
Carisbrooke Dr *SALV* BN13 ...... 187 J7
Carisbrooke Rd *ROTT* BN2 ...... 11 L2
Carleton Rd *CCH* PO19 ...... 6 A1
Carlingford Ct *BOGR* PO21 ...... 12 D4
Carlisle Crs *CCH* PO19 ...... 179 G3
Carlisle Rd *HOVE* BN3 ...... 193 G6
Carlton Av *BOGR* PO21 ...... 220 D1
Carlton Hl *ROTT* BN2 ...... 11 G6
Carlton Ms *WTHG* BN11 ...... 8 A5
Carlton Pl *ROTT* BN2 ...... 11 H6 🔢
Carlton Ter *HOVE* BN3 ...... 192 D4
Carlton Tye *HORL* RH6 ...... 15 L1
Carlyle Av *ROTT* BN2 ...... 194 E3
Carlyle St *ROTT* BN2 ...... 11 K3
Carnegie Cl *CRAWE* RH10 ...... 188 D7
Carnegie Gdns *FIN/BW* BN14 ...... 188 D7
Carnegie Rd *FIN/BW* BN14 ...... 188 D7
Carnforth Rd *LAN/SOMP* BN15 ...... 189 J7
Carol Cl *BRI* BN1 ...... 172 A6
Caron Cl *LAN/SOMP* BN15 ...... 189 M7
Carousel Ct *BOGR* PO21 ...... 12 B2
Carpenters *BRI* BN1 ...... 79 L4
Carpenters Meadow
PUL/STOR RH20 ...... 122 D2 🔢
Carron La *MIDH* GU29 ...... 94 E5
Carse Rd *CCH* PO19 ...... 179 K3
Carter Rd *CRAWE* RH10 ...... 41 L1
Cartersland *LIPH* GU30 ...... 71 J1
Carterslodge La *RHWH* RH17 ...... 62 D4
Carters Wy *BIL* RH14 ...... 78 C4
Carvel Wy *LHPTN* BN17 ...... 207 H2
Carylls Meadow *SWTR* RH13 ...... 104 C5
Casher Rd *CRAWE* RH10 ...... 41 K1
Cassells Rd *CCH* PO19 ...... 179 H3
Cassidy Pl *PUL/STOR* RH20 ...... 143 J3
Castle Av *HAV* PO9 ...... 174 E3
Castle Cl *SALV* BN13 ...... 188 A8
STEY/UB BN44 ...... 167 M2 🔢
Castle Dr *HORL* RH6 ...... 15 K3
Castlegate *PUL/STOR* RH20 ...... 123 J5
Castle La *STEY/UB* BN44 ...... 167 M2
SWTR RH13 ...... 104 A5
Castleman Rd *CCH* PO19 ...... 7 J1
Castlemans La *HISD* PO11 ...... 196 D3
Castlereagh Gn *MIDOS* PO22 ...... 13 M2
Castle Rd *HAV* PO9 ...... 152 D2
HORS RH12 ...... 59 L1
SALV BN13 ...... 188 A8
Castle Sq *BRI* BN1 ...... 10 E7
Castle St *BRI* BN1 ...... 10 D6
The Castle *HORS* RH12 ...... 37 M5
Castleway *HAV* PO9 ...... 174 E3 🔢
Castle Wy *SALV* BN13 ...... 188 A8
STEY/UB BN44 ...... 167 M1
Castlewood Rd *SWTR* RH13 ...... 82 B2
Caterways *HORS* RH12 ...... 60 B1
Cathedral Wy *CCH* PO19 ...... 6 A5
Catherine V *ROTT* BN2 ...... 195 M4
Catherington Wy *HAV* PO9 ...... 152 C8
Cathill La *RDKG* RH5 ...... 16 C1
Catkin Wy *HWH* RH16 ...... 88 C8 🔢
Catsland La *HFD* BN5 ...... 148 D4
Catslands La *HFD* BN5 ...... 148 D4
The Causeway *ARUN* BN18 ...... 184 D2
BOGR PO21 ...... 220 B4
EPSF GU31 ...... 90 B2
FERR BN12 ...... 209 L1
HORS RH12 ...... 4 C9
ROTT BN2 ...... 11 M5
SELS PO20 ...... 199 M6
SELS PO20 ...... 222 F7
Cavalier Cl *MIDH* GU29 ...... 94 F5
Cavalier Wy *EGRIN* RH19 ...... 25 G5
Cavell Wy *CRAWE* RH10 ...... 21 K7
Cavendish Cl *FERR* BN12 ...... 209 L1
HORS RH12 ...... 37 L5
Cavendish Pl *BRI* BN1 ...... 10 A7
Cavendish Rd *BOGR* PO21 ...... 12 C3
Cavendish St *CCH* PO19 ...... 6 C2
ROTT BN2 ...... 11 G7 🔢
Cawley Rd *CCH* PO19 ...... 6 E6
Caxton Cl *CRAWE* RH10 ...... 40 E1 🔢
Caxton Wy *HWH* RH16 ...... 87 M8
Cecilian Av *FIN/BW* BN14 ...... 9 G1
Cecil Rd *LAN/SOMP* BN15 ...... 189 M8
Cedar Av *SALV* BN13 ...... 188 A6
Cedar Cl *BOGR* PO21 ...... 220 E1
BURH RH15 ...... 109 J7
CRAWW RH11 ...... 20 D3
FERR BN12 ...... 208 F3
HORS RH12 ...... 4 B7
LAN/SOMP BN15 ...... 189 J8
SALV BN13 ...... 188 A6
Cedar Cl East *BOGR* PO21 ...... 220 F1 🔢
Cedar Ct *HASM* GU27 ...... 28 B6 🔢
Cedar Dr *CCH* PO19 ...... 6 B3
SWTR RH13 ...... 82 A2
Cedar Gdns *HAV* PO9 ...... 174 D2
Cedars Farm Cl *BIL* RH14 ...... 79 K4
Cedars Gdns *BRI* BN1 ...... 193 L1
The Cedars *ANG/EP* BN16 ...... 207 M2
HWH RH16 ...... 87 L5 🔢
Cedar Wy *HFD* BN5 ...... 128 A8
HWH RH16 ...... 88 C8
Celandine Cl *CRAWW* RH11 ...... 40 B2 🔢
Cemetery La *EMRTH* PO10 ...... 175 M1
PETW GU28 ...... 97 J3
Central Av *ANG/EP* BN16 ...... 207 K4
BOGR PO21 ...... 203 H6
FIN/BW BN14 ...... 188 A1
Central Dr *BOGR* PO21 ...... 203 G6
MIDOS PO22 ...... 205 H7
Centrecourt Cl *FIN/BW* BN14 ...... 8 F2
Centrecourt Rd *FIN/BW* BN14 ...... 8 F2
Centurion Rd *BRI* BN1 ...... 10 D5 🔢
Ceres Pl *MIDOS* PO22 ...... 204 E8 🔢
Chadborn Cl *ROTT* BN2 ...... 11 M8
Chadwick Cl *CRAWW* RH11 ...... 40 C3
Chaffer La *SELS* PO20 ...... 199 L8
Chaffinch Cl *BURH* RH15 ...... 108 E8 🔢
CRAWW RH11 ...... 20 E4 🔢
HORS RH12 ...... 37 L5
SALV BN13 ...... 187 K7 🔢
Chailey Av *ROTT* BN2 ...... 213 H3
Chailey Cl *CRAWW* RH11 ...... 40 B1 🔢

Chailey Crs *ROTT* BN2 ...... 213 M3
Chailey Rd *BRI* BN1 ...... 172 F8
Chainbridge La *SELS* PO20 ...... 222 D3
Chalcraft Cl *LIPH* GU30 ...... 26 B8 🔢
Chalcraft La *BOGR* PO21 ...... 203 G7
Chalder La *SELS* PO20 ...... 219 G1
Chaldon Rd *CRAWW* RH11 ...... 40 D3
Chalet Cl *FERR* BN12 ...... 208 F4 🔢
Chalet Gdns *FERR* BN12 ...... 209 G4 🔢
Chalet Rd *FERR* BN12 ...... 208 F3
Chalfont Cl *MIDOS* PO22 ...... 204 F7
Chalfont Dr *HOVE* BN3 ...... 193 K1
Chalfont La *SALV* BN13 ...... 187 L6
Chalkdock La *SELS* PO20 ...... 199 H7
Chalkers La *HPPT/KEY* BN6 ...... 130 C8
Chalkland Ri *ROTT* BN2 ...... 195 M4
Chalk La *SELS* PO20 ...... 218 F5
Chalk Rd *BIL* RH14 ...... 55 K1
RCCH PO18 ...... 137 H8
Chalky Rd *PTSD* BN41 ...... 192 A1
Challen Cl *SELS* PO20 ...... 180 D5
Challoners *RHWH* RH17 ...... 67 K8
Challoners Cl *ROTT* BN2 ...... 213 G2
Challoners Ms *ROTT* BN2 ...... 213 G2
Challow Cl *HPPT/KEY* BN6 ...... 130 F8 🔢
Chaloner Cl *HWH* RH16 ...... 88 C5
Chaloner Rd *HWH* RH16 ...... 88 C5
Chalton Crs *HAV* PO9 ...... 152 A7
Chalvington Cl *BRI* BN1 ...... 172 F6
Chancellors Pk *HPPT/KEY* BN6 ...... 131 G8
Chanctonbury
PUL/STOR RH20 ...... 125 H8 🔢
Chanctonbury Cl
PUL/STOR RH20 ...... 144 F6
Chanctonbury Dr *SHOR* BN43 ...... 190 F3
Chanctonbury Rd *ANG/EP* BN16 ...... 207 J4
BURH RH15 ...... 131 G3
HOVE BN3 ...... 10 A2
Chanctonbury Vw *HFD* BN5 ...... 127 L8
Chanctonbury Wk
PUL/STOR RH20 ...... 143 L3 🔢
Chanctonbury Wy *CRAWW* RH11 ...... 2 C7
Chancton Cl *PUL/STOR* RH20 ...... 144 C1
WTHG BN11 ...... 210 A1
Chandler Cl *CRAWW* RH11 ...... 2 E8
Chandlers Cl *HISD* PO11 ...... 214 F2 🔢
Chandlers Reach *SELS* PO20 ...... 199 H5 🔢
Chandlers Wy *STEY/UB* BN44 ...... 167 K1
Chandos Rd *WTHG* BN11 ...... 9 F7
Channel Vw *BOGR* PO21 ...... 220 B4 🔢
Channel View Rd *ROTT* BN2 ...... 195 J4
Chantiers Cl *EGRIN* RH19 ...... 24 D2
Chantrey Rd *CRAWE* RH10 ...... 40 F1
Chantry Cl *HFD* BN5 ...... 127 M6
PUL/STOR RH20 ...... 143 M3 🔢
Chantryfield Rd *ANG/EP* BN16 ...... 186 A6
Chantry La *SALV* BN13 ...... 143 L7
Chantry Rd *SALV* BN13 ...... 188 B6
Chapel Cl *BURH* RH15 ...... 109 G7
LHPTN BN17 ...... 206 D2 🔢
Chapelfields *RHWH* RH17 ...... 87 G4
Chapel Hl *MFD/CHID* GU8 ...... 32 A1
Chapel La *EGRIN* RH19 ...... 25 L6
PUL/STOR RH20 ...... 143 H3
RCCH PO18 ...... 178 B1
RHWH RH17 ...... 67 K7
SELS PO20 ...... 217 G2
Chapel Ms *HOVE* BN3 ...... 193 L7 🔢
Chapel Pl *PTSD* BN41 ...... 192 C4
Chapel Rd *PTSD* BN41 ...... 192 B5 🔢
SWTR RH13 ...... 81 G2
WTHG BN11 ...... 9 G4
Chapel Rw *EGRIN* RH19 ...... 43 M5
RCCH PO18 ...... 137 K6
Chapel St *BOGR* PO21 ...... 12 D7
CCH PO19 ...... 6 D3
PSF GU32 ...... 68 C8
ROTT BN2 ...... 11 G7
Chapel Ter *ROTT* BN2 ...... 11 L8
Chapman Rd *CRAWE* RH10 ...... 41 J2
Chapman's La *EGRIN* RH19 ...... 24 E3 🔢
Chappell Cl *LIPH* GU30 ...... 26 D8
Charlecote Rd *WTHG* BN11 ...... 9 J5
Charles Av *BURH* RH15 ...... 130 F2
CCH PO19 ...... 7 K4
Charles Cl *HOVE* BN3 ...... 193 H1
Charles St *PSF* GU32 ...... 90 B1
ROTT BN2 ...... 10 F8
Charleston Cl *HISD* PO11 ...... 214 F2 🔢
Charleston Ct *CRAWE* RH10 ...... 41 J1 🔢
Charlesworth Pk *HWH* RH16 ...... 88 D6
Charlmead *SELS* PO20 ...... 217 G6
Charlock Cl *CRAWW* RH11 ...... 40 B2 🔢
Charlock Wy *SWTR* RH13 ...... 82 K1
Charlotte St *ROTT* BN2 ...... 11 H8
Charlton Mill Wy *RCCH* PO18 ...... 137 G6
Charlton Rd *RCCH* PO18 ...... 136 F5
The Charltons *BRI* BN1 ...... 172 E6 🔢
Charlton St *STEY/UB* BN44 ...... 167 K1
Charlwood Gdns *BURH* RH15 ...... 109 K7
Charlwood Rd *BURH* RH15 ...... 109 K7
CRAWW RH11 ...... 14 D4
HORL RH6 ...... 14 D4
Charlwoods Business Centre
EGRIN ...... 24 E2 🔢
Charlwoods Pl *EGRIN* RH19 ...... 24 F1 🔢
Charlwoods Rd *EGRIN* RH19 ...... 24 E2
Charlwood St *BOGR* PO21 ...... 12 B8
Charlwood Wk *CRAWW* RH11 ...... 20 C3 🔢
Charmandean La
FIN/BW BN14 ...... 188 E4
Charmandean Rd
FIN/BW BN14 ...... 188 E6
Charmans Cl *HORS* RH12 ...... 5 M2
Charnwood Rd *MIDOS* PO22 ...... 12 A1
Charrington Wy *HORS* RH12 ...... 59 K1
Chartfield *HOVE* BN3 ...... 193 H2
Chartwell Dr *HAV* PO9 ...... 174 F1
Chartwell Rd *LAN/SOMP* BN15 ...... 189 L7
Chase Cl *LISS* GU33 ...... 47 K8
Chase La *HASM* GU27 ...... 28 B4
Chase Rd *LISS* GU33 ...... 47 K8
The Chase *CRAWE* RH10 ...... 41 J6
FIN/BW BN14 ...... 165 M7

RHWH RH17 ...... 87 H1
Chatham Pl *BRI* BN1 ...... 10 C
Chatham Rd *WTHG* BN11 ...... 211 H
Chatsmore Crs *FERR* BN12 ...... 209 H
Chatsworth Av *HASM* GU27 ...... 28 D
Chatsworth Cl *ANG/EP* BN16 ...... 207 J1 🔢
Chatsworth Cl *ANG/EP* BN16 ...... 207 J1 🔢
CCH PO19 ...... 7 L
Chatsworth Rd *BRI* BN1 ...... 7 L
Chaucer Av *EGRIN* RH19 ...... 24 D
Chaucer Rd *CRAWE* RH10 ...... 21 J
WTHG BN11 ...... 8 D
Chaucer Av *ANG/EP* BN16 ...... 204 D
Chaucer Av *ANG/EP* BN16 ...... 207 J3
Chawkmare Coppice
BOGR PO21 ...... 220 F2 🔢
Cheal Cl *SHOR* BN43 ...... 191 J6
Cheam Rd *ANG/EP* BN16 ...... 207 L
Cheapside *BRI* BN1 ...... 10 E
Cheeleys *RHWH* RH17 ...... 67 K
Cheesecombe Farm La
LISS GU33 ...... 46 C
Cheesemans La *RCCH* PO18 ...... 154 F
Chelston Av *HOVE* BN3 ...... 192 E
Cheltenham Pl *BRI* BN1 ...... 10 E
Chelwood Av *FERR* BN12 ...... 209 K
Chelwood Cl *BRI* BN1 ...... 172 D
CRAWE RH10 ...... 3 J
Chennells Wy *HORS* RH12 ...... 4 E
Chepstow Cl *CRAWE* RH10 ...... 21 M
Chequer Gra *FROW* RH18 ...... 45 M
Chequer La *RCCH* PO18 ...... 177 L
Chequer Rd *EGRIN* RH19 ...... 25 G3 🔢
Cherington Cl
HPPT/KEY BN6 ...... 130 C7 🔢
Cheriton Cl *HAV* PO9 ...... 152 A8 🔢
Cherrimans Orch *HASM* GU27 ...... 28 A6 🔢
Cherry Av *ARUN* BN18 ...... 205 G
Cherry Cl *BOGR* PO21 ...... 220 E
BURH RH15 ...... 130 F
Cherry Ct *SWTR* RH13 ...... 5 L
Cherry Cft *LHPTN* BN17 ...... 206 F
Cherry Gdns *SALV* BN13 ...... 187 M3 🔢
Cherrylands Cl *HASM* GU27 ...... 51 J6 🔢
Cherry La *CRAWW* RH11 ...... 20 D5
RHWH RH17 ...... 65 G
RHWH RH17 ...... 107 K
SELS PO20 ...... 200 A
Cherry Orchard Rd *CCH* PO19 ...... 7 G
Cherry Tree Av *HASM* GU27 ...... 28 A
Cherry Tree Cl *BIL* RH14 ...... 79 K
CRAWE RH10 ...... 21 L
SALV BN13 ...... 187 L
Cherry Wk *SALV* BN13 ...... 187 M
Cherrywood Gdns *HISD* PO11 ...... 196 D
Cherwell Rd *SALV* BN13 ...... 187 K
Cherwell Wk *CRAWW* RH11 ...... 20 H
FERR BN12 ...... 209 M2
Chesham Pl *ROTT* BN2 ...... 11 M9
Chesham Rd *ROTT* BN2 ...... 11 M9
ROTT BN2 ...... 11 M9
Cheshire Cl *BOGR* PO21 ...... 12 E5
Cheshire Wy *EMRTH* PO10 ...... 176 B2
Chesholt Cl *HASM* GU27 ...... 51 J6
Chesley Cl *SALV* BN13 ...... 187 K6 🔢
Chess Brook Gn *HFD* BN5 ...... 128 A6
Chesswood Av *MIDOS* PO22 ...... 204 D6
Chesswood Cl *WTHG* BN11 ...... 9 M2
Chesswood Rd *WTHG* BN11 ...... 9 L1
Chester Av *LAN/SOMP* BN15 ...... 189 M8
WTHG BN11 ...... 9 M3
Chesterfield Rd *FERR* BN12 ...... 209 L1
Chester Ter *BRI* BN1 ...... 194 B3
Chesterton Cl *EGRIN* RH19 ...... 25 G5
Chestnut Av *CCH* PO19 ...... 179 G1
WTHG GU27 ...... 28 A6
Chestnut Av *ANG/EP* BN16 ...... 186 A8 🔢
BURH RH15 ...... 109 J7
EGRIN RH19 ...... 25 H5
GSHT GU26 ...... 27 J1
LIPH GU30 ...... 49 L1
MIDH GU29 ...... 94 E7
PUL/STOR RH20 ...... 144 C1
Chestnut Ct *CRAWE* RH10 ...... 208 B3 🔢
Chestnut Gdns *HORS* RH12 ...... 4 C3 🔢
HPPT/KEY BN6 ...... 130 A6 🔢
Chestnut Gv *MIDOS* PO22 ...... 12 D1
Chestnut Rdg *PUL/STOR* RH20 ...... 125 K8 🔢
Chestnut Rd *BIL* RH14 ...... 79 L5
Chestnuts Cl *HWH* RH16 ...... 88 B5
The Chestnuts *HPPT/KEY* BN6 ...... 129 L3 🔢
HWH RH16 ...... 88 A5
SELS PO20 ...... 201 H4 🔢
Chestnut Wk *CRAWW* RH11 ...... 20 D3
FERR BN12 ...... 187 J8
PUL/STOR RH20 ...... 122 C2
SELS PO20 ...... 180 D3
Chestnut Wy *HFD* BN5 ...... 127 M6
Chesworth Cl *SWTR* RH13 ...... 60 D4
Chesworth Crs *SWTR* RH13 ...... 60 D3
Chesworth Gdns *SWTR* RH13 ...... 60 D3
Chesworth La *SWTR* RH13 ...... 60 D2
Chetwood Rd *HORS* RH12 ...... 39 L2
Cheveley Gdns *BOGR* PO21 ...... 220 F2 🔢
Chevening Cl *CRAWW* RH11 ...... 40 D3 🔢
Cheviot Cl *ANG/EP* BN16 ...... 208 B2 🔢
SALV BN13 ...... 187 M4
Cheviot Rd *SALV* BN13 ...... 187 M4
Cheyne Wk *HORL* RH6 ...... 15 G3
Chichester Av *HISD* PO11 ...... 214 C2
Chichester By-pass *CCH* PO19 ...... 179 L4
SELS PO20 ...... 6 A7
Chichester Cl *CRAWE* RH10 ...... 40 F2 🔢
HOVE BN3 ...... 170 F8
Chichester Dr *SELS* PO20 ...... 180 D3
Chichester Dr East *ROTT* BN2 ...... 213 K4
Chichester Dr West *ROTT* BN2 ...... 213 J3
Chichester Rd *ROTT* BN2 ...... 11 M9
Chichester Rd *ARUN* BN18 ...... 183 K1
BOGR PO21 ...... 12 B2
BOGR PO21 ...... 203 G5
HISD PO11 ...... 196 F3
MIDH GU29 ...... 95 G7
SELS PO20 ...... 200 E7
SELS PO20 ...... 223 G3
Chichester Ter *HORS* RH12 ...... 4 E8
ROTT BN2 ...... 11 M9

Chichester Wy *BURH* RH15 ...... 109 K7
SELS PO20 ...... 223 J4
Chiddingfold Rd
MFD/CHID GU8 ...... 31 K1
Chiddingley Cl *ROTT* BN2 ...... 195 G7
Chiddingly Cl *CRAWE* RH10 ...... 3 M5
Chidham Cl *HAV* PO9 ...... 174 B2
Chidham Dr *HAV* PO9 ...... 174 B2
Chidham La *RCCH* PO18 ...... 176 F5
Chidham Sq *HAV* PO9 ...... 174 B2 ☑
Chilbolton *BURH* RH15 ...... 131 K3
Chilcomb Cl *HAV* PO9 ...... 174 B1
Chilcroft La *HASM* GU27 ...... 51 J3
Chilcroft Rd *HASM* GU27 ...... 28 A5
Chilcrofts Rd *HASM* GU27 ...... 51 H3
Childerstone Cl *LIPH* GU30 ...... 26 C8 ☑
Chilgrove Cl *FERR* BN12 ...... 209 J1
Chilling St *EGRIN* RH19 ...... 44 E8
EGRIN RH19 ...... 67 J4
Chillis Wood Rd *HWH* RH16 ...... 87 K7
Chiltern Cl *ANG/EP* BN16 ...... 208 B2
CRAWW RH11 ...... 2 B4
HASM GU27 ...... 28 C7
SHOR BN43 ...... 191 J4
Chiltern Crs *SALV* BN13 ...... 187 M4
Chiltington Cl *BURH* RH15 ...... 109 G7 ☑
PUL/STOR RH20 ...... 123 K6
ROTT BN2 ...... 213 K2
Chiltington Wy *ROTT* BN2 ...... 213 K2
Chiltlee Cl *LIPH* GU30 ...... 49 K1
Chiltlee Mnr *LIPH* GU30 ...... 26 D8
Chiltley La *LIPH* GU30 ...... 49 L2
Chiltley Wy *LIPH* GU30 ...... 49 K2
Chilton Cl *CRAN* GU6 ...... 33 G2
The Chine *LHPTN* BN17 ...... 207 H4
Chippendale Rd *CRAWW* RH11 ...... 40 C3
Chippers Cl *SALV* BN13 ...... 188 A8
Chippers Rd *SALV* BN13 ...... 188 A7
Chippers Wk *SALV* BN13 ...... 188 A8 ☑
Chithurst La *LIPH* GU30 ...... 71 J6
Chorley Av *ROTT* BN2 ...... 213 J2
Chownes Mead La *RHWH* RH17 ...... 87 J8
Chrisdory Rd *PTSD* BN41 ...... 191 M1
Christchurch Crs *BOGR* PO21 ...... 220 F1
Christchurch Rd *WTHG* BN11 ...... 9 G4
Christies *EGRIN* RH19 ...... 24 E4 ☑
Christopher Rd *EGRIN* RH19 ...... 24 F3
Christopher Wy *EMRTH* PO10 ...... 175 J2
Christ's Hospital Rd *SWTR* RH13 ...... 59 J6
Church Ap *LHPTN* BN17 ...... 206 F3 ☑
Church Av *HWH* RH16 ...... 87 M6
Church Cl *BOGR* PO21 ...... 219 M4
BRI BN1 ...... 172 A7
BURH RH15 ...... 131 H1
HASM GU27 ...... 29 G2
LAN/SOMP BN15 ...... 189 M4
SALV BN13 ...... 187 G3
STEY/UB BN44 ...... 168 B1 ☑
SWTR RH13 ...... 84 B1
SWTR RH13 ...... 103 L4
Churcher Rd *EMRTH* PO10 ...... 153 L8
Churchfarm La *SELS* PO20 ...... 217 G4
Churchfarm La *SELS* PO20 ...... 218 F2
Church Farm Wk
STEY/UB BN44 ...... 168 B1
Churchfield *PUL/STOR* RH20 ...... 121 H1
Churchfield *EPSF* GU31 ...... 68 E8
Church Gn *SHOR* BN43 ...... 191 K5
Church Gv *PUL/STOR* RH20 ...... 123 J8
Church Hl *ARUN* BN18 ...... 160 D7
BRI BN1 ...... 171 M6
MIDH GU29 ...... 95 G4
POY/PYE BN45 ...... 150 D6
PUL/STOR RH20 ...... 122 C2
Church House Cl *STHW* BN42 ...... 191 M3
Churchill Av *BOGR* PO21 ...... 202 F8
HORS RH12 ...... 4 A5
Churchill Ct *CRAWE* RH10 ...... 21 G3
Churchill Dr *EMRTH* PO10 ...... 153 H4
Churchill Wy *BURH* RH15 ...... 131 K2
Church La *ARUN* BN18 ...... 182 F4
BOGR PO21 ...... 219 L4
CRAWE RH10 ...... 22 B2
EGRIN RH19 ...... 25 G3
FERR BN12 ...... 208 F2
GSHT GU26 ...... 27 K1
HASM GU27 ...... 28 D5
HAV PO9 ...... 174 A4
HFD BN5 ...... 127 M7
HISD PO11 ...... 196 F1
HORL RH6 ...... 15 M6
HORS RH12 ...... 59 L1
HPPT/KEY BN6 ...... 151 J7
HWH RH16 ...... 110 A6
LAN/SOMP BN15 ...... 189 M4
LHPTN BN17 ...... 205 M3
LIPH GU30 ...... 26 C6
LISS GU33 ...... 46 E1
LISS GU33 ...... 47 G2
MIDH GU29 ...... 116 C5
MIDOS PO22 ...... 12 D2
MIDOS PO22 ...... 182 C8
PETW GU28 ...... 96 C2
POY/PYE BN45 ...... 149 L5
POY/PYE BN45 ...... 150 D6
PUL/STOR RH20 ...... 121 K6
PUL/STOR RH20 ...... 125 G8
PUL/STOR RH20 ...... 141 H5
RCCH PO18 ...... 136 A7
RCCH PO18 ...... 155 H7
RCCH PO18 ...... 180 E1
RDKG RH5 ...... 16 A3
RHWH RH17 ...... 66 A4
RHWH RH17 ...... 67 J5
SELS PO20 ...... 180 D3
SELS PO20 ...... 181 M5
SELS PO20 ...... 199 M4
SELS PO20 ...... 201 H4
SELS PO20 ...... 218 F1
STEY/UB BN44 ...... 126 E7
STEY/UB BN44 ...... 146 L8
STEY/UB BN44 ...... 167 L1
STEY/UB BN44 ...... 168 B2
STHW BN42 ...... 191 L5
SWTR RH13 ...... 62 B7
SWTR RH13 ...... 81 L3
SWTR RH13 ...... 127 G1

Church Md *HPPT/KEY* BN6 ...... 151 H1
STEY/UB BN44 ...... 146 E8
Churchmead La *RCCH* PO18 ...... 157 G6
Church Meadow *WTHG* BN11 ...... 177 H7
Church Pth *EMRTH* PO10 ...... 175 J4
RCCH PO18 ...... 134 B8
Church Pl *PUL/STOR* RH20 ...... 122 C2
ROTT BN2 ...... 194 F8
Church Platt *RHWH* RH17 ...... 86 F7
Church Rd *ANG/EP* BN16 ...... 186 A7 ☑
ANG/EP BN16 ...... 207 K3
ARUN BN18 ...... 205 G1
BURH RH15 ...... 131 H1
CCH PO19 ...... 7 L2
CRAWE RH10 ...... 21 M6
CRAWE RH10 ...... 22 C1
CRAWE RH10 ...... 43 G1
EGRIN RH19 ...... 43 M6
EMRTH PO10 ...... 175 L1
EMRTH PO10 ...... 176 A5
EMRTH PO10 ...... 198 A3
HASM GU27 ...... 28 D5
HASM GU27 ...... 51 J7
HISD PO11 ...... 196 D7
HORL RH6 ...... 14 F7
HORL RH6 ...... 15 G2
HORS RH12 ...... 38 C7
HORS RH12 ...... 59 L1
HOVE BN3 ...... 193 H1
HWH RH16 ...... 87 M8
LHPTN BN17 ...... 184 D6
LIPH GU30 ...... 26 D6
MIDH GU29 ...... 95 H6
PSF GU32 ...... 68 B5
PTSD BN41 ...... 192 C5
RHWH RH17 ...... 111 G1
SALV BN13 ...... 188 B7
SELS PO20 ...... 181 H4
SELS PO20 ...... 201 K3
SELS PO20 ...... 217 G5
SELS PO20 ...... 223 G4
SWTR RH13 ...... 61 K7
SWTR RH13 ...... 127 G1
Churchside *CCH* PO19 ...... 6 D2
Church St *ARUN* BN18 ...... 141 L5
BRI BN1 ...... 10 C5
CRAWW RH11 ...... 2 D4 ☑
HFD BN5 ...... 34 E4
HORS RH12 ...... 37 G5
LHPTN BN17 ...... 206 F3 ☑
LISS GU33 ...... 47 H6
PETW GU28 ...... 98 A4
PTSD BN41 ...... 192 C5 ☑
PUL/STOR RH20 ...... 123 H3
PUL/STOR RH20 ...... 143 L3
RHWH RH17 ...... 86 F7
SHOR BN43 ...... 191 G5
STEY/UB BN44 ...... 167 L1
Church Vw *EMRTH* PO10 ...... 175 J4
Church View Cl *HORL* RH6 ...... 15 G2 ☑
Church Wk *HORL* RH6 ...... 15 G2
WTHG BN11 ...... 9 M5
Church Wy *BOGR* PO21 ...... 220 B3
RCCH PO18 ...... 136 C5
SALV BN13 ...... 188 B7
Church Way Cl *SALV* BN13 ...... 188 B7 ☑
PUL/STOR RH20 ...... 99 J8
Churchwood Dr *SELS* PO20 ...... 180 E3
Chute Av *SALV* BN13 ...... 187 M3
Chute Wy *SALV* BN13 ...... 187 M4
Cinder Hl *EGRIN* RH19 ...... 67 J3
The Circle *ANG/EP* BN16 ...... 208 B4 ☑
Circus St *ROTT* BN2 ...... 10 F6
Cissbury Av *CCH* PO19 ...... 6 F6 ☑
Cissbury Av *HORS* RH12 ...... 188 A2
Cissbury Crs *ROTT* BN2 ...... 213 M5
Cissbury Dr *FIN/BW* BN14 ...... 188 A1
Cissbury Gdns *FIN/BW* BN14 ...... 188 B1
Cissbury Hl *CRAWW* RH11 ...... 2 C7
Cissbury Rd *BURH* RH15 ...... 108 F8
FERR BN12 ...... 208 F1
FIN/BW BN14 ...... 188 B6
HOVE BN3 ...... 10 A2
City Fields Wy *SELS* PO20 ...... 180 E2
Civic Centre Rd *HAV* PO9 ...... 174 C2
Civic Wy *BURH* RH15 ...... 131 H1
Claigmar Rd *ANG/EP* BN16 ...... 207 K3
Clair Rd *HWH* RH16 ...... 87 M7
Clapgate La *SWTR* RH13 ...... 35 K7
Clapham Cl *SALV* BN13 ...... 187 G3 ☑
Clapham Common *SALV* BN13 ...... 186 F4
Clappers Ga *CRAWE* RH10 ...... 2 F1 ☑
CRAWW RH11 ...... 2 F1
Clappers La *HFD* BN5 ...... 149 C5
SELS PO20 ...... 217 J4
Clappers Meadow *CRAN* GU6 ...... 33 H2
Clare Cl *CRAWE* RH10 ...... 21 K3
Clare Cl *EPSF* GU31 ...... 90 F1
Claremont Wy *MIDH* GU29 ...... 94 F5
Clarence Av *LHPTN* BN17 ...... 206 D1
Clarence Dr *ANG/EP* BN16 ...... 208 A2
EGRIN RH19 ...... 25 G5
Clarence Rd *BOGR* PO21 ...... 12 F7
SWTR RH13 ...... 4 F9
Clarence Sq *BRI* BN1 ...... 10 C5
Clarence Wy *HORL* RH6 ...... 15 K6
Clarendon Pl *PTSD* BN41 ...... 192 D6 ☑
Clarendon Rd *FIN/BW* BN14 ...... 188 F6
HAV PO9 ...... 174 B3 ☑
HOVE BN3 ...... 193 J4
SHOR BN43 ...... 191 K4
Clarendon Ter *ROTT* BN2 ...... 11 M9 ☑
Clarendon Vls *HOVE* BN3 ...... 193 H5
Clarke Av *HOVE* BN3 ...... 193 G1
Clark Rd *CRAWW* RH11 ...... 40 B3
Clay La *ARUN* BN18 ...... 185 L3
PUL/STOR RH20 ...... 143 H3
RCCH PO18 ...... 177 K3
Claypit La *RCCH* PO18 ...... 179 L1
Clays Cl *EGRIN* RH19 ...... 24 F4 ☑
Clays Hl *STEY/UB* BN44 ...... 167 M2
Clayton Av *HPPT/KEY* BN6 ...... 150 F3
Clayton Dr *BURH* RH15 ...... 131 G3
Clayton Hl *CRAWW* RH11 ...... 2 C7
Clayton La *SELS* PO20 ...... 217 J5
Clayton Rd *HPPT/KEY* BN6 ...... 151 K2
ROTT BN2 ...... 11 J3

SELS PO20 ...... 222 E6
Claytons Cnr *SELS* PO20 ...... 199 M7 ☑
Clayton Wy *HOVE* BN3 ...... 193 G1
Clearwater La *RHWH* RH17 ...... 111 H1
Clearwaters La *RHWH* RH17 ...... 109 L4
Cleaver's La *RHWH* RH17 ...... 86 C2
Cleeves Wy *ANG/EP* BN16 ...... 207 L2
Clerks Acre *HPPT/KEY* BN6 ...... 131 H8 ☑
Clermont Rd *BRI* BN1 ...... 193 L2
Clermont Ter *BRI* BN1 ...... 193 M2
Cleveland Cl *SALV* BN13 ...... 188 A4
Cleveland Gdns *BURH* RH15 ...... 131 J2
Cleveland Rd *BRI* BN1 ...... 194 B3
CCH PO19 ...... 7 H6
SALV BN13 ...... 188 A4
Cleve Wy *BIL* RH14 ...... 79 L4
Cliff Ap *ROTT* BN2 ...... 195 G8
Cliff Rd *ROTT* BN2 ...... 212 A1
Clifton Hl *BRI* BN1 ...... 10 B4
Clifton Ms *BRI* BN1 ...... 10 B4
Clifton Pl *BRI* BN1 ...... 10 B4
Clifton Rd *BOGR* PO21 ...... 12 C5
BRI BN1 ...... 10 C4
BURH RH15 ...... 108 E7
LHPTN BN17 ...... 206 E4
WTHG BN11 ...... 8 F4
Clifton St *BRI* BN1 ...... 10 A4
Clifton Ter *BRI* BN1 ...... 10 C5
Climping Cl *HWH* RH16 ...... 109 L1
Climping Rd *CRAWW* RH11 ...... 20 C4
Climping St *LHPTN* BN17 ...... 205 L4
Clitherow Gdns *CRAWE* RH10 ...... 3 G6
Clive Av *FERR* BN12 ...... 209 L2
Clivedale Gdns *STEY/UB* BN44 ...... 167 L1
Clive Wy *CRAWE* RH10 ...... 21 K6
The Cloisters *LHPTN* BN17 ...... 207 G4 ☑
BIL RH14 ...... 55 K1
BOGR PO21 ...... 220 D3
BRI BN1 ...... 171 L7
BURH RH15 ...... 109 K8
EGRIN RH19 ...... 24 E4
HORL RH6 ...... 15 K3
HPPT/KEY BN6 ...... 131 G8
LAN/SOMP BN15 ...... 190 A8
MIDOS PO22 ...... 205 H7
PUL/STOR RH20 ...... 125 H7
RCCH PO18 ...... 157 G7
RCCH PO18 ...... 180 E1
RHWH RH17 ...... 66 C5
SELS PO20 ...... 222 E4
SHOR BN43 ...... 191 G4
Closewalks *MIDH* GU29 ...... 95 G5
Clothalls La *SWTR* RH13 ...... 104 C7
Clovelly Av *MIDOS* PO22 ...... 204 C7
Clovelly Rd *EMRTH* PO10 ...... 175 H4
EMRTH PO10 ...... 176 A3
HISD PO11 ...... 174 F8
Cloverlands *CRAWE* RH10 ...... 21 G4
Clover La *FERR* BN12 ...... 208 F3
Clovers End *BRI* BN1 ...... 172 C5
HORS RH12 ...... 5 M1
Clovers Wy *HORS* RH12 ...... 38 E5
Clover Wy *PTSD* BN41 ...... 192 C2
Club Wk *ANG/EP* BN16 ...... 208 B4
Clun Rd *LHPTN* BN17 ...... 206 E2 ☑
Clyde Cl *SALV* BN13 ...... 187 K4
Clyde Rd *BRI* BN1 ...... 10 E1
MIDOS PO22 ...... 13 K6
SALV BN13 ...... 187 K5
Clydesdale Av *CCH* PO19 ...... 6 F6 ☑
Clydesdale Rd *MIDOS* PO22 ...... 203 H5
Coach House Cl *SELS* PO20 ...... 223 G5
Coach House Ms *WTHG* BN11 ...... 8 F6
Coachmans Dr *CRAWW* RH11 ...... 40 C2
Coach Rd *RCCH* PO18 ...... 179 M3
SELS PO20 ...... 180 A4
Coastal Rd *ANG/EP* BN16 ...... 208 C4
Coastguard La *SELS* PO20 ...... 216 B3
Coastguard Pde *BOGR* PO21 ...... 220 E3 ☑
Coastguard Rd *LHPTN* BN17 ...... 206 C1
Coates La *PUL/STOR* RH20 ...... 120 E4
Cobbett Cl *CRAWW* RH11 ...... 21 K4
Cobbetts Md *HWH* RH16 ...... 110 C1
Cobbles Crs *CRAWE* RH10 ...... 3 G2
Cobblewood *EMRTH* PO10 ...... 175 J1
Cob Cl *CRAWE* RH10 ...... 23 K4
Cobden La *HASM* GU27 ...... 28 E5
Cobden Rd *MIDH* GU29 ...... 94 F5 ☑
ROTT BN2 ...... 11 J3
WTHG BN11 ...... 8 E5
Cobham Cl *ARUN* BN18 ...... 205 G2
Cobham Wy *CRAWE* RH10 ...... 15 J8
Cob La *RHWH* RH17 ...... 66 C3
Cobnor Cl *CRAWW* RH11 ...... 20 A8
Cobton Dr *HOVE* BN3 ...... 193 H1
Cob Wk *CRAWW* RH11 ...... 20 B7
Cocking Hl *RCCH* PO18 ...... 116 D8
Cohen Cl *SELS* PO20 ...... 181 L7
Cokeham Gdns
LAN/SOMP BN15 ...... 189 K6
Cokeham La *LAN/SOMP* BN15 ...... 189 K6
Cokeham Rd *LAN/SOMP* BN15 ...... 189 K5
Colbourne Av *ROTT* BN2 ...... 194 C3
Colbourne Rd *HOVE* BN3 ...... 10 A3
Colbrook V *FROW* RH18 ...... 45 M2
Colchins *BURH* RH15 ...... 131 G3 ☑
Coldean La *BRI* BN1 ...... 172 D4
Coldharbour Farm Rd
EMRTH PO10 ...... 175 J3
Coldharbour La *SALV* BN13 ...... 186 E3
Coldwaltham La *BURH* RH15 ...... 131 H1
Colebrook Cl *WTHG* BN11 ...... 9 M3
Colebrook La *PUL/STOR* RH20 ...... 121 J7
Colebrook Rd *BRI* BN1 ...... 171 L3
LHPTN BN17 ...... 206 D1
STHW BN42 ...... 192 A5
Cole Cl *CRAWW* RH11 ...... 40 D1
Coleman Av *HOVE* BN3 ...... 192 F5
Coleman St *ROTT* BN2 ...... 11 H3
Colemore Sq *HAV* PO9 ...... 152 C8 ☑
Coleridge Cl *FERR* BN12 ...... 209 J1
HORS RH12 ...... 37 M6 ☑
Coleridge Crs *CRAWW* RH11 ...... 209 H1
Coleridge St *HOVE* BN3 ...... 193 H4
Colet Rd *CRAWE* RH10 ...... 40 E1
Colgate Cl *CRAWW* RH11 ...... 20 C4 ☑
ROTT BN2 ...... 195 G6

Colindale Rd *FERR* BN12 ...... 208 F2
Colindale Rd North
FERR BN12 ...... 208 F2 ☑
Collards La *HASM* GU27 ...... 28 E6
Collard Wy *LISS* GU33 ...... 47 J8 ☑
College Cl *BOGR* PO21 ...... 203 G8
EGRIN RH19 ...... 25 G3
HAV PO9 ...... 152 F3
PTSD BN41 ...... 192 A1
RHWH RH17 ...... 63 K2
College Gdns *ROTT* BN2 ...... 11 K8
WTHG BN11 ...... 8 B5
College Hl *HASM* GU27 ...... 28 D6
STEY/UB BN44 ...... 167 L2
College La *CCH* PO19 ...... 179 H4
EGRIN RH19 ...... 25 G3
HPPT/KEY BN6 ...... 130 D7
College Pl *HPPT/KEY* BN6 ...... 130 D7
ROTT BN2 ...... 11 K8
College Rd *CRAWE* RH10 ...... 3 H4
HWH RH16 ...... 87 M6
HWH RH16 ...... 88 B1
ROTT BN2 ...... 11 K8
STEY/UB BN44 ...... 168 D3
College St *EPSF* GU31 ...... 90 C1
EGRIN RH19 ...... 25 G4
ROTT BN2 ...... 11 K8
College Ter *ROTT* BN2 ...... 11 K6
Collier Rw *CRAWE* RH10 ...... 2 F9
Collingwood
PUL/STOR RH20 ...... 122 D1 ☑
Collingwood Cl *EGRIN* RH19 ...... 25 G5 ☑
Collingwood Ct *SHOR* BN43 ...... 191 G6 ☑
Collingwood Rd *CRAWE* RH10 ...... 21 L7 ☑
FERR BN12 ...... 187 K8 ☑
Collins La *EPSF* GU31 ...... 91 J5
Collins Rd *CRAWW* RH11 ...... 19 M8
Collyer Av *BOGR* PO21 ...... 12 A3
Collyers Crs *LIPH* GU30 ...... 26 F8 ☑
Colmer Ct *BURH* RH15 ...... 130 F1
Colmer Pl *BURH* RH15 ...... 130 F1 ☑
Colne Cl *SALV* BN13 ...... 187 K4
Colonsay Rd *CRAWW* RH11 ...... 2 A9
Coltash Rd *CRAWE* RH10 ...... 3 L6
Colt's Bay *BOGR* PO21 ...... 220 D3
Coltsfoot Dr *HORS* RH12 ...... 5 G1
Coltstaple La *SWTR* RH13 ...... 60 D8
Colt St *SELS* PO20 ...... 222 E4
Columbia Dr *SALV* BN13 ...... 187 K6
Colvill Av *SHOR* BN43 ...... 190 E4
Colwell Cl *HWH* RH16 ...... 110 A1
Colwell Gdns *HWH* RH16 ...... 110 A1
Colwell La *HWH* RH16 ...... 110 A2
RHWH RH17 ...... 110 A3
Colwell Rd *HWH* RH16 ...... 110 A2
Colwood La *RHWH* RH17 ...... 85 J6
Colwyn Cl *CRAWW* RH11 ...... 19 M8
Combe Dr *STEY/UB* BN44 ...... 167 L3
Combe Rd *LISS* GU33 ...... 69 L3
Comley Hl *HAV* PO9 ...... 154 B6
Commerce Wy
LAN/SOMP BN15 ...... 189 K7
Commercial Rd *BURH* RH15 ...... 131 G1 ☑
Common Hl *RCCH* PO18 ...... 125 K5
Common La *HPPT/KEY* BN6 ...... 131 L7
Commonmead La *BOGR* PO21 ...... 220 B1
Common Rd *EMRTH* PO10 ...... 154 C7
Commonside *EMRTH* PO10 ...... 153 L7
The Common *PUL/STOR* RH20 ...... 123 K4
Common Vw *MIDH* GU29 ...... 94 F5
Compass Cl *LHPTN* BN17 ...... 207 H2 ☑
Compassion Cl *CRAWW* RH11 ...... 19 M8 ☑
Comper Cl *CRAWW* RH11 ...... 19 M8 ☑
Compton Av *BRI* BN1 ...... 10 C4
FERR BN12 ...... 209 J2
Compton Cl *CCH* PO19 ...... 179 H1
HAV PO9 ...... 174 C1 ☑
Compton Dr *MIDOS* PO22 ...... 204 E6
Compton Rd *BRI* BN1 ...... 193 L3
HWH RH16 ...... 88 C4
Comptons Brow La *SWTR* RH13 ...... 5 K5
Comptons La *SWTR* RH13 ...... 5 J9
Conbar Av *BRI* BN1 ...... 207 K2
Concorde Cl *PUL/STOR* RH20 ...... 144 A1
Condor Wy *BURH* RH15 ...... 130 F1
Conduit Md *CCH* PO19 ...... 7 J1
Coney Cl *CRAWW* RH11 ...... 20 C4
SELS PO20 ...... 217 G6
Coney Cft *SELS* PO20 ...... 5 M2
Coney Rd *SELS* PO20 ...... 217 G6
Coney Six *SELS* PO20 ...... 217 G6
Conford Ct *SWTR* RH13 ...... 5 J7
Congreve Rd *FIN/BW* BN14 ...... 9 J1
Conifer Dr *CRAWW* RH11 ...... 20 B3
Conifers Cl *HORS* RH12 ...... 38 C6
Conigar Rd *EMRTH* PO10 ...... 19 L8 ☑
Coniston Cl *CRAWW* RH11 ...... 19 L8 ☑
HORS RH12 ...... 38 C7
LAN/SOMP BN15 ...... 189 K6 ☑
MIDOS PO22 ...... 204 C6
Coniston Rd *FERR* BN12 ...... 187 K8
Coniston Wy *ANG/EP* BN16 ...... 207 L1 ☑
Connaught Av *SHOR* BN43 ...... 190 F4
Connaught Gdns
CRAWW RH11 ...... 20 E4 ☑
Connaught Rd *HAV* PO9 ...... 174 D3
HOVE BN3 ...... 193 H6
LHPTN BN17 ...... 206 D1
Connaught Ter *HOVE* BN3 ...... 193 H5
Connell Dr *ROTT* BN2 ...... 195 M5
Consort Wy *BURH* RH15 ...... 130 F2
HORL RH6 ...... 15 H1
Consort Wy East *HORL* RH6 ...... 15 J2
Constable Dr *SELS* PO20 ...... 223 H5
Constable Rd *CRAWE* RH10 ...... 41 G2
Convent La *EMRTH* PO10 ...... 175 H4
Conway Dr *BOGR* PO21 ...... 220 B4
Conway Rd *HOVE* BN3 ...... 193 H5
Conway St *HOVE* BN3 ...... 193 J4
Cook Rd *CRAWE* RH10 ...... 3 M7
HORS RH12 ...... 37 G6
Cooksbridge Rd *ROTT* BN2 ...... 194 F6
Cooks Hl *HORS* RH12 ...... 34 A3
Cooks La *EMRTH* PO10 ...... 176 B3
RCCH PO18 ...... 154 C2
Cooks Md *HORS* RH12 ...... 18 C5
Cook's Pond Rd *LIPH* GU30 ...... 71 H4

Coolham Dr *ROTT* BN2 ...... 194 F6
Coolham Rd *PUL/STOR* RH20 ...... 124 C8
SWTR RH13 ...... 80 E8
Coolhurst La *SWTR* RH13 ...... 5 L9
Coombe Cl *BIL* RH14 ...... 79 L3
CRAWW RH11 ...... 20 C3
Coombe Crs *FERR* BN12 ...... 187 K8 ☑
Coombe Dro *STEY/UB* BN44 ...... 167 L2 ☑
Coombe Hl *BIL* RH14 ...... 79 L3
Coombe Hill Rd *EGRIN* RH19 ...... 24 D6
Coombelands La
PUL/STOR RH20 ...... 122 B1
Coombe La *ARUN* BN18 ...... 163 K5
Coombe Ri *FIN/BW* BN14 ...... 188 B2
ROTT BN2 ...... 213 L1
Coombe Rd *ROTT* BN2 ...... 194 E3
STEY/UB BN44 ...... 167 K3
Coombers *RHWH* RH17 ...... 65 H3
Coombers La *HWH* RH16 ...... 88 C7 ☑
Coombes Rd *LAN/SOMP* BN15 ...... 168 B6
Coombe V *ROTT* BN2 ...... 213 L1
Coomes Wy *LHPTN* BN17 ...... 184 E8
Cooper Rw *CRAWE* RH10 ...... 2 F9
Coopers Cl *BURH* RH15 ...... 109 J7
The Coopers *SWTR* RH13 ...... 58 E8
Cooper St *CCH* PO19 ...... 7 J5
Coopers Wy *HFD* BN5 ...... 128 A7
Coos La *RHWH* RH17 ...... 63 H6
Cootes Av *HORS* RH12 ...... 60 B1
Cootes La *MIDOS* PO22 ...... 205 G7
Cootham Gn *PUL/STOR* RH20 ...... 143 J2
Copeland Rd *MIDOS* PO22 ...... 13 M5
Copestake Dr *BURH* RH15 ...... 131 L1
Copnall Wy *HORS* RH12 ...... 4 D8
Coppards Cl *RHWH* RH17 ...... 110 D8 ☑
Copper Beech Dr *SELS* PO20 ...... 180 D3
Copperfield Pl *HORS* RH12 ...... 4 A4
Copperfields *SWTR* RH13 ...... 61 J4
Copper Hall Cl *ANG/EP* BN16 ...... 207 M2 ☑
Coppice La *SELS* PO20 ...... 222 F4
Coppice Rd *HORS* RH12 ...... 5 M1 ☑
The Coppice *CRAWE* RH10 ...... 23 J4
RHWH RH17 ...... 111 G1 ☑
Coppice Wk *CRAWE* RH10 ...... 3 M1
Coppice Wy *HWH* RH16 ...... 109 L1
Copsale Rd *SWTR* RH13 ...... 82 F7
Copse Cl *CRAWE* RH10 ...... 23 J4
EGRIN RH19 ...... 25 G1
EPSF GU31 ...... 68 F8
HORS RH12 ...... 38 A6
LISS GU33 ...... 47 K8
Copse Crs *CRAWW* RH11 ...... 2 C1
Copse Hl *BRI* BN1 ...... 171 L7
Copse La *ARUN* BN18 ...... 182 D3
HISD PO11 ...... 196 D4
Copse Rd *HASM* GU27 ...... 27 L3
The Copse *CCH* PO19 ...... 179 H2
HWH RH16 ...... 88 C7
SWTR RH13 ...... 82 A2
Copse Vw *ANG/EP* BN16 ...... 208 A2
Copthorne Bank *CRAWE* RH10 ...... 22 C1
Copthorne Cl *SALV* BN13 ...... 188 B4 ☑
Copthorne Common Rd
CRAWE RH10 ...... 22 C2
Copthorne Hl *SALV* BN13 ...... 188 A5
Copthorne Rd *CRAWE* RH10 ...... 21 L4
Copthorne Wy *BOGR* PO21 ...... 202 E8
CRAWE RH10 ...... 22 A2
Copyhold Hl *HASM* GU27 ...... 51 K4
Copyhold La *HWH* RH16 ...... 87 L2
RHWH RH17 ...... 87 G8
Copyhold Rd *EGRIN* RH19 ...... 24 E4
Corbishley Rd *MIDOS* PO22 ...... 12 C1
Corbyn Crs *SHOR* BN43 ...... 191 H5
Cordal Cl *ANG/EP* BN16 ...... 207 J5
Corfe Cl *SALV* BN13 ...... 187 J7
SWTR RH13 ...... 82 B3
Corhampton Crs *HAV* PO9 ...... 152 A8
Cormorant Wy *SELS* PO20 ...... 217 H6
Corner Garth *FERR* BN12 ...... 209 G3
Cornfield Cl *LHPTN* BN17 ...... 206 F1
Cornflower Wy *SWTR* RH13 ...... 82 B1
Cornford Cl *BURH* RH15 ...... 108 F7
PTSD BN41 ...... 192 C2 ☑
Cornwall Gdns *BRI* BN1 ...... 193 H1
EGRIN RH19 ...... 25 G4 ☑
LHPTN BN17 ...... 206 F2 ☑
Cornwall Rd *LHPTN* BN17 ...... 206 F1
Coronation Rd *EGRIN* RH19 ...... 24 F5
HISD PO11 ...... 215 H3
Coronation St *ROTT* BN2 ...... 11 J2 ☑
The Coronet *HORL* RH6 ...... 15 K3 ☑
Corsletts Av *HORS* RH12 ...... 59 L1
Cortis Av *SWTR* RH13 ...... 5 J7
Corunna Dr *SWTR* RH13 ...... 5 J7
Cory Cl *CCH* PO19 ...... 6 E6
Costells Edge *RHWH* RH17 ...... 89 G8
Cote St *SALV* BN13 ...... 187 K3
Cotland Rd *SELS* PO20 ...... 223 H6
Cot La *RCCH* PO18 ...... 176 E7
Cotsford *CRAWW* RH11 ...... 40 C6
HAV PO9 ...... 152 B6 ☑
SALV BN13 ...... 187 M4
Cotswold Cl *CRAWW* RH11 ...... 2 A1
HAV PO9 ...... 152 B6 ☑
SALV BN13 ...... 188 A5
Cotswold Rd *SALV* BN42 ...... 191 M5 ☑
The Cotswolds *STHW* BN42 ...... 191 M5 ☑
Cotswold Wy *ANG/EP* BN16 ...... 208 B2
Cottage Bush Cl *PTSD* BN41 ...... 192 C2 ☑
Cottage Cl *BOGR* PO21 ...... 220 D2 ☑
RCCH PO18 ...... 38 C6
Cottage La *LISS* GU33 ...... 46 C8
Cottage Pl *CRAWE* RH10 ...... 22 F1
Cottenham Rd *WTHG* BN11 ...... 9 L3
Cottingham Av *HORS* RH12 ...... 37 L5
Cotton Dr *EMRTH* PO10 ...... 175 H1
The Cottrells *ANG/EP* BN16 ...... 186 A7
Coulstock Rd *HPPT/KEY* BN6 ...... 108 D8
Coultershaw Br *PETW* GU28 ...... 119 M1
Countisbury Cl *BOGR* PO21 ...... 221 G1 ☑
Countryman La *SWTR* RH13 ...... 103 J5
County Oak Av *BRI* BN1 ...... 172 C6
County Oak La *CRAWW* RH11 ...... 20 B7
County Oak Wy *CRAWW* RH11 ...... 20 B6
Court Barn La *SELS* PO20 ...... 199 M6 ☑
Court Cl *BRI* BN1 ...... 171 M5 ☑
EGRIN RH19 ...... 25 G3
LIPH GU30 ...... 49 J1
Court Crs *EGRIN* RH19 ...... 25 H3
Court Farm Rd *HOVE* BN3 ...... 193 G2
ROTT BN2 ...... 212 F1

Courtlands *HWH* RH16 .... 109 M1
Courtlands Cl *FERR* BN12 ...... 209 M3
Courtlands Wy *FERR* BN12 ...... 209 M3
   MIDOS PO22 .... 204 D6
Courtmead Rd *RHWH* RH17 ...... 87 G6
Court Ord Rd *ROTT* BN2 .... 212 F1
Courts Hill Rd *HASM* GU27 ...... 28 C6
Courts Mount Rd *HASM* GU27 .... 28 C6
The Court *BOGR* PO21 .... 220 B3
Courtwick Cl *LHPTN* BN17 ...... 184 D8
Courtwick Rd *LHPTN* BN17 ...... 206 D1
The Courtyard *EGRIN* RH19 ...... 25 J3
   EPSF GU31 .... 90 C1
Cousins Wy *PUL/STOR* RH20 .... 122 D1
Coventry Cl *BOGR* PO21 .... 202 E3
Coventry St *BRI* BN1 .... 193 M4
Cove Rd *ANG/EP* BN16 .... 207 J4
Covert Cl *CRAWE* RH10 .... 3 C1
Covert Md *PUL/STOR* RH20 ...... 125 G7
   RHWH RH17 .... 63 J5
The Covey *CRAWE* RH10 .... 21 L4
Covington Rd *EMRTH* PO10 ...... 153 L4
Cowden Rd *ROTT* BN2 .... 213 L4
Cowdens Cl *HOVE* BN3 .... 170 E8
Cowdown La *RCCH* PO18 .... 112 F8
Cowdray Cl *ANG/EP* BN16 ...... 207 J1
   CRAWE RH10 .... 21 K7
Cowdray Ct *MIDH* GU29 .... 95 G4
Cowdray Dr *ANG/EP* BN16 ...... 207 J1
   FERR BN12 .... 209 L3
Cowdray Rd *MIDH* GU29 .... 95 H3
Cowfold Cl *CRAWW* RH11 ...... 40 A1
Cowfold Rd *RHWH* RH17 .... 107 L2
   ROTT BN2 .... 194 F7
   SWTR RH13 .... 105 G3
Cow La *EPSF* GU31 .... 91 K8
   SELS PO20 .... 218 E5
Cowley Dr *LAN/SOMP* BN15 .... 190 A7
   ROTT BN2 .... 195 M6
Cowper Rd *WTHG* BN11 .... 8 D5
Cowper St *HOVE* BN3 .... 193 H5
Cowslip Wy *SWTR* RH13 .... 82 B2
Coxes Meadow *PSF* GU32 ...... 68 B7
Coxes Rd *SELS* PO20 .... 222 E4
Cox Green Rd *HORS* RH12 ...... 34 C2
Cox Gv *BURH* RH15 .... 108 F7
Coxham La *STEY/UB* BN44 ...... 146 D8
Coxswain Wy *SELS* PO20 ...... 223 G7
Crabbet Rd *CRAWE* RH10 ...... 21 J5
Crablands *SELS* PO20 .... 222 E5
Crablands Cl *SELS* PO20 ...... 222 E5
Crabtree Av *BRI* BN1 .... 172 E4
Crabtree La *LAN/SOMP* BN15 ... 189 M6
Crabtree Rd *CRAWW* RH11 ...... 2 D2
Crabwood Ct *HAV* PO9 .... 152 A5
Cradock Pl *SALV* BN13 .... 187 L4
Craggits La *HFD* BN5 .... 127 M7
Craigans *CRAWW* RH11 .... 20 B6
Craignair Av *BRI* BN1 .... 172 A5
Craigweil La *BOGR* PO21 ...... 220 F5
Craigwell Mnr *BOGR* PO21 .... 220 E3
Cranborne Wk *CRAWE* RH10 .... 3 K8
Cranford Gdns *MIDOS* PO22 .... 12 D4
Cranford Rd *PSF* GU32 .... 90 B2
Cranham Av *BIL* RH14 .... 79 K6
Cranleigh Av *ROTT* BN2 .... 213 J3
Cranleigh Rd *FIN/BW* BN14 .... 188 C2
Cranmer Av *HOVE* BN3 .... 193 G3
Cranmer Rd *SALV* BN13 .... 8 A3
Cranston Rd *EGRIN* RH19 ...... 24 F2
Cranworth Rd *WTHG* BN11 ...... 9 L3
Craven Rd *CRAWE* RH10 .... 21 J7
   ROTT BN2 .... 11 L6
Crawford Gdns *SWTR* RH13 .... 194 E3
Crawfurd Wy *EGRIN* RH19 ...... 25 G1
Crawley Av *CRAWE* RH10 ...... 20 F4
   CRAWW RH11 .... 2 A6
   HAV PO9 .... 152 D6
Crawley Down Rd *EGRIN* RH19 .. 23 M1
Crawley La *CRAWE* RH10 ...... 21 K5
   RHWH RH17 .... 41 L7
Crawley Rd *BRI* BN1 .... 172 E6
   HORS RH12 .... 5 K4
Crawters Cl *CRAWE* RH10 ...... 3 J2
Crayford Rd *ROTT* BN2 .... 194 E5
Cray La *PUL/STOR* RH20 ...... 100 E7
Cray's La *PUL/STOR* RH20 .... 124 D5
Creasys Dr *CRAWW* RH11 ...... 40 C4
Crede La *RCCH* PO18 .... 177 K6
   EMRTH PO10 .... 175 J5
Creek End *CCH* PO19 .... 178 C6
Creek Rd *HISD* PO11 .... 215 G2
Crescenta Wk *BOGR* PO21 .... 221 H1
Crescent Cl *BURH* RH15 ...... 131 J1
   ROTT BN2 .... 195 M4
Crescent Dr North *ROTT* BN2 .. 195 M4
Crescent Dr South *ROTT* BN2 .. 195 M6
Crescent Pl *ROTT* BN2 .... 11 K9
Crescent Ri *PUL/STOR* RH20 .. 144 B1
Crescent Rd *BOGR* PO21 ...... 12 D7
   BURH RH15 .... 131 H1
   EGRIN RH19 .... 24 E3
   ROTT BN2 .... 11 L1
   WTHG BN11 .... 8 F6
The Crescent *ANG/EP* BN16 .... 207 H4
   BOGR PO21 .... 220 B4
   EMRTH PO10 .... 176 A4
   HORS RH6 .... 15 H3
   HORS RH12 .... 60 B2
   HPPT/KEY BN6 .... 151 J1
   LAN/SOMP BN15 ...... 189 M8
   MIDOS PO22 .... 13 M4
   PUL/STOR RH20 ...... 143 G5
   ROTT BN2 .... 194 F2
   SELS PO20 .... 216 F5
   STEY/UB BN44 ...... 167 L2
   STHW BN42 .... 192 A4
Crescent Wy *BURH* RH15 ...... 131 H1
   HORL RH6 .... 15 H3
Crespin Wy *BRI* BN1 .... 194 D3
Crest Wy *PTSD* BN41 .... 192 C1
The Crestway *BRI* BN1 .... 194 D3
Crewdson Rd *HORL* RH6 ...... 15 J1
Cricket Ct *EGRIN* RH19 ...... 24 F1
Cricket Field Rd *HORS* RH12 .. 60 C1
Crimbourne La *BIL* RH14 ...... 77 K8
Cripland Cl *HWH* RH16 .... 88 C6
Cripplecrutch Hl
   MFD/CHID GU8 .... 30 A6

Cripplegate La *SWTR* RH13 ...... 82 B4
Cripps La *STEY/UB* BN44 ...... 167 M1
Critchel's La *SELS* PO20 ...... 218 D3
Critchfield Rd *RCCH* PO18 ...... 177 J7
Critchmere Dr *SELS* PO20 ...... 182 A5
Critchmere Hl *HASM* GU27 ...... 27 M5
Critchmere V *HASM* GU27 ...... 27 L6
Crockford Rd *EMRTH* PO10 .... 153 L8
Crockham Cl *CRAWW* RH11 .... 2 C7
Crockhurst Cl *SWTR* RH13 ...... 82 B2
Crockhurst Hl *SALV* BN13 ...... 188 A4
Croft Av *STHW* BN42 .... 191 M5
Croft Dr *PTSD* BN41 .... 192 B1
Crofters Wd *STEY/UB* BN44 .... 168 A2
Croft La *HFD* BN5 .... 127 L8
   HISD PO11 .... 196 D3
Croft Md *CCH* PO19 .... 179 H2
Croft Rd *BRI* BN1 .... 171 L8
   SELS PO20 .... 222 F6
The Croft *ARUN* BN18 .... 208 B3
   ARUN BN18 .... 183 G8
   BOGR PO21 .... 203 G7
   CRAWW RH11 .... 20 B6
   HPPT/KEY BN6 .... 131 C7
   MIDH GU29 .... 116 E4
   PETW GU28 .... 96 C1
Croft Wy *HORS* RH12 .... 60 B1
   MIDOS PO22 .... 204 D6
   SELS PO20 .... 222 F5
Cromleigh Wy *STHW* BN42 .... 191 M2
Crompton Flds *CRAWE* RH10 .. 20 F5
Crompton Wy *CRAWE* RH10 .... 20 F4
Cromwell Pl *EGRIN* RH19 ...... 25 G5
   HOVE BN3 .... 193 K5
Cromwell Rd *BURH* RH15 ...... 131 G1
   HOVE BN3 .... 193 K5
Cromwell St *HOVE* BN3 ...... 11 K3
Crondall Av *HAV* PO9 .... 152 B6
Cuckoo La *SELS* PO20 .... 199 M7
Crookthorn La *LHPTN* BN17 .... 205 L4
Crosbie Cl *CCH* PO19 .... 201 G1
Crosby Cl *SALV* BN13 .... 187 L6
Croshaw Cl *LAN/SOMP* BN15 .. 189 J1
Crossbush La *ARUN* BN18 .... 184 F3
Crossbush Rd *MIDOS* PO22 .... 204 D8
   ROTT BN2 .... 194 F6
Cross Colwood La *RHWH* RH17 .. 85 H8
Cross Eels *SELS* PO20 .... 222 D4
Crossfield *HASM* GU27 ...... 51 H7
Cross Keys *CRAWW* RH11 ...... 2 F4
Crossland Dr *HAV* PO9 ...... 174 D1
Cross La *FIN/BW* BN14 ...... 165 M6
   SWTR RH13 .... 81 G3
Cross Rd *ANG/EP* BN16 .... 207 M3
   STHW BN42 .... 191 L4
Crossroad Cl *STHW* BN42 .... 191 L4
Cross St *BRI* BN1 .... 10 E2
   HOVE BN3 .... 193 L7
   WTHG BN11 .... 8 F3
Cross Wy *HAV* PO9 .... 174 B2
Crossways *ANG/EP* BN16 ...... 208 C2
   CRAWE RH10 .... 3 K2
   MIDH GU29 .... 95 H2
   MIDOS PO22 .... 205 G7
   PUL/STOR RH20 ...... 123 L6
   RHWH RH17 .... 107 L2
Crossways Av *EGRIN* RH19 .... 24 D3
   FERR BN12 .... 187 H8
Crossways Cl *CRAWE* RH10 .... 3 K2
Crossways Pk *PUL/STOR* RH20 . 123 L5
The Crossways *LHPTN* BN17 .. 206 D1
The Crossway *BRI* BN1 .... 194 D1
   PTSD BN41 .... 192 B2
Crouch Cross La *RCCH* PO18 .. 180 D1
Crouch Hl *HFD* BN5 .... 128 A5
Crouchlands Farm *RHWH* RH17 .. 86 F4
Crowberry Cl *CRAWW* RH11 .... 40 B2
Crowborough Dr *FERR* BN12 .. 209 J3
Crowborough Rd *ROTT* BN2 .. 213 L4
Crowhurst Cl *CRAWE* RH10 .... 21 M6
Crown Rd *PTSD* BN41 .... 192 B4
   SHOR BN43 .... 191 J4
Crown St *BRI* BN1 .... 10 C6
Crowsbury Cl *EMRTH* PO10 .... 175 H1
Croxton La *HWH* RH16 .... 88 C5
Croy Cl *CCH* PO19 .... 178 C6
Crundens Cnr *ANG/EP* BN16 .. 207 M2
Crundles *EGRIN* RH19 ...... 90 D1
Crypt La *MIDH* GU29 .... 116 D9
Cuckfield Cl *CRAWW* RH11 .... 40 A1
Cuckfield Crs *SALV* BN13 ...... 188 A6
Cuckfield La *RHWH* RH17 ...... 85 J3
Cuckfield Rd *BURH* RH15 ...... 108 F5
   HPPT/KEY BN6 .... 130 B6
   RHWH RH17 .... 86 B3
   RHWH RH17 .... 108 C4
Cuckmere Crs *CRAWW* RH11 .. 20 A7
Cuckmere Wy *BRI* BN1 ...... 172 C6
Cudlow Av *ANG/EP* BN16 ...... 207 K3
Cudlow Gdn *ANG/EP* BN16 .... 207 K4
Cuffs Hl *CRAWE* RH10 ...... 41 M2
Culimore Cl *SELS* PO20 ...... 216 F5
Culimore Rd *SELS* PO20 ...... 216 F5
Culpepper *BURH* RH15 ...... 108 F8
Culpepper Cl *ROTT* BN2 ...... 194 E2
Culross Av *HWH* RH16 ...... 87 L7
Culver Dr *HISD* PO11 .... 214 F3
Culver Rd *LAN/SOMP* BN15 .. 189 M6
   MIDOS PO22 .... 13 L5
Culvers *EPSF* GU31 .... 113 L1
Cumberland Av *EMRTH* PO10 .. 153 H8
   FERR BN12 .... 187 L7
Cumberland Crs
   ANG/EP BN16 .... 186 B7
Cumberland Dr *BRI* BN1 ...... 193 M2
Cumberland Rd *ANG/EP* BN16 . 186 B7
   BRI BN1 .... 193 M2
Cumbrian Cl *SALV* BN13 ...... 187 M5
Cunliffe Cl *SELS* PO20 ...... 216 D2
Cunningham Gdns
   MIDOS PO22 .... 204 D7
Curbey Cl *PUL/STOR* RH20 .. 123 L3
Curdridge Cl *HAV* PO9 ...... 152 D7
Curlescroft *BOGR* PO21 ...... 221 G2
Curlew Cl *EMRTH* PO10 ...... 175 H4
The Curlews *SHOR* BN43 ...... 191 H4
Curvins Wy *LAN/SOMP* BN15 .. 190 A5
Curwen Pl *BRI* BN1 .... 193 M1
Curzon Av *HORS* RH12 ...... 4 A7
Curzon Cl *SALV* BN13 .... 188 A6

Cutfield Cl *CCH* PO19 .... 201 G1
Cuthbert Rd *ROTT* BN2 ...... 11 K6
Cuttinglye La *CRAWE* RH10 .... 23 H3
Cuttinglye Rd *CRAWE* RH10 .... 23 H3
The Cygnets *SHOR* BN43 ...... 191 G4
Cygnet Wk *MIDOS* PO22 ...... 203 J6
The Cylinders *HASM* GU27 .... 51 H7
Cypress Av *SALV* BN13 ...... 187 K7
Cypress Cl *SHOR* BN43 ...... 191 G3
Cypress Wy *BOGR* PO21 ...... 220 D2
   GSHT GU26 .... 27 L2
Cyprus Rd *BURH* RH15 ...... 131 H1

D

Dagbrook La *HFD* BN5 .... 147 M1
Dagmar St *WTHG* BN11 .... 9 H3
Dairyfields *CRAWW* RH11 ...... 20 B7
Dairy La *ARUN* BN18 .... 182 E4
   RCCH PO18 .... 180 A3
The Daisycroft *HFD* BN5 ...... 128 A8
Dakin Cl *CRAWE* RH10 ...... 41 K2
The Dakins *EGRIN* RH19 ...... 24 F4
Dale Av *BRI* BN1 .... 172 A7
Dale Cl *HORS* RH12 .... 5 J2
Dale Crs *BRI* BN1 .... 172 A6
Dale Dr *BRI* BN1 .... 172 A6
Dale Hl *POY/PYE* BN45 ...... 150 B6
Dale Rd *WTHG* BN11 .... 189 J8
Dale Vw *HASM* GU27 ...... 28 A7
   HOVE BN3 .... 192 E2
Dale View Gdns *HOVE* BN3 .. 192 E2
Dalewood Gdns *BURH* RH15 .. 131 K2
   CRAWE RH10 .... 21 G4
Dallaway Gdns *EGRIN* RH19 .. 24 F3
Dallaway Rd *CCH* PO19 ...... 7 H8
Dallington Rd *HOVE* BN3 ...... 192 F4
Dalloway Rd *ARUN* BN18 ...... 183 M3
Dalton Cl *CRAWW* RH11 ...... 40 B3
Daltons Pl *ARUN* BN18 ...... 184 B2
Damer's Br *PETW* GU28 ...... 98 A4
Damian Wy *HPPT/KEY* BN6 .... 131 H4
Danbury Ct *EMRTH* PO10 .... 175 K2
Dances Wy *HISD* PO11 ...... 196 B8
Danebury Cl *HAV* PO9 ...... 152 B6
Danefield Rd *SELS* PO20 ...... 222 E7
Danehill La *RHWH* RH17 ...... 67 M7
Danehill Rd *ROTT* BN2 ...... 195 G2
Danehurst Crs *SWTR* RH13 .... 105 H6
Daniel La *LAN/SOMP* BN15 .. 190 A5
Dankton Gdns
   LAN/SOMP BN15 .... 189 J5
Dankton La *LAN/SOMP* BN15 .. 189 J4
Danley La *HASM* GU27 ...... 50 B1
Danworth La *HPPT/KEY* BN6 .. 130 C1
Dapper's La *ANG/EP* BN16 .... 186 B6
Darcey Dr *BRI* BN1 .... 172 B6
Dark La *BOGR* PO21 .... 220 F2
Darleydale *CRAWW* RH11 ...... 2 C9
Dart Cl *SALV* BN13 .... 187 L4
Dartmouth Cl *ROTT* BN2 ...... 195 G3
Dartmouth Crs *ROTT* BN2 .... 194 F3
Darwin Cl *HORS* RH12 ...... 5 K3
Daux Av *BIL* RH14 .... 79 L6
Daux Hl *HORS* RH12 ...... 37 J6
Daux La *BIL* RH14 .... 79 L5
Daux Wy *BIL* RH14 .... 79 L6
Dauxwood Cl *BIL* RH14 ...... 79 L6
Davenport Rd *MIDOS* PO22 .. 13 M5
Davey Dr *BRI* BN1 .... 194 C3
Davids Cl *BOGR* PO21 ...... 203 G5
Davigdor Rd *HOVE* BN3 ...... 193 L5
Davis Cl *CRAWW* RH11 ...... 40 B3
Davis Dr *LHPTN* BN17 ...... 207 H2
Dawes Av *WTHG* BN11 ...... 9 M3
Dawes Cl *WTHG* BN11 ...... 9 M3
Daw La *HISD* PO11 .... 196 C4
Dawlish Cl *ROTT* BN2 ...... 194 F3
Dawn Cl *STEY/UB* BN44 ...... 168 C3
Dawn Crs *STEY/UB* BN44 .... 168 C3
Dawson Ter *ROTT* BN2 ...... 11 K2
Dawtrey Cl *ANG/EP* BN16 .... 207 M2
Dawtrey Rd *PETW* GU28 .... 98 A5
Daynes Wy *BURH* RH15 ...... 130 F3
Days La *ARUN* BN18 .... 182 A1
Deacons Dr *PTSD* BN41 ...... 192 C2
Deacons Wy *STEY/UB* BN44 .. 168 C3
Deacon Wy *FIN/BW* BN14 .... 189 G7
Deak's La *RHWH* RH17 ...... 86 C6
Dean Cl *LHPTN* BN17 ...... 206 D1
   PTSD BN41 .... 192 D2
Dean Court Rd *ROTT* BN2 .... 213 H2
Deane Ct *HAV* PO9 .... 152 E7
Dean Gdns *PTSD* BN41 ...... 192 D2
Deanland Rd *RHWH* RH17 .... 65 H3
Dean La *HORN* PO8 ...... 132 A7
   PETW GU28 .... 97 G4
Deans Cl *ROTT* BN2 .... 195 M4
Dean St *BRI* BN1 .... 10 B6
Deanway *HOVE* BN3 .... 193 J1
Dean Wy *PUL/STOR* RH20 .. 143 K2
De Braose Wy *STEY/UB* BN44 . 167 M2
Decoy Dr *ANG/EP* BN16 ...... 186 A5
Decoy Rd *FIN/BW* BN14 ...... 189 G7
Dedisham Cl *CRAWE* RH10 .... 3 M5
Deep Dene *HASM* GU27 ...... 27 M6
Deepdene Cl *MIDOS* PO22 .... 205 H7
Deer Pk *HFD* BN5 .... 127 M6
Deer Park La *SELS* PO20 .... 222 C4
Deerswood Cl *CRAWW* RH11 .. 2 B7
   SALV BN13 .... 187 J7
Deerswood Rd *CRAWW* RH11 .. 2 B7
Deeside Av *CCH* PO19 ...... 178 C5
The Deeside *BRI* BN1 ...... 172 B5
Defiance Pl *MIDOS* PO22 ...... 204 D8
De La Warr Rd *EGRIN* RH19 .. 25 G3
Delfont Cl *CRAWE* RH10 ...... 21 L8
Delius Gdns *SWTR* RH13 ...... 38 C8
Dell Cl *HASM* GU27 .... 28 B5
Dell Dr *ANG/EP* BN16 ...... 186 A4
Delling Cl *RCCH* PO18 ...... 177 J6
Delling La *RCCH* PO18 ...... 177 K6
Dell La *BIL* RH14 .... 79 L4
Dellney Av *HWH* RH16 ...... 110 A1
Dell Quay Rd *SELS* PO20 .... 200 C2
The Dell *EGRIN* RH19 ...... 25 J3
   HWH RH16 .... 87 K7

Delta Dr *HORL* RH6 .... 15 H3
De Montfort Rd *ROTT* BN2 .... 11 J2
Dempsey Rd *CCH* PO19 ...... 179 H1
Den Av *BOGR* PO21 .... 12 F6
Denbigh Rd *HASM* GU27 ...... 28 E7
Denchers Plat *CRAWW* RH11 .. 20 E3
Dene Ct *HASM* GU27 ...... 28 D6
Deneside *BRI* BN1 .... 171 L7
The Dene *HOVE* BN3 ...... 192 E1
   SWTR RH13 .... 82 B2
Dene Tye *CRAWE* RH10 ...... 21 K5
Dene V *BRI* BN1 .... 171 L7
The Deneway *BRI* BN1 ...... 171 L8
   LAN/SOMP BN15 ...... 189 K6
Denham Cl *LHPTN* BN17 .... 204 F7
Denham Rd *BURH* RH15 ...... 108 E8
Denhill Cl *HISD* PO11 ...... 196 B7
Denmans *CRAWE* RH10 ...... 21 L5
Denman's Cl *HWH* RH16 ...... 88 A5
Denman's La *HWH* RH16 ...... 88 B5
   SELS PO20 .... 181 M2
Denmark Rd *PTSD* BN41 ...... 192 D5
Denmark Ter *BRI* BN1 ...... 10 B4
Denmark Vls *HOVE* BN3 ...... 193 J5
Denne Pde *HORS* RH12 ...... 4 D9
Denne Rd *CRAWW* RH11 ...... 2 E5
   HORS RH12 .... 60 D3
Dennis Hobden Cl *ROTT* BN2 .. 194 F3
Dennis Wy *LISS* GU33 ...... 69 K1
Denny's Cl *SELS* PO20 ...... 223 G5
Denshare Rd *SELS* PO20 .... 223 G4
Denshire Dr *PUL/STOR* RH20 . 143 H5
Densinale *BOGR* PO21 ...... 221 G1
Denton Cl *FERR* BN12 ...... 209 J1
Denton Dr *BRI* BN1 .... 172 B7
Denvilles Cl *HAV* PO9 ...... 174 E2
Depot Rd *MIDH* GU29 ...... 95 J2
Derby Rd *HASM* GU27 ...... 28 C5
Derek Av *HOVE* BN3 ...... 192 E6
Derek Rd *LAN/SOMP* BN15 .. 189 L4
Derwent Cl *ANG/EP* BN16 .... 207 H2
   CRAWW RH11 .... 20 A7
   HORS RH12 .... 38 C6
   LAN/SOMP BN15 ...... 189 K7
   SELS PO20 .... 180 D3
Derwent Dr *FERR* BN12 ...... 187 L3
Derwent Gv *MIDOS* PO22 .... 204 C6
Desmond Rd *ROTT* BN2 ...... 195 G6
Detling Rd *CRAWW* RH11 .... 40 D3
Devil's Dyke Rd *HOVE* BN3 .. 171 G6
   POY/PYE BN45 ...... 170 C2
   PTSD BN41 .... 170 D3
Devils La *LIPH* GU30 ...... 49 M1
Devonport Pl *WTHG* BN11 .... 211 H1
Devonport Rd *WTHG* BN11 .... 211 H1
Devonshire Pl *ROTT* BN2 .... 11 G7
Devonshire Rd *BOGR* PO21 .. 12 C7
   HORS RH13 .... 194 F4
Dewar Cl *CRAWW* RH11 ...... 19 M7
Dewe Rd *ROTT* BN2 .... 194 D3
Dexter Dr *EGRIN* RH19 ...... 24 F4
Dial Cl *MIDOS* PO22 .... 182 D7
Diana Cl *EMRTH* PO10 ...... 153 H8
Dickens Cl *EGRIN* RH19 ...... 24 D1
The Dingle *CRAWW* RH11 .... 2 A3
Dingley Rd *ANG/EP* BN16 .... 207 J3
Dinsdale Gdns *ANG/EP* BN16 . 205 K2
Dirty La *EGRIN* RH19 ...... 25 M6
Ditcham Crs *HAV* PO9 ...... 152 B6
Ditchfield Rd *MIDOS* PO22 .... 204 E6
Ditchling Bostall
   HPPT/KEY BN6 .... 151 L5
Ditchling Crs *BRI* BN1 ...... 172 D7
Ditchling Gdns *BRI* BN1 ...... 194 B3
Ditchling Hl *CRAWW* RH11 .... 2 D8
Ditchling Ri *BRI* BN1 ...... 10 F1
Ditchling Rd *BRI* BN1 ...... 172 D4
   ROTT BN2 .... 10 F3
Dobbins Pl *CRAWW* RH11 .... 19 M7
Dobson Rd *CRAWW* RH11 .... 40 B3
Dodsley Gv *MIDH* GU29 ...... 95 G2
Dodsley La *MIDH* GU29 ...... 95 H2
Dog La *STEY/UB* BN44 ...... 167 L1
Dollis Cl *CRAWE* RH10 ...... 21 K7
Dolphin Cl *CCH* PO19 ...... 178 C6
   HASM GU27 .... 27 M6
Dolphin Ms *CCH* PO19 ...... 178 C6
Dolphin Rd *SHOR* BN43 ...... 191 J5
Dolphin Wy *ANG/EP* BN16 .... 207 L4
   SHOR BN43 .... 191 J5
Domehouse Cl *SELS* PO20 .. 223 G2
Dominion Cl *FIN/BW* BN14 .... 9 K1
Dominion Rd *ANG/EP* BN16 .. 207 K1
   FIN/BW BN14 .... 187 L2
Dominion Wy West
   FIN/BW BN14 .... 189 G7
Donald Hall Rd *ROTT* BN2 .... 11 M7
Donkey La *HORL* RH6 ...... 15 L8
Donkey Ms *HOVE* BN3 ...... 193 L7
Donne Cl *CRAWE* RH10 ...... 21 L8
Donnington Ct *CRAWW* RH11 . 40 A1
Donnington Pk *SELS* PO20 .. 200 E1
Donnington Rd *ROTT* BN2 .... 195 M6
Doomsday Gdn *SWTR* RH13 .. 61 K7
Doone End *FERR* BN12 ...... 209 G4
Dorchester Gdns *WTHG* BN11 . 8 A5
Dorking Rd *HORS* RH12 ...... 37 H2
Dormans *CRAWW* RH11 ...... 38 E7
Dormans Park Rd *EGRIN* RH19 . 24 E1
Dorothy Rd *HOVE* BN3 ...... 192 E4
Dorset Av *EGRIN* RH19 ...... 24 D1
Dorset Cl *LHPTN* BN17 ...... 206 F3
Dorset Gdns *EGRIN* RH19 .... 24 D1
   ROTT BN2 .... 11 G7
Dorset Pl *ROTT* BN2 .... 11 G7
Dorset Rd *BOGR* PO21 ...... 12 C3
Dorset St *ROTT* BN2 ...... 11 G7
Doubledays *BURH* RH15 ...... 131 J2
Douglas Av *HAV* PO9 ...... 210 A2
Douglas Cl *ARUN* BN18 ...... 205 J7
   MIDOS PO22 .... 205 H7
   WTHG BN11 .... 210 A2
Douglas Martin Rd *CCH* PO19 .. 7 H2
Dove Cl *CRAWE* RH10 ...... 21 L8
Dovecote Ms *LAN/SOMP* BN15 . 189 K4
Dove Ct *MIDOS* PO22 ...... 12 A2

Dovedale Crs *CRAWW* RH11 .... 2 B8
Dover Cl *SHOR* BN43 ...... 82 A4
Dover Ct *HISD* PO11 ...... 196 B5
Dover Rd *BRI* BN1 .... 194 B2
   WTHG BN11 .... 8 B1
Dower Cl *ROTT* BN2 .... 212 C4
Dower Wk *CRAWW* RH11 ...... 20 B7
Downash Cl *ROTT* BN2 ...... 194 F6
Downing Cl *MIDH* GU29 ...... 117 K4
Downing Rd *BOGR* PO21 .... 202 E6
Downland Av *STHW* BN42 .... 191 L5
Downland Cl *FIN/BW* BN14 .. 165 M6
   ROTT BN2 .... 195 L4
   STEY/UB BN44 ...... 168 C3
   WTHG BN11 .... 191 L3
Downland Crs *HOVE* BN3 .... 193 G7
Downland Dr *CRAWW* RH11 .. 2 C8
   HOVE BN3 .... 193 G7
Downland Rd *ROTT* BN2 ...... 195 L4
   STEY/UB BN44 ...... 168 C2
Downlands *PUL/STOR* RH20 .. 122 E2
   SWTR RH13 .... 127 G1
Downlands Av *FIN/BW* BN14 . 188 C5
Downlands Cl *BOGR* PO21 .... 220 B2
   LAN/SOMP BN15 ...... 189 K5
Downlands Gdns
   FIN/BW BN14 .... 188 F5
Downley Rd *HAV* PO9 ...... 152 E8
Downs Cl *LAN/SOMP* BN15 .. 190 C6
Downscroft *BURH* RH15 ...... 109 L2
   STEY/UB BN44 ...... 168 C3
Downside *BRI* BN1 .... 171 L7
   HORS RH13 .... 193 J1
   SHOR BN43 .... 191 H4
Downside Av *FIN/BW* BN14 .. 188 A1
Downside Cl *FIN/BW* BN14 .. 187 M4
   SHOR BN43 .... 191 G3
Downs Link *HFD* BN5 ...... 147 K4
   HORS RH12 .... 34 D4
   STEY/UB BN44 ...... 168 B4
   SWTR RH13 .... 35 H8
   SWTR RH13 .... 59 J4
   SWTR RH13 .... 104 F8
   SWTR RH13 .... 127 L8
Downs Md *LAN/SOMP* BN15 . 189 K4
Downs Rd *BURH* RH15 ...... 108 F8
   RCCH PO18 .... 155 J6
Down St *RCCH* PO18 ...... 177 J7
Downs Valley Rd *ROTT* BN2 .. 195 M4
Downsview *HFD* BN5 ...... 148 A5
   HOVE BN3 .... 192 E1
Downsview Av *PUL/STOR* RH20 . 143 H5
   ROTT BN2 .... 195 K3
Downsview Dr *MIDH* GU29 .... 94 F7
   RHWH RH17 .... 110 D8
Downsview Rd *ANG/EP* BN16 . 208 E4
   HORS RH12 .... 38 C6
Downsview Rd
   HPPT/KEY BN6 .... 151 G1
Downsview Rd *PTSD* BN41 .. 192 B3
Downs Wy *ANG/EP* BN16 ...... 208 A1
   SHOR BN43 .... 191 G3
   STHW BN42 .... 192 A2
Down Ter *ROTT* BN2 .... 11 K4
The Down *HOVE* BN3 ...... 170 E8
Downview Av *FERR* BN12 .... 208 F1
Downview Rd *ARUN* BN18 .... 205 H1
   RCCH PO18 .... 156 F6
   SELS PO20 .... 217 M6
Downview Rd *ARUN* BN18 .... 205 H1
   FERR BN12 .... 208 F1
   FIN/BW BN14 .... 165 M5
   MIDOS PO22 .... 13 L2
   MIDOS PO22 .... 182 B5
   PETW GU28 .... 97 M5
Down View Rd *WTHG* BN11 .. 8 B3
Downview Wy *ARUN* BN18 .... 205 H1
Dragons Green *SWTR* RH13 .. 81 K6
Dragons La *SWTR* RH13 ...... 103 J1
   SWTR RH13 .... 105 M5
Dragon St *EPSF* GU31 ...... 90 C2
Drake Av *FERR* BN12 ...... 187 L8
Drake Cl *HORS* RH12 ...... 37 M6
Drake Gv *ARUN* BN18 ...... 205 J2
Drakeleys Fld *LIPH* GU30 ...... 71 J2
Drake Pk *MIDOS* PO22 ...... 204 D6
Drake Rd *CRAWE* RH10 ...... 3 H9
   HORL RH6 .... 14 F7
Drakes Cl *LAN/SOMP* BN15 .. 190 C6
Draxmont Wy *BRI* BN1 ...... 194 B1
Draycliff Cl *FERR* BN12 ...... 208 F3
Drayton La *SELS* PO20 ...... 180 A5
Drewetts Cl *ANG/EP* BN16 .... 207 J1
Drewitts Ms *SELS* PO20 ...... 180 C5
Drift La *RCCH* PO18 ...... 176 F5
   SELS PO20 .... 222 F5
Drift Rd *BOGR* PO21 ...... 220 C2
   SELS PO20 .... 223 J4
The Drift *HAV* PO9 .... 152 E3
The Driftway *ANG/EP* BN16 .. 207 J1
   STEY/UB BN44 ...... 168 C1
The Drive *ANG/EP* BN16 ...... 208 C4
   BIL RH14 .... 55 J2
   BOGR PO21 .... 220 E3
   BURH RH15 .... 109 J2
   CCH PO19 .... 179 H1
   CRAWE RH10 .... 22 D1
   EMRTH PO10 .... 176 A4
   HAV PO9 .... 174 C1
   HORL RH6 .... 15 J2
   HOVE BN3 .... 193 K5
   LAN/SOMP BN15 ...... 189 L8
   LAN/SOMP BN15 ...... 190 C3
   PETW GU28 .... 118 E6
   RCCH PO18 .... 155 J5
   SHOR BN43 .... 191 G5
   STHW BN42 .... 191 L5
   WTHG BN11 .... 210 A1
The Driveway *SHOR* BN43 .... 191 G4
Droke La *RCCH* PO18 ...... 137 M6
Dropping Holms *HFD* BN5 .... 125 L2
Drove Av *ROTT* BN2 .... 195 L4
Drove Crs *PTSD* BN41 ...... 192 B2
Drove La *ARUN* BN18 ...... 204 D3
   SELS PO20 .... 217 L6
Drove Rd *PTSD* BN41 ...... 192 B3
   ROTT BN2 .... 195 H4

rovers Cl *PTSD* BN41 ... 192 D2
rovers Wy *BURH* RH15 ... 131 K2
he Drove *BRI* BN1 ... 173 K7
BRI BN1 ... 193 L3
he Droveway *HOVE* BN3 ... 193 K3
RHWH RH17 ... 87 K6
rum Rd *PSF* GU32 ... 90 B1
rummond Cl *HWH* RH16 ... 87 L8
rummond Rd *CRAWW* RH11 ... 19 M7
FERR BN12 ... 209 M3
rungewick La *BIL* RH14 ... 56 D6
rury Cl *CRAWE* RH10 ... 21 L8
ryad Wk *MIDOS* PO22 ... 204 E8
ryad Wy *MIDOS* PO22 ... 204 E8
rydens Wy *LIPH* GU30 ... 26 B7
rygrounds La *MIDOS* PO22 ... 13 K3
uck La *MIDOS* GU29 ... 95 G4
SELS PO20 ... 222 D3
uckmead La *LISS* GU33 ... 47 L6
udley Rd *BRI* BN1 ... 194 C3
udwell Rd *MIDOS* BN15 ... 195 M5
uffield La *EMRTH* PO10 ... 176 A1
uke Cl *CRAWE* RH10 ... 41 K2
uke Cl *ARUN* BN18 ... 184 A1
PSF GU32 ... 68 A8
ukes Cl *ARUN* BN18 ... 184 A1
ukes Meadow *BOGR* PO21 ... 220 C1
RCCH PO18 ... 155 H7
uke's Mound *ROTT* BN2 ... 11 L9
ukes Rd *ARUN* BN18 ... 159 M8
HWH RH16 ... 88 C4
uke St *BRI* BN1 ... 10 D7
LHPTN BN17 ... 206 E3
ukes Yd *STEY/UB* BN44 ... 167 L1
umbrells Court Rd *HPPT/KEY* BN6 ... 131 L8
umbrills Cl *BURH* RH15 ... 109 H7
ummer Ct *HAV* PO9 ... 152 A6
umpford La *EPSF* GU31 ... 92 C4
uncan Cl *CCH* PO19 ... 6 B1
uncton Cl *HWH* RH16 ... 87 L8
MIDOS PO22 ... 204 C8
uncton High St *PETW* GU28 ... 119 J6
uncton Wy *ANG/EP* BN16 ... 207 K1
undonald Cl *HISD* PO11 ... 196 D7
he Dunes *BOGR* PO21 ... 220 C4
unford Hollow *MIDH* GU29 ... 94 F8
unhurst Cl *HAV* PO9 ... 174 D1
unlop Cl *HPPT/KEY* BN6 ... 129 L3
unning's Wy *EGRIN* RH19 ... 24 F5
EGRIN RH19 ... 24 F6
unnock Cl *HAV* PO9 ... 152 E3
unsbury Wy *HAV* PO9 ... 152 B7
unsfold Cl *CRAWW* RH11 ... 20 B7
unsfold Rd *BIL* RH14 ... 31 L8
MFD/CHID GU8 ... 31 K5
MFD/CHID GU8 ... 32 F1
unstall Av *BURH* RH15 ... 108 F8
unstall Farm Rd *BURH* RH15 ... 109 G8
unstan Cl *CCH* PO19 ... 179 H1
unster Cl *HAV* PO9 ... 194 C3
urbans Rd *BIL* RH14 ... 78 C3
urfold Cl *HWH* RH12 ... 37 L5
urfold Wd *BIL* RH14 ... 31 K6
urford Ct *HAV* PO9 ... 152 A6
urford La *EPSF* GU31 ... 90 F1
urham Cl *CRAWE* RH10 ... 220 B4
CRAWE RH10 ... 40 F2
ROTT BN2 ... 195 H3
urham Gdns *CCH* PO19 ... 179 G3
urkins Rd *EGRIN* RH19 ... 24 E1
urleston Dr *MIDOS* PO22 ... 203 J6
urnford Cl *CCH* PO19 ... 6 A3
urrants Gdns *HAV* PO9 ... 152 E4
urrants Rd *HAV* PO9 ... 152 E5
urrington Hl *SALV* BN13 ... 187 L5
urrington La *SALV* BN13 ... 187 L5
utchells Copse *HORS* RH12 ... 37 M6
yall Cl *BURH* RH15 ... 108 F8
yers La *ARUN* BN18 ... 160 D7
yke Cl *HOVE* BN3 ... 171 J8
yke Rd *BRI* BN1 ... 10 D6
HOVE BN3 ... 10 D7
yke Road Av *HOVE* BN3 ... 171 J8
yke Road Dr *BRI* BN1 ... 193 M4
yke Road Vl *HOVE* BN3 ... 193 K1
he Dymock's *HPPT/KEY* BN6 ... 151 L1
ymoke St *EMRTH* PO10 ... 153 H8

E

ady Cl *SWTR* RH13 ... 5 J8
agles Cha *LHPTN* BN17 ... 184 D8
ames La *LISS* GU33 ... 46 C4
arles Meadow *HORS* RH12 ... 38 C6
arlswood Cl *SWTR* RH13 ... 5 K4
arly Commons *CRAWE* RH10 ... 3 K2
arnham Manor *LT SELS* PO20 ... 217 L5
arnley Rd *HISD* PO11 ... 215 J3
SELS PO20 ... 217 L5
arwig La *RHWH* RH17 ... 84 F6
asebourne La *MIDH* GU29 ... 95 H3
asebourne St *MIDH* GU29 ... 95 J2
PETW GU28 ... 74 A5
ast Av *FERR* BN12 ... 210 A5
MIDOS PO22 ... 205 G6
ast Bank *SELS* PO20 ... 223 H5
astbank *STHW* BN42 ... 192 A3
ast Beach Rd *SELS* PO20 ... 223 J5
astbourne Rd *ROTT* BN2 ... 194 E8
ast Bracklesham Dr *SELS* PO20 ... 217 J7
astbrook Rd *PTSD* BN41 ... 192 C5
astbrook Wy *STHW* BN42 ... 192 A3
astcourt Rd *FIN/BW* BN14 ... 8 F2
ast Court Wy *ANG/EP* BN16 ... 207 M2
astdale Rd *BURH* RH15 ... 109 K8
astdean Hl *RCCH* PO18 ... 137 K7
ast Dr *ANG/EP* BN16 ... 185 M8
MIDOS PO22 ... 205 H7
ROTT BN2 ... 11 J6
asteds La *SWTR* RH13 ... 82 J6
astergate Cl *FERR* BN12 ... 209 G2
astergate La *ARUN* BN18 ... 182 C5

Eastergate Rd *ROTT* BN2 ... 182 A3
Eastern Av *SHOR* BN43 ... 191 H5
Eastern Cl *ANG/EP* BN16 ... 208 G2
SHOR BN43 ... 191 H5
Eastern Pl *HAV* PO9 ... 174 D2
HWH RH16 ... 88 C5
HWH RH16 ... 110 A1
ROTT BN2 ... 11 K7
ROTT BN2 ... 194 F8
Eastern Ter *ROTT* BN2 ... 11 L9
Eastern Terrace Ms *ROTT* BN2 ... 11 L9
East Field Cl *EMRTH* PO10 ... 176 B2
Eastfield La *EPSF* GU31 ... 114 B1
East Front Rd *BOGR* PO21 ... 220 B5
Eastgate Sq *CCH* PO19 ... 6 F4
East Hampnett La *SELS* PO20 ... 180 F2
East Harting St *EPSF* GU31 ... 114 A1
Easthill Dr *PTSD* BN41 ... 192 C3
Easthill Wy *PTSD* BN41 ... 192 C3
East Lake *BOGR* PO21 ... 214 D1
Eastlake *EPSF* GU31 ... 90 F1
Eastland Rd *CCH* PO19 ... 7 H8
East Leigh Rd *HAV* PO9 ... 174 F1
East Mascalls Rd *HWH* RH16 ... 88 E6
East Md *BOGR* PO21 ... 220 B4
FERR BN12 ... 209 G3
East Meadway *SHOR* BN43 ... 191 H6
Eastoke Av *HISD* PO11 ... 215 G3
Easton Crs *BIL* RH14 ... 79 M4
Easton La *SELS* PO20 ... 218 C6
East Onslow Cl *FERR* BN12 ... 208 F2
Eastover Wy *MIDOS* PO22 ... 13 J5
East Pallant *CCH* PO19 ... 6 E5
East Pk *CRAWW* RH11 ... 2 F5
East Rw *CCH* PO19 ... 6 F4
Eastshaw La *MIDH* GU29 ... 167 L1
East Strd *SELS* PO20 ... 216 C4
East St *ARUN* BN18 ... 141 M5
BIL RH14 ... 79 L4
BRI BN1 ... 10 E7
BRI BN1 ... 173 K6
CCH PO19 ... 6 E6
CRAWE RH10 ... 23 J8
EMRTH PO10 ... 175 L1
HAV PO9 ... 174 C3
HORS RH12 ... 4 D9
HORS RH12 ... 18 F5
LAN/SOMP BN15 ... 189 M8
LHPTN BN17 ... 206 F3
PETW GU28 ... 98 A4
PTSD BN41 ... 192 D6
PUL/STOR RH20 ... 123 M3
SELS PO20 ... 223 G5
SHOR BN43 ... 191 G5
East Tyne *SALV* BN13 ... 187 L6
East View *RCCH* PO18 ... 157 G5
East Walls *CCH* PO19 ... 6 F4
East Wy *SELS* PO20 ... 223 H5
East Wick *HWH* RH16 ... 88 D5
Eastwick Cl *BRI* BN1 ... 172 C5
Eastwood *CRAWE* RH10 ... 3 J4
Eastwood Cl *HISD* PO11 ... 196 B8
Eaton Gdns *HOVE* BN3 ... 193 K5
Eaton Gv *HOVE* BN3 ... 193 K5
Eaton Pl *ROTT* BN2 ... 11 M9
Eaton Rd *HOVE* BN3 ... 193 K6
Eaton Vls *HOVE* BN3 ... 193 J5
Ebburton Av *BRI* BN1 ... 194 B3
Eburton Dro *HFD* BN5 ... 148 E5
Eburton Gdns *SHOR* BN43 ... 191 G3
Eden Rd *CRAWW* RH11 ... 20 A8
Edgar Cl *CRAWE* RH10 ... 21 M7
Edgehill Cl *SALV* BN13 ... 188 A5
Edgehill Wy *PTSD* BN41 ... 192 A2
Edgell Rd *EMRTH* PO10 ... 153 L8
Edgell Dr *BRI* BN1 ... 10 E2
SWTR RH13 ... 82 B3
Edinburgh Cl *BOGR* PO21 ... 220 F2
Edinburgh Rd *ROTT* BN2 ... 11 H1
Edinburgh Sq *MIDH* GU29 ... 95 G5
Edinburgh Wy *EGRIN* RH19 ... 25 G5
Edmonton Rd *SALV* BN13 ... 187 K6
Edrich Rd *CRAWW* RH11 ... 40 B3
Edward Av *HOVE* BN3 ... 193 H1
ROTT BN2 ... 213 L1
Edward Cl *HOVE* BN3 ... 193 H1
Edward Rd *HWH* RH16 ... 109 M1
Edwards Av *SELS* PO20 ... 180 D2
Edward St *ROTT* BN2 ... 11 G7
Edwards Wy *LHPTN* BN17 ... 184 D8
Edwen Cl *BOGR* PO21 ... 220 C1
Edwin Cl *LAN/SOMP* BN15 ... 189 K6
Effingham Cl *ROTT* BN2 ... 213 K2
Egginton Cl *BRI* BN1 ... 173 J1
Egginton Rd *BRI* BN1 ... 173 G8
Egmont Rd *HOVE* BN3 ... 192 E3
MIDH GU29 ... 95 J2
Egremont Pl *ROTT* BN2 ... 11 H7
Eighth Av *LAN/SOMP* BN15 ... 189 M5
Eileen Av *ROTT* BN2 ... 213 J3
Eirene Av *FERR* BN12 ... 209 J3
Eirene Rd *FERR* BN12 ... 209 M3
Elbridge Crs *BOGR* PO21 ... 220 F2
Elcombe Cl *SELS* PO20 ... 217 J7
Elder Cl *PTSD* BN41 ... 192 C3
Elderfield Cl *EMRTH* PO10 ... 175 K1
Elderfield Rd *HAV* PO9 ... 152 E2
Elder Pl *BRI* BN1 ... 10 E2
Elder Rd *HAV* PO9 ... 174 E1
Eldon Cl *PTSD* BN41 ... 192 C3
Eldon Rd *WTHG* BN11 ... 9 L4
Eldon Rd *LHPTN* BN17 ... 206 L1
Eldred Av *BRI* BN1 ... 171 L7
Eleanor Gdns *MIDOS* PO22 ... 204 E7
Eley Cl *ROTT* BN2 ... 212 F1
Eley Dr *ROTT* BN2 ... 195 M8
Elfin Gv *BOGR* PO21 ... 220 D1
Elgar Wy *HORS* RH12 ... 38 C8
Eliot Dr *HASM* GU27 ... 48 A6
Elizabethan Wy *CRAWE* RH10 ... 21 K7
Elizabeth Av *BOGR* PO21 ... 220 D1
HOVE BN3 ... 193 H1
Elizabeth Cl *BOGR* PO21 ... 220 D1

Elizabeth Ct *HORL* RH6 ... 15 H1
Elizabeth Crs *EGRIN* RH19 ... 25 G5
Elizabeth Pl *LAN/SOMP* BN15 ... 189 K7
Elizabeth Rd *CCH* PO19 ... 7 G1
SHOR BN43 ... 191 K4
WTHG BN11 ... 8 F5
Ella Cl *SELS* PO20 ... 216 F5
Ellanore La *SELS* PO20 ... 216 C1
Ellasdale Rd *BOGR* PO21 ... 12 A8
Ellen St *HOVE* BN3 ... 193 J5
PTSD BN41 ... 192 D5
Ellesmere Orch *EMRTH* PO10 ... 153 K6
Elliot Cl *CRAWE* RH10 ... 21 K7
Ellis Av *SALV* BN13 ... 187 M4
Ellis Cl *ARUN* BN18 ... 184 A2
Ellisfield Rd *HAV* PO9 ... 152 B8
Ellis Wy *BOGR* PO21 ... 220 B4
Elman Rd *CRAWW* RH11 ... 20 A8
Elson Rd *CRAWE* RH10 ... 21 K8
Elm Av *ANG/EP* BN16 ... 208 B3
Elm Cl *BOGR* PO21 ... 220 B5
HISD PO11 ... 214 D1
HOVE BN3 ... 193 K2
SELS PO20 ... 217 J6
SHOR BN43 ... 191 G5
Elm Dr *EGRIN* RH19 ... 25 H1
HOVE BN3 ... 192 F3
MIDOS PO22 ... 205 J7
Elmer Cl *MIDOS* PO22 ... 205 J7
Elmer Ct *MIDOS* PO22 ... 205 J7
Elmer Rd *MIDOS* PO22 ... 205 G7
Elm Gv *BOGR* PO21 ... 221 H1
HISD PO11 ... 214 D1
LAN/SOMP BN15 ... 189 L7
MIDOS PO22 ... 182 B5
ROTT BN2 ... 11 J3
SELS PO20 ... 222 F1
SWTR RH13 ... 5 G9
WTHG BN11 ... 210 A1
Elm Grove La *STEY/UB* BN44 ... 167 L1
Elmgrove Rd *LHPTN* BN17 ... 206 F3
Elm Gv South *MIDOS* PO22 ... 182 B6
Elmhurst Cl *ANG/EP* BN16 ... 186 B6
Elmhurst La *SWTR* RH13 ... 58 C6
Elm La *HAV* PO9 ... 174 C3
Elmleigh *MIDH* GU29 ... 94 F4
Elmleigh Rd *HAV* PO9 ... 174 C2
Elmore Rd *ROTT* BN2 ... 11 G5
Elm Pk *FERR* BN12 ... 209 K7
RCCH PO18 ... 177 K6
Elm Park Rd *HAV* PO9 ... 174 C2
Elm Pl *ANG/EP* BN16 ... 207 L3
Elm Ri *FIN/BW* BN14 ... 165 M6
Elm Rd *HAV* PO9 ... 174 D4
PTSD BN41 ... 192 C4
SELS PO20 ... 181 M5
WTHG BN11 ... 9 J6
Elms Dr *LAN/SOMP* BN15 ... 189 L6
Elmsfield *SELS* PO20 ... 223 G5
Elms La *SELS* PO20 ... 216 D3
Elms Lea Av *BRI* BN1 ... 193 M1
Elms Ride *SELS* PO20 ... 216 D2
Elmstead Gdns *SELS* PO20 ... 216 D2
Elmstead Park Rd *SELS* PO20 ... 216 D2
Elmstone Cl *LAN/SOMP* BN15 ... 189 L6
Elms Wy *SELS* PO20 ... 216 D2
Elm Tree Close *BOGR* PO21 ... 203 H6
Elm Tree Cl *SELS* PO20 ... 223 G4
Elmwood Av *MIDOS* PO22 ... 12 F3
Elrington Rd *HOVE* BN3 ... 193 K3
Elsie Rd *WTHG* BN11 ... 8 D7
Elsted Cl *CRAWW* RH11 ... 20 C4
Elsted Crs *BRI* BN1 ... 172 C6
Elsted Rd *MIDH* GU29 ... 92 E8
Elverlands Cl *FERR* BN12 ... 209 G4
Elvin Crs *ROTT* BN2 ... 195 M8
Elwell Gn *HISD* PO11 ... 214 C1
Elwood Cl *BURH* RH15 ... 131 G3
Ely Cl *CRAWE* RH10 ... 41 G2
SALV BN13 ... 188 A4
SELS PO20 ... 217 G4
Ely Gdns *BOGR* PO21 ... 220 E1
Ely Rd *SALV* BN13 ... 188 A4
Emerald Quay *SHOR* BN43 ... 191 H6
Emms La *SWTR* RH13 ... 81 G2
Emsbrook Dr *EMRTH* PO10 ... 175 J2
Emsworth Cl *CRAWE* RH10 ... 41 K1
Emsworth Common Rd *EMRTH* PO10 ... 153 G7
Emsworth House Cl *EMRTH* PO10 ... 175 L8
Emsworth Rd *EMRTH* PO10 ... 175 L8
HAV PO9 ... 174 D3
End La *HFD* BN5 ... 127 H7
Enfield Cl *LIPH* GU30 ... 49 L1
Enfield Rd *CRAWW* RH11 ... 40 C2
Engalee *EGRIN* RH19 ... 24 D2
Englefield *HORS* RH12 ... 60 A3
English Cl *HWH* RH16 ... 192 F4
Ennerdale Cl *CRAWW* RH11 ... 2 B8
Ennerdale Dr *LAN/SOMP* BN15 ... 189 J7
Ensign Wy *ANG/EP* BN16 ... 207 L2
Epping Wk *CRAWE* RH10 ... 3 K8
Epsom Rd *CRAWE* RH10 ... 3 H8
Erica Wy *CRAWE* RH10 ... 22 A1
HORS RH12 ... 4 E1
Eridge Cl *CRAWW* RH11 ... 21 K6
Eridge Rd *HOVE* BN3 ... 193 H4
Erin Wy *BURH* RH15 ... 130 F1
Eriskay Cl *SALV* BN13 ... 187 J4
Eriswell Rd *WTHG* BN11 ... 8 F6
Erles Rd *LIPH* GU30 ... 26 D8
Ernest Cl *EMRTH* PO10 ... 175 J3
Erringham Rd *SHOR* BN43 ... 190 F3
Erroll Rd *HOVE* BN3 ... 192 B6
Erskine Cl *CRAWW* RH11 ... 39 M2
Esher Cl *BOGR* PO21 ... 220 C4
Esher Dr *LAN/SOMP* BN15 ... 189 L4
Eskbank Av *BRI* BN1 ... 172 E5
Esmond Cl *LHPTN* BN17 ... 207 G2
Esmonde Cl *LHPTN* BN17 ... 207 G2
The Esplanade *BOGR* PO21 ... 12 D8
WTHG BN11 ... 9 J6
Essendon Dr *SALV* BN13 ... 187 J6
Essex Rd *BOGR* PO21 ... 12 C3
Essex St *ROTT* BN2 ... 11 H7
Estcots Dr *EGRIN* RH19 ... 25 H7
The Estuary *LHPTN* BN17 ... 207 G3

Ethelred Rd *SALV* BN13 ... 8 A2
Ethel St *HOVE* BN3 ... 193 J5
Ethelwulf Rd *SALV* BN13 ... 8 A2
Eton Cl *BOGR* PO21 ... 202 F8
Eton Dr *SELS* PO20 ... 217 G4
SHOR BN43 ... 191 K4
WTHG BN11 ... 8 F5
Ettrick Cl *CCH* PO19 ... 7 G6
Ettrick Rd *CCH* PO19 ... 7 G6
Evans Cl *CRAWE* RH10 ... 21 L7
Evelyn Av *LAN/SOMP* BN15 ... 207 L4
Evelyn Rd *HOVE* BN3 ... 193 L6
Evelyn Ter *ROTT* BN2 ... 11 K6
Eversfield *SWTR* RH13 ... 82 C3
Eversfield Rd *SWTR* RH13 ... 5 G9
Eversley Crs *HAV* PO9 ... 152 A8
Ewart St *ROTT* BN2 ... 11 H4
Ewens Gdns *MIDOS* PO22 ... 182 B5
Ewhurst Cl *CRAWW* RH11 ... 2 C3
HAV PO9 ... 152 A8
Ewhurst Rd *CRAWW* RH11 ... 2 C3
ROTT BN2 ... 194 D4
Exbury Rd *HAV* PO9 ... 152 D7
Excalibur Cl *CRAWW* RH11 ... 19 M7
Exceat Ct *ROTT* BN2 ... 194 F6
Exchange Rd *CRAWE* RH10 ... 3 H3
Exeter Cl *BOGR* PO21 ... 221 G1
CRAWE RH10 ... 40 F2
EMRTH PO10 ... 175 J1
Exeter Rd *CCH* PO19 ... 178 F3
HOVE BN3 ... 192 F3
MIDOS PO22 ... 205 J7
Exeter St *BRI* BN1 ... 10 E1
Exmoor Cl *SALV* BN13 ... 187 L5
Exmoor Crs *SALV* BN13 ... 187 M5
Exmoor Dr *SALV* BN13 ... 187 M4
Exton Cl *CCH* PO19 ... 7 G8
HAV PO9 ... 152 E7
Eyles Cl *HORS* RH12 ... 4 A3

F

Faber Cl *HAV* PO9 ... 152 D7
Fabians Wy *HFD* BN5 ... 127 L7
Fairbanks *HFD* BN5 ... 87 M8
Fairbridge Wy *BURH* RH15 ... 109 G7
Faircox La *HFD* BN5 ... 127 L7
Fairdene *STHW* BN42 ... 192 A3
Fairfield *HORL* RH6 ... 15 H3
Fairfield Cl *BURH* RH15 ... 109 G8
EMRTH PO10 ... 175 J2
RCCH PO18 ... 177 K7
RHWH RH17 ... 66 B4
SHOR BN43 ... 191 J3
Fairfield Cottages *SWTR* RH13 ... 105 M2
Fairfield Crs *HPPT/KEY* BN6 ... 130 B6
Fairfield Gdns *PTSD* BN41 ... 192 C3
Fairfield Ri *PETW* GU28 ... 98 A5
Fairfield Rd *BURH* RH15 ... 131 G1
EGRIN RH19 ... 25 G4
HAV PO9 ... 174 C3
PUL/STOR RH20 ... 125 H8
RCCH PO18 ... 177 J7
Fairfield Wy *HWH* RH16 ... 87 M7
Fairford Cl *HWH* RH16 ... 87 M7
Fairholme Dr *ARUN* BN18 ... 205 H2
Fairlands *ANG/EP* BN16 ... 207 K2
Fairlawn *ANG/EP* BN16 ... 207 K2
Fairlawn Crs *EGRIN* RH19 ... 24 C2
Fairlawn Dr *EGRIN* RH19 ... 24 C2
FIN/BW BN14 ... 9 H1
Fairlawns *HORL* RH6 ... 15 J1
SHOR BN43 ... 191 H4
Fairlea Cl *BURH* RH15 ... 109 G8
Fairlead *LHPTN* BN17 ... 207 G4
Fairlea Rd *EMRTH* PO10 ... 175 J1
Fairlie Gdns *BRI* BN1 ... 193 M1
Fairlight Pl *ROTT* BN2 ... 11 J1
Fairmead Cl *PUL/STOR* RH20 ... 121 H1
Fairmile Bottom *ARUN* BN18 ... 141 H1
Fair Oak Dr *HAV* PO9 ... 174 C1
Fair Vw *HORS* RH12 ... 60 B1
Fairview Av *FERR* BN12 ... 209 K3
Fairview Ri *BRI* BN1 ... 171 L7
Fairview Rd *LAN/SOMP* BN15 ... 189 M4
Fairway *CRAWE* RH10 ... 22 C2
CRAWW RH11 ... 19 L7
LHPTN BN17 ... 207 G4
Fairway Cl *CRAWE* RH10 ... 22 B2
LIPH GU30 ... 48 E1
Fairway Crs *PTSD* BN41 ... 192 C4
The Fairway *BOGR* PO21 ... 220 C4
HAV PO9 ... 152 C7
LAN/SOMP BN15 ... 190 B7
MIDH GU29 ... 94 F7
Faithfull Crs *PUL/STOR* RH20 ... 143 J2
Falcon Cl *CRAWW* RH11 ... 20 E4
SHOR BN43 ... 191 K6
Falcon Gdns *MIDOS* PO22 ... 184 D8
Falkland Av *LHPTN* BN17 ... 207 G2
Falklands Cl *MIDOS* PO22 ... 12 F2
Falklands Dr *SWTR* RH13 ... 38 C8
Fallow Deer Cl *SWTR* RH13 ... 61 J1
Fallowfield Cl *HOVE* BN3 ... 193 G2
Fallowfield Crs *HOVE* BN3 ... 192 F2
Falmer Av *FERR* BN12 ... 209 J3
ROTT BN2 ... 213 J1
Falmer Cl *CRAWW* RH11 ... 2 E7
FERR BN12 ... 209 K3
Falmer Gdns *ROTT* BN2 ... 195 L4
Falmer House Rd *BRI* BN1 ... 173 K5
Falmer Rd *ROTT* BN2 ... 195 L2
Faraday Av *EGRIN* RH19 ... 24 B2
Faraday Cl *CRAWE* RH10 ... 22 A2
Faraday Rd *SALV* BN13 ... 187 K6
Faresmead *BOGR* PO21 ... 221 G2
Farhalls Crs *HORS* RH12 ... 5 K1
Farleigh Cl *HAV* PO9 ... 152 A7
Farlington Av *HWH* RH16 ... 88 A7
Farlington Cl *HWH* RH16 ... 88 A7
Farm Acre *ANG/EP* BN16 ... 208 A3
Farm Av *HWH* RH16 ... 88 A4
Farm Cl *BIL* RH14 ... 56 B1

Farm Cnr *MIDOS* PO22 ... 205 H7
Far Meadow Wy *EMRTH* PO10 ... 175 G4
Farm Hl *ROTT* BN2 ... 195 M5
Farm La *HPPT/KEY* BN6 ... 151 M1
RCCH PO18 ... 176 C5
Farmleigh Cl *CRAWE* RH10 ... 21 K4
Farm Ms *HOVE* BN3 ... 193 L6
Farm Pl *BIL* RH14 ... 56 A1
Farm Rd *HOVE* BN3 ... 193 L6
SELS PO20 ... 217 J7
Farm Vw *EMRTH* PO10 ... 175 G4
Farm Wy *ANG/EP* BN16 ... 207 K2
BURH RH15 ... 131 K3
STHW BN42 ... 192 B5
Farmway Cl *HOVE* BN3 ... 192 E2
Farncombe Cl *RHWH* RH17 ... 110 E7
Farncombe Rd *WTHG* BN11 ... 9 L4
Fardell Cl *CCH* PO19 ... 7 J2
Farne Cl *SELS* PO20 ... 199 M8
Farne La *SELS* PO20 ... 199 M8
Farnfold Rd *STEY/UB* BN44 ... 146 E8
Farnham Av *HPPT/KEY* BN6 ... 131 K3
Farnham Cl *CRAWW* RH11 ... 20 A4
Farnham La *LISS* GU33 ... 47 H7
PSF GU32 ... 68 A8
Farnhurst Rd *MIDOS* PO22 ... 182 C6
Farnlea Rd *BURH* RH15 ... 109 J7
The Faroes *LHPTN* BN17 ... 207 H1
Farr Cl *RHWH* RH17 ... 87 C4
Farriers Cl *BIL* RH14 ... 79 K5
Farringdon Rd *HAV* PO9 ... 152 B8
Fastnet Wy *LHPTN* BN17 ... 207 H3
Fathoms Reach *HISD* PO11 ... 196 B8
Faulkners Wy *BURH* RH15 ... 109 H7
Fawley Ct *HAV* PO9 ... 152 E7
Fawn Ri *HFD* BN5 ... 127 M6
Faygate La *HORS* RH12 ... 4 D2
Fay Rd *HORS* RH12 ... 4 D2
Felbridge Av *CRAWE* RH10 ... 21 L5
Felbridge Cl *EGRIN* RH19 ... 24 D1
Felbridge Ct *EGRIN* RH19 ... 24 D1
Felbridge Rd *EGRIN* RH19 ... 23 L1
Felcot Rd *EGRIN* RH19 ... 23 J4
Fellcott Wy *HORS* RH12 ... 60 A3
Felpham Gdns *MIDOS* PO22 ... 204 C7
Felpham Rd *MIDOS* PO22 ... 13 K5
Felpham Wy *MIDOS* PO22 ... 13 J5
Felride *HWH* RH16 ... 109 M1
Fenby Cl *SWTR* RH13 ... 5 J8
Fenchurch Rd *CRAWE* RH10 ... 21 J8
Fenhurst Cl *HORS* RH12 ... 60 A3
Fennel Crs *CRAWW* RH11 ... 40 C1
Fereday Cl *LAN/SOMP* BN15 ... 189 M6
Fermandy La *CRAWE* RH10 ... 23 H7
Fern Cl *EPSF* GU31 ... 90 F1
Ferndale Rd *BURH* RH15 ... 131 G3
CCH PO19 ... 179 H2
HOVE BN3 ... 193 L5
Ferndale Wk *ANG/EP* BN16 ... 186 B6
Fernden La *HASM* GU27 ... 51 J1
Ferndown *CRAWE* RH10 ... 21 L2
Ferndown Gdns *MIDOS* PO22 ... 13 M3
Fern Dr *HAV* PO9 ... 174 D2
Fernhill Cl *CRAWE* RH10 ... 23 J3
Fernhill Rd *HORL* RH6 ... 15 L4
Fernhurst Cl *BRI* BN1 ... 172 C6
CRAWW RH11 ... 20 C4
HISD PO11 ... 214 A1
Fernhurst Crs *BRI* BN1 ... 172 C7
Fernhurst Dr *FERR* BN12 ... 209 H2
Fernhurst Gdns *BOGR* PO21 ... 220 E2
Fernhurst La *LIPH* GU30 ... 71 J1
Fern Rd *PUL/STOR* RH20 ... 143 K3
Fern Wy *HORS* RH12 ... 4 E2
Fernwood Ri *BRI* BN1 ... 171 L7
Feroners Cl *CRAWE* RH10 ... 3 M7
Ferring Cl *CRAWW* RH11 ... 2 A1
FERR BN12 ... 208 F4
Ferring Gdns *FERR* BN12 ... 208 F3
Ferring Grange Gdns *FERR* BN12 ... 208 F2
Ferringham La *FERR* BN12 ... 208 F3
Ferringham Wy *FERR* BN12 ... 208 F4
Ferring La *FERR* BN12 ... 209 G1
Ferring Marine *FERR* BN12 ... 208 G4
Ferring St *FERR* BN12 ... 208 F2
Ferry Rd *LHPTN* BN17 ... 207 H2
SHOR BN43 ... 191 G6
Fetherston Rd *LAN/SOMP* BN15 ... 189 L5
Feversham Cl *SHOR* BN43 ... 191 J6
Field Cl *ARUN* BN18 ... 182 C5
BURH RH15 ... 108 F8
LAN/SOMP BN15 ... 189 L6
Fieldend *HORS* RH12 ... 38 C7
Field End *PUL/STOR* RH20 ... 143 M2
Fieldgate Cl *SWTR* RH13 ... 61 K8
The Fieldings *SWTR* RH13 ... 82 A5
Field Pl *LHPTN* BN17 ... 206 E3
LIPH GU30 ... 49 J1
Field Rd *SELS* PO20 ... 217 G5
Fields End *HWH* RH16 ... 88 D8
Fieldway *HASM* GU27 ... 28 D5
HPPT/KEY BN6 ... 151 L1
HWH RH16 ... 88 A4
Fifth Av *FIN/BW* BN14 ... 188 D4
HAV PO9 ... 174 E2
LAN/SOMP BN15 ... 189 M5
Filbert Crs *CRAWW* RH11 ... 20 B6
Filey Cl *CRAWW* RH11 ... 20 B6
Fincham Cl *ANG/EP* BN16 ... 208 A3
Finchdean Rd *HAV* PO9 ... 152 F2
Finches *LAN/SOMP* BN15 ... 189 L6
LHPTN BN17 ... 184 D8
SWTR RH13 ... 127 H1
Finches Gdns *HWH* RH16 ... 88 B3
Finches La *HWH* RH16 ... 88 B3
PUL/STOR RH20 ... 123 K4
Finches Park Rd *HWH* RH16 ... 88 B3
The Finches *SHOR* BN43 ... 191 H5
Finch Gdns *MIDOS* PO22 ... 203 J5
Findon Av *ROTT* BN2 ... 195 M3
Findon By-pass *FIN/BW* BN14 ... 165 L6
Findon Dr *MIDOS* PO22 ... 204 E6
Findon Rd *CRAWW* RH11 ... 20 A6
FIN/BW BN14 ... 166 A8
ROTT BN2 ... 195 G7

Findon Wy *HORS* RH12 .... 59 L1
Finians Fld *SWTR* RH13 .... 81 G2
Finisterre Wy *LHPTN* BN17 .... 207 H4
Finsbury Cl *CRAWW* RH11 .... 40 D2 🔢
Finsbury Rd *ROTT* BN2 .... 11 H4
Fircroft Av *LAN/SOMP* BN15 .. 189 L4
Fircroft Crs *ANG/EP* BN16 .... 207 L2
Firlands *HORS* RH16 .... 88 A8 🔢
Firle Cl *CRAWE* RH10 .... 20 F4
Firle Rd *LAN/SOMP* BN15 ...... 189 L3
  ROTT BN2 .... 11 M3
Firs Av *MIDOS* PO22 .... 204 C7
Firs Av West *MIDOS* PO22 .... 204 C7
Firsdown Cl *SALV* BN13 ...... 187 M2 🔢
Firsdown Rd *SALV* BN13 ...... 187 M2 🔢
First Av *HOR/PO10 .... 176 A4
  FIN/BW BN14 .... 188 D4
  HAV PO9 .... 174 E2
  HOVE BN3 .... 193 H5
  LAN/SOMP BN15 ...... 189 M6
  MIDOS PO22 .... 204 F6
  SELS PO20 .... 217 J7
  SELS PO20 .... 218 A2
The Firs *LIPH* GU30 .... 49 J1
Firtoft Cl *BURH* RH15 .... 131 M1
Fir Tree Av *HASM* GU27 ...... 27 L6
Fir Tree Cl *CRAWW* RH11....... 20 C3
  PUL/STOR RH20 .... 125 L6
  SWTR RH13 .... 84 B1
Fir Tree La *PUL/STOR* RH20 .. 125 L6
Fir Tree Rd *HISD* PO11 ...... 214 D1
Fir Tree Wy *HPPT/KEY* BN6 .. 131 H8
  MIDOS PO22 .... 203 K5
Fishbourne Rd (East)
  CCH PO19 .... 178 D6
Fishbourne Rd (West)
  CCH PO19 .... 178 C6
Fisher Cl *CRAWE* RH10 .... 3 G1
Fishergate Cl *PTSD* BN41 .... 192 B5 🔢
Fisher La *MFD/CHID* GU8 ...... 31 H5
  SELS PO20 .... 201 K5
The Fishermans
  EMRTH PO10 .... 175 K4 🔢
Fisherman's Wk *BOGR* PO21 .. 220 E3 🔢
  HISD PO11 .... 215 H2
  SELS PO20 .... 223 G6
  SHOR BN43 .... 190 E7 🔢
Fishers Cl *ANG/EP* BN16 ...... 207 H4
Fishers Ct *HORS* RH12.......... 4 C3
Fishersgate Ter *PTSD* BN41 .. 192 B5
Fishery La *HISD* PO11 .... 214 F2
Fish La *BOGR* PO21 .... 221 G2
  SELS PO20 .... 222 D4
Fitch Dr *ROTT* BN2 .... 194 F3
Fitchet Cl *CRAWW* RH11 ...... 20 C4
Fittleworth Cl *FERR* BN12 .... 187 J8 🔢
Fittleworth Dr *MIDOS* PO22 .. 204 D6
Fittleworth Rd *BIL* RH14 ...... 78 A6
Fitzalan Rd *ARUN* BN18 ...... 184 C2
  HORS RH12 .... 5 L3
  LHPTN BN17 .... 206 F3
Fitzherbert Dr *ROTT* BN2 .... 194 E4
Fitzwilliam Cl *BOGR* PO21 .. 203 G8 🔢
Fitzwygram Crs *HAV* PO9 .... 174 C1
Five Acres *CRAWE* RH10 ...... 20 F4
  RCCH PO18 .... 155 H7
Five Oaks Rd *SWTR* RH13 .... 58 F4
Flag Sq *SHOR* BN43 .... 191 G6
Flansham La *MIDOS* PO22 .... 204 D5
Flansham Pk *MIDOS* PO22 .... 204 D6
Flatt Rd *RCCH* PO18 .... 176 E4
Flaxman Av *CCH* PO19 ...... 178 C6
Flax Mean *MIDOS* PO22 ...... 204 C7
Fleet Cl *LHPTN* BN17 .... 207 H2
Fleetend *HAV* PO9 .... 152 B6 🔢
The Fleet *PUL/STOR* RH20 .... 121 J1
Fleming Wy *CRAWE* RH10 .... 20 F1
  CRAWE RH10 .... 3 G8
Fletcher Cl *BOGR* PO21 ...... 220 C2
Fletcher Pl *SELS* PO20 ...... 201 K5
Fletcher Rd *FIN/BW* BN14 .... 188 E7
Fletchers *SWTR* RH13 .... 82 A1 🔢
Fletchers Cl *SWTR* RH13 ...... 60 F3
Fletchers Fld *LIPH* GU30 ...... 49 J1
Fletcher's La *RCCH* PO18 .... 199 L3
  SELS PO20 .... 218 E1
Fletcher Wy *ANG/EP* BN16 .. 186 A6
  BOGR PO21 .... 12 C3
Fletching Cl *ROTT* BN2 ...... 195 G6
Flexford Gdns *HAV* PO9 ...... 174 D1 🔢
Flimwell Cl *ROTT* BN2 ...... 194 F7 🔢
Flint Cl *ANG/EP* BN16 ...... 208 A2 🔢
  CRAWE RH10 .... 41 J1
  PTSD BN41 .... 192 C2
Florence Av *HOVE* BN3 ...... 192 K4
Florence Cl *SELS* PO20 ...... 199 L8
Florence Pl *BRI* BN1 .... 194 C3
Florence Rd *BRI* BN1 .... 194 B4
  CCH PO19 .... 7 K4
The Florets *STEY/UB* BN44 .. 168 C3 🔢
Florida Cl *FERR* BN12 .... 209 J4
Florida Gdns *FERR* BN12 .... 209 G4 🔢
Florida Rd *FERR* BN12 .... 209 G4
Florlandia Cl *LAN/SOMP* BN15 .. 189 J7
Flower Farm Cl *HFD* BN5 .... 127 L1
Foamcourt Waye *FERR* BN12 .. 208 F3
Folders Cl *BURH* RH15 ...... 131 L3
Folders La *BURH* RH15 ...... 131 K3
Follett Cl *BOGR* PO21 ...... 220 F3
Follis Gdns *CCH* PO19 ...... 178 C5
Folly La *EPSF* GU31 .... 90 C1
  PUL/STOR RH20 .... 139 M1
Fonthill Rd *HOVE* BN3 .... 193 J4
Fontwell Av *SELS* PO20 ...... 182 A3
Fontwell Cl *ANG/EP* BN16 .. 207 J4
  ARUN BN18 .... 182 B2
  FIN/BW BN14 .... 188 B4
Fontwell Rd *CRAWE* RH10 .... 3 J4
  SELS PO20 .... 223 J4
Forbes Cl *CRAWE* RH10 ...... 41 J2 🔢
Fordingbridge Cl *HORS* RH12 .. 60 D3
Ford La *ARUN* BN18 .... 183 L4
  SWTR RH13 .... 126 K5
Ford Rd *ARUN* BN18 .... 183 M8
Fordwater Gdns *ARUN* BN18 .. 205 J1
Fordwater La *CCH* PO19 .... 179 H2
Fordwater Rd *CCH* PO19 .... 179 H1
  RCCH PO18 .... 157 H7
Foredown Cl *PTSD* BN41 .... 192 C2 🔢

Foredown Dr *PTSD* BN41 ...... 192 C3
Foredown Rd *PTSD* BN41 .... 192 C1
Foreland Ct *HISD* PO11 ...... 214 F2
Forest Cl *CRAWE* RH10 ...... 23 J4
  SWTR RH13 .... 38 C3
  SWTR RH13 .... 61 K6
Forest Cnr *LISS* GU33 .... 47 K5
Forestdale *GSHT* GU26 .... 27 L1
Forester Rd *CRAWE* RH10 ...... 3 G8
Forestfield *CRAWE* RH10 ...... 21 J8
  SWTR RH13 .... 5 L6
Forest Lane Cl *LIPH* GU30 .... 26 B8
Forest Oaks *SWTR* RH13 .... 38 C8 🔢
Forest Ri *LISS* GU33 .... 47 K6
Forest Rd *BRI* BN1 .... 172 F7
  FIN/BW BN14 .... 188 E6
  LISS GU33 .... 47 H3
  MIDH GU29 .... 94 E6
Forestside Av *HAV* PO9 ...... 152 D7
Forest Vw *CRAWE* RH10 ...... 3 L9
Forest View Rd *EGRIN* RH19 .. 24 F6
Forest Wy *EGRIN* RH19 ...... 25 J7
Forge Cl *ANG/EP* BN16 ...... 208 A2
  CCH PO19 .... 200 F1
  HORS RH12 .... 36 F3
  PTSD BN41 .... 192 C2
Forge La *CRAWE* RH10 .... 3 L1
  HORS RH12 .... 36 E8
Forge Rd *CRAWE* RH10 .... 3 L1
The Forge *HORS* RH12 .... 36 F5
  SWTR RH13 .... 82 A3
Forge Wy *BIL* RH14 .... 79 K4
  BURH RH15 .... 109 G8
Forge Wd *CRAWE* RH10 ...... 21 L1
Forrester Rd *SWTR* RH13 .... 127 C1
Forsythia Cl *HAV* PO9 ...... 152 E8
Fort Hvn *SHOR* BN43 .... 191 K6
Fort Rd *LHPTN* BN17 .... 206 F1
Forty Acre La *EPSF* GU31 .... 112 E1
Foster Cl *PUL/STOR* RH20 .... 125 C7
Fosters Cl *ANG/EP* BN16 .... 207 M4
Foundry Cl *SWTR* RH13 ...... 5 G4
Foundry La *HASM* GU27 ...... 28 B6
  SWTR RH13 .... 5 G5
Foundry Rd *ARUN* BN18........ 205 G1
Foundry St *BRI* BN1 .... 10 E5
Fountains Cl *BRI* BN1 ...... 194 C2 🔢
  CRAWW RH11 .... 20 B8 🔢
Founthill Av *ROTT* BN2 ...... 213 J3
Founthill Rd *ROTT* BN2 ...... 213 J3
Fourth Av *FIN/BW* BN14 ...... 188 E5
  HAV PO9 .... 174 E2
  HOVE BN3 .... 193 J7
  LAN/SOMP BN15 ...... 189 M5
  MIDOS PO22 .... 204 D8 🔢
Fowey Cl *SHOR* BN43 .... 191 J6
Fowler Cl *CRAWE* RH10 ...... 21 K8
Foxbridge La *BIL* RH14 ...... 55 K3
Foxbury La *EMRTH* PO10 .... 153 M8
Fox Cl *BURH* RH15 .... 131 G3 🔢
  CRAWW RH11 .... 20 C4
Foxcott Gv *HAV* PO9 .... 152 C7
Fox Ct *PUL/STOR* RH20 ...... 143 J3
Foxdale Dr *ANG/EP* BN16 .... 186 A8
Fox Dell *PUL/STOR* RH20 .... 143 J3
Foxes Cl *SWTR* RH13 .... 82 A5
Foxes Cft *MIDOS* PO22 ...... 182 D6
Foxfield Cottages *SWTR* RH13 .. 82 A5
Foxfields *PUL/STOR* RH20 .... 123 K4
Foxglove Av *HORS* RH12 ...... 37 M6
Foxglove Wy *ANG/EP* BN16 .. 207 H1 🔢
Fox HI *HWH* RH16 .... 109 M3
Fox Hill *HWH* RH16 .... 109 M3
Fox Hill Village *HWH* RH16.. 110 A4
Foxhole La *RHWH* RH17 ...... 107 J2
Foxholes *HORS* RH12 .... 34 E4
Foxhunters Rd *PTSD* BN41 .. 192 A1 🔢
Fox Lea *HHs *CRAWE* RH10 .. 165 M7
Foxleigh Cha *HORS* RH12........ 5 J3
Foxley La *SALV* BN13 .... 188 A4
Fox Rd *HASM* GU27 .... 27 M6
  MIDH GU29 .... 94 D4
Foxwarren *HWH* RH16 ...... 87 K7 🔢
Foxwarren Cl *SELS* PO20 .... 217 G5
Fox Wy *PTSD* BN41 .... 192 B1
Foxwells *RHWH* RH17 ...... 65 H3
Framfield Cl *BRI* BN1 .... 172 K6
  CRAWW RH11 .... 20 B4
The Framptons *ANG/EP* BN16 .. 208 C3
France La *SALV* BN13 .... 186 E4
Franciscan Wy *LHPTN* BN17 .. 206 E3
Francis Edwards Wy
  CRAWW RH11 .... 39 M2 🔢
Francis Rd *HWH* RH16 ...... 88 C4 🔢
Francis St *BRI* BN1 .... 10 E4
Frandor Rd *BOGR* PO21 ...... 203 G7
Frankland Md
  PUL/STOR RH20 .... 144 F6 🔢
Franklands Cl *BURH* RH15 .. 131 J3 🔢
  FIN/BW BN14 .... 188 A3
Franklands Gdns *BURH* RH15 .. 131 H4
Franklands Wy *BURH* RH15 .. 131 H4
Frankland Ter *EMRTH* PO10 .. 175 K4 🔢
Franklin Pl *CCH* PO19 .... 6 E3
Franklin Rd *CCH* PO19 ...... 21 K7
  PTSD BN41 .... 192 D5
  ROTT BN2 .... 11 J1
  SALV BN13 .... 187 M5
  SHOR BN43 .... 191 K4
Franklin St *ROTT* BN2 .... 11 J2
Franklynn Rd *HWH* RH16 .... 110 A1
Frankton Av *HWH* RH16 .... 110 B1 🔢
Frant Rd *HOVE* BN3 .... 193 H2
Frarydene *EMRTH* PO10 ...... 176 A4
Fraser Cl *SELS* PO20 .... 223 H5
Fraser Gdns *EMRTH* PO10 .... 176 B3
Fraser Rd *HAV* PO9 .... 174 A2
Frederick Pl *BRI* BN1 .... 10 E4
Frederick Rd *CCH* PO19 ...... 178 D5 🔢
Frederick St *BRI* BN1 .... 10 E4
Freehold St *SHOR* BN43 ...... 190 F5
Freehold Ter *ROTT* BN2 ...... 194 C4
Freek's La *BURH* RH15 ...... 109 H4
Freeland Cl *SELS* PO20 ...... 178 D6
Freeman Cl *SELS* PO20 ...... 182 C3
Freeman Rd *HORS* RH12 .... 36 K4
Freemans Cl *BIL* RH14 ...... 79 K4 🔢
Freemans Rd *PTSD* BN41 .... 192 B4

Freeways *SELS* PO20 .... 222 E4
Frenches Cl *RHWH* RH17 .... 143 L2 🔢
Frenches Md *BIL* RH14 ...... 79 K4
French Gdns *HWH* RH16 ...... 88 A6
Frenchmans Rd *PSF* GU32 ...... 68 B8
French Rd *LISS* GU33 .... 48 A1
Freshbrook Cl
  LAN/SOMP BN15 .... 189 M7 🔢
Freshbrook Rd
  LAN/SOMP BN15 .... 190 A7
Freshfield Bank *FROW* RH18 .. 45 M2
Freshfield Cl *CRAWE* RH10 ...... 3 M5
Freshfield La *RHWH* RH17 .... 89 K4
Freshfield Pl *ROTT* BN2 ...... 11 J6
Freshfield Rd *ROTT* BN2 ...... 11 J7
Freshfields Cl *LAN/SOMP* BN15.. 189 L6
Freshfields Dr
  LAN/SOMP BN15 .... 189 L6
Freshfield St *ROTT* BN2 ...... 11 K4
Freshfield Wy *ROTT* BN2 ...... 11 J7
Freya Cl *MIDOS* PO22 ...... 205 G8
Friar Cl *HPPT/KEY* BN6 ...... 130 F8
Friar Rd *BRI* BN1 .... 194 A1
Friar's Rd *BRI* BN1 .... 172 B8
Friars Cl *HPPT/KEY* BN6 ...... 130 F8
Friars Oak Rd *HPPT/KEY* BN6 .. 130 F7
Friars Rookery *CRAWE* RH10 .... 3 J3
  SALV BN13 .... 210 A1
Friary Cl *MIDOS* PO22 ...... 204 F7
Friary La *CCH* PO19 .... 203 K3
Friary Wy *CRAWE* RH10 ...... 2 F5
Friday St *HORS* RH12 .... 17 M7
  HORS RH12 .... 36 F5
Friends Cl *CRAWW* RH11 .... 20 E3 🔢
Frimley Cl *ROTT* BN2 .... 195 M5
Friston Cl *ROTT* BN2 .... 173 G8
Friston Wk *CRAWW* RH11...... 20 B5
Frith Pk *EGRIN* RH19 .... 24 F1
Frith Rd *BOGR* PO21 .... 203 H7
  HOVE BN3 .... 193 H4
Frobisher Cl *BRI* BN1 .... 172 B8
Frobisher Gdns *EMRTH* PO10 .. 175 J4 🔢
Frobisher Rd *BOGR* PO21 .... 220 C2
Frobisher Wy *ANG/EP* BN16 .. 207 M4
  FERR BN12 .... 187 L8
Froxfield Rd *HAV* PO9 ...... 152 E7
Froyle Cl *HAV* PO9 .... 152 E7
Fry Cl *CRAWW* RH11 .... 40 C3
Fry Crs *BURH* RH15 .... 108 F7
Fryern Cl *PUL/STOR* RH20 .. 143 K2
Fryern Rd *PUL/STOR* RH20 .. 143 L1
Fryland La *HFD* BN5 .... 106 C8
Fulbeck Av *SALV* BN13 ...... 187 J6
Fulflood Rd *HAV* PO9 .... 152 B7
Fulham Cl *CRAWW* RH11 .... 40 C2
Fullers Wk *LHPTN* BN17 .... 184 E7
Fullerton Cl *HAV* PO9 ...... 152 E7 🔢
Fulmar Cl *CRAWW* RH11 .... 19 L7 🔢
  HOVE BN3 .... 193 L3
Fulmar Dr *EGRIN* RH19 ...... 25 H1
Fulmar Wy *SELS* PO20 ...... 180 F3
The Furlongs *STEY/UB* BN44 .. 167 L2
Furnace Dr *CRAWE* RH10 ...... 3 K1
Furnace Farm Rd *CRAWE* RH10 ... 3 M8
Furnace Pde *CRAWE* RH10 ...... 3 M7
Furnace Pl *CRAWE* RH10 ...... 3 M7
Furners La *HFD* BN5 .... 128 B7
Furners Md *HFD* BN5 .... 128 A8
Furniss Wy *HISD* PO11 ...... 196 A8
Furnston Gv *EMRTH* PO10 .... 176 B3
Furse Feld *BOGR* PO21 ...... 221 H2
Furze Cl *SALV* BN13 .... 187 L2
Furze Common Rd
  PUL/STOR RH20 .... 124 A6
Furzedown *LHPTN* BN17 .... 206 F4
Furzedown Crs *HAV* PO9 .... 152 D7
Furzefield *CRAWW* RH11 ...... 2 B1
  SELS PO20 .... 217 G3
Furzefield Cl *ANG/EP* BN16 .. 186 A5
Furzefield Rd *HORS* RH12 .... 38 C7
Furze HI *HOVE* BN3 .... 193 H4
Furzeholme *SALV* BN13 ...... 187 M2 🔢
Furzeland Wy *HPPT/KEY* BN6 .. 129 L4
Furze Meadow *EPSF* GU31 .. 92 B4
Furzen La *EGRIN* RH19 ...... 24 C7
Furze Rd *HORS* RH12 .... 35 H1
  SALV BN13 .... 187 L2
Furze Vw *BIL* RH14 .... 58 C6
Fushia Cl *HAV* PO9 .... 152 F8

G

Gableson Av *BRI* BN1 .... 171 J8
The Gables *HORS* RH12.......... 4 E3
  SWTR RH13 .... 82 A4
Gabriel La *CRAWE* RH10 ...... 41 K2
Gage Cl *CRAWE* RH10 .... 23 K3
Gage Rdg *FROW* RH18 .... 45 M3
Gaggle Wd *SWTR* RH13.......... 61 K6
Gainsboro Rd *BOGR* PO21 .... 12 C7
Gainsborough Av
  FIN/BW BN14 .... 188 F5
Gainsborough Dr *SELS* PO20 .. 223 G5
Gainsborough Rd *CRAWE* RH10 .. 41 G2
Gaisford Cl *FIN/BW* BN14 .... 8 E2
Gaisford Rd *FIN/BW* BN14 .... 8 D1
Galahad Rd *CRAWW* RH11 .. 19 M6 🔢
Gales Dr *CRAWE* RH10 .... 3 L3
  CRAWE RH10 .... 3 L3 🔢
Gales Pl *CRAWE* RH10 .... 3 K3
Galliers Cl *BRI* BN1 .... 172 C6
Galsworthy Rd *FERR* BN12 .. 209 J1
Gamecock Ter *SELS* PO20 .... 222 A2
Gander Cl *BURH* RH15 ...... 109 H7 🔢
Gander Gn *HWH* RH16 ...... 88 A5
Gander HI *HWH* RH16 ...... 88 A5
Gandersgate La *BIL* RH14 .... 77 H5
Gannon Rd *WTHG* BN11 ...... 9 M4
Garbitts La *EPSF* GU31 ...... 92 C1
Garden Av *SELS* PO20 ...... 217 J6
Garden Cl *ANG/EP* BN16 ...... 186 B5
  EGRIN RH19 .... 25 H3
  HISD PO11 .... 214 D1

  LAN/SOMP BN15 .... 189 K6
  PTSD BN41 .... 192 D4
  PUL/STOR RH20 .... 143 L2
  SHOR BN43 .... 191 J3
Garden Ct *BOGR* PO21 ...... 220 F2
Garden Crs *MIDOS* PO22 .... 182 D7
Gardeners La *HORS* RH12 .... 36 F4
Gardeners Gn *BURH* RH12 .. 18 D6
Gardner St *PTSD* BN41 ...... 192 D4
Garden House La *EGRIN* RH19.. 24 F5
The Gardens *HAV* PO9.......... 174 E4
  PTSD BN41 .... 192 D4
  PUL/STOR RH20 .... 121 H1
  RCCH PO18 .... 177 J1
  STHW BN42 .... 192 A5
Garden Wk *HORS* RH12 .... 4 D3
Garden Wood Cl
  PUL/STOR RH20 .... 123 L6
Garden Wood Rd *EGRIN* RH19 .. 24 C2
Gardner Rd *PTSD* BN41 ...... 192 D4
Gardner St *BRI* BN1 .... 10 E6
Garland Av *HOR/PO10 ...... 175 J1
Garland Cl *CCH* PO19 .... 7 G7
Garland Rd *EGRIN* RH19 ...... 24 E5
Garland Sq *SELS* PO20 ...... 180 C2
Garrett Cl *CRAWE* RH10 ...... 21 K8 🔢
Garrick Rd *FIN/BW* BN14 ...... 9 H1
The Garrones *CRAWE* RH10 .. 21 M5 🔢
Garsons Rd *EMRTH* PO10 .... 176 A4
Garton Cl *CRAWW* RH11 .... 19 M7 🔢
Gaskyns Cl *HORS* RH12 .... 34 E5
Gasson Wood Rd *CRAWW* RH11 .. 19 M8
Gaston Av *RCCH* PO18 ...... 156 F5
Gatcombe Cl *SALV* BN13 .... 187 J7 🔢
Gateford Dr *HAV* PO9 .... 38 A6
Gatehouse La *BURH* RH15 .. 108 D8
  EPSF GU31 .... 71 G6
  HPPT/KEY BN6 .... 108 C7
Gates Cl *CRAWE* RH10 .... 41 K2 🔢
Gatesmead *HWH* RH16 ...... 87 M4
The Gattons *BURH* RH15 .... 130 F1
Gatwick Rd *CRAWE* RH10 .... 21 H2
  HORL RH6 .... 15 H8
Gatwick Wy *HORL* RH6 ...... 15 G4
Gaugemaster Wy *ARUN* BN18.. 183 M7
Gaulter Rd *HAV* PO9 .... 174 D1
Gay St *PUL/STOR* RH20 ...... 101 K7
Gay Street La *PUL/STOR* RH20 .. 101 H5
Geddes Wy *EPSF* GU31 ...... 68 F8
Gemini Cl *CRAWW* RH11 .... 19 L8
Genoa Cl *ANG/EP* BN16 ...... 207 H2
Gentles La *LIPH* GU30 .... 26 B3
George Denyer Cl
  HASM GU27 .... 28 D5 🔢
George Iv Wk *MIDOS* PO22 .. 13 L2
Georges La *PUL/STOR* RH20 .. 144 D3
George St *CCH* PO19 .... 6 E2 🔢
  HOVE BN3 .... 193 J6
  PTSD BN41 .... 192 D5 🔢
  ROTT BN2 .... 11 G7
George V Av *FERR* BN12 .... 210 A2
  LAN/SOMP BN15 ...... 189 M5
  WTHG BN11 .... 209 M1
Georgia Av *FIN/BW* BN14 ...... 9 G1
Georgian Cl *CRAWE* RH10 .... 21 L7
Georgian Gdns
  ANG/EP BN16 .... 207 M2 🔢
Gerald Cl *BURH* RH15 ...... 131 L1
Gerald Rd *WTHG* BN11 ...... 210 A3
Gerard St *BRI* BN1 .... 10 E1
Ghyllside *BURH* RH15 ...... 131 G3
Gibbons Cl *CRAWE* RH10 .... 41 K1 🔢
Giblets La *HORS* RH12 .... 38 A5
Giblets Wy *HORS* RH12 ...... 37 M5
Gibson Rd *SELS* PO20 ...... 180 D2
Gibson Wy *BOGR* PO21 ...... 12 E5
Giffards Cl *EGRIN* RH19 ...... 25 G3 🔢
Gifford Rd *RCCH* PO18 ...... 177 K5
Gilbert Md *HISD* PO11 ...... 196 B8
Gilbert Rd *CCH* PO19 .... 6 A1
The Gilberts *ANG/EP* BN16 .. 207 J5 🔢
Giles Cl *ARUN* BN18 .... 205 G2
Gilham La *FROW* RH18 .... 45 M2
Gillett Ct *SWTR* RH13 .... 38 C8 🔢
Gillham's La *HASM* GU27 .... 27 H8
The Gilligans *BURH* RH15 .. 109 G7
Gillway *SELS* PO20 .... 223 J4
Gilmore Rd *CCH* PO19 .... 7 K4
Gilpin Cl *CCH* PO19 .... 178 C6
Gilwynes *BOGR* PO21 ...... 221 G2
Ginhams Rd *CRAWW* RH11...... 2 B3
The Glades *EGRIN* RH19 ...... 25 J3
The Glade *BOGR* PO21 ...... 220 B4
  CRAWE RH10 .... 3 L7
  HISD PO11 .... 214 F2
  SWTR RH13 .... 5 L5
Gladionian Rd *LHPTN* BN17 .. 206 E1
Gladstone Pl *ROTT* BN2 ...... 194 D4
Gladstone Rd *ARUN* BN18 .... 205 G2
  BURH RH15 .... 109 K7
  HORS RH12 .... 4 E3
  PTSD BN41 .... 192 D5 🔢
Gladstone Ter *LHPTN* BN17 .. 206 E1 🔢
Gladys Rd *HOVE* BN3 .... 192 E4
Glamis Cl *BOGR* PO21 ...... 12 F6
Glamis St *BOGR* PO21 ...... 12 F6
Glaseby La *PUL/STOR* RH20 .. 144 D3
Glasshouse La *BIL* RH14 ...... 77 H7
Glastonbury Rd *HOVE* BN3 .. 192 E6
Glatting La *PUL/STOR* RH20 .. 139 M3
Glaziers La *MIDH* GU29 ...... 95 H2
Gleave Cl *EGRIN* RH19 ...... 25 H2
Glebe Cl *CRAWE* RH10 .... 3 G1
  HISD PO11 .... 196 B1
  LAN/SOMP BN15 ...... 189 M5 🔢
  SELS PO20 .... 181 J3
  STHW BN42 .... 192 A5
Glebe Field Rd *SELS* PO20 .. 199 H7
Glebelands *BIL* RH14 .... 33 G8
  CRAWE RH10 .... 23 H4
  PUL/STOR RH20 .... 122 C1
Glebe Rd *EPSF* GU31 .... 90 A7
The Glebe *CRAWE* RH10 ...... 22 C1

  HORL RH6 .... 15 G1 🔢
  HWH RH16 .... 88 B4
  SELS PO20 .... 180 D2
Glebe Vw *RHWH* RH17 ...... 65 H3
Glebe Vls *HOVE* BN3 .... 192 E6
Glebe Wy *BIL* RH14 .... 78 D4
  LAN/SOMP BN15 ...... 189 M5
Glenbarrie Wy *FERR* BN12 .. 208 L1
Glencathara Rd *BOGR* PO21.. 12 A7
Glen Crs *SELS* PO20 .... 223 G5
Glen Dl *HAV* PO9 .... 153 G3
Glendale Cl *HORS* RH12 ...... 38 B6
Glendale Rd *BURH* RH15 .... 131 J2
  HOVE BN3 .... 193 L5
Glendor Rd *HOVE* BN3 ...... 192 F6
Glendyne Cl *EGRIN* RH19 .... 25 H4
Glendyne Wy *EGRIN* RH19 .. 25 H4
Glenelg Cl *BOGR* PO21 ...... 203 G6
Glenfalls Av *BRI* BN1 .... 172 B5
Glen Gdns *FERR* BN12 ...... 209 G2
Glenlea *GSHT* GU26 .... 27 M3
Glenlea Hollow *GSHT* GU26 .. 27 M3
Glenleigh Pk *HAV* PO9 ...... 174 E2
Glen Ri *BRI* BN1 .... 171 J7
Glen Rise Cl *BRI* BN1 .... 171 J7
Glen Rd *GSHT* GU26 .... 27 L1
The Glen *SALV* BN13 .... 188 B5
  SWTR RH13 .... 82 B2 🔢
Glenview Cl *CRAWE* RH10 .... 21 G4
Glenville Rd *ANG/EP* BN16 .. 207 K4
Glen Vue *EGRIN* RH19 ...... 24 F3
Glenway *MIDOS* PO22 ...... 12 F4
Glenwood Av *MIDOS* PO22 .. 12 F4
Glenwood Rd *EMRTH* PO10 .. 176 A3
Gleton Av *HOVE* BN3 .... 192 C4
Globe Pl *LHPTN* BN17 ...... 206 E1
Gloster Dr *BOGR* PO21 ...... 220 C2
Gloucester Cl *PSF* GU32 ...... 90 A1
Gloucester La *LHPTN* BN17 .. 206 E1
Gloucester Pas *BRI* BN1 ...... 10 F5 🔢
Gloucester Pl *LHPTN* BN17 .. 206 E1
  ROTT BN2 .... 10 F5
Gloucester Rd *BOGR* PO21 .. 13 G5
  BRI BN1 .... 10 E5 🔢
  BURH RH15 .... 131 G1 🔢
  CRAWE RH10 .... 40 F2
  LHPTN BN17 .... 206 D3
Gloucester St *BRI* BN1 ...... 10 F5
Gloucester Wy *CCH* PO19 .... 179 G3
Glynde Av *FERR* BN12 ...... 209 G2
  ROTT BN2 .... 213 K2
Glyndebourne Av *ROTT* BN2.. 213 K3
Glynde Cl *FERR* BN12 ...... 209 G2
Glynde Crs *MIDOS* PO22 ...... 13 L2
Glynde Pl *HORS* RH12 .... 4 C8 🔢
Glynde Rd *LHPTN* BN17 ...... 206 F3
Goda Rd *LHPTN* BN17 ...... 206 F3
Goddard Cl *CRAWE* RH10 .... 41 J1
Godman Rd *BOGR* PO21 .... 220 E3 🔢
Godstalls La *STEY/UB* BN44 .. 167 K1
Godwin Cl *EMRTH* PO10 .... 175 H1
Godwin Rd *HOVE* BN3 ...... 192 E5
Godwin Wy *RCCH* PO18 .... 178 B4
Goffs Cl *CRAWW* RH11 .... 2 C7
Goffs La *CRAWW* RH11 .... 2 C7
Goffs Park Rd *CRAWW* RH11 .... 2 C7
Goldcrest Av *LHPTN* BN17 .. 184 D8
Golden Acre *ANG/EP* BN16 .. 208 C4
  BOGR PO21 .... 220 B4
Golden Av *ANG/EP* BN16 .... 208 C3
Golden Avenue Cl
  ANG/EP BN16 .... 208 C4
Golden Flds *LIPH* GU30 .... 49 L1
Golden HI *BURH* RH15 ...... 131 G1
Golden La *SWTR* RH13 ...... 126 E6
Goldfinch Cl *CRAWW* RH11 .. 20 E4
  HORS RH12 .... 37 K5
Golding Cl *CRAWE* RH10 .... 21 K7 🔢
Golding La *SWTR* RH13 ...... 61 L3
Goldring Cl *HISD* PO11 ...... 214 D1
Goldsmid Rd *HOVE* BN3 ...... 10 B3
Goldsmith Rd *FIN/BW* BN14 .... 9 J1
Goldstone Cl *HOVE* BN3 .... 193 H2
Goldstone Crs *HOVE* BN3 .. 193 H2
Goldstone La *HOVE* BN3 .... 193 H2
Goldstone Rd *HOVE* BN3 .... 193 H2
Goldstone St *HOVE* BN3 .... 193 H2
Goldstone Vls *HOVE* BN3 .. 193 H2
Goldstone Wy *HOVE* BN3 .... 193 H2
Golf Club La *PUL/STOR* RH20.. 123 G5
Golf Dr *BRI* BN1 .... 194 C1
Golf Links La *SELS* PO20 .... 223 G3
Golf Links Rd *MIDOS* PO22 .. 204 B6
Goodacres *MIDOS* PO22 .... 182 D7
Goodhew Cl *ARUN* BN18 .... 205 H4
Goodwin Cl *CRAWW* RH11 .. 39 M1
Goodwins Cl *EGRIN* RH19 .... 24 E1
Goodwood Av *MIDOS* PO22 .. 13 G3
Goodwood Cl *ANG/EP* BN16 .. 207 M2
  CRAWE RH10 .... 3 L9
  MIDH GU29 .... 94 F7
Goodwood Ct *EMRTH* PO10 .. 176 B4
Goodwood Gdns *SELS* PO20 .. 201 M3
Goodwood Rd *SALV* BN13 .. 188 B5
Goodwood Wy *ROTT* BN2 .. 194 F1
Goose Green Cl *HORS* RH12 .... 4 F1
Goosegreen La
  PUL/STOR RH20 .... 124 D1
Gordon Av *BOGR* PO21 ...... 12 E4
  CCH PO19 .... 200 F1
  MIDOS PO22 .... 13 G3
  SHOR BN43 .... 191 H5
Gordon Av West *MIDOS* PO22 .. 12 E3
Gordon Cl *HWH* RH16 ...... 87 H4
Gordon Rd *BRI* BN1 .... 194 A2
  BURH RH15 .... 109 K8
  EMRTH PO10 .... 175 L5
  HORS RH12 .... 4 E3
  HWH RH16 .... 87 M6
  LAN/SOMP BN15 ...... 189 L6
  PTSD BN41 .... 192 C3
  SHOR BN43 .... 191 G5
  WTHG BN11 .... 9 H4
Goreside La *RHWH* RH17 .... 213 G4
Gorham Av *ROTT* BN2 .... 213 G2
Gorham Cl *ROTT* BN2 .... 213 H2
Gorham Wy *PEAHV* BN10 .. 213 M3
Goring Cha *FERR* BN12 ...... 187 K8
Goring Rd *FERR* BN12 ...... 209 K2 🔢
  STEY/UB BN44 .... 167 L2

WTHG BN11 ...... 210 A2
aring's Md SWTR RH13 ...... 60 E3
ring St FERR BN12 ...... 209 H1
ring Wy FERR BN12 ...... 209 H2
SWTR RH13 ...... 105 H8
rling CI CRAWW RH11 ...... 19 M7
rringe CI SHOR BN43 ...... 191 L5
rringes Brook HORS RH12 ...... 37 L6
rrange Av ANG/EP BN16 ...... 208 D3
FIN/BW BN14 ...... 188 C6
MIDOS PO22 ...... 204 E6
rse Bank CI PUL/STOR RH20 ...... 144 D1
CRAWW RH11 ...... 40 C4
PTSD BN41 ...... 170 A8
rse End HORS RH12 ...... 4 F2
rselands BIL RH14 ...... 79 M4
rse La SALV BN13 ...... 187 M2
rse Rd EPSF GU31 ...... 90 F1
sden CI CRAWW RH10 ...... 3 M5
sden Rd LHPTN BN17 ...... 207 G2
spond Rd MIDOS PO22 ...... 182 B7
ssamer La BOGR PO21 ...... 220 E1
ssops Dr CRAWW RH11 ...... 20 B7
ssops Green La CRAWW RH11.. 20 B7
strode La MFD/CHID GU8 ...... 30 B6
udhurst CI CRAWE RH10 ...... 21 M6
HWH RH16 ...... 87 M8
wer Rd HORL RH6 ...... 14 F1
HWH RH16 ...... 87 M8
wers CI RHWH RH17 ...... 66 C4
ace Rd CRAWW RH11 ...... 40 B3
affham CI CCH PO19 ...... 179 H1
CRAWW RH11 ...... 20 C4
ROTT BN2 ...... 194 F6
rafton Av MIDOS PO22 ...... 204 D6
rafton CI ANG/EP BN16 ...... 207 H4
rafton Dr LAN/SOMP BN15 ...... 189 K6
rafton Gdns LAN/SOMP BN15.. 189 K6
rafton PI WTHG BN11 ...... 9 G6
rafton Rd SELS PO20 ...... 223 G7
WTHG BN11 ...... 9 G6
rafton St ROTT BN2 ...... 11 H8
raham Av BRI BN1 ...... 171 M8
PTSD BN41 ...... 170 A8
raham Crs PTSD BN41 ...... 170 A8
raham Rd ARUN BN18 ...... 205 G2
WTHG BN11 ...... 9 G6
railands CI HASM GU27 ...... 51 K6
anary La SELS PO20 ...... 222 F4
anary's Md HORS RH12 ...... 184 E8
LHPTN BN17 ...... 184 E8
and HOVE BN3 ...... 193 K6
HPPT/KEY BN6 ...... 131 G8
LAN/SOMP BN15 ...... 189 M5
LHPTN BN17 ...... 206 D1
WTHG BN11 ...... 8 A4
and Crs ROTT BN2 ...... 213 H3
and Junction Rd BRI BN1 ...... 10 E4
and Pde HISD PO11 ...... 214 D2
ROTT BN2 ...... 10 F5
rand Parade Ms ROTT BN2 .. 10 F6
ange CI BRI BN1 ...... 193 M3
BURH RH15 ...... 109 K7
CRAWE RH10 ...... 21 H4
FERR BN12 ...... 208 F3
HAV PO9 ...... 174 E2
ange Ct BOGR PO21 ...... 220 F3
ange Crs CRAWE RH10 ...... 23 J5
ange Field Wy BOGR PO21 .. 220 E2
ange La SELS PO20 ...... 223 J2
ange Park Rd FERR BN12 ...... 208 F3
ange Rd CRAWE RH10 ...... 23 H5
SHOR BN43 ...... 192 F5
MIDH GU29 ...... 95 G5
PSF GU32 ...... 90 B2
STHW BN42 ...... 191 M5
range Wy SWTR RH13 ...... 82 A2
rangeways BRI BN1 ...... 171 M7
he Grangeway ANG/EP BN16 .. 207 K3
rangewood Dr BOGR PO21 .. 220 E2
ranston Wy CRAWE RH10 ...... 25 K4
rant CI SELS PO20 ...... 222 F5
antham Rd BRI BN1 ...... 194 B3
antsmead
LAN/SOMP BN15 ...... 189 M5
ant St ROTT BN2 ...... 11 H3
anville Ct HAV PO9 ...... 174 D3
anville Rd HOVE BN3 ...... 10 A3
LHPTN BN17 ...... 206 F4
asmere La LAN/SOMP BN15 .. 189 J4
asmere Gdns HORS RH12 ...... 38 C6
assmere CI LHPTN BN17 ...... 207 H1
MIDOS PO22 ...... 13 K4
atten La HFD BN5 ...... 129 C1
attons Dr CRAWE RH10 ...... 21 K3
he Grattons SWTR RH13 ...... 58 F1
atwicke CI BIL RH14 ...... 79 L4
atwicke Rd HWH RH16 ...... 8 F6
avelly Crs LAN/SOMP BN15 .. 190 A6
ravelye CI HWH RH16 ...... 88 C7
ravelye La HWH RH16 ...... 88 B7
aveney Rd CRAWE RH10 ...... 21 K7
avett CI BURH RH15 ...... 131 G2
avetye CI CRAWE RH10 ...... 3 M8
avits La BOGR PO21 ...... 203 H8
ayland CI HISD PO11 ...... 196 B3
ays CI HASM GU27 ...... 28 F4
rays Wd HORL RH6 ...... 15 K1
rayswood Av SELS PO20 ...... 217 G6
rayswood Rd HASM GU27 ...... 28 E4
reat College St ROTT BN2 .. 11 H4
reatfield Wy HAV PO9 ...... 152 D2
reatham Br FIN/BW BN14 ...... 121 M7
reatham Rd CRAWE RH10 ...... 41 K1
FIN/BW BN14 ...... 188 A3
reat Hanger EPSF GU31 ...... 90 F1
reatpin Cft PUL/STOR RH20 .. 121 H1
rebe Crs SWTR RH13 ...... 61 H3
reenacre CI PUL/STOR RH20 .. 143 J5
reenacres CRAWE RH10 ...... 3 M6
HORS RH12 ...... 4 D3
PUL/STOR RH20 ...... 125 H6
SHOR BN43 ...... 190 F4
STEY/UB BN44 ...... 167 L2
reenacres Ring
ANG/EP BN16 ...... 186 A6
reenbank MIDOS PO22 ...... 182 D7
reenbank Av ROTT BN2 ...... 213 K3

Green Bushes CI
LAN/SOMP BN16 ...... 207 J4
Green CI STHW BN42 ...... 191 M5
SWTR RH13 ...... 82 A2
Greencourt Dr BOGR PO21 .. 203 H7
Greenfield PUL/STOR RH20 .. 140 A2
Green Field CI BRI BN1 ...... 172 B7
LIPH GU30 ...... 26 D7
Greenfield CI BRI BN1 ...... 172 A7
Greenfield Crs BRI BN1 ...... 172 A7
SWTR RH13 ...... 58 L1
Greenfields EPSF GU31 ...... 92 B5
LHPTN BN17 ...... 206 C1
LISS GU33 ...... 47 K8
Greenfields CI EPSF GU31 ...... 92 B4
HORS RH12 ...... 38 B6
Greenfields Rd HORS RH12 ...... 5 L1
Greenfield Wy PUL/STOR RH20.. 143 M2
Greenfinch Wy HORS RH12 ...... 37 L5
Greenhill Pk HWH RH16 ...... 110 B2
Greenhill Pk HWH RH16 ...... 110 B2
Greenhurst La PUL/STOR RH20.. 123 M7
Greenland Rd SALV BN13 ...... 187 M6
Greenlands Rd SALV BN13 ...... 187 M6
Greenlands CI BURH RH15 ...... 131 J4
Greenlands Dr BURH RH15 ...... 131 J4
Green La CCH PO19 ...... 7 H3
CRAWE RH10 ...... 20 F4
CRAWE RH10 ...... 21 L6
HASM GU27 ...... 28 C8
HASM GU27 ...... 51 J1
HISD PO11 ...... 214 B2
HORS RH12 ...... 17 M8
RCCH PO18 ...... 177 C4
RCCH PO18 ...... 177 K6
ROTT BN2 ...... 195 M6
SELS PO20 ...... 180 A8
SELS PO20 ...... 202 A2
SELS PO20 ...... 218 D3
SELS PO20 ...... 222 F6
SWTR RH13 ...... 104 C3
Green Lane CI ARUN BN18 .. 184 A2
Greenlea Av BOGR PO21 ...... 220 E2
Greenleas HOVE BN3 ...... 192 E3
Green Mdw HWH RH16 ...... 88 C4
Greenoaks LAN/SOMP BN15 .. 189 L4
Green Pk FERR BN12 ...... 209 G1
Green Pond Cnr HAV PO9 .. 174 E3
Green Rdg BRI BN1 ...... 171 J7
Green Rd RHWH RH17 ...... 110 B7
Greensand Wy GSHT GU26 ...... 28 B2
HASM GU27 ...... 28 D5
Greenstede Av EGRIN RH19 ...... 25 C1
The Green BOGR PO21 ...... 220 B4
CRAWE RH10 ...... 22 C1
HOVE BN3 ...... 193 K2
LISS GU33 ...... 47 H7
MFD/CHID GU8 ...... 30 D1
PUL/STOR RH20 ...... 144 A2
ROTT BN2 ...... 213 G2
SWTR RH13 ...... 105 K7
Greentree La SWTR RH13 .. 105 K7
Greentrees CI
LAN/SOMP BN15 ...... 189 K6
Greentrees Crs
LAN/SOMP BN15 ...... 189 K6
Green Wk CRAWE RH10 ...... 20 F4
Greenway HORS RH12 ...... 4 A5
Green Wy MIDOS PO22 ...... 205 G7
Greenways BOGR PO21 ...... 220 C3
HWH RH16 ...... 88 A6
ROTT BN2 ...... 195 L8
STHW BN42 ...... 192 A3
Greenways Crs FERR BN12 .. 209 G3
SHOR BN43 ...... 191 H3
The Green Wy FERR BN12 .. 187 J8
Greenwich CI CRAWW RH11 .. 40 D2
Greenwood Av MIDOS PO22 .. 12 B1
Greenwood CI MIDOS PO22 .. 12 B1
Greenwood Dr ANG/EP BN16 .. 208 A1
Greet Rd LAN/SOMP BN15 .. 189 L5
Gregory CI CRAWE RH10 ...... 41 K2
Gregsons HORS RH12 ...... 36 F4
Grenehurst Wy EPSF GU31 ...... 90 C1
Grenville Av FERR BN12 ...... 209 L1
Grenville CI FERR BN12 ...... 209 K1
LIPH GU30 ...... 26 D8
Grenville Gdns CCH PO19 ...... 6 C9
Grenville St BRI BN1 ...... 10 C6
Gresham PI BOGR PO21 ...... 220 C2
Gresham Wk CRAWE RH10 .. 40 F1
Grevatt's La LHPTN BN17 ...... 205 H5
Grevatt's La East ARUN BN18 .. 205 G4
Greville Gn EMRTH PO10 ...... 153 H8
Grey Alders HWH RH16 ...... 88 C6
Greyfriars HOVE BN3 ...... 193 L4
Greyfriars CI BOGR PO21 ...... 221 G1
SALV BN13 ...... 188 B6
Greyfriars La PUL/STOR RH20 .. 143 K4
Greyhound Slip CRAWE RH10 .. 21 L5
Greylands CI BOGR PO21 ...... 220 D2
Greystoke Ms FERR BN12 .. 208 F2
Greystoke Rd FERR BN12 ...... 208 F2
Greystone Av BOGR PO21 ...... 203 G5
SALV BN13 ...... 188 A7
Gribble La SELS PO20 ...... 180 A7
Grier CI CRAWW RH11 ...... 19 M7
Griffin Crs LHPTN BN17 ...... 206 F2
Griffith's Av LAN/SOMP BN15 .. 189 L4
Grinstead Av LAN/SOMP BN15 .. 189 M6
Grinstead La EGRIN RH19 ...... 44 D6
Grisedale CI CRAWW RH11 ...... 2 C8
Groombridge Wy HORS RH12 .. 4 A5
Groomsdale Dr BIL RH14 ...... 79 K6
The Grooms CRAWE RH10 ...... 21 L4
Grosvenor Gdns BOGR PO21 .. 220 D1
Grosvenor Rd CCH PO19 ...... 201 G4
EGRIN RH19 ...... 24 E3
WTHG BN11 ...... 9 G5
Grosvenor St ROTT BN2 ...... 11 G7
Grosvenor Wy BOGR PO21 .. 220 D1
Grove Crs LHPTN BN17 ...... 206 F2
Grove HI ROTT BN2 ...... 11 G5
Grovelands CI BURH RH15 .. 131 G3

The Grovelands
LAN/SOMP BN15 ...... 189 M8
Grove La PETW GU28 ...... 98 B2
PUL/STOR RH20 ...... 123 L6
Grove Pk CCH PO19 ...... 178 C6
Grover Av LAN/SOMP BN15 .. 189 L5
Grove Rd BURH RH15 ...... 131 J3
CCH PO19 ...... 7 G6
FIN/BW BN14 ...... 188 D6
HAV PO9 ...... 174 C3
SELS PO20 ...... 222 F4
Grove St PETW GU28 ...... 98 A5
ROTT BN2 ...... 11 H4
The Grove CRAWW RH11 ...... 2 C3
EMRTH PO10 ...... 175 L1
FERR BN12 ...... 208 F2
HORL RH6 ...... 15 J2
HWH RH16 ...... 110 C1
LIPH GU30 ...... 26 C8
MIDOS PO22 ...... 13 M4
Guernsey CI CRAWW RH11 ...... 40 B2
Guernsey Farm La
MIDOS PO22 ...... 204 D7
Guernsey Rd FERR BN12 ...... 209 G4
Guilden CI CCH PO19 ...... 7 H4
Guildford CI EMRTH PO10 ...... 176 A3
FIN/BW BN14 ...... 8 B3
Guildford PI CCH PO19 ...... 179 G3
Guildford Rd ANG/EP BN16 .. 207 M2
BRI BN1 ...... 10 D4
FIN/BW BN14 ...... 8 B3
HORS RH12 ...... 34 A4
HORS RH12 ...... 60 B2
Guildford St BRI BN1 ...... 10 D4
Guildhall St BRI BN1 ...... 6 C3
Guillards Oak MIDH GU29 ...... 94 F5
Guinevere Rd CRAWW RH11 .. 19 M6
Gunning CI CRAWW RH11 ...... 40 B3
Gunns Farm LIPH GU30 ...... 49 K2
Gunwin Ct BOGR PO21 ...... 220 E2
Gutner La HISD PO11 ...... 196 F3
Gwynne Gdns EGRIN RH19 ...... 24 D2

H

Habin HI EPSF GU31 ...... 70 L2
Hackenden CI EGRIN RH19 ...... 24 F1
Hackenden La EGRIN RH19 ...... 24 F1
Haddington CI HOVE BN3 ...... 193 J6
Haddington St HOVE BN3 ...... 193 J5
Hadlands BOGR PO21 ...... 220 B3
Hadley Av FIN/BW BN14 ...... 188 E5
Hadley CI MIDOS PO22 ...... 204 F6
Hadlow CI ROTT BN2 ...... 11 L5
Hadlow Wy LAN/SOMP BN15 .. 190 A6
Hadmans CI HORS RH12 ...... 4 C9
Hadrian Av STHW BN42 ...... 192 A4
Haglands Copse
PUL/STOR RH20 ...... 123 L5
Haglands La PUL/STOR RH20 .. 123 L5
Haig Av BRI BN1 ...... 172 E6
Haigh CI LAN/SOMP BN15 ...... 190 C6
Hailsham Av ROTT BN2 ...... 213 L1
Hailsham CI ANG/EP BN16 .. 208 C1
Hailsham Rd WTHG BN11 ...... 210 A3
Hale CI SELS PO20 ...... 217 J6
Hales Fld HASM GU27 ...... 28 D6
Halewick CI LAN/SOMP BN15 .. 189 K4
Halewick La LAN/SOMP BN15 .. 189 K4
Haleybridge Wk SELS PO20.. 180 E3
Half Moon La HASM GU27 ...... 28 D6
Half Moon La SALV BN13 ...... 188 A4
Halfrey CI RCCH PO18 ...... 178 B5
Halfrey Rd RCCH PO18 ...... 178 B5
Halifax CI CRAWE RH10 ...... 21 M3
Halifax Dr SALV BN13 ...... 187 K6
Halland CI CRAWE RH10 ...... 3 L1
Halland Rd ROTT BN2 ...... 173 M8
Hall Av FIN/BW BN14 ...... 188 B5
Hall CI FIN/BW BN14 ...... 188 B5
Hallett Rd HAV PO9 ...... 174 C4
ROTT BN2 ...... 11 J3
Halley CI CRAWW RH11 ...... 40 C1
Halliford Dr MIDOS PO22 ...... 182 D7
Halliwick Gdns MIDOS PO22 .. 204 D3
Hallsland CRAWE RH10 ...... 23 K4
Hallyburton Rd HOVE BN3 ...... 192 E4
Halnaker Barn La RCCH PO18 .. 159 H8
Halnaker Gdns BOGR PO21 .. 220 D2
Halsbury CI WTHG BN11 ...... 9 K3
Halsbury Rd WTHG BN11 ...... 9 K3
Halsford CI EGRIN RH19 ...... 24 C2
Halsford Park Rd EGRIN RH19.. 24 D2
Halson CI BOGR PO21 ...... 12 B4
Halters End GSHT GU26 ...... 27 H1
Hambledon PI BOGR PO21.... 12 B7
Hamble Gdns SALV BN13 ...... 187 J5
Hamble Rd LAN/SOMP BN15 .. 189 J6
Hambleton CI CRAWW RH11 .. 2 C1
Hamble Wy SALV BN13 ...... 187 K5
Hambrook Rd BURH RH15 .. 131 K3
Hambrook HI (North)
RCCH PO18 ...... 176 E1
Hambrook HI (South)
RCCH PO18 ...... 176 E1
Ham CI WTHG BN11 ...... 189 H8
Hamfield Dr HISD PO11 ...... 196 B8
Hamilton CI ANG/EP BN16 .. 207 J1
FIN/BW BN14 ...... 188 F7
HAV PO9 ...... 174 C1
PTSD BN41 ...... 192 B1
Hamilton Dr ANG/EP BN16 .. 207 J1
Hamilton Gdns BOGR PO21 .. 220 E2
RCCH PO18 ...... 177 K5
Hamilton Rd BRI BN1 ...... 10 C1
HORS RH12 ...... 4 B3
LAN/SOMP BN15 ...... 189 M6
LISS GU33 ...... 48 A2
Ham La EMRTH PO10 ...... 176 A5
RHWH RH17 ...... 110 F1
SELS PO20 ...... 180 E5
Ham Manor CI MIDOS PO22 .. 185 L4
Ham Manor Wy ANG/EP BN16 .. 185 M8
Hammer HI HASM GU27 ...... 27 K8
RHWH RH17 ...... 86 B1
Hammer La GSHT GU26 ...... 27 K4
HASM GU27 ...... 27 K7
LIPH GU30 ...... 27 H6

MIDH GU29 ...... 71 L8
Hammerpond Rd
SWTR RH13 ...... 61 H4
SWTR RH13 ...... 62 C6
Hammerwood Copse
HASM GU27 ...... 27 L7
Hammerwood Rd EGRIN RH19 .. 25 M6
Hammingden La EGRIN RH19 .. 66 F1
RHWH RH17 ...... 66 F5
Hammond Dr SALV BN13 ...... 187 L4
Hammonds Gdns
BURH RH15 ...... 131 G3
Hammonds Rdg BURH RH15.. 130 F3
Hammy CI SHOR BN43 ...... 191 J4
Hammy La SHOR BN43 ...... 191 J4
Hammy Wy SHOR BN43 ...... 191 J4
Hampden CI CRAWE RH10 .. 21 M3
MIDOS PO22 ...... 205 G7
Hampden Rd ROTT BN2 ...... 11 J3
Hampers La PUL/STOR RH20.. 144 C4
SWTR RH13 ...... 5 L8
Hampshire Av BOGR PO21 .. 12 A3
Hampstead CI BRI BN1 ...... 193 L3
Hampstead Rd BRI BN1 ...... 193 L3
Hampton Ct BOGR PO21 ...... 203 G8
Hampton Flds LHPTN BN17 .. 206 E2
Hampton PI BRI BN1 ...... 10 B6
Hampton St BRI BN1 ...... 10 B6
Hampton Wy EGRIN RH19 ...... 25 C5
Ham Rd SELS PO20 ...... 218 D6
SHOR BN43 ...... 191 G6
WTHG BN11 ...... 211 H1
Hamsey CI ROTT BN2 ...... 195 C2
Hamsey Rd EGRIN RH19 ...... 44 B6
ROTT BN2 ...... 213 L4
Hamshire HI RHWH RH17 ...... 63 C8
Hamsland RHWH RH17 ...... 67 K8
Hamstead Meadow
RCCH PO18 ...... 176 B5
Ham Wy WTHG BN11 ...... 189 H8
Hanbury La HWH RH16 ...... 88 B7
Hanbury Rd CRAWW RH11 ...... 19 M7
Handcross Rd RHWH RH17 ...... 64 D1
SWTR RH13 ...... 62 C8
Handford Wy RHWH RH17 ...... 62 C6
Hanger Wy EPSF GU31 ...... 90 E1
Hangleton CI HOVE BN3 ...... 192 E2
Hangleton Gdns HOVE BN3 .. 192 E3
Hangleton Gra FERR BN12 .. 208 F3
HOVE BN3 ...... 192 D2
PTSD BN41 ...... 192 C2
Hangleton La FERR BN12 ...... 186 E8
HOVE BN3 ...... 192 D2
PTSD BN41 ...... 192 C2
Hangleton Manor CI
HOVE BN3 ...... 192 D2
Hangleton Rd HOVE BN3 ...... 192 F2
Hangleton Valley Dr
HOVE BN3 ...... 192 D1
Hangleton Wy HOVE BN3 ...... 192 C2
Hanlye La RHWH RH17 ...... 87 H4
Hannah Sq CCH PO19 ...... 178 C5
Hannington PI HPPT/KEY BN6 .. 130 F3
Hannington Rd HAV PO9 .. 152 A5
Hanover CI CRAWE RH10 ...... 3 J8
PUL/STOR RH20 ...... 141 H5
SELS PO20 ...... 223 H5
Hanover Ct MIDH GU29 ...... 95 H2
Hanover Crs ROTT BN2 ...... 11 G3
Hanover Gdns SWTR RH13 .. 105 M2
Hanover Ms ROTT BN2 ...... 11 H3
Hanover St ROTT BN2 ...... 11 H3
Hanover Ter ROTT BN2 ...... 11 H3
Hanover Wk CRAWE RH10 .. 143 L3
Harberton Crs CCH PO19 ...... 179 H1
Harbolets Rd BIL RH14 ...... 102 A5
PUL/STOR RH20 ...... 102 B3
Harborough CI
PUL/STOR RH20 ...... 123 J4
Harborough Dr
PUL/STOR RH20 ...... 123 J4
Harborough Gorse
PUL/STOR RH20 ...... 123 J4
Harborough HI
PUL/STOR RH20 ...... 123 H5
Harborough Meadow
PUL/STOR RH20 ...... 123 J4
Harbour Ct RCCH PO18 ...... 177 K7
Harbour Rd BOGR PO21 ...... 220 A6
RCCH PO18 ...... 177 J8
Harbourside HAV PO9 ...... 174 C6
Harbour View Rd BOGR PO21 .. 220 B4
Harbour Wy EMRTH PO10 .. 175 K4
RCCH PO18 ...... 176 F7
RCCH PO18 ...... 177 K8
SHOR BN43 ...... 191 J6
Harbridge Ct HAV PO9 ...... 152 A5
Harcourt Wy SELS PO20 ...... 223 H4
Hardbarrow Woods
PUL/STOR RH20 ...... 124 B6
Hardham CI ANG/EP BN16 .. 207 J4
CRAWW RH11 ...... 20 B4
Hardham Rd CCH PO19 ...... 7 G8
Hard's HI SWTR RH13 ...... 60 E7
The Hard MIDOS PO22 ...... 205 K7
Hardwick Rd HOVE BN3 ...... 192 F1
Hardwick Wy HOVE BN3 ...... 170 F8
Hardy CI CRAWE RH10 ...... 21 K5
HORL RH6 ...... 14 F1
HORS RH12 ...... 4 B4
MIDOS PO22 ...... 204 E7
SHOR BN43 ...... 191 G6
Harebell CI ANG/EP BN16 .. 207 J1
Harebell CI PTSD BN41 ...... 192 B1
Harefield Av SALV BN13 ...... 188 A8
Harefield Rd MIDOS PO22 ...... 205 G6
Hare La CRAWW RH11 ...... 20 D3
SELS PO20 ...... 222 D4
Haresfield Ter SELS PO20 ...... 180 A3
Haresfoot CI RCCH PO18 ...... 155 G7
Hares La RCCH PO18 ...... 154 C5
Harestock Rd HAV PO9 ...... 174 A1
Harewood CI CRAWE RH10 .. 21 H3
Harlands Rd HWH RH16 ...... 87 K6
Harland Rd FIN/BW BN14 .. 188 E6
Harlech CI SALV BN13 ...... 187 J7
Harmans Md EGRIN RH19 ...... 25 H1
Harmony CI CRAWW RH11 .. 19 M8
Harmony Dr SELS PO20 ...... 223 H4
Harmsworth Crs HOVE BN3 .. 192 F1
Harold CI CRAWE RH10 ...... 21 M7
EMRTH PO10 ...... 153 L4
HISD PO11 ...... 214 D1

Haroldslea HORL RH6 ...... 15 M2
Haroldslea CI HORL RH6 ...... 15 K3
Haroldslea Dr HORL RH6 ...... 15 K3
Harper Dr MIDOS PO22 ...... 41 K2
Harrier Wy EPSF GU31 ...... 90 F2
Harrington PI BRI BN1 ...... 194 C2
Harrington Rd BRI BN1 ...... 193 M2
Harriots CI SWTR RH13 ...... 83 H4
Harris CI CRAWW RH11 ...... 40 C1
Harris La HORN PO8 ...... 112 A7
Harrison Ct FIN/BW BN14 ...... 188 F7
Harrison Rd FIN/BW BN14 ...... 188 F7
Harrow Dr SELS PO20 ...... 217 G5
Harrow La PSF GU32 ...... 68 C6
Harrow Rd WTHG BN11 ...... 8 C3
Harsfold Av ANG/EP BN16 .. 207 H4
Harsfold CI ANG/EP BN16 .. 207 J4
Hartfield Av BRI BN1 ...... 172 B8
Hartfield Rd ROTT BN2 ...... 213 L3
Harting CI FERR BN12 ...... 187 J8
Harting CI CRAWW RH11 ...... 40 A1
Harting Down EPSF GU31 ...... 90 E1
Harting Rd LHPTN BN17 ...... 206 E1
The Hartings MIDOS PO22 .. 204 E6
Hartington PI ROTT BN2 ...... 11 K1
Hartington Rd ROTT BN2 ...... 11 K1
Hartington Ter ROTT BN2 ...... 11 K1
Hartington Vls HOVE BN3 ...... 193 J4
Hartland CI EMRTH PO10 ...... 176 A3
Harvest CI HWH RH16 ...... 88 C5
Harvester CI CCH PO19 ...... 7 H2
Harvesters HORS RH12 ...... 4 F3
HORS RH12 ...... 109 L2
Harvest HI EGRIN RH19 ...... 25 C5
RHWH RH17 ...... 108 D2
Harvest Rd CRAWE RH10 ...... 21 K8
Harvey CI CRAWW RH11 ...... 40 B3
Harvey Rd FERR BN12 ...... 209 M3
Harwarden CI CRAWE RH10 .. 23 K4
Harwood Av FERR BN12 ...... 187 L8
Harwood Rd LHPTN BN17 .. 206 D2
SWTR RH13 ...... 5 H6
Harwoods CI EGRIN RH19 ...... 25 C5
Harwoods' La EGRIN RH19 ...... 25 C4
EGRIN RH19 ...... 25 C6
Hasle Dr HASM GU27 ...... 28 C7
Haslemere Gdns HISD PO11 .. 215 J2
Haslemere Rd EMRTH PO10 .. 176 A2
HASM GU27 ...... 51 J6
LIPH GU30 ...... 26 E8
Hasler's La RCCH PO18 ...... 135 M7
Haslett Av East CRAWE RH10 .. 3 H4
Haslett Av West CRAWE RH10.. 2 E4
CRAWW RH11 ...... 2 E4
Haslingbourne La PETW GU28 .. 97 M7
Hassocks Ct CRAWW RH11 .. 40 A1
Hassocks Rd HPPT/KEY BN6 .. 130 C7
Haste HI HASM GU27 ...... 28 E7
Hastings Ct BOGR PO21 ...... 203 G8
Hastings Rd CRAWE RH10 ...... 21 J6
ROTT BN2 ...... 11 J1
WTHG BN11 ...... 10 A2
Hatch CI CRAN GU6 ...... 33 H1
Hatchetts Dr HASM GU27 ...... 27 K6
Hatchgate HORL RH6 ...... 15 G2
Hatchgate CI RHWH RH17 ...... 87 H6
Hatchgate La RHWH RH17 ...... 87 H6
Hatch HI HASM GU27 ...... 51 J3
Hatchlands HORS RH12 ...... 38 B5
RHWH RH17 ...... 87 C6
Hatch La HASM GU27 ...... 51 J2
LISS GU33 ...... 47 M8
Hatherleigh CI BOGR PO21 .. 203 G8
Hatherleigh Gdns BOGR PO21.. 203 H7
Havant Farm CI HAV PO9 .. 174 C1
Havant Rd EMRTH PO10 ...... 175 C4
HISD PO11 ...... 196 C1
Havelock Rd MIDOS PO22 ...... 13 K6
Havelock Rd BOGR PO21 ...... 12 D5
BRI BN1 ...... 194 A3
Haven Gdns CRAWE RH10 .. 23 H3
Havengate HORS RH12 ...... 4 F3
The Haven ANG/EP BN16 .. 207 H3
Haversham CI CRAWW RH11 .. 19 M8
Hawke CI ANG/EP BN16 ...... 207 M3
Hawkesbourne Rd HORS RH12.. 4 F3
Hawkesmoor Rd CRAWW RH11.. 19 M8
Hawkhurst Rd BRI BN1 ...... 172 E6
Hawkhurst Wk CRAWE RH10 .. 21 J8
Hawkins CI BOGR PO21 ...... 220 C2
SHOR BN43 ...... 191 L3
Hawkins Crs SHOR BN43 ...... 191 L2
Hawkins Rd CRAWE RH10 ...... 3 H8
SHOR BN43 ...... 191 L3
Hawkley CI HAV PO9 ...... 152 B6
Hawkley Rd LISS GU33 ...... 46 C5
Hawksfold La East HASM GU27.. 51 H6
Hawksfold La West HASM GU27.. 51 H6
Hawkshaw CI LIPH GU30 ...... 26 E8
Hawks PI MIDOS PO22 ...... 203 J6
Hawley Rd ANG/EP BN16 ...... 207 J4
Hawmead CRAWE RH10 ...... 23 K4
Haworth Rd CRAWE RH10 ...... 21 J7
Hawth Av CRAWE RH10 ...... 3 J7
Hawth CI CRAWE RH10 ...... 3 J7
Hawthorn CI BURH RH15 .. 109 L7
CCH PO19 ...... 6 C5
CRAWW RH11 ...... 20 D3
HORS RH12 ...... 4 D3
MIDH GU29 ...... 94 E6
ROTT BN2 ...... 213 K2
Hawthorn Crs FIN/BW BN14 .. 188 E6
Hawthorne Gv HISD PO11 .. 214 D1
Hawthorn Gdns FIN/BW BN14 .. 188 E6
Hawthorn Rd FIN/BW BN14 .. 188 E6
LHPTN BN17 ...... 184 E8
The Hawthorns BURH RH15 .. 109 H7
PUL/STOR RH20 ...... 123 M5
Hawthorn Wy PTSD BN41 .. 192 B1
PUL/STOR RH20 ...... 143 L2
Haybarn Dr HORS RH12 ...... 37 M5
Haybourne CI ROTT BN2 ...... 194 F5
Haybourne Rd ROTT BN2 ...... 194 F5
Haydon CI BOGR PO21 ...... 220 D2

Hayes Cl *PTSD* BN41 .... 192 D4
  RCCH PO18 .... 156 F5
Hayes La *SWTR* RH13 .... 58 D3
Hayes Wood Rd RH14 .... 58 A7
Hayley Rd *LAN/SOMP* BN15 .. 190 A5
Hayley's Gdns *MIDOS* PO22 ... 13 L4
Hayland Rd *HWH* RH16 .... 88 C7
Hayling Gdns *SALV* BN13 ...... 187 M3
Hayling Ri *SALV* BN13 .... 187 M3
Haynes Rd *FIN/BW* BN14 .... 8 C1
Haynes Wy *FIN/BW* BN14 .... 8 C1
Hay Rd *CCH* PO19 .... 7 G8
Haywards *CRAWE* RH10 .... 21 L3
Haywards *CRAWW* RH11 .... 13 M2
Haywards Heath Rd
  RHWH RH17 .... 65 H2
Haywards Rd *BRI* BN1 .... 172 B6
  HWH RH16 .... 109 M1
Hazelbank Cl *EPSF* GU31 .... 68 E8
  LIPH GU30 .... 26 E8
Hazel Cl *CRAWE* RH10 .... 23 K4
  CRAWW RH11 .... 20 D3
  PTSD BN41 .... 192 C1
  SWTR RH13 .... 82 B3
Hazeldean Dr *HAV* PO9 .... 152 E3
Hazeldene Meads *BRI* BN1 .... 193 L1
Hazel Gv *ARUN* BN18 .... 183 M2
  BURH RH15 .... 131 J3
  GSHT GU26 .... 27 M2
Hazelgrove Rd *HWH* RH16 .... 87 M8
Hazelhurst Crs *FIN/BW* BN14 .. 188 A1
  HORS RH12 .... 60 A3
Hazelhurst Dr *CRAWE* RH10 .. 21 M6
Hazelmead Dr *ANG/EP* BN16... 208 B3
Hazel Wy *CRAWE* RH10 .... 23 J4
Hazelwick Av *CRAWE* RH10 .... 21 H4
Hazelwick Mill La
  CRAWE RH10 .... 21 H4
Hazelwick Rd *CRAWE* RH10 .... 3 M2
Hazelwood *CRAWW* RH11 .... 20 D3
Hazelwood Cl *CRAWE* RH10 .. 23 C4
  FIN/BW BN14 .... 9 H1
  MIDH GU29 .... 95 C1
  PUL/STOR RH20 .... 144 C2
Hazelwood Rd *SWTR* RH13 .... 127 H1
Head Down *EPSF* GU31 .... 90 E1
Headley Cl *CRAWE* RH10 .... 21 L3
Headley Rd *LIPH* GU30 .... 26 B6
Hearn Cl *SELS* PO20 .... 180 D3
Hearnfield Rd *LHPTN* BN17 .. 184 E8
Heath Cl *HORS* RH12 .... 59 M1
  HPPT/KEY BN6 .... 129 L3
  SELS PO20 .... 201 H4
  SWTR RH13 .... 61 L6
Heathcote Dr *EGRIN* RH19 .... 24 C1
Heather Bank *HWH* RH16 .... 87 K7
Heather Cl *CRAWE* RH10 .... 22 C2
  HORS RH12 .... 4 F2
  RCCH PO18 .... 177 J1
Heatherfield *EPSF* GU31 .... 90 A7
Heatherlands
  PUL/STOR RH20 .... 144 A2
Heather La *PUL/STOR* RH20 .. 123 J7
  SALV BN13 .... 187 M2
Heather Rd *EPSF* GU31 .... 90 F1
Heatherstone Rd *WTHG* BN11 .. 211 H1
Heatherton Ms *EMRTH* PO10 .. 175 J1
Heather Wy *PUL/STOR* RH20 .. 144 A3
Heatherwood *MIDH* GU29 .... 94 E4
Heathfield *CRAWE* RH10 .... 21 L3
Heathfield Av *ANG/EP* BN16 .. 208 A1
  ROTT BN2 .... 213 L2
Heathfield Cl *MIDH* GU29 .... 94 F5
  SALV BN13 .... 188 A7
Heathfield Copse
  PUL/STOR RH20 .... 123 J5
Heathfield Crs *PTSD* BN41 .. 170 A8
Heathfield Dr *PTSD* BN41 .... 192 A1
Heathfield Gdns *MIDH* GU29 .. 94 F5
Heathfield Pk *MIDH* GU29 .... 94 E5
Heathfield Rd *EPSF* GU31 .... 90 F1
Heath Hill Av *ROTT* BN2 .... 195 G3
Heath Pl *MIDOS* PO22 .... 203 L5
Heath Rd *EPSF* GU31 .... 90 D1
  HASM GU27 .... 27 L7
  HWH RH16 .... 87 M7
Heath Rd East *EPSF* GU31 .... 90 E2
Heath Rd West *EPSF* GU31 .... 90 D1
Heath Wy *HORS* RH12 .... 4 L1
Hebe La *SHOR* BN43 .... 190 F5
Hechle Wd *BOGR* PO21 .... 221 G2
Heckfield Pl *HAV* PO9 .... 152 E7
Hedge End Rd *MIDOS* PO22 .. 182 D6
Hedgehog La *HASM* GU27 .... 28 C7
Hedgerow Gdns *EMRTH* PO10 .. 175 J1
Hedgers Hl *ARUN* BN18 .... 183 G3
Hedgeside *CRAWW* RH11 .... 40 D3
Hedgeway *MIDOS* PO22 .... 204 E7
Heene Pl *WTHG* BN11 .... 8 D7
Heene Rd *WTHG* BN11 .... 8 D4
Heene Ter *WTHG* BN11 .... 8 D8
Heene Wy *WTHG* BN11 .... 8 C6
Heghbrok Wy *BOGR* PO21 .... 221 H2
The Heights *BRI* BN1 .... 171 J7
  FIN/BW BN14 .... 188 B3
Helena Cl *PTSD* BN41 .... 192 D3
Helena Rd *ROTT* BN2 .... 195 L3
Hellingly Cl *HWH* RH16 .... 194 F7
Helston Dr *EMRTH* PO10 .... 175 H4
Helyer's Gn *LHPTN* BN17 .... 206 D2
Hempstead Rd *ROTT* BN2 .... 213 L4
Henderson Rd *CRAWW* RH11... 40 C3
Henderson Wk
  STEY/UB BN44 .... 146 F8
Hendon Av *ANG/EP* BN16 .... 207 H5
Hendon St *BRI* BN1 .... 11 L6
Henfield Cl *FERR* BN12 .... 187 J8
  ROTT BN2 .... 195 G8
Henfield Rd *HFD* BN5 .... 147 M8
  STEY/UB BN44 .... 168 C3
Henfield Wy *HOVE* BN3 .... 193 G1
  MIDOS PO22 .... 204 E6
Henge Wy *PTSD* BN41 .... 192 D3
Hengist Cl *HWH* RH16 .... 60 B3
Henley Cl *CRAWE* RH10 .... 41 L1
Henley Rd *ROTT* BN2 .... 195 G8
Henry Av *ANG/EP* BN16 .... 207 H3
Henry Burt Wy *BURH* RH15 .. 130 F3
Henry Cl *CCH* PO19 .... 7 L4

Henry St *BOGR* PO21 .... 12 E5
Henshaw Cl *CRAWW* RH11 .... 20 B3
Henson Rd *CRAWE* RH10 .... 21 J5
Henty Cl *ARUN* BN18 .... 183 G4
  CRAWW RH11 .... 39 M1
Henty Gdns *CCH* PO19 .... 6 C4
Henty Rd *FERR* BN12 .... 209 G4
  .... 8 E2
Henwood Down *EPSF* GU31 .. 90 D1
Hepplewhite Cl *CRAWW* RH11.. 40 C3
Herald Dr *CCH* PO19 .... 6 F7
Herbert Rd *BRI* BN1 .... 194 A2
  LAN/SOMP BN15 .... 189 J3
Hercules Pl *MIDOS* PO22 .... 204 E7
Hereford Cl *CCH* PO19 .... 179 G3
  .... 40 F2
Hereford St *ROTT* BN2 .... 11 H7
Herington La *PETW* GU28 ....
Herington Rd *ARUN* BN18 .... 184 A2
Herm Cl *CRAWW* RH11 .... 40 B2
Hermione Cl *FERR* BN12 .... 208 L1
Hermitage Cl *HAV* PO9 .... 152 B8
  SELS PO20 .... 201 L3
Hermitage Rd *EGRIN* RH19 .... 25 C4
Hermitage St *CRAWE* RH10 .... 3 K1
Hermonger La *HORS* RH12 .... 35 G2
Herne Gdns *ANG/EP* BN16 .... 207 L2
Herne Rd *ANG/EP* BN16 .... 207 L2
Herne Rd *EPSF* GU31 .... 90 D1
Herne Ct *CRAWW* RH11 .... 20 D4
  MIDOS PO22 .... 203 J5
  RCCH PO18 .... 156 F5
  SELS PO20 .... 222 D4
Herondale *HASM* GU27 .... 27 M6
Heron Md *BOGR* PO21 .... 220 A5
Heron Pl *EGRIN* RH19 .... 25 C4
Heron Quay *EMRTH* PO10 .... 175 K5
Herons Cl *BIL* RH14 .... 77 J2
Herontye Dr *EGRIN* RH19 .... 25 C4
Heron Wy *SWTR* RH13 .... 5 L8
Herrick Cl *CRAWE* RH10 .... 21 K4
Hersee Wy *SELS* PO20 .... 222 E5
Hertford Dr *BOGR* PO21 .... 203 G8
Hertford Rd *BRI* BN1 .... 194 C2
  .... 9 G4
Heston Av *BRI* BN1 .... 172 A5
Heston Gv *BOGR* PO21 .... 220 D3
Hewart's La *BOGR* PO21 .... 220 E1
Hewitts *HFD* BN5 .... 127 M8
Hewitts End *HFD* BN5 .... 127 M8
Hewshott Gv *LIPH* GU30 .... 26 F7
Hewshott La *LIPH* GU30 .... 26 E7
Hexham Cl *HWH* RH16 .... 88 C4
Heyshott Cl *LAN/SOMP* BN15 .. 189 M4
Hickman's Cl *HWH* RH16 .... 88 C4
Hickman's La *HWH* RH16 .... 88 B4
Hickstead La *RHWH* RH17 .... 107 K7
Hide Gdns *ANG/EP* BN16 .... 207 J2
Highams Hl *CRAWW* RH11 .... 20 A7
Highbank *BRI* BN1 .... 171 K7
High Bar La *RHWH* RH17 .... 63 L2
Highbarn *FIN/BW* BN14 .... 165 M5
High Beeches La *RHWH* RH17 .. 63 L2
High Beech La *HWH* RH16 .... 88 A4
Highbrook Cl *ROTT* BN2 .... 194 E2
Highbury Gv *HASM* GU27 .... 28 D4
Highclere Rd *HAV* PO9 .... 152 A8
Highclere Wy *SALV* BN13 .... 187 J7
High Cl *PTSD* BN41 .... 192 B3
Highcroft Av *MIDOS* PO22 .... 12 F3
Highcroft Cl *MIDOS* PO22 .... 13 C3
Highcroft Crs *MIDOS* PO22 .... 13 C2
Highcroft Dr *HORS* RH12 .... 34 F3
Highcroft Rd *EGRIN* RH19 .... 44 B6
Highcroft Vls *BRI* BN1 .... 193 M3
Highdown *STHW* BN42 .... 192 A3
Highdown Av *SALV* BN13 .... 188 B7
Highdown Cl *FERR* BN12 .... 208 F1
  STHW BN42 .... 192 A3
Highdown Ct *CRAWE* RH10 .... 41 J1
Highdown Dr *LHPTN* BN17 .... 206 F1
Highdown Rd *HOVE* BN3 .... 10 A2
Highdown Wy *FERR* BN12 .... 208 F1
  HORS RH12 .... 38 A5
Highercombe Rd *HASM* GU27 .. 28 F4
Highfield *LHPTN* BN17 .... 206 F1
Highfield Cl *ANG/EP* BN16 .... 186 B7
  MIDH GU29 .... 95 H2
Highfield Crs *BRI* BN1 .... 172 B7
Highfield Dr *HPPT/KEY* BN6 .. 130 C7
Highfield Gdns *ANG/EP* BN16 .. 207 J3
  LISS GU33 .... 47 L8
  MIDOS PO22 .... 12 F3
Highfield La *LIPH* GU30 .... 49 L2
  SELS PO20 .... 180 D5
Highfield Rd *EGRIN* RH19 .... 24 E1
  MIDOS PO22 .... 12 F4
  PSF GU32 .... 68 C3
  SALV BN13 .... 188 B6
Highfields *BRI* BN1 .... 172 F7
Highgate Dr *BOGR* PO21 .... 203 C5
Highground La *MIDOS* PO22 .. 182 C8
Highgrove Gdns *WTHG* BN11 .. 8 D6
Highland Av *BOGR* PO21 .... 12 B4
Highland Cl *EMRTH* PO10 .... 175 H4
Highland Ct *HWH* RH16 .... 87 M8
Highland Rd *CCH* PO19 .... 179 C2
  EMRTH PO10 .... 175 H3
  HWH RH16 .... 110 A1
Highlands Av *FIN/BW* BN14 .. 188 C5
Highlands Cl *CRAWW* RH11 .... 2 B7
  EGRIN RH19 .... 24 F1
Highlands Crs *ANG/EP* BN16 .. 186 B7
Highlands Dr *BURH* RH15 .... 109 H8
Highlands Rd *PTSD* BN41 .... 192 C3
The Highlands *RHWH* RH17 .... 87 G4
High Lawn Wy *HAV* PO9 .... 152 E7
Highleigh Rd *SELS* PO20 .... 218 D2
High Meadow *MIDH* GU29 .... 116 L4
High Oaks *CRAWW* RH11 .... 2 B7
High Park Av *HOVE* BN3 .... 192 F1
High Ridge Cl *BRI* BN1 .... 184 A3
High Seat Gdns *BIL* RH14 .... 79 L3
High Spinney
  PUL/STOR RH20 .... 123 M7

Highstanding La *MIDH* GU29 .. 95 H6
Highstead La *PETW* GU28 .... 74 C2
High St *ANG/EP* BN16 .... 186 A7
  ARUN BN18 .... 141 M5
  ARUN BN18 .... 184 C1
  BIL RH14 .... 79 L3
  BOGR PO21 .... 12 E7
  CCH PO19 .... 6 D2
  CRAWW RH11 .... 2 E5
  EGRIN RH19 .... 175 J4
  EMRTH PO10 .... 90 A7
  EPSF GU31 ....
  FIN/BW BN14 .... 165 M7
  HASM GU27 .... 28 A4
  HFD BN5 .... 128 A8
  HORL RH6 .... 15 J1
  HORS RH12 .... 18 D4
  HPPT/KEY BN6 .... 130 A6
  HPPT/KEY BN6 .... 151 L1
  HWH RH16 .... 88 C4
  LHPTN BN17 .... 206 E3
  PETW GU28 .... 98 B5
  PTSD BN41 .... 192 B3
  PUL/STOR RH20 .... 143 L3
  RCCH PO18 .... 177 H8
  RHWH RH17 .... 41 J8
  RHWH RH17 .... 41 M6
  RHWH RH17 .... 63 K4
  RHWH RH17 .... 66 C4
  RHWH RH17 .... 86 F6
  ROTT BN2 .... 11 G7
  ROTT BN2 .... 213 G3
  SALV BN13 .... 188 B7
  SELS PO20 .... 180 D6
  SELS PO20 .... 222 F5
  SHOR BN43 .... 190 F5
  STEY/UB BN44 .... 167 L1
  STEY/UB BN44 .... 168 B2
  SWTR RH13 .... 127 H1
  WTHG BN11 .... 9 J4
High Street Gn *MFD/CHID* GU8 .. 30 F3
  MFD/CHID GU8 .... 31 H1
The High St *CRAWW* RH11 .... 2 F3
High Titten *ARUN* BN18 .... 141 K1
High Trees *BOGR* PO21 .... 221 G2
  HWH RH16 .... 88 A7
  SELS PO20 .... 201 H3
Highview *LAN/SOMP* BN15 .... 189 L3
High Vw *SALV* BN13 .... 188 A7
Highview Av North *BRI* BN1 .... 171 M6
Highview Av South *BRI* BN1 .... 171 M7
Highview Rd *BRI* BN1 .... 171 M6
  PEAHV BN10 .... 213 M5
  SELS PO20 .... 182 A5
Highview Wy *BRI* BN1 .... 171 M6
Highway Cl *ROTT* BN2 .... 194 E2
Highways *PTSD* BN41 .... 192 C2
The Highway *ROTT* BN2 .... 194 E1
High Weald Landscape Trail
  EGRIN RH19 .... 24 E5
  EGRIN RH19 .... 43 L7
  RHWH RH17 .... 87 J3
Higworth La *HISD* PO11 .... 196 C7
Hilary Rd *CCH* PO19 .... 6 A2
Hildon Cl *SALV* BN13 .... 187 L2
Hilgrove Rd *ROTT* BN2 .... 213 L1
Hillary Cl *EGRIN* RH19 .... 25 H2
Hillbank Cl *PTSD* BN41 .... 192 A1
Hill Barn Av *LAN/SOMP* BN15 .. 189 L3
Hill Barn La *FIN/BW* BN14 .... 188 D5
Hill Barn La *RCCH* PO18 .... 116 D6
Hill Brow *HOVE* BN3 .... 171 J8
Hill Brow Cl *HAV* PO9 .... 152 E3
Hillbrow Rd *BRI* BN1 .... 171 K8
Hill Brow Rd *LISS* GU33 .... 69 J1
Hillcrest *BRI* BN1 .... 171 K7
Hillcrest Cl *CRAWE* RH10 .... 21 L6
  PUL/STOR RH20 .... 125 H7
  RHWH RH17 .... 111 C2
Hillcrest Dr *PUL/STOR* RH20 .. 125 H7
Hillcrest La *RHWH* RH17 .... 111 C1
Hillcrest Pk *PUL/STOR* RH20 .. 122 E2
Hillcroft *PTSD* BN41 .... 192 A2
Hill Dr *HOVE* BN3 .... 193 J1
Hill Farm Cl *HASM* GU27 .... 28 A7
Hill Farm La *PUL/STOR* RH20 .. 100 B7
Hill Farm Wy *STHW* BN42 .... 191 L2
Hillfield Rd *SELS* PO20 .... 222 F6
Hill House Cl *CRAWE* RH10 .... 23 H8
Hill House Hl *LIPH* GU30 .... 26 A5
Hillhouse La *HORS* RH12 .... 33 M3
Hillingdale *CRAWW* RH11 .... 40 D3
Hill La *EPSF* GU31 .... 113 M2
  MIDOS PO22 .... 182 D8
Hillmead *CRAWW* RH11 .... 40 C4
Hill Md *HORS* RH12 .... 60 B1
Hill Pl *CRAWW* RH11 .... 2 A5
Hillrise Av *LAN/SOMP* BN15 .. 189 K4
Hill Rd *GSHT* GU26 .... 27 K1
  HASM GU27 .... 28 D6
  LHPTN BN17 .... 206 F2
  ROTT BN2 .... 213 J3
Hillsboro Rd *BOGR* PO21 .... 12 C4
Hills Farm La *HORS* RH12 .... 60 A3
Hillside *CRAWE* RH10 .... 23 J4
  HORS RH12 .... 60 B2
  PTSD BN41 .... 192 D3
  ROTT BN2 .... 194 E2
  STHW BN42 .... 192 A3
Hillside Av *SWTR* RH13 .... 188 C5
Hillside Cl *CRAWW* RH11 .... 2 B7
  EGRIN RH19 .... 24 F1
Hillside Crs *ANG/EP* BN16 .... 186 B7
Hillside La *HFD* BN5 .... 147 M7
Hillside Rd *HASM* GU27 .... 28 A7
  LAN/SOMP BN15 .... 189 K4
  PUL/STOR RH20 .... 144 A2
Hillside Wk *PUL/STOR* RH20 .. 87 K6
  RHWH RH17 ....
Hillside Wy *BRI* BN1 .... 171 K8
Hills Pl *HORS* RH12 .... 60 B2
Hills Rd *STEY/UB* BN44 .... 167 K2
Hill Ter *ARUN* BN18 .... 184 A1
Hill Top Cl *BRI* BN1 .... 171 J7
Hill Top Dr *PTSD* BN41 .... 192 A2
Hilltop Rd *EGRIN* RH19 .... 43 M6
Hill View Cl *HASM* GU27 .... 28 A7
Hillview Gdns *CRAWW* RH11 .. 40 D4
Hillview Ri *FIN/BW* BN14 .... 188 A3

Hillview Rd *FIN/BW* BN14 .... 188 A2
  ROTT BN2 .... 195 H4
Hillybarn Rd *CRAWW* RH11 .... 19 K3
Hiltingbury Av *HAV* PO9 .... 152 D7
Hilton Pk *SELS* PO20 .... 217 H4
Hinde Rd *MIDOS* PO22 .... 204 D7
Hindhead *CRAWW* RH11 .... 2 C7
Hindhead Rd *HASM* GU27 .... 28 A6
Hindle Cl *PUL/STOR* RH20 .... 123 L5
Hinton Cl *BRI* BN1 .... 194 D2
Hipley Rd *HAV* PO9 .... 174 D1
Hislop Wk *BOGR* PO21 .... 12 F7
Hither Gn *EMRTH* PO10 .... 176 B2
Hoadlands *EPSF* GU31 .... 68 D8
Hoad La *HWH* RH16 .... 66 D8
Hobart Cl *SALV* BN13 .... 187 K5
Hobbs Rd *CRAWW* RH11 .... 40 B7
Hobbs Wy *ANG/EP* BN16 .... 207 K3
Hobdens La *RHWH* RH17 .... 66 B5
Hoblands *HWH* RH16 .... 88 C8
Hobs Acre *STEY/UB* BN44 .... 168 C3
Hocken Md *CRAWE* RH10 .... 21 L4
Hodges Cl *HAV* PO9 .... 174 D1
Hodgkin Cl *CRAWE* RH10 .... 21 J7
Hodshrove Rd *ROTT* BN2 .... 194 F1
Hoe Ct *LAN/SOMP* BN15 .... 190 B4
Hoefield La *RCCH* PO18 .... 116 D7
Hoe La *ARUN* BN18 .... 183 K5
  MIDOS PO22 .... 204 B4
  RCCH PO18 .... 199 K3
Hoewood Rd *HFD* BN5 .... 147 M5
Hogarth Rd *CRAWE* RH10 .... 41 G5
  HOVE BN3 .... 193 G5
Hoggarth Cl *EPSF* GU31 .... 68 D8
Hog La *ARUN* BN18 .... 141 M5
Hogwood Rd *BIL* RH14 .... 55 K1
Holbein Rd *CRAWE* RH10 .... 41 G4
Holbrook School La *HORS* RH12.. 37 L5
Holbury Ct *HAV* PO9 .... 152 E7
The Holdens *RCCH* PO18 .... 177 H7
Holder Rd *CRAWE* RH10 .... 41 J1
Holders *HPPT/KEY* BN6 .... 129 K6
Holdfast La *HASM* GU27 .... 29 G4
Hole St *PUL/STOR* RH20 .... 145 J2
Holford Gn *SELS* PO20 .... 223 H5
Holland Cl *BOGR* PO21 .... 203 G7
Holland Ms *HOVE* BN3 .... 193 L6
Holland Rd *HOVE* BN3 .... 193 L6
  STEY/UB BN44 .... 167 L1
Hollands Fld *HORS* RH12 .... 36 F8
Hollands La *HFD* BN5 .... 127 K8
Holland St *ROTT* BN2 .... 11 H5
Hollands Wy *HORS* RH12 .... 37 G4
Hollin Ct *CRAWW* RH11 .... 20 F3
Hollingbourne Crs
  CRAWW RH11 .... 40 D4
Hollingbury Copse *BRI* BN1... 172 B8
Hollingbury Crs *BRI* BN1 .... 194 C3
Hollingbury Gdns
  FIN/BW BN14 .... 188 B1
Hollingbury Park Av *BRI* BN1.. 194 B1
Hollingbury Pl *BRI* BN1 .... 194 C2
Hollingbury Ri West *BRI* BN1 .. 194 B2
Hollingbury Rd *BRI* BN1 .... 194 C3
Hollingbury Ter *BRI* BN1 .... 194 B2
Hollingdean La *BRI* BN1 .... 194 C4
Hollingdean Rd *ROTT* BN2 .... 194 C4
Hollingdean St *BRI* BN1 .... 194 C4
Hollingdean Ter *BRI* BN1 .... 194 C3
Hollist La *EPSF* GU31 .... 92 B8
  MIDH GU29 .... 94 E1
Hollow La *HISD* PO11 .... 214 C1
The Hollow *CRAWW* RH11 .... 20 A7
  EGRIN RH19 .... 44 A6
  HWH RH16 .... 88 C7
  PUL/STOR RH20 .... 123 L3
  PUL/STOR RH20 .... 141 H4
  PUL/STOR RH20 .... 144 A2
Hollybank La *EMRTH* PO10 .... 153 J8
Hollybush Rd *CRAWE* RH10 .... 3 M1
Holly Cl *BRI* BN1 .... 193 M1
  CRAWE RH10 .... 21 H4
  HORS RH12 .... 38 C7
  PUL/STOR RH20 .... 123 L3
  PUL/STOR RH20 .... 143 K3
  SALV BN13 .... 187 K2
Hollycombe Cl *LIPH* GU30 .... 49 K2
Holly Ct *PUL/STOR* RH20 .... 143 K2
Holly Dr *LHPTN* BN17 .... 184 F8
Hollyhock Wy *ANG/EP* BN16 .. 207 K1
Hollyridge *HASM* GU27 .... 28 D6
Holly Rd *HWH* RH16 .... 88 A1
Holman Cl *CRAWW* RH11 .... 40 C4
Holmans *RHWH* RH17 .... 66 B4
Holmbury Cl *CRAWW* RH11 .... 2 B7
Holmbush Cl *HWH* RH16 .... 109 M2
  SHOR BN43 .... 191 L2
Holmbush La *HFD* BN5 .... 148 F4
Holmbush Wy *MIDH* GU29 .... 94 E6
  STHW BN42 .... 191 L3
Holmcroft *CRAWE* RH10 .... 3 G6
Holmcroft Gdns *FIN/BW* BN14 .. 165 M7
Holmes Av *HOVE* BN3 .... 193 C2
Holmes La *ANG/EP* BN16 .... 207 J4
Holmesdale Rd *BURH* RH15 .. 131 G5
Holmfield Cl *ANG/EP* BN16 .. 207 K2
Holming End *HORS* RH12 .... 38 C7
Holm Oaks *SWTR* RH13 .... 106 A3
Holmsted Hl *RHWH* RH17 .... 86 B2
Holt Down *EPSF* GU31 .... 90 D1
Holt Gdns *HAV* PO9 .... 152 E1
Holton Hl *ROTT* BN2 .... 195 M5
The Holt *BURH* RH15 .... 131 K2
  PUL/STOR RH20 .... 144 F6
Holtveiw Rd *ROTT* BN2 .... 195 J4
Holtye Av *EGRIN* RH19 .... 25 G1
Holtye Rd *EGRIN* RH19 .... 25 J1
  EGRIN RH19 .... 25 M1
Holybourne Rd *HAV* PO9 .... 174 C1
Holyrood Pl *CRAWW* RH11 .... 40 C2
Homebush Av *ROTT* BN2 .... 213 L3
Home Cl *CRAWE* RH10 .... 21 K4
Homefield Av *MIDOS* PO22 .. 204 D6
Homefield Crs *ARUN* BN18 .. 182 E3
Homefield Rd *EMRTH* PO10 .. 153 L8
  WTHG BN11 .... 9 K3
Homelands Av *ANG/EP* BN16 .. 208 B4

Homelands Copse *HASM* GU27 73
Home Platt *EGRIN* RH19 44
Home Rd *BRI* BN1 193
Homestall Rd *EGRIN* RH19 25
Homestead La *BURH* RH15 109
Home Wy *EPSF* GU31 90
Homewell *HAV* PO9 174
Homewood *FIN/BW* BN14 165
Homing Gdns *MIDOS* PO22 203
Honer La *SELS* PO20 201
Honeysuckle Cl
  ANG/EP BN16 207
  LAN/SOMP BN15 189
  SALV BN13 165
Honeysuckle La *CRAWW* RH11 .. 20
Honeysuckle Wk *HORS* RH12 .. 5
Honeywood Cl *SWTR* RH13 5
The Hooe *LHPTN* BN17 207
Hooklands La *SWTR* RH13 125
Hook La *BOGR* PO21 220
  EGRIN RH19 66
  MIDOS PO22 12
  RCCH PO18 199
  RH17 ....
  SELS PO20 181
Hook Lane Cl *BOGR* PO21 220
Hook's Farm Wy *HAV* PO9 174
Hook's La *HAV* PO9 174
The Hooks *HFD* BN5 127
Hopewood *LISS* GU33 47
Hop Garden La *SELS* PO20 201
The Hop Gdn *EPSF* GU31 113
The Hopgarton *BOGR* PO21 .. 220
Hophurst Cl *CRAWE* RH10 23
Hophurst Dr *CRAWE* RH10 23
Hophurst Hl *CRAWE* RH10 23
The Hordens *SWTR* RH13 81
Horley Pl *ROTT* BN2 194
Horley Rd *HORL* RH6 14
Hormare Crs *PUL/STOR* RH20 .. 143
Hornbeam Cl *BOGR* PO21 221
  SWTR RH13 ....
Hornbeam Rd *HAV* PO9 174
Hornbeam Wy *MIDH* GU29 94
Hornby Rd *ROTT* BN2 195
Horndean Cl *CRAWW* RH11 21
Horndean Rd *EMRTH* PO10 153
Hornet Rd *EMRTH* PO10 197
The Hornet *CCH* PO19 7
Horn La *HFD* BN5 148
Hornshill La *HORS* RH12 34
Horns La *BOGR* PO21 220
Horsebridge Hl *BIL* RH14 99
Horsebridge Rd *HAV* PO9 152
Horsefield Rd *SELS* PO20 222
Horsemere Green La
  LHPTN BN17 205
Horseshoe Bend *GSHT* GU26 .. 27
Horseshoe Cl *CRAWE* RH10 21
The Horse Shoe *SELS* PO20 222
Horsgate La *RHWH* RH17 87
Horsham Cl *ROTT* BN2 195
Horsham Rd *BIL* RH14 33
  BIL RH14 58
  CRAWW RH11 2
  FIN/BW BN14 165
  HORS RH12 18
  HORS RH12 39
  HORS RH17 207
  PETW GU28 98
  RDKG RH5 17
  RHWH RH17 63
  STEY/UB BN44 146
Horsham Rd West
  LHPTN BN17 207
Horsted La *EGRIN* RH19 44
Horton Rd *BRI* BN1 194
Hospital Vls *HWH* RH16 110
Hotham Gdns *MIDOS* PO22 13
Hotham Wy *BOGR* PO21 12
Houghton Br *ARUN* BN18 141
Houghton Cl *HAV* PO9 152
Houghton La *PUL/STOR* RH20 .. 141
Houghton Rd *CRAWE* RH10 41
Hova Vls *HOVE* BN3 193
Hove Park Gdns *HOVE* BN3 193
Hove Park Rd *HOVE* BN3 193
Hove Park Vls *HOVE* BN3 193
Hove Pl *HOVE* BN3 193
Hove St *HOVE* BN3 193
Howard Av *BURH* RH15 108
  SELS PO20 216
Howard Pl *BRI* BN1 10
  LHPTN BN17 206
Howard Rd *ARUN* BN18 184
  CRAWW RH11 39
  LAN/SOMP BN15 189
  ROTT BN2 11
  SWTR RH13 5
Howard St *WTHG* BN11 8
Howards Wy *ANG/EP* BN16 207
Howard Ter *BRI* BN1 10
Hoylake Cl *CRAWW* RH11 19
Hoyle La *MIDH* GU29 117
Hudson Cl *SALV* BN13 187
Hudson Dr *ANG/EP* BN16 207
Hughes Cl *BOGR* PO21 203
Hughes Rd *ROTT* BN2 194
Humber Cl *SALV* BN13 187
Humber Ct *LHPTN* BN17 187
  SALV BN13 187
Humphrey's Gap *SHOR* BN43 .. 191
Humphrys Wy *WTHG* BN11 ....
Hundredsteddle La *SELS* PO20 .. 217
Hunston Cl *CRAWW* RH11 19
Hunter Rd *CRAWE* RH10 2
  CRAWW RH11 39
  EMRTH PO10 175
Hunters Cha *LIPH* GU30 26
Hunters Cl *BOGR* PO21 220
Hunters Md *SWTR* RH13 125

unters Race *CCH* PO19............. 178 E1
unters Rd *LISS* GU33............ 48 A2
unters Wy *CCH* PO19............. 179 G1
untingdon Wy *BURH* RH15... 109 L7
urlands *MFD/CHID* GU8 ...... 32 A3
urley Rd *SALV* BN13............ 187 M6
urn Ct *HAV* PO9................ 152 E6
ursley Rd *HAV* PO9............. 152 A7
urst Av *HORS* RH11............... 4 E5
 WTHG BN11.................. 210 A2
urstbourne Cl *HAV* PO9 .... 152 A6 ⬛
urst Cl *ARUN* BN18........... 141 M5
 CRAWW RH11............... 20 A8
 LIPH GU30.................. 26 B7
urst Cottages *ARUN* BN18... 141 M5
urst Crs *PTSD* BN41......... 192 E6
urst Farm Rd *EGRIN* RH19... 24 E4
urstfield *LAN/SOMP* BN15.. 189 L7 ⬛
 LAN/SOMP BN15........ 189 L7 ⬛
urstfield Cl *HWH* RH16 ...... 110 B2 ⬛
urst Gdns *HPPT/KEY* BN6 .. 130 A6
urst Hl *BRI* BN1.............. 172 D7
urstlands *BIL* RH14............ 79 K5
urstmere Cl *GSHT* GU26 ...... 27 L1
urston Cl *FIN/BW* BN14 ...... 188 B4
urst Gv *PUL/STOR* RH20 .... 143 J2
urston Rd *FIN/BW* BN14.... 123 H8
urst Rd *ANG/EP* BN16....... 207 M2
 HORS RH12.................. 4 E5
 HPPT/KEY BN6.............. 130 E5
urstwood Rd *EMRTH* PO10.. 176 B3
urstwood La *HWH* RH16 .... 110 A4 ⬛
 RHWH RH17................. 67 L3
utton Rd *BRI* BN1............. 194 C1
yde Dr *CRAWW* RH11 .... 19 M7
yde La *STEY/UB* BN44........ 168 A5
yde Sq *STEY/UB* BN44........ 168 C2 ⬛
yde St *STEY/UB* BN44......... 168 C2 ⬛
he Hyde *ROTT* BN2............. 195 G3
ylands Cl *CRAWE* RH10........ 3 M6
ylden Cl *ROTT* BN2............ 195 J4 ⬛
ylters's La *RCCH* PO18........ 135 K3
ylton Rd *PSF* GU32............ 90 C1
yperion Ct *CRAWW* RH11 .... 19 M8 ⬛
ythe La *STEY/UB* BN44........ 168 A5 ⬛
ythe Rd *BRI* BN1.............. 194 D2
 WTHG BN11.................. 8 A7

I

bsley Gv *HAV* PO9.............. 174 A1
carus Cl *ROTT* BN2............ 194 F7
den Cl *ROTT* BN2.............. 194 F7
den Hurst *HPPT/KEY* BN6.. 130 B5
field Av *CRAWW* RH11.......... 2 D1
field Cl *ROTT* BN2............ 213 M2
field Dr *CRAWW* RH11 .... 20 B5
field Gn *CRAWW* RH11 .... 20 B3
field Rd *CRAWW* RH11.......... 2 B2
field St *CRAWW* RH11.......... 20 A4
field Wd *CRAWW* RH11........ 19 L3
fold Bridge La *BIL* RH14...... 32 D8
foldhurst *BIL* RH14............ 55 K2
ford Ct *HAV* PO9............. 152 E6 ⬛
lex Cl *ANG/EP* BN16.......... 207 J4
lex Wk *HISD* PO11............ 214 F1
lex Wy *FERR* BN12............ 209 J2
 MIDOS PO22................. 204 F6
mberhorne Wy *EGRIN* RH19... 24 C1
nfirmary Dr *SWTR* RH13...... 59 M6
nfirmary Ter *CCH* PO19......... 6 D1
ngham Dr *BRI* BN1........... 172 D7
 HAV PO9.................... 174 A2
ngledene Cl *HAV* PO9......... 174 A2
ngle Green Cl *FERR* BN12.... 208 F4 ⬛
ngleside Crs *LAN/SOMP* BN15.. 189 M7
ngleside Rd
 LAN/SOMP BN15.......... 189 M7 ⬛
nglewood Dr *BOGR* PO21.... 220 C3
ngram Cl *ANG/EP* BN16...... 207 J3
 HORS RH12.................. 60 B2
ngram Crs *HOVE* BN3........ 192 F5 ⬛
ngram Crs East *HOVE* BN3.. 192 F5
ngram Crs West *HOVE* BN3.. 192 F5
ngram Rd *STEY/UB* BN44.... 167 K2
ngram's Green La *MIDH* GU29... 93 K6
 MIDH GU29................. 115 J2
nholmes Cl *BURH* RH15...... 131 J2
nholmes Park Rd *BURH* RH15 .. 131 J1
nlands Rd *RCCH* PO18....... 176 C3
nmans La *PSF* GU32........... 68 E7
nnerwyke Cl *MIDOS* PO22.... 204 C7 ⬛
nnes Rd *HORS* RH12............ 5 K3
nnovation Dr *HPPT/KEY* BN6.. 130 C3
nval Hl *HASM* GU27............ 28 D4
nverness Rd *ROTT* BN2....... 11 J1 ⬛
nwood Cl *BRI* BN1............ 193 L3
nwood Rd *LISS* GU33........ 47 K8
ona Cl *CRAWW* RH11............ 2 B9
ona Wy *HWH* RH16............ 87 M8 ⬛
ping Av *HAV* PO9............. 152 A7
ping La *MIDH* GU29........... 71 M8
rene Av *LAN/SOMP* BN15.... 189 L5
rvine Rd *LHPTN* BN17........ 206 E4
rving Wk *CRAWE* RH10........ 40 F1
rwin Dr *HORS* RH12........... 60 B1
saac's La *BURH* RH15......... 109 G6
sabel Crs *HOVE* BN3......... 192 F4
sfield Rd *BRI* BN1............ 194 D2
sland Cl *HISD* PO11........... 196 D1
sland La *SELS* PO20.......... 222 D4
sland Loop *SELS* PO20....... 222 D4
slingword Pl *ROTT* BN2....... 11 J4
slingword Rd *ROTT* BN2 .... 11 H3
tchen Cl *PSF* GU32............ 90 B2
 SELS PO20................. 199 G5
tchen Rd *HAV* PO9........... 152 E6
tchingfield Rd *SWTR* RH13.. 59 H4 ⬛
thica Cl *HISD* PO11.......... 196 D8
vanhoe Cl *CRAWW* RH11....... 20 E3
vanhoe Pl *MIDOS* PO22...... 204 D7
veagh Cl *CRAWW* RH11.......... 40 D3
ver Rd *ROTT* BN2............. 195 K3
vory Pl *ROTT* BN2............. 11 G5

Ivory Wk *CRAWW* RH11 .... 39 M1 ⬛
Ivy Arch Cl *FIN/BW* BN14..... 166 A6
Ivy Arch Rd *FIN/BW* BN14..... 9 H3
Ivy Cl *PUL/STOR* RH20....... 125 H7
 SELS PO20.................. 181 L5
 SHOR BN43................. 81 M3
Ivy Crs *MIDOS* PO22........... 12 F2
Ivydale Rd *BOGR* PO21....... 203 H8
Ivydene Crs *RCCH* PO18...... 176 E3
Ivy Dene La *EGRIN* RH19...... 25 L2
Ivydore Av *SALV* BN13........ 187 L4
Ivydore Cl *SALV* BN13........ 187 L5
Ivy La *MIDOS* PO22............ 12 F3
 PUL/STOR RH20........... 125 H6
 SELS PO20.................. 181 L5
Ivy Pl *HOVE* BN3............. 193 L7 ⬛
 WTHG BN11................... 8 D7

J

Jackdaw Cl *CRAWW* RH11....... 20 D4
Jackdaw La *HORS* RH12.......... 5 H1
Jacken Cl *MIDOS* PO22....... 204 D8
Jackrells La *SWTR* RH13....... 82 C1
Jackson Rd *CRAWE* RH10........ 40 C4
Jackson St *ROTT* BN2.......... 11 H4
Jacobean Cl *CRAWE* RH10...... 21 K7
James Cl *HISD* PO11.......... 214 B1
 SALV BN13................. 188 A6
James Rd *HAV* PO9........... 174 A2
James St *SELS* PO20.......... 223 G6
Jane Murray Wy *BURH* RH15.. 130 F5
 HPPT/KEY BN6............. 108 D3
Janes Cl *BURH* RH15......... 109 K7
Janes La *BURH* RH15......... 109 K7
 PETW GU28................. 96 F1
Jan Smuts Cl *LISS* GU33....... 48 A3
Japonica Cl *SHOR* BN43...... 191 J3
Japonica Wy *HAV* PO9......... 152 F8
Jarvis La *STEY/UB* BN44...... 167 L1
Jarvis Rd *ARUN* BN18......... 184 A1
Jasmine Cl *ANG/EP* BN16..... 207 H1 ⬛
Jasmine Rd *EMRTH* PO10...... 197 K1
Jay Cl *SWTR* RH13............. 82 B2
Jays Cl *LHPTN* BN17.......... 206 E2
Jay's La *HASM* GU27........... 52 C1
The Jays *ROTT* BN2........... 108 F8
Jefferies La *CRAWE* RH10...... 21 C1
Jeremy's La *RHWH* RH17....... 85 J6
Jerrard Rd *SELS* PO20........ 180 D2
Jersey Rd *CRAWW* RH11......... 40 B2
 FERR BN12................. 209 G3
Jersey St *ROTT* BN2........... 11 G4
Jervis Av *ANG/EP* BN16...... 207 L3
Jesmond Rd *HOVE* BN3........ 192 F5
Jesters *BURH* RH15........... 109 K5
The Jetty *MIDOS* PO22........ 205 H8
Jevington Cl *SALV* BN13...... 187 J7
Jevington Dr *ROTT* BN2...... 194 E3
Jew St *BRI* BN1................ 10 E6
Jib *ANG/EP* BN16............. 207 H1 ⬛
Jobes *RHWH* RH17.............. 65 G3
Job's La *HPPT/KEY* BN6....... 108 B6
Jobson's La *HASM* GU27........ 52 D4
John Arundel Rd *CCH* PO19..... 6 A7
Johnson Dr *BURH* RH15....... 131 L1
Johnson Wk *CRAWE* RH10....... 40 E1
Johnson Wy *ARUN* BN18...... 205 J2
John St *BOGR* PO21............ 12 E7
 ROTT BN2................... 11 G6
 SHOR BN43................. 190 F5
Joiesfield *CRAWW* RH11........ 40 A1
 SWTR RH13................. 105 G8
Jolliffe Rd *SELS* PO20........ 216 E5
Jones Sq *SELS* PO20.......... 223 G6
Jordans Cl *CRAWW* RH11....... 20 E4
Jordans Crs *CRAWW* RH11...... 20 L3
The Jordans *EGRIN* RH19...... 24 E4
Joyce Cl *LHPTN* BN17........ 206 D1
Joys Cft *CCH* PO19............. 7 H2
Jubilee Av *ANG/EP* BN16..... 207 K2
Jubilee Cl *HWH* RH16.......... 88 D8
Jubilee La *GSHT* GU26......... 27 L1 ⬛
Jubilee Rd *CRAWW* RH11....... 20 D3
 CCH PO19.................... 6 F3
 HORS RH12.................. 34 E4
 PTSD BN41................. 192 B4
Jubilee St *BRI* BN1........... 10 E6
Jubilee Ter *CCH* PO19.......... 6 F2
Jubilee Wk *CRAWE* RH10........ 3 M3
Jubilee Wy *PUL/STOR* RH20.. 144 A1
Judge's Ter *EGRIN* RH19...... 24 E4
Juggs La *PUL/STOR* RH20.... 123 M3
The Juggs *PUL/STOR* RH20.. 123 M3
Julian Rd *HOVE* BN3.......... 10 B3
Junction Cl *ARUN* BN18...... 205 J2
 BURH RH15................. 109 K8
Junction Rd *BRI* BN1......... 10 D4 ⬛
 BURH RH15................. 131 J2
June Cl *BOGR* PO21.......... 220 A4
June La *MIDH* GU29............ 94 A4
June Mdw *MIDH* GU29.......... 94 A4
Juniper Cl *MIDOS* PO22...... 204 F6 ⬛
 PTSD BN41................. 192 B3
 SALV BN13................. 187 K7
Juniper Rd *CRAWW* RH11....... 20 D3
Juniper Sq *HAV* PO9.......... 174 C4
Jupp's La *FERR* BN12......... 209 J1
Jura Cl *CRAWW* RH11........... 40 C1
Jury La *SELS* PO20........... 200 E7
Juxon Cl *CCH* PO19............. 6 C7
 CRAWW RH11................ 20 A8

K

Katrina Gdns *HISD* PO11...... 196 D7
Kearsley Dr *FIN/BW* BN14.... 188 B3
Keats Cl *HORS* RH12........... 37 M5
Keats Pl *EGRIN* RH19......... 24 E3 ⬛
Keats Wk *BOGR* PO21.......... 12 A7
Keble Cl *BOGR* PO21.......... 221 G1

 CRAWE RH10................ 21 L3
Keelson Wy *ANG/EP* BN16.... 207 H2
Keepers Wd *CCH* PO19....... 179 G1
Kelly Rd *HOVE* BN3........... 193 L3
Kelsey Av *EMRTH* PO10....... 176 B3
Kelsey Cl *HORL* RH6.......... 15 G1 ⬛
 LISS GU33.................. 47 K7
Kelso Cl *CRAWE* RH10......... 21 M5
 SALV BN13................. 187 M8
Kelvin Cl *CRAWW* RH11......... 21 G2
Kelvin Wy *CRAWW* RH11........ 21 G2
Kemnal Pk *HASM* GU27......... 28 E4
Kemps *HPPT/KEY* BN6......... 130 A6
Kempshott Rd *HORS* RH12...... 4 B4
Kemp St *BRI* BN1............. 10 E5
Kemp Town Pl *ROTT* BN2..... 11 M9 ⬛
Kemshott Rd *HAV* PO9........ 152 A6
Ken Berry Ct *HAV* PO9........ 152 E7
Kendal Cl *LHPTN* BN17....... 207 H1 ⬛
Kendale Cl *CRAWE* RH10...... 41 K2 ⬛
Kendal Rd *HOVE* BN3......... 193 G4
 LAN/SOMP BN15........... 189 K6
Kenilworth Cl *CRAWW* RH11... 40 C2 ⬛
 ROTT BN2.................. 195 H2
Kenilworth Ct *BOGR* PO21.... 203 H8
Kenlegh *BOGR* PO21.......... 221 G2
Kenmara Cl *CRAWW* RH11...... 21 J3
Kenmara Ct *CRAWW* RH11...... 21 J3
Kenmure Av *BRI* BN1......... 172 B5
Kennedy Av *EMRTH* PO10..... 175 H4
Kennedy Rd *SWTR* RH13....... 60 E3
Kennel Hl *RCCH* PO18........ 157 M5
Kennel La *HORL* RH6.......... 14 E2
 SWTR RH13................. 104 F2
Kennet Cl *CRAWW* RH11....... 187 L5 ⬛
 SALV BN13................. 187 L5 ⬛
Kennet Rd *PSF* GU32........... 90 B2
Kensington Gdns *BRI* BN1..... 10 E5
Kensington Pl *BRI* BN1....... 10 E5
Kensington Rd *CCH* PO19....... 7 K5
 CRAWW RH11................ 40 C2
Kensington St *BRI* BN1....... 10 E5
Kent Cl *SHOR* BN43.......... 191 K5
Kenton Rd *HOVE* BN3......... 192 E5
Kent Rd *CCH* PO19............. 7 H3
 LHPTN BN17................ 206 E2
Kents Rd *HWH* RH16.......... 110 A1
Kent St *SWTR* RH13.......... 106 D6
Kentstreet La *SWTR* RH13.... 106 D3
Kenwards *BRI* BN1........... 172 E5
Kerves La *SWTR* RH13......... 60 F6
Kestrel Cl *CRAWW* RH11....... 20 D4 ⬛
 HORS RH12................... 5 G1
 HOVE BN3.................. 193 L4
 SELS PO20................. 217 H6
Kestrel Cl *BOGR* PO21....... 203 A8 ⬛
 HORS RH12.................. 5 G1
Kestrel Wy *LHPTN* BN17...... 184 D8 ⬛
Keswick Cl *CRAWW* RH11....... 19 L8
 FERR BN12................. 187 L7
Ketches La *RHWH* RH17........ 89 M5
Ketch Rd *LHPTN* BN17........ 207 H4
Kevin Gdns *ROTT* BN2........ 195 M4
Kewell's Cnr *SELS* PO20...... 199 M7 ⬛
Kew Gdns *BOGR* PO21........ 203 G8 ⬛
Kew St *BRI* BN1............... 10 D5
Keymer Ct *BURH* RH15........ 131 J2 ⬛
Keymer Crs *FERR* BN12....... 209 K3
Keymer Gdns *BURH* RH15..... 131 J3
Keymer Pde *BURH* RH15...... 131 J2 ⬛
Keymer Pk *HPPT/KEY* BN6.... 151 J1
Keymer Rd *BURH* RH15........ 131 J4
 CRAWW RH11................ 40 C1
 HPPT/KEY BN6............. 151 G1 ⬛
Keymer Wy *FERR* BN12........ 209 K3
Keynor La *SELS* PO20........ 218 F4
Keysford La *HWH* RH16........ 88 F1
Kidborough Rd *CRAWW* RH11... 20 A8
Kidbrook *HWH* RH16........... 88 D6 ⬛
Kidders La *HFD* BN5.......... 127 L4
Kidd Rd *CCH* PO19........... 179 J3
Kidmans Cl *HORS* RH12........ 38 A6 ⬛
Kilmore Cl *FIN/BW* BN14..... 165 M6
Kilnbarn Wy *HWH* RH16....... 109 L2
Kiln Cl *LISS* GU33............ 47 H7
Kilnfield Rd *HORS* RH12....... 34 E4
Kiln Flds *HASM* GU27.......... 28 D4
Kiln La *HWH* RH16............. 88 C7
Kilnmead *CRAWE* RH10.......... 2 F7
Kilnmead Cl *CRAWE* RH10...... 3 G2
Kiln Rd *CRAWE* RH10.......... 23 J5
The Kiln *BURH* RH15.......... 131 K1
Kilnwood Cl *SELS* PO20...... 223 H5 ⬛
Kilnwood La *HORS* RH12....... 39 H1
Kilwich Cl *HORS* RH12........ 204 E6
Kimber Cl *LAN/SOMP* BN15.. 189 L1
Kimberley Cl *HORL* RH6....... 14 F1 ⬛
Kimberley Rd *CRAWE* RH10.... 21 J5 ⬛
 LISS GU33.................. 47 M2
 ROTT BN2.................. 194 E4
Kimbers *PSF* GU32............ 68 B8
Kimbridge Crs *HAV* PO9...... 152 D6
Kimbridge Rd *SELS* PO20..... 217 H6
Kimpton Ct *HAV* PO9......... 152 E6 ⬛
Kindersley Cl *EGRIN* RH19.... 25 J1 ⬛
Kinfauns Dr *SALV* BN13...... 187 L2
King Alfred Cl *STEY/UB* BN44.. 167 L1
King Edward Av *FIN/BW* BN14.. 9 J3
King Edward Cl *FIN/BW* BN14.. 9 J3
 SWTR RH13................. 59 L6
King Edward Rd *SWTR* RH13.. 59 L6
Kingfisher Cl *CRAWE* RH10.... 21 H3 ⬛
 HAV PO9................... 152 B3
 HISD PO11................. 196 E3
 SALV BN13................. 187 K7 ⬛
Kingfisher Ri *EGRIN* RH19..... 25 G4
Kingfisher Wy *HORS* RH12...... 4 F1 ⬛
King George Av *EGRIN* RH19... 24 D1
King George Gdns *CCH* PO19... 6 C8
 EPSH GU31................. 68 C8
King George Gdns *CCH* PO19... 6 C8
King George Rd *SHOR* BN43.. 191 K4
King George Vl *HOVE* BN3.... 193 J3
King George Vl Dr *HOVE* BN3.. 193 H7
King Pl *BRI* BN1.............. 10 D6
King's Arms Hl *ARUN* BN18.. 184 C1 ⬛
King's Av *CCH* PO19............ 6 D8
King's Barn La *STEY/UB* BN44.. 167 L1
King's Barn Vls *STEY/UB* BN44.. 167 M1
Kingsbridge Ms *SALV* BN13.. 187 L5 ⬛

Kingsbury Rd *BRI* BN1......... 10 F2
Kingsclere Av *HAV* PO9....... 152 A7
Kings Cl *ARUN* BN18.......... 205 G1
 HAV PO9................... 152 D2
 LAN/SOMP BN15........... 190 A7
Kings Copse *EGRIN* RH19..... 25 G4 ⬛
Kingscote Hl *CRAWW* RH11...... 2 F1
Kings Crs *SELS* PO20......... 223 G4
Kingscroft Ct *HAV* PO9...... 174 A3
Kings Dr *BOGR* PO21......... 220 C4
 HPPT/KEY BN6............. 131 G8
 MIDH GU29................. 72 E5
Kingsey Av *EMRTH* PO10...... 175 H4
Kingsfernsden La *PSF* GU32... 68 D7
Kingsfold *BIL* RH14........... 79 L6
Kingsfold Cl *BIL* RH14........ 79 L6
Kings Gap *SHOR* BN43........ 190 E7
King's Gdns *HOVE* BN3....... 193 J7
Kingsham Av *CCH* PO19........ 7 G3
Kingsham Rd *CCH* PO19........ 6 F6 ⬛
 CCH PO19................... 6 F6
Kingsland Cl *PUL/STOR* RH20.. 143 M2
 SHOR BN43................ 191 K5
Kingsland Rd *FIN/BW* BN14.. 188 E6
Kings La *PUL/STOR* RH20..... 121 K5
 PUL/STOR RH20........... 123 G2
 SWTR RH13................. 60 B8
 SWTR RH13................. 106 C4
Kingslea *SWTR* RH13............ 5 H5
Kingsley Cl *FIN/BW* BN14...... 9 H4
Kingsley Rd *BRI* BN1......... 193 L3
 CRAWW RH11................ 40 B1
Kingsmead *LHPTN* BN17....... 184 D7
 MIDOS PO22................ 205 H6
Kingsmead Cl *STEY/UB* BN44.. 167 L3
Kingsmead Pl *HORS* RH12..... 59 L1 ⬛
Kingsmead Rd *HORS* RH12.... 59 K1
 MIDOS PO22................ 205 H6
Kings Ms *HOVE* BN3.......... 193 J6 ⬛
Kingsmill Rd *MIDOS* PO22.... 182 D6
Kings Pde *BOGR* PO21........ 221 H1 ⬛
Kingspit La *PETW* GU28....... 98 D5
Kings Platt *SWTR* RH13...... 103 K4
Kings Ride *BURH* RH15....... 131 L3
Kings Rd *BRI* BN1............ 10 A7
 EMRTH PO10............... 175 H4
 HASM GU27................. 28 B6
 HISD PO11................. 196 D1
 HORL RH6.................. 15 H1
 HWH RH16................. 110 A2
 LAN/SOMP BN15........... 189 M7
 PSF GU32.................. 68 A8
 SWTR RH13................. 191 L3
 SWTR RH13................... 5 H5
King's Stone Av *STEY/UB* BN44.. 168 A2
Kingsthorpe Rd *HOVE* BN3... 192 F4
Kingston Bay Rd *SHOR* BN43.. 191 K6
Kingston Broadway
 SHOR BN43................ 191 K3
Kingston Cl *BRI* BN1......... 172 F6
 HOVE BN3.................. 192 F2
 SHOR BN43................ 191 K4
Kingston La *ANG/EP* BN16.... 208 C3
 SHOR BN43................ 191 K3
Kingston Wy *SHOR* BN43..... 191 K3
King St *ARUN* BN18........... 184 B1
 BRI BN1................... 10 E6 ⬛
 EMRTH PO10............... 175 H4
 FIN/BW BN14................ 9 G1
Kings Wk *SHOR* BN43......... 190 E7
Kings Wy *BURH* RH15......... 131 K3
Kingsway *BOGR* PO21......... 220 E3
 HISD PO11................. 196 D1
 HOVE BN3.................. 193 G6
 SELS PO20................. 223 H6
Kingswood *PUL/STOR* RH20.. 123 K5 ⬛
Kingswood Cl *CRAWW* RH11... 40 D4 ⬛
Kingswood Firs *GSHT* GU26... 27 K2
Kingswood La *GSHT* GU26..... 27 K2
Kingswood St *ROTT* BN2..... 10 F7
Kingsworthy Rd *HAV* PO9.... 174 C1
Kinnell Cl *EMRTH* PO10...... 175 J4
Kipling Av *FERR* BN12........ 209 J1
 ROTT BN2.................. 195 M4
Kipling Cl *CRAWW* RH11....... 21 K4 ⬛
Kipling Ct *SWTR* RH13........ 5 M4 ⬛
Kipling Wy *EGRIN* RH19...... 24 D3
Kirdford Cl *ANG/EP* BN16.... 207 J3
 BURH RH15................. 131 K3 ⬛
 CRAWW RH11................ 20 B4
Kirdford Rd *ARUN* BN18...... 184 B2
Kirkby Cl *RCCH* PO18......... 180 E1
Kirkland Cl *ANG/EP* BN16.... 207 J3
Kitchener Rd *LISS* GU33....... 47 M3
Kites Cl *CRAWW* RH11.......... 2 E7 ⬛
 CRAWW RH11................ 20 E6 ⬛
 FERR BN12................. 187 J8
Kithurst Crs *FERR* BN12...... 187 J8
Kithurst Farm Rd
 PUL/STOR RH20........... 143 J4
Kithurst La *PUL/STOR* RH20.. 143 K3
Kithurst Pk *PUL/STOR* RH20.. 143 J3
Kitsmead *CRAWE* RH10......... 22 B2
Kittiwake Cl *CRAWW* RH11.... 19 L8 ⬛
Knepp Cl *CRAWE* RH10......... 21 K6
 ROTT BN2.................. 195 G2
Knighton Cl *CRAWE* RH10..... 40 D4
Knightscroft Av *ANG/EP* BN16.. 207 K4
Knightscroft Cl
 ANG/EP BN16.............. 207 J4 ⬛
Knight's Hl *RCCH* PO18....... 136 F7
Knightwood Av *HAV* PO9..... 152 C6
Knob Hl *HWH* RH16............ 88 C8
Knockhundred La *GSHT* GU26.. 27 J4
Knockhundred Rw *MIDH* GU29.. 93 K3 ⬛
Knole Cl *CRAWE* RH10......... 21 L5 ⬛
Knole Gv *EGRIN* RH19......... 24 D1
Knole Rd *ROTT* BN2.......... 213 H5
Knoll Cl *HORS* RH12.......... 192 E5
Knowle Cl *CRAWE* RH10........ 22 D1
Knowle Dr *CRAWE* RH10....... 22 C1
Knowles Meadow *LISS* GU33.. 69 L3
The Knowle *RHWH* RH17...... 86 F5
Knox Rd *HAV* PO9............ 174 A3

Knoyle Rd *BRI* BN1........... 193 M2
Kymer Gdns *HPPT/KEY* BN6.. 151 H1
Kynon Gdns *MIDOS* PO22.... 204 E6
Kyoto Ct *BOGR* PO21......... 221 H1

L

Laburnum Av *HOVE* BN3...... 192 F3
Laburnum Cl *FERR* BN12..... 209 G3 ⬛
 LAN/SOMP BN15........... 189 L8 ⬛
Laburnum Gv *CCH* PO19........ 6 F5
 HISD PO11................. 196 E8
 MIDOS PO22................ 12 C1
Laburnum Wy *HWH* RH16...... 88 C8
Lackenhurst La *SWTR* RH13... 81 G6
Lacock Cl *SELS* PO20......... 217 K7
Ladies Mile Cl *BRI* BN1...... 172 A6
Ladies' Mile Rd *BRI* BN1..... 171 M6
Laddell Rd *WTHG* BN11......... 9 L2
Ladygate Dr *GSHT* GU26...... 27 H1
Lady Margaret Rd
 CRAWW RH11................ 20 B5
Ladymead *BURH* RH15........ 109 K7 ⬛
Ladymead Cl *CRAWE* RH10.... 41 K1 ⬛
Ladysmith Rd *ROTT* BN2..... 194 E4
Lagness Rd *SELS* PO20....... 201 L3
Lagoon Rd *BOGR* PO21....... 220 A6
Lagwood Cl *HPPT/KEY* BN6.. 150 F1
Laine Cl *BRI* BN1............ 193 M1
Laines Rd *STEY/UB* BN44..... 167 K2
Lake La *ARUN* BN18........... 183 G7
 MIDOS PO22................ 182 G5
Lake Rd *BOGR* PO21............ 7 K5
Lakers Meadow *BIL* RH14..... 79 L4
Lakeside *HORS* RH12............ 4 C1
 MIDH GU29................. 94 F6
Lakeside Dr *SWTR* RH13....... 82 B3
Lakeside Gdns *HAV* PO9...... 174 D2
Lake Vw *BOGR* PO21.......... 220 B3
Lake View Rd *CRAWE* RH10.... 23 J1
Lakers Meadow *BIL* RH14..... 79 L4
Lambert's La *MIDH* GU29...... 95 G4
Lambeth Cl *CRAWW* RH11...... 40 C2
Lambleys La *FIN/BW* BN14... 189 G5 ⬛
Lambourn Cl *EGRIN* RH19..... 24 F1 ⬛
Lambourne Cl *BRI* BN1....... 194 D2
 CRAWE RH10................. 3 K7
Lambourne La *LIPH* GU30..... 71 J3
Lambourne Rd *BRI* BN1....... 194 D2
Lambs Crs *HORS* RH12.......... 5 K1
Lambs Farm Cl *HORS* RH12.... 5 L1
Lambs Farm Rd *HORS* RH12... 5 K1
Lambs Green Rd *HORS* RH12.. 38 B2 ⬛
Lammas Cl *LHPTN* BN17...... 206 F1
Lamorna Gdns *FERR* BN12... 209 G4 ⬛
 SELS PO20................. 181 L6 ⬛
Lamorna Gv *FIN/BW* BN14... 188 D6
Lanark Cl *SWTR* RH13.......... 5 H7
Lancaster Cl *CRAWE* RH10.... 21 L3 ⬛
Lancaster Dr *EGRIN* RH19..... 25 H1
Lancaster Pl *MIDOS* PO22.... 12 C1
Lancaster Rd *BRI* BN1.......... 10 C2
 FERR BN12................. 209 H3
Lancastrian Gra *CCH* PO19.... 6 D3 ⬛
Lancelot Cl *CRAWW* RH11..... 19 M6 ⬛
Lancing Cl *CRAWW* RH11...... 20 B5
 LAN/SOMP BN15........... 189 G1
Lancing Ct *HORS* RH12......... 5 M3
Lancing Pk *LAN/SOMP* BN15.. 189 K7 ⬛
Landseer Dr *SELS* PO20...... 223 H5
Landseer Rd *HOVE* BN3....... 193 H4
Lane End Dr *EMRTH* PO10.... 175 H4
Lane End Rd *MIDOS* PO22.... 205 H7
Lanercost Rd *CRAWW* RH11.... 2 D6
The Lane *BIL* RH14............ 32 D8
 CCH PO19.................. 179 G2
Lanfranc Rd *FIN/BW* BN14..... 8 C2
Langbrook Cl *HAV* PO9....... 174 C4
Langbury Cl *FERR* BN12...... 208 F1
Langbury La *FERR* BN12...... 208 F1
Langdale Av *CCH* PO19......... 7 J9
Langdale Cl *LAN/SOMP* BN15.. 189 K7 ⬛
Langdale Gdns *HOVE* BN3.... 192 E5
Langdale Rd *CRAWW* RH11.... 19 L8 ⬛
 HOVE BN3.................. 193 G6
Langham Gdns *WTHG* BN11..... 8 B6
Langhurst Cl *HORS* RH12...... 17 L8
Langhurst La *HORS* RH12...... 19 H4
Langhurstwood Rd *HORS* RH12.. 17 L8
Langley Crs *ROTT* BN2........ 195 L3
Langley Dr *CRAWW* RH11...... 20 D4
Langley Gv *BOGR* PO21....... 220 D3
Langley La *CRAWW* RH11...... 20 D4
Langley Pde *CRAWW* RH11.... 20 D3
Langley Pl *CRAWW* RH11...... 20 D3 ⬛
Langley Wk *CRAWW* RH11...... 20 D4
Langmead Cl *LHPTN* BN17... 205 M4 ⬛
Langridge Dr *EGRIN* RH19.... 24 F4 ⬛
 PTSD BN41................. 192 C2
Langridge La *HWH* RH16...... 88 B7 ⬛
Langridge Wy *BURH* RH15.... 108 F7 ⬛
Langrish La *HAV* PO9......... 152 D6 ⬛
Langshott Cl *HORL* RH6....... 15 K1
Langstone Av *HAV* PO9....... 174 C5
Langstone Cl *CRAWE* RH10.... 41 L1
Langstone High St *HAV* PO9.. 174 C6
Langstone Rd *HAV* PO9....... 174 C5
Langton Cl *SELS* PO20........ 223 H2
Langton La *HPPT/KEY* BN6... 129 M4
Langton Rd *CCH* PO19.......... 6 A3
 FIN/BW BN14................ 9 G2
Lansbury Rd *CRAWW* RH11.... 40 C3
Lansdown Cl *HORS* RH12...... 38 C6 ⬛
Lansdowne Av *ANG/EP* BN16.. 186 A6
 WTHG BN11.................. 8 A6
Lansdowne Ct *WTHG* BN11..... 8 A6 ⬛
Lansdowne Ms *HOVE* BN3.... 193 L6 ⬛
Lansdowne Pl *HOVE* BN3..... 193 L6
Lansdowne Rd *ANG/EP* BN16.. 186 A4
 HOVE BN3.................. 193 L5
 LHPTN BN17............... 206 E1
Lansdowne Sq *HOVE* BN3.... 193 L6 ⬛
Lansdowne St *HOVE* BN3..... 193 L6
Lansdowne Wy *ANG/EP* BN16.. 186 A6
Lanyards *ANG/EP* BN16...... 207 H1
Lanyon Cl *HORS* RH12......... 38 B6
Lapwing Cl *SWTR* RH13......... 5 K5
Larch Cl *ANG/EP* BN16....... 207 L3 ⬛
 CCH PO19.................. 179 G2

LIPH GU30 ... 49 J1
MIDOS PO22 ... 203 K5
Larch End *HORS* RH12 ... 4 A5
PUL/STOR PO20 ... 123 L5
The Larches *HORS* RH12 ... 38 D6 ⊡
Larches Wy *CRAWE* RH10 ... 23 K4
Larchfield CI *BOGR* PO21 ... 220 E3
Larch Wy *HAV* PO9 ... 88 C8
Larcombe Rd *PSF* GU32 ... 90 A3
Large Acres *SELS* PO20 ... 222 F5
Larke CI *SHOR* BN43 ... 191 K5
Larkfield CI *LAN/SOMP* BN15 ... 190 A7
Larkfield Wy *BRI* BN1 ... 172 B8
Lark HI *HOVE* BN3 ... 192 F1
Larkins Rd *HORL* RH6 ... 14 E5
Lark Ri *CRAWW* RH11 ... 20 D4
  LIPH GU30 ... 26 B7
Larkspur Wy *HORS* RH12 ... 82 B1
Lashmar Rd *ANG/EP* BN16 ... 208 B3
Lashmere *CRAWE* RH10 ... 22 E1
Latham Rd *SELS* PO20 ... 222 F6
Latimer CI *CRAWW* RH11 ... 20 E3
Latimer Rd *WTHG* BN11 ... 210 A3
Laud Dr *CRAWE* RH10 ... 21 L7
Lauder CI *EMRTH* PO10 ... 176 A2
Laughton Rd *HORS* RH12 ... 5 K2
Laurel CI *BURH* RH15 ... 109 L7 ⊡
  CRAWE RH10 ... 3 M9
  SALV BN13 ... 187 K7
Laurel Dene *EGRIN* RH19 ... 25 G3
Laurel Gv *MIDOS* PO22 ... 203 K6 ⊡
Laurel Mt *PUL/STOR* RH20 ... 122 D2 ⊡
The Laurels *HFD* BN5 ... 127 M7
  SWTR RH13 ... 82 A2
Laurel Wk *SWTR* RH13 ... 9 J9
Lauriston Rd *BRI* BN1 ... 193 M2
Lavant CI *CRAWW* RH11 ... 20 A7
  FERR BN12 ... 187 H8 ⊡
Lavant Down Rd *RCCH* PO18... 156 F5
Lavant Rd *HAV* PO9 ... 174 C1
Lavant Rd *CCH* PO19 ... 179 C1
Lavant *PSF* GU32 ... 68 B8
Lavender HI *SHOR* BN43 ... 191 J3
Lavender St *ROTT* BN2 ... 11 H8
Lavington CI *CRAWW* RH11 ... 20 A5
Lavington Rd *FIN/BW* BN14 ... 188 B2 ⊡
Lavinia Ct *FERR* BN12 ... 209 K1
Lavinia Wy *ANG/EP* BN16 ... 208 B3
Lawns *HORS* RH12 ... 34 B1
The Lawns *ANG/EP* BN16 ... 208 B5
  LAN/SOMP BN15 ... 189 K5
The Lawn *BOGR* PO21 ... 220 F2
Lawrence Av *ANG/EP* BN16 ... 207 L2
Lawrence CI *SELS* PO20 ... 223 C6
Lawrence Rd *HOVE* BN3 ... 193 C5
Lawrie La *HWH* RH16 ... 88 C7
Laws CI *CRAWW* RH11 ... 19 M7
Lawyer's La *HFD* BN5 ... 127 K7
Laylands Rd *PTSD* BN41 ... 192 B5
The Layne *MIDOS* PO22 ... 205 H7
Lazy Acre *EMRTH* PO10 ... 176 A4
Lea CI *CRAWW* RH11 ... 20 A7
Lea Farm La *PUL/STOR* RH20.. 121 J2
Leahurst Court Rd *BRI* BN1... 193 M1
Leaman CI *MIDOS* PO22 ... 205 C7 ⊡
Leander Rd *RCCH* PO18 ... 177 K7
Leas Ct *MIDOS* PO22 ... 12 D2
The Leas *ANG/EP* BN16 ... 207 M1
Leatherbottle La *CCH* PO19 ... 7 K4 ⊡
Lechford Rd *HORL* RH6 ... 15 G3
Leckford Rd *HAV* PO9 ... 152 E6
Leconfield Rd
  LAN/SOMP BN15 ... 189 K7
Ledbury Wy *BOGR* PO21 ... 220 C2
Ledgers Meadow
  RHWH RH17 ... 87 G6
Ledra Dr *BOGR* PO21 ... 220 C4
Leechpond HI *SWTR* RH13 ... 84 B2
Leechpool La *SWTR* RH13 ... 5 M3
Leecroft Rd *BOGR* PO21 ... 220 F2
Leeds CI *SALV* BN13 ... 187 J7
  SWTR RH13 ... 82 B2
Leeward CI *SALV* BN13 ... 188 A7 ⊡
Leeward CI *LHPTN* BN17 ... 207 C3
  SALV BN13 ... 188 A7
Legion Rd *HISD* PO11 ... 196 B8
Legion Wy *SELS* PO20 ... 217 H6
Legsheath La *EGRIN* RH19 ... 45 C5
Leicester St *ROTT* BN2 ... 11 H7
Leicester Vls *HOVE* BN3 ... 192 E5
Leighlands *CRAWE* RH10 ... 21 K4
  HAV PO9 ... 174 C2
Leighton Av *FIN/BW* BN14 ... 188 E6
Leighton Rd *HOVE* BN3 ... 193 H4
  RHWH RH17 ... 67 K7
Leinster Gdns *MIDOS* PO22 ... 204 C3
Leith View Rd *HORS* RH12 ... 5 L2
Lemmington Wy *HORS* RH12 ... 38 A5
Lenham Av *ROTT* BN2 ... 213 J5
Lenham Rd East *ROTT* BN2 ... 213 J3
Lenham Rd West *ROTT* BN2 ... 213 J4
Lenhurst Wy *SALV* BN13 ... 188 A7
Lennox CI *CCH* PO19 ... 7 K2
  HOVE BN3 ... 193 G4
  SHOR BN43 ... 191 J4
  WTHG BN11 ... 9 H4
Lennox St *BOGR* PO21 ... 12 E8
  ROTT BN2 ... 11 H6
Leonardslee Ct *CRAWE* RH10 ... 41 J1 ⊡
Leonard Wy *SWTR* RH13 ... 5 J8
Leonora Dr *BOGR* PO21 ... 220 C4
Leopold CI *MIDOS* PO22 ... 13 M2
Leopold Rd *BRI* BN1 ... 10 C5
  CRAWW RH11 ... 2 C4
Lesser Foxholes *SHOR* BN43 ... 190 F4
Letchworth CI *CRAWW* RH11 ... 2 A9
Level Mare La *SELS* PO20 ... 181 L1
Leveret La *CRAWW* RH11 ... 2 C4
Leverton Av *MIDOS* PO22 ... 204 D8
Lewes CI *BOGR* PO21 ... 220 D2
  CRAWE RH10 ... 21 K6
  ROTT BN2 ... 213 J3
Lewes Crs *ROTT* BN2 ... 194 F8
Lewes Rd *BRI* BN1 ... 173 H6
  EGRIN RH19 ... 25 C4
  FROW RH18 ... 45 M1
  HPPT/KEY BN6 ... 131 M2
  HWH RH16 ... 88 C5
  HWH RH16 ... 110 C1

RHWH RH17 ... 67 K8
ROTT BN2 ... 11 H2
Lewes St *ROTT* BN2 ... 11 G4
Lewin CI *LAN/SOMP* BN15 ... 190 A5
Lewis Ct *SALV* BN13 ... 187 J1
Lewisham CI *CRAWW* RH11 ... 40 D2 ⊡
Lewis La *ARUN* BN18 ... 205 J1
Lewis Rd *CCH* PO19 ... 7 G3
  EMRTH PO10 ... 175 K1
  LAN/SOMP BN15 ... 189 L4
  SELS PO20 ... 222 F6
Lexden Gdns *HISD* PO11 ... 196 B8
Leybourne CI *CRAWW* RH11 ... 40 D3 ⊡
  ROTT BN2 ... 195 H3 ⊡
Leybourne Rd *ROTT* BN2 ... 195 H2
Leyfield *CRAWE* RH10 ... 129 L7 ⊡
Leylands Pk *BURH* RH15 ... 109 J7
Leylands Rd *BURH* RH15 ... 109 H8
The Leys *HASM* GU27 ... 51 H7
  RCCH PO18 ... 136 F5
Leyton Lea *RHWH* RH17 ... 86 F6
Liam CI *HAV* PO9 ... 152 D8
Library HI *WTHG* BN11 ... 9 J6
Lichfield Gdns *BOGR* PO21 ... 220 F1
Lidsey CI *CRAWE* RH10 ... 21 K8
Lidsey Rd *MIDOS* PO22 ... 181 L8
Lifeboat Wy *SELS* PO20 ... 223 G7
Lilac CI *HAV* PO9 ... 174 F1
  MIDOS PO22 ... 204 F6
  SALV BN13 ... 187 J7 ⊡
Lillywhite CI *BURH* RH15 ... 109 G7
Limbourne La *PUL/STOR* RH20 .. 121 J1
Limbrick CI *FERR* BN12 ... 209 K1
Limbrick La *FERR* BN12 ... 187 K8
Limbrick Wy *FERR* BN12 ... 187 J8
Lime Av *HORS* RH12 ... 5 L3
Lime Cha *PUL/STOR* RH20 ... 143 L2
Lime CI *CCH* PO19 ... 7 L2
  CRAWE RH10 ... 22 C1
  CRAWW RH11 ... 20 D3
Lime Kiln La *ROTT* BN2 ... 11 L6 ⊡
Lime Rd *FIN/BW* BN14 ... 165 M5
Limes Av *HORL* RH6 ... 15 J3
Limes CI *LIPH* GU30 ... 26 D5
  LISS GU33 ... 47 J8
The Limes *ARUN* BN18 ... 205 G1
Lime Tree Av *FIN/BW* BN14 ... 188 B2 ⊡
Lime Tree CI *ANG/EP* BN16 ... 208 A2 ⊡
Limmard Wy *MIDOS* PO22 ... 204 D8
Limmer La *MIDOS* PO22 ... 204 D8
Limney La *ROTT* BN2 ... 194 F5
Linacre Dr *HASM* GU27 ... 34 D1
Lincett Av *SALV* BN13 ... 188 A8
Lincett Dr *SALV* BN13 ... 210 A1
Linchmere Av *ROTT* BN2 ... 213 K3
Linchmere PI *CRAWW* RH11 ... 20 B5
Linchmere Rd *HASM* GU27 ... 50 D1
Linch Rd *HASM* GU27 ... 72 B1
  MIDH GU29 ... 72 C7
Lincoln Av *BOGR* PO21 ... 202 D8
Lincoln CI *CRAWE* RH10 ... 40 F1
Lincoln Cottages *ROTT* BN2 ... 11 H4 ⊡
Lincoln Gn *CCH* PO19 ... 179 G3
Lincoln Rd *PTSD* BN41 ... 192 C5
  SALV BN13 ... 188 A8
Lincoln St *ROTT* BN2 ... 11 H4
Lincoln Wd *RHWH* RH17 ... 87 K7
Linden Av *EGRIN* RH19 ... 24 D2
Linden CI *CRAWE* RH10 ... 3 M9
  HORS RH12 ... 5 H3
Linden Dr *LISS* GU33 ... 47 J8
Linden Gv *HISD* PO11 ... 214 D1
  HWH RH16 ... 88 B6
Linden Pk *LHPTN* BN17 ... 206 D3
Linden Rd *BOGR* PO21 ... 12 B4
  LHPTN BN17 ... 206 D3
Lindens CI *EMRTH* PO10 ... 175 J1
The Lindens *CRAWE* RH10 ... 22 C1 ⊡
Linden Wy *HAV* PO9 ... 174 C1 ⊡
Lindfield CI *ROTT* BN2 ... 213 J2
Lindfield Rd *RHWH* RH17 ... 66 D6
Lindsey Rd *MIDOS* PO22 ... 13 M1
Lindum Rd *SALV* BN13 ... 188 A4
Lindum Wy *SALV* BN13 ... 188 A7 ⊡
Lineside Wy *LHPTN* BN17 ... 206 C2
Linfield Copse *PUL/STOR* RH20.. 124 A6
Linford Ct *HAV* PO9 ... 152 A6
Lingfield CI *SALV* BN13 ... 188 A6
Lingfield Dr *CRAWE* RH10 ... 21 M5
Lingfield Rd *EGRIN* RH19 ... 24 E1 ⊡
Lingfield Wy *SELS* PO20 ... 223 H5
Link HI *PUL/STOR* RH20 ... 143 J3
Link La *PUL/STOR* RH20 ... 122 D2
Links Av *MIDOS* PO22 ... 13 J5
Links CI *PTSD* BN41 ... 192 B1
Links La *HAV* PO9 ... 152 E1
Links Rd *FIN/BW* BN14 ... 188 E1
  LAN/SOMP BN15 ... 190 A6
  PTSD BN41 ... 192 D4
The Link *CRAWW* RH11 ... 2 E2
Link Wy *BOGR* PO21 ... 220 B3
The Linkway *BRI* BN1 ... 194 C3
Linnet CI *EPSF* GU31 ... 90 F2
Linton Rd *HOVE* BN3 ... 193 G4
Lintott Gdns *SWTR* RH13 ... 5 H5
Lionel Av *MIDOS* PO22 ... 204 D6
Lion La *CRAWE* RH10 ... 23 H4
  GSHT GU26 ... 28 A3
Lion Md *HASM* GU27 ... 28 A6
Lion Rd *BOGR* PO21 ... 220 B2
Lion St *CCH* PO19 ... 6 E4
Liphook CI *BRI* BN1 ... 194 D3 ⊡
Liphook Rd *HASM* GU27 ... 27 H8
Lisher Rd *LAN/SOMP* BN15 ... 190 A5
Lisle Wy *EMRTH* PO10 ... 175 H1
Lismore Crs *CRAWW* RH11 ... 2 A9
Lister Av *EGRIN* RH19 ... 24 F6
Listers *RHWH* RH17 ... 85 G3
Litten Ter *CCH* PO19 ... 6 F3
Little Ashfield *MIDH* GU29 ... 94 F4
Little Babbsham *BOGR* PO21 .. 220 F2 ⊡
Little Barn PI *LISS* GU33 ... 47 L8
Little Bentswood *HWH* RH16 .. 88 A7 ⊡
Little Black HI *HWH* RH16 ... 88 B6 ⊡
Little Boultons *SELS* PO20 ... 201 G4
Little Breach *CCH* PO19 ... 6 C5
Little Bridges *SWTR* RH13 ... 82 A3
Little CI *SWTR* RH13 ... 82 A1
Little Comptons *SWTR* RH13 ... 5 K8
Little Copse Rd *HPPT/KEY* BN6.. 130 F7

Littlecote *PETW* GU28 ... 98 A5
Little Crabtree *CRAWW* RH11 ... 2 D2
Little Crs *ROTT* BN2 ... 213 J3
Little Dipper's
  PUL/STOR RH20 ... 122 D2 ⊡
Little Dr *FERR* BN12 ... 208 F3
Little Dro *STEY/UB* BN44 ... 167 L3
Little East St *BIL* RH14 ... 79 L3
Littlefield CI *SELS* PO20 ... 223 C5
Littlefield Rd *CCH* PO19 ... 7 H6
Little Finches *SWTR* RH13 ... 127 H1
Little Gables *SALV* BN13 ... 188 A6 ⊡
Little Grebe *HORS* RH12 ... 4 D2
Littlegreen Av *HAV* PO9 ... 174 D1
Littlehampton Rd
  ANG/EP BN16 ... 208 D1
  FERR BN12 ... 187 J8
  SALV BN13 ... 187 M7 ⊡
Little Hatch *HORS* RH12 ... 5 J2
Little Haven La *HORS* RH12 ... 5 K2 ⊡
Littleheath Rd *ARUN* BN18 ... 181 M1
Little High St *BOGR* PO21 ... 12 D8 ⊡
  SHOR BN43 ... 190 F5 ⊡
  WTHG BN11 ... 9 H4
Little London
  FERR BN12 ... 187 H8 ⊡
  WTHG BN11 ... 9 H4
Little King St *EGRIN* RH19 ... 24 F3 ⊡
Little London *CCH* PO19 ... 6 F4
Little Pembrokes *WTHG* BN11 ... 9 H6
Little Preston St *BRI* BN1 ... 10 C8
Littlestone Rd *SALV* BN13 ... 187 M6 ⊡
Littleworth La *SWTR* RH13 ... 105 H4
Liverpool Gdns *WTHG* BN11 ... 9 H6
Liverpool Rd *WTHG* BN11 ... 9 H6
Liverpool Ter *HWH* RH16 ... 9 H6
Livesay Crs *FIN/BW* BN14 ... 9 H1
Livingstone Rd *BURH* RH15 ... 131 G1
  CRAWE RH10 ... 3 H7
  HOVE BN3 ... 193 J5
  SWTR RH13 ... 4 E3
Livingstone St *ROTT* BN2 ... 11 L6 ⊡
Lizard Head *LHPTN* BN17 ... 207 H2
Lloyd CI *HOVE* BN3 ... 193 K4
Lloyd Goring CI *ANG/EP* BN16 .. 186 A6
Lloyd Rd *HOVE* BN3 ... 193 K4
Loats La *SELS* PO20 ... 205 G5
Lobster La *SELS* PO20 ... 222 D4
Lobs Wood La *PUL/STOR* RH20.. 143 L2
Lockerley Rd *HAV* PO9 ... 174 D1
Locke CI *LIPH* GU30 ... 26 E8
Lockgate Rd *SELS* PO20 ... 218 D1
Lock La *SELS* PO20 ... 200 A6
Locksash CI *SELS* PO20 ... 216 C2
Locksash La *RCCH* PO18 ... 133 H4
Locks Crs *PTSD* BN41 ... 192 C4
Locksheath CI *HAV* PO9 ... 152 A6 ⊡
Locks HI *PTSD* BN41 ... 192 C3
Lockwood CI *HORS* RH12 ... 5 M2
  ROTT BN2 ... 195 M5
Lockwood Crs *ROTT* BN2 ... 195 M5
Loddon CI *SALV* BN13 ... 187 K4
Loder Gdns *FIN/BW* BN14 ... 188 D7
Loder PI *BRI* BN1 ... 194 A2
Loder Rd *BRI* BN1 ... 194 A2
Lodgebury CI *EMRTH* PO10 ... 176 B4
Lodge CI *CRAWW* RH11 ... 2 C4
  EGRIN RH19 ... 24 D3
  MIDOS PO22 ... 205 H7
  PTSD BN41 ... 192 A2 ⊡
Lodge Ct *BOGR* PO21 ... 220 F2
  SHOR BN43 ... 190 F3
Lodge Hill La *HPPT/KEY* BN6 ... 131 K8
Lodgelands *RHWH* RH17 ... 66 C6
Lodge La *HAV* PO9 ... 133 G6
  HPPT/KEY BN6 ... 151 H1
Lodsworth CI *ROTT* BN2 ... 195 C5
Lodsworth Rd *BOGR* PO21 ... 220 C1
Lombard St *PETW* GU28 ... 98 A4 ⊡
Lomond Av *BRI* BN1 ... 172 B5
London Av *HAV* PO9 ... 174 C5
London La *RHWH* RH17 ... 87 L7
London Rd *ARUN* BN18 ... 161 M6
  ARUN BN18 ... 182 B1
  BOGR PO21 ... 12 E6
  BRI BN1 ... 10 F2
  BRI BN1 ... 171 L4
  BRI BN1 ... 193 M1
  BURH RH15 ... 131 G1 ⊡
  CRAWE RH10 ... 42 B3
  CRAWW RH11 ... 2 F1
  CRAWW RH11 ... 20 F1
  EGRIN RH19 ... 24 E2
  EPSF GU31 ... 69 H6
  FROW RH18 ... 25 M8
  HFD BN5 ... 127 M5
  HORL RH6 ... 15 H4
  HORS RH12 ... 4 C7
  HPPT/KEY BN6 ... 130 F7
  HPPT/KEY BN6 ... 149 L2
  LIPH GU30 ... 26 D8
  PUL/STOR RH20 ... 121 J7
  PUL/STOR RH20 ... 125 H8
  PUL/STOR RH20 ... 144 F5
  RHWH RH17 ... 65 G1
  SWTR RH13 ... 86 F4
London St *WTHG* BN11 ... 8 E3
London Ter *BRI* BN1 ... 10 F2
Long Acre *CRAWE* RH10 ... 23 H4
Longacre *SELS* PO20 ... 222 F6
Longacre CI *LISS* GU33 ... 47 K8
Longacre Crs *RHWH* RH17 ... 87 G4
Longacre La *SELS* PO20 ... 222 F6
Longbridge Rd *HORL* RH6 ... 15 G4
Longbridge Wk *HORL* RH6 ... 15 G3 ⊡
Longbrook *BOGR* PO21 ... 13 J6
Longchamp CI *HORL* RH6 ... 15 K1 ⊡
Long Copse La *EMRTH* PO10 ... 153 J3
Longdene Rd *HASM* GU27 ... 28 C6
Long Down *EPSF* GU31 ... 68 E8
Longfellow Rd *WTHG* BN11 ... 8 D2
Longfield Rd *EMRTH* PO10 ... 175 H1
Longford Rd *BOGR* PO21 ... 12 D5
Long Furlong *SALV* BN13 ... 165 G3
Longfurlong La *SALV* BN13 ... 164 F3
Long HI *SWTR* RH13 ... 84 A4
Longhill CI *ROTT* BN2 ... 195 M8
Longhill Rd *ROTT* BN2 ... 195 L8
Longhurst *BURH* RH15 ... 131 L2
Longhurst Rd *CRAWW* RH11 ... 40 B3
Longland Av *PUL/STOR* RH20 .... 143 J2

Longlands *FIN/BW* BN14 ... 188 D4
Longlands Gld *FIN/BW* BN14 ... 188 E4
Longlands Rd *EMRTH* PO10 ... 176 A4
  SELS PO20 ... 217 G6
Longlands Spinney
  FIN/BW BN14 ... 188 E4
Long La *ARUN* BN18 ... 161 K7
  RCCH PO18 ... 134 A1
Long Md *ARUN* BN18 ... 182 B3
Longmead *LISS* GU33 ... 69 J1
Longmead Gdns *HAV* PO9 ... 174 C5
Long Meadow *FIN/BW* BN14 ... 166 A8
Longmeadow Gdns *SELS* PO20.. 199 M8
Longmere Rd *CRAWW* RH11 ... 20 E4
Longmoor Rd *LISS* GU33 ... 47 K2
Long Park Cnr *HPPT/KEY* BN6 .. 151 L2
Longport Rd *MIDOS* PO22 ... 204 C8
Longridge Av *ROTT* BN2 ... 213 K4
Long Rd *PSF* GU32 ... 68 D7
Longships *BOGR* PO21 ... 207 H2
Longstock Rd *HAV* PO9 ... 152 E6
Longwood Vw *CRAWE* RH10 ... 3 J8
Longwood Gdns *MIDOS* PO22 ... 204 D8
The Loop *MIDOS* PO22 ... 204 C8
Loose La *FIN/BW* BN14 ... 189 H7
  LAN/SOMP BN15 ... 189 J6
Loppets Rd *CRAWE* RH10 ... 3 J8
Lordings La *PUL/STOR* RH20 ... 123 L5
Lordings Rd *BIL* RH14 ... 79 G7
Loriners *CRAWE* RH10 ... 2 E5
Lorna Rd *HOVE* BN3 ... 193 L5
Lorne Rd *BRI* BN1 ... 10 F1
Lotts La *LAN/SOMP* BN15 ... 189 K6
Loudoun Rd *LHPTN* BN17 ... 206 D3 ⊡
Love CI *EPSF* GU31 ... 68 D8
Loveletts *CRAWW* RH11 ... 20 B7
Lovells CI *BOGR* PO21 ... 220 C2
Lover's Wk *BRI* BN1 ... 194 A4
Loveys Rd *ARUN* BN18 ... 205 G2 ⊡
Lowdells La *EGRIN* RH19 ... 24 D1
Lowe CI *CRAWW* RH11 ... 40 C4
Lower Barn CI *HORS* RH12 ... 5 L2
Lower Beach Rd *SHOR* BN43 ... 191 G6
Lower Bevendean Av
  ROTT BN2 ... 194 F3
Lower Bognor Rd *BOGR* PO21 .. 202 F8
  SELS PO20 ... 202 C6
Lower Chalvington PI
  FIN/BW BN14 ... 194 F7 ⊡
Lower Church Rd *BURH* RH15 .. 131 G1
Lower Dene *EGRIN* RH19 ... 25 H3
Lower Dr *STHW* BN42 ... 191 M3
Lower Faircox *HFD* BN5 ... 127 L7
Lower Grove Rd *HAV* PO9 ... 174 D4
Lower Hanger *LIPH* GU30 ... 26 A8
Lower Heyshott *EPSF* GU31 ... 68 D8
Lower Hone La *ROTT* BN2 ... 195 L7
Lower Market St *HOVE* BN3 ... 193 L7 ⊡
Lower Md *EPSF* GU31 ... 90 E1
Lower Mere *EGRIN* RH19 ... 25 E1
Lower Rd *HASM* GU27 ... 29 G2
  RCCH PO18 ... 157 H7
Lower Rock Gdns *ROTT* BN2 ... 11 H8
Lower Station Rd *BIL* RH14 ... 79 L6
  HFD BN5 ... 127 L8
Lower St *HASM* GU27 ... 28 C6
  PUL/STOR RH20 ... 121 G3
Lower Tanbridge Wy *HORS* RH12... 4 B8
Lower Wardown *EPSF* GU31 ... 68 E7
Lowfield Heath Rd *HORL* RH6 ... 14 A6
  SWTR RH13 ... 58 E1
Lowfield Wy *HORL* RH6 ... 14 F7 ⊡
Lowlands Rd *BURH* RH15 ... 109 J7
Lowther Rd *BRI* BN1 ... 194 B2
  SALV BN13 ... 188 A5
Loxwood Av *FIN/BW* BN14 ... 208 C1 ⊡
Loxwood CI *BIL* RH14 ... 33 L8
  BIL RH14 ... 55 H2
  CRAN GU6 ... 33 G5
Loxwood Wk *CRAWW* RH11 ... 20 A5 ⊡
Luard Ct *HAV* PO9 ... 174 E3
Lucas *RHWH* RH17 ... 67 L7
Lucas CI *EGRIN* RH19 ... 25 G3 ⊡
Lucas Fld *HASM* GU27 ... 27 M6 ⊡
Lucas Gra *HWH* RH16 ... 87 L7
Lucas Rd *HORS* RH12 ... 36 F4
Lucastes Av *HWH* RH16 ... 87 K6
Lucastes La *RHWH* RH17 ... 87 K7
Lucastes Rd *HWH* RH16 ... 87 K6
Lucerne CI *PTSD* BN41 ... 192 C3
Lucerne Ct *BOGR* PO21 ... 220 F2
Lucerne Dr *CRAWE* RH10 ... 21 L8
Lucerne Rd *BRI* BN1 ... 194 A3
Lucking La *MIDOS* PO22 ... 205 J2
Lucraft Rd *ROTT* BN2 ... 173 G7
Ludlow CI *BOGR* PO21 ... 220 F2 ⊡
Ludlow Ri *ROTT* BN2 ... 195 H3
Luffs Meadow *PETW* GU28 ... 53 H5
Lullington Av *HOVE* BN3 ... 193 G4
Lulworth CI *CRAWW* RH11 ... 40 B1 ⊡
  HISD PO11 ... 196 D7
Lumley Rd *EMRTH* PO10 ... 175 K3
  HORL RH6 ... 15 H1
Lunce's HI *RHWH* RH17 ... 110 A4
Lundy CI *ANG/EP* BN16 ... 207 H4
  CRAWW RH11 ... 40 D1
Lupin CI *ANG/EP* BN16 ... 207 H3
Lurgashall *BURH* RH15 ... 131 K3
Lustrells CI *ROTT* BN2 ... 213 J3
Lustrells Crs *ROTT* BN2 ... 213 J2
Lustrells V *ROTT* BN2 ... 213 J2
Lutener Rd *EGRIN* RH19 ... 24 E4
Luther St *ROTT* BN2 ... 11 J3
The Luth *BIL* RH14 ... 78 B8
Lutman St *EMRTH* PO10 ... 153 H8
Lutyens CI *CRAWW* RH11 ... 19 M8
Luxford CI *HORS* RH12 ... 5 J1
Luxford Rd *HWH* RH16 ... 88 B3
Luxford's La *EGRIN* RH19 ... 25 H3
Luxford Wy *BIL* RH14 ... 79 K5
The Lychgates *ARUN* BN18 ... 183 G8
Lye La *RCCH* PO18 ... 156 A8
Lymbourn Rd *HAV* PO9 ... 174 D3
Lyminster Av *BRI* BN1 ... 172 B7
Lyminster Rd *ARUN* BN18 ... 184 E3
  LHPTN BN17 ... 184 E7

Lynch Down *RCCH* PO18 ... 155 G6
Lynchet CI *BRI* BN1 ... 194 D2
Lynchet Down *BRI* BN1 ... 194 D2
Lynchets Crs *HOVE* BN3 ... 192 E1
The Lynchette *SHOR* BN43 ... 191 G3
Lynchet Wk *BRI* BN1 ... 194 D2
Lynchmere Av
  LAN/SOMP BN15 ... 189 L4
Lyndhurst CI *CRAWW* RH11 ... 2 E6 ⊡
  HISD PO11 ... 214 D2
Lyndhurst Rd *CCH* PO19 ... 7 G6
  HOVE BN3 ... 193 L5
  WTHG BN11 ... 9 J3
Lyndum CI *EPSF* GU31 ... 90 C1
Lyn Rd *SALV* BN13 ... 187 K6
Lynton CI *HPPT/KEY* BN6 ... 130 C7
Lynton Park Av *EGRIN* RH19 ... 25 H2
Lynton Rd *PSF* GU32 ... 68 B8
Lyntons *PUL/STOR* RH20 ... 122 D2
Lynton St *ROTT* BN2 ... 11 K3
Lynwick St *HORS* RH12 ... 34 E5
Lynwood Ct *HORS* RH12 ... 4 C5
Lynwood Rd *ROTT* BN2 ... 213 K4
Lyon CI *CRAWE* RH10 ... 41 K2
  HOVE BN3 ... 193 L5
Lyons CI *SWTR* RH13 ... 58 E1
Lyons Rd *SWTR* RH13 ... 58 F1
Lyon St *BOGR* PO21 ... 12 E8
Lyon St West *BOGR* PO21 ... 12 D6
Lyons Wy *FIN/BW* BN14 ... 188 D4
Lyoth La *HWH* RH16 ... 88 C7
Lyric CI *CRAWE* RH10 ... 21 L8
Lysander Wy *SELS* PO20 ... 180 E3
Lytton Dr *CRAWE* RH10 ... 21 L5

M

Mackerel La *SELS* PO20 ... 222 D4
Mackie Av *BRI* BN1 ... 172 A6
  HPPT/KEY BN6 ... 131 H7
Macklin Rd *MIDOS* PO22 ... 13 G4
Macleod Rd *SWTR* RH13 ... 5 H9
Madehurst CI *ANG/EP* BN16 ... 207 M4
  ROTT BN2 ... 213 J4
Madehurst Ct *CRAWW* RH11 ... 40 A1 ⊡
Madehurst Wy *LHPTN* BN17 ... 206 E2
Madeira Av *HORS* RH12 ... 4 D7
  MIDOS PO22 ... 13 G4
  WTHG BN11 ... 9 K5
Madeira Dr *ROTT* BN2 ... 11 G8
Madeira PI *ROTT* BN2 ... 11 G8
Madeline Rd *EPSF* GU31 ... 68 C8
Madgwick La *RCCH* PO18 ... 179 L3
Mafeking Rd *ROTT* BN2 ... 194 D4
Magdala Rd *HISD* PO11 ... 214 B1
Magdalene CI *CRAWE* RH10 ... 21 K3 ⊡
Magnolia CI *SALV* BN13 ... 187 J7 ⊡
Magpie La *SELS* PO20 ... 222 E3
  SWTR RH13 ... 61 G3
Maidenbower Dr *CRAWE* RH10 ... 21 K8
Maidenbower La
  CRAWE RH10 ... 21 K8 ⊡
Maidenbower PI *CRAWE* RH10 .. 21 K8 ⊡
Maiden La *CRAWW* RH11 ... 20 D4
Maidment CI *HFD* BN5 ... 128 A6
Main Dr *MIDOS* PO22 ... 205 G1
Main Rd *ARUN* BN18 ... 205 G1
  EMRTH PO10 ... 175 M4
  RCCH PO18 ... 137 K6
  RCCH PO18 ... 176 F5
  SELS PO20 ... 200 A7
Mainstone Rd *HOVE* BN3 ... 193 G5 ⊡
Maisemore Gdns *EMRTH* PO10.. 175 G4
Major CI *BRI* BN1 ... 194 C3
Major's HI *CRAWE* RH10 ... 22 E8
Malcolm CI *FERR* BN12 ... 208 F3
Malcolm Gdns *HORL* RH6 ... 14 E3
Malcolm Rd *SELS* PO20 ... 180 D2
Maldon Rd *BRI* BN1 ... 193 L2
Malham CI *CRAWE* RH10 ... 41 K1
Malin Rd *ANG/EP* BN16 ... 207 H3
Mallard CI *HASM* GU27 ... 27 M6 ⊡
  HORS RH12 ... 4 D2
Mallard Crs *BOGR* PO21 ... 220 A5
Mallard PI *EGRIN* RH19 ... 25 G4
Mallard Rd *HAV* PO9 ... 152 E3
The Mallards *HAV* PO9 ... 174 C5
Mallard Wy *HFD* BN5 ... 127 M6
Mallion's La *RHWH* RH17 ... 85 M2
Mallon Dene *ANG/EP* BN16 ... 207 K4
Mallory Rd *HOVE* BN3 ... 193 K2
Mallow CI *HORS* RH12 ... 37 M6
Malthouse CI *ARUN* BN18 ... 184 B2
  LAN/SOMP BN15 ... 189 J5
Malthouse La *HPPT/KEY* BN6 ... 130 D1
  RCCH PO18 ... 157 H7
  ROTT BN2 ... 11 G4 ⊡
Malthouse Mdw *LIPH* GU30 ... 26 D8
Malthouse Pas *LHPTN* BN17 ... 206 E2 ⊡
Malthouse Rd *CRAWW* RH11 ... 2 E2 ⊡
  SELS PO20 ... 223 G5
The Maltings *BURH* RH15 ... 108 E8
  EPSF GU31 ... 90 C1
  LIPH GU30 ... 26 E8
Maltravers Dr *LHPTN* BN17 ... 206 F4
Maltravers Rd *LHPTN* BN17 ... 206 F3
Maltravers St *ARUN* BN18 ... 184 B2
Malvern CI *WTHG* BN11 ... 211 J1
Malvern Ms *EMRTH* PO10 ... 175 J3
Malvern Rd *CRAWW* RH11 ... 2 F1
  LISS GU33 ... 47 J8
Malvern St *HOVE* BN3 ... 193 J5 ⊡
Malvern Wy *BOGR* PO21 ... 220 C3 ⊡
Malwood CI *HAV* PO9 ... 152 D6
Manaton CI *HWH* RH16 ... 88 A8
Manchester St *ROTT* BN2 ... 10 F8
Manet Sq *MIDOS* PO22 ... 203 J6
Manhood La *SELS* PO20 ... 219 G4
Manitoba Wy *SALV* BN13 ... 187 K6
Manley's HI *PUL/STOR* RH20 ... 143 L3
Manning CI *EGRIN* RH19 ... 24 E2
Manning Rd *CCH* PO19 ... 7 J2
  LHPTN BN17 ... 206 D2
Mannings CI *CRAWE* RH10 ... 21 L3
Manor Av *HPPT/KEY* BN6 ... 131 H7
Manor CI *ANG/EP* BN16 ... 208 A3
  BURH RH15 ... 109 L8
  CCH PO19 ... 201 G1

HASM GU27 ... 27 M6
HFD BN5 ... 128 A7
HORL RH6 ... 15 G1
LAN/SOMP BN15 ... 190 C6
MIDOS PO22 ... 13 L4
PUL/STOR RH20 ... 143 L3⑤
ROTT BN2 ... 194 F7
STHW BN42 ... 192 B4
WTHG BN11 ... 8 C6
Manor Dr HORL RH6 ... 15 G1
RHWH RH17 ... 86 F5
Manor Farm Cl SELS PO20 ... 223 G4
Manor Farm Ct SELS PO20 ... 223 G4
Manorfields CRAWW RH11 ... 39 L2
Manor Flds LIPH GU30 ... 26 E8
SWTR RH13 ... 5 M4
Manor Gdns EMRTH PO10 ... 176 A3
HPPT/KEY BN6 ... 130 A6
ROTT BN2 ... 194 F7
Manor Gn ROTT BN2 ... 194 F7
Manor Hall STHW BN42 ... 191 M4
Manor Hl ROTT BN2 ... 194 F6
Manor La SELS PO20 ... 223 H3
SWTR RH13 ... 61 J4
Manor Lodge Rd HAV PO9 ... 152 D3
Manor Paddock ROTT BN2 ... 194 F8
Manor Pk BOGR PO21 ... 220 B3
Manor Pl BOGR PO21 ... 12 D8
Manor Pl ... 194 F8
Manor Rd ANG/EP BN16 ... 207 J2
ANG/EP BN16 ... 208 B4
BURH RH15 ... 109 K7
EGRIN RH19 ... 24 D2
EMRTH PO10 ... 176 A3
HISD PO11 ... 196 B8
HORS RH12 ... 5 L2
HPPT/KEY BN6 ... 130 A6
LAN/SOMP BN15 ... 189 L4
PTSD BN41 ... 192 C3
ROTT BN2 ... 194 F8
SELS PO20 ... 223 G5
STEY/UB BN44 ... 168 D2
WTHG BN11 ... 8 C6
Manor Royal CRAWE RH10 ... 20 F3
Manor Vis RCCH PO18 ... 177 K7
Manor Wy BOGR PO21 ... 220 C3
EMRTH PO10 ... 176 A3
HFD BN5 ... 128 A7
HISD PO11 ... 214 D2
LAN/SOMP BN15 ... 190 A5
MIDOS PO22 ... 205 J7
ROTT BN2 ... 194 F7
Mansbergh Rd CCH PO19 ... 179 J3
Mansell Rd SHOR BN43 ... 191 J4
Manser Rd ARUN BN18 ... 183 C4
Mansfield Cl WTHG BN13 ... 189 H8
Mansfield Rd HOVE BN3 ... 192 D1⑦
MIDOS PO22 ... 12 A2
WTHG BN11 ... 211 H1
Mansion Cl BURH RH15 ... 131 L1
Mant Cl PUL/STOR RH20 ... 143 L3⑧
Mantling Rd LHPTN BN17 ... 206 E2
Manton Cl SELS PO20 ... 217 K7
Manton Rd ROTT BN2 ... 194 F3
Mant Rd PETW GU28 ... 98 A5
Maple Cl BIL RH14 ... 79 K3
BURH RH15 ... 109 J7
CRAWW RH11 ... 20 D3
EMRTH PO10 ... 175 J2
HORS RH12 ... 5 M2
HWH RH16 ... 110 C1
MIDOS PO22 ... 204 F6
ROTT BN2 ... 195 M5
SALV BN13 ... 187 M3
Mapledown Rd SWTR RH13 ... 82 K2
Maple Dr BURH RH15 ... 109 C8
EGRIN RH19 ... 25 H3
Maple Gdns HOVE BN3 ... 192 E5
MIDOS PO22 ... 203 K5①
Maplehurst Rd CCH PO19 ... 179 J4
PTSD BN41 ... 192 B3
SWTR RH13 ... 83 G8
Maple Leaf PUL/STOR RH20 ... 121 K6
Maple Rd ARUN BN18 ... 182 F4
BIL RH14 ... 79 L5
The Maples FERR BN12 ... 209 G4
Maple Wk LAN/SOMP BN15 ... 189 J5
Mapsons La SELS PO20 ... 218 B1
Marama Gdns ANG/EP BN16 ... 207 J5
Marchants Cl HPPT/KEY BN6 ... 130 B6
Marchants Rd HPPT/KEY BN6 ... 130 B6
Marchants Wy BURH RH15 ... 109 G7
Marches Rd HORS RH12 ... 16 E8
The Marches HASM GU27 ... 51 J7
HORS RH12 ... 17 J7
Marchwood CCH PO19 ... 179 H1
Marchwood Rd HAV PO9 ... 152 B6
Marcuse Flds RCCH PO18 ... 177 H6
Mardale Rd SALV BN13 ... 188 A6
Marden Av SELS PO20 ... 200 F1
The Mardens CRAWW RH11 ... 2 A1
Marden Wy EPSF GU31 ... 90 D1
Mardyke SHOR BN43 ... 190 E6
Mare Hill Rd PUL/STOR RH20 ... 122 F2
Maresfield Rd ROTT BN2 ... 194 F1
Margaret Cl BOGR PO21 ... 220 F1
Margaret St ROTT BN2 ... 11 G8
Margery Rd HOVE BN3 ... 192 E4
Marian Wy BOGR PO21 ... 13 G6
Marina Cl EMRTH PO10 ... 175 K4①
Marina Wy ROTT BN2 ... 212 A1
Marine Av HOVE BN3 ... 192 E6
Marine Cl ROTT BN2 ... 213 J3
SELS PO20 ... 216 F6
WTHG BN11 ... 8 A8
Marine Crs FERR BN12 ... 209 L3
Marine Dr FERR BN12 ... 209 H4
ROTT BN2 ... 212 A1
SELS PO20 ... 216 G5
SELS PO20 ... 223 H5
Marine Dr West BOGR PO21 ... 221 H2
SELS PO20 ... 216 G3
Marine Gdns ROTT BN2 ... 11 H8
SELS PO20 ... 222 G4
Marine Pde BOGR PO21 ... 11 G8
ROTT BN2 ... 11 G8
WTHG BN11 ... 9 J7
Marine Pl WTHG BN11 ... 9 J7
Mariners Cl SHOR BN43 ... 190 E7②
Mariners Wk ANG/EP BN16 ... 207 L5

Marineside SELS PO20 ... 217 J7
Marine Sq ROTT BN2 ... 11 K9
Marine Terrace Ms ROTT BN2 ... 11 J8
Marine Vw ROTT BN2 ... 11 J6
Marine Wk HISD PO11 ... 215 G1
Marion Rd BRI BN1 ... 41 J1
Marisfield Pl SELS PO20 ... 223 H4
Marjoram Pl SHOR BN43 ... 191 J3②
Market Av CCH PO19 ... 6 E6
Market Cl MIDOS PO22 ... 182 C6
Market Fld STEY/UB BN44 ... 167 L1
Market Pde HAV PO9 ... 174 C3
Market Pl HWH RH16 ... 87 L7
Market Rd CCH PO19 ... 6 D6
Market Sq HORS RH12 ... 4 C9①
MIDH GU29 ... 95 G5②
Market St BOGR PO21 ... 12 D8
BRI BN1 ... 10 E7
WTHG BN11 ... 9 H6
Markfield MIDOS PO22 ... 203 J6
Markway Cl EMRTH PO10 ... 175 G3
Markwick Ms WTHG BN11 ... 9 J4
Marlborough Cl CCH PO19 ... 7 L5②
CRAWW RH11 ... 40 D2②
HORS RH12 ... 4 E2
Marlborough Dr BOGR PO21 ... 203 G8②
Marlborough Dr BURH RH15 ... 131 K1
Marlborough Ms BRI BN1 ... 10 C6①
Marlborough Pk HAV PO9 ... 174 F1②
Marlborough Pl BRI BN1 ... 10 F6②
Marlborough Rd FERR BN12 ... 209 L2
LAN/SOMP BN15 ... 189 K8
Marlborough St BRI BN1 ... 10 D6①
Marlborough Wy FERR BN12 ... 209 L2①
Marldell Cl HAV PO9 ... 152 D7
Marles La BIL RH14 ... 57 K3
Marley Combe Rd HASM GU27 ... 28 A7
Marley Hanger HASM GU27 ... 51 H1
Marley La HASM GU27 ... 27 M7
Marley Wy PUL/STOR RH20 ... 143 M2
The Marlinspike SHOR BN43 ... 191 H6
Marlow Ct CRAWW RH11 ... 2 F1
Marlowe Cl MIDOS PO22 ... 204 E6
Marlowe Dr HWH RH16 ... 88 B8
Marlow Rd ROTT BN2 ... 195 G8
Marlpit Cl EGRIN RH19 ... 24 F1
Marlpit La EMRTH PO10 ... 154 D8
SELS PO20 ... 180 C6
Marlpit Rd EGRIN RH19 ... 44 B6
Marlpost Rd SWTR RH13 ... 81 K3
Marmion Rd HOVE BN3 ... 193 G5
Marples Wy HAV PO9 ... 174 A3
Marquis Wy BOGR PO21 ... 220 F3
Marringdean Rd BIL RH14 ... 101 L2
Marshall Av BOGR PO21 ... 12 A5
FIN/BW BN14 ... 188 A1
Marshall Cl MIDOS PO22 ... 182 C7
Marshall Rd CRAWE RH10 ... 21 K8
HISD PO11 ... 214 D2
Marshalls Rw BRI BN1 ... 10 F3
Marshall Wy HOVE BN3 ... 193 G5
Marsh La RCCH PO18 ... 157 C5
RCCH PO18 ... 176 D3
SELS PO20 ... 181 H2
SELS PO20 ... 202 A3
SELS PO20 ... 202 B1
Marston Rd FIN/BW BN14 ... 9 H1
Martha Gunn Rd ROTT BN2 ... 194 E3
Martin Cl CRAWW RH11 ... 20 E4③
Martin Rd HAV PO9 ... 152 D8
HOVE BN3 ... 192 E3
Martins La SELS PO20 ... 200 A7
The Martins CRAWE RH10 ... 23 K4
Martlet Cl CCH PO19 ... 6 F7
Martlet Rd PETW GU28 ... 97 M5
Martlets PUL/STOR RH20 ... 123 K4
Martlets Cl HORS RH12 ... 4 C2
The Martlets ANG/EP BN16 ... 207 H4
CRAWE RH10 ... 3 G4
LAN/SOMP BN15 ... 189 K6
SHOR BN43 ... 191 G4
Martlets Wy FERR BN12 ... 209 K1
The Martlet HOVE BN3 ... 193 L4
Martlet Wy BOGR PO21 ... 220 A5
The Marts HORS RH12 ... 34 E5
Martyn Cl HFD BN5 ... 127 M1
Martyn's Cl ROTT BN2 ... 195 M4
Martyns Pl EGRIN RH19 ... 25 H4
Martyrs Av CRAWW RH11 ... 20 D3③
Marvell Cl CRAWE RH10 ... 21 K4
Marvic Ct HAV PO9 ... 152 B6③
Marylands HWH RH16 ... 88 A7③
Marylands Crs MIDOS PO22 ... 13 C8
Masefield Rd CRAWW RH11 ... 39 M1
Mash Barn La LAN/SOMP BN15.. 190 B5
Mason Cl EGRIN RH19 ... 24 F2
Mason Rd CRAWE RH10 ... 3 C4
Masons Fld SWTR RH13 ... 61 K6
Masons Wy PUL/STOR RH20 ... 100 D7
Massetts Rd HORL RH6 ... 15 G2
Matlock Rd BRI BN1 ... 193 L3
Matthews Dr CRAWE RH10 ... 41 K2
Matthey Pl CRAWE RH10 ... 21 L3
Maudlin La HASM GU27 ... 167 L3
Maudlyn Pk STEY/UB BN44 ... 167 L3
Maudlyn Pkwy STEY/UB BN44 .. 167 L3
Mauldmare Ct BOGR PO21 ... 221 G2①
Maunsell Pk CRAWE RH10 ... 21 J6①
Mavis Crs HAV PO9 ... 174 C2
Maxwell Rd ARUN BN18 ... 184 A3
LHPTN BN17 ... 206 D3
Maxwell Wy CRAWE RH10 ... 21 H3
Maybridge Crs FERR BN12 ... 209 K1
Maybridge Sq FERR BN12 ... 187 K8
Maybush Cl RCCH PO18 ... 176 D5
May Cl FERR BN12 ... 187 K8
MIDOS PO22 ... 12 E3
SELS PO20 ... 219 G4
Maydwell Av SWTR RH13 ... 58 C2
Mayes Cl HORS RH12 ... 21 K7
Mayes La HORS RH12 ... 36 F3
HORS RH12 ... 37 G1
Mayfield ANG/EP BN16 ... 208 B1
CRAWE RH10 ... 21 L6
Mayfield Cl BOGR PO21 ... 220 C2
BRI BN1 ... 172 A7
FIN/BW BN14 ... 188 B3

Mayfield Crs BRI BN1 ... 172 A7
Mayfield Rd BOGR PO21 ... 203 H8
Mayfields RHWH RH17 ... 85 K8①
Mayflower Cl CRAWE RH10 ... 21 L7②
Mayflower Ct HWH RH16 ... 88 A8①
Mayflower Rd HWH RH16 ... 88 A8
Mayhouse Rd BURH RH15 ... 131 G3①
Mayo Rd ROTT BN2 ... 194 C4
Maypole La ARUN BN18 ... 183 G7
Maypole Rd EGRIN RH19 ... 24 E2
EGRIN RH19 ... 25 M6
Mayridge SELS PO20 ... 222 D4②
May Rd ROTT BN2 ... 11 M2
May Tree Av FIN/BW BN14 ... 188 A1
Maytree Cl ANG/EP BN16 ... 186 A8①
LAN/SOMP BN15 ... 189 J7
Maytree Wk HOVE BN3 ... 192 F3
Mcindoe Rd EGRIN RH19 ... 24 E1
Mckerchar Cl
LAN/SOMP BN15 ... 190 A5①
Mcnair Cl SELS PO20 ... 222 F4
Mcwilliam Rd ROTT BN2 ... 195 K3
Meadend Cl HWH RH16 ... 152 E7②
Mead La MIDOS PO22 ... 12 F4
PUL/STOR RH20 ... 143 M2
Meadow Ap CRAWE RH10 ... 22 B1
Meadowbank BIL RH14 ... 78 C4
Meadow Cl CRAWE RH10 ... 22 B1
HISD PO11 ... 196 C1
HORS RH12 ... 5 M2
HOVE BN3 ... 193 J1
LIPH GU30 ... 26 D8
PTSD BN41 ... 192 C2③
ROTT BN2 ... 212 F1
SELS PO20 ... 201 H4
STHW BN42 ... 192 B4
WTHG BN11 ... 211 J1
Meadow Crs WTHG BN11 ... 211 H1
Meadowcroft Cl
CRAWW RH11 ... 20 A7②
EGRIN RH19 ... 24 D2
Meadow Croft Cl HORL RH6 ... 15 K4①
Meadow Dr HWH RH16 ... 88 C6
Meadow Farm La HORS RH12 ... 38 A5
Meadowfield Dr CCH PO19 ... 7 H1
Meadowland SELS PO20 ... 222 F4
Meadowlands CRAWW RH11.. 2 C3
HAV PO9 ... 152 F1
HAV PO9 ... 174 D3
Meadow La BURH RH15 ... 131 G3
HWH RH16 ... 88 C6
LAN/SOMP BN15 ... 189 M7③
SELS PO20 ... 216 E2
Meadow Pde ANG/EP BN16 ... 208 C3
Meadow Pk ANG/EP BN16 ... 208 C3
Meadow Rd WTHG BN11 ... 211 H1
Meadows HPPT/KEY BN6 ... 130 F7
Meadowside ANG/EP BN16 ... 186 B6
PUL/STOR RH20 ... 143 L3
Meadows Rd SELS PO20 ... 217 H5
The Meadows ARUN BN18 ... 182 E3
HOVE BN3 ... 192 D1
Meadow Sweet Cl
SALV BN13 ... 187 H7①
The Meadow CRAWE RH10 ... 22 B1
Meadow V HASM GU27 ... 28 B6
Meadowview ROTT BN2 ... 194 F3
Meadowview
LAN/SOMP BN15 ... 189 L4
Meadow Wk LISS GU33 ... 47 J8
MIDOS PO22 ... 205 H7
Meadow Wy BOGR PO21 ... 220 C3
FERR BN12 ... 208 F2
LHPTN BN17 ... 207 G3
LIPH GU30 ... 26 D7
MIDOS PO22 ... 203 H6
PETW GU28 ... 97 M5
SELS PO20 ... 180 C3
SELS PO20 ... 181 L6
Mead Rd CRAWE RH10 ... 3 J7
Meads Av HOVE BN3 ... 192 D1
Meads Rd HOVE BN3 ... 192 D1①
The Meads BRI BN1 ... 172 E7
EGRIN RH19 ... 24 F5
HASM GU27 ... 28 A6
Mead Sway ARUN BN18 ... 160 E8
The Mead LIPH GU30 ... 26 C7
Meadway ANG/EP BN16 ... 207 L3
HASM GU27 ... 28 A6
Mead Wy MIDH GU29 ... 94 E6
Meadway Ct STHW BN42 ... 191 L4
Meadway Crs HOVE BN3 ... 193 J3
The Meadway HORL RH6 ... 15 K1
ROTT BN2 ... 195 G7
SHOR BN43 ... 191 G6
Measham Cl FERR BN12 ... 209 G2
Meath Cl HISD PO11 ... 214 F3
Medina Pl HOVE BN3 ... 193 J7
Medina Ter HOVE BN3 ... 193 J7②
Medina Vis HOVE BN3 ... 193 J7
Medlar Cl CRAWW RH11 ... 20 D3
Medmerry Hl SELS PO20 ... 222 F4
Medmerry Hl SELS PO20 ... 222 F4
Medstead Rd HAV PO9 ... 174 C1
Medway CRAWE RH10 ... 23 H7
Medway Cl SALV BN13 ... 187 L5②
Medway Dr EGRIN RH19 ... 24 E6
Medway Rd CRAWW RH11 ... 20 A7
Medwin Wy HORS RH12 ... 4 C8
Meeds Rd BURH RH15 ... 131 H2
Meeting House La BRI BN1 ... 10 E7②
Meiros Wy PUL/STOR RH20 ... 125 G7
Melbourne Av FERR BN12 ... 209 K2
Melbourne Rd CCH PO19 ... 7 G3
FERR BN12 ... 209 K2
Melbourne St ROTT BN2 ... 11 J1
Melbourne Wy HORS RH12 ... 5 K2②
Melksham Cl SWTR RH13 ... 5 G9
Melksham Av PTSD BN41 ... 192 B3
SALV BN13 ... 187 M8
Melrose Av BRI BN1 ... 194 C3
SALV BN13 ... 187 M8
Melrose Cl CRAWW RH11 ... 40 A2①
HISD PO11 ... 196 C2
POY/PYE BN45 ... 149 K7
Melrose Pl PUL/STOR RH20 ... 144 A7②
Melton Av PUL/STOR RH20 ... 143 L1
Melton Cl PUL/STOR RH20 ... 143 M1

Melton Dr PUL/STOR RH20 ... 143 L1
Melville Rd HOVE BN3 ... 10 B3
Melville Wy FERR BN12 ... 187 K8
Mendip Cl ANG/EP BN16 ... 208 B2①
Mendip Crs SALV BN13 ... 187 M5
Mendip Rd SALV BN13 ... 187 M5
Mengham Av HISD PO11 ... 214 D2
Mengham La HISD PO11 ... 214 D1
Mengham Rd HISD PO11 ... 214 D1
Meon Cl PSF GU32 ... 68 B8
Meon Rd HOVE BN3 ... 10 B3
Mercer Rd HORS RH12 ... 37 K4
Mercers Md SWTR RH13 ... 105 M3②
Merchant St BOGR PO21 ... 12 D6
Mercury Cl CRAWW RH11 ... 39 M1
Meredith Rd CRAWW RH14 ... 9 L2
Merevale BRI BN1 ... 194 C2
Mereworth Dr CRAWE RH10 ... 21 L4
Meridian Wy EGRIN RH19 ... 25 G3
Merle Wy HASM GU27 ... 51 H6
Merlin Cl CRAWW RH11 ... 19 M6②
HOVE BN3 ... 193 L4
Merlin Wy EGRIN RH19 ... 25 H1
MIDOS PO22 ... 204 E6
Merrion Av MIDOS PO22 ... 12 B2
Merry End MIDOS PO22 ... 204 F7
Merryfield Crs ANG/EP BN16 ... 186 B6
Merryfield Dr HORS RH12 ... 60 B1
SELS PO20 ... 223 H5
Merryfield Rd EPSF GU31 ... 68 E8
Merryfield Wy PUL/STOR RH20.. 143 L2
Merryhills La BIL RH14 ... 33 H7
Merryweather Rd RCCH PO18 ... 177 J3
Merrywood La
PUL/STOR RH20 ... 124 B8
Mersey Cl SALV BN13 ... 187 K5
Mersey Rd SALV BN13 ... 187 K5
Mersham Gdns FERR BN12 ... 209 K2③
Merston Cl ROTT BN2 ... 195 M6
Merston Rd ANG/EP BN16 ... 207 K4
Merton Av MIDOS PO22 ... 202 F8①
Merton Cl CRAWE RH10 ... 41 K1
Merton Dr LHPTN BN17 ... 206 E2②
Merton Rd WTHG BN11 ... 9 L6
Metcalf Wy CRAWW RH11 ... 20 E2
Meteor Rd EMRTH PO10 ... 197 K1
Methuen Rd LISS GU33 ... 47 M1
Mews Ct EGRIN RH19 ... 25 G6
Mewsey Ct HAV PO9 ... 152 A5
The Mews HAV PO9 ... 152 B8
Meynell Wd SWTR RH13 ... 127 G1
Meyners Cl HOVE BN3 ... 192 D1②
Meyrick Rd HAV PO9 ... 174 A3
Michael Crs HORL RH6 ... 15 H3
Michael Flds FROW RH18 ... 45 M2
Michelbourne Cl BURH RH15 ... 130 F3①
Michel Gv ANG/EP BN16 ... 207 M3
Michel Gv HORS RH12 ... 60 B2①
Micklam Cl BOGR PO21 ... 220 D2
Middelfield La RCCH PO18 ... 157 J4
Middle Md STEY/UB BN44 ... 146 E8
Middle Meadow LISS GU33 ... 47 K8
Middle Onslow Cl
FERR BN12 ... 208 F1②
Middle Rd BRI BN1 ... 193 M3
LAN/SOMP BN15 ... 189 L7
SHOR BN43 ... 191 J5
SWTR RH13 ... 127 H1
Middle St BRI BN1 ... 10 D8
BRI BN1 ... 173 K6
HORS RH12 ... 4 C4
PETW GU28 ... 98 A4③
PTSD BN41 ... 192 C6
SHOR BN43 ... 191 G5
Middleton Av HOVE BN3 ... 192 E6
Middleton Cl SELS PO20 ... 217 J6
Middleton Gdns SELS PO20 ... 180 E2
Middleton Ri HORS RH12 ... 172 F7
Middleton Rd HORS RH12 ... 60 B2
MIDOS PO22 ... 204 D7
Middleton Wy CRAWW RH11 ... 19 M7
BURH RH15 ... 131 J1
Middle Tyne SALV BN13 ... 187 L7
Middle Wy ANG/EP BN16 ... 208 E4
BURH RH15 ... 131 J1
Midfields Cl BURH RH15 ... 109 J8③
Midfields Dr BURH RH15 ... 131 J1
Midfields Wk BURH RH15 ... 109 J8②
Midgley Rd CRAWE RH10 ... 21 G4③
Midhurst Cl CRAWW RH11 ... 20 B5①
FERR BN12 ... 209 G2
Midhurst Dr FERR BN12 ... 209 G2
Midhurst Ri BRI BN1 ... 172 C6
Midhurst Rd HASM GU27 ... 51 J8
HASM GU27 ... 51 J8
LIPH GU30 ... 49 K1
PETW GU28 ... 97 L5
Midhurst Wk HOVE BN3 ... 193 G1②
Midway ROTT BN2 ... 195 M4
The Midway MIDOS PO22 ... 13 M4
Mighell St ROTT BN2 ... 11 G4
Milborne Rd CRAWE RH10 ... 41 K2
Milbury Cl FERR BN12 ... 209 G4③
Milcote Av HOVE BN3 ... 193 G4
Mile End La SELS PO20 ... 200 D2
Mile Oak Crs STHW BN42 ... 192 A3
Mile Oak Gdns PTSD BN41 ... 192 B3
Mile Oak Rd PTSD BN41 ... 192 A1
Miles Cl ARUN BN18 ... 205 J3
Milford Cl HAV PO9 ... 174 A1②
Millais SWTR RH13 ... 5 L5
Millais Cl CRAWW RH11 ... 40 A2③
Millais Ct SWTR RH13 ... 5 L4
Milland La LIPH GU30 ... 49 H6
Milland Rd MIDH GU29 ... 94 B2
Mill Av SHOR BN43 ... 191 G3②
Millbank BURH RH15 ... 109 J8
The Millbank CRAWW RH11 ... 20 A6
Mill Bay La HORS RH12 ... 4 B9
Millbrook Cl LISS GU33 ... 47 M8
Millbrook Rd HAV PO9 ... 152 D6
Mill Cl ANG/EP BN16 ... 207 L3
CCH PO19 ... 178 C6
EGRIN RH19 ... 24 F5
HASM GU27 ... 27 M6④
HISD PO11 ... 196 C2
POY/PYE BN45 ... 149 K7
PTSD BN41 ... 192 D3

SWTR RH13 ... 84 B5
Mill Copse Rd HASM GU27 ... 28 C8
Millcroft BRI BN1 ... 172 B1
Millcroft Av STHW BN42 ... 191 M3
Millcroft Gdns STHW BN42 ... 191 M3
Millcross Rd PTSD BN41 ... 192 C3
Mill Dr HFD BN5 ... 128 A8
HOVE BN3 ... 193 H1
Mill End EMRTH PO10 ... 175 L4
HFD BN5 ... 127 M8
PUL/STOR RH20 ... 123 K5
Millennium Vw LAN/SOMP BN15.. 190 C6
Miller Rd BRI BN1 ... 193 M3
Millers Cl ANG/EP BN16 ... 207 L2
Millers Ga HORS RH12 ... 4 E1
Miller's Rd BRI BN1 ... 193 M3①
The Millers ARUN BN18 ... 205 G4
Millers Wy BURH RH15 ... 109 H8
Mill Farm Rd SWTR RH13 ... 5 M4
Millfield LAN/SOMP BN15 ... 189 K5
SWTR RH13 ... 82 B4
Millfield Cl ANG/EP BN16 ... 207 J5
CCH PO19 ... 179 K4
Millfield Cottages ROTT BN2 ... 11 L9
Mill Gdns SELS PO20 ... 217 G5
Mill Green Rd HWH RH16 ... 87 M6
Mill Hi SHOR BN43 ... 168 F7
Mill Hill Cl HWH RH16 ... 87 M5
SHOR BN43 ... 190 F5
Mill Hill Dr SHOR BN43 ... 190 F5
Mill Hill Gdns SHOR BN43 ... 190 F5
Mill House Gdns WTHG BN11 ... 8 B5
Mill La ANG/EP BN16 ... 207 L2
ARUN BN18 ... 141 M6
ARUN BN18 ... 160 D6
ARUN BN18 ... 182 E3
ARUN BN18 ... 184 B8
CCH PO19 ... 178 C6
CRAWE RH10 ... 22 F1
CRAWW RH11 ... 20 B4
EMRTH PO10 ... 175 G2
EPSF GU31 ... 93 G4
EPSF GU31 ... 113 L1
HASM GU27 ... 28 D8
HAV PO9 ... 152 D5
HORL RH6 ... 14 E1
HPPT/KEY BN6 ... 129 M2
HPPT/KEY BN6 ... 130 B1
HPPT/KEY BN6 ... 150 F5
LHPTN BN17 ... 184 F1
LISS GU33 ... 46 C2
MFD/CHID GU8 ... 30 B1
MIDH GU29 ... 94 B2
MIDH GU29 ... 116 E4
MIDH GU29 ... 117 G2
POY/PYE BN45 ... 149 K7
PSF GU32 ... 68 B4
PSF GU32 ... 68 E6
PTSD BN41 ... 192 C2
PUL/STOR RH20 ... 125 G8
PUL/STOR RH20 ... 125 G8
PUL/STOR RH20 ... 145 G1
RHWH RH17 ... 65 K3
SALV BN13 ... 188 C3
SELS PO20 ... 201 M3
SELS PO20 ... 219 G5
SELS PO20 ... 222 D5
SHOR BN43 ... 190 F4
SWTR RH13 ... 84 B5
SWTR RH13 ... 102 E1
SWTR RH13 ... 105 G7
Mill Md PUL/STOR RH20 ... 125 H8
Mill Park Rd BURH RH15 ... 220 B2
Mill Pond Wy ANG/EP BN16.. 208 A2
Mill Quay EMRTH PO10 ... 175 K5
Mill Race HPPT/KEY BN6 ... 130 F4
Mill Ri BRI BN1 ... 171 K7
Mill Rd ANG/EP BN16 ... 186 A7
ARUN BN18 ... 182 E4
ARUN BN18 ... 184 C1
BRI BN1 ... 171 K6
BURH RH15 ... 109 J8
CRAWE RH10 ... 21 J8
EMRTH PO10 ... 175 G2
LAN/SOMP BN15 ... 189 M4
LISS GU33 ... 47 K7
PTSD BN41 ... 192 C5
PUL/STOR RH20 ... 123 K4
STEY/UB BN44 ... 167 K1
WTHG BN11 ... 8 A5
Mill Road Av ANG/EP BN16 ... 186 A7
Mill Rythe La HISD PO11 ... 196 D5
Mill Straight SWTR RH13 ... 82 A4
Mill Stream Meadow
HWH RH16 ... 87 L5②
The Millstream HASM GU27 ... 27 M7
Millthorpe Rd HORS RH12 ... 5 J3
Mill Vale Mdw LIPH GU30 ... 71 J1
Millview Cl BOGR PO21 ... 220 B2
Mill View Rd ARUN BN18 ... 205 G2
Mill Wy BIL RH14 ... 79 K3
EGRIN RH19 ... 24 F5
Mill Wd BURH RH15 ... 131 J1
Millwood EGRIN RH19 ... 23 M7
Millyard Crs ROTT BN2 ... 195 L3
Milne Cl CRAWW RH11 ... 39 M1③
Milner Rd ROTT BN2 ... 194 D3
Milnthorpe Rd HOVE BN3 ... 192 F4
Milnwood Rd HORS RH12 ... 4 C5
Milton Av ANG/EP BN16 ... 207 J3③
LAN/SOMP BN15 ... 189 M7
Milton Crs EGRIN RH19 ... 24 C5
Milton Dr STHW BN42 ... 192 A4
Milton Mount Av
CRAWE RH10 ... 21 K4③
CRAWE RH10 ... 21 L1①
Milton Rd CRAWE RH10 ... 21 K5
HORS RH12 ... 4 C7
HWH RH16 ... 87 L7
ROTT BN2 ... 11 H3
WTHG BN11 ... 8 E7
Milton St WTHG BN11 ... 8 E7
Mimmack Cl STEY/UB BN44 ... 146 E8①
Mindleheim Av EGRIN RH19 ... 25 J2
Minley Ct HAV PO9 ... 152 F7
The Minnels HPPT/KEY BN6 ... 151 G1
Minsted Rd MIDH GU29 ... 93 M7

Minton Rd MIDOS PO22 13 M5
Mint Rd LISS GU33 47 L6
Mitchell Gdns SWTR RH13 58 F1
Mitchells Rd CRAWE RH10 3 J3
Mixon Cl SELS PO20 223 G6
Moatfield La SWTR RH13 106 B4
Moat La PUL/STOR RH20 122 D2
Moat Rd EGRIN RH19 24 F3 2
The Moat PUL/STOR RH20 122 D2
Moat Wk CRAWE RH10 21 K5
Moat Wy FERR BN12 209 M3
Mocatta Wy BURH RH15 108 E7
Modena Rd HOVE BN3 193 C5
Moggs Md EPSF GU31 90 D1
Mole Cl CRAWW RH11 20 C4 4
Molecomb Broadwalk
RCCH PO18 158 B2
Molesworth St HOVE BN3 193 C4
The Mole LHPTN BN17 207 H3
Monarch Cl CRAWW RH11 40 B1
Monarch's Wy ARUN BN18 162 B3
HAV PO9 153 J3
HOVE BN3 193 K5
PTSD BN41 170 E6
PUL/STOR RH20 123 L3
RCCH PO18 134 A8
RCCH PO18 134 E8
RCCH PO18 137 J8
SALV BN13 164 E6
SALV BN13 165 J6
SHOR BN43 169 H5
STEY/UB BN44 167 H4
STEY/UB BN44 167 M3
STHW BN42 191 M1
Monastery La PUL/STOR RH20 143 K3
Monk Cl BRI BN1 172 F6
Monkmead Copse
PUL/STOR RH20 123 K6
Monkmead La PUL/STOR RH20 123 J5
Monks Av LAN/SOMP BN15 190 A6
Monks Cl LAN/SOMP BN15 189 M6
Monksfield CRAWE RH10 3 J3
Monk's Hl EMRTH PO10 153 K6
Monks La RDKG RH5 16 A7
Monks Orch PSF GU32 68 C7
Monks Wk STEY/UB BN44 168 C2
Monks Wd PSF GU32 68 C7
Monkwood Cl HAV PO9 152 A7 2
Monmouth St HOVE BN3 193 J5 5
Mons Av BOGR PO21 12 A3
Montague Cl SHOR BN43 191 L5 1
Montague Gdns EPSF GU31 90 F1
Montague Pl ROTT BN2 11 J8
WTHG BN11 9 H7
Montague Rd MIDH GU29 95 H2
Montague St ROTT BN2 11 J8
WTHG BN11 8 F7
Montagu Rd CCH PO19 178 F4
Montalan Crs SELS PO20 222 D4
Montefiore Rd HOVE BN3 10 A3
Monterey Dr HAV PO9 152 D8
Monterey Pines MIDOS PO22 13 M4
Montes Hl HWH RH16 89 G4
Monteswood La RHWH RH17 89 J4
Montford Cl SHOR BN43 191 L4
Montgomeri Dr ANG/EP BN16 207 J1
Montgomery Dr MIDOS PO22 204 E6
Montgomery Rd HAV PO9 174 D3
Montgomery St HOVE BN3 193 G5
Montpelier Crs BRI BN1 10 B4
Montpelier Gdns
PUL/STOR RH20 144 F4
Montpelier Pl BRI BN1 10 A5
Montpelier Rd ANG/EP BN16 208 B3
BRI BN1 10 A6
Montpelier St BRI BN1 10 B5
Montpelier Ter BRI BN1 10 B5
Montpelier Vls BRI BN1 10 B5
Montreal Rd ROTT BN2 11 H5
Montreal Wy SALV BN13 187 K6
Montrose Cl FERR BN12 209 K1
Monument La RCCH PO18 154 C5
Monument Vw ROTT BN2 11 M5
Moorcroft Cl CRAWW RH11 2 B2 1
Moore Cl SALV BN13 187 J6
Moorfield HASM GU27 28 A7
Moorfoot Rd SALV BN13 188 A5
Moorgreen Rd HAV PO9 152 D7
Moorhead Rd HORS RH12 38 C7
Moorhen Wy MIDOS PO22 203 J6 1
Moorhouse La MIDH GU29 71 K6
The Moorings EGRIN RH19 24 B1
LAN/SOMP BN15 190 A4
SHOR BN43 191 K6
Moorland Rd CRAWE RH10 41 K1
Moor Park Crs CRAWW RH11 19 L7 4
Moor Pl EGRIN RH19 24 A2
Moor Rd HASM GU27 27 K7
LISS GU33 47 L3
Moraunt Dr MIDOS PO22 204 E6
Morecambe Cl CRAWW RH11 20 A8 2
Morecambe Rd BRI BN1 172 B6
Moreton Rd RCCH PO18 177 H7
Morland Av FIN/BW BN14 188 F5
Morleys PUL/STOR RH20 125 H8
Morley St ROTT BN2 10 F5
Mornington Crs HOVE BN3 192 E5 1
MIDOS PO22 13 M2
Morrell Av HORS RH12 5 K1
Morris Wy PUL/STOR RH20 123 K5
Mortimer Rd HOVE BN3 193 G4
Morton Cl CRAWW RH11 40 C4 2
Morton Rd EGRIN RH19 24 F5
Mosdell Rd EMRTH PO10 176 A4
Moss Cl LISS GU33 47 K8
Mosse Gdns CCH PO19 178 C5
Moulsecoomb Wy ROTT BN2 194 F1
Mountbatten Cl
CRAWW RH11 40 D2 5
Mount Cl CRAWE RH10 21 K5
Mount Dr ROTT BN2 213 L2
Mountfields BRI BN1 194 D2
Mount La CCH PO19 6 C5
CRAWE RH10 23 H8
Mount Noddy RHWH RH17 108 D1
Mount Pleasant ARUN BN18 184 B1
ROTT BN2 11 H7 1
The Mount HASM GU27 29 G2
HORS RH12 19 J3
Mountview Rd
LAN/SOMP BN15 189 K4
Mountway LAN/SOMP BN15 189 M3
Mountwood Rd EMRTH PO10 176 A3
SELS PO20 223 H4
Mount Zion Pl BRI BN1 10 D5 2
Mouse La STEY/UB BN44 145 M5
STEY/UB BN44 146 C8
Mouthey's La RCCH PO18 177 M2
Mowbray Dr CRAWW RH11 20 A8
Moyne Cl HOVE BN3 192 F3
Moyne Rd CRAWW RH11 40 D2
Muccleshell Cl HAV PO9 152 D8 2
Mudberry La RCCH PO18 177 H4
Muggeridge's Hl RDKG RH5 17 M4
Muirfield Cl CRAWW RH11 19 L7
SALV BN13 187 M6 2
Muirfield Rd SALV BN13 187 L6
Mulberry Cl BRI BN1 194 A1 1
FERR BN12 208 F2
FERR BN12 209 K1
HORS RH12 4 C2
LAN/SOMP BN15 189 M6 3
SHOR BN43 191 L3
Mulberry Gdns FERR BN12 209 K2 4
Mulberry La FERR BN12 209 K1
HPPT/KEY BN6 151 L1
Mulberry Rd CRAWW RH11 20 C3 2
Mumford Pl CCH PO19 7 H8
Munmere Wy ANG/EP BN16 207 M2 6
Munnion Rd RHWH RH17 66 C5
Munns Dr BURH RH15 109 J8
Muntham Dr SWTR RH13 80 F1
Murina Av BOGR PO21 12 C3
Murray Ct SWTR RH13 38 C8
Murray Rd SELS PO20 222 E6
Muscliffe Ct HAV PO9 152 E7 10
Museum Hl HASM GU27 28 E6
Musgrave Av EGRIN RH19 24 F5
Mustang Cl ARUN BN18 205 J1
Muster Gn North HWH RH16 87 L8
Muster Gn South HWH RH16 87 L8
Mutton's La PUL/STOR RH20 144 E1
My Lords La HISD PO11 214 E1
Myrtle Crs LAN/SOMP BN15 189 K7
Myrtle Gv ANG/EP BN16 207 M3
Myrtle La BIL RH14 79 L5
Myrtle Rd LAN/SOMP BN15 189 L7
Mytten Bank RHWH RH17 87 G6 2
Mytten Cl RHWH RH17 87 G6

N

Nab Tower La SELS PO20 222 C4
Nab Wk SELS PO20 217 G6
Nagels Cl SELS PO20 217 H6
Naiad Gdns MIDOS PO22 204 E8 4
Naldrett Cl HORS RH12 5 J3
Naldretts La HORS RH12 34 D7
Namrik Ms HOVE BN3 193 H6
Nanson Rd BRI BN1 172 E6
Napier Wy CRAWE RH10 21 G3
Nappers Wd HASM GU27 51 H6
Nash La RHWH RH17 89 J8
Nash Rd CRAWE RH10 40 F1
Nash Wy ARUN BN18 182 E3
Natal Rd ROTT BN2 194 D2
Natts La BIL RH14 79 K5
Navarino Rd WTHG BN11 211 H1
Neale Cl EGRIN RH19 24 C1
Needlemakers CCH PO19 7 G4 1
Needles Cl HORS RH12 60 C3 1
Need's Hl SWTR RH13 104 F6
Nell Ball BIL RH14 54 F2
Nelson Cl CRAWE RH10 21 K7
LAN/SOMP BN15 189 L4
SELS PO20 180 E3
Nelson Rd BOGR PO21 221 H1
FERR BN12 187 L8
HORS RH12 4 B5
Nelson Rw ARUN BN18 205 M1
ROTT BN2 11 G6
Nepcote La FIN/BW BN14 165 M6
Nepfield Cl FIN/BW BN14 165 M7
Nep Town Rd HFD BN5 127 M8
Neptune Cl CRAWW RH11 19 M8 5
Neptune Ct MIDOS PO22 204 E8 5
Neptune Wy ANG/EP BN16 207 H4
Nesbitt Rd ROTT BN2 194 E3
Netherfield Cl HAV PO9 174 D4
Netherton Cl SELS PO20 223 G5
SWTR RH13 60 A8 1
Netherwood CRAWW RH11 2 A8
Netherwoods Rd SWTR RH13 81 J6
Netley Cl CRAWW RH11 40 D4 4
Nettleton Av SELS PO20 180 D2
Nevile Cl CRAWW RH11 40 B1
Nevill Av HOVE BN3 193 G3
Nevill Cl HOVE BN3 193 H2
Neville Gdns EMRTH PO10 175 H1
Neville Rd CCH PO19 178 E5
MIDOS PO22 12 F4
Nevill Gdns HOVE BN3 193 H2
Nevill Pl HOVE BN3 193 H2
Nevill Rd HOVE BN3 193 H2
ROTT BN2 213 G3
Nevill Wy HOVE BN3 193 H2
Newark Pl ROTT BN2 11 G4
Newark Rd CRAWE RH10 21 G4
New Barn Cl PTSD BN41 192 C2
SHOR BN43 191 J3 3
New Barn Hl RCCH PO18 158 B7
New Barn La PUL/STOR RH20 123 J4
New Barn La RDKG RH5 16 B1
Newbarn La BOGR PO21 203 G5
HFD BN5 147 M2
MIDOS PO22 204 C6
Newbarn La RCCH PO18 154 C4
New Barn Rd ARUN BN18 141 L7
ROTT BN2 212 F1
SHOR BN43 191 J3
New Br BIL RH14 79 G4
Newbridge Cl HORS RH12 59 K1 1
Newbridge Rd BIL RH14 79 H4
New Brighton Rd
EMRTH PO10 175 J2
Newbury La RHWH RH17 86 F7
Newbury Rd CRAWE RH10 21 L6
New Church Rd HOVE BN3 192 E5
New Courtwick La
LHPTN BN17 184 D8 3
New Cut ARUN BN18 184 C1 3
HISD PO11 196 C1
Newdigate Rd HORS RH12 18 E4
New Dorset St BRI BN1 10 D5
Newells Cl ROTT BN2 195 M3
Newells La RCCH PO18 177 G2
SWTR RH13 83 L2
New England Ri PTSD BN41 170 B8
New England Rd BRI BN1 10 D2
HWH RH16 87 M8
New England St BRI BN1 10 E2
Newfield Rd LISS GU33 47 K6
SELS PO20 223 J4
Newhall Cl BOGR PO21 221 G1
New Hall La HFD BN5 147 L5
Newham Cl STEY/UB BN44 167 K1
Newham La STEY/UB BN44 167 J2
Newhaven St ROTT BN2 11 G4
Newhouse La PUL/STOR RH20 144 D1
RCCH PO18 137 L5
Newick Rd BRI BN1 172 F8
Newland Rd STEY/UB BN44 168 C2
WTHG BN11 9 H3
Newlands RHWH RH17 65 G3
Newlands Cl HPPT/KEY BN6 151 H1
Newlands Crs EGRIN RH19 24 E2
Newlands La CCH PO19 178 E4
Newlands Pk CRAWE RH10 22 F1
Newlands Rd CRAWW RH11 2 D5
HORS RH12 4 C4
ROTT BN2 213 H3
Newland St WTHG BN11 9 H3
New La EPSF GU31 113 L2
HAV PO9 152 E8
HAV PO9 174 D2
Newling Wy SALV BN13 187 M3
Newman Cl CRAWE RH10 21 K8 7
Newman's Gdns
LAN/SOMP BN15 189 J5 1
Newmarket Rd CRAWE RH10 3 L9
ROTT BN2 194 D4 3
New Moorhead Dr HORS RH12 38 D6
Newnham Ct HAV PO9 152 E7 11
New Pde WTHG BN11 9 L6
New Park Rd CCH PO19 6 F3
New Place Rd PUL/STOR RH20 122 D1
Newport Dr CCH PO19 178 C5
Newport Ms WTHG BN11 211 J1
Newport Rd BURH RH15 131 G1
Newport St ROTT BN2 11 H2
Newpound BIL RH14 78 F1
Newpound La BIL RH14 78 D3
New Rd ANG/EP BN16 207 L1
BIL RH14 79 M2
BIL RH14 80 C2
BRI BN1 10 E6
EMRTH PO10 175 L1
HASM GU27 28 A7
HAV PO9 174 A2
HPPT/KEY BN6 151 G3
LHPTN BN17 206 E4
MIDH GU29 94 F6
MIDH GU29 95 M7
PETW GU28 97 H3
RCCH PO18 138 A3
RCCH PO18 158 B8
SALV BN13 187 K5
SHOR BN43 191 G5
STEY/UB BN44 168 C3
SWTR RH13 60 A8
Newstead Hall HORL RH6 15 L2
New Steine ROTT BN2 11 G8
New Steine Ms ROTT BN2 11 G8
New St CRAWE RH10 3 M2
SWTR RH13 4 F9
WTHG BN11 9 G7
Newtimber Av FERR BN12 209 J1
Newtimber Dr PTSD BN41 192 B3
Newtimber Gdns
SHOR BN43 191 G3 5
Newton Av EGRIN RH19 25 G6
Newton Cl HWH RH16 88 C5
Newton Rd CRAWE RH10 21 G2
HWH RH16 88 C5
New Town CCH PO19 6 F5
CRAWE RH10 22 C1
Newtown Av BOGR PO21 203 H6
Newtown La HISD PO11 196 B8 4
Newtown Rd HOVE BN3 193 J4
LIPH GU30 49 J1
New Town Rd PUL/STOR RH20 143 J3
New Way La HPPT/KEY BN6 150 C2
Nicholsfield BIL RH14 33 G8
Nicholson Wy HAV PO9 174 B1
Nicolson Dr SHOR BN43 191 G4
Nightingale Cl CRAWW RH11 20 D4
EGRIN RH19 24 E5 1
HAV PO9 152 D3
PUL/STOR RH20 143 M3
Nightingale La BURH RH15 131 G4
PUL/STOR RH20 143 M3
RCCH PO18 176 D1
Nightingale Pk HAV PO9 174 E3 5
PUL/STOR RH20 143 M3
Nightingale Rd HORS RH12 4 F6
PSF GU32 90 A2 1
Nightingales FIN/BW BN14 165 M5
PUL/STOR RH20 123 L5
Nightingales Cl SWTR RH13 5 J8
Nightingale Wk BIL RH14 79 L4
Nile St BRI BN1 10 E7
EMRTH PO10 175 J4
Nimbus Cl LHPTN BN17 207 H2
Ninfield Pl ROTT BN2 194 F5
Niven Cl CRAWE RH10 21 L7 6
Nizells Av HOVE BN3 193 L5
Noahs Ark La HWH RH16 88 D5
Noel Gn BURH RH15 109 J8
Noel Ri BURH RH15 109 J8
Nolan Rd ROTT BN2 195 M5
Nonnington La PETW GU28 118 C3
The Nookery ANG/EP BN16 208 B3
Nor'bren Av BOGR PO21 203 H7
Norbury Cl LAN/SOMP BN15 190 A4
Norbury Dr LAN/SOMP BN15 189 M4
Nore Crs EMRTH PO10 175 G3
Nore Down Wy RCCH PO18 133 H4
Nore Farm Av EMRTH PO10 175 G3
Noreuil Rd PSF GU32 90 A1
Norfolk Buildings BRI BN1 10 A6 1
Norfolk Cl BOGR PO21 12 B8
CRAWW RH11 39 M2 5
HORL RH6 15 H2
Norfolk Gdns LHPTN BN17 207 G4
Norfolk Ms BRI BN1 10 A6 2
Norfolk Pl LHPTN BN17 207 G4 2
Norfolk Rd BRI BN1 10 A6
HORS RH12 4 E8
LHPTN BN17 207 G4
Norfolk Sq BOGR PO21 12 B8
BRI BN1 10 A6 3
Norfolk St BOGR PO21 12 D8
BRI BN1 10 A7
WTHG BN11 8 E4
Norfolk Ter BRI BN1 10 A5
SWTR RH13 4 E8
Norfolk Wy MIDOS PO22 205 H7
Norley Cl HAV PO9 152 B7
Norman Cl BIL RH14 79 M3
LHPTN BN17 207 G3
Norman Crs SHOR BN43 191 G3
Normandy HORS RH12 60 D3 2
Normandy Cl CRAWE RH10 21 J8 3
EGRIN RH19 25 G4 4
Normandy Dr ANG/EP BN16 208 A4
Normandy Gdns HORS RH12 4 C9
Normandy La ANG/EP BN16 208 B4
Normandy Rd FIN/BW BN14 8 F1
Normanhurst Cl
ANG/EP BN16 207 K4 2
CRAWE RH10 3 K4
Norman Rd BURH RH15 131 G1
HISD PO11 214 E2
HOVE BN3 192 F6
Norman's Dr MIDOS PO22 204 C6
Normanton Av BOGR PO21 12 A6
Normanton St ROTT BN2 11 J2
Norman Wy MIDOS PO22 205 G7
STEY/UB BN44 146 E8
Norris Gdns HAV PO9 174 D4
North Av FERR BN12 209 M3
MIDOS PO22 205 G7
North Av South MIDOS PO22 205 G7
North Bank HPPT/KEY BN6 130 F8
North Bay EMRTH PO10 197 K1
North Bersted St MIDOS PO22 203 H5
Northbourne Cl SHOR BN43 191 G4 2
Northbrook Cl FIN/BW BN14 188 F6 1
Northbrook Rd FIN/BW BN14 188 F6
Northcliffe Rd MIDOS PO22 13 G4
North Cl CRAWE RH10 3 J1
HAV PO9 174 D4
PTSD BN41 192 B2
North Common Rd
RHWH RH17 110 E7
Northcote Rd BOGR PO21 203 H8
North Ct HPPT/KEY BN6 130 F8
Northcourt Cl ANG/EP BN16 207 L2
Northcourt Rd FIN/BW BN14 8 F2
North Crs HISD PO11 214 E1
Northcroft HFD BN5 127 L7
Northdown Cl HORS RH12 5 J3
North Dr ANG/EP BN16 186 A8
ROTT BN2 11 J5
Northease Cl HOVE BN3 192 E2 2
Northease Dr HOVE BN3 192 E2
Northease Gdns HOVE BN3 192 F1 3
North End HPPT/KEY BN6 131 L8
North End Cl PETW GU28 98 A3
Northend La HPPT/KEY BN6 130 A1
North End Rd ARUN BN18 183 G8
Northern Crs SELS PO20 216 F5
North Farm Rd
LAN/SOMP BN15 189 M6 4
Northfield SELS PO20 223 H5
Northfield Ri HOVE BN3 170 E8
ROTT BN2 213 H2
Northfield Rd SALV BN13 188 B6 1
Northfields La SELS PO20 181 L4
Northfield Wy BRI BN1 172 B8
North Gdns BRI BN1 10 D5
Northgate CCH PO19 6 E3
Northgate Av CRAWE RH10 3 J2
Northgate Cl
LAN/SOMP BN15 189 K6 4
ROTT BN2 213 G2
Northgate Pl CRAWE RH10 3 H1
Northgate Rd CRAWE RH10 2 F3
North Ham Rd LHPTN BN17 206 E3
North Heath Cl HORS RH12 4 F1
North Heath La HORS RH12 4 F2
North Holmes Cl HORS RH12 5 M2
Northlands Av HWH RH16 110 B1
Northlands La PUL/STOR RH20 123 M8
Northlands Rd HORS RH12 36 E3
HORS RH12 37 M5
North La ANG/EP BN16 207 J2
ANG/EP BN16 208 B3
EGRIN RH19 43 M7
EPSF GU31 90 B7
EPSF GU31 91 L7
PTSD BN41 192 B2
RCCH PO18 137 H3
STEY/UB BN44 145 K2
North Md CRAWE RH10 20 F4
Northney La HISD PO11 174 F8
Northney Rd HISD PO11 174 D7
North Pallant CCH PO19 6 E5
North Pde HORS RH12 4 C3
North Pl BRI BN1 10 F6
LHPTN BN17 206 F4
North Pound ARUN BN18 182 E3
North Rd BRI BN1 10 E5
BRI BN1 193 M3
CRAWE RH10 3 L1
HWH RH16 88 B8
LAN/SOMP BN15 189 M7
PSF GU32 68 C8
PTSD BN41 192 B2
RCCH PO18 177 K5
SELS PO20 223 G5
North Shore Rd HISD PO11 196 A7
Northside RCCH PO18 156 F5
North St BRI BN1 10 D6
CCH PO19 6 E3
CRAWE RH10 3 H8
EMRTH PO10 153 L8
EMRTH PO10 175 J3
HAV PO9 174 A2
HORS RH12 4 E7
LHPTN BN17 206 E1
MIDH GU29 95 G4
PETW GU28 98 A3
PTSD BN41 192 C5
PUL/STOR RH20 143 L3
SHOR BN43 190 F5
WTHG BN11 9 H4
North Walls CCH PO19 6 C4
Northway BURH RH15 109 K8
North Wy HAV PO9 174 B3
PETW GU28 97 M5
Northway Rd LHPTN BN17 184 E8
Northwood Av ROTT BN2 213 M3
Northwood La HISD PO11 196 D3
Northwyke Cl MIDOS PO22 204 D7
Northwyke Rd MIDOS PO22 204 D7
Norton Cl HOVE BN3 193 J6 2
Norton Dr ROTT BN2 195 L3
Norton La SELS PO20 181 J3
Norton Rd HOVE BN3 193 J6
LAN/SOMP BN15 189 L7
Norway La LHPTN BN17 207 G1
Norway St PTSD BN41 192 D5
Norwich Cl ROTT BN2 195 H2
Norwich Dr ROTT BN2 195 H2
Norwich Rd CCH PO19 179 G4
Norwoodhill Rd HORL RH6 14 A3
Norwood La PETW GU28 118 F4
Norwood La South
PETW GU28 118 F7
Nowhurst La HORS RH12 36 B7
Nuffield Cl BOGR PO21 220 F1 3
The Nurseries BOGR PO21 220 D1 2
Nursery Cl ANG/EP BN16 208 B4
EMRTH PO10 175 J1
HPPT/KEY BN6 130 A5
HWH RH16 87 L7
LAN/SOMP BN15 189 L4
MIDOS PO22 182 C6
PTSD BN41 169 M8 1
SHOR BN43 191 J4
Nursery Fld LISS GU33 69 H1
Nursery Gdns LHPTN BN17 206 E1 2
Nurserylands CRAWW RH11 20 B6
Nursery La HORL RH6 14 E2
RCCH PO18 178 C5
WTHG BN11 8 E7
The Nursery BURH RH15 109 K8
Nursling Crs HAV PO9 152 D7
Nutbourne La PUL/STOR RH20 101 H8
Nutbourne Rd FIN/BW BN14 8 C1
HISD PO11 215 H3
PUL/STOR RH20 123 H3
Nutcombe La GSHT GU26 27 M3
Nutcroft PUL/STOR RH20 122 D1 2
Nutham La SWTR RH13 82 B3
Nuthatch Cl HAV PO9 152 E3
Nuthurst Cl CRAWW RH11 20 B5
ROTT BN2 195 G6
Nuthurst Pl ROTT BN2 195 G7
Nuthurst Rd SWTR RH13 83 G7
SWTR RH13 83 K1
Nuthurst St SWTR RH13 83 H4
Nutley Av FERR BN12 209 K3
ROTT BN2 213 L4
Nutley Cl FERR BN12 209 K3
HOVE BN3 193 G1 3
Nutley Crs FERR BN12 209 K3
Nutley Dr FERR BN12 209 K3
Nutley Rd HAV PO9 152 A7
Nutwick Rd HAV PO9 174 E1
Nye La HPPT/KEY BN6 151 L3
Nye Rd BURH RH15 131 J1
Nyes Cl HFD BN5 128 A7
Nyes La SWTR RH13 82 A1
Nyetimber Cl PUL/STOR RH20 123 K6
Nyetimber Copse
PUL/STOR RH20 123 K5
Nyetimber Crs BOGR PO21 220 C2
Nyetimber Hl ROTT BN2 194 F2
Nyetimber La BOGR PO21 220 C2
PUL/STOR RH20 123 J5
Nyetimber Ml BOGR PO21 220 B2
The Nyetimbers BOGR PO21 220 B2
Nyewood Gdns BOGR PO21 12 B6 1
Nyewood La BOGR PO21 12 A5
Nymans Cl HORS RH12 38 B5
Nymans Ct CRAWE RH10 41 J1 4
Nyton Rd SELS PO20 181 H2
SELS PO20 181 M4

O

Oakapple Cl CRAWW RH11 40 C3 1
SWTR RH13 105 M3
Oakapple Rd STHW BN42 191 L2
Oak Av CCH PO19 6 B2
PUL/STOR RH20 144 C1
Oak Bank HWH RH16 88 A5
Oak Cl BRI BN1 193 M1
CCH PO19 6 B2
CRAWE RH10 22 A1
MIDOS PO22 203 K6
PUL/STOR RH20 144 A2
SALV BN13 187 M3
SWTR RH13 82 A5
Oak Cft EGRIN RH19 25 H4
Oakcroft Gdns LHPTN BN17 207 G1
Oakdale Rd HWH RH16 110 A1 1
Oak Dell CRAWE RH10 21 K5
Oakdene Av PTSD BN41 191 M1
Oakdene Cl PTSD BN41 191 M1
Oakdene Crs PTSD BN41 169 M8
Oakdene Gdns PTSD BN41 191 M1
Oakdene Ri PTSD BN41 169 M8
Oakdene Wy PTSD BN41 191 M1
Oak End ARUN BN18 183 M2
PUL/STOR RH20 123 L5
Oakenfield BURH RH15 109 G7
Oakfield BIL RH14 54 F2
Oakfield Av SELS PO20 217 G5
Oakfield Cl HWH RH16 88 B5
Oakfield Ct HAV PO9 152 E7 12
Oakfield Rd SELS PO20 217 G5
SWTR RH13 105 M3

Oakfields *CRAWE* RH10.............. 21 L5
Oakfield Wy *EGRIN* RH19.............. 25 G1
Oak Gv *BIL* RH14.............. 33 H8 ②
MIDOS P022.............. 203 K6
Oak Hall Pk *BURH* RH15.............. 131 J3
Oakhaven *CRAWW* RH11.............. 2 E7 ②
Oakhill Rd *SWTR* RH13.............. 4 F7
Oakhurst *GSHT* GU26.............. 27 L1
HFD BN5.............. 127 M6
MIDH GU29.............. 94 E4
Oakhurst Gdns *ANG/EP* BN16.............. 207 M2
EGRIN RH19.............. 24 D2
Oakhurst La *BIL* RH14.............. 87 L5
Oakhurst Rd *HOVE* BN3.............. 192 F1
Oaklands *BIL* RH14.............. 79 L5
HASM GU27.............. 28 D5 ④
HORL RH6.............. 15 K1
RHWH RH17.............. 66 C4
Oaklands Av *ROTT* BN2.............. 213 K3
Oaklands La *MIDH* GU29.............. 94 F4
Oaklands Rd *HAV* P09.............. 174 D3
HWH RH16.............. 87 L7
PSF GU32.............. 68 B8
Oaklands Wy *CCH* P019.............. 6 E2
Oak La *HORS* RH12.............. 59 M1
Oakleigh Cl *WTHG* BN11.............. 189 L6
Oakleigh Cl *FIN/BW* BN14.............. 189 M8
HORS RH12.............. 5 K3
Oakley Cl *BRI* BN1.............. 25 J5
Oakley Gdns *ANG/EP* BN16.............. 208 B4
Oakley Rd *HAV* P09.............. 152 A7
Oak Little *SWTR* RH13.............. 127 G1
Oak Meadow *SELS* P020.............. 199 M7
Oakmeadow Cl *EMRTH* P010.............. 175 K1
Oakmead Rd *BURH* RH15.............. 131 G3
Oak Park Dr *HAV* P09.............. 174 D1
Oak Rd *CRAWW* RH11.............. 2 D5
SWTR RH13.............. 81 M3
Oakroyd Cl *BURH* RH15.............. 109 K7
Oaks Cl *HORS* RH12.............. 38 C6
SELS P020.............. 181 L6
Oakshott Dr *HAV* P09.............. 152 D7
The Oaks *ANG/EP* BN16.............. 207 M3
BURH RH15.............. 108 D8
EGRIN RH19.............. 25 H4
HWH RH16.............. 88 B8 ①
Oak Tree Dr *EMRTH* P010.............. 153 H8
LISS GU33.............. 47 K8
Oak Tree Farm *RCCH* P018.............. 176 E3
Oak Tree La *HASM* GU27.............. 27 L6
SELS P020.............. 181 L7
Oak Tree Wy *SWTR* RH13.............. 5 K4
Oak Wk *HORS* RH12.............. 39 C5
Oak Wy *CRAWW* RH10.............. 20 F4
Oakway *SWTR* RH13.............. 61 K5
Oakwood *SWTR* RH13.............. 127 N1
Oakwood Cl *BURH* RH15.............. 131 J2
MIDH GU29.............. 94 E5
SELS P020.............. 180 E2
Oakwood Gdns *BOGR* P021.............. 12 C4
Oakwood Rd *BURH* RH15.............. 131 J2
HISD P011.............. 214 C1
HWH RH16.............. 87 L8
Oathall Av *HWH* RH16.............. 88 A6
Oathall Rd *HWH* RH16.............. 87 M7
Oatlands *CRAWW* RH11.............. 20 B7
Oberon Wy *CRAWW* RH11.............. 39 M1 ③
Ocean Cl *FERR* BN12.............. 208 F4
Ocean Dr *FERR* BN12.............. 208 F4
Ockenden La *RHWH* RH17.............. 86 F6
Ockenden Wy *HPPT/KEY* BN6.............. 150 F1
Ockley Ct *BOGR* P021.............. 12 D7
Ockley Hl *HPPT/KEY* BN6.............. 131 K8
Ockley La *HORS* RH15.............. 131 J5
HPPT/KEY BN6.............. 131 K8
Ockley Rd *BOGR* P021.............. 12 C7
Ockley Wy *HPPT/KEY* BN6.............. 131 H7
Offington Av *FIN/BW* BN14.............. 188 C5
Offington Dr *FIN/BW* BN14.............. 188 D6
Offington Gdns *FIN/BW* BN14.............. 188 B5
Offington La *FIN/BW* BN14.............. 188 B6
Okehurst La *BIL* RH14.............. 57 K8
Okehurst Rd *BIL* RH14.............. 57 J7
Old Arundel Rd *RCCH* P018.............. 180 A2
Old Barn Cl *BOGR* P021.............. 220 B2
Old Barn Wy *STHW* BN42.............. 192 B5
Old Boat Wk *BRI* BN1.............. 172 C5
Old Bridge Rd *RCCH* P018.............. 177 K5
Old Brighton Rd (North)
CRAWW RH11.............. 40 D5
Old Brighton Rd South
CRAWE.............. 14 F8
Old Brighton Rd (South)
CRAWW RH11.............. 40 C7
CCH P019.............. 178 D2
Old Broyle Rd *CCH* P019.............. 6 D2
Old Buddington La *MIDH* GU29.............. 94 F2
Oldbury Cl *RHWH* RH17.............. 38 B5
Old Coastguards *MIDOS* P022.............. 13 K5
Old Copse Rd *HAV* P09.............. 174 D2
Old Cottage Cl *SELS* P020.............. 180 D3 ①
Old Court Cl *BRI* BN1.............. 172 A8
Old Crawley Rd *HORS* RH12.............. 38 D6
Old Denne Gdns *HORS* RH12.............. 60 D3 ①
Olde Place Ms *ROTT* BN2.............. 213 G3
Older Wy *ANG/EP* BN16.............. 186 A6 ①
Old Farm Cl *BOGR* P021.............. 220 E2
Old Farm Dr *SELS* P020.............. 181 L5
Old Farm La *EMRTH* P010.............. 175 L1
Old Farm Rd *BRI* BN1.............. 172 A7
SELS P020.............. 222 A4
Oldfield Crs *STHW* BN42.............. 191 L5
Oldfield Rd *HORL* RH6.............. 15 G3
Old Fort Rd *SHOR* BN43.............. 191 H6
Old Glebe *HASM* GU27.............. 51 J6
Old Guildford Rd *HORS* RH12.............. 59 M1
RHWH RH17.............. 65 G3
Old London Rd *BRI* BN1.............. 171 M7
PUL/STOR RH20.............. 121 G1
PUL/STOR RH20.............. 144 F4

Old Manor Cl *CRAWW* RH11.............. 20 B4
Old Manor House Gdns
MIDOS P022.............. 204 C7
Old Manor Rd *ANG/EP* BN16.............. 207 J2
Old Market Av *CCH* P019.............. 6 E5
Old Martyrs *CRAWW* RH11.............. 20 D3
Old Mead Rd *LHPTN* BN17.............. 184 D7
Old Mill *BRI* BN1.............. 171 M7
Old Mill Dr *PUL/STOR* RH20.............. 143 L3
Old Mill La *EPSF* GU31.............. 68 E7
Old Millmeads *HORS* RH12.............. 4 C2
Old Mill Pl *HASM* GU27.............. 28 A5
PUL/STOR RH20.............. 122 E3
Old Orchards *CRAWE* RH10.............. 21 M6
Old Parish La *ROTT* BN2.............. 195 L4
Old Park Cl *RHWH* RH17.............. 87 H6 ①
Old Park La *RCCH* P018.............. 199 M1
Old Patcham Ms *BRI* BN1.............. 171 M6
Old Pl *BOGR* P021.............. 220 F2
Old Point *MIDOS* P022.............. 204 F8
The Old Quarry *HASM* GU27.............. 28 A8
Old Rectory Cl *EMRTH* P010.............. 175 L1 ①
Old Rectory Dr *SELS* P020.............. 181 M5
Old Rectory Gdns *MIDOS* P022.............. 13 L4
STHW BN42.............. 191 L5
The Old Rectory *MIDOS* P022.............. 13 L5
EGRIN RH19.............. 25 G4
Old Salts Farm Rd
LAN/SOMP BN15.............. 190 B6
Old School Cl *SELS* P020.............. 199 L8 ①
Old School Dr *HISD* P011.............. 214 E2
Old School Ms *MIDOS* P022.............. 13 L3
Old School Pl *BURH* RH15.............. 131 G2
Old School Rd *LISS* GU33.............. 47 J8
Old Shoreham Rd *HOVE* BN3.............. 191 K4
LAN/SOMP BN15.............. 190 B4 ①
STHW BN42.............. 192 A4
Old Station Cl *CRAWE* RH10.............. 23 J5
Old Steine *BRI* BN1.............. 10 F7
ROTT BN2.............. 10 F6
Old Timbers *HISD* P011.............. 214 C1
Old Wickham La *HWH* RH16.............. 87 L5
Old Wickhurst La *HORS* RH12.............. 59 L3
Oldwick Mdw *RCCH* P018.............. 157 G7
Old Worthing Rd
ANG/EP BN16.............. 208 C2
Oliver Cl *ROTT* BN2.............. 11 K6
Olive Rd *HOVE* BN3.............. 192 F4
Oliver Rd *HORS* RH12.............. 60 B5
Olivers Meadow *SELS* P020.............. 181 L5
Oliver Whitby Rd *CCH* P019.............. 6 A4
Olivier Rd *CRAWE* RH10.............. 21 L7
Onslow Dr *FERR* BN12.............. 208 F2
Onslow Rd *HOVE* BN3.............. 193 K3
Ontario Cl *SALV* BN13.............. 187 K8
Ontario Gdns *SALV* BN13.............. 187 K6
Ophir Rd *WTHG* BN11.............. 211 H1
Orange Rw *EMRTH* P010.............. 175 J4 ①
Orchard Av *CCH* P019.............. 6 D2
FIN/BW BN14.............. 188 B7
HOVE BN3.............. 193 H3
LAN/SOMP BN15.............. 189 M5
SELS P020.............. 223 G6
Orchard Cl *BOGR* P021.............. 12 B7
EPSF GU31.............. 92 B8
FERR BN12.............. 208 F1
FIN/BW BN14.............. 188 C7 ①
HFD BN5.............. 148 A2
HWH RH16.............. 87 L4
PETW GU28.............. 98 A5
RHWH RH17.............. 111 G1 ①
SHOR BN43.............. 190 F4
STHW BN42.............. 192 A4
Orchard Cnr *HWH* RH16.............. 88 D7
Orchard Crs *ARUN* BN18.............. 182 B1
Orchard Dell *PUL/STOR* RH20.............. 123 J4
Orchard Gdns *ANG/EP* BN16.............. 207 L2
CCH P019.............. 6 D3
HOVE BN3.............. 193 J3
SELS P020.............. 181 L1
Orchard Hl *HORS* RH12.............. 34 D5
Orchard La *EMRTH* P010.............. 175 K4
HPPT/KEY BN6.............. 131 K8
SELS P020.............. 199 G5
Orchard Pl *ARUN* BN18.............. 184 D1
Orchard Rd *ANG/EP* BN16.............. 208 B2
BURH RH15.............. 130 F1
HAV P09.............. 174 C4
HISD P011.............. 214 D2
HOVE BN3.............. 193 H3
SWTR RH13.............. 5 H9
Orchard Side *SELS* P020.............. 201 G4
The Orchards *CRAWW* RH11.............. 19 L7 ②
Orchard St *CCH* P019.............. 6 D3 ①
CRAWW RH11.............. 2 E3
The Orchard *BOGR* P021.............. 220 D3 ①
HASM GU27.............. 28 A7
Orchard Wy *ARUN* BN18.............. 182 B1
BURH RH15.............. 131 G1 ①
EGRIN RH19.............. 24 F3
HPPT/KEY BN6.............. 130 A6
HWH RH16.............. 87 L4
LAN/SOMP BN15.............. 189 M5
MIDH GU29.............. 95 G4
MIDOS P022.............. 12 C2
MIDOS P022.............. 182 C6
PUL/STOR RH20.............. 122 D1
RHWH RH17.............. 85 L1
Orchid Pk *HWH* RH16.............. 88 D6
Orchid Vw *BRI* BN1.............. 172 D6
Orde Cl *CRAWE* RH10.............. 21 K3 ①
Oriel Cl *CRAWE* RH10.............. 21 K3 ②
MIDOS P022.............. 182 C6
Oriental Pl *BRI* BN1.............. 10 A7
Orient Rd *LAN/SOMP* BN15.............. 190 D7
Orkney Ct *SALV* BN13.............. 187 J7 ②
Orltons La *HORS* RH12.............. 19 G2
Orme Rd *WTHG* BN11.............. 8 E5
Ormesby Crs *MIDOS* P022.............. 13 K1
Ormonde Av *CCH* P019.............. 7 H5
Ormonde Wy *SHOR* BN43.............. 190 E6
Orpen Pl *SELS* P020.............. 220 B5
Orpen Rd *HOVE* BN3.............. 193 L3
Orwell Rd *PSF* GU32.............. 90 B2
Osborn Crs *CCH* P019.............. 179 H5
Osborne Crs *LAN/SOMP* BN15.............. 189 K6
Osborne Crs *CCH* P019.............. 7 H5
Osborne Dr *LAN/SOMP* BN15.............. 189 K6
Osborne Rd *BRI* BN1.............. 194 A2
PSF GU32.............. 68 C8

Osborne Vls *HOVE* BN3.............. 193 J7
Osmonde Cl *FIN/BW* BN14.............. 8 F2
Osmond Rd *HOVE* BN3.............. 10 A3
Osmund Cl *CRAWW* RH10.............. 21 M6
Osney Cl *CRAWW* RH11.............. 2 D6
Osprey Dr *HISD* P011.............. 214 E1
Osprey Gdns *MIDOS* P022.............. 203 K5
Osprey Quay *EMRTH* P010.............. 175 L5
Ostlers Cl *BIL* RH14.............. 79 K5
Otard Cl *SELS* P020.............. 223 G5
Otford Cl *CRAWW* RH11.............. 40 D4
Otterbourne Crs *HAV* P09.............. 152 A7
Otter Cl *CCH* P019.............. 178 F4
Otway Cl *CRAWW* RH11.............. 20 A8 ③
Otway Rd *CCH* P019.............. 179 G3
Outerwyke Av *MIDOS* P022.............. 13 M1
Outerwyke Gdns *MIDOS* P022.............. 13 M1
MIDOS P022.............. 204 C6 ①
Outerwyke Rd *MIDOS* P022.............. 13 L1
Outram Rd *FIN/BW* BN14.............. 165 M5
The Oval *FIN/BW* BN14.............. 165 M5
LISS GU33.............. 47 J8
SALV BN13.............. 188 A7
Oval Waye *FERR* BN12.............. 208 F4
Overdene Dr *CRAWW* RH11.............. 20 B6
Overdown Ri *PTSD* BN41.............. 170 A8
Overdown Rd *MIDOS* P022.............. 204 C7
Overhill *STHW* BN42.............. 191 M3
Overhill Dr *BRI* BN1.............. 171 M7
Overhill Gdns *BRI* BN1.............. 171 M7
Overhill Wy *BRI* BN1.............. 171 M6
Overmead *SHOR* BN43.............. 190 F4
Overstrand Av *ANG/EP* BN16.............. 207 J5
Over St *BRI* BN1.............. 10 E5
Overton Crs *HAV* P09.............. 152 A7
Overton Shaw *EGRIN* RH19.............. 24 F1
Ovingdean Cl *ROTT* BN2.............. 195 L7
Ovingdean Rd *ROTT* BN2.............. 195 L8
Oving Rd *CCH* P019.............. 7 J4
Owen Cl *BURH* RH15.............. 131 G3
Owers Wy *SELS* P020.............. 216 F5
Owlbeech Wy *SWTR* RH13.............. 38 C8
Owletts *CRAWE* RH10.............. 21 L5 ④
Owlscastle Cl *HORS* RH12.............. 4 F1
Owslebury Gv *HAV* P09.............. 152 C7
Oxen Av *SHOR* BN43.............. 191 G4
Oxford Cl *SELS* P020.............. 217 G5
Oxford Ct *BRI* BN1.............. 10 F3 ②
Oxford Dr *BOGR* P021.............. 220 F1
Oxford Ms *HOVE* BN3.............. 193 K5
Oxford Pl *BRI* BN1.............. 10 F3
Oxford Rd *CRAWE* RH10.............. 40 F2
SWTR RH13.............. 4 F5
WTHG BN11.............. 8 F3
Oxford St *BOGR* P021.............. 12 A8
BRI BN1.............. 10 F3 ①

P

Pacific Wy *SELS* P020.............. 223 G7
Packham Wy *BURH* RH15.............. 109 G8 ①
Paddock Cl *HASM* GU27.............. 51 H7
Paddock Gdns *EGRIN* RH19.............. 24 D1
Paddock Gn *ANG/EP* BN16.............. 207 M2
Paddockhall Rd *HWH* RH16.............. 87 L8
Paddockhurst La *RHWH* RH17.............. 42 E8
Paddockhurst Rd *CRAWE* RH10.............. 42 D7
CRAWW RH11.............. 20 B7
Paddock La *SELS* P020.............. 222 F5
Paddocks *MIDOS* P022.............. 182 A5
The Paddocks
LAN/SOMP BN15.............. 190 A4
STEY/UB BN44.............. 168 C1
Paddock Wy *FIN/BW* BN14.............. 165 M6
HASM GU27.............. 29 H2
LIPH GU30.............. 26 C7
PSF GU32.............. 90 A2
Padwick Rd *SWTR* RH13.............. 5 L7
Pages La *WTHG* BN11.............. 211 H1
Pagewood Cl *CRAWE* RH10.............. 21 L8
Pagham Cl *EMRTH* P010.............. 175 K4
Pagham Gdns *HISD* P011.............. 215 G3
Pagham Rd *BOGR* P021.............. 220 A4
SELS P020.............. 202 B7
Pain's Flat *RHWH* RH17.............. 108 E4
Palace Pl *BRI* BN1.............. 10 F7
Palatine Rd *FIN/BW* BN12.............. 187 K8
Palings Wy *HASM* GU27.............. 51 H7
Palk Rd *HAV* P09.............. 174 A2
The Pallant *BRI* BN1.............. 187 J8
HAV P09.............. 174 C3
Pallingham Dr *CRAWW* RH11.............. 41 K1
Pallingham La *BIL* RH14.............. 100 A2
Palm Ct *SALV* BN13.............. 187 M5
Palmeira Av *HOVE* BN3.............. 193 K6
Palmeira Sq *HOVE* BN3.............. 193 K7
Palmer Cl *PUL/STOR* RH20.............. 144 A2
Palmer Rd *SELS* P020.............. 201 L3
Palmer Rd *ANG/EP* BN16.............. 185 M6
CRAWE RH10.............. 41 K1
Palmers Field Av *CCH* P019.............. 179 J4
Palmer's Rd *EMRTH* P010.............. 175 J3
Palmerston Av *FERR* BN12.............. 209 K2
Palmerston Rd *HISD* P011.............. 196 D8
Palmers Wy *SALV* BN13.............. 187 L3
Pangdean La *HPPT/KEY* BN6.............. 108 D8
Pangdene Cl *BURH* RH15.............. 130 F3
Pankhurst Av *ROTT* BN2.............. 11 K4
Pannell Cl *EGRIN* RH19.............. 24 D1
Pannett *BURH* RH15.............. 108 F8 ①
Panton Cl *EMRTH* P010.............. 175 H1 ①
The Parade *BIL* RH14.............. 33 G8
BOGR P021.............. 220 B5
CRAWE RH10.............. 3 H1
Paradise La *SWTR* RH13.............. 153 L8
Parchment St *CCH* P019.............. 6 C2
The Parchment *HAV* P09.............. 174 C3 ②
Parham Cl *ANG/EP* BN16.............. 207 J4 ②
FIN/BW BN14.............. 188 A3
LHPTN BN17.............. 206 E2
ROTT BN2.............. 11 J6

Parham Rd *CRAWW* RH11.............. 20 A5
FIN/BW BN14.............. 188 A3
Parish La *CRAWE* RH10.............. 41 G6
Park Av *HOVE* BN3.............. 192 F5
HPPT/KEY BN6.............. 151 H2
SELS P020.............. 223 H5
SHOR BN43.............. 191 H4
WTHG BN11.............. 9 K3
Park Cl *BRI* BN1.............. 172 F1
BURH RH15.............. 131 G1
FIN/BW BN14.............. 188 B5
HASM GU27.............. 29 G3
HOVE BN3.............. 192 F1
PTSD BN41.............. 192 C3
Park Copse *SELS* P020.............. 223 K3
Park Crs *EMRTH* P010.............. 175 G3
MIDH GU29.............. 94 F4
PTSD BN41.............. 192 B4
ROTT BN2.............. 213 G3
SELS P020.............. 223 J4
WTHG BN11.............. 8 E5
Park Crescent Pl *ROTT* BN2.............. 11 H2 ①
Park Crescent Rd *ROTT* BN2.............. 11 G2
Park Crescent Ter *ROTT* BN2.............. 11 G2
Park Dr *ANG/EP* BN16.............. 207 L2
ARUN BN18.............. 205 H2
FERR BN12.............. 209 G2
MIDOS P022.............. 204 E7
Parker Cl *CRAWE* RH10.............. 21 L8
Park Farm Cl *HORS* RH12.............. 37 L5
Parkfield *HORS* RH12.............. 4 D5
Parkfield Av *FIN/BW* BN14.............. 20 A6
SALV BN13.............. 8 A2
Parkfield Ct *SALV* BN13.............. 8 A2
Parkfield Rd *SALV* BN13.............. 8 A2
Park Hl *ROTT* BN2.............. 11 H6
Parklands *SHOR* BN43.............. 191 K4
Parklands Av *BOGR* P021.............. 12 B5
FERR BN12.............. 209 L3
Parklands Rd *CCH* P019.............. 6 B4
HPPT/KEY BN6.............. 151 G1
Park La *ARUN* BN18.............. 160 D8
EMRTH P010.............. 153 L4
HASM GU27.............. 51 J6
HWH RH16.............. 88 E2
PUL/STOR RH20.............. 124 E7
RCCH P018.............. 158 E7
RCCH P018.............. 199 L2
SELS P020.............. 181 J6
SELS P020.............. 223 H3
STHW BN42.............. 191 L5
SWTR RH13.............. 83 H6
SWTR RH13.............. 104 E4
Park Pde *HAV* P09.............. 152 B8 ③
Park Pl *ARUN* BN18.............. 184 B1
Park Ri *HORS* RH12.............. 4 A4
HOVE BN3.............. 192 F1
PETW GU28.............. 97 M5
Park Rd *ARUN* BN18.............. 205 H1
BRI BN1.............. 172 F1
BURH RH15.............. 131 G1
EGRIN RH19.............. 24 E3
EMRTH P010.............. 176 A3
HASM GU27.............. 28 D6
HFD BN5.............. 127 M8
HORS RH12.............. 39 G3
HWH RH16.............. 87 L8
MIDOS P022.............. 182 E6
PETW GU28.............. 98 A4
PSF GU32.............. 90 C1
RCCH P018.............. 158 A6
RHWH RH17.............. 63 J5
ROTT BN2.............. 213 G3
SELS P020.............. 223 J4
SHOR BN43.............. 191 H4
WTHG BN11.............. 9 J3
Park Rd North *HAV* P09.............. 174 B2
Park Rd South *HAV* P09.............. 174 C3
Park Road Ter *ROTT* BN2.............. 11 H6
Parkside *CRAWE* RH10.............. 3 G4
EGRIN RH19.............. 24 D3
HPPT/KEY BN6.............. 151 H1
SHOR BN43.............. 191 H3
Parkside Av *LHPTN* BN17.............. 207 G3
Parkside Ms *HORS* RH12.............. 4 E7
The Parks *PTSD* BN41.............. 192 C1 ②
Park St *BRI* BN1.............. 173 K5
HORS RH12.............. 11 H7
ROTT BN2.............. 11 H7
SELS P020.............. 58 D1
Park Ter *BOGR* P021.............. 12 B9
Park Ter East *SWTR* RH13.............. 4 E9
Park Ter West *SWTR* RH13.............. 4 E9
Park Trott *ROTT* BN2.............. 213 H3
Park Vw *CRAWW* RH11.............. 2 C5
HORL RH6.............. 15 H1
HWH RH16.............. 87 M6
Park View Rd *HOVE* BN3.............. 193 J3
Parkway *BOGR* P021.............. 221 H1
Park Wy *CRAWE* RH10.............. 21 K4
HAV P09.............. 174 B3
HORS RH12.............. 4 A4
MIDH GU29.............. 95 J2
STHW BN42.............. 192 A4
Park Way Cl *STHW* BN42.............. 192 A4
The Parkway *ANG/EP* BN16.............. 207 L2
Parry Cl *SWTR* RH13.............. 38 C8
Parry Dr *ANG/EP* BN16.............. 207 J3
Parsonage Est *EPSF* GU31.............. 70 B8
Parsonage Rd *HFD* BN5.............. 127 M7
HORS RH12.............. 4 F3
Parsonage Wy *HORS* RH12.............. 5 L8
Parsons Cl *HASM* GU27.............. 28 D4
Parsons Gn *HASM* GU27.............. 28 D4
Parson's Hl *ARUN* BN18.............. 184 C1
Parsons Wk *ARUN* BN18.............. 184 B1
Parthings La *HORS* RH12.............. 60 A4
Partridge La *HORS* RH12.............. 63 H9
Paston Pl *ROTT* BN2.............. 11 L9
Pasture Hill Rd *HWH* RH16.............. 87 M2
The Pasture *CRAWE* RH10.............. 21 K6
Patcham By-pass *BRI* BN1.............. 171 M6
Patcham Gra *BRI* BN1.............. 172 A7
Patchdean *BRI* BN1.............. 172 A7
Patching Cl *CRAWW* RH11.............. 20 A3 ①
FERR BN12.............. 187 J8
Patchings *SWTR* RH13.............. 5 J6

Paterson Rd *LISS* GU33.............. 47 M2
Paterson Wilson Rd
LHPTN BN17.............. 206 F3 ②
Pathfield Cl *HORS* RH12.............. 34 E5 ②
Pathfield Rd *HORS* RH12.............. 34 E5 ②
Pathfields *LHPTN* BN17.............. 28 C5
Path Link *CRAWE* RH10.............. 3 H2
Patricia Av *HOVE* BN3.............. 209 L3
Patricia Cl *FERR* BN12.............. 209 L3
Patrick's Cl *LISS* GU33.............. 47 K8
Patrington Cl *CRAWW* RH11.............. 40 B1
Patterdale Cl *CRAWW* RH11.............. 2 B9
Pavilion Buildings *BRI* BN1.............. 10 F7
Pavilion Cl *HPPT/KEY* BN6.............. 130 F7
Pavilion Pde *ROTT* BN2.............. 10 F7
Pavilion Rd *FIN/BW* BN14.............. 188 D5
Pavilion St *ROTT* BN2.............. 10 F7 ②
Pavilion Wy *EGRIN* RH19.............. 24 F4
Pax Cl *CRAWW* RH11.............. 19 K3
Paxmead Crs *FIN/BW* BN14.............. 189 G6
Payne Av *HOVE* BN3.............. 193 G4
Payne Cl *BOGR* P021.............. 220 B4
CRAWE RH10.............. 21 L4
Paynesfield *RHWH* RH17.............. 107 K1
Paythorne Cl *STHW* BN42.............. 191 L3 ①
Paythorne Dro *HFD* BN5.............. 148 E2
Payton Dr *BURH* RH15.............. 131 G2
Peace Cl *BRI* BN1.............. 194 D3
Peacemaker Cl *CRAWW* RH11.............. 19 M8 ②
Peace Rd *MIDH* GU29.............. 117 H2
The Peacheries *CCH* P019.............. 7 K6
Peachey Rd *SELS* P020.............. 222 F6
Peacock Cl *CCH* P019.............. 178 F4
Peacock La *BRI* BN1.............. 171 M8
Peacock's Hl *SWTR* RH13.............. 83 K6
Peacocks La *PUL/STOR* RH20.............. 124 D2
Peak La *ANG/EP* BN16.............. 208 D4
The Peak *HAV* P09.............. 152 F2
Pearson Rd *ARUN* BN18.............. 184 A2
CRAWE RH10.............. 21 J6
Peartree Cl *BURH* RH15.............. 130 F1
Peary Cl *HORS* RH12.............. 37 L6
Pease Cft *EPSF* GU31.............. 113 L1
Pebble Cl *HISD* P011.............. 214 E2 ①
Pebble Wk *ANG/EP* BN16.............. 207 H1 ①
Peckhams Copse La
SELS P020.............. 201 L3
Peeks Brook La *HORL* RH6.............. 15 M5
Peel Cl *LHPTN* BN17.............. 206 D2
Peel Rd *ROTT* BN2.............. 195 G8
Peerley Cl *SELS* P020.............. 217 H6
Peerley Rd *SELS* P020.............. 217 H6
Pegasus Cl *HASM* GU27.............. 27 L1
Pegasus Wy *EGRIN* RH19.............. 25 H1
Pegler Wy *CRAWW* RH11.............. 2 E5
Pegwell Cl *CRAWW* RH11.............. 20 A8
Pelham Ct *CRAWE* RH10.............. 40 C2
Pelham Dr *CRAWW* RH11.............. 40 B2
Pelham Pl *CRAWW* RH11.............. 40 C2
Pelham Rd *HWH* RH16.............. 88 B6
SALV BN13.............. 188 A7
Pelham Sq *BRI* BN1.............. 10 F4 ②
Pelham St *BRI* BN1.............. 10 F4
Pelham Ter *EMRTH* P010.............. 175 K4 ②
Pemberton Cl
LAN/SOMP BN15.............. 189 M5 ②
Pembley Gn *CRAWE* RH10.............. 21 L5
Pembroke Av *HOVE* BN3.............. 193 H6
WTHG BN11.............. 210 A2
Pembroke Crs *HOVE* BN3.............. 193 H6
Pembroke Gdns *HOVE* BN3.............. 193 H6
Pembroke Rd *CRAWE* RH10.............. 21 K3
Pembroke Wy *BOGR* P021.............. 202 F8
Pembury Cl *FIN/BW* BN14.............. 9 G2
HWH RH16.............. 110 C1
Pembury Rd *FIN/BW* BN14.............. 9 G1
HAV P09.............. 174 D4
Penarth Gdns *LHPTN* BN17.............. 184 D4
Pendean Burh *BURH* RH15.............. 131 K3 ②
Pende Cl *LAN/SOMP* BN15.............. 189 L4 ①
Pendine Av *WTHG* BN11.............. 211 H1
Penfold La *ANG/EP* BN16.............. 207 K1
Penfold Rd *CRAWE* RH10.............. 41 J2
FIN/BW BN14.............. 188 B2
Penfolds Pl *ARUN* BN18.............. 184 B2
Penfold Wy *STEY/UB* BN44.............. 167 L2
Penhill Rd *LAN/SOMP* BN15.............. 190 A4
Penhurst Pl *ROTT* BN2.............. 195 G6
Penland Cl *HWH* RH16.............. 87 L5
Penland Rd *HWH* RH16.............. 87 L6
Penland's Cl *STEY/UB* BN44.............. 167 L2
Penlands Ri *STEY/UB* BN44.............. 167 K2
Penlands V *STEY/UB* BN44.............. 167 K2
Penlands Wy *STEY/UB* BN44.............. 167 L2
Penleigh Cl *LAN/SOMP* BN15.............. 190 A4
Penn Cl *CRAWW* RH11.............. 20 E3 ②
MIDOS P022.............. 204 D7
Penn Crs *HWH* RH16.............. 88 B7
Pennels Cl *LIPH* GU30.............. 71 J2
Pennerly Ct *HAV* P09.............. 152 A5
Penner Rd *HAV* P09.............. 174 D3
Pennine Cl *CRAWW* RH11.............. 2 A3 ②
Penns Ct *STEY/UB* BN44.............. 146 E8
Penns Pl *EPSF* GU31.............. 91 G1
Penns Rd *PSF* GU32.............. 68 B8
Pennycord Cl *SELS* P020.............. 223 G7
Pennycress Av *FERR* BN12.............. 187 H1
Pennyfields *MIDOS* P022.............. 204 D7
Penny La *EMRTH* P010.............. 175 L4
Pensfold La *HORS* RH12.............. 34 F7
Penshurst Cl *CRAWE* RH10.............. 21 L5 ②
Penstone Pk *LAN/SOMP* BN15.............. 189 L8
Pentland Rd *SALV* BN13.............. 187 M4 ①
Penton Ct *HAV* P09.............. 152 E6
Penwarden Wy *RCCH* P018.............. 177 K5
Penwith Dr *HASM* GU27.............. 27 L3
Peperham Rd *HASM* GU27.............. 28 D4
Peppard *CRAWE* RH10.............. 21 L5
Pepper Dr *BURH* RH15.............. 130 F2 ②
BURH RH15.............. 131 G3 ②
Peppering La *ARUN* BN18.............. 163 H4
Pepperscoombe La
STEY/UB BN44.............. 168 B1
Peppersgate *SWTR* RH13.............. 84 B5
Pepper's La *STEY/UB* BN44.............. 146 F7
Perche Ct *MIDH* GU29.............. 94 E6 ①
Perching Dro *HFD* BN5.............. 148 F7
Percival Ter *ROTT* BN2.............. 11 M9
Percy Rd *HORS* RH12.............. 4 B5
Peregrine Rd *LHPTN* BN17.............. 207 G2

Perimeter Rd East HORL RH6.... 15 J5
Perimeter Rd North HORL RH6.... 15 G4
Perimeter Rd South HORL RH6.... 15 G7
Perrots La STEY/UB BN44.... 167 K2
Perry Av EGRIN RH19.... 24 F1
Perryfield La SWTR RH13.... 84 D6
Perryfield Rd CRAWW RH11.... 2 D6
Perryfields BURH RH15.... 108 F8
Perry HI ROTT BN2.... 213 K2
Perrylands HORL RH6.... 14 A5
Perrymount Rd HWH RH16.... 87 M7
Perth CI CRAWW RH11.... 20 E3
Perth Wy HORS RH12.... 5 K3
Pescott's CI SELS PO20.... 199 M7
Peskett CI SWTR RH13.... 81 C1
Peterborough Rd CRAWE RH10.... 40 F7
Peterhouse CI PUL/STOR RH20.... 203 G8
Peter Rd LAN/SOMP BN15.... 189 M6
Petersfield Rd EPSF GU31.... 90 A7
  HAV PO9.... 174 C1
  LISS GU33.... 47 H3
  MIDH GU29.... 94 A3
Peter's La SELS PO20.... 222 C4
Peter's PI SELS PO20.... 222 C4
Peter Weston CI CCH PO19.... 7 C4
Petlands Gdns HWH RH16.... 110 H4
Petlands Rd HWH RH16.... 109 M1
Pett CI ROTT BN2.... 195 G6
Petworth Av FERR BN12.... 209 K4
Petworth Ct CRAWW RH11.... 40 A1
Petworth Dr BURH RH15.... 109 H8
  HORS RH12.... 38 A5
Petworth Rd BIL RH14.... 78 C4
  BRI BN1.... 172 C6
  HASM GU27.... 28 E7
Pevensey CI CRAWE RH10.... 21 K7
  SALV BN13.... 8 A2
Pevensey Gdn WTHG BN11.... 8 A7
Pevensey Rd BOGR PO21.... 203 G8
  ROTT BN2.... 11 J1
  SWTR BN13.... 82 A3
  WTHG BN11.... 210 A3
Peverel Rd CRAWW RH11.... 19 M7
  SALV BN13.... 8 A2
Peveril La LAN/SOMP BN15.... 189 H6
Peveril Dr LAN/SOMP BN15.... 189 H6
Phillips CI CRAWE RH10.... 41 J2
Philliswood La RCCH PO18.... 134 E2
Phoenix CI CCH PO19.... 6 F7
Phoenix Crs STHW BN42.... 191 M4
Phoenix La EGRIN RH19.... 25 M6
Phoenix PI ROTT BN2.... 11 C4
Phoenix Ri BRI BN1.... 11 C4
Phoenix Wy STHW BN42.... 191 L4
Phrosso Rd WTHG BN11.... 210 A3
Pickers Gn HWH RH16.... 88 B4
Pickhurst La PUL/STOR RH20.... 100 C5
Pickhurst Rd MFD/CHID GU8.... 30 D1
Pickwell La RHWH RH17.... 86 A4
Picton St ROTT BN2.... 11 J2
Picts La SWTR RH13.... 84 A7
Pier Rd LHPTN BN17.... 206 E4
Piers Secombe CI
  PUL/STOR RH20.... 121 L7
Pigbush La BIL RH14.... 33 G5
Pigeonhouse La ANG/EP
  BN16.... 207 M3
Piggery Hall La SELS PO20.... 217 G3
Pilgrims CI FIN/BW BN14.... 8 B2
Pilgrims Wk SALV BN13.... 8 A3
Pilgrims Wy BOGR PO21.... 220 C3
Piltdown Rd ROTT BN2.... 195 G6
Pine CI BIL RH14.... 79 K3
  CRAWW RH11.... 20 D3
  MIDH GU29.... 95 C1
  PUL/STOR RH20.... 144 C1
Pine Gdns HORL RH6.... 15 H2
Pine Gv CCH PO19.... 178 D3
  EGRIN RH19.... 24 C1
  HAV PO9.... 174 D3
Pineham Copse HWH RH16.... 88 A8
Pinehurst BURH RH15.... 131 K5
  HORS.... 4 D4
Pinehurst Pk BOGR PO21.... 202 F3
Pines Av FIN/BW BN14.... 188 C5
Pine Shaw CRAWE RH10.... 21 K5
The Pines ANG/EP BN16.... 186 A8
  ARUN BN18.... 205 C1
  HORS.... 38 D7
  HWH.... 88 C8
Pine Tree CI HPPT/KEY BN6.... 130 C7
Pine Trees CI ANG/EP BN16.... 186 A5
Pinetrees CI CRAWE RH10.... 22 C1
Pine View CI HASM GU27.... 28 D4
Pine Wk BOGR PO21.... 202 E8
  LISS GU33.... 47 K6
Pine Way CI EGRIN RH19.... 24 F5
Pinewood ANG/EP BN16.... 208 B2
  HORS RH12.... 59 L1
Pinewood Ct MIDH GU29.... 95 H6
Pinewood Gdns BOGR PO21.... 221 H1
Pinewood Wy HWH RH16.... 109 L2
  MIDH GU29.... 94 F7
Pinfold CI ROTT BN2.... 195 M6
Pinkhurst La SWTR RH13.... 59 H2
Pinks La SELS PO20.... 217 L1
Pinland Rd SWTR RH13.... 127 G3
Pipers CI HOVE BN3.... 192 D1
Pipers End SWTR RH13.... 58 F1
Pipers La PETW GU28.... 53 J5
  PETW.... 54 B8
Pitcroft La EPSF GU31.... 90 C7
The Pitcroft CCH PO19.... 179 K4
Pitfold Av HASM GU27.... 27 L6
Pitfold La HASM GU27.... 27 M6
Pit Rd HPPT/KEY BN6.... 130 B7
Pitsham La MIDH GU29.... 94 E7
Pitsham Wd MIDH GU29.... 94 E6
Pitt Gdns ROTT BN2.... 195 M4
Plainfields La HORS RH12.... 172 B5
Plainwood CI CCH PO19.... 179 G2
Plaistow CI ROTT BN2.... 195 G6
Plaistow La BIL RH14.... 55 M3
  BIL.... 77 H1
  MFD/CHID GU8.... 30 E7
Plantain Crs CRAWW RH11.... 40 A1
Plantation CI SALV BN13.... 188 A5
Plantation Ri SALV BN13.... 188 B5
Plantation La LISS GU33.... 69 L2
The Plantation ANG/EP BN16.... 208 B3

PUL/STOR RH20.... 143 J3
  SALV BN13.... 188 A5
Plantation Wy PUL/STOR RH20.... 143 K3
  SALV BN13.... 188 A5
The Plat HORS RH12.... 60 B2
Platts Meadow BIL RH14.... 79 K4
The Platt HWH RH16.... 88 C7
Plaw Hatch La EGRIN RH19.... 44 F7
Playden CI ROTT BN2.... 194 F8
Pleasant La EMRTH PO10.... 198 A3
Plough CI CRAWW RH11.... 20 A4
Plough La HORS RH12.... 5 G2
Plover CI CRAWW RH11.... 20 D4
  MIDOS PO22.... 203 J3
  SELS PO20.... 217 H6
Plovers Rd SWTR RH13.... 5 K5
Plumer CI LISS GU33.... 47 M1
Plummerden La HWH RH16.... 88 C7
Plumpton Rd ROTT BN2.... 11 L4
Plumtree Cross La SWTR RH13.... 59 G8
Plymouth Av ROTT BN2.... 195 G3
Pococks La LISS GU33.... 46 C5
Polecat La SWTR RH13.... 82 D3
Poles La CRAWW RH11.... 14 D8
Polestub La RHWH RH17.... 87 G5
Poling CI CRAWW RH11.... 20 B7
Poling St ARUN BN18.... 185 H6
Pollards CRAWW RH11.... 20 B7
Pollards Dr SWTR RH13.... 5 J7
Pollard's HI SWTR RH13.... 82 B7
Polperro CI FERR BN12.... 208 E3
Pomper La HPPT/KEY BN6.... 130 E2
Pond CI BIL RH14.... 33 G8
  HWH.... 79 K4
Pond Copse La BIL RH14.... 33 G8
Pondcroft Rd HWH RH16.... 88 C5
Pondfield Rd HORS RH12.... 34 E4
Pond La SALV BN13.... 187 L6
Pond Ms SALV BN13.... 187 L6
Pond Ri PUL/STOR RH20.... 123 M3
Pond Rd SELS PO20.... 217 J7
  SHOR BN43.... 191 G5
Pondtail CI HORS RH12.... 4 E1
Pondtail Copse HORS RH12.... 37 L6
Pondtail Dr HORS RH12.... 37 L5
Pondtail Rd HORS RH12.... 4 D2
Pond Wy EGRIN RH19.... 25 J3
Pond Wood Rd CRAWE RH10.... 21 H4
Pony Farm FIN/BW BN14.... 166 A4
Pookbourne La RHWH RH17.... 107 M7
Pook La HAV PO9.... 174 E4
  RCCH PO18.... 157 H7
Pool Va BRI BN1.... 10 E8
Popes Md HASM GU27.... 28 D5
Poplar Av HOVE BN3.... 192 F1
Poplar CI BRI BN1.... 194 A2
  CRAWW RH11.... 20 D3
  HOVE BN3.... 192 F1
Poplar Gv HISD PO11.... 196 D8
Poplar Rd SALV BN13.... 187 K7
The Poplars ARUN BN18.... 183 H8
  HPPT/KEY BN6.... 151 H1
  SWTR RH13.... 5 G6
Poplar Wy MIDH GU29.... 94 F7
Poppy CI SWTR RH13.... 82 B1
Porchester CI SWTR RH13.... 82 B3
Portfield Av BRI BN1.... 172 B6
Portfield Wy CCH PO19.... 7 L1
Port Hall Av BRI BN1.... 193 M4
Port Hall Ms BRI BN1.... 10 A1
Port Hall PI BRI BN1.... 193 M4
Port Hall Rd BRI BN1.... 10 B1
Port Hall St BRI BN1.... 193 M4
Portland Av HOVE BN3.... 192 F5
Portland CI ANG/EP BN16.... 207 H2
  EGRIN RH19.... 24 F4
  HOVE BN3.... 192 G5
  WTHG BN11.... 9 G6
Portland's CI PSF GU32.... 68 E7
Portland Sq LISS GU33.... 47 J8
Portland St BRI BN1.... 10 D6
Portland Vls HOVE BN3.... 192 F5
Portsmouth La HWH RH16.... 88 A5
Portsmouth Rd LIPH GU30.... 27 L5
  LIPH GU30.... 48 C1
  LIPH GU30.... 49 H4
Portsmouth Wd HWH RH16.... 88 A4
Portsmouth Wood CI
  HWH RH16.... 88 A4
Portwood Rd HAV PO9.... 152 A4
Portway STEY/UB BN44.... 167 K2
Post Office La SELS PO20.... 201 L3
Post Vw PUL/STOR RH20.... 143 M4
Potters Cft SWTR RH13.... 5 H8
Potters Fld LISS GU33.... 47 K8
Potters Gn HWH RH16.... 88 C7
Potters La BURH RH15.... 131 G5
Potters Md LHPTN BN17.... 206 D1
Pottery La RCCH PO18.... 176 C5
Poulner CI MIDOS PO22.... 13 L3
Poulter's La FIN/BW BN14.... 188 C6
Pound CI BIL RH14.... 33 G7
  PETW.... 98 A5
Pound Farm Rd CCH PO19.... 7 J4
Poundfield La BIL RH14.... 55 J1
Pound Hill PI CRAWE RH10.... 21 K6
Pound La STEY/UB BN44.... 168 C2
  SWTR RH13.... 61 K6
  SWTR.... 103 L4
  SWTR.... 105 L4
Pound Lea HISD PO11.... 196 D7
Pound Rd ARUN BN18.... 182 A3
  SELS PO20.... 216 C3
Pound St PETW GU28.... 98 A4
The Pound BURH RH15.... 109 G8
Povey Cross Rd HORL RH6.... 14 F3
Poveys Rd BURH RH15.... 130 E1
Powell Gdns HORL RH6.... 15 L1
Powis Gv BRI BN1.... 10 B5
Powis Rd BRI BN1.... 10 B5
Powis Sq BRI BN1.... 10 B5
Powis Vls BRI BN1.... 10 C5
Poynings Dr HOVE BN3.... 193 G1
Poynings Rd CRAWW RH11.... 19 L7
Poynter Rd HOVE BN3.... 193 H4
Poyntz CI CCH PO19.... 201 G1
Pratton Av LAN/SOMP BN15.... 189 L5
Prawn CI SELS PO20.... 222 E4

Preston Av ANG/EP BN16.... 207 L3
Preston Dro BRI BN1.... 194 A2
Preston Paddock
  ANG/EP BN16.... 207 M3
Preston Park Av BRI BN1.... 194 A1
Preston Rd BRI BN1.... 193 M2
Preston St BRI BN1.... 10 B7
Prestonville Rd BRI BN1.... 10 C3
Prestwick CI CRAWW RH11.... 19 L7
Prestwick La HASM GU27.... 29 H2
Prestwood CI CRAWW RH11.... 20 D5
Prestwood La CRAWW RH11.... 19 K2
Pretoria CI LISS GU33.... 47 M2
Pretoria Rd MIDH GU29.... 94 F5
Price Wy RHWH RH17.... 66 C5
Priest Croft CI CRAWW RH11.... 20 B6
Priestley Wy CRAWE RH10.... 21 H1
  MIDOS PO22.... 204 E7
Prime CI ARUN BN18.... 182 F4
Primrose Av BURH RH15.... 108 E8
  CRAWW RH11.... 40 C1
Primrose Copse HORS RH12.... 37 L5
Primrose La LISS GU33.... 48 A8
Prince Albert St BRI BN1.... 10 E7
Prince Charles Rd STHW BN42.... 192 A4
Prince George's St HAV PO9.... 174 C3
Prince Regent's CI ROTT BN2.... 194 F8
Princes Av HOVE BN3.... 193 H6
Princes Crs HOVE BN3.... 193 H6
  ROTT BN2.... 11 C1
Princes Cft BOGR PO21.... 220 B3
Prince's Dr RCCH PO18.... 157 M3
Princes Pi BRI BN1.... 10 E7
Princes Rd PSF GU32.... 68 A8
  ROTT BN2.... 194 C4
Princess Anne Rd HORS RH12.... 34 E5
Princess Av BOGR PO21.... 221 H2
  SALV BN13.... 210 A1
Princess Margaret Rd
  HORS RH12.... 34 E5
Princes Sq HOVE BN3.... 193 H6
Princess Rd CRAWW RH11.... 2 C4
Prince's St ROTT BN2.... 10 F7
Prince's Ter ROTT BN2.... 194 F8
Prince William CI
  FIN/BW BN14.... 188 B4
Prings La SWTR RH13.... 83 L4
Prinsep Rd HOVE BN3.... 193 H4
Prinsted CI EMRTH PO10.... 176 A5
Priors Acre RCCH PO18.... 180 E1
Priors CI EMRTH PO10.... 176 B3
Priorsdean Crs HAV PO9.... 152 A8
Priors Leaze La RCCH PO18.... 176 C3
Priors Wk CRAWE RH10.... 3 H3
Priors Waye BOGR PO21.... 220 B2
Priors Wd HASM GU27.... 28 A6
Priory CI BOGR PO21.... 220 C4
  LAN/SOMP BN15.... 189 J5
  RCCH PO18.... 180 E1
  SWTR.... 8 A1
Priory Fld STEY/UB BN44.... 168 B2
Priory La CCH PO19.... 6 E3
Priory Rd ANG/EP BN16.... 207 J2
  ARUN BN18.... 184 A2
  BURH RH15.... 131 H3
  CCH PO19.... 6 E3
  FROW.... 45 H6
  HPPT/KEY BN6.... 130 F7
Priory Wy HWH RH16.... 88 A8
Proctor CI CRAWE RH10.... 21 K8
The Promenade EMRTH PO10.... 175 J5
Prospect La HAV PO9.... 152 E6
Prospect PI CRAWW RH11.... 2 C4
  WTHG BN11.... 9 G7
Providence PI BRI BN1.... 10 E5
Providence Ter WTHG BN11.... 9 J5
The Providence CCH PO19.... 6 D3
Pruetts La LISS GU33.... 69 J3
Pryors La BOGR PO21.... 220 D2
Puckshott Wy HASM GU27.... 28 E4
Puffin Rd CRAWW RH11.... 19 L7
Pulborough CI ROTT BN2.... 195 G5
Pulborough Rd
  PUL/STOR RH20.... 143 J2
Pulborough Wy MIDOS PO22.... 204 E6
Pulens Crs EPSF GU31.... 68 F8
Pulens La EPSF GU31.... 68 F8
Punch Copse La CRAWE RH10.... 3 K2
Punches La SELS PO20.... 201 L7
Purbeck PI LHPTN BN17.... 206 D3
Purbeck Wy HAV PO9.... 152 A8
Purcell Rd CRAWW RH11.... 40 A1
Purley CI CRAWW RH11.... 41 L1
The Purrocks PSF GU32.... 68 C7
Purton Rd HORS RH12.... 4 B4
Putmans La EPSF GU31.... 91 J6
Puttock CI HASM GU27.... 27 L7
Pycroft CI HISD PO11.... 196 F1
Pyecombe St CRAWW RH11.... 40 A1
Pyecombe St POY/PYE BN45.... 150 B6
Pyrford CI BOGR PO21.... 220 C2

Q

The Quadrangle FIN/BW BN14.... 165 M7
The Quadrant FERR BN12.... 209 K1
  HPPT/KEY BN6.... 131 H8
Quail CI HORS RH12.... 37 L5
Quakers La HWH RH16.... 88 B7
Quantock CI CRAWW RH11.... 2 A3
  SALV BN13.... 188 A4
Quantock Rd SALV BN13.... 188 A4
The Quarries SWTR RH13.... 61 L6
Quarry Bank Rd BRI BN1.... 194 C2
Quarry CI BURH RH15.... 131 L1
  HORS RH12.... 38 A6
Quarry HI RHWH RH17.... 87 K6
Quarry La CCH PO19.... 7 J7
Quarry Ri EGRIN RH19.... 25 H1
Quarry Wy SWTR RH13.... 82 A3
Quarterbrass Farm Rd
  HORS RH12.... 37 L5
The Quashetts FIN/BW BN14.... 9 H1
  FIN/BW BN14.... 188 E7
Quayside LHPTN BN17.... 206 C3

Q

Quebec St ROTT BN2.... 11 H5
Queen Alexandra Av
  HOVE BN3.... 193 H1
Queen Caroline CI
  HOVE BN3.... 193 H1
Queen Elizabeth Av
  BURH.... 131 G2
Queen Elizabeth Rd HORS RH12.... 34 E5
Queen Mary Av HOVE BN3.... 193 H1
Queen's Av CCH PO19.... 6 C9
Queensbury Ms BRI BN1.... 10 B7
Queensdown School Rd
  BRI BN1.... 194 D1
Queens Dr HPPT/KEY BN6.... 131 G8
Queens Flds East BOGR PO21.... 203 G8
Queens Flds West BOGR PO21.... 202 F8
Queen's Gdns BRI BN1.... 10 E5
  CCH PO19.... 6 C9
  HOVE BN3.... 193 K7
Queens Ga SHOR BN43.... 191 K5
Queens La ARUN BN18.... 184 C1
Queensmead BOGR PO21.... 220 A4
Queen's Park Ri ROTT BN2.... 11 K5
Queen's Park Ter ROTT BN2.... 11 J4
Queen's PI BRI BN1.... 10 F3
  HOVE BN3.... 193 K6
  SHOR BN43.... 191 G5
Queen Sq BRI BN1.... 10 D6
Queens Sq MIDH GU29.... 94 B2
Queen St ARUN BN18.... 184 C1
Queensway BOGR PO21.... 12 D7
  CRAWE RH10.... 3 G4
  EGRIN RH19.... 24 F4
  HISD PO11.... 196 D1
  LAN/SOMP BN15.... 189 M6
  ROTT BN2.... 11 L5
  SWTR.... 60 D3
Queen Victoria Av HOVE BN3.... 193 H1
Querneby CI SHOR BN43.... 191 L5
Quest CI CCH PO19.... 7 H5

R

Racecourse Wy HORL RH6.... 15 G5
Rackfield HASM GU27.... 27 L5
Rackham CI CRAWW RH11.... 2 E8
  SALV BN13.... 188 A2
Rackham Rd ANG/EP BN16.... 207 J5
  ARUN BN18.... 142 A5
  SALV BN13.... 188 A7
Rackham St ARUN BN18.... 142 A5
  PUL/STOR RH20.... 142 D4
Racton Rd EMRTH PO10.... 175 J1
Radford Rd CRAWE RH10.... 15 K8
  MIDOS PO22.... 12 B2
Radinden Dr HOVE BN3.... 193 L3
Radinden Manor Rd
  HOVE BN3.... 193 K4
Radnor CI SALV BN13.... 188 A8
Radnor Rd SALV BN13.... 188 A8
Raglan Av SALV BN13.... 187 M7
Railey Rd CRAWE RH10.... 3 H2
Rails La HISD PO11.... 214 E2
Railway Ap EGRIN RH19.... 24 E3
  WTHG BN11.... 8 F3
Railway Rd LISS GU33.... 48 A3
Railway St BRI BN1.... 10 D4
Rainbow Wy
  PUL/STOR RH20.... 144 A1
Rake Rd LIPH GU30.... 71 G2
  LISS GU33.... 47 K8
Rakers Rdg HORS RH12.... 4 E2
Raleigh CI SHOR BN43.... 190 F6
Raleigh Crs FERR BN12.... 209 L1
Raleigh Rd BOGR PO21.... 220 D1
Raleigh Wk CRAWE RH10.... 3 H9
Raleigh Wy FERR BN12.... 187 K8
Rambledown La
  PUL/STOR RH20.... 123 K6
Ramblers Wy CRAWW RH11.... 40 C3
Ramilies Gdns MIDOS PO22.... 204 D7
Ramsey CI HORL RH6.... 15 L1
  HORS.... 4 D1
Ramsey Rd HISD PO11.... 214 D1
Ramshill EPSF GU31.... 68 D8
Rams La MFD/CHID GU8.... 32 B2
Ranelagh Rd HAV PO9.... 174 A3
Ranelagh Vls HOVE BN3.... 193 H3
Ranmore CI CRAWW RH11.... 40 C4
Ransome CI CRAWW RH11.... 39 L1
Ranville CI PETW GU28.... 97 M5
Ranworth CI MIDOS PO22.... 13 K2
Raphael Rd HOVE BN3.... 193 G5
Rapley Av PUL/STOR RH20.... 143 J2
Rascals CI SWTR RH13.... 82 B1
Rastrick CI BURH RH15.... 131 G3
Ratham La RCCH PO18.... 177 K4
Rathlin Rd CRAWW RH11.... 40 C1
Raughmere Dr CCH PO19.... 157 G8
Raven La CRAWW RH11.... 20 D4
Ravensbourne Av SHOR BN43.... 191 G3
Ravensbourne CI
  SHOR BN43.... 191 G3
Ravenscroft PUL/STOR RH20.... 143 L4
Ravenscroft Ct HORS RH12.... 4 C5
Raven's Rd BOGR PO21.... 220 D1
Ravens Wy MIDOS PO22.... 203 J6
Ravenswood Rd BURH RH15.... 131 J1
Raworth CI CRAWE RH10.... 21 K8
Raycroft CI BOGR PO21.... 221 G2
Rayden CI LHPTN BN17.... 206 F3
Reading Rd ROTT BN2.... 195 G8

Readon CI EPSF GU31.... 68 D8
Reapers CI HORS RH12.... 4 F2
Record Rd EMRTH PO10.... 175 H5
Rectory CI PUL/STOR RH20.... 122 D2
  PUL/STOR RH20.... 125 H1
  PUL/STOR RH20.... 143 L3
  RDKG RH5.... 16 C1
  SHOR BN43.... 191 H5
Rectory Farm Rd
  LAN/SOMP BN15.... 189 J5
Rectory Gdns FIN/BW BN14.... 188 D7
Rectory La ANG/EP BN16.... 186 A7
  CRAWW RH11.... 20 A4
  LIPH GU30.... 26 E5
  PUL/STOR RH20.... 122 C2
  PUL/STOR RH20.... 124 E6
  SELS PO20.... 223 H2
Rectory Rd FIN/BW BN14.... 8 B1
  HAV PO9.... 174 B1
  PUL/STOR RH20.... 143 L3
  SHOR BN43.... 191 K5
Rectory Wk LAN/SOMP BN15.... 189 J5
  PUL/STOR RH20.... 143 L3
Red Admiral St HORS RH12.... 5 H1
Redbridge Gv HAV PO9.... 174 A1
Redbridge La RHWH RH17.... 64 C5
Redcross St BRI BN1.... 10 F4
Red Deer CI SWTR RH13.... 61 L3
Redditch CI CRAWW RH11.... 39 M2
Redford Av HORS RH12.... 4 A4
Redgarth Ct EGRIN RH19.... 24 C1
Redhill CI BRI BN1.... 171 K7
Redhill Dr BRI BN1.... 171 K8
Redhill Rd HAV PO9.... 152 C3
Red House Ct EPSF GU31.... 70 C8
Redkiln CI SWTR RH13.... 5 J5
Redkiln Wy HORS RH12.... 5 J5
Redlands La EMRTH PO10.... 153 J8
  SELS PO20.... 217 G1
Red La SWTR RH13.... 103 L3
Red Lion St MIDH GU29.... 95 G5
Redlynch CI HAV PO9.... 152 A8
Redvers Rd ROTT BN2.... 195 G1
Redwing CI LHPTN BN17.... 184 D8
  SWTR RH13.... 5 K6
Redwood CI CRAWE RH10.... 20 F4
  SALV BN13.... 187 K7
Redwood Dr HWH RH16.... 109 L2
Redwood Gv HAV PO9.... 152 C8
Redwood PI BOGR PO21.... 220 F2
Reed CI PUL/STOR RH20.... 143 K3
Reedings CRAWW RH11.... 19 L8
Reed Pond Wk HWH RH16.... 88 B8
Reed's La HPPT/KEY BN6.... 129 L2
  LISS GU33.... 48 A6
  SWTR RH13.... 82 C1
Reef CI LHPTN BN17.... 207 G4
Reeves HI BRI BN1.... 172 C7
Regal Dr EGRIN RH19.... 25 C4
Regency Ms BRI BN1.... 10 B6
Regency Rd BRI BN1.... 10 C7
Regency Sq BRI BN1.... 10 C7
Regent La LAN/SOMP BN15.... 190 C6
Regent HI BRI BN1.... 10 C6
Regent Rw BRI BN1.... 10 C6
Regents CI CRAWW RH11.... 40 D2
Regents Ct HAV PO9.... 174 C4
Regent St BRI BN1.... 10 E6
Regents Wy BOGR PO21.... 203 G8
Regis Av BOGR PO21.... 220 C3
Regis Ct BOGR PO21.... 12 F6
Reigate CI CRAWE RH10.... 21 L3
Reigate Rd BRI BN1.... 193 L3
  HORL RH6.... 14 E2
  WTHG BN11.... 210 A2
Renn Gdns PUL/STOR RH20.... 124 F7
Renoir Ct MIDOS PO22.... 203 H6
Renoir Ms MIDOS PO22.... 203 H6
Renton CI BIL RH14.... 79 L4
Reservoir La PSF GU32.... 68 C7
Rest-a-wyle Av HISD PO11.... 196 D7
Rew La CCH PO19.... 179 G1
Reynard CI HORS RH12.... 38 C7
Reynolds La ARUN BN18.... 160 E3
Reynolds Rd CRAWW RH11.... 2 C2
  HOVE BN3.... 193 G5
Rhodes Wy CRAWE RH10.... 3 J8
Rice Br RHWH RH17.... 107 L5
Rices HI EGRIN RH19.... 24 F3
Richardson Rd HOVE BN3.... 193 G5
Richmond Av BOGR PO21.... 221 H1
  CCH PO19.... 179 G1
Richmond CI ANG/EP BN16.... 207 M2
  HISD PO11.... 196 D3
Richmond Ct CRAWE RH10.... 3 G6
  WTHG BN11.... 8 E5
Richmond Dr HISD PO11.... 196 D3
Richmond Pde ROTT BN2.... 10 F5
Richmond PI ROTT BN2.... 10 F4
Richmond Rd BOGR PO21.... 12 D6
  HORS RH12.... 4 D6
  RCCH PO18.... 179 M1
  WTHG BN11.... 8 D6
Richmond Rd North
  BOGR.... 12 E5
Richmond St ROTT BN2.... 11 H5
Richmond Wy EGRIN RH19.... 25 G4
Rickfield CRAWW RH11.... 20 B7
Rickman's La BIL RH14.... 55 J4
Riders La HAV PO9.... 152 B8
The Ride BIL RH14.... 55 K2
  BRI BN1.... 171 K8
Ridge CI PTSD BN41.... 170 B8
Ridgehurst Dr HORS RH12.... 60 A3
Ridge Rd BRI BN1.... 173 J4
Ridgeside CRAWE RH10.... 3 J3
Ridgeside Av BRI BN1.... 171 M7
The Ridge HORS RH12.... 34 C1
Ridge Vw BRI BN1.... 172 F7
Ridge Wy EGRIN RH19.... 24 F5
Ridge Wy HWH RH16.... 110 C2
Ridgeway PTSD BN41.... 192 A3
Ridgeway SU STHW BN42.... 192 A3
Ridgeway Gdns ROTT BN2.... 195 M5
The Ridgeway BURH RH15.... 109 J8
  HASM GU27.... 51 J6
  HORL RH6.... 15 H3
  HORS RH12.... 4 A4
Ridgewood Av ROTT BN2.... 213 K1

Ridgway HAV PO9 174 A3
Ridgway Cl ROTT BN2 195 L4
The Ridgway MIDOS PO22 204 C8 1
ROTT BN2 195 L4
The Ridings ANG/EP BN16 208 A3
ARUN BN18 182 B2
BOGR PO21 220 D3
BURH RH15 131 K3
CRAWE RH10 21 L5
LISS GU33 47 L8
STEY/UB BN44 167 L3
Ridleys EGRIN RH19 43 M6
Rife La SELS PO20 222 D4
Rifeside Gdns FERR BN12 208 F1 4
Rife Wy FERR BN12 208 F2
MIDOS PO22 13 J4
Rigden Rd HOVE BN3 193 K4
Riley Rd ROTT BN2 194 D3
Rillside CRAWE RH10 41 H1
Rill Wk EGRIN RH19 25 J3
Rimmer Cl CRAWW RH11 40 C4 3
Ringley Av HORL RH6 15 H2
Ringley Rd HORS RH12 5 H4
Ringmer Cl BRI BN1 172 F8
Ringmer Rd BRI BN1 172 F8
SALV BN13 187 M7
Ring Rd LAN/SOMP BN15 189 M3
Ringwood Cl CRAWE RH10 3 H7
Ripley Rd WTHG BN11 210 A1
Ripon Gdns BOGR PO21 220 F1 4
The Rise CRAWE RH10 21 K6
EGRIN RH19 24 F4
HWH RH16 88 C7
PTSD BN41 192 A2
SWTR RH13 127 H1
Ritchie Cl CRAWE RH10 41 K2 5
Rival Moor Rd EPSF GU31 90 E2
River Cl SHOR BN43 190 F6
Riverhill La PUL/STOR RH20 98 E6
River La PETW GU28 74 D8
PUL/STOR RH20 121 H8
River Md CRAWW RH11 20 B3
HORS RH12 4 A9
Rivermead PUL/STOR RH20 122 E3
River Rd ARUN BN18 184 C2
LHPTN BN17 206 D3
Riverside CCH PO19 7 H3
FROW RH18 45 M1
HORL RH6 15 H3
HORS RH12 60 B2
PTSD BN41 191 M6
PUL/STOR RH20 143 L2 2
SHOR BN43 191 G6
STEY/UB BN44 168 B2
Riverside Cl LISS GU33 47 J8
Riverside Rd SHOR BN43 191 G6
River's Rd HWH RH16 87 L1
River St EMRTH PO10 153 L8
River Wy HAV PO9 174 D1
Rixons Cl RHWH RH17 67 K7
Rixons Orch RHWH RH17 67 K7
Robell Wy PUL/STOR RH20 143 M1
Roberts Cl SWTR RH13 60 A8
Robertson Rd BRI BN1 193 L2
Roberts Rd LAN/SOMP BN15 189 M8
LISS GU33 47 M2
Robert St BRI BN1 10 E5
Robert Wy HORS RH12 38 A5
Robin Cl CRAWW RH11 20 D4
EGRIN RH19 24 F2
LHPTN BN17 184 D8
SWTR RH13 82 B2
Robin Davis Cl ROTT BN2 194 F4
Robin Dene ROTT BN2 194 F8
Robin Hood La HORS RH12 36 F7
Robin Rd HPPT/KEY BN6 130 E2
Robin's Cl SELS PO20 223 G4
Robins Dr BOGR PO21 220 E1
Robins La MIDH GU29 71 L5
Robinson Cl
LAN/SOMP BN15 189 M6 6
Robinson Rd CRAWW RH11 2 E5
Robson Rd WTHG BN11 209 M2
Rochester Cl CCH PO19 179 G3
SALV BN13 187 J7 10
Rochester Gdns HOVE BN3 193 L6
Rochester St ROTT BN2 11 L6
Rochester Wy BOGR PO21 220 E1
Rockall Cl ANG/EP BN16 207 H1 12
Rockdale Dr GSHT GU26 27 L1 1
Rock Gdns BOGR PO21 12 C9
Rock Gv ROTT BN2 11 M9
Rockingham Cl SALV BN13 187 M6
Rock La PUL/STOR RH20 144 F3
Rock Pl ROTT BN2 11 H8
Rock Rd PUL/STOR RH20 144 B1
Rocks La RHWH RH17 65 G3
The Rocks EGRIN RH19 25 K6
Rock St ROTT BN2 194 F8
Rocky La HWH RH16 109 K3
Rodmell Av ROTT BN2 213 L3
Rodmell Rd SALV BN13 187 M7
Rodney Cl BOGR PO21 220 D1 5
Rodney Crs ARUN BN18 205 L1
Roebuck Cl SWTR RH13 38 C8
Roedale Rd BRI BN1 194 C3
Roedean Crs ROTT BN2 195 H8
Roedean Hts ROTT BN2 195 H8
Roedean Pth ROTT BN2 212 C1
Roedean Rd ROTT BN2 195 G8
SALV BN13 187 M6
Roedean V ROTT BN2 212 C1
Roedeer Copse HASM GU27 27 M6
Roffey Cl HORL RH6 15 G1
Roffye Ct HORS RH12 5 L3
Rogate Cl LAN/SOMP BN15 189 J5
SALV BN13 188 B6
Rogate Rd SALV BN13 188 B6
Roger's La FIN/BW BN14 165 M8
Rogers Md HISD PO11 196 C1
Rolfe Dr BURH RH15 131 L1
Rollaston Pk ARUN BN18 205 J2
Romaine Cl BURH RH15 109 L7
Roman Acre LHPTN BN17 206 D2
Roman Crs STHW BN42 191 M4
Roman Landing SELS PO20 216 B2
Roman Rd HOVE BN3 192 E6
STEY/UB BN44 167 M2
STHW BN42 191 M4
Roman Wk LAN/SOMP BN15 189 J5
Roman Wy BIL RH14 79 M3
CCH PO19 178 C6
STHW BN42 191 M4
Romany Cl PTSD BN41 192 C4
Romany Rd SALV BN13 187 J7
Romney Broadwalk
MIDOS PO22 203 H6
Romney Garth SELS PO20 223 H5 4
Romney Rd ROTT BN2 213 H3
WTHG BN11 210 A3
Romsey Cl BRI BN1 194 C2
Rona Cl CRAWW RH11 2 A9
Rookcross La SWTR RH13 104 B8
Rookery Cl BRI BN1 193 M3
Rookery La SELS PO20 219 G4
The Rookery EMRTH PO10 175 K3
Rookery Wy HWH RH16 109 M3
Rooksbury Cft HAV PO9 152 D7 3
Rook Wy HORS RH12 37 M6
Rookwood La SELS PO20 198 D8
Rookwood Pk HORS RH12 60 B1
Rookwood Rd SELS PO20 216 D2
Ropeland Wy HORS RH12 37 M5
Ropes La HASM GU27 51 K7
Ropetackle SHOR BN43 190 F5
Rope Wk LHPTN BN17 206 D3
SHOR BN43 190 F5
Ropley Rd HAV PO9 152 E7
Rosamund Rd CRAWE RH10 21 J8
Rose Av MIDOS PO22 205 G7
Rosebarn Cl BURH RH15 131 K3
Rosebery Av FERR BN12 209 M2
ROTT BN2 195 K4
Rose Cottage La RHWH RH17 64 B8
Rosecroft Cl
LAN/SOMP BN15 189 M7 4
Rosedale Cl CRAWW RH11 20 B8
Rosedene Cl ROTT BN2 195 M6
Rose Green Rd BOGR PO21 220 C1
Rosehill BIL RH14 79 L3
Rose Hl ROTT BN2 11 G2
Rose Hill Cl BRI BN1 10 F2
Rose Hill Ter BRI BN1 10 E2
Roseleigh Gdns RHWH RH17 111 G1
Rosemary Av STEY/UB BN44 167 M1
Rosemary Cl BOGR PO21 220 D1 4
PUL/STOR RH20 143 L3 7
RHWH RH17 87 J6
STEY/UB BN44 167 M1
Rosemary Dr SHOR BN43 191 J3
Rosemary La CRAN GU6 32 E4
HORL RH6 15 J2
PETW GU28 98 A4
Rosemead LHPTN BN17 206 F3
Rose Wk FERR BN12 209 M2
Rosier Wy BIL RH14 79 M6
Rossalyn Cl BOGR PO21 220 C1
Ross Cl BOGR PO21 220 C2
CRAWE RH10 3 J9
Rossiter Rd LAN/SOMP BN15 189 M4
Rosslyn Av SHOR BN43 191 H5
Rosslyn Ct SHOR BN43 191 G4
Rosslyn Rd SHOR BN43 191 G5
Rossmore Cl CRAWE RH10 21 L2 2
Rothbury Rd HOVE BN3 192 E5
Rotherbank Farm La LISS GU33 47 J6
Rotherbridge La PETW GU28 97 L7
Rother Cl EPSF GU31 68 F8
PUL/STOR RH20 144 A1
Rother Crs CRAWW RH11 19 M8
Rotherfield Cl BRI BN1 172 C6
Rotherfield Crs BRI BN1 172 C7
Rother La EPSF GU31 93 H3
Rothermead PETW GU28 97 M5
Rotherwick Cl HAV PO9 152 E7
Rothesay Cl SALV BN13 187 M8
Rothley Cha HWH RH16 88 A8
Rotten Rw SELS PO20 218 E1
The Rotyngs ROTT BN2 213 G2
Rough Wy HORS RH12 5 K1
Roundabout Copse
PUL/STOR RH20 123 L7
Roundabout La
PUL/STOR RH20 123 L7
The Roundabouts LISS GU33 47 K7 1
Roundhill Crs ROTT BN2 11 H1
Round Hill Rd BRI BN1 11 G1
Roundhouse Meadow
EMRTH PO10 175 K5
Roundle Av MIDOS PO22 204 C6
Roundle Rd MIDOS PO22 204 D6
Roundle Square Rd
MIDOS PO22 204 C7
Round Piece SELS PO20 222 E4
Round Piece La SELS PO20 222 D4
Roundstone By-pass Rd
ANG/EP BN16 208 A1
Roundstone Crs ANG/EP BN16 208 A2
Roundstone Dr ANG/EP BN16 208 B2
Roundstone La ANG/EP BN16 208 B1
Roundstone Wy SELS PO20 223 H4
Roundway BRI BN1 172 F7
The Roundway ANG/EP BN16 207 L4
Roundwood La HWH RH16 88 A4
Rowan Av HOVE BN3 192 F3
Rowan Cl CRAWE RH10 3 J4
HORS RH12 38 C7
HWH RH16 88 C8
PTSD BN41 192 A3
Rowan Dr BIL RH14 79 K3
Rowan Rd HAV PO9 174 D1
The Rowans GSHT GU26 27 L2 1
WTHG BN11 8 A6
Rowan Wy HORS RH12 38 D7
MIDOS PO22 203 K5
ROTT BN2 195 M8
Rowbury Rd HAV PO9 152 A6
Rowfant Cl CRAWE RH10 21 M6
Rowhill La RHWH RH17 64 F5
Rowhook Rd HORS RH12 36 A3
Rowin Cl HISD PO11 215 G2
Rowlands Rd HORS RH12 38 B6
WTHG BN11 8 C7
Rowner Rd BIL RH14 79 H4
Rownhams Rd HAV PO9 152 A7
Rowplatt La EGRIN RH19 23 M1
Roxburgh Cl SALV BN13 188 A5 3
Royal Cl CCH PO19 7 J5
Royal Crs ROTT BN2 11 J8
Royal Crescent Ms ROTT BN2 11 J8
Royal Gdns HAV PO9 152 D3
Royal George Pde SHOR BN43 191 J3
Royal George Rd BURH RH15 130 F1
Royce Cl SELS PO20 216 D3
Royce Rd CRAWE RH10 21 H1
Royce Wy SELS PO20 216 D3
Royles Cl ROTT BN2 213 H2
Royston Cl CRAWE RH10 21 H2 1
The Roystons ANG/EP BN16 208 A3
Ruckmans La RDKG RH5 16 B6
Rucrofts Cl BOGR PO21 221 G1
Rudgwick Av FERR BN12 209 H2
Rudgwick Cl ANG/EP BN16 207 J4 5
Rudgwick Rd CRAWW RH11 20 A5 3
Rudwick's Cl MIDOS PO22 204 D8
Rudwick Wy MIDOS PO22 204 D8
Rudyard Cl ROTT BN2 195 M4
Rudyard Rd ROTT BN2 195 M4
Rufwood CRAWE RH10 23 G4
Rugby Pl ROTT BN2 194 F8
Rugby Rd BRI BN1 194 B3
Ruislip Gdns BOGR PO21 220 D2
Rumbolds Cl CCH PO19 7 J6
Rumbolds Hl MIDH GU29 95 G5
Rumbolds La HWH RH16 109 L2
Runcorn Cl CRAWW RH11 39 M2
Runcton La SELS PO20 201 M6
Runnymede Ct BOGR PO21 203 G7 1
Rusbridge Cl BOGR PO21 202 E8
Rushams Rd HORS RH12 4 A7
Rushes Rd PSF GU32 68 B8
The Rushes HWH RH16 88 D8 1
Rushetts Pl CRAWW RH11 20 D3
Rushetts Rd CRAWW RH11 20 C3
Rushfield Rd LISS GU33 69 J1
Rushlake Cl BRI BN1 172 F7
Rushlake Rd BRI BN1 172 F6
Rushwood Cl HWH RH16 88 C8 2
Ruskin Cl CRAWE RH10 21 K3 3
SELS PO20 223 H5
Ruskin Rd FIN/BW BN14 9 L1
HOVE BN3 193 G4
Rusper Rd BRI BN1 172 E6
CRAWW RH11 20 A6
HORS RH12 5 J3
HORS RH12 18 E3
HORS RH12 38 A5
RDKG RH5 17 L1
SALV BN13 188 A7
Rusper Rd South SALV BN13 188 A7
Ruspers BURH RH15 131 L2
Ruspers Keep CRAWW RH11 20 A5 4
Russell Cl FIN/BW BN14 188 F7
Russell Crs BRI BN1 10 B2
Russell Pl BRI BN1 10 C7
Russell Rd BRI BN1 10 C7
HAV PO9 174 C1
SELS PO20 216 F5
Russell's Cl ANG/EP BN16 208 C2
Russells Crs HORL RH6 15 H2
Russells Dr LAN/SOMP BN15 189 M7
Russell Sq BRI BN1 10 B6
Russell St CCH PO19 7 J4
Russell Wy CRAWE RH10 3 L5
EPSF GU31 90 D2
Russet Cl HORL RH6 15 K1 3
Russet Gdns EMRTH PO10 175 L4
Rustington Rd BRI BN1 172 B7
Rustlings Cl HWH RH16 88 C7 2
Ruston Av ANG/EP BN16 207 L3
Ruston Cl CRAWE RH10 41 K1 3
Ruston Pk ANG/EP BN16 207 M3
Rutherford Wy CRAWE RH10 21 H1
Rutherwick Cl HORL RH6 15 G1
Rutland Gdns HOVE BN3 193 G5
Rutland Rd HOVE BN3 193 H5
Rutland Wy SELS PO20 7 M1
Rycroft Cl FERR BN12 209 K3
Rydal Cl ANG/EP BN16 207 H2 5
CRAWW RH11 19 L8
Ryde Rd ROTT BN2 11 L2
Ryders Wy HORS RH12 38 A5 1
Rye Ash CRAWE RH10 3 M1
Rye Cl ROTT BN2 213 M2
WTHG BN11 8 A8
Ryecroft HAV PO9 174 E3 4
HWH RH16 109 L1
Ryecroft Dr HORS RH12 60 B1
Ryecroft Gdns FERR BN12 209 K2 5
Ryecroft La PUL/STOR RH20 143 L3
Ryecroft Meadow SWTR RH13 61 K6
Ryecroft Rd RHWH RH17 107 K1
Rye Farm La SWTR RH13 81 H2
Ryefield Cl EPSF GU31 90 F1
Ryelands CRAWW RH11 20 B7 4
Ryelands Dr ROTT BN2 194 E1

S

Sabre Rd EMRTH PO10 197 K1
Sack La MIDOS PO22 203 M2
Sackville Cl EGRIN RH19 24 D1
Sackville Crs FIN/BW BN14 9 K1
Sackville Gdns HOVE BN3 193 G6
Sackville La EGRIN RH19 24 C1
Sackville Rd FIN/BW BN14 9 J2
HOVE BN3 193 H6
Sackville Wy FIN/BW BN14 9 K2
Saddle La SELS PO20 222 F4
Saddler Rw CRAWE RH10 2 F9
Saddlers Cl BURH RH15 131 L3
Sadler St BOGR PO21 12 D8
Sadlers Wk EMRTH PO10 175 K4
Sadler Wy ROTT BN2 195 G6
Saffron Cl CRAWW RH11 40 B1 3
SHOR BN43 191 K3
The Saffrons BURH RH15 108 F7
St Agnes Rd EGRIN RH19 24 F2
St Alban's Rd HAV PO9 152 D8
St Andrew's Cl FERR BN12 208 F2
SELS PO20 180 D6
St Andrew's Rd BRI BN1 194 B3 1
BURH RH15 131 L1 1
CRAWW RH11 19 L7
HISD PO11 214 E2
PTSD BN41 192 C5
SALV BN13 188 A8
St Annes Rd CRAWE RH10 21 K2
St Ann's Hl MIDH GU29 95 G5 3
St Anselm's Rd FIN/BW BN14 8 C2
St Anthony's Wk BOGR PO21 220 E1 3
St Anthony's Wy
ANG/EP BN16 207 L2 1
St Aubin Cl CRAWW RH11 40 A2 2
St Aubin's Pk HISD PO11 214 A1
St Aubins Rd FERR BN12 209 G4
St Aubyns HOVE BN3 193 H6
St Aubyn's Crs PTSD BN41 192 C5 2
St Aubyn's Md ROTT BN2 213 H3
St Aubyn's Rd PTSD BN41 192 B5
St Aubyns South HOVE BN3 193 H7 1
St Augustine Cl RHWH RH17 111 G1 4
St Augustine Rd LHPTN BN17 206 F4
St Bartholomews Cl CCH PO19 6 B4 1
St Bernards Ct
LAN/SOMP BN15 189 M7 5
St Blaises Rd RCCH PO18 158 D8
St Botolph's Rd WTHG BN11 8 C3
St Brelades Rd CRAWW RH11 40 A2
St Catherines Rd CRAWE RH10 21 K3
LHPTN BN17 206 E4
St Christopher's Cl
CCH PO19 178 D6 2
HORS RH12 4 D4
St Christopher's Rd HASM GU27 28 B6
St Clares Av HAV PO9 152 A5
St Clement Rd CRAWW RH11 40 A2
St Cuthmans Cl ROTT BN2 194 F6
St Cuthman's Rd
STEY/UB BN44 146 E7
St Cyriacs CCH PO19 6 D3
St Dunstan's Rd SALV BN13 8 A3
St Edmund Cl CRAWW RH11 20 E3 8
St Edmund's Rd HWH RH16 110 A1
St Edward's Cl EGRIN RH19 24 D3
St Elmo Rd FIN/BW BN14 8 D2
St Flora's Cl LHPTN BN17 207 G3 1
St Flora's Rd LHPTN BN17 207 G3
St Francis Cl HWH RH16 109 M2
St Francis Pl HAV PO9 174 B1
St Gabriels Rd BIL RH14 79 L4
St George's Av HAV PO9 174 E3
St Georges Cl HORL RH6 15 J1
St Georges Ct CRAWW RH11 2 F1
St George's Dr CCH PO19 201 G1
St George's Gdns SWTR RH13 5 H4
St George's La HPPT/KEY BN6 130 C7
St George's Ms BRI BN1 10 F5
St George's Pl BRI BN1 10 F4
HPPT/KEY BN6 130 C7
St George's Rd HISD PO11 214 A1
ROTT BN2 11 M9 3
SWTR RH13 127 G1 1
WTHG BN11 9 L4
St Georges's Cl SELS PO20 223 H4
St George's Ter ROTT BN2 11 J8
St Georges Wk SELS PO20 182 A5
St Giles Cl SHOR BN43 191 J4
St Helen's Crs HOVE BN3 192 E1
St Helen's Dr HOVE BN3 192 E1
St Helen's Rd HISD PO11 214 A1
ROTT BN2 11 L2
St Helier Cl CRAWW RH11 40 B2 7
St Helier Rd FERR BN12 209 G4
St Heliers Av HOVE BN3 192 F5
St Hermans Rd HISD PO11 214 F2
St Hilda's Cl CRAWE RH10 21 K3 4
HORL RH6 15 J1
Saint Hill Rd EGRIN RH19 24 C6
St Hugh's Cl CRAWE RH10 21 K3
St Itha Cl SELS PO20 223 G6
St Itha Rd SELS PO20 223 G6
St James Av LAN/SOMP BN15 189 M4
St James' Rd CCH PO19 7 J3
EMRTH PO10 175 J4
St James's Av ROTT BN2 11 H8
St James's Cl SELS PO20 199 M7
St James's Rd EGRIN RH19 24 E3
St James's Sq CCH PO19 7 J3
St James's St ROTT BN2 10 F7 2
St James's Street Ms ROTT BN2 11 G7
St Joan Cl CRAWW RH11 20 E3
St John Cl SWTR RH13 5 G9
St John's Av BURH RH15 131 G1
FERR BN12 209 L3
St John's Cl BOGR PO21 203 G8
EGRIN RH19 24 F2
FERR BN12 209 K3
HISD PO11 214 B1
MIDH GU29 94 F5 4
SELS PO20 181 L6
St John's Crs HORS RH12 59 M1 2
St John's Pl HOVE BN3 193 K6 1
ROTT BN2 11 G6
St Johns Rd BURH RH15 131 H1
CRAWW RH11 2 D4 2
EGRIN RH19 24 F2
EMRTH PO10 175 M3
HOVE BN3 193 K7
HWH RH16 109 M1
St John's St CCH PO19 6 F5
St Joseph's Cl HOVE BN3 193 H4
St Josephs Wy HWH RH16 87 M8
St Julians Cl SHOR BN43 191 K5
St Julian's La SHOR BN43 191 K5
St Keyna Av HOVE BN3 192 E6
St Lawrence Av FIN/BW BN14 8 C1
SALV BN13 8 B1
St Lawrence Wy
HPPT/KEY BN6 130 B5
St Leodegar's Wy SELS PO20 201 H3
St Leonard's Av HISD PO11 214 D1
HOVE BN3 192 D6
St Leonards Dr CRAWE RH10 3 M8
St Leonard's Gdns HOVE BN3 192 E6
St Leonard's Rd HOVE BN3 192 D6
ROTT BN2 11 J1 3
SWTR RH13 60 F4
St Louie Cl STHW BN42 192 B4 1
St Luke's Cl WTHG BN11 189 J8
St Luke's Rd ROTT BN2 11 K4
St Luke's Ter ROTT BN2 11 J4
St Malo Cl FERR BN12 209 G4
St Margaret's Pl BRI BN1 10 B7
St Margaret's Rd EGRIN RH19 25 G1 2
HISD PO11 214 D1
St Mark's Crs WTHG BN11 189 J8
St Mark's La HORS RH12 37 M6
St Mark's St ROTT BN2 194 F8
St Martin's La LHPTN BN17 206 E3 3
St Martin's Pl ROTT BN2 11 H2
St Martins Rd LHPTN BN17 206 E3 4
St Martin's Sq CCH PO19 6 E4
St Martin's St CCH PO19 6 E4
ROTT BN2 11 H1
St Mary Magdalene St
ROTT BN2 11 H1
St Mary's Cl BIL RH14 79 L4
LAN/SOMP BN15 189 H5
LHPTN BN17 206 F3
MIDOS PO22 12 E2
PUL/STOR RH20 122 D2
RCCH PO18 156 F5
SHOR BN43 191 G5 1
St Mary's Dr ANG/EP BN16 208 A3
CRAWE RH10 21 J4
St Mary's Gdns HORS RH12 60 D3
LHPTN BN17 206 F3 3
St Marys Meadow ARUN BN18 205 G1
St Mary's Pl ROTT BN2 11 H7
St Mary's Rd HISD PO11 196 D8
LISS GU33 47 J8
RCCH PO18 158 D8
SHOR BN43 191 G5
St Mary's Rd West BURH RH15 108 F8
St Mary's Sq ROTT BN2 11 M9
St Mary's Wy LHPTN BN17 207 G3 2
St Matthew's Rd WTHG BN11 8 E4
St Maur's Rd FERR BN12 208 F2
St Michaels Cl PETW GU28 53 H5
St Michael's Ct WTHG BN11 8 C6
St Michael's Pl BRI BN1 10 B5
St Michaels Rd EGRIN RH19 24 F2
PTSD BN41 192 C5
WTHG BN11 8 C6
St Michaels Wy SWTR RH13 127 G1
St Nicholas' La MIDOS PO22 205 G7
St Nicholas Rd BRI BN1 10 D5
PTSD BN41 192 C5
RCCH PO18 156 F5
St Nicolas La SHOR BN43 190 E4
St Osmund Rd FERR BN12 208 E2
St Pancras CCH PO19 6 F4
St Patrick's La LISS GU33 47 M7
St Patrick's Rd HOVE BN3 193 H5
St Paul's Av WTHG BN11 189 J8
St Paul's Cl HWH RH16 88 A7
St Paul's Gdns CCH PO19 6 D2 2
St Paul's Rd CCH PO19 6 D2
St Paul's St ROTT BN2 11 H1
St Peter's CCH PO19 6 E3
St Peter's Av HISD PO11 196 F2
St Peters Cl BOGR PO21 202 F8
HOVE BN3 193 G2
SWTR RH13 105 M3
St Peter's Crs SELS PO20 223 G4
St Peter's Pl BRI BN1 10 F4
St Peters Rd BURH RH15 109 H8
CRAWW RH11 2 D4
HISD PO11 196 F2
PSF GU32 90 C1
PTSD BN41 192 C5
St Peter's Sq EMRTH PO10 175 J4
St Peter's St BRI BN1 10 F3
St Philips Ms HOVE BN3 193 G5
St Raphael's Rd WTHG BN11 210 A2 1
St Richard's Dr BOGR PO21 220 E1
St Richard's Rd PTSD BN41 192 C5
SELS PO20 181 M5
St Richard's Wy BOGR PO21 220 E1
St Roche's Cl RCCH PO18 157 G5
St Sampson Rd CRAWW RH11 40 A2
St Stephens Cl HASM GU27 28 D5
St Swithun's Cl EGRIN RH19 25 G3 5
St Thomas Av HISD PO11 196 A8
St Thomas Dr BOGR PO21 220 A4
St Valerie Rd WTHG BN11 8 B7
St Vincent Cl CRAWE RH10 21 L7 7
St Wilfreds Cl SELS PO20 223 J4 1
St Wilfreds Rd BURH RH15 109 J8
FIN/BW BN14 9 H1
St Wilfrid Rd CCH PO19 178 E5
St Wilfrid's Wy HWH RH16 87 M8
St Winefride's Rd LHPTN BN17 206 F4
St Winifred's Cl BOGR PO21 12 B8
Sake Ride La HFD BN5 128 C3
Salehurst Rd CRAWE RH10 21 M6
Salisbury Rd CRAWE RH10 40 F2
HOVE BN3 193 K6
WTHG BN11 9 G5
Salisbury Wy CCH PO19 179 G3 2
Salt Box Cl SWTR RH13 81 G2
Saltdean Cl CRAWW RH11 2 E9 2
Saltdean Dr ROTT BN2 213 J3
Saltdean Park Rd ROTT BN2 213 K3
Saltdean V ROTT BN2 213 K2
Salterns Cl HISD PO11 214 F1
Salterns La HISD PO11 214 E1
Salterns Rd CRAWE RH10 41 K1
Saltham La SELS PO20 201 M3
Salthill La CCH PO19 178 D4
Salthill Rd CCH PO19 178 C5
The Saltings ANG/EP BN16 207 H2
HAV PO9 174 C6
LAN/SOMP BN15 190 A7 2
SELS PO20 199 M8
SHOR BN43 190 E6
Saltings Wy STEY/UB BN44 168 B2
Saltmarsh La HISD PO11 196 B7
Salvington Cl SALV BN13 187 L5 4
Salvington Gdns SALV BN13 188 A6
Salvington Hl SALV BN13 187 M3
Salvington Rd CRAWW RH11 40 A1
SALV BN13 187 M5
Samaritan Cl CRAWW RH11 19 M8 7
Samphire Cl CRAWW RH11 40 B1 5
Samphire Dr SALV BN13 187 H7
Sampsons Dr SELS PO20 180 D5 1
Sanctuary La PUL/STOR RH20 144 D3
The Sanderlings HISD PO11 214 D2 1
Sandfield Av LHPTN BN17 184 E8
Sandgate La PUL/STOR RH20 144 B2
Sandgate Rd BRI BN1 194 B2
Sandhill La CRAWE RH10 23 J5
PUL/STOR RH20 144 F4
Sandhills Rd SWTR RH13 81 G1
Sandhurst Av ROTT BN2 195 L3
Sandleford Rd HAV PO9 152 A5

Sandown Av *FERR* BN12 .... 209 K3
Sandown Cl *FERR* BN12 .... 209 K3
Sandown Rd *ROTT* BN2 .... 11 L2
   STHW BN42 .... 191 L4
Sandpiper Cl *CRAWW* RH11 .... 19 L8 ▣
Sandridge La *HWH* RH16 .... 88 A3
Sandringham Cl *HOVE* BN3 .... 193 H3 ▣
   SELS PO20 .... 217 J2
Sandringham Dr *HOVE* BN3 .... 193 H3
Sandringham Ms *SALV* BN13 .... 187 L5 ▣
Sandringham Rd *CCH* PO19 .... 7 K5
   CRAWW RH11 .... 40 C2
   PSF GU32 .... 68 C8
Sandringham Wy *BOGR* PO21 .... 12 A4
Sandrock *HASM* GU27 .... 28 D6
   MIDH GU29 .... 94 E4
Sandrocks Wy *HWH* RH16 .... 109 M2
The Sands *PUL/STOR* RH20 .... 125 C7
Sandwich Rd *WTHG* BN11 .... 210 A3
Sandy *EPSF* GU31 .... 90 F1
Sandygate La *CRAWE* RH10 .... 23 H4
Sandy La *CRAWE* RH10 .... 23 H4
   EGRIN RH19 .... 24 F3
   EGRIN RH19 .... 43 M6
   GSHT GU26 .... 28 A2
   HASM GU27 .... 27 K5
   HASM GU27 .... 28 F3
   HFD BN5 .... 127 L8
   LISS GU33 .... 70 B1
   MIDH GU29 .... 94 D4
   PUL/STOR RH20 .... 121 H7
   PUL/STOR RH20 .... 144 C3
   RCCH PO18 .... 155 J7
Sandymount Av *BOGR* PO21 .... 12 B2
Sandymount Cl *MIDOS* PO22 .... 12 C1
Sandy Point La *SELS* PO20 .... 222 D4
Sandy Point Rd *HISD* PO11 .... 215 H3
Sandy V *BOGR* PO21 .... 220 B5
Sandy V *HWH* RH16 .... 109 L2
San Feliu Ct *EGRIN* RH19 .... 25 J2
Sangers Dr *HORL* RH6 .... 15 C2
Sanyhills Av *BRI* BN1 .... 172 A5
Sargent Cl *CRAWE* RH10 .... 41 G2 ▣
Sarisbury Cl *MIDOS* PO22 .... 13 M3
Sark Cl *CRAWW* RH11 .... 40 B2 ▣
Sark Gdns *FERR* BN12 .... 209 K3
Satinwood Cl *MIDOS* PO22 .... 19 M8 ▣
Saturn Cl *CRAWW* RH11 .... 19 M8 ▣
Saucelands Rd *SWTR* RH13 .... 102 F5
Saunders Cl *CRAWE* RH10 .... 21 J6
Saunders Hl *BRI* BN1 .... 172 E5
Saunders Park Vw *ROTT* BN2 .... 194 B3
Savernake Wk *CRAWE* RH10 .... 3 K9
Saville Gdns *BIL* RH14 .... 79 L5
Savill Rd *HWH* RH16 .... 88 B4
Sawyers Cl *BURH* RH15 .... 131 L5
Saxby Rd *BURH* RH15 .... 108 E8
Saxifrage Wy *SALV* BN13 .... 187 H7
Saxon Cl *ANG/EP* BN16 .... 208 C1
   BIL RH14 .... 79 L3
   BOGR PO21 .... 220 A4
   ROTT BN2 .... 213 K2
Saxon Crs *HORS* RH12 .... 4 A5
Saxon Rd *CRAWE* RH10 .... 21 M7
   HOVE BN3 .... 192 M4
   STEY/UB BN44 .... 168 A1
Saxons *SHOR* BN43 .... 191 C3
Saxony Rd *FIN/BW* BN14 .... 8 E1
Sayers Cl *SWTR* RH13 .... 5 H7
The Sayers *EGRIN* RH19 .... 24 D3
Scallows Cl *CRAWE* RH10 .... 3 L2
Scallows Rd *CRAWE* RH10 .... 3 L2
Scamps Hl *HWH* RH16 .... 88 D6
Scant Rd *RCCH* PO18 .... 177 C1
Scant Rd (East) *RCCH* PO18 .... 176 F2
Scant Rd (West) *RCCH* PO18 .... 176 F2
Scarborough Rd *BRI* BN1 .... 193 L3 ▣
School Cl *BURH* RH15 .... 131 C2
   HORS RH12 .... 38 B6 ▣
   PUL/STOR RH20 .... 121 H1
   STHW BN42 .... 191 M5 ▣
School Dell *RCCH* PO18 .... 177 H1
School Hl *ARUN* BN18 .... 160 D7
   FIN/BW BN14 .... 165 M4
   HORS RH12 .... 37 G4
   PUL/STOR RH20 .... 143 L3
School La *ARUN* BN18 .... 184 C2 ▣
   EGRIN RH19 .... 25 L6
   EMRTH PO10 .... 153 L7
   EMRTH PO10 .... 175 J4
   LISS GU33 .... 47 J8
   MIDH GU29 .... 94 A3
   PETW GU28 .... 96 C1
   POY/PYE BN45 .... 150 D9
   PSF GU32 .... 68 D6
   PUL/STOR RH20 .... 120 A8
   PUL/STOR RH20 .... 121 H7
   PUL/STOR RH20 .... 143 K3
   PUL/STOR RH20 .... 144 F6
   RCCH PO18 .... 133 J2
   RCCH PO18 .... 176 C5
   RCCH PO18 .... 177 K7
   SELS PO20 .... 182 A5
   SELS PO20 .... 201 L2
   SELS PO20 .... 222 F4
   STEY/UB BN44 .... 167 L1
   STEY/UB BN44 .... 167 L1
   SWTR RH13 .... 103 K3
School Ri *ROTT* BN2 .... 194 F6 ▣
School Rd *ARUN* BN18 .... 141 M5
   BIL RH14 .... 78 D3
   GSHT GU26 .... 27 J1
   HASM GU27 .... 28 A7
   HAV PO9 .... 174 B3
   HOVE BN3 .... 193 G5
   STEY/UB BN44 .... 168 B2
Scory Cl *CRAWW* RH11 .... 40 B1
Scotland La *HASM* GU27 .... 28 C7
Scotlands Cl *HASM* GU27 .... 28 C7
Scotlands Dr *HASM* GU27 .... 28 C7 ▣
   CRAWE RH10 .... 21 K3
Scotland St *ROTT* BN2 .... 11 H5
Scotney Cl *SALV* BN13 .... 187 J7 ▣ ▣
Scotney Ter *HAV* PO9 .... 152 E6 ▣
Scott Rd *CRAWE* RH10 .... 3 J9
   HOVE BN3 .... 193 G5 ▣
Scott St *BOGR* PO21 .... 12 C8
Scratchings La *PETW* GU28 .... 54 B7
Sea Av *ANG/EP* BN16 .... 207 L3
Seabrook Cl *BOGR* PO21 .... 220 E1

Sea Cl *FERR* BN12 .... 209 M2
   MIDOS PO22 .... 204 F8
Seacourt Cl *BOGR* PO21 .... 220 E3 ▣
Sea Dr *FERR* BN12 .... 209 G4
   MIDOS PO22 .... 204 E8
Seafield Av *FERR* BN12 .... 209 L4
Seafield Rd *SELS* PO20 .... 217 G6
   HOVE BN3 .... 193 J7
Seafields *EMRTH* PO10 .... 175 H4
   SELS PO20 .... 217 J8
Seafield Wy *SELS* PO20 .... 217 H6
Seaford Rd *CRAWW* RH11 .... 40 B3
   HOVE BN3 .... 192 D6
Sea Front *HISD* PO11 .... 214 C2
Sea Gv *SELS* PO20 .... 222 E6
Sea Grove Av *HISD* PO11 .... 214 D2
Seagull Cl *SELS* PO20 .... 222 D3
Seagull La *EMRTH* PO10 .... 175 J5
Sea La *ANG/EP* BN16 .... 207 J4
   BOGR PO21 .... 220 A4
   FERR BN12 .... 209 G2
   FERR BN12 .... 209 K3
   MIDOS PO22 .... 204 F7
Sea Lane Cl *ANG/EP* BN16 .... 208 A3
   FERR BN12 .... 209 G2
Sea Lane Gdns *FERR* BN12 .... 209 G3
Seal Rd *SELS* PO20 .... 222 F7
Seal Sq *SELS* PO20 .... 222 F7
Seamill Park Av *WTHG* BN11 .... 211 K1
Seamill Park Crs *WTHG* BN11 .... 211 J1
Seamill Wy *WTHG* BN11 .... 211 J1
Sea Pl *FERR* BN12 .... 209 M3
Searle's Vw *HORS* RH12 .... 5 H2
Sea Rd *ANG/EP* BN16 .... 208 B3
   LHPTN BN17 .... 207 G5
   MIDOS PO22 .... 13 K7
Seasaw Wy *ROTT* BN2 .... 195 G5
Seaside Av *LAN/SOMP* BN15 .... 190 A4
Seaside Cl *LAN/SOMP* BN15 .... 190 A4
Seaside La *LAN/SOMP* BN15 .... 190 A4
Seaview Av *ANG/EP* BN16 .... 208 A4
Seaview Ct *LAN/SOMP* BN15 .... 189 L8
Seaview Rd *ANG/EP* BN16 .... 208 A4
   HISD PO11 .... 214 F1
   ROTT BN2 .... 195 J4
Sea View Rd *WTHG* BN11 .... 8 C8
Seaward Dr *SELS* PO20 .... 216 D3
Seawaves Cl *ANG/EP* BN16 .... 208 B3
Sea Wy *BOGR* PO21 .... 220 A4
   MIDOS PO22 .... 204 E8
   MIDOS PO22 .... 205 J7
Second Av *EMRTH* PO10 .... 176 A4
   FERR BN12 .... 188 E5
   HAV PO9 .... 174 E2
   HOVE BN3 .... 193 K7
   LAN/SOMP BN15 .... 189 M5
   MIDOS PO22 .... 204 C8
   SELS PO20 .... 217 J7
   SELS PO20 .... 218 A3
Sedbury Rd *LAN/SOMP* BN15 .... 189 K4
Sedgefield Cl *CRAWE* RH10 .... 21 M6
Sedgewick Cl *CRAWE* RH10 .... 21 K6 ▣
Sedgewick Rd *BRI* BN1 .... 172 D6
Sedgwick La *SWTR* RH13 .... 60 F1
Sefter Rd *BOGR* PO21 .... 202 C8
Sefton Av *BOGR* PO21 .... 220 D5
Sefton Cl *SALV* BN13 .... 187 L6
Sefton Rd *PTSD* BN41 .... 192 A1
Selangor Av *EMRTH* PO10 .... 175 G3
Selba Dr *ROTT* BN2 .... 194 F2
Selborne Av *HAV* PO9 .... 152 A7
Selborne Pl *HOVE* BN3 .... 193 K5 ▣
Selborne Rd *HOVE* BN3 .... 193 K6
   LHPTN BN17 .... 206 F4
   LISS GU33 .... 46 F2
   WTHG BN11 .... 9 J1
Selborne Wy *ANG/EP* BN16 .... 208 A3
Selbourne Cl *CRAWE* RH10 .... 21 L2
Selbourne Rd *HAV* PO9 .... 174 B3 ▣
Selby Ct *HWH* RH16 .... 109 M1
Selden La *SALV* BN13 .... 186 C3
   WTHG BN11 .... 9 L4
Selden Rd *WTHG* BN11 .... 9 L4
Selden's Ms *SALV* BN13 .... 188 A6 ▣
Selden's Wy *SALV* BN13 .... 188 A6
Selham Cl *BRI* BN1 .... 172 F6 ▣
   CCH PO19 .... 179 H1
   CRAWW RH11 .... 20 B5
Selham Dr *BRI* BN1 .... 172 E6
Selham Rd *MIDH* GU29 .... 95 C8
Selhurst Cl *ANG/EP* BN16 .... 207 M3
Selhurstpark Rd *RCCH* PO18 .... 137 L8
Selhurst Rd *ROTT* BN2 .... 195 M6
Selkirk Cl *SALV* BN13 .... 187 M8
Selmeston Rd *ROTT* BN2 .... 195 G7 ▣
Selmestone Rd *ROTT* BN2 .... 195 G6 ▣
Selsey Av *BOGR* PO21 .... 221 H2
Selsey Cl *BRI* BN1 .... 172 F6
   HISD PO11 .... 215 J1
   SALV BN13 .... 188 A1
Selsey Rd *CCH* PO19 .... 200 F1
   CRAWW RH11 .... 40 B2
   SELS PO20 .... 200 E5
   SELS PO20 .... 218 F2
Selsfield Dr *ROTT* BN2 .... 194 E1
Selsfield Rd *CRAWE* RH10 .... 43 H1
   EGRIN RH19 .... 43 J4
   RHWH RH17 .... 66 C3
Selsmore Av *HISD* PO11 .... 214 D1
Selsmore Rd *HISD* PO11 .... 214 D1
Selway La *LHPTN* BN17 .... 207 G5
Selwyn Av *LHPTN* BN17 .... 206 E1
Selwyn Cl *BOGR* PO21 .... 203 G8
   CRAWE RH10 .... 21 K3
Semley Rd *BRI* BN1 .... 194 B3
   HPPT/KEY BN6 .... 87 K7
Sergison Cl *HWH* RH16 .... 87 L7
Sergison Rd *HWH* RH16 .... 87 L7
Serrin Wy *HORS* RH12 .... 5 H1
Service Rd *HORL* RH6 .... 15 G4
Servite Cl *BOGR* PO21 .... 221 H3
Sevelands Cl *ROTT* BN2 .... 195 G5 ▣
Seventh Av *LAN/SOMP* BN15 .... 189 M4

Severals Rd *MIDH* GU29 .... 94 C4
Severn Rd *CRAWE* RH10 .... 21 K7
Seville St *ROTT* BN2 .... 11 J6
Sewill Cl *HORL* RH6 .... 14 A5
Seymour Av *CRAWW* RH11 .... 40 B2
Seymour St *ROTT* BN2 .... 11 L9
Shackleton Rd *CRAWE* RH10 .... 3 H9
Shadwells Cl *LAN/SOMP* BN15 .... 190 A5
Shadwells Rd *LAN/SOMP* BN15 .... 190 A5
Shaftesbury Av *FERR* BN12 .... 209 M1
Shaftesbury Pl *BRI* BN1 .... 10 F1 ▣
Shaftesbury Rd *ANG/EP* BN16 .... 207 K4
   BRI BN1 .... 10 F1
   CRAWE RH10 .... 21 L8
Shakespeare Rd *WTHG* BN11 .... 8 D4
Shakespeare St *HOVE* BN3 .... 193 H4
Shalbourne Crs *SELS* PO20 .... 217 K7
Shaldon Rd *HAV* PO9 .... 152 E6 ▣
   RCCH PO18 .... 177 H1
Shamrock Cl *CCH* PO19 .... 7 H1
Shandon Gdns *FIN/BW* BN14 .... 188 E6
Shandon Rd *FIN/BW* BN14 .... 188 E6
Shandon Wy *FIN/BW* BN14 .... 188 E6
Shandys *HORS* RH12 .... 60 B3
Shanklin Rd *ROTT* BN2 .... 11 K1
Shannon Cl *ANG/EP* BN16 .... 207 H4
Shardeloes Rd *ANG/EP* BN16 .... 186 A6
Sharon Cl *CRAWE* RH10 .... 3 M9
Sharps Rd *HAV* PO9 .... 152 E7
Sharpthorne Cl *CRAWW* RH11 .... 20 A6 ▣
   PTSD BN41 .... 192 D2
Shaves Wood La
   HPPT/KEY BN6 .... 149 M7
Shaw Cl *MIDOS* PO22 .... 205 H7
Shawfield Rd *HAV* PO9 .... 174 D4
Shaw's La *SWTR* RH13 .... 81 L4
Shaws Rd *CRAWE* RH10 .... 3 H1
Shear Hl *EPSF* GU31 .... 68 E7
Shearwater Dr *MIDOS* PO22 .... 203 K6
Sheddingdean Cl
   BURH RH15 .... 109 H8 ▣
Sheepbell Cl *PTSD* BN41 .... 192 C1
Sheepdown Cl *PETW* GU28 .... 98 B5
Sheepdown Dr *PETW* GU28 .... 98 A5
Sheep Fold Av *ANG/EP* BN16 .... 207 M2
Sheep La *MIDH* GU29 .... 95 G4
Sheep Pen La *STEY/UB* BN44 .... 167 L1
Sheep St *PSF* GU32 .... 90 C1
Sheep Wk *ROTT* BN2 .... 213 G3
Sheepwash La *RCCH* PO18 .... 157 C7
   SELS PO20 .... 216 D1
Sheffield Cl *CRAWE* RH10 .... 21 J8 ▣
Shelby Rd *SALV* BN13 .... 187 K6
Sheldon Cl *CRAWE* RH10 .... 21 L7
Shellbridge Rd *ARUN* BN18 .... 160 F8
Shelldale Av *PTSD* BN41 .... 192 C5
Shelldale Crs *PTSD* BN41 .... 192 C5
Shelldale Rd *PTSD* BN41 .... 192 B4
Shelley Cl *CRAWE* RH10 .... 21 K4 ▣
Shelley Dr *HORS* RH12 .... 59 L3
Shelley Rd *BOGR* PO21 .... 221 H1
   EGRIN RH19 .... 24 E3 ▣
   HORS RH12 .... 4 B5
   HOVE BN3 .... 193 J5
   WTHG BN11 .... 8 E6
Shelleys La *STEY/UB* BN44 .... 167 L1
Shell La *RHWH* RH17 .... 65 K3
Shellys Ct *SWTR* RH13 .... 5 M5 ▣
Shenfield Wy *BRI* BN1 .... 194 C1
Shenstone *HWH* RH16 .... 88 C4
Shepham Av *ROTT* BN2 .... 213 K3
Shepherd Cl *CRAWE* RH10 .... 2 F9
Shepherds Cft *BRI* BN1 .... 193 K1
Shepherd's Hl *HASM* GU27 .... 28 D6
Shepherds La *PETW* GU28 .... 96 C1
Shepherds Md *BURH* RH15 .... 109 G8 ▣
   FIN/BW BN14 .... 188 B1
Shepherds Wk *HPPT/KEY* BN6 .... 130 F7
Shepherds Wy *HORS* RH12 .... 5 M1
   LIPH GU30 .... 49 L1
Sheppard Wy *PTSD* BN41 .... 192 B1
Sheppey Cl *CRAWW* RH11 .... 40 C1
Sheppeys *HWH* RH16 .... 109 L2
Sherborne Cl *HOVE* BN3 .... 192 E1
Sherborne La *SELS* PO20 .... 222 D4
Sherbourne Rd *HOVE* BN3 .... 192 E1
Sherbourne La *HOVE* BN3 .... 192 E1
Sherbrooke Cl *SALV* BN13 .... 187 L6 ▣
Sherfield Av *HAV* PO9 .... 152 D7
Sheridan Cl *EGRIN* RH19 .... 24 D3
Sheridan Rd *FIN/BW* BN14 .... 188 D7
Sheridan Ter *HOVE* BN3 .... 193 H4
Sherlock Cl *CCH* PO19 .... 6 A2
Shermanbury Dr
   PUL/STOR RH20 .... 143 K2 ▣
Shermanbury Rd *FIN/BW* BN14 .... 8 F2 ▣
Sherwood Cl *LISS* GU33 .... 47 K5
Sherwood Dr *HWH* RH16 .... 87 K7
Sherwood Rd *MIDOS* PO22 .... 12 A3 ▣
Sherwood Wk *CRAWE* RH10 .... 3 K9
Shetland Ct *SALV* BN13 .... 187 J7 ▣
Shillinglee Rd *BIL* RH14 .... 54 L1
   MFD/CHID GU8 .... 30 C7
Shingle Rd *SHOR* BN43 .... 191 H6
Shingle Wk *SELS* PO20 .... 217 G6
Shipfield *BOGR* PO21 .... 221 G2 ▣
Shipley La *LIPH* GU30 .... 49 J1 ▣
Shipley Paygate *SWTR* RH13 .... 103 L3
Shipley Rd *CRAWW* RH11 .... 20 B6
   ROTT BN2 .... 195 M5
   SWTR RH13 .... 103 M1
Ship St *BRI* BN1 .... 10 D7
   EGRIN RH19 .... 24 F4
   SHOR BN43 .... 190 F5
Shipton Green La *SELS* PO20 .... 199 H8
Shire Pde *CRAWE* RH10 .... 21 L5 ▣
Shirley Av *HOVE* BN3 .... 193 J4
Shirley Cl *ANG/EP* BN16 .... 207 J1 ▣
   BOGR PO21 .... 220 B4
   FIN/BW BN14 .... 188 C5
   SHOR BN43 .... 191 K4
Shirley Dr *FIN/BW* BN14 .... 188 C5
   HOVE BN3 .... 193 K3
   MIDOS PO22 .... 204 B6
Shirley Rd *HOVE* BN3 .... 193 K4
Shirleys *HPPT/KEY* BN6 .... 151 M2
Shirley St *HOVE* BN3 .... 193 J5
Sholing Ct *HAV* PO9 .... 152 B7

Shooting Fld *STEY/UB* BN44 .... 146 E7
Shopfield Cl *ANG/EP* BN16 .... 207 K3 ▣
Shop La *RCCH* PO18 .... 157 H7
Shopsdam Rd
   LAN/SOMP BN15 .... 190 A8
Shopwhyke Rd *SELS* PO20 .... 179 M5
Shorecroft *BOGR* PO21 .... 221 G3
Shoreham By-pass
   LAN/SOMP BN15 .... 190 D3
Shoreham Rd *CRAWE* RH10 .... 41 K1
   HFD BN5 .... 147 M5
   STEY/UB BN44 .... 168 C4
Shore Rd *RCCH* PO18 .... 177 J8
   SELS PO20 .... 216 F6
Shoreside Wk *SELS* PO20 .... 216 F6
Short Cl *CRAWW* RH11 .... 20 E4 ▣
Short Furlong *LHPTN* BN17 .... 207 G3
Short Gallop *CRAWE* RH10 .... 21 L5 ▣
Shortgate Rd *ROTT* BN2 .... 173 G8
Shortsfield Cl *HORS* RH12 .... 4 C2
Shotterfield Ter *LISS* GU33 .... 47 J8
Shottermill *HORS* RH12 .... 38 B5
Shovelstrode La *EGRIN* RH19 .... 25 M2
Shripney La *MIDOS* PO22 .... 203 J4
Shripney Rd *MIDOS* PO22 .... 12 F1
   MIDOS PO22 .... 203 L3
Shrubbs Dr *MIDOS* PO22 .... 204 F7
Sickle Rd *HASM* GU27 .... 28 A7
Sidehill Dr *PTSD* BN41 .... 192 A2
Sideways La *HORL* RH6 .... 14 D3
Sidlesham Cl *HISD* PO11 .... 215 J2
Sidlesham La *SELS* PO20 .... 200 A7
Silchester Dr *CRAWW* RH11 .... 2 E3
Silkstead Av *HAV* PO9 .... 152 C6
Sillwood Pl *BRI* BN1 .... 10 A6
Sillwood Rd *BRI* BN1 .... 10 B6
Sillwood St *BRI* BN1 .... 10 A6
Silver Birch Cl *LISS* GU33 .... 47 K8
Silver Birch Dr *MIDOS* PO22 .... 204 F6
   SALV BN13 .... 187 J7
Silver Birches *HFD* BN5 .... 148 A5
   HWH RH16 .... 88 B8
Silverdale *HPPT/KEY* BN6 .... 151 J1
   PUL/STOR RH20 .... 123 M6
Silverdale Av *HOVE* BN3 .... 193 L5
Silverdale Cl *BOGR* PO21 .... 220 B4
Silverdale Dr *LAN/SOMP* BN15 .... 189 K7
Silverdale Rd *BURH* RH15 .... 131 J2
   HOVE BN3 .... 193 L5
Silver Gld *PUL/STOR* RH20 .... 123 M6
Silver La *BIL* RH14 .... 79 L5
Silverlea Gdns *HORL* RH6 .... 15 K2
Silversands Gdns *HISD* PO11 .... 214 E2
Silverston Av *BOGR* PO21 .... 221 H2
Silvertrees *EMRTH* PO10 .... 175 J2
Silver Wy *SELS* PO20 .... 217 K7
Silver Wd *PUL/STOR* RH20 .... 123 J5
Silver Wood Copse
   PUL/STOR RH20 .... 123 J5
Simmons Gn *HISD* PO11 .... 214 F1
Sinclair Cl *CRAWE* RH10 .... 21 K8 ▣
Sincox La *SWTR* RH13 .... 102 F6
Singleton Cl *BOGR* PO21 .... 220 D3 ▣
   FERR BN12 .... 209 G3
Singleton Crs *FERR* BN12 .... 209 G3
Singleton Rd *BRI* BN1 .... 172 B6
   HORS RH12 .... 59 L1 ▣
Singleton Wy *BURH* RH15 .... 131 K5
Sir George's Pl
   STEY/UB BN44 .... 167 K1 ▣
Siskin Cl *HORS* RH12 .... 5 H1
Sissinghurst Cl *CRAWE* RH10 .... 21 L5
Six Acres Cl *SWTR* RH13 .... 81 G2
Skeyne Dr *PUL/STOR* RH20 .... 122 D2 ▣
Skiff La *BIL* RH14 .... 56 A6
Skye Cluan Cl *MIDOS* PO22 .... 182 C6
Skylark Vw *HORS* RH12 .... 37 L5
Slade La *EPSF* GU31 .... 69 M8
Slattsfield Cl *SELS* PO20 .... 223 H5
Slaugham Ct *CRAWW* RH11 .... 40 A1 ▣
Slaugham La *RHWH* RH17 .... 63 H8
Sleets Rd *HORS* RH12 .... 59 M1
Slimbridge Rd *BURH* RH15 .... 131 C1
Slindon Bottom Rd
   ARUN BN18 .... 160 B8
Slindon Gdns *HAV* PO9 .... 174 C4
Slindon Rd *FIN/BW* BN14 .... 188 E6
Slinfold Wk *CRAWW* RH11 .... 20 B5
Slinford Cl *ROTT* BN2 .... 11 M7
Slipper Rd *EMRTH* PO10 .... 175 H3
Slonk Hill Rd *SHOR* BN43 .... 191 H2
Sloughbrook Cl *HORS* RH12 .... 38 A6
Sloughgreen La *RHWH* RH17 .... 86 A3
Slugwash La *RHWH* RH17 .... 110 C7
Smallcroft Cl *LHPTN* BN17 .... 206 D3 ▣
Smallcutts Av *EMRTH* PO10 .... 176 A3
Smallfield Rd *HORL* RH6 .... 15 J1
Smallmead *HORL* RH6 .... 15 J1
Smalls Md *CRAWW* RH11 .... 2 D4
Smithbarn *SWTR* RH13 .... 5 L6
Smith Cl *CRAWE* RH10 .... 2 F9
Smithers Hill La *SWTR* RH13 .... 103 J4
Smith La *EMRTH* PO10 .... 197 M3
Smock Aly *PUL/STOR* RH20 .... 123 M6
Smokyhouse La *PETW* GU28 .... 96 C7
Smolletts *EGRIN* RH19 .... 24 D4 ▣
Smugglers End *RHWH* RH17 .... 63 K4
Smuggler's La *RCCH* PO18 .... 199 H3
   RDKG RH5 .... 16 F5
   SWTR RH13 .... 80 E1
Smugglers Wk *FERR* BN12 .... 209 M3
Smugglers Wy *SWTR* RH13 .... 81 G2
Snailing La *LISS* GU33 .... 46 E6
Snapes Rd *PUL/STOR* RH20 .... 144 A1 ▣
Snell Hatch *CRAWW* RH11 .... 2 A3
Snipe La *HASM* GU27 .... 51 H1
Snowberry Crs *HAV* PO9 .... 174 L1
Snowdrop Cl *ANG/EP* BN16 .... 207 J1 ▣
   CRAWW RH11 .... 40 B2
Snowdrop La *HWH* RH16 .... 88 D6
Snowflakes La *HWH* RH16 .... 88 E6
Snow Hl *CRAWE* RH10 .... 23 G1
Soane Cl *CRAWW* RH11 .... 19 M1 ▣
Soberton Rd *HAV* PO9 .... 174 B1
Soldridge Cl *HAV* PO9 .... 152 E6 ▣
Solent Cl *ANG/EP* BN16 .... 207 H1 ▣
Solent Dr *HISD* PO11 .... 214 C3
Solent Rd *HAV* PO9 .... 174 B3
   SELS PO20 .... 217 G6

Solent Wy *EMRTH* PO10 .... 174 F5
   HAV PO9 .... 174 D5
   SELS PO20 .... 222 F7
Solway Av *BRI* BN1 .... 172 A5
Solway Cl *LHPTN* BN17 .... 207 H2
Somborne Dr *HAV* PO9 .... 152 C7
Somergate *HORS* RH12 .... 60 A2
Somerhill Av *HOVE* BN3 .... 193 L5
Somerhill Rd *HOVE* BN3 .... 193 L6
Somerley La *SELS* PO20 .... 217 L3
Somerset Cl *SALV* BN13 .... 188 B7
Somerset Gdns *MIDOS* PO22 .... 12 D3
Somerset Rd *ANG/EP* BN16 .... 208 C2
   FERR BN12 .... 209 G4
Somerset St *ROTT* BN2 .... 11 J7 ▣
Somerston Gn *MIDOS* PO22 .... 13 K2
Somerton Rd *MIDOS* PO22 .... 13 K2
Somerville Dr *CRAWE* RH10 .... 21 K3
Sompting Av *FIN/BW* BN14 .... 188 E7
Sompting By-pass
   FIN/BW BN14 .... 188 E5
Sompting Cl *ROTT* BN2 .... 195 G5 ▣
Sompting Rd *FIN/BW* BN14 .... 188 F7
   LAN/SOMP BN15 .... 189 L6
Sopers La *STEY/UB* BN44 .... 167 J5
Sopley Ct *HAV* PO9 .... 152 E6 ▣
Sorrel Cl *CRAWW* RH11 .... 40 B2
Sorrel Rd *HORS* RH12 .... 5 G1
South Acre *EPSF* GU31 .... 113 L1
Southall Av *ROTT* BN2 .... 194 E2
Southampton St *ROTT* BN2 .... 11 H4
South Ash *STEY/UB* BN44 .... 146 E7
South Av *BOGR* PO21 .... 220 F1
   FERR BN12 .... 209 M3
   HPPT/KEY BN6 .... 130 B7
   ROTT BN2 .... 11 J6
South Bank *CCH* PO19 .... 6 D8
   HPPT/KEY BN6 .... 150 F1
South Bay *EMRTH* PO10 .... 197 K4
Southbourne Av *EMRTH* PO10 .... 175 H5
Southbrook *CRAWW* RH11 .... 40 D3 ▣
Southbrook Rd *HAV* PO9 .... 174 C4
   RCCH PO18 .... 177 H1
South Cl *BURH* RH15 .... 130 F1
   CRAWE RH10 .... 3 J1
   HAV PO9 .... 174 D4
South Coast Rd *PEAHV* BN10 .... 213 M4
   ROTT BN2 .... 213 L4
Southcote Av *SELS* PO20 .... 216 F5
Southcourt Rd *ANG/EP* BN16 .... 207 M2
Southcourt Rd *FIN/BW* BN14 .... 8 F3
Southdean Cl *MIDOS* PO22 .... 205 G7 ▣
Southdean Rd *MIDOS* PO22 .... 205 G7
Southdown Av *BRI* BN1 .... 194 B3
   PTSD BN41 .... 192 C4 ▣
Southdown Cl *HORS* RH12 .... 5 M1
   HWH RH16 .... 109 L2
   MIDH GU29 .... 94 E6
Southdown Pl *BRI* BN1 .... 194 B3 ▣
Southdown Rd *BOGR* PO21 .... 12 C7
   BRI BN1 .... 194 B3
   PTSD BN41 .... 192 B2
   SHOR BN43 .... 191 G5
   STHW BN42 .... 191 M5
South Downs Wy *ARUN* BN18 .... 141 M4
   EPSF GU31 .... 114 B3
   HFD BN5 .... 170 A4
   HPPT/KEY BN6 .... 151 K5
   PETW GU28 .... 118 F8
   POY/PYE BN45 .... 150 F6
   PUL/STOR RH20 .... 140 A3
   PUL/STOR RH20 .... 145 G8
   SHOR BN43 .... 169 J2
   STEY/UB BN44 .... 167 H5
   STEY/UB BN44 .... 168 C2
Southdown Ter
   STEY/UB BN44 .... 167 M1 ▣
Southdown View Cl
   FIN/BW BN14 .... 189 G7 ▣
Southdown View Rd
   FIN/BW BN14 .... 188 F7
Southdown View Wy
   FIN/BW BN14 .... 188 F6
Southdown Wy
   PUL/STOR RH20 .... 144 A1
South Dr *ANG/EP* BN16 .... 207 L3
   BURH RH15 .... 130 F1
   FERR BN12 .... 208 F4
   MIDOS PO22 .... 204 D7
Southern Rd *SELS* PO20 .... 223 H5
Southey Rd *WTHG* BN11 .... 8 E7
South Farm Rd *FIN/BW* BN14 .... 188 C6
Southfield Rd *FIN/BW* BN14 .... 188 E7
Southfields Cl *CCH* PO19 .... 201 G4
Southfields Rd *LHPTN* BN17 .... 207 G3
Southgate *CCH* PO19 .... 6 D6
Southgate Av *CRAWE* RH10 .... 3 G9
   CRAWE RH10 .... 40 E1
Southgate Dr *CRAWE* RH10 .... 2 E8
Southgate Rd *CRAWW* RH11 .... 2 E7
South Gv *PETW* GU28 .... 98 A5 ▣
   SWTR RH13 .... 60 C8
South Holmes Rd *SWTR* RH13 .... 38 C8
Southlands *EGRIN* RH19 .... 24 F5
Southlands La *PUL/STOR* RH20 .... 123 M5
Southlands Pk *MIDH* GU29 .... 94 F7
South La *ARUN* BN18 .... 162 C1
   EMRTH PO10 .... 176 B1
   EPSF GU31 .... 90 A4
   PETW GU28 .... 97 G5
Southleigh Gv *HISD* PO11 .... 196 C8
Southleigh Rd *EMRTH* PO10 .... 175 J1
   HAV PO9 .... 174 E3
Southleys *HASM* GU27 .... 51 H7
South Lodge Cl *BURH* RH15 .... 109 G8 ▣
Southmoor La *HAV* PO9 .... 174 A5
Southmount *ROTT* BN2 .... 194 C3
Southon Cl *PTSD* BN41 .... 192 A1
Southover Pl *ROTT* BN2 .... 11 G3
Southover Rd *BOGR* PO21 .... 12 C7
Southover St *ROTT* BN2 .... 11 G3
Southover Wy *SELS* PO20 .... 201 H4
South Pas *LHPTN* BN17 .... 207 G4
South Pier Rd *HORL* RH6 .... 15 H5
South Rd *BRI* BN1 .... 193 M1
   HISD PO11 .... 214 C1
   HWH RH16 .... 87 M1
   LIPH GU30 .... 49 K3

MIDOS PO22 .... 13 K3
RHWH RH17 .... 110 D8
Southsea Av *FERR* BN12 .... 209 M2
Southside *PUL/STOR* RH20 .... 122 E2
South Strd *ANG/EP* BN16 .... 208 B4
South St *BRI* BN1 .... 10 D7
BRI BN1 .... 173 K6
CCH PO19 .... 6 E5
EMRTH PO10 .... 175 J4
HAV PO9 .... 174 C3
HORS RH12 .... 4 C8
HPPT/KEY BN6 .... 151 L1
LAN/SOMP BN15 .... 189 M7
MIDH GU29 .... 95 G5
PTSD BN41 .... 192 B3
RHWH RH17 .... 86 F7
SALV BN13 .... 8 A1
SWTR RH13 .... 127 H1
WTHG BN11 .... 9 H6
South Ter *LHPTN* BN17 .... 206 E4
South Vw *ANG/EP* BN16 .... 208 C4
HPPT/KEY BN6 .... 131 L7
South View CI *CRAWE* RH10 .... 22 F1
STHW RH42 .... 191 M3
Southview CI *SHOR* BN43 .... 191 K5
STHW RH42 .... 191 M3
Southview Dr *WTHG* BN11 .... 8 A6
Southview Gdns *WTHG* BN11 .... 8 A6
Southview Rd *MIDOS* PO22 .... 204 C8
STHW RH42 .... 191 M4
South View Ter *HFD* BN5 .... 127 M8
South Wk *MIDOS* PO22 .... 204 E7
Southwark Wk *BOGR* PO21 .... 202 F8
Southwater CI *FERR* BN12 .... 209 J1
ROTT BN2 .... 11 L5
Southwater St *SWTR* RH13 .... 82 B1
South Wy *BOGR* PO21 .... 203 H7
Southway *BURH* RH15 .... 130 E1
LHPTN BN17 .... 207 G4
Southways Av *FIN/BW* BN14 .... 188 F6
Southwick CI *EGRIN* RH19 .... 24 E2
Southwick Sq *STHW* RH42 .... 191 M5
Southwick St *STHW* RH42 .... 191 M5
Southwold CI *SALV* BN13 .... 187 M3
South Woodlands *BRI* BN1 .... 171 M8
Southwood Rd *EMRTH* PO10 .... 214 F2
The Spain *PSF* GU32 .... 90 B1
Sparks Ct *LHPTN* BN17 .... 206 E3
Spark's La *RHWH* RH17 .... 86 F2
Sparrow Wy *HPPT/KEY* BN6 .... 131 J7
Sparshott Rd *SELS* PO20 .... 223 G7
Spartan CI *EMRTH* PO10 .... 197 K1
Spear HI *PUL/STOR* RH20 .... 125 H5
Speedwell CI *SALV* BN13 .... 187 H7
Speedwell Wy *HORS* RH12 .... 5 G2
Spencer Av *HOVE* BN3 .... 192 E1
Spencer CI *HISD* PO11 .... 214 D1
Spencer Rd *EMRTH* PO10 .... 153 H8
LAN/SOMP BN15 .... 189 L7
Spencers La *HORL* RH6 .... 14 A3
Spencers PI *HORS* RH12 .... 4 A3
Spencers Rd *CRAWW* RH11 .... 2 D5
HORS RH12 .... 4 B6
Spencer St *BOGR* PO21 .... 12 E5
Spey CI *SALV* BN13 .... 187 K4
Spicers CI *BURH* RH15 .... 109 G7
Spierbridge Rd
PUL/STOR RH20 .... 143 K2
Spiers Wy *HORL* RH6 .... 15 J3
Spindle CI *HAV* PO9 .... 174 F1
Spindle Wy *CRAWE* RH10 .... 3 J4
Spinnaker CI *HISD* PO11 .... 196 B8
LHPTN BN17 .... 207 H3
Spinnaker Gra *HISD* PO11 .... 174 F8
Spinnals Gv *STHW* RH42 .... 191 L5
Spinney CI *CRAWE* RH10 .... 23 K4
HORS RH12 .... 38 C6
HPPT/KEY BN6 .... 130 D7
SELS PO20 .... 222 F4
Spinney La *PUL/STOR* RH20 .... 123 K7
SELS PO20 .... 199 H6
Spinney North
PUL/STOR RH20 .... 122 E2
The Spinney *ANG/EP* BN16 .... 208 B4
BOGR PO21 .... 220 F1
CRAWW RH11 .... 2 B7
HASM GU27 .... 28 D4
HOVE BN3 .... 193 K1
HPPT/KEY BN6 .... 131 C7
PUL/STOR RH20 .... 122 D2
RHWH RH17 .... 87 L5
SELS PO20 .... 199 G4
Spinney Wk *MIDOS* PO22 .... 182 C5
Spitalfield La *CCH* PO19 .... 7 J5
Spithandle La *STEY/UB* BN44 .... 145 L3
Spooners Rd *HORS* RH12 .... 5 L3
Springate Rd *STHW* RH42 .... 192 A4
Springbank *PSF* GU32 .... 179 G3
Spring Copse *CRAWE* RH10 .... 22 F2
Springfarm *HASM* GU27 .... 27 M7
Springfield *BOGR* PO21 .... 220 B2
Springfield CI *ANG/EP* BN16 .... 207 M3
RCCH PO18 .... 157 G5
RHWH RH17 .... 85 K8
SELS PO20 .... 200 A7
Springfield Crs *HORS* RH12 .... 4 B7
Springfield La *SWTR* RH13 .... 39 J8
Springfield Park Rd *HORS* RH12 .... 4 B7
Springfield Rd *BRI* BN1 .... 194 B4
CRAWW RH11 .... 2 D5
HORS RH12 .... 4 C7
Spring Gdns *BRI* BN1 .... 10 E6
CRAWE RH10 .... 22 D1
EMRTH PO10 .... 175 J4
PUL/STOR RH20 .... 144 F2
HWH RH16 .... 88 C3
SWTR RH13 .... 58 D1
Spring Plat *CRAWE* RH10 .... 21 K6
Spring St *BRI* BN1 .... 10 B6
Spronkett's La *RHWH* RH17 .... 84 F1
Sproule CI *ARUN* BN18 .... 205 J2
Sproutes La *SWTR* RH13 .... 102 D4
Spurgeon CI *CRAWW* RH11 .... 2 C1
EMRTH PO10 .... 175 L1

EPSF GU31 .... 91 L8
MIDOS PO22 .... 182 C6
PSF GU32 .... 90 C1
Squires St *BRI* BN1 .... 23 H4
Squirrel CI *CRAWW* RH11 .... 20 C3
Squirrels Copse
PUL/STOR RH20 .... 144 D1
Stable CI *CRAWE* RH10 .... 41 L1
Stable Fld *MIDOS* PO22 .... 205 J7
Stable La *FIN/BW* BN14 .... 165 M6
Stacey Ct *HAV* PO9 .... 152 A5
Stackfield Rd *CRAWW* RH11 .... 19 M7
CRAWW RH11 .... 20 A7
PSF GU32 .... 68 C7
Stafford Rd *BRI* BN1 .... 10 B1
CRAWW RH11 .... 19 M7
Staffords CI *ANG/EP* BN16 .... 207 J2
Staffords PI *HORL* RH6 .... 15 J2
Stafford Wy *HPPT/KEY* BN6 .... 151 H1
Stag CI *HFD* BN5 .... 127 M6
Stagelands *CRAWW* RH11 .... 20 C4
Stairbridge La *RHWH* RH17 .... 107 M4
Stakers La *SWTR* RH13 .... 82 B4
Stalham Wy *MIDOS* PO22 .... 13 L1
Stallard CI *EMRTH* PO10 .... 175 H5
Stall House La
PUL/STOR RH20 .... 101 H5
Stamford CI *BRI* BN1 .... 214 B1
Stammers HI *HFD* BN5 .... 149 G8
Stanbridge Rd *HAV* PO9 .... 152 E8
Stanbridge Wy *RHWH* RH17 .... 66 B5
Stanbrok CI *BOGR* PO21 .... 220 F1
Stanbury CI *RCCH* PO18 .... 177 J3
Standean CI *BRI* BN1 .... 172 E6
Standen CI *EGRIN* RH19 .... 24 B1
Standen PI *HORS* RH12 .... 38 B5
Standgrove Rd *RHWH* RH17 .... 66 B6
Standinghall La *CRAWE* RH10 .... 22 B8
Stane St *BIL* RH14 .... 58 B5
BIL RH14 .... 79 K6
PUL/STOR RH20 .... 100 D8
RDKG RH5 .... 16 D2
SWTR RH13 .... 58 C3
Stane Street CI
PUL/STOR RH20 .... 100 D8
Stanford CI *BRI* BN1 .... 194 B4
HPPT/KEY BN6 .... 130 F8
Stanford CI *HOVE* BN3 .... 193 K3
HPPT/KEY BN6 .... 130 F8
MIDOS PO22 .... 12 F2
Stanford Ct *HAV* PO9 .... 152 E7
Stanford Orch *HORS* RH12 .... 37 G4
Stanford Rd *BRI* BN1 .... 193 M4
HORS RH12 .... 59 L1
Stanhope Rd *LHPTN* BN17 .... 206 F2
WTHG BN11 .... 9 G4
Stanier CI *CRAWE* RH10 .... 21 J7
Stanley Av *PTSD* BN41 .... 170 A8
Stanley CI *BOGR* PO21 .... 12 E5
CRAWE RH10 .... 1 G8
Stanley Rd *BRI* BN1 .... 10 E2
EMRTH PO10 .... 175 K4
LHPTN BN17 .... 206 E1
PTSD BN41 .... 192 B4
WTHG BN11 .... 9 H3
Stanley St *ROTT* BN2 .... 11 H6
Stanmer Av *ROTT* BN2 .... 213 L1
Stanmer Park Rd *BRI* BN1 .... 194 B2
Stanmer St *BRI* BN1 .... 194 C2
Stanmer Vls *BRI* BN1 .... 194 C1
Stanmore Gdns *BOGR* PO21 .... 220 F2
Stanover La *MIDOS* PO22 .... 204 B5
Stanstead CI *HAV* PO9 .... 152 F2
Stansted Crs *HAV* PO9 .... 152 E6
Stanswood Rd *HAV* PO9 .... 152 A6
Stanton Dr *CCH* PO19 .... 179 G1
Stanton Rd *PSF* GU32 .... 68 B8
Stanwater La *MIDH* GU29 .... 71 M8
Staplecross Ct *CRAWW* RH11 .... 40 A2
Staplefield Dr *ROTT* BN2 .... 195 C1
Staplefield Rd *RHWH* RH17 .... 85 M1
RHWH RH17 .... 86 D4
Staple La *RCCH* PO18 .... 157 G4
Staples Barn *HFD* BN5 .... 127 M1
Staples Barn La *HFD* BN5 .... 127 L1
Staples HI *SWTR* RH13 .... 127 L1
Stapleton Ct *BOGR* PO21 .... 220 E1
Stapley Rd *HOVE* BN3 .... 192 E4
Starling CI *HPPT/KEY* BN6 .... 130 D1
Star Rd *SWTR* RH13 .... 127 H2
Station Ap *BRI* BN1 .... 173 J6
HORL RH6 .... 15 J1
HPPT/KEY BN6 .... 130 F8
RHWH RH17 .... 67 K8
Station Approach Rd
HORL RH6 .... 15 J4
Station CI *SWTR* RH13 .... 4 F7
Station HI *CRAWE* RH10 .... 21 J5
Station Rd *ANG/EP* BN16 .... 186 A8
ARUN BN18 .... 184 E3
BIL RH14 .... 56 A1
BIL RH14 .... 79 L4
BOGR PO21 .... 12 D6
BRI BN1 .... 193 L1
BURH RH15 .... 131 G2
CRAWE RH10 .... 2 F5
CRAWE RH10 .... 23 J4
EGRIN RH19 .... 24 E3
EGRIN RH19 .... 68 C8
EPSF GU31 .... 196 B8
HFD BN5 .... 127 M8
HISD PO11 .... 196 B8
HORL RH6 .... 15 J1
HORS RH12 .... 34 C2
HORS RH12 .... 34 E5
HORS RH12 .... 37 J4
LIPH GU30 .... 49 J2
LISS GU33 .... 47 J8
MIDH GU29 .... 94 E5
PETW GU28 .... 97 M6
PSF GU32 .... 68 B8
PUL/STOR RH20 .... 122 B2
RCCH PO18 .... 177 K5
RHWH RH17 .... 67 K7
RING/NEW BN8 .... 111 M5
STEY/UB BN44 .... 167 M1
STHW BN42 .... 191 M5
SWTR RH13 .... 4 F7
SWTR RH13 .... 59 L5
SWTR RH13 .... 82 A3

SWTR RH13 .... 105 H2
SWTR RH13 .... 105 M2
WTHG BN11 .... 9 H3
Station St *BRI* BN1 .... 10 E4
Station Wy *CRAWE* RH10 .... 2 F5
CRAWW RH11 .... 2 E5
Staunton Av *HISD* PO11 .... 214 A1
Staunton Rd *HAV* PO9 .... 174 B3
Staunton Wy *HAV* PO9 .... 174 B1
Stavely Gdns *CCH* PO19 .... 179 G1
Stead CI *HISD* PO11 .... 214 E1
Stean Furlong *LHPTN* BN17 .... 206 D1
Stedham La *MIDH* GU29 .... 94 B1
Steele CI *PUL/STOR* RH20 .... 123 M3
Steels La *RCCH* PO18 .... 176 F7
Steep CI *FIN/BW* BN14 .... 165 M7
Steepdown Rd
LAN/SOMP BN15 .... 189 K4
Steep La *FIN/BW* BN14 .... 165 M1
Steeple Vw *SALV* BN13 .... 188 B7
Steeres HI *HORS* RH12 .... 18 D5
Steers La *CRAWE* RH10 .... 15 K8
Steine Gdns *ROTT* BN2 .... 10 E7
Steine La *BRI* BN1 .... 10 E7
Steine St *ROTT* BN2 .... 10 F8
Stein Rd *EMRTH* PO10 .... 176 A2
Stempo Dr *BIL* RH14 .... 79 K4
Stempswood Wy
MIDOS PO22 .... 182 D6
Stephen CI *CRAWW* RH11 .... 20 E3
Stephenson Dr *EGRIN* RH19 .... 25 G6
Stephenson PI *CRAWE* RH10 .... 21 J6
Stephenson Wy *CRAWE* RH10 .... 3 M4
Stephens Rd *BRI* BN1 .... 194 C2
Stepney CI *CRAWE* RH10 .... 21 K8
Sternway *LHPTN* BN17 .... 207 H3
Stevenage Rd *CRAWW* RH11 .... 39 M2
Stevenson Rd *ROTT* BN2 .... 11 K7
Stewards Ri *ARUN* BN18 .... 184 A3
Steyne Gdns *WTHG* BN11 .... 9 A6
Steyne St *BOGR* PO21 .... 12 D7
The Steyne *BOGR* PO21 .... 12 D8
WTHG BN11 .... 9 J6
Steyning Av *HOVE* BN3 .... 193 G1
Steyning By-pass
STEY/UB BN44 .... 168 A3
Steyning CI *CRAWE* RH10 .... 209 J1
FERR BN12 .... 209 J1
LAN/SOMP BN15 .... 189 L4
Steyning Crs *PUL/STOR* RH20 .... 143 K2
Steyning Rd *ROTT* BN2 .... 213 G3
SHOR BN43 .... 168 C6
SWTR RH13 .... 104 D5
Stile Gdns *HASM* GU27 .... 28 A4
Stirling CI *BURH* RH15 .... 109 K8
CRAWE RH10 .... 21 J7
Stirling PI *HOVE* BN3 .... 193 H6
Stirling Rd *CCH* PO19 .... 6 F6
Stirling Wy *BOGR* PO21 .... 220 F2
EGRIN RH19 .... 25 J1
SWTR RH13 .... 5 H7
Stirrup Wy *CRAWE* RH10 .... 21 L5
Stoatley Hollow *HASM* GU27 .... 28 B4
Stoatley Ri *HASM* GU27 .... 28 B4
Stockbridge Dr *HAV* PO9 .... 152 E7
Stockbridge Gdns *CCH* PO19 .... 6 B9
Stockbridge Rd *CCH* PO19 .... 6 D8
Stockcroft Rd *RHWH* RH17 .... 65 H5
Stocker Rd *BOGR* PO21 .... 12 A9
Stockheath La *HAV* PO9 .... 174 B1
Stockheath Rd *HAV* PO9 .... 152 B8
Stockheath Wy *HAV* PO9 .... 174 C1
Stocklands CI *RHWH* RH17 .... 87 G4
Stocks La *HORL* RH6 .... 15 J3
Stocks La *RCCH* PO18 .... 157 J8
SELS PO20 .... 217 G5
Stocks Md *PUL/STOR* RH20 .... 144 F6
Stockwell Rd *EGRIN* RH19 .... 24 F6
Stodham La *EPSF* GU31 .... 69 H4
LISS GU33 .... 69 H2
Stoke Abbott Rd *WTHG* BN11 .... 9 G5
Stoke Rd *ARUN* BN18 .... 162 D2
Stokes CI *CRAWE* RH10 .... 21 K8
Stoneage CI *MIDOS* PO22 .... 203 K6
Stone CI *SALV* BN13 .... 188 A4
Stonecourt CI *HORL* RH6 .... 15 K1
Stonecroft CI *HOVE* BN3 .... 170 F8
Stonecrop CI *CRAWW* RH11 .... 40 C1
Stonecross La *RHWH* RH16 .... 88 E1
Stonecross Rd *ROTT* BN2 .... 173 G8
Stonefield CI *CRAWW* RH11 .... 1 J4
Stonefields *ANG/EP* BN16 .... 207 K3
Stonefield Wy *BURH* RH15 .... 109 G7
Stonehall La *RHWH* RH17 .... 65 J5
Stoneham Pk *PSF* GU32 .... 68 A8
Stoneham Rd *HOVE* BN3 .... 193 G5
Stonehill Crs *BOGR* PO21 .... 220 C1
Stonehouse La *LIPH* GU30 .... 26 E8
Stonehurst Rd *SALV* BN13 .... 188 A7
Stonehurst Ct *ROTT* BN2 .... 11 K4
Stone La *SALV* BN13 .... 188 A1
Stoneleigh Av *BRI* BN1 .... 172 A6
Stoneleigh CI *BRI* BN1 .... 172 A6
EGRIN RH19 .... 25 G2
Stonepit La *HFD* BN5 .... 127 J7
Stonepound Rd
HPPT/KEY BN6 .... 130 F8
Stoners CI *HORL* RH6 .... 14 E4
Stonery CI *PTSD* BN41 .... 192 B2
Stonery Rd *PTSD* BN41 .... 192 B2
Stone Sq *HAV* PO9 .... 152 C8
Stone St *BRI* BN1 .... 10 C6
Stoney Bottom *GSHT* GU26 .... 27 K1
Stone La *RHWH* RH17 .... 42 B7
SELS PO20 .... 217 L8
SHOR BN43 .... 191 K4
Stoney Stile La *BOGR* PO21 .... 220 D2
Stoney Stile La *BOGR* PO21 .... 220 D3
Stopham CI *FIN/BW* BN14 .... 188 C2
Stopham Rd *CRAWE* RH10 .... 41 K1
PUL/STOR RH20 .... 121 M3
Stor Meadow *PUL/STOR* RH20 .... 143 L2
Storrington CI *HOVE* BN3 .... 192 F2

RCCH PO18 .... 178 C5
Storrington Ri *FIN/BW* BN14 .... 166 A8
Storrington Rd
PUL/STOR RH20 .... 144 B1
Story Rd *CCH* PO19 .... 7 J2
Stour CI *PSF* GU32 .... 90 B2
Stour Rd *SALV* BN13 .... 187 K4
Strand CI *CRAWE* RH10 .... 21 L8
The Strand *FERR* BN12 .... 208 F4
FERR BN12 .... 209 K1
HISD PO11 .... 214 F3
ROTT BN2 .... 212 B1
Strand Wy *MIDOS* PO22 .... 204 C8
Strange Gdn *BOGR* PO21 .... 220 F3
Strathfield CI *FIN/BW* BN14 .... 88 A3
Strathmoor Gdns *MIDH* GU29 .... 95 G3
Strathmore CI *SALV* BN13 .... 187 M8
Strathmore Rd *CRAWW* RH11 .... 20 B3
Stratton Ct *MIDOS* PO22 .... 13 H3
Strawberry La *PUL/STOR* RH20 .... 124 C8
Stream CI *RCCH* PO18 .... 177 J7
Stream La *PUL/STOR* RH20 .... 123 J3
Stream Pk *EGRIN* RH19 .... 24 B1
Streel's La *PETW* GU28 .... 54 A7
Street End La *SELS* PO20 .... 218 F1
Street End Rd *SELS* PO20 .... 218 F1
Streetfield Rd *SWTR* RH13 .... 58 L1
Street HI *CRAWE* RH10 .... 21 M7
Street La *RHWH* RH17 .... 66 B4
The Street *ANG/EP* BN16 .... 207 J3
ARUN BN18 .... 182 E3
BIL RH14 .... 54 F2
HPPT/KEY BN6 .... 129 K6
LAN/SOMP BN15 .... 189 M4
MIDH GU29 .... 94 B3
PUL/STOR RH20 .... 123 H2
PUL/STOR RH20 .... 124 C5
PUL/STOR RH20 .... 141 H5
PUL/STOR RH20 .... 144 E6
RCCH PO18 .... 158 E8
RHWH RH17 .... 85 G4
SALV BN13 .... 186 E2
SELS PO20 .... 199 C5
SHOR BN43 .... 190 E3
STEY/UB BN44 .... 168 A2
SWTR RH13 .... 35 L8
SWTR RH13 .... 105 M2
Stretch HI *PUL/STOR* RH20 .... 99 H7
Strettington La *RCCH* PO18 .... 180 B1
Strettons Copse *LIPH* GU30 .... 71 J1
Strickland CI *CRAWW* RH11 .... 19 M7
Stride CI *PSF* GU32 .... 7 J4
Stringer Wy *BRI* BN1 .... 194 A1
Strood Ga *RHWH* RH17 .... 110 D7
Strood Rd *HORS* RH12 .... 36 D5
Strouden Ct *HAV* PO9 .... 152 A5
Stroud Green Dr *BOGR* PO21 .... 203 G7
Stroudley CI *CRAWE* RH10 .... 21 J7
Stroudwood Rd *HAV* PO9 .... 174 D1
Strudgate CI *CRAWE* RH10 .... 21 J8
Stuart CI *CRAWE* RH10 .... 21 L7
WTHG BN11 .... 9 M2
Stuart Wy *EGRIN* RH19 .... 25 J1
Stubcroft La *SELS* PO20 .... 217 J3
Stubfield *HORS* RH12 .... 60 B1
Stumblemead *RHWH* RH17 .... 65 H3
Stumblets *CRAWE* RH10 .... 21 K5
Stumps La *RCCH* PO18 .... 177 K8
Sturges Rd *BOGR* PO21 .... 12 C6
Sturt Av *HASM* GU27 .... 28 A7
Sturt Rd *HASM* GU27 .... 28 B8
Sudbury CI *BOGR* PO21 .... 220 D3
Sudeley PI *ROTT* BN2 .... 11 M9
Sudeley St *ROTT* BN2 .... 11 L8
Sudeley Ter *ROTT* BN2 .... 11 L8
Sudley Gdns *BOGR* PO21 .... 12 F6
Sudley Rd *BOGR* PO21 .... 12 F6
Suffolk CI *HORL* RH6 .... 15 H2
Suffolk St *HOVE* BN3 .... 193 C4
Sugar La *RHWH* RH17 .... 67 J7
Sugden Rd *WTHG* BN11 .... 9 J3
Sugworth CI *HWH* RH16 .... 87 L5
Sullivan CI *ROTT* BN2 .... 173 C8
Sullington Copse
PUL/STOR RH20 .... 143 M2
Sullington Gdns *FIN/BW* BN14 .... 166 A8
Sullington HI *CRAWW* RH11 .... 2 E8
Sullington La *PUL/STOR* RH20 .... 144 A4
Sullington Md *HORS* RH12 .... 59 M1
Sullington Wy *SHOR* BN43 .... 191 H4
Sullivan Dr *CRAWW* RH11 .... 39 M1
Sultan Rd *EMRTH* PO10 .... 175 J3
Summer La *PTSD* BN41 .... 192 B5
Summerdale Rd *HOVE* BN3 .... 192 F2
Summerdown CI *SALV* BN13 .... 187 J7
Summerfield Rd *SELS* PO20 .... 216 C2
Summerfields *FIN/BW* BN14 .... 165 M6
Summerhill CI *HWH* RH16 .... 87 M1
MIDOS PO22 .... 204 D6
Summerhill Dr *HWH* RH16 .... 88 A5
MIDOS PO22 .... 204 D6
Summerhill Gra *HWH* RH16 .... 88 A5
Summerhill La *HWH* RH16 .... 88 A5
Summer La *BOGR* PO21 .... 220 A3
Summerley La *MIDOS* PO22 .... 204 C7
Summersdeane *STHW* BN42 .... 192 A3
Summersvere CI *CRAWE* RH10 .... 21 H3
Sumners Rd *RHWH* RH17 .... 66 B5
Sun Brow *HASM* GU27 .... 28 B7
Sundale La *MIDOS* PO22 .... 204 F7
Sunderland CI *SELS* PO20 .... 180 E2
Sundew CI *CRAWW* RH11 .... 40 B2
Sunneymead CI *SELS* PO20 .... 223 G6
Sunningdale Ct *CRAWW* RH11 .... 2 E7
Sunningdale Gdns
MIDOS PO22 .... 203 J5
Sunningdale Rd *SALV* BN13 .... 187 L8
Sunninghill Av *HOVE* BN3 .... 192 F1
Sunninghill CI *HOVE* BN3 .... 192 F2
Sunny Av *CRAWE* RH10 .... 23 H4
Sunnybox La *ARUN* BN18 .... 160 E8
Sunny CI *FERR* BN12 .... 209 M3
Sunnycroft CI *RHWH* RH17 .... 110 F2
Sunnydale Av *BRI* BN1 .... 172 B6
Sunnydale CI *BRI* BN1 .... 172 B6
Sunnyheath *HAV* PO9 .... 152 B8

Sunnyhill CI *CRAWE* RH10 .... 23 H4
Sunnymead *CRAWW* RH11 .... 2 E3
Sunnymead CI *MIDOS* PO22 .... 205 H7
Sunnymead Dr *SELS* PO20 .... 223 G6
Sunny Wy *RCCH* PO18 .... 177 J7
Sun Park CI *HWH* RH16 .... 109 J2
Sun Park CI *BOGR* PO21 .... 203 H6
Sunset La *PUL/STOR* RH20 .... 123 K7
Sunshine Av *HISD* PO11 .... 214 E2
Sunte Av *HWH* RH16 .... 88 A5
Sunte CI *HWH* RH16 .... 87 M5
Sunvale Av *HASM* GU27 .... 27 L6
Sunvale CI *HASM* GU27 .... 27 L6
Sunwood Rd *HAV* PO9 .... 152 A7
Surrenden CI *BRI* BN1 .... 172 A1
Surrenden Crs *BRI* BN1 .... 193 M1
Surrenden Holt *BRI* BN1 .... 194 A1
Surrenden Pk *BRI* BN1 .... 172 B8
Surrenden Ri *CRAWW* RH11 .... 40 D4
Surrenden Rd *BRI* BN1 .... 172 A4
Surrey St *ARUN* BN18 .... 184 E2
BRI BN1 .... 10 D4
LHPTN BN17 .... 206 E4
WTHG BN11 .... 8 F7
Surrey Whf *ARUN* BN18 .... 184 E2
Surry St *SHOR* BN43 .... 191 G5
Sussex Border Pth *BRI* BN1 .... 171 G2
CRAWE RH10 .... 22 E2
EGRIN RH19 .... 25 L5
EMRTH PO10 .... 175 K1
EMRTH PO10 .... 177 J1
EPSF GU31 .... 91 J7
HASM GU27 .... 52 A3
HAV PO9 .... 132 A8
HORL RH6 .... 14 D4
HORS RH12 .... 18 D5
LIPH GU30 .... 48 C6
LISS GU33 .... 48 C6
MFD/CHID GU8 .... 30 A7
MFD/CHID GU8 .... 31 M6
PTSD BN41 .... 169 M6
RDKG RH5 .... 17 J4
RHWH RH17 .... 67 L4
Sussex Dr *BOGR* PO21 .... 220 B3
Sussex Gdns *ANG/EP* BN16 .... 207 K2
EPSF GU31 .... 90 C2
HWH RH16 .... 110 C1
Sussex Gv *SELS* PO20 .... 217 K7
Sussex PI *ROTT* BN2 .... 11 G5
Sussex Rd *EPSF* GU31 .... 90 D2
HOVE BN3 .... 193 J7
HWH RH16 .... 109 M1
LAN/SOMP BN15 .... 190 D6
WTHG BN11 .... 9 H4
Sussex Sq *ROTT* BN2 .... 194 F3
Sussex St *BOGR* PO21 .... 12 E7
LHPTN BN17 .... 206 E2
ROTT BN2 .... 11 G6
Sussex Wy *BURH* RH15 .... 108 F7
Sutherland CI *ANG/EP* BN16 .... 207 J3
BOGR PO21 .... 12 C7
Sutherland Rd *ROTT* BN2 .... 11 K7
Sutton Av *ANG/EP* BN16 .... 207 K4
Sutton CI *MIDOS* PO22 .... 195 M2
ROTT BN2 .... 195 M3
Swainsthorpe CI *HWH* RH16 .... 110 A1
Swaledale CI *CRAWW* RH11 .... 2 C9
Swallow CI *HAV* PO9 .... 174 E1
Swallowfield CI *SWTR* RH13 .... 61 K7
Swallow Rd *CRAWW* RH11 .... 20 D4
Swallows CI *LAN/SOMP* BN15 .... 190 D7
Swallows Green Dr *SALV* BN13 .... 187 K7
Swallows La *SWTR* RH13 .... 104 A3
Swallowtail Rd *HORS* RH12 .... 37 M6
Swan Barn Rd *HASM* GU27 .... 28 E6
Swanborough Dr *ROTT* BN2 .... 195 C6
Swanborough PI *ROTT* BN2 .... 195 G5
Swanbourne CI
LAN/SOMP BN15 .... 190 A4
Swanbourne Rd *LHPTN* BN17 .... 206 E1
Swan CI *EMRTH* PO10 .... 175 K4
PUL/STOR RH20 .... 143 K2
SWTR RH13 .... 82 B2
Swan Dene *BOGR* PO21 .... 220 A5
Swanfield Dr *CCH* PO19 .... 7 H2
Swan La *HORL* RH6 .... 14 A5
Swanmore Rd *HAV* PO9 .... 152 A5
Swann CI *BURH* RH15 .... 131 L1
Swann Wy *HORS* RH12 .... 59 M1
Swansea Gdns *BOGR* PO21 .... 12 B8
Swans Ghyll *FROW* RH18 .... 45 M1
Swan St *PSF* GU32 .... 90 B1
Swan Vw *PUL/STOR* RH20 .... 122 D3
Swarraton Rd *HAV* PO9 .... 152 B8
Sway Ct *HAV* PO9 .... 152 E7
Swaything Rd *HAV* PO9 .... 152 A6
Sweetlands *HPPT/KEY* BN6 .... 131 J7
Swift CI *HPPT/KEY* BN6 .... 130 E1
Swift La *CRAWW* RH11 .... 20 E4
Swift Rd *EMRTH* PO10 .... 197 K1
Swift Wy *LHPTN* BN17 .... 184 D1
Swillage La *ANG/EP* BN16 .... 186 B3
Swindon Rd *HORS* RH12 .... 4 A4
Swiss Gdns *SHOR* BN43 .... 190 F5
Sycamore Av *HORS* RH12 .... 38 C7
Sycamore CI *ANG/EP* BN16 .... 186 A8
CRAWW RH11 .... 20 B3
PTSD BN41 .... 192 D1
ROTT BN2 .... 195 M4
Sycamore Dr *EGRIN* RH19 .... 25 H3
HISD PO11 .... 196 B8
Sycamore Rd *MIDOS* PO22 .... 203 K5
Sydmonton Ct *HAV* PO9 .... 152 E6
Sydney Rd *HWH* RH16 .... 87 M6
Sydney St *BRI* BN1 .... 10 E5
Syers Rd *LISS* GU33 .... 47 J8
Sylvan CI *HWH* RH16 .... 88 C8
Sylvan Rd *CRAWE* RH10 .... 3 L8
LAN/SOMP BN15 .... 189 L6
Sylvan Wy *BOGR* PO21 .... 12 A7
Sylvester Wy *HWH* RH16 .... 88 D3
Sylvia CI *BOGR* PO21 .... 220 B5
Symbister Rd *PTSD* BN41 .... 192 D5
Syresham Gdns *HWH* RH16 .... 87 M8

T

Tabard Ga *BOGR* PO21 .... 220 C3

Tack Lee Rd *ARUN* BN18......205 C1
Talbot Crs *BRI* BN1......172 E6
Talbot La *HORS* RH12......4 A9
Talbot Rd *HOV* PO9......174 A1
 LHPTN BN17......206 D3
Tallis Cl *CRAWW* RH11......40 A1
Talman Cl *CRAWW* RH11......19 M7
Tamar Av *SALV* BN13......187 K4
Tamar Cl *CRAWE* RH10......21 K7
 SALV BN13......187 K5
Tamarisk Cl *MIDOS* PO22......203 K5
Tamarisk Wk *SELS* PO20......217 G6
Tamarisk Wy *ANG/EP* BN16......207 M4
 FERR BN12......209 G4
Tamar Wy *SELS* PO20......180 D2
Tamplin Ter *ROTT* BN2......11 G4
Tamworth Dr *HORS* RH12......4 A9
Tanbridge Pl *HORS* RH12......60 C3
Tandridge Rd *HORS* RH12......192 F6
Tangmere Gdns *BOGR* PO21......220 E2
Tangmere Rd *BRI* BN1......172 B6
 CRAWW RH11......20 A6
 SELS PO20......180 A5
Tankerdale La......68 F4
Tanners Fld *RHWH* RH17......110 B7
Tanners La *HASM* GU27......28 D5
Tanners Md *HWH* RH16......63 M7
Tannery Cl *SWTR* RH13......58 D1
Tansy Md *PUL/STOR* RH20......143 J2
Tanyard Av *EGRIN* RH19......25 H4
Tanyard Cl *CRAWE* RH10......41 K1
 SWTR RH13......60 F3
Tanyard La *STEY/UB* BN44......167 L1
Tarmount La *SHOR* BN43......191 G5
Tarner Rd *ROTT* BN2......11 H6
Tarn Rd *GSHT* GU26......27 L1
Tarragon Wy *SHOR* BN43......191 K3
Tarrant Gdns *HAV* PO9......174 A1
Tarrant St *ARUN* BN18......184 C2
Tarrant Whf *ARUN* BN18......184 C2
Tarring Rd *WTHG* BN11......8 C3
Tasman Cl *ANG/EP* BN16......207 L4
Tasman Wy *SALV* BN13......187 K5
Tate Crs *BURH* RH15......109 G7
Tates Wy *HORS* RH12......34 E5
Taunton Rd *ROTT* BN2......195 G3
Taunton Wy *ROTT* BN2......195 H5
Tavern Ct *HASM* GU27......51 J6
Taverner Pl *CCH* PO19......7 G8
Tavistock Down *BRI* BN1......194 D2
Tavistock Gdns *HAV* PO9......174 A1
Tavy Cl *SALV* BN13......187 K6
Tavy Rd *SALV* BN13......187 K6
Taw Cl *SALV* BN13......187 L5
Taylors Fld *MIDH* GU29......94 F6
Taylor's La *RCCH* PO18......177 K8
Taylors Ri *MIDH* GU29......94 F6
Teal Cl *HISD* PO11......214 E1
 HORS RH12......4 D1
Teal La *SELS* PO20......222 D4
Teasel Cl *CRAWW* RH11......40 C1
Teazle Cl *EPSF* GU31......90 F2
Teesdale *CRAWW* RH11......2 D2
Teg Cl *PTSD* BN41......192 D2
Telegraph La *EPSF* GU31......114 B2
Telegraph St *ROTT* BN2......11 K8
Telford Pl *CRAWE* RH10......3 H5
Telgarth Rd *FERR* BN12......208 F4
Telham Ct *CRAWW* RH11......40 A1
Templars Cl *MIDOS* PO22......204 E6
The Templars *FIN/BW* BN14......188 F5
Temple Cl *CRAWE* RH10......21 L7
Temple Gdns *HOVE* BN3......10 A6
Temple Gv *BURH* RH15......108 E8
Temple La *LISS* GU33......47 K6
Templesheen Rd *MIDOS* PO22......205 J7
Temple St *BRI* BN1......10 A6
Tenacre Cl *CCH* PO19......179 J4
Ten Acres *WTHG* BN11......211 H1
Tenantry Down Rd *ROTT* BN2......194 F5
Tenantry Rd *ROTT* BN2......194 E4
Tennis Rd *HOVE* BN3......192 F6
Tennyson Av *ANG/EP* BN16......207 H3
Tennyson Cl *CRAWE* RH10......21 J4
 HORS RH12......37 M6
Tennyson Ri *EGRIN* RH19......24 D3
Tennyson Rd *BOGR* PO21......221 H1
 WTHG BN11......8 F3
Tennyson's La *HASM* GU27......28 F8
Terminus Pl *BRI* BN1......10 D3
 LHPTN BN17......206 E3
Terminus Rd *BRI* BN1......10 D3
 CCH PO19......6 C7
 LHPTN BN17......206 D3
Terminus St *BRI* BN1......10 D4
Tern Rd *CRAWW* RH11......19 L7
The Terrace *LAN/SOMP* BN15......189 M8
Terringes Av *SALV* BN13......187 M7
Terry Rd *CRAWW* RH11......40 C3
Terwick La *EPSF* GU31......93 H4
Test Cl *PSF* GU32......90 B3
Testers Cl *SWTR* RH13......82 B5
Test Rd *LAN/SOMP* BN15......189 J6
Testwood Rd *HAV* PO9......152 A7
Teville Gdns *WTHG* BN11......8 F3
Teville Rd *WTHG* BN11......8 F3
Thackeray Rd *FIN/BW* BN14......9 M1
Thakeham Cl *ANG/EP* BN16......208 C1
 FERR BN12......209 H2
Thakeham Copse
 PUL/STOR RH20......144 C2
Thakeham Dr *FERR* BN12......209 H2
Thakeham Rd *PUL/STOR* RH20......144 A2
Thalassa Rd *WTHG* BN11......211 J1
Thames Cl *LHPTN* BN17......207 H4
 ROTT BN2......11 H6
Thames Wy *SALV* BN13......187 L5
Thatcher Cl *CRAWE* RH10......41 K1
Thatchers Ct *BURH* RH15......131 L3
 HORS RH12......5 G2
Thatchway Cl *LHPTN* BN17......206 E3
The Thatchway *ANG/EP* BN16......185 M7
 ANG/EP BN16......207 L4
Theatre La *CCH* PO19......7 G6
The Denture *ARUN* BN18......140 C8
Thelton Av *HORS* RH12......59 L1
Theobalds Rd *BURH* RH15......109 K6
Thesiger Cl *WTHG* BN11......189 H8
Thesiger Rd *WTHG* BN11......189 H8

Theydon Cl *CRAWE* RH10......3 L7
Thicket La *RCCH* PO18......159 J7
Third Av *FIN/BW* BN14......188 E5
 HAV PO9......174 D2
 HOVE BN3......193 J7
 LAN/SOMP BN15......189 M5
 MIDOS PO22......204 C8
 SELS PO20......217 J7
 SELS PO20......217 M4
Thirlmere Crs *FIN/BW* BN14......189 J7
Thirlmere Rd *CRAWW* RH11......19 L8
Thirlmere Wy *MIDOS* PO22......204 D8
Thistledowne Gdns
 EMRTH PO10......175 L4
Thistle Wy *SWTR* RH13......82 B1
Thistledown V *BIL* RH14......32 E8
Thompson Rd *BRI* BN1......194 D3
 MIDOS PO22......205 G7
Thomson Cl *SALV* BN13......187 J6
Thorgate Rd *LHPTN* BN17......206 C1
Thornbush Crs *PTSD* BN41......192 C1
Thorn Cl *EPSF* GU31......90 F2
Thorncroft Rd *LHPTN* BN17......206 F2
Thorndean Dr *RHWH* RH17......85 L5
Thorndean Rd *ROTT* BN2......194 E1
Thorndon *SWTR* RH13......105 M2
Thorney Cl *BOGR* PO21......12 A5
Thorney Dr *SELS* PO20......222 E6
Thorney Old Pk *EMRTH* PO10......198 A3
Thorney Rd *EMRTH* PO10......175 L7
Thornham La *EMRTH* PO10......175 L6
Thornhill Av *BRI* BN1......172 B5
Thornhill Cl *HOVE* BN3......192 F7
Thornhill Ri *PTSD* BN41......170 B8
Thornhill Wy *PTSD* BN41......192 B1
Thornhill Rd *WTHG* BN11......8 E7
Thornscroft *STEY/UB* BN44......146 E8
Thornton Cl *HORL* RH6......14 F1
Thornton Pl *HORL* RH6......15 G1
Threals Copse *PUL/STOR* RH20......123 M7
Threal's La *PUL/STOR* RH20......123 M6
Three Acres *HORS* RH12......60 B3
Three Bridges Rd *CRAWE* RH10......3 L4
 CRAWE RH10......21 J6
Three Gates La *HASM* GU27......28 E5
Threestile Rd *HORS* RH12......37 G3
Thrusloes *BOGR* PO21......221 G2
Thurlow Rd *WTHG* BN11......9 K3
Thurne Wy *HORS* RH12......34 E5
Thyme Cl *SHOR* BN43......191 K3
Ticehurst Cl *CRAWE* RH10......21 M6
Ticehurst Rd *ROTT* BN2......195 G7
Tichborne Gv *HAV* PO9......152 A7
Tichborne St *BRI* BN1......10 E6
Tideway *ANG/EP* BN16......207 H4
Tidworth Rd *SALV* BN13......187 M6
Tidy St *BRI* BN1......10 E5
Tilbury Pl *ROTT* BN2......11 G6
Tilbury Wy *ROTT* BN2......11 H5
Tile Barn La *SELS* PO20......217 K3
Tilers Cl *BURH* RH15......131 L1
Tilgate Cl *ROTT* BN2......11 L5
Tilgate Dr *CRAWE* RH10......40 F3
Tilgate Pde *CRAWE* RH10......40 F1
Tilgate Pl *CRAWE* RH10......40 F1
Tilgate Wy *CRAWE* RH10......3 G9
Tilletts La *HORS* RH12......36 F4
Tillinghurst La *RHWH* RH17......66 A2
Tillotson Ct *LHPTN* BN17......21 L7
Tillstone Cl *ROTT* BN2......194 E2
Tillstone St *ROTT* BN2......11 H7
Tilmore Gdns *PSF* GU32......68 C7
Tilmore Rd *PSF* GU32......68 B8
Tiltwood Dr *CRAWE* RH10......23 K2
Timber Cl *SALV* BN13......187 K7
Timber Ct *HORS* RH12......4 C5
Timberham Farm Rd *HORL* RH6......14 E4
Timberlands *CRAWW* RH11......40 C3
 PUL/STOR RH20......143 M2
Timberlea Cl *PUL/STOR* RH20......125 H7
Timberleys *LHPTN* BN17......207 G1
Timber Ml *SWTR* RH13......82 A2
Timbermill Ct *HASM* GU27......28 A6
The Timbers *SWTR* RH13......61 K6
Timsbury Crs *HAV* PO9......152 A6
Tindal Cl *BURH* RH15......131 L1
Tinghall *BOGR* PO21......220 F1
Tinsley Gn *CRAWE* RH10......21 J1
Tinsley La *CRAWE* RH10......21 H3
Tinsley La North *CRAWE* RH10......21 J1
Tinsley La South *CRAWE* RH10......21 H4
Tintern Cl *BRI* BN1......194 C3
Tintern Rd *CRAWW* RH11......20 B8
Tinwood La *RCCH* PO18......158 F7
Tipper La *EPSF* GU31......113 L1
Tisbury Rd *HOVE* BN3......193 K6
Tisted Cl *HAV* PO9......152 E7
Titchfield Cl *BURH* RH15......131 L1
Titch Hl *LAN/SOMP* BN15......167 H8
Tithe Barn La *BOGR* PO21......220 D3
Tithe Barn Wy *BOGR* PO21......220 C3
Tithe Gn *ANG/EP* BN16......207 J3
Titian Rd *HOVE* BN3......193 G5
Titmus Dr *CRAWE* RH10......41 G1
Titnore La *FERR* BN12......187 H6
 SALV BN13......187 G5
Titnore Wy *FERR* BN12......187 H7
Tivoli Cls *BRI* BN1......193 L3
Tivoli Crs North *BRI* BN1......193 L2
Tivoli Pl *BRI* BN1......193 L2
Tivoli Rd *BRI* BN1......193 L2
Toat La *PUL/STOR* RH20......100 B5
Toddington La *LHPTN* BN17......184 D8
Toddington Pk *LHPTN* BN17......184 F8
Todmore *LISS* GU33......47 J1
Toftwood Cl *CRAWE* RH10......21 K7
Tollgate Hl *CRAWW* RH11......40 C3
Tollgate La *RHWH* RH17......86 E1
Tollhouse La *CCH* PO19......6 C5
Tomtits La *FROW* RH18......45 M3
Tongdean Av *HOVE* BN3......193 K1
Tongdean La *BRI* BN1......171 L8
Tongdean Ri *BRI* BN1......171 K8
Tongdean Rd *HOVE* BN3......193 J1
Toomey Rd *STEY/UB* BN44......146 E7
Top Rd *ARUN* BN18......160 D7
 EGRIN RH19......44 A7
Top St *RHWH* RH17......85 K8
Torberry Dr *EPSF* GU31......90 E2

Torcross Cl *ROTT* BN2......194 F3
Toronto Cl *SALV* BN13......187 L6
Toronto Ter *ROTT* BN2......11 H5
Torrance Cl *HOVE* BN3......193 G3
Torridge Cl *SALV* BN13......187 K5
Torton Hill Rd *ARUN* BN18......184 A2
Tor Wy *EPSF* GU31......90 D1
Tote La *MIDH* GU29......72 B6
Totland Rd *ROTT* BN2......11 L2
Tottington Dr *HFD* BN5......147 M6
Tottington La *SHOR* BN43......191 J3
Tournerbury La *HISD* PO11......196 D8
Tower Cl *CCH* PO19......6 D3
 EGRIN RH19......24 F2
 HORL RH6......15 G1
Tower Gdns *HAV* PO9......174 C6
Towergate *BRI* BN1......193 M2
Tower House Cl *RHWH* RH17......86 F5
Tower Rd *HORS* RH12......39 H4
 LAN/SOMP BN15......189 K7
 LIPH GU30......26 C8
 ROTT BN2......11 J4
 WTHG BN11......9 J4
Town Barn Rd *CRAWW* RH11......2 C8
Town Cross Av *BOGR* PO21......12 C5
Town Hall Rd *HAV* PO9......174 C3
Town La *EPSF* GU31......68 E7
 RCCH PO18......136 D7
Town Md *CRAWW* RH11......2 D7
Townsend Crs *LHPTN* BN17......207 G2
Tozer Wy *CCH* PO19......7 G3
Trafalgar Cl *BRI* BN1......10 F4
Trafalgar Ga *ROTT* BN2......212 A1
Trafalgar Pl *BRI* BN1......10 E5
Trafalgar Rd *HORS* RH12......4 C4
Trafalgar St *BRI* BN1......10 E4
Tramway La *SELS* PO20......201 G4
Trap La *EGRIN* RH19......16 A2
Treadcroft Dr *HORS* RH12......5 H2
Tredcroft Rd *HOVE* BN3......193 J2
Tree Av *HASM* GU27......28 A4
Treemans Rd *RHWH* RH17......89 J2
Treetops *SWTR* RH13......82 A5
Treeview *CRAWW* RH11......40 D3
Trefoil Cl *HWH* RH16......5 G1
Trefoil Crs *CRAWW* RH11......40 C1
Tregarth Rd *CCH* PO19......179 H2
Treharne Cl *SALV* BN13......187 L5
Treloar Rd *HISD* PO11......215 H3
Tremola Av *ROTT* BN2......213 J2
Trendle Gn *BOGR* PO21......221 G1
Trenear Cl *SWTR* RH13......5 C8
Trent Cl *CRAWW* RH11......20 A8
 LAN/SOMP BN15......189 K6
Trent Rd *WTHG* BN11......209 M2
Tretawn Gdns *SELS* PO20......223 H6
Trevanne Plat *CRAWE* RH10......21 L5
Treveor Cl *WTHG* BN11......8 F5
Treyford Cl *CRAWW* RH11......20 A6
 ROTT BN2......195 M3
Triangle Rd *HWH* RH16......109 M1
Trinity Cl *CRAWW* RH11......21 K4
Trinity Rd *HPPT/KEY* BN6......130 B6
Trinity St *ROTT* BN2......11 H2
Trinity Wy *BOGR* PO21......203 C8
 LHPTN BN17......207 G4
Tripp Hl *PUL/STOR* RH20......121 G5
Tristram Cl *LAN/SOMP* BN15......189 H5
Triton Pl *MIDOS* PO22......204 D7
Troon Cl *CRAWW* RH11......19 L7
Trosnant Rd *HAV* PO9......174 D2
Trotton Cl *CRAWE* RH10......41 K1
Trotton Rd *EPSF* GU31......93 G4
Trout La *SWTR* RH13......81 H4
Trout Rd *HASM* GU27......27 M6
Troymede *RHWH* RH17......65 H3
True Blue Prec *LHPTN* BN17......206 E1
Truggers *RHWH* RH17......63 J4
Truleigh Dr *PTSD* BN41......170 B8
Truleigh Rd *STEY/UB* BN44......168 C2
Truleigh Wy *SHOR* BN43......191 H3
Trundle Cl *RCCH* PO18......156 F6
Trundle Md *HORS* RH12......4 D1
Trundle View Cl *MIDOS* PO22......182 C6
Truro Cl *CCH* PO19......179 C3
Truro Crs *BOGR* PO21......220 F1
Trusler's Hl *HPPT/KEY* BN6......129 G5
Tryndel Wy *MIDOS* PO22......204 D4
Tudor Av *EMRTH* PO10......153 H8
Tudor Cl *CCH* PO19......179 G2
 CRAWE RH10......21 L7
 EGRIN RH19......25 G5
 FIN/BW BN14......165 M6
 GSHT GU26......27 L2
 HISD PO11......214 C2
 HOVE BN3......193 G2
 MIDOS PO22......204 E7
 PUL/STOR RH20......123 G3
Tudor Dr *SELS* PO20......181 L4
 STEY/UB BN44......167 H8
Tudor Gdns *BURH* RH15......109 G8
Tudor Village *PUL/STOR* RH20......144 D1
Tufts Fld *MIDH* GU29......94 E6
Tufts Meadow *MIDH* GU29......94 F6
Tuggles Plat *HORS* RH12......36 F5
Tullett Rd *CRAWE* RH10......41 J2
Tumulus Rd *ROTT* BN2......213 K2
Tunbridge Crs *LIPH* GU30......26 C7
Tunbridge La *LIPH* GU30......26 C6
Tunnmeade *CRAWW* RH11......19 M7
Tunsgate *STEY/UB* BN44......167 L1
Tunworth Ct *HAV* PO9......152 E7
Tuppenny La *EMRTH* PO10......175 M4
Turkey La *BURH* RH15......131 J1
Turnbull Rd *CCH* PO19......7 G2
Turner Ct *FIN/BW* BN14......188 F6
Turner Rd *FIN/BW* BN14......188 F6
Turners Hill Rd *CRAWE* RH10......21 M6
 CRAWE RH10......23 G1
 EGRIN RH19......24 B7
Turners Md *MFD/CHID* GU8......30 D1
 PUL/STOR RH20......143 J2
Turners Mill Cl *HWH* RH16......87 L6
Turners Mill Rd *HWH* RH16......87 L6
Turners Wy *BURH* RH15......109 G8

Turner Wy *SELS* PO20......223 H5
Turnpike Cl *CCH* PO19......201 G1
Turnpike Pk *CRAWW* RH11......20 E4
Turnpike Rd *ARUN* BN18......142 A6
Turton Cl *ROTT* BN2......11 J7
Tuscan Av *SALV* BN13......205 G7
Tuscany Gdns *CRAWE* RH10......20 F3
Tushmore Av *CRAWW* RH11......20 F3
Tushmore Crs *CRAWW* RH11......20 F3
Tushmore La *CRAWE* RH10......20 F4
Tussock Cl *CRAWW* RH11......20 B8
Tuxford Cl *CRAWE* RH10......21 K8
Tweed La *CRAWW* RH11......20 A3
Twineham Cl *ROTT* BN2......195 G5
Twineham La *FIN/BW* BN14......188 C5
Twineham La *HPPT/KEY* BN6......129 H3
Twitten Cl *STHW* BN42......191 M5
The Twitten *BURH* RH15......109 J8
 HPPT/KEY BN6......129 K6
 STHW BN42......191 M5
Twitten Wy *FIN/BW* BN14......8 B1
Two Barns La *RCCH* PO18......156 E6
Two Mile Ash Rd *SWTR* RH13......81 C1
Two Ways *BIL* RH14......33 H8
Twyford Cl *SALV* BN13......187 M6
Twyford Gdns *SALV* BN13......187 M6
Twyford Rd *BRI* BN1......172 E6
 SALV BN13......187 M6
Twyhurst Ct *EGRIN* RH19......24 E1
Twyne Cl *CRAWW* RH11......20 A8
Tye Cl *ROTT* BN2......213 L4
Tye La *ARUN* BN18......182 F3
Tylden Wy *HORS* RH12......38 A6
Tyler Rd *CRAWE* RH10......2 F9
Tyler's Gn *RHWH* RH17......87 J8
Tylston Meadow *LIPH* GU30......26 C7
Tyne Cl *CRAWE* RH10......21 K7
 SALV BN13......187 K6
Tyne Wy *BOGR* PO21......202 E8
The Tynings
 LAN/SOMP BN15......189 M7
Tythe Barn *RHWH* RH17......107 K1
Tythe Barn Rd *SELS* PO20......223 G6

U

Uckfield Cl *ROTT* BN2......195 G6
Ullswater Dr *ANG/EP* BN16......207 H1
Ullswater Gv *MIDOS* PO22......204 C8
Ullswater Rd *LAN/SOMP* BN15......189 J7
Underdown Rd *STHW* BN42......191 M4
Underhill La *HPPT/KEY* BN6......150 F4
Undermill Rd *STEY/UB* BN44......168 C2
Underwood Cl *CRAWE* RH10......23 J4
Underwood Rd *HASM* GU27......28 A5
Union Pl *WTHG* BN11......9 H5
Union Ri *LISS* GU33......48 A2
Union Rd *HAV* PO9......174 B3
 ROTT BN2......11 G3
Union St *BRI* BN1......10 D7
Upfield *HORL* RH6......15 H2
Upfield Cl *HORL* RH6......15 H3
Uphill Wy *SELS* PO20......201 G4
Upland Cl *LISS* GU33......46 D5
Uplands Av *SALV* BN13......188 A3
Uplands Cl *HASM* GU27......28 E4
Uplands Rd *BRI* BN1......194 D2
 HAV PO9......152 F2
Uppark Gdns *HORS* RH12......38 A6
Uppark Wy *MIDOS* PO22......204 D8
Upper Abbey Rd *ROTT* BN2......11 L8
Upper Bannings Rd *ROTT* BN2......213 M1
Upper Bedford St *ROTT* BN2......11 J8
Upper Bevendean Av
 ROTT BN2......194 F3
Upper Bognor Rd *BOGR* PO21......12 C4
 MIDOS PO22......13 J6
Upper Boundstone La
 LAN/SOMP BN15......189 L4
Upper Brighton Rd
 FIN/BW BN14......188 F5
 LAN/SOMP BN15......189 H5
Upper Chalvington Pl
 ROTT BN2......194 F7
Upper Dr *ANG/EP* BN16......208 C4
The Upper Dr *HOVE* BN3......193 K4
Upperfield *MIDH* GU29......95 G2
Upper Gardner St *BRI* BN1......10 D6
Upper Gloucester Rd *BRI* BN1......10 D5
Upper Hamilton Rd *BRI* BN1......10 B1
Upper Heyshott *EPSF* GU31......90 D1
Upper High St *WTHG* BN11......9 J3
Upper Hollingdean Rd
 BRI BN1......194 C3
Upper Kingston La
 STHW BN42......191 L3
Upper Lewes Rd *ROTT* BN2......11 G2
Upper Market St *HOVE* BN3......193 L7
Upper Mt *HASM* GU27......29 G3
 LISS GU33......69 H1
Upper North St *BRI* BN1......10 B5
Upper Park Pl *ROTT* BN2......11 H6
Upper Rock Gdns *ROTT* BN2......11 H8
Upper St James's St *ROTT* BN2......11 J8
Upper St Johns Rd *BURH* RH15......131 H1
Upper Shoreham Rd
 SHOR BN43......190 F4
 STHW BN42......191 L5
Upper Station Rd *HFD* BN5......127 L7
Upper St *PUL/STOR* RH20......121 G1
Upper Sudeley St *ROTT* BN2......11 L8
Upperton Rd *PETW* GU28......97 J2
Upper Wardown *EPSF* GU31......68 E8
Upper Wellington Rd *ROTT* BN2......11 J2
Upper West Dr *FERR* BN12......208 F3
Upper West La
 LAN/SOMP BN15......189 H5
Upton Av *STHW* BN42......191 M3
Upton Cl *HAV* PO9......152 A5
Upton Gdns *SALV* BN13......188 A3
Upton Rd *CCH* PO19......6 C8
 SALV BN13......188 A3
Upways Cl *SELS* PO20......222 F6
Ursula Av *SELS* PO20......222 F6
Ursula Av North *SELS* PO20......222 F6
Ursula Sq *SELS* PO20......222 F7

V

Vale Av *BRI* BN1......171 H5
 FIN/BW BN14......188 F5
Valebridge Cl *BURH* RH15......109 K6
Valebridge Dr *BURH* RH15......109 K7
Valebridge Rd *BURH* RH15......109 K6
Vale Dr *FIN/BW* BN14......188 A4
 HORS RH12......4 A1
Vale Gdns *PTSD* BN41......192 C1
Valencia Rd *WTHG* BN11......8 B1
Valentine Cl *FIN/BW* BN14......188 C5
Valentine Dr *BURH* RH15......108 F7
Valentines Gdns *BOGR* PO21......220 D2
Valentines Lea *PETW* GU28......53 H4
Valerie Cl *PTSD* BN41......192 C1
Vale Rd *HWH* RH16......109 L1
 PTSD BN41......192 D1
 ROTT BN2......213 L1
The Vale *ROTT* BN2......195 M4
Valetta Pk *EMRTH* PO10......175 H4
Valetta Rd *EMRTH* PO10......198 A5
Vale Wk *FIN/BW* BN14......188 A4
Valewood Cl *BIL* RH14......80 F3
Valewood La *BIL* RH14......80 F5
Valewood Rd *HASM* GU27......28 D5
Valiant Rd *EMRTH* PO10......198 A5
Vallance Cl *BURH* RH15......108 F7
Vallance Gdns *HOVE* BN3......193 G5
Vallance Rd *HOVE* BN3......193 G6
Valley Cl *BRI* BN1......171 K4
Valley Dr *BRI* BN1......171 K4
Valley Rd *LAN/SOMP* BN15......189 K4
 PTSD BN41......192 D2
Valley Side *LIPH* GU30......26 C6
Vanbrugh Cl *CRAWW* RH11......39 M1
Vancouver Cl *SALV* BN13......187 L6
Vancouver Dr *CRAWW* RH11......20 E4
Vancouver Rd *SALV* BN13......187 K6
Van Dyck Pl *MIDOS* PO22......203 H6
Van Gogh Pl *MIDOS* PO22......203 J4
Vann Bridge Cl *HASM* GU27......51 H6
Vanners *CRAWE* RH10......3 G1
Vann Lake Rd *RDKG* RH5......17 G2
Vann Rd *HASM* GU27......51 H6
Vanzell Rd *MIDH* GU29......95 H7
Varey Rd *SALV* BN13......187 J3
Varndean Cl *BRI* BN1......193 M1
Varndean Dr *BRI* BN1......193 M1
Varndean Gdns *BRI* BN1......193 M1
Varndean Holt *BRI* BN1......194 A1
Varndean Rd *BRI* BN1......193 M1
Varsity Rd *EMRTH* PO10......198 A3
Vauxhall Wy *PSF* GU32......90 B3
Velyn Av *CCH* PO19......7 G5
Ventnor Vls *HOVE* BN3......193 J4
Venus La *BOGR* PO21......219 M1
Veras Wk *PUL/STOR* RH20......144 D2
Verbania Wy *EGRIN* RH19......25 J3
Verdley Pl *HASM* GU27......73 K4
Vere Rd *BRI* BN1......10 F7
Vermont Dr *ANG/EP* BN16......208 D5
Vermont Wy *ANG/EP* BN16......208 B3
Vernon Av *ROTT* BN2......195 K5
Vernon Cl *ANG/EP* BN16......207 K3
 HORS RH12......5 L1
Vernon Ter *BRI* BN1......10 B6
Veronica Cl *ANG/EP* BN16......208 B4
Veronica Wy *ROTT* BN2......11 J3
Verwood Rd *HAV* PO9......152 E6
Viaduct Rd *BRI* BN1......10 E2
Vicarage Flds *SALV* BN13......187 L3
Vicarage Gdns *CSHT* GU26......27 K1
Vicarage La *ANG/EP* BN16......208 A1
 HASM GU27......28 A6
 MIDOS PO22......13 K5
 PETW GU28......96 C2
 RHWH RH17......111 G2
 ROTT BN2......213 G3
 STEY/UB BN44......167 L2
Vicarage Rd *CRAWE* RH10......23 H1
Vicarage Ter *ROTT* BN2......213 G3
Victoria Av *BURH* RH15......130 F1
 HISD PO11......214 C2
 MIDH GU29......95 H7
Victoria Cl *BURH* RH15......130 F1
 HORL RH6......15 H1
 MIDOS PO22......94 F5
Victoria Dr *BOGR* PO21......12 B8
 SELS PO20......181 L5
Victoria Gv *HOVE* BN3......193 K6
Victoria Park Gdns *WTHG* BN11......8 E4
Victoria Pl *BRI* BN1......10 B5
Victoria Rd *BOGR* PO21......12 B8
 BRI BN1......10 B5
 BURH RH15......130 F2
 CCH PO19......7 K4
 CRAWW RH11......2 D2
 EMRTH PO10......175 H3
 HISD PO11......196 C2
 HORL RH6......15 H1
 HWH RH16......110 A1
 PTSD BN41......192 C4
 RHWH RH17......65 H7
 SHOR BN43......190 F5
 STHW BN42......191 L5
 WTHG BN11......8 F4
Victoria Rd South *BOGR* PO21......12 B9
Victoria St *BOGR* PO21......10 B8
 SWTR RH13
Victoria Wy *BURH* RH15......131 G2
 EGRIN RH19......25 G5
Victor Rd *EMRTH* PO10......198 A4
Victory Ms *ROTT* BN2......212 B6
Victory Rd *HORS* RH12......4 B5
The View *BOGR* PO21......220 B4
The Village Barn *BRI* BN1......171 M4
Village St *PSF* GU32......68 C6
Village Wy *BRI* BN1......173 K6
Villiers Cl *ROTT* BN2......195 M4
Vinall Gdns *HORS* RH12......36 E5
Vincent Cl *LAN/SOMP* BN15......189 L6
 SWTR RH13
Vincent Rd *SELS* PO20......222 L8
Vineries Cl *SALV* BN13......188 B6
The Vineries *BURH* RH15......131 G1
Vines Cross Rd *ROTT* BN2......195 G3

Vine St *BRI* BN1 .... 10 F5
Vinnetrow Rd *SELS* PO20 .... 7 M8
Vinson Rd *LISS* GU33 .... 47 K8
Viscount Dr *BOGR* PO21 .... 220 C4
Vivienne Cl *CRAWW* RH11 .... 20 E3
Vowels La *EGRIN* RH19 .... 43 L2
Vulcan Cl *CRAWW* RH11 .... 40 D2
Vulcan Rd *EMRTH* PO10 .... 198 A3

W

Waddington Cl *CRAWW* RH11 .... 40 B1
Wade Court Rd *HAV* PO9 .... 174 D4
Wade End *SELS* PO20 .... 222 E4
Wade La *HAV* PO9 .... 174 D5
The Wadeway *SELS* PO20 .... 222 F4
The Wadeys *BIL* RH14 .... 79 K4
Wadham Cl *CRAWE* RH10 .... 21 K3
Wadhurst Cl *BOGR* PO21 .... 12 A3
Wadhurst Dr *BRI* BN12 .... 209 J2
Wadhurst Ri *ROTT* BN2 .... 195 C7
The Wad *SELS* PO20 .... 216 C3
Wagg Cl *EGRIN* RH19 .... 25 H3
Waggoners Wy *GSHT* GU26 .... 27 H1
Waggoners Wells Rd
  GSHT GU26 .... 27 H2
Wagtail Cl *HORS* RH12 .... 37 K5
Wain End *HORS* RH12 .... 4 F2
Wainwrights *CRAWW* RH11 .... 2 E9
Wakefield Cl *ROTT* BN2 .... 11 G1
Wakefield Wy *BOGR* PO21 .... 202 F8
Wakefords Wy *HAV* PO9 .... 152 E6
Wakehams Green Dr
  CRAWE RH10 .... 21 L3
Wakehurst Dr *CRAWE* RH10 .... 2 F9
Wakehurst La *RHWH* RH17 .... 66 A3
Wakehurst Ms *HORS* RH12 .... 60 A3
Wakehurst Pl *ANG/EP* BN16 .... 207 J2
Wakestone La *PUL/STOR* RH20 .... 99 H3
Walberton Cl *MIDOS* PO22 .... 13 M2
Waldegrave Rd *BRI* BN1 .... 194 E1
Walders Rd *ANG/EP* BN16 .... 207 L2
Waldron Av *BRI* BN1 .... 172 E6
Walesbeech *CRAWE* RH10 .... 3 M6
Walesbeech Rd *ROTT* BN2 .... 213 L4
Waley's Cl *RDKG* RH5 .... 16 E3
Walker Rd *CRAWE* RH10 .... 21 J8
Wallace Av *WTHG* BN11 .... 210 A2
Wallace Cl *ANG/EP* BN16 .... 207 K2
Wallage La *CRAWE* RH10 .... 22 E6
The Walled Gdn *BIL* RH14 .... 33 G5
Wallfield *BOGR* PO21 .... 221 G2
Wall Hill Rd *FROW* RH18 .... 25 L7
Wallis Wy *BURH* RH15 .... 108 F3
  SWTR RH13 .... 5 M4
Walmer Crs *MIDOS* PO22 .... 204 D7
Walmer Cl *SWTR* RH13 .... 82 B2
Walmer Crs *ROTT* BN2 .... 195 H3
Walmsleys Wy *SELS* PO20 .... 217 K8
Walnut Av *ANG/EP* BN16 .... 207 J3
  CCH PO19 .... 6 B1
Walnut Cl *BRI* BN1 .... 193 M1
Walnut La *CRAWW* RH11 .... 20 C3
Walnut Pk *HWH* RH16 .... 88 C8
Walnut Tree Cl *HISD* PO11 .... 214 C1
Walnut Tree Dr *EMRTH* PO10 .... 176 E1
Walnut Tree Wy *SALV* BN13 .... 187 J7
Walpole Av *FERR* BN12 .... 209 L2
Walpole Rd *ROTT* BN2 .... 11 K8
Walpole Ter *ROTT* BN2 .... 11 L7
Walsham Cl *MIDOS* PO22 .... 13 K1
Walsingham Rd *HOVE* BN3 .... 193 G6
Waltham Park Rd
  PUL/STOR RH20 .... 121 J6
Walton Av *BOGR* PO21 .... 13 G7
Walton Bank *BRI* BN1 .... 172 F7
Walton Cl *SALV* BN13 .... 188 A6
Walton Dr *SWTR* RH13 .... 38 D8
Walton Heath *CRAWE* RH10 .... 21 L4
Walton La *RCCH* PO18 .... 177 K7
Walton Rd *BOGR* PO21 .... 12 F7
Wanderdown Cl *ROTT* BN2 .... 195 M8
Wanderdown Dr *ROTT* BN2 .... 195 L8
Wanderdown Rd *ROTT* BN2 .... 195 L8
Wanderdown Wy *ROTT* BN2 .... 195 M8
Wandle Cl *CRAWE* RH10 .... 21 K7
Wandleys Cl *SELS* PO20 .... 182 A3
Wandleys Dr *SELS* PO20 .... 182 A3
Wandleys La *SELS* PO20 .... 182 A3
Wansford Wy *MIDOS* PO22 .... 204 D8
Wantage Cl *CRAWE* RH10 .... 41 K1
Wantley Hill Est *HFD* BN5 .... 128 A4
Wantley La *PUL/STOR* RH20 .... 143 M2
Wantley Rd *FIN/BW* BN14 .... 188 B3
Warble Heath Rd *RCCH* PO18 .... 157 C6
Warblers Wy *MIDOS* PO22 .... 203 J5
Warbleton Cl *ROTT* BN2 .... 194 F7
Warblington Av *HAV* PO9 .... 174 E3
Warblington Rd *EMRTH* PO10 .... 175 H5
Warbrook Ct *HAV* PO9 .... 152 E7
Warburton Cl *EGRIN* RH19 .... 25 H3
Ward Ct *EMRTH* PO10 .... 175 K1
Warden Ct *RHWH* RH17 .... 87 C6
Wardens Cl *HISD* PO11 .... 196 C7
Warelands *BURH* RH15 .... 131 C3
Warenne Rd *HOVE* BN3 .... 192 D1
Warleigh Rd *BRI* BN1 .... 10 F1
Warltersville Wy *HORL* RH6 .... 15 K3
Warmdene Av *BRI* BN1 .... 172 A6
Warmdene Cl *BRI* BN1 .... 172 A7
Warmdene Rd *BRI* BN1 .... 172 A6
Warmdene Wy *BRI* BN1 .... 172 A6
Warminghurst Cl
  PUL/STOR RH20 .... 125 G7
Warner Cl *CRAWE* RH10 .... 41 K7
Warner Rd *FIN/BW* BN14 .... 9 L1
  SELS PO20 .... 222 E4
Warner's La *SELS* PO20 .... 222 A7
Warnford Crs *HAV* PO9 .... 152 A7
Warnham Cl *FERR* BN12 .... 209 L3
Warnham Ri *BRI* BN1 .... 10 B1
Warnham Rd *CRAWE* RH10 .... 3 M8
  FERR BN12 .... 209 L2
  HORS RH12 .... 4 B1
  HORS RH12 .... 36 E8
  HORS RH12 .... 60 C5
Warninglid La *SWTR* RH13 .... 62 D8

Warren Av *ROTT* BN2 .... 195 K3
Warren Cl *EGRIN* RH19 .... 23 M1
  ROTT BN2 .... 195 J4
Warren Cft *PUL/STOR* RH20 .... 143 J3
Warren Dr *CRAWW* RH11 .... 20 B5
  SWTR RH13 .... 82 B1
Warren Farm La *CCH* PO19 .... 179 G2
Warren Gdns *FIN/BW* BN14 .... 188 C5
Warren La *RING/NEW* BN8 .... 111 M4
Warren Ri *ROTT* BN2 .... 195 J4
Warren Rd *FIN/BW* BN14 .... 188 C5
  LISS GU33 .... 47 K5
  LISS GU33 .... 47 A4
  ROTT BN2 .... 194 F5
  ROTT BN2 .... 195 K4
Warren Side *EPSF* GU31 .... 113 L1
The Warren *BURH* RH15 .... 131 K3
  FERR BN12 .... 209 G4
Warren Wy *MIDOS* PO22 .... 182 C6
  ROTT BN2 .... 195 L4
Warrington Cl *CRAWW* RH11 .... 39 M2
Warrior Cl *PTSD* BN41 .... 192 C2
Warrs Hill La *RING/NEW* BN8 .... 111 M3
Warsash Rd *HAV* PO9 .... 152 B6
Warwick Gdns *WTHG* BN11 .... 9 J6
Warwick Pl *MIDOS* PO22 .... 204 E7
  WTHG BN11 .... 9 K5
Warwick Rd *WTHG* BN11 .... 9 K6
Warwick St *WTHG* BN11 .... 9 K6
Washington Bostal
  PUL/STOR RH20 .... 144 F7
Washington Rd *CRAWW* RH11 .... 39 M1
  EMRTH PO10 .... 175 J3
  HWH RH16 .... 88 A7
  PUL/STOR RH20 .... 144 B4
  STEY/UB BN44 .... 145 L5
Washington St *CCH* PO19 .... 6 D1
  ROTT BN2 .... 11 H4
Wassand Cl *CRAWE* RH10 .... 3 M3
Waterbury HI *RHWH* RH17 .... 67 G4
Waterdyke Av *STHW* BN42 .... 191 M5
Waterfield Cl *SWTR* RH13 .... 5 H6
Waterfield Gdns *CRAWW* RH11 .... 19 M8
Waterhall Rd *BRI* BN1 .... 171 K6
Waterlands La *HORS* RH12 .... 35 M4
Water La *ANG/EP* BN16 .... 186 B6
  LHPTN BN17 .... 206 E2
  PUL/STOR RH20 .... 143 M1
  STEY/UB BN44 .... 145 K3
Water Lea *CRAWE* RH10 .... 3 M6
Waterloo Rd *HAV* PO9 .... 174 C2
  MIDOS PO22 .... 13 L4
Waterloo Sq *BOGR* PO21 .... 12 D8
Waterloo St *HOVE* BN3 .... 193 L7
The Waterplat *CCH* PO19 .... 179 K4
Waters Edge *BOGR* PO21 .... 220 F3
  PUL/STOR RH20 .... 122 B3
Waters Edge Gdns
  EMRTH PO10 .... 175 J4
Watersedge Gdns *SELS* PO20 .... 216 F6
Watersfield Rd *FIN/BW* BN14 .... 188 C7
Waterside *EGRIN* RH19 .... 25 J3
Waterside Dr *CCH* PO19 .... 201 G1
Waterside *CRAWW* RH11 .... 19 M8
Waterstone Cl *SELS* PO20 .... 199 H5
Waterworks Rd *PSF* GU32 .... 68 D6
Watery La *RCCH* PO18 .... 155 H7
  SELS PO20 .... 6 F9
Watling Cl *STHW* BN42 .... 191 M5
Watson Cl *CRAWE* RH10 .... 41 K1
Watson Wy *SELS* PO20 .... 181 L5
Waverley Crs *BRI* BN1 .... 194 C3
Waverley Rd *ANG/EP* BN16 .... 207 K3
  BOGR PO21 .... 203 H8
Wavertree Rd *FERR* BN12 .... 209 L1
Wayfarer's Wk *EMRTH* PO10 .... 175 H5
Wayfield Cl *HOVE* BN3 .... 192 F3
Wayfield Cl *HOVE* BN3 .... 193 G3
Wayland Av *BRI* BN1 .... 171 K8
Wayland Hts *BRI* BN1 .... 171 K8
Wayside *BRI* BN1 .... 171 L6
  CRAWW RH11 .... 19 M8
Wayside Av *SALV* BN13 .... 187 L5
The Way *ANG/EP* BN16 .... 208 B4
Weald Av *HOVE* BN3 .... 193 G3
Weald Cl *HPPT/KEY* BN6 .... 130 A6
Weald Dr *CRAWE* RH10 .... 3 L6
Weald Dyke *SHOR* BN43 .... 191 G6
Wealden Wy *HWH* RH16 .... 87 L8
Wealdon Cl *SWTR* RH13 .... 82 A4
Weald Ri *HWH* RH16 .... 109 M3
Weald Rd *BURH* RH15 .... 130 F1
The Weald *EGRIN* RH19 .... 25 G1
Wear Cl *SALV* BN13 .... 187 K5
Weare St *RDKG* RH5 .... 16 D5
Wear Rd *SALV* BN13 .... 187 K5
Weaver Cl *CRAWW* RH11 .... 19 M7
Weavers Cl *BURH* RH15 .... 131 L3
  MIDH GU29 .... 95 G2
Weavers Gn *HAV* PO9 .... 174 F1
Weavers HI *HAV* PO9 .... 186 B6
Weavers Ring *ANG/EP* BN16 .... 186 B7
Webb Cl *BOGR* PO21 .... 220 B5
  CRAWW RH11 .... 40 C3
  HISD PO11 .... 214 D1
Webb La *HISD* PO11 .... 214 D2
Weddell Rd *CRAWE* RH10 .... 3 J9
The Wedges *SWTR* RH13 .... 58 E7
Wedgwood Rd *MIDOS* PO22 .... 13 M5
Weirbrook *CRAWE* RH10 .... 3 L9
Welbeck Av *HOVE* BN3 .... 192 F6
Welbeck Cl *BURH* RH15 .... 109 L8
Welbeck Dr *BURH* RH15 .... 109 K7
Welesmere Rd *ROTT* BN2 .... 213 H1
The Welkin *HWH* RH16 .... 88 B6
Welland Cl *SALV* BN13 .... 187 L4
Welland Rd *SALV* BN13 .... 187 L4
Wellcroft Cottages
  HPPT/KEY BN6 .... 129 K7
Weller Cl *EMRTH* PO10 .... 21 L7
Wellesley Av *FERR* BN12 .... 209 L2
Wellfield *SELS* PO20 .... 25 K5
Wellhouse La *BURH* RH15 .... 131 J5
Wellingham La *SALV* BN13 .... 187 M3
Wellington Cl *CRAWE* RH10 .... 21 M3
Wellington Gdns *SELS* PO20 .... 223 G4
Wellington Rd *BOGR* PO21 .... 12 B7
  CCH PO19 .... 179 H1
  HORS RH12 .... 4 E8

  PTSD BN41 .... 192 C6
  ROTT BN2 .... 11 H2
Wellington St *ROTT* BN2 .... 11 J3
Wellington Town Rd
  EGRIN RH19 .... 24 E1
Well La *HASM* GU27 .... 28 C6
Well Meadow *HAV* PO9 .... 152 B6
Wellow Cl *HAV* PO9 .... 174 A1
Well Rd *BOGR* PO21 .... 220 A5
Wells Crs *BOGR* PO21 .... 220 E1
Wells Rd *CRAWE* RH10 .... 21 M3
Wellsfield *SELS* PO20 .... 216 D3
Wells Lea *EGRIN* RH19 .... 24 E1
Wells Meadow *EGRIN* RH19 .... 24 E1
Wells Rd *CRAWE* RH10 .... 40 F2
Wellswood Gdns *HAV* PO9 .... 152 F1
Wellsworth La *HAV* PO9 .... 152 F1
Wellwood Cl *SWTR* RH13 .... 38 C8
Welwyn Cl *CRAWW* RH11 .... 39 M1
Wembley Av *LAN/SOMP* BN15 .... 189 L6
Wembley Gdns
  LAN/SOMP BN15 .... 189 L6
Wenban Rd *WTHG* BN11 .... 9 G4
Wenceling Cottages
  LAN/SOMP BN15 .... 190 D7
Wendover Rd *HAV* PO9 .... 174 B2
Wendy Rdg *ANG/EP* BN16 .... 207 J2
Wenlock Cl *CRAWW* RH11 .... 20 B8
Wensleydale *CRAWW* RH11 .... 40 D3
Wensley Gdns *EMRTH* PO10 .... 175 J1
Wentworth Cl *MIDOS* PO22 .... 182 C5
  SALV BN13 .... 188 A4
Wentworth Dr *CRAWE* RH10 .... 21 L5
Wentworth St *ROTT* BN2 .... 11 G8
Wesley Cl *CRAWW* RH11 .... 39 M1
Wessex Av *BOGR* PO21 .... 221 H2
  SELS PO20 .... 217 H5
West Ashling Rd *RCCH* PO18 .... 176 E1
West Av *BOGR* PO21 .... 221 G1
  CRAWE RH10 .... 21 G4
  LAN/SOMP BN15 .... 190 B7
  MIDOS PO22 .... 205 G6
  WTHG BN11 .... 8 A5
West Beach Rd
  LAN/SOMP BN15 .... 190 D7
Westbourne Av *EMRTH* PO10 .... 175 K2
  FIN/BW BN14 .... 9 G2
Westbourne Cl *EMRTH* PO10 .... 175 K2
Westbourne Gdns *HOVE* BN3 .... 193 H6
Westbourne Pl *HOVE* BN3 .... 193 H6
Westbourne Rd *EMRTH* PO10 .... 175 K1
Westbourne St *HOVE* BN3 .... 193 H6
Westbourne Vls *HOVE* BN3 .... 193 H6
West Bracklesham Dr
  SELS PO20 .... 217 H6
West Brook Cl *RCCH* PO18 .... 177 J7
Westbrooke *WTHG* BN11 .... 9 G5
Westbrook Fld *RCCH* PO18 .... 177 H1
Westbrook Wy *STHW* BN42 .... 192 A5
West Broyle Dr *CCH* PO19 .... 178 D3
West Buildings *WTHG* BN11 .... 8 A5
West Burton La
  PUL/STOR RH20 .... 140 E4
West Chiltington La *BIL* RH14 .... 80 C7
  BIL RH14 .... 102 A2
  SWTR RH13 .... 58 F6
West Chiltington Rd
  PUL/STOR RH20 .... 123 G3
  PUL/STOR RH20 .... 124 B3
West Cl *HASM* GU27 .... 51 J6
  MIDOS PO22 .... 204 C7
West Common *HWH* RH16 .... 88 A5
West Common Dr *HWH* RH16 .... 88 B5
Westcott Cl *CRAWW* RH11 .... 40 D4
Westcourt Pl *FIN/BW* BN14 .... 8 F3
Westcourt Rd *FIN/BW* BN14 .... 8 F3
Westdean Rd *FIN/BW* BN14 .... 188 C7
Westdene Dr *BRI* BN1 .... 171 K7
West Dr *ANG/EP* BN16 .... 185 L8
  BOGR PO21 .... 220 C3
  FERR BN12 .... 208 F4
  MIDOS PO22 .... 205 H7
  ROTT BN2 .... 11 H6
West End La *HASM* GU27 .... 29 L4
  HFD BN5 .... 127 K7
West End Wy *LAN/SOMP* BN15 .... 189 L8
Westergate Cl *FERR* BN12 .... 209 G2
Westergate Ms *SELS* PO20 .... 181 L4
Westergate Rd *ROTT* BN2 .... 172 F8
Westergate St *SELS* PO20 .... 181 L6
Western Av *EMRTH* PO10 .... 175 G4
Western Cl *LAN/SOMP* BN15 .... 189 K8
Western Pde *EMRTH* PO10 .... 175 H5
Western Pl *WTHG* BN11 .... 8 F7
Western Rd *BURH* RH15 .... 130 F1
  HAV PO9 .... 174 B2
  HPPT/KEY BN6 .... 130 A6
  HWH RH16 .... 110 A1
  LAN/SOMP BN15 .... 189 K8
  LHPTN BN17 .... 206 F4
  LISS GU33 .... 47 J8
  SELS PO20 .... 223 G6
  SHOR BN43 .... 190 F5
Western Rd North
  LAN/SOMP BN15 .... 189 K5
Western Rw *WTHG* BN11 .... 8 F7
Western Ter *BRI* BN1 .... 10 A6
Westfield Av *ANG/EP* BN16 .... 208 B4
  HISD PO11 .... 214 B1
  ROTT BN2 .... 213 L1
Westfield Av North *ROTT* BN2 .... 213 L1
Westfield Av South *ROTT* BN2 .... 213 L1
Westfield Cl *BRI* BN1 .... 172 B8
Westfield Crs *BRI* BN1 .... 172 B7
Westfield Ri *ROTT* BN2 .... 213 L1
Westfield Rd *CRAWW* RH11 .... 2 B4
West Front Rd *BOGR* PO21 .... 220 A5
West Furlong La
  HPPT/KEY BN6 .... 130 B7
Westgate *CCH* PO19 .... 6 A5
West Green Dr *CRAWW* RH11 .... 2 C3
Westhampnett Rd *CCH* PO19 .... 7 J2
West Haye Rd *HISD* PO11 .... 215 G3
West Head *LHPTN* BN17 .... 207 G4
West HI *EGRIN* RH19 .... 24 E4
West Hill Cl *SALV* BN13 .... 187 M2

Westhill Dr *BURH* RH15 .... 130 F1
West Hill Pl *BRI* BN1 .... 10 C4
West Hill Rd *BRI* BN1 .... 10 C4
West Hoathly Rd *EGRIN* RH19 .... 44 D1
Westingway *BOGR* PO21 .... 221 H1
Westlake Cl *SALV* BN13 .... 188 A7
Westland Av *ROTT* BN2 .... 8 B2
Westlands *ANG/EP* BN16 .... 207 H4
Westlands Rd *HWH* RH16 .... 88 C7
  SELS PO20 .... 201 H4
West La *EGRIN* RH19 .... 24 E4
  HISD PO11 .... 196 B7
  LAN/SOMP BN15 .... 189 M6
West Leigh *EGRIN* RH19 .... 25 G5
Westloats Gdns *BOGR* PO21 .... 203 H7
Westloats La *BOGR* PO21 .... 12 A3
West Mare La *PUL/STOR* RH20 .... 122 F3
West Md *ANG/EP* BN16 .... 207 M4
Westmead Cl *HISD* PO11 .... 214 A1
West Meade *LIPH* GU30 .... 71 J2
Westmead Rd *CCH* PO19 .... 178 D6
West Meads Dr *BOGR* PO21 .... 203 G7
Westmeston Av *ROTT* BN2 .... 213 J2
Westminster Dr *BOGR* PO21 .... 220 E1
Westminster Rd *CRAWE* RH10 .... 21 K7
Westmorland Dr *MIDOS* PO22 .... 204 C6
Westmount Cl *STHW* BN42 .... 191 L4
Weston La *RCCH* PO18 .... 155 C7
Weston Rd *EPSF* GU31 .... 90 D1
Westons HI *SWTR* RH13 .... 59 J7
West Onslow Cl *FERR* BN12 .... 208 F3
West Pallant *CCH* PO19 .... 6 E5
West Pde *HORS* RH12 .... 4 C4
  WTHG BN11 .... 8 A8
West Park La *BURH* RH15 .... 108 E8
  RCCH PO18 .... 178 D1
West Park Rd *CRAWE* RH10 .... 23 C1
  RHWH RH17 .... 63 J5
West Ridings *ANG/EP* BN16 .... 207 M4
West Rd *EMRTH* PO10 .... 175 H4
  POY/PYE BN45 .... 149 L6
  PTSD BN41 .... 192 B5
West Stoke Rd *CCH* PO19 .... 178 E2
  RCCH PO18 .... 178 D1
West Strd *SELS* PO20 .... 216 B4
West St *BIL* RH14 .... 79 K4
  BOGR PO21 .... 12 D8
  BRI BN1 .... 10 D7
  BURH RH15 .... 108 F7
  CCH PO19 .... 6 C5
  CRAWW RH11 .... 2 E5
  EGRIN RH19 .... 25 G4
  EMRTH PO10 .... 175 J4
  HASM GU27 .... 28 D6
  HAV PO9 .... 174 B3
  HORS RH12 .... 4 C5
  HPPT/KEY BN6 .... 151 K1
  LAN/SOMP BN15 .... 189 J5
  MIDH GU29 .... 95 G2
  PTSD BN41 .... 192 D5
  PUL/STOR RH20 .... 143 K3
  ROTT BN2 .... 213 G3
  SELS PO20 .... 222 E6
  SHOR BN43 .... 190 F5
  WTHG BN11 .... 8 F7
West Tyne *SALV* BN13 .... 187 L7
Westup Rd *RHWH* RH17 .... 64 F2
West Vw *HWH* RH16 .... 88 C6
West View Dr *ARUN* BN18 .... 205 G2
West View Gdns *EGRIN* RH19 .... 24 F4
Westview Ter *FIN/BW* BN14 .... 165 M6
West Walberton La
  ARUN BN18 .... 182 C2
Westward Cl *RCCH* PO18 .... 177 K7
Westward La *PUL/STOR* RH20 .... 123 K6
West Wy *CCH* PO19 .... 178 D3
  CRAWE RH10 .... 3 L2
  HOVE BN3 .... 192 E2
  LAN/SOMP BN15 .... 190 B7
  LHPTN BN17 .... 206 D1
  SALV BN13 .... 187 L3
  SWTR RH13 .... 58 E1
Westway *CRAWE* RH10 .... 22 B1
  MIDOS PO22 .... 205 H7
Westway Cl *PTSD* BN41 .... 169 M8
Westway Gdns *PTSD* BN41 .... 169 M8
Westwood Cl *EMRTH* PO10 .... 175 K1
Wetherdown *EPSF* GU31 .... 90 D1
Weycombe Rd *HASM* GU27 .... 28 A4
Weydown Rd *HASM* GU27 .... 28 B6
Wey HI *HASM* GU27 .... 28 B6
Weyhill Cl *HAV* PO9 .... 152 A7
Weyland Dr *LIPH* GU30 .... 26 D7
Wey Lodge Cl *LIPH* GU30 .... 26 E8
Wey South Pth *MFD/CHID* GU8... .... 32 D2
  PUL/STOR RH20 .... 99 L4
  PUL/STOR RH20 .... 141 M2
Weysprings *HASM* GU27 .... 28 A5
Wharf Cl *LHPTN* BN17 .... 206 D5
The Wharf *MIDH* GU29 .... 95 C5
Wheatcroft *LHPTN* BN17 .... 206 D1
Wheatear Dr *EPSF* GU31 .... 90 F1
Wheatfield Rd *SELS* PO20 .... 223 H4
Wheatfield Wy *ROTT* BN2 .... 195 C1
Wheatlands Av *HISD* PO11 .... 215 H3
Wheatlands Crs *HISD* PO11 .... 215 H3
Wheatsheaf Cl *BURH* RH15 .... 108 F7
  HORS RH12 .... 5 G2
Wheatsheaf La *RHWH* RH17 .... 87 H6
Wheatstone Cl *CRAWE* RH10 .... 21 J4
Wheelbarrow Castle
  MIDH GU29 .... 95 H2
Wheeler Rd *CRAWE* RH10 .... 21 J8
Wheelers Wy *EGRIN* RH19 .... 23 M1
Wheelwright La *BURH* RH15 .... 131 L3
Wheelwrights
  PUL/STOR RH20 .... 123 M3
Wherwell Ct *HAV* PO9 .... 152 E7
Whichelo Pl *ROTT* BN2 .... 11 J4
Whichers Cl *HAV* PO9 .... 152 E4
Whichers Gate Rd *HAV* PO9 .... 152 E4
Whippingham Rd *ROTT* BN2 .... 11 K1
Whippingham St *ROTT* BN2 .... 11 K1
Whipping Post La *ROTT* BN2 .... 213 G3

Whistler Av *CCH* PO19 .... 179 H3
Whistler Cl *CRAWE* RH10 .... 41 G1
Whitebeam Rd *SALV* BN13 .... 187 K7
Whitebeam Wy *MIDOS* PO22 .... 204 E6
  SELS PO20 .... 180 E3
Whitechimney Rw
  EMRTH PO10 .... 175 L1
White City *MIDH* GU29 .... 94 F5
Whitecross St *BRI* BN1 .... 10 F4
Whitehall Dr *CRAWW* RH11 .... 19 M6
White Hart Ct *HORS* RH12 .... 4 C4
Whitehawk Cl *ROTT* BN2 .... 194 F7
Whitehawk Crs *ROTT* BN2 .... 194 F7
Whitehawk Hill Rd *ROTT* BN2 .... 11 L8
Whitehawk Rd *ROTT* BN2 .... 194 F6
Whitehawk Wy *ROTT* BN2 .... 195 G6
Whitehorse Rd *HORS* RH12 .... 38 C6
White Horses Wy
  ANG/EP BN16 .... 207 H3
Whitehouse Gdns *BOGR* PO21 .... 12 A3
White Ladies Cl *HAV* PO9 .... 174 D3
Whitelands *MIDOS* PO22 .... 13 M1
Whitelea Rd *LHPTN* BN17 .... 206 E2
Whitelot Cl *STHW* BN42 .... 191 M3
Whitelot Wy *STHW* BN42 .... 191 M3
Whiteman's Cl *RHWH* RH17 .... 86 F4
Whitemans Gn *RHWH* RH17 .... 86 E4
Whiterock Pl *STHW* BN42 .... 191 M5
White's Cl *HPPT/KEY* BN6 .... 130 B5
Whiteside Cl *CCH* PO19 .... 7 G2
Whites La *HASM* GU27 .... 72 F1
White St *ROTT* BN2 .... 11 G7
Whitethorn Dr *BRI* BN1 .... 171 J8
Whitethorn Rd *HISD* PO11 .... 214 A1
Whitethroat La *RHWH* RH17 .... 64 D6
Whiteway La *ROTT* BN2 .... 213 H2
Whiteways *MIDOS* PO22 .... 203 H6
Whiteways Cl *LHPTN* BN17 .... 206 E2
  MIDOS PO22 .... 203 H6
Whitfield Cl *HASM* GU27 .... 28 D5
  MIDOS PO22 .... 13 G2
Whitfield Rd *HASM* GU27 .... 28 D4
Whitley Cl *EMRTH* PO10 .... 153 L7
Whitley HI *CRAWE* RH10 .... 42 A3
Whitsbury Rd *HAV* PO9 .... 152 D7
Whittingehame Gdns *BRI* BN1 .... 194 A1
Whittington Ct *EMRTH* PO10 .... 175 J4
Whittington Rd *CRAWW* RH11 .... 40 E1
Whittle Wy *CRAWE* RH10 .... 15 H8
Whitworth Rd *CRAWW* RH11 .... 20 C1
Whyke Cl *CCH* PO19 .... 7 H8
Whyke La *CCH* PO19 .... 7 H7
Whyke Rd *CCH* PO19 .... 7 H8
Whylands Av *SALV* BN13 .... 187 L4
Whylands Cl *SALV* BN13 .... 187 L4
Whylands Crs *SALV* BN13 .... 187 L4
Whytings *SWTR* RH13 .... 61 K6
Wick Cl *MIDOS* PO22 .... 204 C7
The Wickets *BURH* RH15 .... 109 G7
Wick Farm Rd *LHPTN* BN17 .... 206 D2
Wickham Cl *HWH* RH16 .... 87 M5
Wickham Dr *HPPT/KEY* BN6 .... 130 C7
Wickham HI *HPPT/KEY* BN6 .... 130 D8
Wickham Wy *HWH* RH16 .... 87 M5
Wickhurst Cl *PTSD* BN41 .... 192 A3
Wickhurst La *HORS* RH12 .... 59 M1
Wickhurst Ri *PTSD* BN41 .... 192 A1
Wickhurst Rd *PTSD* BN41 .... 192 A2
Wicklands Av *ROTT* BN2 .... 213 L3
Wick La *MIDH* GU29 .... 73 K8
  MIDOS PO22 .... 204 C7
Wickor Cl *EMRTH* PO10 .... 175 K2
Wickor Wy *EMRTH* PO10 .... 175 J1
Wicks Rd *BIL* RH14 .... 79 K4
Wick St *LHPTN* BN17 .... 206 E1
Widdicombe Wy *ROTT* BN2 .... 194 F7
Widewater Cl
  LAN/SOMP BN15 .... 190 D7
Widgeon Cl *SELS* PO20 .... 222 E4
Widgeon Wy *HORS* RH12 .... 4 D1
Wight Wy *SELS* PO20 .... 223 G7
Wigmore Cl *BRI* BN1 .... 194 C3
Wigmore Rd *FIN/BW* BN14 .... 188 E6
Wilberforce Cl *CRAWW* RH11 .... 40 D4
Wilbury Av *HOVE* BN3 .... 193 K4
Wilbury Crs *HOVE* BN3 .... 193 L5
Wilbury Gdns *HOVE* BN3 .... 193 K4
Wilbury Gv *HOVE* BN3 .... 193 K6
Wilbury Rd *HOVE* BN3 .... 193 K5
Wilbury Vls *HOVE* BN3 .... 193 K5
Wilby Av *STHW* BN42 .... 191 M3
Wildacre Cl *BIL* RH14 .... 55 L1
Wilderness Rd *HPPT/KEY* BN6 .... 130 B6
The Wilderness *HWH* RH16 .... 88 C4
Wildgoose Dr *HORS* RH12 .... 60 A1
Wild Orchid Wy *SWTR* RH13 .... 82 B1
Wild Park Cl *ROTT* BN2 .... 194 F1
Wilfrid Rd *HOVE* BN3 .... 192 E4
Wilkinson Cl *ROTT* BN2 .... 213 G1
Willard Wy *PUL/STOR* RH20 .... 125 G7
Willett Cl *PETW* GU28 .... 119 J5
William Allen La *HWH* RH16 .... 88 C6
William Morris Wy
  CRAWW RH11 .... 40 C4
William Rd *CCH* PO19 .... 7 L4
Williamson Cl *HASM* GU27 .... 29 G3
Williams Rd *RCCH* PO18 .... 177 K5
  SHOR BN43 .... 191 J4
William St *BOGR* PO21 .... 12 E6
  PTSD BN41 .... 192 C5
  ROTT BN2 .... 10 F6
Williams Wy *CRAWE* RH10 .... 21 J6
Willingdon Rd *ROTT* BN2 .... 194 F3
Willow Av *ANG/EP* BN16 .... 207 M3
Willowbed Av *CCH* PO19 .... 7 J8
Willowbed Dr *CCH* PO19 .... 7 H8
Willow Brook *LHPTN* BN17 .... 206 D1
Willowbrook Rd *FIN/BW* BN14 .... 9 M1
Willowbrook Wy
  HPPT/KEY BN6 .... 151 H1
Willow Cl *CRAWE* RH10 .... 20 F4
  EGRIN RH19 .... 24 E1
  HAV PO9 .... 174 D3
  LAN/SOMP BN15 .... 190 D7
  LIPH GU30 .... 49 L1
  PUL/STOR RH20 .... 123 L6
  ROTT BN2 .... 195 M4

STEY/UB BN44 .... 146 E8
Willow Cnr HORL RH6 .... 14 A5
Willow Ct WTHG BN11 .... 8 A4
Willow Crs SALV BN13 .... 187 K7
Willow Dr BIL RH14 .... 79 L4
Willow Gdns EMRTH PO10 .... 153 L8
HPPT/KEY BN6 .... 130 A5
LIPH GU30 .... 49 L1
Willowhale Av BOGR PO21 .... 220 E2
Willowhayne Av ANG/EP BN16 .. 208 B4
Willowhayne Cl
ANG/EP BN16 .... 208 B4 ⬛
Willowhayne Crs
ANG/EP BN16 .... 208 B4
Willow Md EGRIN RH19 .... 25 G4
Willow Pk HWH RH16 .... 88 C8
Willow Rdg CRAWE RH10 .... 43 H1
Willow Rd HORS RH12 .... 38 C7
LISS GU33 .... 47 J8
The Willows ANG/EP BN16 .... 207 L3
BURH RH12 .... 109 J7
HORS RH12 .... 4 B3
PUL/STOR RH20 .... 122 B3 ⬛
SELS PO20 .... 223 G4
Willow Wy BOGR PO21 .... 220 C3
HPPT/KEY BN6 .... 130 A4
PUL/STOR RH20 .... 122 B3 ⬛
Willow Wood Rd HISD PO11 .. 214 D1 ⬛
Wills Cl ARUN BN18 .... 205 J2
Wilman Gdns BOGR PO21 ...... 220 E2
Wilmington Cl BRI BN1 .... 172 B7
CRAWW RH11 .... 40 D5 ⬛
HPPT/KEY BN6 .... 151 C1
Wilmington Pde BRI BN1 ..... 172 A7 ⬛
Wilmington Wy BRI BN1 .... 172 A7
HWH RH16 .... 88 A7
Wilmot Rd SHOR BN43 .... 191 K4
Wilson Av ROTT BN2 .... 195 M4
Wilson Cl CCH PO19 .... 178 E5
CRAWE RH10 .... 41 L1 ⬛
Wilson Ct ARUN BN18 .... 205 J2 ⬛
Wilton Cl ANG/EP BN16 ...... 207 J1 ⬛
SELS PO20 .... 217 J7
SWTR RH13 .... 127 H1
Wilton Dr ANG/EP BN16 ...... 207 J1
Wilverley Av HAV PO9 .... 152 D8
Wimblehurst Rd HORS RH12 ..... 4 D4
Wimland Hl HORS RH12 .... 38 E2
Wimland Rd HORS RH12 .... 18 C7
HORS RH12 .... 38 E3
Wimlands La HORS RH12 .... 38 E1
Wincanton Cl CRAWE RH10 .. 21 L6 ⬛
Winchelsea Gdns WTHG BN11 .... 8 A8
Winchester Dr CCH PO19 ..... 179 G4
Winchester Rd ANG/EP BN16 .. 207 M2
CRAWE RH10 .... 40 F2
PSF GU32 .... 68 A8
WTHG BN11 .... 8 D6
Winchester St BRI BN1 .... 10 E1
Wincombe Rd BRI BN1 .... 193 L3 ⬛
Winden Av CCH PO19 .... 7 H5
Windermere Crs FERR BN12 .. 187 L7
Windermere Rd HWH RH16 ..... 88 A7
Windlesham Av HOVE BN3 ...... 10 A4
Windlesham Cl PTSD BN41 ... 192 B3
Windlesham Gdns
ANG/EP BN16 .... 208 B2 ⬛
BRI BN1 .... 10 B4
SHOR BN43 .... 191 G4
Windlesham Rd BRI BN1 .... 10 A4
SHOR BN43 .... 191 G4
Windmill SELS PO20 .... 180 E3
Windmill Av HPPT/KEY BN6 .. 151 C1
Windmill Cl BOGR PO21 .... 220 C3
HORL RH6 .... 15 J1 ⬛
HOVE BN3 .... 193 G2
PUL/STOR RH20 .... 125 H7
STEY/UB BN44 .... 168 C2
SWTR RH13 .... 5 L5
Windmill Copse
PUL/STOR RH20 .... 143 L2
Windmill Ct CRAWW RH11 ..... 20 E4
SELS PO20 .... 217 G5
Windmill Dr ANG/EP BN16 ... 207 L2
BRI BN1 .... 171 K6
BURH RH15 .... 109 H8
Windmill Fld RCCH PO18 .... 177 H7
Windmill La EGRIN RH19 ...... 24 E1
EGRIN RH19 .... 25 K5

HFD BN5 .... 147 L1
Windmill Platt RHWH RH17 .... 63 K4
Windmill Rd LHPTN BN17 .... 206 E5
STHW BN42 .... 191 M3
Windmill St ROTT BN2 .... 11 H6
Windmill Ter ROTT BN2 .... 11 H5
Windrush Cl CRAWW RH11..... 20 A8
SALV BN13 .... 187 K4 ⬛
Windsor Cl ANG/EP BN16 .... 207 J1 ⬛
BOGR PO21 .... 202 F8
CRAWW RH11 .... 40 D2
HOVE BN3 .... 193 H1
HWH RH16 .... 109 M2
SWTR RH13 .... 82 B3
Windsor Dr ANG/EP BN16 .... 207 J1
SELS PO20 .... 216 F5
Windsor Rd CCH PO19 .... 7 L5 ⬛
PSF GU32 .... 90 C1
SELS PO20 .... 223 G6
WTHG BN11 .... 9 M4
Windsor St BRI BN1 .... 10 D6
Windsor Wy LAN/SOMP BN15 . 190 C6
Windward Cl LHPTN BN17 .... 207 H3
Windyridge CRAWW RH11 .... 20 B7 ⬛
Wineham La HFD BN5 .... 128 E1
Winfield Av BRI BN1 .... 172 A6
Winfield Cl BRI BN1 .... 172 A7 ⬛
PTSD BN41 .... 170 B8
Winfield Wy EMRTH PO10 .... 153 J8 ⬛
Wingle Tye Rd BURH RH15 ... 131 H4
Winguard Wy CCH PO19 .... 6 E6
Winkhurst Wy BURH RH15 ... 131 L3
Winkton Cl HAV PO9 .... 174 B1 ⬛
Winnet Wy SWTR RH13 .... 82 B2
Winslade Rd HAV PO9 .... 152 A7 ⬛
Winsor Cl HISD PO11 .... 215 G3
Winston Cl BOGR PO21 .... 203 G5
HISD PO11 .... 214 B1
Winston Crs BOGR PO21 ..... 203 G6
Winston Rd LAN/SOMP BN15 . 211 K1
Winterbourne HORS RH12 ..... 38 A5
Winterbourne Cl SALV BN13 . 187 J7 ⬛
Winterbourne Rd CCH PO19 . 179 H2
Winterbourne Wy SALV BN13 . 187 J7
Winterfold CRAWE RH10 ..... 41 H1 ⬛
The Winter Knoll LHPTN BN17 . 207 G3
Winterpit Cl SWTR RH13...... 61 L6
Winterpit La SWTR RH13 ..... 61 L6
Winters La MIDH GU29 .... 95 H1
Winterslow Dr HAV PO9 ..... 152 B6 ⬛
Winterton Cl HAV PO9 .... 4 F8 ⬛
Winterton Wy SHOR BN43 ... 191 H6
Winton Av ROTT BN2 .... 213 K2
Winton Pl WTHG BN11 .... 9 G5
Winton Rd PSF GU32 .... 90 C1
Wisborough Cl CRAWW RH11 . 40 A1 ⬛
Wisborough Gdns BIL RH14... 78 E4
Wisborough La
PUL/STOR RH20 .... 143 M3 ⬛
Wisden Av BURH RH15 .... 108 F7
Wish Rd HOVE BN3 .... 192 F6
Wisteria Gdns HAV PO9 ...... 152 E8
Wiston Av CCH PO19 .... 6 B9
FIN/BW BN14 .... 188 C7
Wiston Cl FIN/BW BN14 ...... 188 C7
Wiston Ct CRAWW RH11 ...... 40 A1 ⬛
Wiston Rd ROTT BN2 .... 195 G5
Wiston Wy ROTT BN2 .... 195 G5
Witchampton Cl HAV PO9 ... 152 D7 ⬛
Withdean Av BRI BN1 .... 193 L2
FERR BN12 .... 209 J4
Withdean Cl BRI BN1 .... 193 L1
Withdean Court Av BRI BN1 . 193 L1
Withdean Crs BRI BN1 .... 193 M1
Withdean Ri BRI BN1 .... 193 L1
Withdean Rd BRI BN1 .... 193 L1
Withey Brook HORL RH6 ..... 14 E5 ⬛
Withey Mdw HORL RH6 .... 14 E3
Withy Bush BURH RH15 ..... 108 F7 ⬛
BURH RH15 .... 108 F8 ⬛
Witham Av ROTT BN2 .... 213 K4
Withypitts CRAWE RH10...... 43 H1
Withypitts East CRAWE RH10 . 43 H1
Wittering Rd HISD PO11 .... 215 J2
Wivelsfield Rd HWH RH16 ... 109 M2
ROTT BN2 .... 213 K1
Woburn Pl BRI BN1 .... 173 G7

Woburn Rd CRAWW RH11 .... 20 B8
Wold Cl CRAWW RH11 .... 20 A8
Woldhurstlea Cl CRAWW RH11 . 20 B8
Wolfe La LISS GU33 .... 47 K2
Wolseley Rd BRI BN1 .... 172 E6
BRI BN1 .... 192 B4
Wolsey Cl BOGR PO21 .... 220 C3
Wolstonbury Cl CRAWW RH16 . 2 D7
Wolstonbury Rd HOVE BN3 ... 10 A2
Wolstonbury Wy
BURH RH15 .... 131 H2 ⬛
Wolverstone Dr BRI BN1 .... 194 D2
Wolverton Cl HORL RH6 ...... 15 G3
Wolverton Gdns HORL RH6 ... 15 G2
Wolverton Rd HAV PO9 ...... 152 B7
Wonston Ct HAV PO9 ...... 152 E6 ⬛
Woodard Rd LAN/SOMP BN15 . 190 E7
Woodards Vw SHOR BN43 .... 190 E7
Woodberry La EMRTH PO10 . 153 J5
HAV PO9 .... 153 G3
Woodborough Cl SELS PO20 . 217 K6
Woodbourne Av BRI BN1 ..... 172 A8
Woodbourne Cl LISS GU33 ... 47 K8 ⬛
Woodbridge Pk ANG/EP BN16 . 208 B3
Woodbury Av EGRIN RH19 ..... 25 J4
HAV PO9 .... 174 C4
PSF GU32 .... 68 B7
Woodbury Cl EGRIN RH19 .... 25 J4
Woodcot Crs HAV PO9 ...... 152 D6
Woodcote La LHPTN BN17 ... 184 E7
PUL/STOR RH20 .... 99 L7
Woodcote Rd FROW RH18 .... 45 M2
Woodcourt CRAWW RH11 .... 40 D3 ⬛
Woodcrest Rd BURH RH15 ... 131 G3
Woodcroft BURH RH15 ...... 109 G7 ⬛
Woodcroft BURH CRAWW RH11 . 19 L8 ⬛
Woodale La BIL RH14 .... 80 B3
Wood End HORS RH12 .... 38 D7
Woodend Cl CRAWE RH10 .... 21 H4 ⬛
Woodfield SWTR RH13 .... 81 M3
Woodfield Cl BOGR PO21 .... 220 B5
CRAWE RH10 .... 3 H1
SELS PO20 .... 180 E3
Woodfield Park Rd
EMRTH PO10 .... 153 L8
Woodfield Rd CRAWE RH10 .... 3 H1
HWH RH16 .... 34 E5
Woodgason La HISD PO11 ... 196 F3
Woodgate Cl SELS PO20 .... 181 L7
Woodgate Pk SELS PO20 .... 181 L7
Woodgate Rd SELS PO20 .... 181 L7
Woodgates Cl SWTR RH13 ..... 5 H6
Woodgreen Av HAV PO9 ..... 174 A2
Woodhall Cl RHWH RH17 ..... 87 G5
Woodhatch SWTR RH13 .... 82 A2
Woodhorn La SELS PO20 .... 180 E5
Woodhouse Rd HOVE BN3 ... 192 F5
Wooding Gv CRAWW RH11 ... 40 C3 ⬛
Woodington Cl HAV PO9 .... 152 D6 ⬛
Woodland Av BURH RH15 .... 109 K8
HOVE BN3 .... 171 J8
SALV BN13 .... 187 M3
Woodland Cl BIL RH14 .... 57 M6
BURH RH15 .... 109 K8 ⬛
HOVE BN3 .... 193 J2 ⬛
SWTR RH13 .... 38 C8
Woodland Dr CRAWE RH10 ... 23 J4
HOVE BN3 .... 193 J1
Woodland La SWTR RH13...... 62 C1
Woodland Rd SELS PO20 .... 222 F7
Woodlands CRAWE RH10 ..... 21 L4
HOVE BN3 .... 193 K2
Woodlands Av ANG/EP BN16 . 207 K2
EMRTH PO10 .... 175 H1
Woodlands Cl ANG/EP BN16 . 186 B5
CRAWE RH10 .... 21 H1 ⬛
HPPT/KEY BN6 .... 131 G8 ⬛
SALV BN13 .... 187 G3 ⬛
Woodlands La CCH PO19 ...... 6 C1
HASM GU27 .... 28 A5
HISD PO11 .... 196 B7
LISS GU33 .... 69 L2
RCCH PO18 .... 154 B2
Woodlands Rd HPPT/KEY BN6 . 131 G8
HWH RH16 .... 88 A4
LHPTN BN17 .... 206 F4
MIDOS PO22 .... 203 J6
The Woodlands BRI BN1 .... 171 M7

Woodlands Wk SWTR RH13 ... 61 K7
Woodlands Wy BIL RH14 ..... 79 M6
HAV PO9 .... 152 C8 ⬛
SWTR RH13 .... 81 M4
Woodland Wk ROTT BN2 .... 195 L8
Woodland Wy BRI BN1 .... 172 A8
BRI BN1 .... 5 M4
Wood La HFD BN5 .... 148 A6
Woodlark Gdns EPSF GU31 ... 90 F1
Woodlea Rd SALV BN13 .... 8 A2
Woodleigh Cl HAV PO9 ...... 174 F1
Woodleigh Rd BURH RH15 ... 109 K8
Woodmancote La
EMRTH PO10 .... 154 B8
Woodmancote Rd FIN/BW BN14 . 8 C1
Woodmans Hl CRAWW RH11 .. 40 D3
Woodpecker Cl HAV PO9 .... 174 E3 ⬛
Woodpecker Crs
HPPT/KEY BN6 .... 130 E1
Woodpecker La
PUL/STOR RH20 .... 143 M3
Woodpecker Rd PETW GU28 . 98 A5 ⬛
Woodpecker Wy SALV BN13 . 187 G3
Wood Ride HWH RH16 .... 109 L1
Woodridge Cl HWH RH16 ... 110 B1 ⬛
Woodroyd Av HORL RH6 ..... 15 G2
Woodroyd Gdns HORL RH6 ... 15 G1
Woodruff Av HOVE BN3 ..... 193 K2
Woods Hill Cl EGRIN RH19 ... 25 L6
Woods Hill La EGRIN RH19 ... 25 L6
Woodside MIDOS PO22 ...... 182 C6
SWTR RH13 .... 38 C8
Woodside Av BRI BN1 .... 193 L2
Woodside Cl PUL/STOR RH20 . 143 M2
SWTR RH13 .... 105 L8
Woodside Rd CRAWE RH10 ... 21 G4
FIN/BW BN14 .... 8 C1
Woodstock EGRIN RH19 ...... 24 D2
Woodstock Cl HORS RH12 ..... 4 E2
Woodstock Gdns
BOGR PO21 .... 221 G2 ⬛
Wood St BOGR PO21 .... 12 A8
EGRIN RH19 .... 24 E3
Woods Wy FERR BN12 .... 209 K1
Wood Vw ARUN BN18 .... 184 B2
Woodview SHOR BN43 ...... 191 G3
Woodview Cl BRI BN1 .... 172 E6
Woodwards CRAWW RH11..... 40 C3
Woodwards Cl BURH RH15 .. 131 J3 ⬛
Woolbeding La MIDH GU29 ... 94 C1
Woolborough Cl CRAWE RH10 . 3 G1 ⬛
Woolborough La
CRAWE RH10 .... 21 H4 ⬛
Woolborough Rd CRAWE RH10.. 2 F2
Wool La MIDH GU29 .... 95 G4
Woolmer Cl HAV PO9 ...... 152 E7 ⬛
Woolmer Hill Rd HASM GU27 . 27 K5
Woolmer La LIPH GU30 .... 26 D4
Woolmer Rd LISS GU33 ...... 47 L1
Woolmer St EMRTH PO10 ... 153 H8
Wooller Av PSF GU32 .... 68 C8
The Woolstaplers CCH PO19 ... 6 E4
Woolven Cl BURH RH15 ...... 130 F3
Wophams La SELS PO20 .... 200 D5
Worcester Rd CRAWE RH10 .. 40 F2
Worcester Vls HOVE BN3 ... 192 D5
Wordsworth Cl CRAWE RH10 . 21 J4 ⬛
Wordsworth Gdns
MIDOS PO22 .... 204 E6
Wordsworth Pl HORS RH12 . 37 M5 ⬛
Wordsworth Ri EGRIN RH19 . 24 D3 ⬛
Wordsworth Rd WTHG BN11 ... 8 D6
Wordsworth St HOVE BN3 ... 193 H5
Worldham Rd HAV PO9 ...... 152 E6
Worms La MIDOS PO22 ...... 204 D5
Worsted La EGRIN RH19 ...... 25 J5
Worthing Rd ANG/EP BN16 . 207 K1
HORS RH12 .... 4 B9
LHPTN BN17 .... 206 F1
LHPTN BN17 .... 207 G1 ⬛
SWTR RH13 .... 60 A8
SWTR RH13 .... 82 A2
SWTR RH13 .... 104 B6
SWTR RH13 .... 125 M1
Worthing Road Picts Hl
HORS RH12 .... 60 C1
Worth Park Av CRAWE RH10 . 21 K5
Worth Rd CRAWE RH10 ...... 21 K6
Worth Wy CRAWE RH10 .... 21 L7 ⬛

CRAWE RH10 .... 22 C6
Worthy Ct HAV PO9 .... 152 E7 ⬛
Wray Cl EGRIN RH19 .... 25 L6
Wraysbury Park Dr
EMRTH PO10 .... 153 ...
Wren Cl HORS RH12 .... 37 L5
Wren Crs MIDOS PO22 ...... 203 G4
Wright Cl CRAWE RH10 ..... 41 J2 ⬛
Wrotham Hl MFD/CHID GU8 .. 31 M1
Wroxham Wy MIDOS PO22 ... 13 K1
Wyatt Cl BIL RH14 .... 78 C4
Wyatts La RHWH RH17 .... 67 L7
Wyberlye Rd BURH RH15 .... 109 H8
Wyborn Cl HISD PO11 ...... 214 D2
Wycherry Rd HWH RH16 ..... 87 L7
Wychwood BIL RH14 .... 55 L1
Wychwood Cl BOGR PO21 ... 220 E3
Wychwood Gdns WTHG BN11 . 211 J1 ⬛
Wychwood Wk BOGR PO21 .. 220 F5
Wyde Feld BOGR PO21 ...... 221 G2
Wye Cl CRAWW RH11 .... 40 D4
Wyeford Cl HAV PO9 .... 152 E6 ⬛
Wyke Av WTHG BN11 .... 9 J6
Wykeham Cl STEY/UB BN44 . 167 L1
Wykeham Rd WTHG BN11 ...... 8 C4
Wykeham Wy BURH RH15 .... 131 K2 ⬛
Wyke La North MIDOS PO22 . 204 D7
Wykwood LIPH GU30 .... 26 E8 ⬛
Wylde Green La LISS GU33 ... 47 K7
Wyncombe Cl PUL/STOR RH20 . 121 H1
Wyndham Lea PUL/STOR RH20 . 123 K6
Wyndham Rd PETW GU28 .... 98 A5
Wyndham St ROTT BN2 ...... 11 H8
Wynlea Cl CRAWE RH10 ...... 23 H4
Wynnes Ms HOVE BN3 ...... 193 H5 ⬛
The Wyshe POY/PYE BN45 ... 150 D4
Wythering Cl BOGR PO21 ... 220 A5
Wythwood HWH RH16 .... 109 M3
Wyvern Cl SELS PO20 .... 180 F5

Y

Yaldhurst Ct HAV PO9 ..... 152 E6 ⬛
Yapton La ARUN BN18 ...... 183 G4
Yapton Rd MIDOS PO22 ..... 182 E7
Yardlea Cl HAV PO9 .... 152 E3
Yardley St BRI BN1 .... 10 E1
Yarmouth Cl CRAWE RH10 .... 3 M7
Yarrow Cl HORS RH12 .... 5 G1
Yattendon Rd HORL RH6 ..... 15 J1
Yeoman Rd SALV BN13 ..... 187 J7
Yeomans Acre BOGR PO21 . 221 G1
Yeomans Fld RCCH PO18 ... 176 B5
Yeomans La LIPH GU30 ...... 26 B8
Yeoman Wy SALV BN13 ..... 187 J8
Yew La EGRIN RH19 .... 24 C1
Yew Tree Cl MIDOS PO22 .... 12 B1
Yewtree Cl SWTR RH13...... 105 M2
Yew Tree Pl LISS GU33 ...... 47 K8
Yew Tree Rd HISD PO11 .... 196 D4
York Av EGRIN RH19 .... 25 H4
HOVE BN3 .... 10 A4
York Cha CCH PO19 .... 179 G2
York Cl PSF GU32 .... 90 A1
SWTR RH13 .... 5 K5
SWTR RH13 .... 82 B3
York Gdns LHPTN BN17 ..... 206 E3
York Gv BRI BN1 .... 10 C2
York Hl BRI BN1 .... 10 E3
Yorkhurst Hl RCCH PO18 ... 137 G3
York Pl BRI BN1 .... 10 F4
York Rd BOGR PO21 .... 12 B7
CCH PO19 .... 7 J6
CRAWE RH10 .... 40 F2
HOVE BN3 .... 10 A5
LHPTN BN17 .... 206 E3
SELS PO20 .... 223 G7
WTHG BN11 .... 9 J6
York Vls BRI BN1 .... 10 C2
Yorkwood LISS GU33 .... 47 J8
Youngsmere Cl BRI BN1 .... 172 C6 ⬛

Index - featured places

Abbotsford School
BURH RH15 .... 109 G6
Adur District Council
LAN/SOMP BN15 .... 189 M6
Adur District Council
STHW BN42 .... 191 M5
Aids Positive Underground
Theatre
ROTT BN2 .... 11 J7
Albion Doctors Surgery
ROTT BN2 .... 11 G4
Albourne C of E Primary
School
HPPT/KEY BN6 .... 129 K6
Aldingbourne County
Primary School
SELS PO20 .... 181 L6
Aldrington House Hospital
HOVE BN3 .... 193 G6
Allman Business Park
SELS PO20 .... 200 C6
Amberley Museum
ARUN BN18 .... 141 L8
Amberley School
ARUN BN18 .... 141 M5
Amesbury School
GSHT GU26 .... 27 M3
Amey Industrial Estate
PSF GU32 .... 90 B1
A M F Bowling
CRAWW RH11 .... 2 F3
A M F Bowling
WTHG BN11 .... 9 G7

Angmering School
ANG/EP BN16 .... 208 A1
Aquarena Swimming Pool
WTHG BN11 .... 9 L6
Archway Theatre
HORL RH6 .... 15 J2
The Arden Foot
& Health Clinic
ROTT BN2 .... 10 F7
Ardingly College
RHWH RH17 .... 66 A6
Ardmore School
WTHG BN11 .... 9 G5
Art Gallery
BRI BN1 .... 10 E5
The Art Gallery
EMRTH PO10 .... 153 L8
Arthur Griffiths Clinic
BOGR PO21 .... 220 B5
Arundale School
PUL/STOR RH20 .... 122 E2
Arundel Castle
ARUN BN18 .... 184 C1
Arundel C of E Primary School
ARUN BN18 .... 183 M2
Arundel & District Hospital
ARUN BN18 .... 184 B1
Arundel Football Club
ARUN BN18 .... 184 D1
Arundel Toy & Military
Museum
ARUN BN18 .... 184 D1

Arun District Council
ARUN BN18 .... 184 C1
Arun District Council
LHPTN BN17 .... 206 E4
Arun Fitzalan Swimming Pool
ARUN BN18 .... 184 D2
Arun Leisure Centre
MIDOS PO22 .... 13 J3
Arunside CP School
HORS RH12 .... 60 A2
Ashdown Forest Health Centre
FROW RH18 .... 45 M1
The Ashdown Hospital
HWH RH16 .... 87 L6
Ashington C of E School
PUL/STOR RH20 .... 125 G7
Ashurst Primary School
STEY/UB BN44 .... 126 E7
Ashwyn Business Centre
BURH RH15 .... 109 H7
Assembly Hall
WTHG BN11 .... 9 G5
Atlas Medical Centre
HORL RH6 .... 15 H5
Avalon Health Centre
ANG/EP BN16 .... 207 L2
The Avenue Surgery
BURH RH15 .... 131 G2
Bacchus Gallery
PETW GU28 .... 98 A4
Balcombe Primary School
RHWH RH17 .... 65 G2

Baldwins Hill CP School
EGRIN RH19 .... 24 D1
Balfour Junior School
BRI BN1 .... 194 B1
Barncroft Infant School
HAV PO9 .... 152 A8
Barnham Medical Centre
MIDOS PO22 .... 182 C5
Barnham Primary School
MIDOS PO22 .... 182 C6
Bartholomews Tutorial College
BRI BN1 .... 10 E7
Barton County Infants School
MIDOS PO22 .... 203 J6
Beach House Surgery
FERR BN12 .... 209 K3
The Bear Museum
EPSF GU31 .... 90 C2
Beaver Industrial Estate
LIPH GU30 .... 49 K2
Bedales School
PSF GU32 .... 68 B5
Bellerbys College
HOVE BN3 .... 193 K5
Bell Tower Industrial Estate
ROTT BN2 .... 195 G8
Benfield County Junior School
PTSD BN41 .... 192 D4
Benfield Valley Golf Course
PTSD BN41 .... 192 D1
Ben Turner Industrial Estate
CCH PO19 .... 7 M4

Bersted Green Surgery
MIDOS PO22 .... 12 C1
Bevendean County
Primary School
ROTT BN2 .... 195 G3
Bewbush Community
Middle School
CRAWW RH11 .... 39 M8
Bewbush Leisure Centre
CRAWW RH11 .... 40 A2
Bewbush Medical Centre
CRAWW RH11 .... 39 M1
Bewhurst County First School
CRAWW RH11 .... 40 A1
Bidbury Junior & Infant School
HAV PO9 .... 174 A2
Billingshurst County
Infant School
BIL RH14 .... 79 L5
Birdham C of E Primary School
SELS PO20 .... 199 M7
The Birman Gallery
HWH RH16 .... 88 C4
Bishop Luffa C of E School
CCH PO19 .... 178 E5
Bishop Tufnell C of E
Junior & Infant School
MIDOS PO22 .... 204 D6
Blackwell CP School
EGRIN RH19 .... 24 F1
Blatchington Mill School
HOVE BN3 .... 193 H3

ognor Health Centre
BOGR PO21 .... 12 D7
ognor Lawn Tennis Club
BOGR PO21 .... 221 H1
ognor Regis Community
College
BOGR PO21 .... 203 H7
ognor Regis Golf Club
MIDOS PO22 .... 204 B6
ognor Regis Town
Football Club
BOGR PO21 .... 12 A5
ognor Regis Town
Football Club
BOGR PO21 .... 203 H8
ognor Regis War
Memorial Hospital
MIDOS PO22 .... 12 D3
ognor Regis Yacht Club
BOGR PO21 .... 12 B9
ognor Rugby Club
BOGR PO21 .... 12 B3
ohunt Community School
LIPH GU30 .... 26 C8
ohunt Manor
LIPH GU30 .... 49 J1
olney Ct (Sch)
RHWH RH17 .... 107 L2
ooth Museum
of Natural History
BRI BN1 .... 193 M4
orers Business Park
CRAWE RH10 .... 22 D1
osham Abbey
RCCH PO18 .... 177 H8
osham County
Primary School
RCCH PO18 .... 177 K7
osham Football Club
RCCH PO18 .... 177 K7
osham Sailing Club
RCCH PO18 .... 177 H8
osmere Junior School
HAV PO9 .... 174 C3
he Bourne Community
College
EMRTH PO10 .... 175 M3
oxgrove C of E
Primary School
RCCH PO18 .... 158 E8
ramber Castle
STEY/UB BN44 .... 168 A2
ramber First School
FIN/BW BN14 .... 188 F6
rambletye School
EGRIN RH19 .... 25 K7
rantridge School
RHWH RH17 .... 63 M7
raybon Business Park
BURH RH15 .... 130 F2
rickyards Industrial Estate
PSF GU32 .... 68 C3
ridge Industrial Estate
HORL RH6 .... 15 J1
ridge Medical Centre
CRAWE RH10 .... 3 M3
ridge Road Business Park
HWH RH16 .... 87 M5
righton Business Centre
BRI BN1 .... 10 F2
righton Business Centre
BRI BN1 .... 194 A4
he Brighton Centre
BRI BN1 .... 10 C7
righton College
ROTT BN2 .... 11 K7
righton College of
Technology
BRI BN1 .... 10 F4
righton College of
Technology
HOVE BN3 .... 192 A4
righton College of
Technology
HOVE BN3 .... 193 J6
righton College of
Technology
ROTT BN2 .... 11 G3
righton County Court
ROTT BN2 .... 10 F6
righton Fishing Museum
BRI BN1 .... 10 D8
righton Framing Gallery
ROTT BN2 .... 11 K8
righton General Hospital
ROTT BN2 .... 11 M3
righton & Hove Council
BRI BN1 .... 10 F3
righton & Hove Council
BRI BN1 .... 172 C6
righton & Hove Council
HOVE BN3 .... 193 G3
righton & Hove Council
HOVE BN3 .... 193 J5
righton & Hove Council
HOVE BN3 .... 193 K6
righton & Hove Council
PTSD BN41 .... 192 B3
righton & Hove Council
PTSD BN41 .... 192 D4
righton & Hove Council
ROTT BN2 .... 11 K2
righton & Hove Council
ROTT BN2 .... 194 F1
righton & Hove Girls
Day School
BRI BN1 .... 10 A5
righton & Hove Golf Course
HOVE BN3 .... 170 F6
righton & Hove High Schools
BRI BN1 .... 10 A4
righton & Hove Islamic
Centre & Mosque
HOVE BN3 .... 10 D3
righton & Hove Progressive
Synagogue
HOVE BN3 .... 193 L6

Brighton Hove & Sussex
6th Form College
HOVE BN3 .... 10 B1
Brighton Library & Museum
BRI BN1 .... 10 E6
Brighton Media Centre
BRI BN1 .... 10 D7
Brighton Municipal Market
ROTT BN2 .... 10 F5
Brighton Racecourse
ROTT BN2 .... 195 H4
Brighton Rugby Club
BRI BN1 .... 171 J6
Brighton Technical College
BRI BN1 .... 10 D1
Brighton Youth Centre
BRI BN1 .... 11 H7
Broadbridge Heath
Leisure Centre
HORS RH12 .... 59 M2
Broadfield East First School
CRAWW RH11 .... 40 D2
Broadfield Health Centre
CRAWW RH11 .... 40 C2
Broadwater C of E School
FIN/BW BN14 .... 188 D7
Broadwater Manor School
FIN/BW BN14 .... 188 E7
Broadway Surgery
FIN/BW BN14 .... 195 G8
Brookers Road
Industrial Estate
BIL RH14 .... 79 M5
Brookham School
LIPH GU30 .... 49 M2
Brooklands Trading Estate
FIN/BW BN14 .... 8 D3
Buckingham Middle School
SHOR BN43 .... 191 H4
Burgess Hill Clinic
BURH RH15 .... 131 G2
Burgess Hill School
BURH RH15 .... 131 J2
Burgess Hill Town
Football Club
BURH RH15 .... 109 J7
Buriton CP School
EPSF GU31 .... 90 A7
Bury School
PUL/STOR RH20 ..... 141 G5
Business Centre
ANG/EP BN16 .... 207 K3
Camelsdale County
First School
HASM GU27 .... 28 A7
Canon Gallery
PETW GU28 .... 98 A4
Cardinal Newman School
HOVE BN3 .... 193 L4
Carlton Hill CP School
ROTT BN2 .... 11 G6
The Car Surgery
LHPTN BN17 .... 206 E1
Castledean School
BRI BN1 .... 194 C2
Catherine Corbett Clinic
HAV PO9 .... 174 C2
Catherington School
CRAWW RH11 .... 20 E2
Centenary Industrial Estate
BRI BN1 .... 194 C3
Central C of E Junior School
CCH PO19 .... 6 C3
The Central Hove Surgery
HOVE BN3 .... 193 J6
Chailey Heritage
Clinical Services
RING/NEW BN8 ...... 111 K5
Chailey Heritage School
RING/NEW BN8 ...... 111 K5
Chanctonbury Leisure Centre
PUL/STOR RH20 ..... 143 J2
Charlwoods Industrial Estate
EGRIN RH19 .... 24 F1
Charlwood Village School
HORL RH6 .... 14 A5
Charter Medical Centre
HOVE BN3 .... 193 L5
Chelsea College
SHOR BN43 .... 190 E5
Chesswood Middle School
WTHG BN11 .... 9 K2
Chesworth Junior School
SWTR RH13 .... 5 H6
Chichester Cathedral
CCH PO19 .... 6 D5
Chichester College of
Arts Science & Tech
BOGR PO21 .... 12 E7
Chichester College of
Arts Science & Tech
CCH PO19 .... 6 B5
Chichester College of
Arts Science & Tech
CCH PO19 .... 6 E4
Chichester College
of Technology
CCH PO19 .... 6 B5
Chichester District Council
MIDH GU29 .... 95 G4
Chichester District Museum
CCH PO19 .... 6 E4
Chichester Festival Theatre
CCH PO19 .... 6 E1
Chichester Gallery
CCH PO19 .... 6 E4
Chichester Health Authority
CCH PO19 .... 179 H3
Chichester High
School for Boys
CCH PO19 .... 6 E7
Chichester High
School for Girls
CCH PO19 .... 6 C7
Chichester High
School for Girls
CCH PO19 .... 6 F8

Chichester Homoeopathic
Medical Practice
CCH PO19 .... 6 E7
Chichester Lawn Tennis
& Squash Club
CCH PO19 .... 6 F2
Chichester Priory Park Cricket &
Hockey Club
CCH PO19 .... 6 F3
Chichester Rugby Club
CCH PO19 .... 179 H4
Chichester School of English
CCH PO19 .... 6 F4
Chichester Yacht Club
SELS PO20 .... 200 A5
Chiddingford Golf Club
MFD/CHID GU8 .... 30 C3
Chidham Parochial
Primary School
RCCH PO18 .... 176 F6
Child Clinic
ROTT BN2 .... 10 F6
Christchurch Medical Centre
HAV PO9 .... 174 F1
Christs Hospital Infirmary
SWTR RH13 .... 59 M6
Christ's Hospital (school)
SWTR RH13 .... 59 L7
The Christs Hospital
Sports Centre
SWTR RH13 .... 59 L6
Churchers College
EPSF GU31 .... 68 D8
Churchers College
Junior School
PSF GU32 .... 90 B1
Churchill Square
Shopping Centre
BRI BN1 .... 10 C7
Church Surgery
ROTT BN2 .... 194 D3
Cinema
BOGR PO21 .... 12 D6
City Business Centre
CCH PO19 .... 6 E7
City Business Centre
SWTR RH13 .... 4 E9
The City Business Centre
CRAWW RH11 .... 20 E2
City Fields Business Park
SELS PO20 .... 180 E2
Civic Centre
LHPTN BN17 .... 206 F3
Civic Centre
SHOR BN43 .... 191 G5
Clairmonte Galleries
BRI BN1 .... 10 E6
Clapham & Patching
C of E Primary School
SALV BN13 .... 186 F3
Clarence Road School
SWTR RH13 .... 4 F9
Clerklands Surgery
HORL RH6 .... 15 G1
Clermont C P U School
BRI BN1 .... 193 M2
The Clockhouse
Business Centre
MIDH GU29 .... 95 G4
Club House
FIN/BW BN14 .... 188 C3
The Club House
LISS GU33 .... 48 B8
Coldean Junior
& Infant School
BRI BN1 .... 172 E6
Colgate School
SWTR RH13 .... 39 K6
Collyers Sixth Form College
HORS RH12 .... 4 E4
Coin Gallery
CCH PO19 .... 6 E3
Community Mental
Health Centre
BURH RH15 .... 109 H8
Compton & Upmarden
C of E Primary School
RCCH PO18 .... 133 J2
Connaught Theatre
WTHG BN11 .... 9 H5
The Constable Gallery Artshop
WTHG BN11 .... 8 E7
Contour Gallery
LIPH GU30 .... 26 C8
Conway Court Clinic
HOVE BN3 .... 193 J4
Coombe Road County
Primary School
ROTT BN2 .... 194 E3
The Coppice Surgery
ANG/EP BN16 .... 207 L2
The Copthorne
Business Centre
CRAWE RH10 .... 22 C1
Copthorne Fairway
Infant School
CRAWE RH10 .... 22 C1
Copthorne Golf Club
CRAWE RH10 .... 22 D1
Copthorne Junior School
CRAWE RH10 .... 22 C1
Copthorne Squash Club
CRAWE RH10 .... 22 B2
The Corner Gallery
HWH RH16 .... 88 C4
Cornerstones Independent
School
HOVE BN3 .... 193 L6
Corn Exchange Theatre
BRI BN1 .... 10 E6
Cornfield School
LHPTN BN17 .... 206 F1
Cottesmore Golf
& Country Club
CRAWW RH11 .... 39 M5
Cottesmore St Marys
RC Primary School
HOVE BN3 .... 193 L4

Cottesmore School
CRAWW RH11 .... 40 A4
Council Offices
EPSF GU31 .... 69 G8
Count Primary School
BURH RH15 .... 131 K3
County First School
SALV BN13 .... 187 J6
County Middle School
STHW BN42 .... 192 A4
County Oak Retail Park
CRAWW RH11 .... 20 E2
County Primary School
BRI BN1 .... 194 C2
Court Lodge First School
HORL RH6 .... 15 G1
Court Meadow School
RHWH RH17 .... 87 H4
The Courtyard Surgery
HORS RH12 .... 4 C7
Cowdray Park Golf Club
MIDH GU29 .... 95 J2
The Craftsman Gallery
HPPT/KEY BN6 .... 151 L1
Craftwork Gallery
CCH PO19 .... 6 F4
Crawley College
CRAWE RH10 .... 3 H3
Crawley College
HORS RH12 .... 4 E6
Crawley College Annexe
CRAWE RH10 .... 2 D2
Crawley Down C of E
Infant School
CRAWE RH10 .... 23 J4
Crawley Down C of E School
CRAWE RH10 .... 23 J4
Crawley Down Health Centre
CRAWE RH10 .... 23 H4
Crawley Health Clinic
CRAWE RH10 .... 3 H3
Crawley Hospital
CRAWW RH11 .... 2 C3
The Crawley Lawn Tennis Club
CRAWE RH10 .... 21 J5
Crawley Leisure Centre
CRAWE RH10 .... 3 K5
Crawley Rugby Club
CRAWW RH11 .... 20 B2
Crawley Town Football Club
CRAWW RH11 .... 40 D2
The Croft Surgery
SELS PO20 .... 182 A4
Crosspost Industrial Estate
RHWH RH17 .... 107 J3
Crown Court
HOVE BN3 .... 193 L6
Crow Place Doctors Surgery
CRAWW RH11 .... 2 E5
Cuckfield Medical Practice
RHWH RH17 .... 87 G6
The Cyril Richings
Business Centre
SHOR BN43 .... 191 H5
Davigdor County
Infants School
HOVE BN3 .... 193 L5
Davison C of E Secondary
School for Girls
WTHG BN11 .... 9 M3
Deerswood School
CRAWW RH11 .... 20 B4
Dell Quay Sailing Club
SELS PO20 .... 200 B2
Desmond Anderson School
CRAWE RH10 .... 40 E2
Ditcham Park Sch
EPSF GU31 .... 112 C4
Ditchling Gallery
HPPT/KEY BN6 .... 151 K1
Ditchling Health Centre
HPPT/KEY BN6 .... 151 L1
Ditchling Museum
HPPT/KEY BN6 .... 151 L1
Ditchling Primary School
HPPT/KEY BN6 .... 151 L1
Ditton Place (School)
RHWH RH17 .... 64 B4
Doll House Museum
PETW GU28 .... 98 A5
Dolphin House Clinic
for Adults
BRI BN1 .... 10 E6
Dolphin Leisure Centre
HWH RH16 .... 87 L6
Dorset House School
PUL/STOR RH20 ..... 141 J5
Downlands School
HPPT/KEY BN6 .... 151 L4
Downlands School
PETW GU28 .... 118 C6
Downsbrook CP School
FIN/BW BN14 .... 188 F7
Downsbrook Middle School
FIN/BW BN14 .... 188 F7
Downsbrook Trading Estate
FIN/BW BN14 .... 188 F6
Downs County First School
BRI BN1 .... 194 B4
Downs Junior School
BRI BN1 .... 194 B3
Downs Park School
PTSD BN41 .... 192 C4
Downs View School
ROTT BN2 .... 195 K4
Downview County
Primary School
MIDOS PO22 .... 13 K1
The Dr Jan De Winter Clinic
for Cancer Prevention Advice
BRI BN1 .... 10 E6
DSS
ROTT BN2 .... 11 G7
Duncton C of E First School
PETW GU28 .... 119 J5
Dunhurst School
PSF GU32 .... 68 D3

Dunnings Squash Club
EGRIN RH19 .... 24 F6
Durrington First &
Middle School
SALV BN13 .... 187 M5
Durrington Health Centre
SALV BN13 .... 187 L6
Durrington High School
SALV BN13 .... 187 M7
Eagle Estate
BIL RH14 .... 79 L5
Easebourne Primary School
MIDH GU29 .... 95 J1
East Court
EGRIN RH19 .... 25 G2
Eastgate C of E Primary
School
SELS PO20 .... 181 M5
Eastgate Gallery
CCH PO19 .... 7 G4
East Grinstead Health Clinic
EGRIN RH19 .... 24 F2
East Grinstead Sports Club
EGRIN RH19 .... 24 D7
East Hants District Council
PSF GU32 .... 90 A1
Eastmead Industrial Estate
RCCH PO18 .... 156 F5
East Preston CP School
ANG/EP BN16 .... 208 B2
East Street Medical Centre
LHPTN BN17 .... 206 E3
East Sussex County Council
BRI BN1 .... 10 E6
East Sussex County Council
HOVE BN3 .... 192 F1
East Sussex County Council
ROTT BN2 .... 194 F6
East Wittering County
Primary School
SELS PO20 .... 217 G5
Eaton Place Surgery
ROTT BN2 .... 11 M9
Edward Bryant County Primary
School
BOGR PO21 .... 12 E6
Elm Grove County First School
WTHG BN11 .... 210 A1
Elm Grove County
Infants School
LHPTN BN17 .... 206 F2
Elm Grove CP School
BRI BN1 .... 11 K2
Emsworth Museum
EMRTH PO10 .... 175 J3
Emsworth Primary School
EMRTH PO10 .... 175 H3
Emsworth Surgery
EMRTH PO10 .... 175 J4
English Gallery
HAV PO9 .... 152 F2
English Martyrs RC School
FERR BN12 .... 187 L7
Escotts County Primary School
EGRIN RH19 .... 25 H3
Evolution Health Centre
BRI BN1 .... 10 B5
Fairfield Infant School
HAV PO9 .... 174 D3
Fairfield Medical Centre
PETW GU28 .... 98 A5
Fairlight County
Primary School
ROTT BN2 .... 11 J1
Faques Gallery
ROTT BN2 .... 11 J8
Far Horizons Gallery
PSF GU32 .... 90 B1
Faringdon Gallery
ARUN BN18 .... 184 C1
Farlington School
HORS RH12 .... 36 C6
Faygate Business Centre
HORS RH12 .... 39 G3
Felpham Community College
MIDOS PO22 .... 13 K3
Felpham & Middleton
Health Centre
MIDOS PO22 .... 204 E7
Felpham Sailing Club
MIDOS PO22 .... 13 L6
Ferring C of E Primary School
FERR BN12 .... 209 G2
Ferring Football Club
FERR BN12 .... 208 F2
Fireside Gallery
BOGR PO21 .... 220 D1
Firsland Park Estate
HFD BN5 .... 129 G3
Fishbourne C of E
Primary School
RCCH PO18 .... 178 C5
Fishersgate First School
PTSD BN41 .... 192 B5
Fittleworth C of E First School
PUL/STOR RH20 ..... 121 H1
Flansham Business Centre
MIDOS PO22 .... 204 C5
Flora Mcdonald County
Junior School
LHPTN BN17 .... 206 D2
The Fold School
HOVE BN3 .... 192 E5
Fonthill Lodge School
EGRIN RH19 .... 24 D6
Fontwell Medical Centre
ARUN BN18 .... 182 B1
Fontwell Park Race Course
ARUN BN18 .... 182 A1
Fordwater School
CCH PO19 .... 179 H3
Forest Community School
SWTR RH13 .... 5 K9
Forge Wood Industrial Estate
CRAWE RH10 .... 21 J2
Forum House Business Centre
CCH PO19 .... 6 F5

Fowlers Business Centre
SWTR RH13 .... 105 M3
Foxbridge Golf Club
BIL RH14 .... 55 K3
The Framing Studio & Gallery
LAN/SOMP BN15 .... 189 M7
Freshbrook County
First School
LAN/SOMP BN15 .... 189 M6
Freshbrook School
LAN/SOMP BN15 .... 189 M6
Friends of Arundel
Castle Cricket Club
ARUN BN18 .... 162 B8
Front Lawn Gm Junior School
HAV PO9 .... 152 C6
Front Lawn Infant School
HAV PO9 .... 152 C7
Funtington County
Primary School
RCCH PO18 .... 177 J1
Furnace Green Surgery
CRAWE RH10 .... 3 K7
The Gallery
BRI BN1 .... 10 C6
The Gallery
HOVE BN3 .... 193 H5
The Gallery
PETW GU28 .... 98 A4
The Gallery
WTHG BN11 .... 8 C8
Gattons CP School
BURH RH15 .... 130 F1
Gatwick Medical Centre
HORL RH6 .... 15 J5
Gatwick Park Hospital
HORL RH6 .... 14 F2
Gemini Business Centre
HOVE BN3 .... 193 H4
Genesis Business Centre
SWTR RH13 .... 5 J5
George & Dragon Surgery
EMRTH PO10 .... 175 L1
George House Gallery
PETW GU28 .... 98 A4
George Pringle School
FERR BN12 .... 187 L7
George Street Gallery
ROTT BN2 .... 10 F7
Georgian Gardens CP School
ANG/EP BN16 .... 207 M2
Georgian House
Business Centre
ROTT BN2 .... 10 F7
Gerald Daniel Sailing Club
RCCH PO18 .... 198 F2
Gerrard House
Business Centre
ANG/EP BN16 .... 208 A2
Gerston Business Park
PUL/STOR RH20 .... 143 K4
Ghyll House Farm Estate
SWTR RH13 .... 82 E3
Gillets Surgery
RHWH RH17 .... 65 H3
Glade County Infant School
BOGR PO21 .... 203 H7
Glebe CP School
STHW BN42 .... 191 L5
The Glebe Surgery
PUL/STOR RH20 .... 143 K3
Glenhurst School
HAV PO9 .... 174 D3
Glenwood School
EMRTH PO10 .... 175 H3
Goldstone Junior School
HOVE BN3 .... 192 F3
Golf Club Bungalow
MIDH GU29 .... 95 J3
The Good Start School
POY/PYE BN45 .... 149 K7
Goodwood Golf Club
RCCH PO18 .... 157 M5
Goring C of E School
FERR BN12 .... 209 K2
Goring Cricket Club
FERR BN12 .... 209 H2
Gossops Green Clinic
CRAWW RH11 .... 20 A8
Gossops Green First
& Middle School
CRAWW RH11 .... 20 B7
Graham Whitehouse Practice
BURH RH15 .... 108 F8
The Grange Leisure Centre
MIDH GU29 .... 94 F5
Graylingwell Hospital
CCH PO19 .... 179 J3
Grayshott Council Office
GSHT GU26 .... 27 L1
Grayshott Primary School
GSHT GU26 .... 27 J1
Grayshott Surgery
GSHT GU26 .... 27 L1
Grayswood C of E School
HASM GU27 .... 29 G2
Great Ballard School
RCCH PO18 .... 159 L5
Greatham Primary School
LISS GU33 .... 47 J2
Great Walstead School
HWH RH16 .... 89 G6
Greenfield School
FROW RH18 .... 45 K3
Greenway School
HORS RH12 .... 4 A5
Grey Welles Surgery
HAV PO9 .... 152 C8
Grove House Surgery
BOGR PO21 .... 220 D2
Guildbourne Shopping Centre
WTHG BN11 .... 9 H6
Halsford Park Primary School
EGRIN RH19 .... 24 C2
Ham Bridge Trading Estate
FIN/BW BN14 .... 189 H8
Hambrook Business Centre
RCCH PO18 .... 154 E8

Ham Business Centre
SHOR BN43 .... 191 H5
Hamilton Lodge School
ROTT BN2 .... 11 L7
Ham Manor Golf Club
ANG/EP BN16 .... 185 L8
Ham Manor Golf Course
ANG/EP BN16 .... 185 K7
Hampshire County Council
HAV PO9 .... 174 D3
Handcross Park School
RHWH RH17 .... 63 L2
Handcross Primary School
RHWH RH17 .... 63 K3
Hangleton County Junior
& Infant School
HOVE BN3 .... 192 F2
Hapstead Business Centre
RHWH RH17 .... 66 C4
Harlands CP School
RHWH RH17 .... 87 L5
Haslemere District Hospital
HASM GU27 .... 28 E5
Haslemere Health Centre
HASM GU27 .... 28 E5
Haslemere Museum
HASM GU27 .... 28 E5
Haslemere Preparatory School
HASM GU27 .... 28 E7
Hassocks County Infant School
HPPT/KEY BN6 .... 131 G8
Hassocks Golf Club
HPPT/KEY BN6 .... 130 F7
Havant Business Centre
HAV PO9 .... 174 A4
Havant College
HAV PO9 .... 174 B2
Havant Leisure Centre
HAV PO9 .... 174 C2
Havant Museum
HAV PO9 .... 174 D3
Havant Rugby Football Club
HAV PO9 .... 174 A2
Havant Sports Club
HAV PO9 .... 174 C2
Havant Town Football Club
HAV PO9 .... 152 D7
Havant War
Memorial Hospital
HAV PO9 .... 174 B2
The Hawthorns School
SALV BN13 .... 187 K7
The Hawth Theatre
& Conference Complex
CRAWE RH10 .... 3 K5
Hayling Billy Business Centre
HISD PO11 .... 196 A8
Hayling Island Health Centre
HISD PO11 .... 214 D1
Hayward Business Centre
HAV PO9 .... 174 E1
Haywards Heath College
HWH RH16 .... 87 L6
Haywards Heath Football Club
HWH RH16 .... 88 B7
Haywards Heath Golf Club
HWH RH16 .... 88 A3
Haywards Heath Hospital
HWH RH16 .... 87 K7
Hazel Cottage Clinic
ROTT BN2 .... 195 K4
Hazelwick School
CRAWE RH10 .... 21 H4
Hazelwood Trading Estate
FIN/BW BN14 .... 9 L1
Heene C of E First School
WTHG BN11 .... 8 E4
The Henfield Business Park
HFD BN5 .... 148 B3
Henfield C of E
Primary School
HFD BN5 .... 127 L6
Henfield & District
Leisure Centre
HFD BN5 .... 127 M6
Herbert Hone Clinic
ROTT BN2 .... 11 G2
Herbert Shiner School
PETW GU28 .... 98 A5
Herne County Junior School
EPSF GU31 .... 68 D8
The Herne Farm Leisure Centre
EPSF GU31 .... 68 D8
Herons Dale School
SHOR BN43 .... 191 K3
The Herons Swimming
and Fitness Centre
HASM GU27 .... 28 A6
Heron Way CP School
SWTR RH13 .... 5 L9
Heyworth County
Primary School
HWH RH16 .... 87 M7
Highdown School
SALV BN13 .... 187 M7
Highdown Surgery
SALV BN13 .... 188 B7
Highfield School
LIPH GU30 .... 49 M2
Hillside School
PTSD BN41 .... 192 C1
Hippodrome Bingo
BRI BN1 .... 10 D7
Holbrook CP School
HORS RH12 .... 37 M5
Holbrook Recreation Centre
HORS RH12 .... 37 M5
Holiday Village
BOGR PO21 .... 13 H6
Hollycombe School
LIPH GU30 .... 49 K8
Hollywood Bowl
CRAWW RH11 .... 2 E1
Holmbush County
Infants School
SHOR BN43 .... 191 K3
Holy Cross Hospital
HASM GU27 .... 28 A5

Holy Trinity C of E School
CRAWW RH11 .... 20 B8
Holy Trinity School
RHWH RH17 .... 87 G5
Home Farm Business Centre
BRI BN1 .... 194 E1
Horley Health Centre
HORL RH6 .... 15 H1
Horsham Cricket & Sports Club
HORS RH12 .... 60 C3
Horsham District Council
HORS RH12 .... 4 E7
Horsham Football Club
SWTR RH13 .... 60 E3
Horsham Hospital
HORS RH12 .... 4 D5
Horsham Museum
HORS RH12 .... 4 C9
Horsham Trading Estate
SWTR RH13 .... 5 G4
Horsham Ymca Football Club
SWTR RH13 .... 60 E3
Horsted Keynes C of E School
RHWH RH17 .... 67 K6
Hove Business Centre
HOVE BN3 .... 193 J4
Hove General Hospital
HOVE BN3 .... 193 H5
Hove Medical Centre
HOVE BN3 .... 192 E1
Hove Metal Galleries
BRI BN1 .... 10 C3
Hove Park Upper School
HOVE BN3 .... 193 H3
Hove Polyclinic
HOVE BN3 .... 193 G3
Hove Rugby Football Club
HOVE BN3 .... 193 J3
Hubbard School
EGRIN RH19 .... 24 F3
Hurstpierpoint College
HPPT/KEY BN6 .... 130 C4
Hurstwood Park Hospital
HWH RH16 .... 110 B2
The Hutchinson Gallery
HWH RH16 .... 87 M7
Ice Rink
BRI BN1 .... 10 D6
Ifield Community College
CRAWW RH11 .... 20 B5
Ifield First School
CRAWW RH11 .... 20 A4
Ifield Golf & Country Club
CRAWW RH11 .... 19 M6
Ifield Middle School
CRAWW RH11 .... 20 B6
Imberhorne School
EGRIN RH19 .... 24 C2
The Imber Sports Centre
EGRIN RH19 .... 24 E1
Independent Business Centre
EGRIN RH19 .... 24 B1
Industrial Estate
PUL/STOR RH20 .... 122 B2
Industrial Estate
SWTR RH13 .... 82 A3
Ingfield Manor School
BIL RH14 .... 57 M6
Itchenor Sailing Club
SELS PO20 .... 199 H5
Itchingfield County
Primary School
SWTR RH13 .... 59 H6
James Searle Industrial Estate
HORS RH12 .... 5 H3
Jessie Younghusband
County Primary School
CCH PO19 .... 179 G4
J & G Gallery
CCH PO19 .... 6 C4
The John Horniman School
WTHG BN11 .... 9 K5
John Selden County
First School
FERR BN12 .... 187 L8
Jolesfild C of E Primary School
SWTR RH13 .... 105 H8
Jubilee Hall Clinic
CRAWE RH10 .... 3 M3
Kelseys Doctors Surgery
LISS GU33 .... 47 K8
Kelvin Business Centre
CRAWE RH10 .... 21 G3
King Business Centre
HPPT/KEY BN6 .... 129 K3
King Edward Vii Hospital
MIDH GU29 .... 72 E6
Kingsham County
Primary School
CCH PO19 .... 6 F8
Kings Manor School
SHOR BN43 .... 191 L4
Kingston Buci School
SHOR BN43 .... 191 H4
Kirdford County Junior School
BIL RH14 .... 77 H2
Knoll Business Centre
HOVE BN3 .... 192 E4
Laburnum Grove
County Junior School
MIDOS PO22 .... 12 C1
Lancastrian County
Infants School
CCH PO19 .... 6 C2
Lancing College Chapel
LAN/SOMP BN15 .... 190 B2
Lancing Health Centre
LAN/SOMP BN15 .... 189 L4
Lancing Parish Council
LAN/SOMP BN15 .... 189 M1
Landerry Industrial Estate
SELS PO20 .... 222 F4
Langley Corner Surgery
CRAWW RH11 .... 20 A4
Langley Green First School
CRAWW RH11 .... 20 E2
Langley House Surgery
CCH PO19 .... 6 D4

Holy Trinity C of E School
Langshott County Infant School
HORL RH6 .... 15 J1
Lannards Gallery
BIL RH14 .... 57 L8
Lavant C of E Primary School
RCCH PO18 .... 156 F6
Lavant House School
RCCH PO18 .... 156 F7
Lavant Road Surgery
CCH PO19 .... 179 G2
Law Courts
ROTT BN2 .... 11 G6
Lawn Tennis Club
HORL RH6 .... 15 G1
Lawson Hunt Industrial Park
HORS RH12 .... 36 E8
Leacroft Medical Practice
CRAWW RH11 .... 2 C3
Leacroft Medical Practice
CRAWW RH11 .... 20 D4
Leechpool Lane
County Primary School
SWTR RH13 .... 5 M4
Limes Business Centre
BURH RH15 .... 131 H3
Limetree Surgery
FIN/BW BN14 .... 188 B2
Lindfield Infant School
HWH RH16 .... 88 B5
Lindfield Junior School
HWH RH16 .... 88 C5
Lindfield Medical Centre
HWH RH16 .... 88 C4
Lion Hotel & Country Club
BOGR PO21 .... 220 B2
Liphook County Infant School
LIPH GU30 .... 26 C8
Liphook Golf Club
LIPH GU30 .... 49 H4
Liphook Junior School
LIPH GU30 .... 26 B8
Liss Business Centre
LISS GU33 .... 47 H7
Liss County Infant
& Junior School
LISS GU33 .... 69 J1
Littlefield School
LIPH GU30 .... 49 L2
Little Green School
RCCH PO18 .... 113 H8
Littlehampton
Community School
LHPTN BN17 .... 206 F2
Littlehampton Health Centre
LHPTN BN17 .... 206 F4
Littlehampton Hospital
LHPTN BN17 .... 206 F3
Littlehampton
Swimming Centre
LHPTN BN17 .... 207 G5
Littlehampton Town Council
LHPTN BN17 .... 206 E3
Littlehaven School
HORS RH12 .... 5 K2
Littlemead Grammar School
SELS PO20 .... 180 B5
The Lombard Gallery
PETW GU28 .... 98 A4
London Gatwick Airport
HORL RH6 .... 14 E5
London Gatwick Airport
HORL RH6 .... 15 K5
London Meed CP School
BURH RH15 .... 131 H3
Longhill School
ROTT BN2 .... 195 M8
Longley Industrial Estate
BRI BN1 .... 10 E2
Longley Trading Estate
CRAWE RH10 .... 3 G5
Lower Beeding C of E
Primary School
SWTR RH13 .... 84 B1
Loxwood Primary School
BIL RH14 .... 33 H8
Lyminster County
Infant School
LHPTN BN17 .... 206 E1
Lyndhurst CP School
WTHG BN11 .... 9 M3
Lyons Farm Estate
SWTR RH13 .... 59 H2
Mackley Industrial Estate
HFD BN5 .... 148 A6
Madison Gallery
PETW GU28 .... 97 M4
Maidenbower First School
CRAWE RH10 .... 21 K8
Mainline Business Centre
LISS GU33 .... 47 J8
The Manhood
Community College
SELS PO20 .... 222 F4
Mannings Heath Golf Club
SWTR RH13 .... 61 M5
Manor Farm Business Centre
POY/PYE BN45 .... 149 L7
Manor Field CP School
BURH RH15 .... 109 K8
Manor House Hospital
HOVE BN3 .... 193 H5
Manor Sports Ground Pavilion
FIN/BW BN14 .... 188 E7
March C of E Primary School
RCCH PO18 .... 179 L3
Marchwell Industrial Estate
CCH PO19 .... 179 J3
Marine Clinic
ROTT BN2 .... 213 H2
Market Place
BURH RH15 .... 131 H2
Marlborough Business Centre
LAN/SOMP BN15 .... 189 K8
Marlipins Museum
SHOR BN43 .... 190 F6
Marriott Goodwood
Park Hotel & Country Club
RCCH PO18 .... 158 A6

Marriott Goodwood
Park Hotel & Country Club
RCCH PO18 .... 158 B7
Maywood Surgery
BOGR PO21 .... 12 A5
The Meadows Surgery
BURH RH15 .... 108 E8
Meads School
EGRIN RH19 .... 24 F5
Mechanical Music
& Doll Collection
CCH PO19 .... 7 L2
Medmerry County
Primary School
SELS PO20 .... 222 F5
Mengham Infant School
HISD PO11 .... 196 D8
Mengham Junior School
HISD PO11 .... 196 D8
Michael Ayres County
Junior School
BOGR PO21 .... 203 H7
Michael Hall School
FROW RH18 .... 45 L7
Middle Street Primary School
BRI BN1 .... 10 D7
Middleton Business Park
MIDOS PO22 .... 204 F6
Middleton Medical Centre
MIDOS PO22 .... 204 F7
Midhurst C of E
Primary School
MIDH GU29 .... 94 F5
Midhurst Gallery
MIDH GU29 .... 95 J3
Midhurst Grammar School
MIDH GU29 .... 94 F4
Midhurst Intermediate School
MIDH GU29 .... 95 H2
Mile Oak Clinic
PTSD BN41 .... 192 A1
Mile Oak Junior School
PTSD BN41 .... 192 A1
Millais School
SWTR RH13 .... 5 J8
Mill Green Industrial Estate
HWH RH16 .... 87 M6
Mill View Hospital
HOVE BN3 .... 192 F3
Milton Mount School
CRAWE RH10 .... 21 K4
Moatfield Surgery
EGRIN RH19 .... 24 F2
Modern Mould Business Centre
LHPTN BN17 .... 206 C2
Modern Moulds
Business Centre
WTHG BN11 .... 189 K8
Montague Shopping Centre
WTHG BN11 .... 9 H6
Moreton House School
PSF GU32 .... 90 A4
Morley Street Health Centre
ROTT BN2 .... 11 G5
Moulscoomb Clinic
ROTT BN2 .... 194 F1
Moulsecoomb County
Junior School
ROTT BN2 .... 194 F1
Mowden School
HOVE BN3 .... 193 L3
Muntham House School
SWTR RH13 .... 58 F8
Museum
BOGR PO21 .... 12 D8
Museum
SHOR BN43 .... 190 E5
The Museum
STEY/UB BN44 .... 167 L1
Natural Health Centre
CCH PO19 .... 6 D7
Newhouse Farm
Business Centre
HORS RH12 .... 38 D5
Newick House Special School
BURH RH15 .... 131 K3
Newlands Health Clinic
HWH RH16 .... 87 K8
New Life School
EGRIN RH19 .... 24 E2
Newmans Loner School
HOVE BN3 .... 193 L4
New Pond Row Surgery
LAN/SOMP BN15 .... 189 M5
Newtown Surgery
LIPH GU30 .... 49 J2
The Nicholas Rowe Practice
RHWH RH17 .... 86 F6
Norfolk Square Surgery
BOGR PO21 .... 12 C8
Northbourne Medical Centre
SHOR BN43 .... 191 H4
Northbrook College
FIN/BW BN14 .... 188 D7
Northbrook College
SALV BN13 .... 187 J8
Northbrook College
WTHG BN11 .... 9 H5
Northbrook College Design
& Technology
HORS RH12 .... 4 D4
Northbrook Trading Estate
FIN/BW BN14 .... 188 F6
Northchapel Primary School
PETW GU28 .... 53 H5
Northgate First
& Middle School
CRAWE RH10 .... 20 F4
Northgate First School
CRAWE RH10 .... 3 G1
Northgate House School
CCH PO19 .... 6 E3
Northgate Surgery
CRAWE RH10 .... 3 G2
North Heath CP School
HORS RH12 .... 4 F1
Northlands Business Park
HORS RH12 .... 16 D8

orthlands Wood CP School
HWH RH16 .... 88 C8

orthlands Wood Surgery
HWH RH16 .... 88 C8

orth Mundham
County Primary School
SELS PO20 .... 201 L2

ortholmes County
Junior School
HORS RH12 .... 5 M2

uffield Hospital
SELS PO20 .... 180 A7

yewood C of E Junior
& Infant School
BOGR PO21 .... 203 H8

akendene Industrial Estate
SWTR RH13 .... 106 C3

akley Surgery
SWTR RH13 .... 127 H1

ukmeads Community School
BURH RH15 .... 131 H2

he Oaks First & Middle School
CRAWE RH10 .... 3 K9

akwood Industrial Park
CRAWE RH10 .... 21 H3

akwood Preparatory School
RCCH PO18 .... 178 A2

athall Community College
HWH RH16 .... 88 A6

deon Cinema
BRI BN1 .... 10 C4

ld Barn Theatre
CRAWW RH11 .... 20 A4

ld Club House
CRAWE RH10 .... 23 G8

ld Club House
RHWH RH17 .... 63 K3

ld Darlington Mushroom
Farm Industrial Estate
ANG/EP BN16 .... 186 B7

ld Thorns Golf
& Country Club
LIPH GU30 .... 48 E1

he Old Town Hall Gallery
MIDH GU29 .... 95 G5

he Open University
EGRIN RH19 .... 24 F3

rchards Middle School
FERR BN12 .... 187 L8

ur Lady of Lourdes School
ROTT BN2 .... 213 G2

ur Lady of Sion Junior School
WTHG BN11 .... 9 G5

ur Lady of Sion School
WTHG BN11 .... 8 F6

vingdean Hall School
ROTT BN2 .... 195 L8

agham Cricket Club
BOGR PO21 .... 220 B3

agham Football Club
BOGR PO21 .... 220 B3

agham Yacht Club
BOGR PO21 .... 220 B5

alace Pier
ROTT BN2 .... 10 F9

allant House Gallery
CCH PO19 .... 6 E5

arham Historic House
PUL/STOR RH20 .... 142 E3

ark Ho (Hotel)
MIDH GU29 .... 116 B2

arkland Business Centre
LAN/SOMP BN15 .... 189 L8

arklands County
Primary School
CCH PO19 .... 6 A3

arklands Surgery
CCH PO19 .... 6 B4

ark Surgery
HORS RH12 .... 4 D7

he Park Surgery
LHPTN BN17 .... 207 G3

ark View Leisure Centre
HOVE BN3 .... 192 F5

atcham CP School
BRI BN1 .... 172 A6

atcham First School
BRI BN1 .... 171 M6

atcham High School
BRI BN1 .... 172 A6

atcham House School
BRI BN1 .... 171 M6

aul Cooper Galleries
ANG/EP BN16 .... 207 K3

he Pavilion Clinic
BRI BN1 .... 10 B6

avilion Theatre
BRI BN1 .... 10 E6

avilion Theatre
WTHG BN11 .... 9 H7

axton Business Centre
HOVE BN3 .... 192 E4

eacock Industrial Estate
HOVE BN3 .... 193 L5

ennthorpe School
HORS RH12 .... 34 D5

eregrine Gallery
FERR BN12 .... 208 F3

eter Gladwin School
PTSD BN41 .... 192 B2

etersfield Business Park
PSF GU32 .... 90 A1

etersfield
ommunity Hospital
PSF GU32 .... 90 B1

etersfield County
Infant School
EPSF GU31 .... 90 C1

etersfield Golf Club
PSF GU32 .... 68 F4

etersfield Rugby
Football Club
EPSF GU31 .... 69 G8

etersfield School
PSF GU32 .... 90 B2

etersfield Swimming Pool
EPSF GU31 .... 90 C1

Petersfield Town Council
EPSF GU31 .... 90 D1

Petersfield Town
Football Club Ltd
EPSF GU31 .... 68 D8

Petworth C of E Primary
School
PETW GU28 .... 98 A5

Petworth Cottage Museum
PETW GU28 .... 98 A4

Petworth House
PETW GU28 .... 98 A4

Phillips Business Centre
CCH PO19 .... 6 A6

Phillips Business Centre
CCH PO19 .... 178 E7

Philpots Manor School
EGRIN RH19 .... 43 K7

Pier
BOGR PO21 .... 12 D9

Plaistow Primary School
BIL RH14 .... 55 G1

Platform Theatre
RHWH RH17 .... 86 B6

Portfield Football Club
CCH PO19 .... 7 K2

Portfolio Studio Gallery
HOVE BN3 .... 10 E7

Portland Business Park
HOVE BN3 .... 192 E5

Portland Industrial Estate
HOVE BN3 .... 192 E4

Portland Road
Industrial Estate
HOVE BN3 .... 192 E4

Portland Surgery
HOVE BN3 .... 193 G5

Portslade Community College
PTSD BN41 .... 192 B1

Portslade Community College
PTSD BN41 .... 192 B3

Portslade Community College
STHW BN42 .... 192 A2

Portslade Health Centre
PTSD BN41 .... 192 C5

Portsmouth City Council
HAV PO9 .... 152 C8

Pound Hill First
& Middle School
CRAWE RH10 .... 21 K5

Pound Hill Surgery
CRAWE RH10 .... 21 K5

Prebendal School
CCH PO19 .... 6 C4

Preston Furniture Gallery
BRI BN1 .... 194 A2

Preston Park Clinic
BRI BN1 .... 194 B3

Preston Park Surgery
BRI BN1 .... 194 B4

Priest House
EGRIN RH19 .... 43 M6

Primary School
BOGR PO21 .... 12 F7

Primary School
STEY/UB BN44 .... 168 B2

Prince Regent Swimming
Complex
BRI BN1 .... 10 F6

The Princes Royal Hospital
HWH RH16 .... 110 A2

Prinnys Antique Gallery
BRI BN1 .... 10 D7

Queen Alexandra
Hospital Home
WTHG BN11 .... 8 D6

Queen Elizabeth Ii Silver Jubilee
School
SWTR RH13 .... 5 K9

Queensdown School
BRI BN1 .... 194 D1

Queens Park County
Primary School
ROTT BN2 .... 11 J7

Queen Victoria Hospital
N H S Trust
EGRIN RH19 .... 25 C1

Quell Farm Industrial Estate
PUL/STOR RH20 .... 121 M8

Rake C of E Controlled
First School
LISS GU33 .... 48 C7

Rapha House Surgery
RHWH RH17 .... 65 C3

Regent Business Centre
BURH RH15 .... 130 F2

Register Office
WTHG BN11 .... 8 C5

Richards Osteopathic Clinic
& Natural Health Centre
CRAWE RH10 .... 3 H4

Riders Junior & Infant School
HAV PO9 .... 152 A7

Rikkyo Sch
BIL RH14 .... 33 L4

Riverbank Business Centre
SHOR BN43 .... 190 E5

River Gallery
ARUN BN18 .... 184 C2

Riverside Business Centre
SHOR BN43 .... 191 G6

Riverside Close Surgery
LISS GU33 .... 47 J8

Riverside Gallery
PETW GU28 .... 98 A4

Riverside Industrial Estate
LHPTN BN17 .... 206 C3

Rock & Bowl Bowling Alley
EGRIN RH19 .... 24 F3

Roedean School
ROTT BN2 .... 212 D1

Roffey Social & Sports Club
HORS RH12 .... 5 L2

Rogate C of E Controlled School
EPSF GU31 .... 70 C8

Rose Green County
Infant School
BOGR PO21 .... 220 D2

Rose Green County
Junior School
BOGR PO21 .... 220 D1

The Rotherfield Sports Ground
MIDH GU29 .... 95 G3

Rottingdean Football Club
ROTT BN2 .... 213 G1

Rottingdean Primary School
ROTT BN2 .... 213 H2

Rottingdean Surgery
ROTT BN2 .... 212 F1

Rowfant Business Centre
CRAWE RH10 .... 22 F6

Royal Alexandra Hospital
BRI BN1 .... 10 C4

Royal George Clinic
BURH RH15 .... 130 F1

Royal Pavilion
BRI BN1 .... 10 F6

The Royal School
HASM GU27 .... 28 B2

Royal & Sunalliance Sports Club
HORS RH12 .... 37 M6

Royal Sussex County
Hospital N H S Trust
ROTT BN2 .... 11 L8

Rudford Industrial Estate
ARUN BN18 .... 205 L2

Rudgwick Medical Centre
HORS RH12 .... 34 D5

Rudgwick School
HORS RH12 .... 34 E5

Rudyard Kipling
Primary School
ROTT BN2 .... 195 M5

Rugby Club
EGRIN RH19 .... 24 D7

Rugby Football Club
RHWH RH17 .... 86 E4

Rumboldswyke C of E
Infant School
CCH PO19 .... 7 J6

Rusper School
HORS RH12 .... 18 D5

Rustington Primary School
ANG/EP BN16 .... 207 J2

Rustington Retail Park
ANG/EP BN16 .... 207 L1

The Rydon
Community School
PUL/STOR RH20 .... 144 A2

Sackville Road First School
FIN/BW BN14 .... 9 K1

Sackville School
EGRIN RH19 .... 25 H3

St Albans C of E
Primary School
HAV PO9 .... 174 D1

St Andrews C of E
(aided) School
SWTR RH13 .... 83 G3

St Andrews C of E
High School for Boys
FIN/BW BN14 .... 9 J1

St Andrews C of E School
HOVE BN3 .... 193 J6

St Andrews Primary School
CRAWE RH10 .... 3 M7

St Anthonys School
CCH PO19 .... 179 G4

St Aubyns School
ROTT BN2 .... 213 H3

St Bartholomews
C of E Primary School
BRI BN1 .... 10 E3

St Bartholomews C of E School
HASM GU27 .... 28 D4

St Bartholomews Middle School
HASM GU27 .... 28 D5

St Bernadettes First Middle
Va School
BRI BN1 .... 193 M2

St Catherines RC
Primary School
LHPTN BN17 .... 206 E2

St Christophers School
HOVE BN3 .... 193 H5

St Cuthmans School
MIDH GU29 .... 72 B6

St Dominics Gallery
HPPT/KEY BN6 .... 151 K1

St Edmunds School
GSHT GU26 .... 27 L1

St Faith Clinic
ROTT BN2 .... 194 F8

St Francis Middle School
CRAWE RH10 .... 3 G6

St James C of E Primary School
EMRTH PO10 .... 175 J2

St James C of E School
PUL/STOR RH20 .... 121 K6

St James County
Primary School
CCH PO19 .... 7 J3

St James Industrial Estate
CCH PO19 .... 7 K2

St John Baptist Primary School
FIN/BW BN14 .... 165 L6

St Johns C of E Primary School
HAV PO9 .... 152 E4

St Johns RC Primary School
HORS RH12 .... 60 B2

St Johns Residential School
ROTT BN2 .... 11 L7

St John the Baptist RC
Primary School
ROTT BN2 .... 11 M6

St Josephs R C Primary School
HWH RH16 .... 87 M8

St Lawrence Surgery
FIN/BW BN14 .... 8 B1

St Leonards County
Infants School
SWTR RH13 .... 4 F9

St Lukes Junior & Infant School
ROTT BN2 .... 11 K5

St Lukes Swimming Pool
ROTT BN2 .... 11 K4

St Margarets C of E
Primary School
CRAWW RH11 .... 2 A1

St Margarets C of E School
ANG/EP BN16 .... 186 A5

St Marks C of E
Primary School
ROTT BN2 .... 194 F7

St Marks School
RHWH RH17 .... 64 A7

St Martins C of E
Primary School
ROTT BN2 .... 11 J1

St Martins C of E
Primary School
ROTT BN2 .... 194 D4

St Mary Magdalene School
BRI BN1 .... 10 B6

St Marys C of E (aided)
Primary School
PUL/STOR RH20 .... 122 D1

St Marys C of E First School
MFD/CHID GU8 .... 30 C1

St Marys C of E First School
PUL/STOR RH20 .... 144 E6

St Marys C of E Primary School
LHPTN BN17 .... 205 M4

St Marys C of E School
EGRIN RH19 .... 24 E2

St Marys Hospital
CCH PO19 .... 6 E4

St Marys Primary School
HORS RH12 .... 60 C3

St Marys RC Primary School
BOGR PO21 .... 12 F7

St Marys RC Primary School
WTHG BN11 .... 8 C5

St Marys RC Primary School
PTSD BN41 .... 192 C5

St Nicholas & St. Mary School
SHOR BN43 .... 191 H4

St Pauls C of E School
BRI BN1 .... 10 D5

St Pauls RC Comprehensive
School
HWH RH16 .... 88 A7

St Peters C of E Primary School
SWTR RH13 .... 105 L2

St Peters C of E School
RHWH RH17 .... 66 B4

St Peters County Infant School
PTSD BN41 .... 192 C6

St Peters Medical Centre
BRI BN1 .... 10 F3

St Peters Primary School
RING/NEW BN8 .... 111 M8

St Peters RC School
EGRIN RH19 .... 24 D3

St Peters R C School
SHOR BN43 .... 191 H4

The St Philip Howard
High School
MIDOS PO22 .... 182 B6

St Philips RC Primary School
ARUN BN18 .... 184 B1

St Richards Hospital
CCH PO19 .... 7 G1

St Richards RC Primary School
CCH PO19 .... 6 E6

St Robert Southwell RC
First School
HORS RH12 .... 38 B6

St Thomas Mores RC
Primary School
HAV PO9 .... 174 A1

St Wilfrids C of E School
HWH RH16 .... 110 B1

St Wilfrids R C Primary School
ANG/EP BN16 .... 186 A6

St Wilfrids RC School
BURH RH15 .... 131 H2

St Wilfrids RC School
CRAWW RH11 .... 2 B6

Saltdean County
Primary School
ROTT BN2 .... 213 K2

Sandhurst School
WTHG BN11 .... 9 L5

Sangers County Middle School
HORL RH6 .... 15 G1

The Scott Gallery
HORL RH6 .... 15 L5

Seaford College
PETW GU28 .... 118 F7

Seal County Primary School
SELS PO20 .... 223 G5

Sea Life Centre
ROTT BN2 .... 10 F8

Secondary School
ROTT BN2 .... 194 F6

Selsey Business Centre
SELS PO20 .... 222 F5

Selsey Country Club Ltd
SELS PO20 .... 222 F2

Selsey Cricket Club
SELS PO20 .... 222 F4

Selsey Golf Club
SELS PO20 .... 222 F2

Selsey Health Centre
SELS PO20 .... 222 F4

Selsey Indoor Market
SELS PO20 .... 222 F5

The Seven Dials
Medical Centre
BRI BN1 .... 10 C4

Seymour First & Middle School
CRAWW RH11 .... 40 C2

Sharps Copse Junior
& Infant School
HAV PO9 .... 152 E7

Sheddindean Business Centre
BURH RH15 .... 109 G7

Sheddingdean First School
BURH RH15 .... 109 H7

Sheet Cp School
PSF GU32 .... 68 E8

Sheila Cashin Gallery
BRI BN1 .... 10 C5

Shelley Surgery
WTHG BN11 .... 8 F6

Shelly Primary School
HORS RH12 .... 59 M1

The Sherburne Hospital
CCH PO19 .... 179 G3

Shillinglee Park Golf Club
MFD/CHID GU8 .... 30 E6

The Ship House Surgery
LIPH GU30 .... 49 J1

The Ship Street Surgery
EGRIN RH19 .... 24 F4

Shopwhyke Industrial Centre
SELS PO20 .... 7 M3

Shoreham Beach
County First School
SHOR BN43 .... 191 H6

Shoreham College
SHOR BN43 .... 191 L5

Shoreham County First School
SHOR BN43 .... 190 F4

Shoreham Football Club
PTSD BN41 .... 192 C5

Shoreham Health Centre
SHOR BN43 .... 190 F5

Shottermill County
Middle School
HASM GU27 .... 28 A5

Sidlesham County
Primary School
SELS PO20 .... 218 E4

Sidlesham Football Club
SELS PO20 .... 219 G4

Singleton C of E
Primary School
RCCH PO18 .... 136 E5

Slindon C of E School
ARUN BN18 .... 160 E8

Slindon College
ARUN BN18 .... 160 C7

Slinfold C of E Primary School
SWTR RH13 .... 35 L8

Slinfold Park Golf
& Country Club
SWTR RH13 .... 58 C1

Somerhill County
Junior School
HOVE BN3 .... 193 L6

Somerset Hospital
PETW GU28 .... 98 A3

South Bersted C of E
Primary School
MIDOS PO22 .... 12 D2

Southbourne County
Junior & Infant School
EMRTH PO10 .... 176 B4

Southbourne Surgery
EMRTH PO10 .... 176 B4

South Downs Health Clinic
BRI BN1 .... 10 D4

Southfields Industrial Estate
RCCH PO18 .... 177 J6

Southgate First School
CRAWE RH10 .... 2 F8

Southgate Middle School
CRAWE RH10 .... 2 F8

Southgate School
CRAWW RH11 .... 2 D8

Southwater Business Park
SWTR RH13 .... 82 A3

Southwater County
Junior & Infant School
SWTR RH13 .... 82 A2

Southway County
Junior School
HPPT/KEY BN6 .... 130 E1

Southwick Business Centre
PTSD BN41 .... 191 M6

Southwick Manor Hall
County First School
STHW BN42 .... 192 A5

Springfield Industrial Estate
RHWH RH17 .... 110 A7

Stammerham Business Centre
HORS RH12 .... 17 M5

Stanford Junior School
BRI BN1 .... 10 C1

Stanley Deason
Leisure Centre
ROTT BN2 .... 195 G7

Stanstead House
HAV PO9 .... 153 M3

Star Road Trading Estate
SWTR RH13 .... 127 H1

Station Theatre
HISD PO11 .... 196 A8

Staunton Park
Community School
HAV PO9 .... 152 E5

Stedham CP School
MIDH GU29 .... 94 A3

Steep School
PSF GU32 .... 68 B5

Steyning Athletic Club
STEY/UB BN44 .... 167 K1

Steyning Grammar School
STEY/UB BN44 .... 146 E8

Steyning Grammar School
STEY/UB BN44 .... 167 L1

Steyning Health Centre
STEY/UB BN44 .... 167 L1

Steyning St Andrews
C of E Primary School
STEY/UB BN44 .... 146 D8

Steyning Sports Centre
STEY/UB BN44 .... 146 D8

Steyning Town Football Club
STEY/UB BN44 .... 146 L8

Stonelands School
of Ballet & Theatre
HOVE BN3 .... 193 J6

Storrington Cp School
PUL/STOR RH20 .... 143 K2

Storrington Gallery
PUL/STOR RH20 .... 143 L3

Storrington Lawn Tennis Club
PUL/STOR RH20 .... 143 K3

The Strand Surgery
FERR BN12 .... 187 L8
Summerlea County
Primary School
ANG/EP BN16 .... 207 J1
Sussex Clinic Ltd
WTHG BN11 .... 8 E6
Sussex County Cricket Club
HOVE BN3 .... 193 K5
Sussex Eye Hospital
ROTT BN2 .... 11 L8
Sussex House Industrial Estate
HOVE BN3 .... 193 G4
Sussex Manor Business Park
CRAWE RH10 .... 21 H2
Sussex Nuffield Hospital
HOVE BN3 .... 193 G6
Sussex Nuffield Hospital
ROTT BN2 .... 195 K4
The Sussex Toy
& Model Museum
BRI BN1 .... 10 D4
Swandean Hospital
SALV BN13 .... 187 L4
Swan Street Surgery
PSF GU32 .... 90 B1
Swedish School
CRAWE RH10 .... 3 K8
Sydney West Sports Centre
BURH RH15 .... 109 H8
Synagogue
BRI BN1 .... 10 D7
Tadds Cottage Gallery
SELS PO20 .... 222 F5
Tanbridge House School
HORS RH12 .... 4 A9
Tanbridge Retail Park
HORS RH12 .... 4 A8
Tangmere County
Primary School
SELS PO20 .... 180 E2
Tangmere Military
Aviation Museum Trust Co
SELS PO20 .... 180 E3
Tavistock & Summerhill School
HWH RH16 .... 88 Á5
Templars County
Infants School
LAN/SOMP BN15 .... 189 J6
Thakeham C P School
PUL/STOR RH20 .... 124 C5
Theatre Royal
BRI BN1 .... 10 E6
Thomas A Becket First School
SALV BN13 .... 188 B7
Thomas A Becket
Middle School
FIN/BW BN14 .... 188 C7
Thomas Bennett
Community College
CRAWW RH11 .... 40 E1
Thornberry Middle School
LAN/SOMP BN15 .... 190 A7
Thorney County
Primary School
EMRTH PO10 .... 197 K1

Three Bridges County
Middle School
CRAWE RH10 .... 3 K3
Three Bridges Cricket Club
CRAWE RH10 .... 3 L4
Three Bridges First School
CRAWE RH10 .... 3 L2
Three Bridges Football Club
CRAWE RH10 .... 3 M4
Ticehurst Clinic
HOVE BN3 .... 193 H6
Tilgate Forest Business Centre
CRAWW RH11 .... 40 E3
Tilgate Forest Golf Club
CRAWE RH10 .... 41 H2
Tobias School of Art
EGRIN RH19 .... 24 F6
Touch for Health Centre
BOGR PO21 .... 12 B6
Touch for Health Centre
BOGR PO21 .... 12 B6
Trafalgar County Infant School
HORS RH12 .... 4 B4
Tristar Business Centre
SWTR RH13 .... 127 H2
Turners Hill C of E School
CRAWE RH10 .... 43 H1
Turnpike Gallery
EPSF GU31 .... 90 C1
Unicorn Trading Estate
HASM GU27 .... 28 C6
University of Brighton
BRI BN1 .... 172 F6
University of Brighton
BRI BN1 .... 173 H7
University of Brighton
ROTT BN2 .... 10 F6
University of Brighton
ROTT BN2 .... 194 D2
University of Sussex
BRI BN1 .... 173 J5
Uplands School
BRI BN1 .... 194 D2
Upper Beeding Surgery
STEY/UB BN44 .... 168 B2
Vale CP School
SALV BN13 .... 188 A2
Varndean College
BRI BN1 .... 194 A1
Varndean High School
BRI BN1 .... 194 B1
Vicarage Lane Clinic
HASM GU27 .... 28 A6
Victoria Cottage Hospital
EMRTH PO10 .... 175 J4
Victoria Recreation Ground
WTHG BN11 .... 8 E4
Victoria Road Surgery
WTHG BN11 .... 8 F4
Vinnetrow Farm
Business Centre
SELS PO20 .... 201 M1
Virgin Multiplex Cinema
CRAWW RH11 .... 2 F1
Walberton & Binstead
C of E Primary
ARUN BN18 .... 182 F3

Warblington School
HAV PO9 .... 174 E3
Warden Park School
RHWH RH17 .... 87 H7
Warnham C of E School
HORS RH12 .... 37 G4
Warnham Court School
HORS RH12 .... 37 G6
Warninglid Primary School
RHWH RH17 .... 85 H2
Warren Park Primary School
HAV PO9 .... 152 A5
Waterfield School
CRAWW RH11 .... 19 M8
Waterhall Golf Course
BRI BN1 .... 171 J5
Watershed Theatre
and Exibition Centre
BOGR PO21 .... 12 E8
Waytefield Clinic
BRI BN1 .... 193 M2
Weald & Downland
Open Air Museum
RCCH PO18 .... 136 E6
Weald School
HOVE BN3 .... 79 K5
Welfare Clinic
HOVE BN3 .... 192 F2
Westbourne County
Primary School
EMRTH PO10 .... 153 L8
Westbourne House School
SELS PO20 .... 180 A5
Westbourne Surgery
EMRTH PO10 .... 175 L1
West Chiltington Golf Club
PUL/STOR RH20 .... 123 L2
West Chiltington School
PUL/STOR RH20 .... 123 M3
West Dean C of E
Primary School
RCCH PO18 .... 135 M7
West Dean College
RCCH PO18 .... 136 B6
Westdene Primary School
BRI BN1 .... 171 K7
Westergate Community
College
SELS PO20 .... 181 M5
Westgate Leisure Centre
CCH PO19 .... 6 C5
Westgate Surgery
CCH PO19 .... 6 C4
West Green County
First School
CRAWW RH11 .... 2 C2
West Hoathly School
EGRIN RH19 .... 43 M6
Westholme Clinic Ltd
FERR BN12 .... 209 L2
Westholme Clinic Ltd
WTHG BN11 .... 8 E6
West Hove Middle School
HOVE BN3 .... 192 F5
West Lavington C of E School
MIDH GU29 .... 95 H7

West Park C of E Controlled
First & Middle School
FERR BN12 .... 209 L2
West Pier (Under Repair)
BRI BN1 .... 10 B8
West Sands Leisure Centre
SELS PO20 .... 222 D5
West Sussex Area
Health Authority
WTHG BN11 .... 9 M5
West Sussex County Council
ANG/EP BN16 .... 207 L2
West Sussex County Council
ANG/EP BN16 .... 208 A2
West Sussex County Council
FERR BN12 .... 209 K2
West Sussex County Council
SHOR BN43 .... 191 J5
West Sussex County Council
WTHG BN11 .... 9 G4
West Sussex Golf Club
PUL/STOR RH20 .... 123 H6
West Sussex Health Authority
FERR BN12 .... 209 M1
West Wittering
Parochial School
SELS PO20 .... 216 C3
Weydown Industrial Estate
HASM GU27 .... 28 C5
The White Gallery
HOVE BN3 .... 193 K6
Whitehawk Clinic
ROTT BN2 .... 195 G7
Whitehawk Infant School
ROTT BN2 .... 194 F6
Whitehawk Junior School
ROTT BN2 .... 194 F6
White Styles County
Junior School
LAN/SOMP BN15 .... 189 J6
Whytemead CP School
FIN/BW BN14 .... 188 F7
Wickbourne Primary School
LHPTN BN17 .... 206 D2
Wick Football Club
LHPTN BN17 .... 184 F8
Wigmore Athletic
Football Club
FIN/BW BN14 .... 188 E5
The Wildwood Golf Club PLC
CRAN GU6 .... 33 H2
William Penn Primary School
SWTR RH13 .... 102 F2
Willow Green
Doctors Surgery
ANG/EP BN16 .... 207 M2
The Willow Surgery
ROTT BN2 .... 195 G3
Windlesham House School
FIN/BW BN14 .... 165 K1
Windmills County
Junior School
HPPT/KEY BN6 .... 151 G1
Window Gallery
BRI BN1 .... 10 C3
Window Gallery
BRI BN1 .... 10 D7

Winston Business Centre
LAN/SOMP BN15 .... 189 K
Wisborough Green C P School
BIL RH14 .... 78 D
Wispers School
HASM GU27 .... 28 D
Witterings Health Centre
SELS PO20 .... 216 F
Woodingdean Primary School
ROTT BN2 .... 195 K
Woodlands Surgery
CRAWE RH10 .... 3 G
Woodlawn Surgery
SWTR RH13 .... 127 H
Woodruff Business Centre
CCH PO19 .... 6 A
Woolmer Hill School
HASM GU27 .... 27 L
Worthing Auction Galleries
WTHG BN11 .... 9 G
Worthing Borough Council
WTHG BN11 .... 9 G
Worthing Borough Council
WTHG BN11 .... 9 H
Worthing District
Health Authority
LHPTN BN17 .... 206 C
Worthing District
Health Authority
SHOR BN43 .... 191 G
Worthing & District
Magistrates Court
WTHG BN11 .... 8 H
Worthing Football Club
FIN/BW BN14 .... 8 D
Worthing Golf Course
FIN/BW BN14 .... 188 C
Worthing Health Authority
WTHG BN11 .... 9 K
Worthing High School
FIN/BW BN14 .... 8 E
Worthing Leisure Centre
WTHG BN11 .... 209 M
Worthing Museum
WTHG BN11 .... 9 H
Worthing Priority Care
N H S Trust
ANG/EP BN16 .... 207 L
Worthing Rugby Club
ANG/EP BN16 .... 186 C
Worthing Sixth Form College
SALV BN13 .... 209 M
Worthing & Southlands
Hospitals N H S Trust
SHOR BN43 .... 191 J
Worthing & Southlands
Hospitals N H S Trust
WTHG BN11 .... 9 K
Wych Cross Place
FROW RH18 .... 45 K
Yapton C of E School
ARUN BN18 .... 183 G
YMCA
BRI BN1 .... 10 E
Zoo
WTHG BN11 .... 8 F

Page 19

1 Arnfield Cl
2 Beaumont Cl
3 Behenna Cl
4 Bitmead Cl
5 Compassion Cl
6 Dewar Cl
7 Dobbins Pl
8 Excalibur Cl
9 Garton Cl
10 Gorling Cl
11 Grier Cl
12 Strickland Cl
13 Talman Cl
14 Tunnmeade
15 Weaver Cl

Page 20

A4
1 Plough Cl
A5
1 Loxwood Wk
2 Patching Cl
3 Rudgwick Rd
4 Ruspers Keep
A6
1 Sharpthorne Cl
A7
1 Derwent Cl
2 Meadowcroft Cl
A8
1 Henshaw Cl
2 Morecambe Cl
3 Otway Cl
B5
1 Midhurst Cl
B7
1 Almond Cl
2 Dairyfields
3 Richfield
4 Ryelands
5 Windyridge
B8
1 Fountains Cl
C3
1 Charlwood Wk
2 Mulberry Rd
3 Squirrel Cl
C4
1 Binstead Cl
2 Birdham Cl
3 Colgate Cl
4 Mole Cl
C5
1 Deerswood Cl
C6
1 Cotswold Cl
2 Ginhams Rd
3 Pennine Cl
4 Quantock Cl
5 Snell Hatch
C8
1 Borrowdale Cl
2 Calderdale Cl
3 Ennerdale Cl
D3
1 Hawthorn Cl
2 Langley Pl
3 Martyrs Av
D4
1 Heron Cl
2 Kestrel Cl
D5
1 Reynolds Pl
2 Spurgeon Cl
D6
1 Church St
2 Lodge Cl
3 Prospect Pl
4 St John's Rd
5 St Peter's Rd
D7
1 Hill Pl
D8
1 Biggin Cl
2 Blackcap Cl
3 Crockham Cl
4 Grisedale Cl
5 Hindhead Cl
6 Patterdale Cl
E3
1 Adelaide Cl
2 Auckland Cl
3 Brisbane Cl
4 Canberra Cl
5 Friends Cl
6 Old Martyrs
7 Penn Cl
8 St Edmund Cl
9 Stephen Cl
E4
1 Chaffinch Cl
2 Connaught Gdns
3 Martin Cl
4 Short Cl
E5
1 Beech Tree Cl
2 Clappers Ga
3 Marlow Ct
E6
1 High St
2 The Square
E7
1 Station Rd
E8
1 Falmer Cl
2 Kithurst Cl
3 Oakhaven
4 Sullington Hl
5 Sunningdale Ct
F3
1 Tuscany Gdns
2 Tushmore Crs
F4
1 Black Dog Wk
2 Bramber Cl
F5
1 Covert Cl
2 Northgate Pl
3 The Parade
4 Vanners
5 Woolborough Cl
F6
1 Parkside
F7
1 Beechside
2 Friary Wy
3 Richmond Ct
F8
1 Fletcher Cl
2 Raleigh Wk

Page 21

G4
1 Midgley Rd
G5
1 Crawters Cl
2 Early Commons
G6
1 Haversham Cl
2 Ridgeside
3 Rowan Cl

G8
1 Cranborne Wk
H1
1 Priestley Wy
H2
1 Royston Cl
H3
1 Kingfisher Cl
H4
1 Hazelwick Mill La
2 Tinsley La South
3 Woodend Cl
4 Woolborough La
H5
1 The Birches
2 Coppice Wk
3 Forge La
4 Halland Cl
H6
1 Hawth Av
2 Jubilee Wk
H7
1 Beverley Ms
2 Blackfold Rd
3 Brambletye Rd
4 Burwash Rd
5 Dedisham Cl
6 Freshfield Cl
7 Gosden Cl
8 Walesbeech
H8
1 Brunswick Cl
2 Feroners Cl
3 Furnace Farm Rd
4 Graveye Cl
J4
1 Wordsworth Cl
J5
1 Kimberley Rd
J6
1 Maunsell Pk
2 Three Bridges Rd
3 Williams Wy
J7
1 Stanier Cl
2 Stroudley Cl
J8
1 Baxter Cl
2 Hawkhurst Wk
3 Normandy Cl
4 Sheffield Cl
5 Strudgate Cl
K3
1 Magdalene Cl
2 Oriel Cl
3 Ruskin Cl
4 St Hilda's Cl
K4
1 Farmleigh Cl
2 Kipling Cl
3 Milton Mount Av
4 Shelley Cl
K5
1 Hardy Cl
2 Stumblets
K6
1 Sedgewick Cl
K7
1 Dollis Cl
2 Elliot Cl
3 Golding Cl
4 Graveney Rd
5 Pevensey Cl
6 Tamar Cl
7 Wandle Cl
K8
1 Atkinson Rd
2 Aveling Cl
3 Ellson Cl
4 Garrett Cl
5 Maidenbower La
6 Maidenbower Pl
7 Newman Cl
8 Raworth Cl
9 Sinclair Cl
10 Stepney Cl
11 Stokes Cl
L2
1 Horndean Cl
2 Rossmore Cl
L3
1 Balliol Cl
2 Blenheim Cl
3 Blindley Rd
4 Heathfield
5 Lancaster Cl
6 Milton Mount Av
L4
1 Cherry Tree Cl
2 The Covey
3 Walton Heath
L5
1 The Cackstones
2 Denmans
3 Greyhound Slip
4 Knole Cl
5 Owletts
6 The Paddock
7 Penshurst Cl
8 Shire Pde
9 Short Gallop
10 Trevanne Plat
L6
1 Wincanton Cl
L7
1 Albion Cl
2 Bethune Cl
3 Burdett Cl
4 Collingwood Rd
5 Mayflower Cl
6 Niven Cl
7 St Vincent Cl
8 Stuart Cl
9 Thorndyke Cl
10 Worth Wy
L8
1 Adelphi Cl
2 Benjamin Cl
3 Bray Cl
4 Delfont Cl
5 Drury Cl
6 Strand Cl
M3
1 Binney Ct
2 Hampden Cl
3 Wellington Ct
M5
1 The Garrones
2 Horseshoe Cl
3 Shetland Cl

Page 40

A1
1 Donnington Ct
2 Hassocks Ct
3 Madehurst Ct
4 Petworth Ct
5 Pyecombe Ct
6 Slaugham Ct
7 Telham Ct
8 Wisborough Ct
9 Wiston Ct

B2
1 Borage Cl
2 Burdock Cl
3 Celandine Cl
4 Charlock Cl
5 Crowberry Cl
6 Herm Cl
7 St Helier Cl
8 Sark Cl
9 Sundew Cl
C1
1 Bilberry Cl
2 Bluebell Cl
3 Burbeach Cl
4 Harris Cl
5 Primrose Cl
6 Stonecrop Cl
D3
1 Chevening Cl
2 Hedgeside
3 Leybourne Cl
4 Southbrook
5 Willmington Cl
6 Woodcourt
E1
1 Caxton Cl
2 Loriners
3 Saddler Rw
4 Smith Cl
5 Wainwrights

Page 152

E6
1 Blissford Cl
2 Burley Cl
3 Chilbolton Ct
4 Houghton Cl
5 Iford Ct
6 Kimpton Ct
7 Scotney Cl
8 Shaldon Rd
9 Soldridge Cl
10 Sopley Cl
11 Sydmonton Cl
12 Verwood Rd
13 Wonston Ct
14 Wyeford Cl
15 Yaldhurst Ct
E7
1 Ashe Rd
2 Bentley Ct
3 Bramshaw Ct
4 Deane Ct
5 Fawley Cl
6 Fullerton Ct
7 Heckfield Cl
8 Holbury Ct
9 Meadend Cl
10 Muscliffe Ct
11 Newnham Ct
12 Oakfield Ct
13 Stanford Ct
14 Stockbridge Cl
15 Sway Ct
16 Tisted Ct
17 Tunworth Ct
18 Warbrook Ct
19 Wherwell Ct
20 Woolmer Ct
21 Worthy Ct

Page 187

J7
1 Ashburnham Cl
2 Batemans Cl
3 Beckworth Cl
4 Deerswood Cl
5 Gatcombe Cl
6 Highclere Wy
7 Lilac Cl
8 Magnolia Cl
9 Orkney Cl
10 Rochester Cl
11 Scotney Cl
12 Shetland Ct
13 Summerdown Cl
14 Walnut Tree Wy
15 Winterbourne Cl
K6
1 Chesley Cl
2 Tavy Cl
K7
1 Chaffinch Cl
2 Kingfisher Cl
3 Redwood Cl
4 Timber Cl
L6
1 Pond Ms
2 Sherbrooke Cl
3 Toronto Cl
4 Vancouver Cl

Page 188

A6
1 Butler Ct
2 Little Cables
3 Selden's Ms
4 Walton Lodge
F6
1 Northbrook Cl
2 Southdown View Wy
F8
1 King Edward Cl
2 Marston Rd

Page 189

K6
1 Coniston Cl
2 The Deneway
3 Greentrees Cl
4 Northgate Cl
L7
1 Hurstfield
M7
1 Freshbrook Cl
2 Ingleside Rd
3 Meadow La
4 Rosecroft Cl
5 St Bernards Cl
6 The Tynings

Page 191

M5
1 The Cotswolds
2 Green Cl
3 School Cl
4 Twitten Cl
5 Waterdyke Av
6 Watling Cl

Page 192

C2
1 Blackthorn Cl
2 Brackenbury Cl
3 Comford Cl
4 Foredown Cl
5 Highways
6 Meadow Cl
B5
1 Mornington Crs
F1
1 Harmsworth Crs
2 Northease Dr
3 Northease Gdns
F2
1 Ashlings Wy
2 Storrington Cl
3 Sunninghill Cl
4 Thornhill Cl
F5
1 Ingram Crs

Page 193

M2
1 Cumberland Dr
M3
1 Miller's Rd
M4
1 Port Hall Av
2 Port Hall Ms
M5
1 Belmont
2 Caburn Rd
3 Chanctonbury Rd
4 Wolstonbury Rd
M6
1 Victoria Pl
M7
1 Bedford Pl
2 Bedford Sq
3 Hampton St
4 Little Western St
5 Norfolk Buildings
6 Norfolk Ms
7 Queensbury Ms
8 Sillwood Pl
9 Sillwood Rd
10 Spring St
11 Western St
12 Western Ter

Page 194

A6
1 Buckingham St
2 Clifton Rd
3 Guildford St
4 Kew St
5 Mount Zion Pl
6 North Rd
7 Railway St
8 Surrey St
9 Terminus St
10 Upper Gloucester Rd
A7
1 Cannon Pl
2 Crown St
3 Marlborough Rd
4 Marlborough St
5 Middle St
6 Portland St
7 Regent Rw
8 Russell Pl
9 Russell Rd
10 St Margaret's Pl
11 Ship St
12 Upper North St
13 Windsor St
B6
1 Blackman St
2 Cheltenham Pl
3 Gloucester St
4 Kensington Gdns
5 Kensington St
6 Pelham Sq
7 Robert St
8 St George's Ms
9 St George's Pl
10 Station St
11 Trafalgar Pl
12 Trafalgar St
13 Upper Gardner St
14 Vine St
15 Whitecross St
B7
1 Bartholomews
2 Bond St
3 Brighton Pl
4 Dorset St
5 East St
6 Gardner St
7 Grand Parade Ms
8 Jew St
9 King Pl
10 King St
11 Kingswood St
12 Market St
13 Marlborough Pl
14 Meeting House La
15 New Rd
16 Nile St
17 North Pl
18 North St
19 Old Steine
20 Orange Rw
21 Palace Pl
22 Pavilion Buildings
23 Pavilion Pde
24 Pavilion St
25 Prince Albert St
26 Prince's Pl
27 Prince's St
28 Regent St
29 St James's St
30 Steine Gdns
31 Steine La
32 Tichborne St
33 Union St
34 William St
C7
1 Carlton Pl
2 Cavendish St
3 Dorset Pl
4 Egremont Pl
5 George St
6 Grosvenor St
7 Mighell St
8 Mount Pleasant
9 Nelson Rw
10 St James's Street Ms
11 St John's Pl
12 Tilbury Pl
13 Upper Park Pl
14 White St
C8
1 Atlingworth St
2 Camelford St
3 Charlotte St
4 Grafton St
5 Lower Rock Gdns
6 Madeira Pl
7 Margaret St
8 Marine Gdns
9 New Steine
10 Wentworth St
11 Wyndham St
D4
1 Bembridge St
2 Fairlight Pl
3 Inverness Rd
4 Newmarket Rd
5 Pevensey Rd
6 St Leonard's Rd
7 Whippingham St
D5
1 Bernard Pl
2 Coronation St
3 Cromwell St
4 Normanton St
D6
1 Barn Field Gdns
2 Barry Wk
3 Beaufort Ter
4 Stonehurst Ct
D8
1 Bloomsbury Pl
2 Bloomsbury St
3 Marine Terrace Ms
4 Royal Crescent Ms
5 Telegraph St
E2
1 Culpepper Cl
2 Tillstone Cl
E3
1 Borrow King Cl
2 Canfield Rd
E7
1 Livingstone St

Page 207

E8
1 Belgrave Pl
2 Chapel Ter
3 Chesham Pl
4 Chichester Pl
5 Clarendon Ter
6 Eastern Ter
7 Eastern Terrace Ms
8 Kemp Town Pl
9 Millfield Cottages
10 Percival Ter
11 St Mary's Sq
12 Seymour Sq
13 Seymour St
14 Sudeley Ter
15 Upper Sudeley St
F1
1 Broadfields
2 Broadfields Rd
F5
1 Haybourne Cl
F6
1 Exceat Cl
2 School Ri
F7
1 Flimwell Cl
2 Lower Chalvington Pl
F8
1 Eastern Rd

H1
1 Bailey Cl
2 Buttermere Wy
3 Coniston Wy
4 Foxglove Wy
5 Grassmere Cl
6 Hollyhock Wy
7 Honeysuckle Cl
8 Jasmine Cl
9 Jib Cl
10 Kendal Cl
11 Pebble Wk
12 Rockall Cl
13 Solent Cl
J1
1 Blenheim Cl
2 Brookenbee Cl
3 Chatsworth Cl
4 Chatsworth Dr
5 Cowdray Cl
6 Hamilton Cl
7 Harebell Cl
8 Snowdrop Cl
9 Wilton Cl
10 Windsor Cl
J2
1 Staffords Cl
J3
1 Highfield Gdns
2 Milton Cl
3 Sutherland Cl
J5
1 Aldwick Cl
2 The Gilberts
3 Howards Wy
4 Rackham Rd
M2
1 Copper Hall Cl
2 Crundens Cnr
3 Dawtrey Cl
4 East Court Wy
5 Georgian Gdns
6 Munmere Wy
7 Richmond Cl

Page 210

B2
1 Dorchester Gdns
2 Lansdowne Ct
3 The Rowans
4 West Av
E1
1 Gordon Rd
2 Hertford Rd
3 Newland St
4 Railway Ap
5 Stanhope Rd
6 Wenban Rd
E2
1 Chapel Rd
2 Grafton Pl
3 Grosvenor Rd
4 Humphrys Rd
5 Stoke Abbott Rd

Page 220

F3
1 Aldwick Hundred
2 Strange Gdn